ולזך

אשל לזך לממן

Michael
Lockman

DEVELOPING MULTICULTURAL COUNSELING COMPETENCE

A SYSTEMS APPROACH

Danica G. Hays
Old Dominion University

Bradley T. Erford
Loyola University Maryland

Boston Columbus Indianapolis New York San Francisco Upper Saddle River
Amsterdam Cape Town Dubai London Madrid Milan Munich Paris Montreal Toronto
Delhi Mexico City Sao Paulo Sydney Hong Kong Seoul Singapore Taipei Tokyo

Vice President and Editor in Chief: Jeffery W. Johnston
Acquisitions Editor: Meredith D. Fossel
Editorial Assistant: Nancy Holstein
Vice President, Director of Marketing and Sales
  Strategies: Emily Williams Knight
Vice President, Director of Marketing: Quinn Perkson
Marketing Manager: Amanda Stedke
Marketing Coordinator: Brian Mounts
Senior Managing Editor: Pamela D. Bennett

Operations Manager: Renata Butera
Creative Art Director: Jayne Conte
Cover Designer: Diane Ernsberger
Cover Art: SuperStock
Composition: GGS Higher Education Resources, A division of
  PreMedia Global, Inc.
Printer/Binder: Courier Corporation, Inc.
Cover Printer: Lehigh-Phoenix Color
Text Font: Minion

Credits and acknowledgments borrowed from other sources and reproduced, with permission, in this textbook appear on appropriate page within text.

Every effort has been made to provide accurate and current Internet information in this book. However, the Internet and information posted on it are constantly changing, so it is inevitable that some of the Internet addresses listed in this textbook will change.

Library of Congress Cataloging-in-Publication Data

Developing multicultural counseling competence : a systems approach / [edited by] Danica G. Hays, Bradley T. Erford.
  p. cm.
Includes bibliographical references and index.
ISBN-13: 978-0-13-243241-2
ISBN-10: 0-13-243241-2
  1. Cross-cultural counseling—United States.   2. Multiculturalism—United States.   3. Minorities—Counseling
  of—United States.   I. Hays, Danica G.   II. Erford, Bradley T.

BF636.7.C76D48 2010
158'.308—dc22

2009015063

10 9 8 7 6 5 4 3   V013

ISBN 13: 978-0-13-243241-2
ISBN 10:   0-13-243241-2

*In memory of those in New Orleans and the Gulf Coast region
who were tragically impacted by Hurricane Katrina in 2005.
May we never forget the lives lost and changed, the social
injustices they continue to face, and the extraordinary ways
they exemplify resilience, community, and culture.*

—dgh

*This effort is dedicated to The One: the Giver of energy,
passion, and understanding; Who makes life worth living
and endeavors worth pursuing and accomplishing; the Teacher
of love and forgiveness.*

—bte

PREFACE

Becoming culturally competent is a lifelong process. It is both a personal and professional journey of cultural understanding and political changes. It is a personal as well as a professional journey in that we are constantly striving for meaning as cultural beings. We define culture in terms of our race, ethnicity, nationality, geographic origin, gender, sexual orientation, education level, family values, language, immigration history, socioeconomic level, ability status, and spirituality, to name only a few ways. At times culture may be visible: our race or gender might be quite apparent to others. However, culture is not always visible; it may be a shared history of kinship, community practices and norms, discrimination, historical and political power, or resilience. Developing multicultural competence is a professional journey in that it involves promoting optimal counseling relationships, processes, and outcomes among individuals of unique cultural identities. This practice may occur in the counseling session and in the larger community.

There are many concepts related to the process of developing multicultural counseling competence: self-awareness, sensitivity to diversity, knowledge of cultural values, and social advocacy. The core of developing multicultural competence is possessing awareness, knowledge, and skills related to each of these concepts. It is also recognizing resilience in our clients as well as ourselves. Resilience grows from adversity, which can result from interacting with others in a multicultural world. Oftentimes, the cultural values and identities we possess are partly a product of our resilience from systemic barriers. We build community by identifying with others with similar social, political, and historical experiences.

Developing multicultural counseling competence challenges us to do what we ask of our clients: to aspire to greater personal insight about what makes us members of various cultures and to examine the ways we grow from adversity borne from familial, community, and historical systems. Multicultural counseling competence involves allowing ourselves to be vulnerable and to reflect on our personal wounds, addressing mixed emotions of anger, grief, sadness, guilt, shame, and many others that accompany our privilege and oppression experiences. To this end, developing multicultural counseling competence means acknowledging our resistance to engage in lifelong cultural learning and reveal how our privilege and oppression experiences affect our relationships with others. Only after we engage in self-exploration, experience the consequences, and begin to change because of these consequences can we be free to understand and counsel others. Social advocacy starts when we can connect our personal growth and initiative to change the status quo for those unjustly affected within various social systems by forms of oppression such as structural racism, sexism, heterosexism, classism, ableism, and ageism.

This text is intended to facilitate the journey of developing multicultural counseling competence. The 18 chapters are infused with several self-development opportunities that foster an increase in awareness, knowledge, and skills for understanding cultural makeup, understanding others of diverse identities and experiences, and engaging in facilitative counseling relationships. These opportunities are outlined in boxes inset throughout the text and include case studies, classroom and outside activities, self-reflection activities, tables, figures, and knowledge-building exercises.

The text is divided into four sections that build upon one another. Foundational aspects of multicultural competence are presented in Section One. Some of the major constructs described in multicultural counseling scholarship over the past several decades are described. The authors of Chapter 1 (Hays & McLeod) provide an overview of key multicultural terms and the processes that competent counselors should be aware of as they work toward a systems approach in developing multicultural competence: culture, cultural encapsulation, individualism and collectivism, race and ethnicity, generational status, gender, sexual orientation, socioeconomic status, disability, spirituality, advocacy, privilege, oppression, and worldview. The unique manifestations in counseling of clients' cultural experiences are introduced, including the role of communication and contextual variables such as prejudice and discrimination, acculturation, and violence and trauma. After presenting an approach to multicultural counseling competence that incorporates individual, family, community, and historical systems, key considerations and challenges to developing multicultural competence are presented. Moore-Thomas (Chapter 2) integrates some of these foundational aspects of multicultural competence and presents several cultural identity development models. These models highlight racial, ethnic, gender, sexual, and spiritual identity development among counselors as well as clients. This chapter specifically highlights that cultural identity can develop only in reflection of one's social, political, and historical contexts.

With a fundamental knowledge of key multicultural constructs and interpersonal processes relevant to counseling, the reader is presented in Section Two with scholarship of how differential amounts of power, access, advantage, and social status are available to clients based on cultural makeup. Because shared contemporary and historical experiences of privilege and oppression partly guide our personal development and thus cultural values for the cultural groups to which we belong, it is imperative the origins of and rationale for social injustices and subsequently social advocacy are discussed. Specifically, Section Two opens with a discussion of social advocacy, the fifth force of counseling (Chapter 3, Chang & Gnilka) and continues with a focus on racism and White privilege (Chapter 4, Hays & Grimmett), gender and sexism (Chapter 5, Cannon & Singh), sexual orientation and heterosexism (Chapter 6, Chaney & Marszalek), social class and classism (Chapter 7, Newton) and disability, ableism, and ageism (Chapter 8, Berens). Discourse for each newly presented form of privilege and oppression integrates that of previous chapters so the reader can better understand how clients may have unique combinations of privileged and oppressed statuses.

Section Three incorporates various privilege and oppression experiences into the framework of counseling multicultural populations that include individuals and families of those of African, Arab, Asian, Latin, Native American, and European backgrounds. Specifically, common cultural values, support systems, mental health concerns, and culturally specific interventions are presented in Chapters 9 through 14 . The authors of Chapter 9 (Helm & James) outline African American culture and values that characterize families, couples, children, Black middle-class individuals, males and females, elderly people, and Black gays and lesbians. Common mental health issues and support systems are presented and an Afrocentric psychological perspective is described. Nassar-McMillan, Gonzalez, and Mohamed (Chapter 10) provide information about the immigration history, cultural values, role of Islam, discrimination and resilience experiences, and individual differences in acculturation, ethnicity, and gender identity of Arab Americans. Additionally, best practices for working with individuals and families of Arab descent are provided.

Inman and Alvarez (Chapter 11) outline heterogeneity among Asian Americans, shared cultural values, individual differences based in differential experiences of immigration, enculturation and acculturation, ethnicity and race, gender roles, and sexual identity. Guidelines for working with individuals and families of Asian descent are presented in the context of common mental health concerns and help-seeking and coping behaviors. In articulating multiculturally competent practice with individuals and families of Latin descent, Villalba (Chapter 12) discusses the four major Latin American groups, Latina/o values, and individual differences with respect to immigration, generational, and socioeconomic statuses. After articulating mental health issues related specifically to Latin Americans negotiating their cultural identities, counseling considerations across the life span are discussed. The final commonly presented racial/ethnic minority group, Native Americans, is described in Chapter 13 (Garrett). Garrett presents an account of Native American history, common social and political issues, Native American values, and guidelines for counseling Native American clients. Finally, McMahon, Paisley, and Molina (Chapter 14) offer the reader a conceptualization of the evolution and maintenance of the "White American ethnic," describing European American history and heterogeneity, experiences of European immigrants, and counseling considerations for European descent individuals and families and recent European immigrants. Section Three closes with a chapter on spiritual diversity (Chapter 15, Cashwell). Cashwell highlights important cultural dimensions universal to individuals and families of racially and ethnically diverse backgrounds.

The final section of the text is intended to challenge the reader to think about how multicultural client concerns can be conceptualized. With an understanding of current social and political issues as well as racially and ethnically specific cultural values and counseling practices, it is imperative to consider how cultural awareness, knowledge, and skills manifest in counseling practice. Chapter 16 (Orr) connects the concept of worldview and introduces alternative approaches to the development of theory in multicultural counseling. Specifically, applications of counseling theory across cultures are presented. In Chapter 17 (Eriksen, Kress, Dixon, & Ford) concerns of misdiagnosis and ethnocentric views on normality and psychopathology are raised to challenge the reader to be cautious when applying a diagnostic label for culturally diverse groups that typically experience social injustices, including racial and ethnic minorities and females. The authors provide some solutions for culturally competent case conceptualization and diagnosis. The text concludes with Chapter 18 (Hays & Milliken), which outlines themes across the text and future directions for developing multicultural competence with respect to counseling theory, practice, and research.

SUPPLEMENTAL INSTRUCTIONAL FEATURES

Supplemental to this book are pedagogical tools helpful to counselor educators choosing to use this book as a course textbook. The companion Instructor's Manual contains at least 25 multiple-choice questions and 10 essay questions per chapter. PowerPoint slides are available to help instructors prepare presentations focusing on chapter content. Numerous case studies and activities included in the text can stimulate lively classroom discussions.

ACKNOWLEDGMENTS

We thank Lacey Wallace and Katie Tasch, graduate assistants extraordinaire, for their tireless assistance in the preparation of the original manuscript and ancillary materials. All of the contributing authors are to be commended for lending their expertise in the various topical areas. As always, Kevin Davis and Meredith Fossel of Pearson have been wonderfully responsive and supportive. Their production staff included Nancy Holstein and Renata Butera. Finally, special thanks go to the outside reviewers whose comments helped provide substantive improvement to the original manuscript: Tony W. Cawthon, Clemson University; Timothy B. Smith, Brigham Young University; and Regine Mylene Talleyrand, George Mason University.

BRIEF CONTENTS

CONTENTS

ABOUT THE EDITORS

Danica G. Hays, PhD, LPC, NCC, is an associate professor in the Department of Counseling and Human Services at Old Dominion University in Norfolk, Virginia. She is the recipient of the American Counseling Association (ACA) Research Award, the ACA Counselor Educator Advocacy Award and the Glen E. Hubele National Graduate Student Award. In addition, she has received the Association for Assessment in Counseling and Education (AACE) AACE/MECD Award, AACE President's Special Merit Award, Southern Association of Counselor Education and Supervision (SACES) Pre-tenure Counselor Educator Award Association for Counselor Education and Supervision (ACES) Outstanding Graduate Student Leadership Award, Chi Sigma Iota International (CSI) Outstanding Doctoral Student Award, and CSI Fellow. Dr. Hays's professional service includes AACE member-at-large membership, AACE member-at-large publications, AACE secretary, SACES cochair of the Multicultural Interest Network, and the ACES Best Practices in Supervision Task Force. She also serves as the founding editor of the *Counseling Outcome Research and Evaluation* journal, an editorial board member of the *Counselor Education and Supervision* journal, and an ad hoc reviewer for the *Measurement and Evaluation in Counseling and Development* journal. Dr. Hays's research interests include qualitative methodology, assessment and diagnosis, trauma and gender issues, and multicultural and social justice concerns in counselor preparation and community mental health. She has published numerous refereed journal articles and book chapters. She is associate editor of the text *American Counseling Association Encyclopedia of Counseling* (ACA, 2009), as well as coauthor of the upcoming text *Qualitative Inquiry in Clinical and Education Settings* (Guilford Publications). Dr. Hays has been a faculty member at Old Dominion University since 2006, with prior teaching experience at the University of New Orleans, Argosy University, Atlanta, and Georgia State University. Her primary teaching responsibilities are master's- and doctoral-level research methods courses, assessment, and doctoral supervision.

Bradley T. Erford, PhD, is a professor in the school counseling program in the Education Specialties Department at Loyola University Maryland. He is an American Counseling Association (ACA) Fellow, and the recipient of several ACA awards, including the Research Award, Professional Development Award, and the Carl Perkins Government Relations Award. He has received the Association for Assessment in Counseling and Education (AACE) Exemplary Practices Award; Association for Counselor Education and Supervision (ACES) Robert O. Stripling Award for Excellence in Standards; and the Maryland Association for Counseling and Development (MACD) Maryland Counselor of the Year, Professional Development, Counselor Visibility, and Counselor Advocacy Awards. His research specialization falls primarily in development and technical analysis of psychoeducational tests and has resulted in the publication of numerous books, journal articles, book chapters, and psychoeducational tests. He is an ACA Governing Council representative; past chair of the ACA, Southern Region; past president of the AACE, the MACD, the Maryland Association for Counselor Education and Supervision (MACES), the Maryland Association for Mental Health Counselors (MAMHC), and the Maryland Association for Measurement and Evaluation (MAME). Dr. Erford is the past chair of the ACA Task Force on High Stakes Testing, Task Force on Standards for Test Users, Public Awareness and Support Committee, and Interprofessional Committee. Dr. Erford is a Licensed Clinical Professional Counselor, Licensed Professional Counselor, Nationally Certified Counselor, Licensed Psychologist, and Licensed School Psychologist. He teaches courses primarily in the areas of assessment, human development, research and evaluation, school counseling, and stress management.

ABOUT THE CONTRIBUTING AUTHORS

Alvin Alvarez, PhD, is an associate professor and coordinator of the College Counseling Program at San Francisco State University, where he trains master's-level students to be college counselors and student affairs practitioners. He completed his graduate degree in counseling psychology from the University of Maryland at College Park and his undergraduate work at the University of California at Irvine. His professional interests focus on Asian Americans, racial identity, and the psychological impact of racism.

Debra E. Berens, MS, CRC, CCM, CLCP, is a Certified Rehabilitation Counselor, Certified Case Manager, and Certified Life Care Planner in private practice in Atlanta, Georgia. She also is a counselor educator in the graduate Rehabilitation Counseling program at Georgia State University and is a doctoral student with an emphasis on counselor education and practice and a cognate on rehabilitation practices. Since entering the counseling field in 1989, Berens has lectured and contributed to publications and presentations in the field of rehabilitation counseling, rehabilitation ethics, catastrophic case management, and life care planning. She currently serves as editor of the *Journal of Life Care Planning.*

Edward Cannon, PhD, is an assistant professor in the Department of Counseling at Marymount University in Arlington, Virginia. He completed his doctoral studies in counselor education at the College of William and Mary, with a cognate in family–school collaboration. Prior to completing his doctorate, he worked as a substance abuse counselor, as well as a crisis counselor for a local community mental health center. Dr. Cannon currently teaches both graduate and undergraduate courses, including research methods, practicum, and the psychology of addictions. Research interests include cultural competence in the training of counselors, including LGBT issues, as well as promoting the moral and ego development of counselor trainees. He is personally interested in advocacy work for children of same-sex parents.

Craig Cashwell, PhD, LPC, NCC, ACS, is professor and codirector of graduate studies at the University of North Carolina at Greensboro. He has served as president of the Association for Spiritual, Ethical, and Religious Values in Counseling (ASERVIC) and was recognized with the ASERVIC Meritorious Service Award. Dr. Cashwell is coauthor of *Integrating Spirituality into Counseling: A Guide to Competent Practice*, published by the American Counseling Association.

Michael P. Chaney, PhD, is an assistant professor at Oakland University in Rochester, Michigan. He received his doctorate in counseling from Georgia State University. His doctoral studies focused on psychosocial variables associated with Internet sex addicted men who have sex with men. A Licensed Professional Counselor and National Certified Counselor, he has provided mental health services to LGBT individuals struggling with addictions and to people living with HIV/AIDS in clinical and governmental agencies. Dr. Chaney is an editorial board member for the *Journal of Addictions and Offender Counseling* and the *Journal of Gay, Lesbian, and Bisexual Issues in Counseling.* He serves as a regional trainer for the American Psychological Association's HIV Office for Psychology Education (HOPE) Program. His research interests include sexual and chemical addictions, HIV/AIDS prevention, sexual orientation/gender-identity development, Adlerian theory, and social justice and social advocacy in counseling.

Catherine Y. Chang, PhD, is an associate professor and program coordinator of the counselor education and practice doctoral program in the Counseling and Psychological Services Department at Georgia State University. Her research interests include multicultural issues in counselor training and supervision and Asian American and Korean American concerns. More specifically, she has published articles related to racial identity development, privilege and oppression issues, and multicultural counseling competence. Dr. Chang has been honored with the Alumni Excellence Award from the University of North Carolina at Greensboro, the American Counseling Association Research Award, and the Pre-tenure Counselor Educator Award from the Southern Association for Counselor Education and Supervision.

Andrea Dixon, PhD, is an assistant professor of counseling/counseling psychology at Arizona State University. She has been a school counselor and a professional counselor in private practice. She is an active member of the American Counseling Association and the Association for Multicultural Counseling and Development, and specializes in diversity issues in counseling. Dr. Dixon conducts research and publishes in the areas of racial/ethnic and gender identity and wellness across the lifespan, mattering and meaning in life, adolescence, and school counseling.

Karen Eriksen, PhD, received her doctorate from George Mason University and her master's degree from California State University, Fullerton. Her doctoral study emphasized family therapy, counselor education, supervision, and counselor advocacy. She practiced most recently in Virginia while licensed as a Professional Counselor and Marriage and Family Counselor. She spent 18 years as a mental health and community agency counselor, gaining specialties in family therapy, addictions, survivors of sexual abuse, and the intersection of spirituality and counseling. She then re-careered and began teaching counseling in 1993. Dr. Eriksen is a Nationally Certified Counselor and an American Association for Marriage and Family Therapy (AAMFT) clinical member and approved supervisor. She has written five books. Her research areas are counselor preparation, constructive development, multiculturalism, and spirituality. Dr. Eriksen has been active in leadership of several state and national professional associations, including the American Counseling Association, International Association of Marriage and Family Counselors, American Mental Health Counselors Association, Virginia Association of American and Family Counselors, Virginia Counselors Association, Virginia Association of Clinical Counselors, and Northern Virginia Christian Children's Center. Dr. Eriksen regularly presents workshops on advocacy, counselor preparation, and constructive development at local, state, and national conferences.

Stephanie J. W. Ford is the coordinator of field experience for the masters of science mental health counseling program at Walden University. She is a Licensed Professional Counselor and has practiced in numerous settings including college/university counseling and psychological service centers, hospitals, private practice, and community-based organizations. She has presented and written on multiculturalism in counseling and supervision, diversity-competence in leadership, mental health severity on college/university campuses, and organizational strategies for nonmajorative students.

Michael Tlanusta Garrett, Eastern Band of Cherokee, is professor of counseling and faculty of the University of Florida. He holds a PhD in counseling and counselor education and a MEd in counseling and development from the University of North Carolina at Greensboro, and a BA in psychology from North Carolina State University. He is the author and coauthor of four books and more than 50 articles and chapters dealing with multiculturalism, group work, wellness and spirituality, school counseling, working with youth, and counseling Native Americans. He has also been an editorial board member of several counseling journals. Dr. Garrett has worked as a school counselor at the middle and high school levels, as a college student personnel worker with Native American and other minority students in the university setting, as an individual and group therapist in a family services agency setting, and as a project director in an urban Indian center serving the local Indian community. He grew up on the Cherokee Indian reservation in the mountains of western North Carolina.

Philip B. Gnilka, MS, is a doctoral student at Georgia State University in the counselor education and practice program. He received his master's degree in counseling from Wake Forest University. In Atlanta, he is working with CHRIS Kids, a free residential and mental health program for homeless children and youth. Before transitioning into the field of counseling, he graduated with a BA in economics from the University of North Carolina at Chapel Hill and worked as a stock and municipal bond analyst in New York City for over 4 years.

Laura McLaughlin Gonzalez, PhD, is an adjunct assistant professor and instructional technologist at North Carolina State University, where she works primarily with master's-level students preparing to become college counselors and student affairs practitioners. She completed her doctoral degree in counselor education at North Carolina State as well, with support from an American Educational Research Association dissertation grant. Her professional interests focus on Latina/o students and their pathways into postsecondary education, including college-level choice and experiences in higher education, along with a broader interest in multicultural diversity.

Marc Grimmett, PhD, earned his BS in biology and MA in counseling from the University of Alabama at Birmingham, while his PhD in counseling psychology was earned from the University of Georgia. He is an assistant professor and the coordinator for community agency counseling in the counselor education program at North Carolina State University. His research focuses on the career development of African American boys. Dr. Grimmett was awarded a University Extension and Engagement Grant to develop a program called "Brothers in Excellence" (BE) based on his own "Nurturing Aspirations and Potential Theory of Excellence" (NAP theory). He works with African American boys and their families as an outpatient therapist for Family and Youth Services of Easter Seals UCP in Raleigh, North Carolina.

Katherine M. Helm, PhD, is professor at Lewis University and a Licensed Psychologist in Illinois. Her job includes curriculum and program development for master's-level graduate and undergraduate psychology students. She has developed several courses, workshops, and seminars in the areas of multiculturalism, race and ethnicity, clinical skill development, clinical supervision, group therapy, ethical issues in psychology, psychopathology, contemporary issues in psychology, relationship building, human sexuality, working with sexual issues in a clinical setting, and practicum and internship. Dr. Helm is also in clinical practice and works with a diverse range of clinical issues in a multicultural population.

Arpana Inman received her PhD in counseling psychology from Temple University and is an assistant professor at Lehigh University in Pennsylvania in the counseling psychology program. Her scholastic and research interests are in the areas of multicultural issues and Asian American concerns. Specifically, these interests span several topics including acculturation, South Asian immigrant and second-generation cultural experiences, ethnic and racial identities, the psychology of women, and supervision and training. She has presented nationally and internationally and published in these areas. Dr. Inman is also the recipient of the Jeffrey S. Tanaka Memorial Dissertation Award in Psychology, from the American Psychological Association Committee on Ethnic Minority Affairs (CEMA). She recently cofounded a listserv for South Asian Concerns called South Asian Psychological Networking Association (SAPNA). Dr. Inman was cochair for the Division on Women, and vice president for the Asian American Psychological Association. She also served as vice president for the Association for Multicultural Counseling and Development, and coordinates the Asian American Pacific Islander Special Interest group in the American Counseling Association.

Lawrence James Jr., PhD, is a licensed clinical psychologist with over 18 years of experience in providing mental health services in direct care and administration. Dr. James received his doctoral degree in clinical psychology from Southern Illinois University at Carbondale in 1996. His doctorate dissertation focused on racial disparities in neuropsychological testing. His postdoctoral training was in rehabilitation psychology with an emphasis on the assessment and treatment of persons with acquired brain injuries, stroke, and spinal cord injury. His range of clinical experience has included working with persons with developmental disabilities, and runaway/homeless and abused children. Currently, he has his own multisite private practice where he works with a wide range of clients from childhood to adulthood. Over 50% of his clients are persons of color. He has presented on culturally congruent treatment with ethnic minority populations, especially African Americans.

Victoria E. Kress, PhD, is an associate professor in the Department of Counseling at Youngstown State University in Ohio. She is a Licensed Professional Clinical Counselor, and has more than 15 years of clinical experience working in various settings, such as community mental health centers, hospitals, residential treatment facilities, private practice, and college counseling centers. She has numerous refereed publications in the areas of self-injurious behavior, the *DSM,* sexual assault and trauma, and strength-based counseling approaches.

John Marszalek received his BA from Canisius College in Buffalo, New York. He received an MS in elementary education, MS in counselor education, and PhD in counselor education all at Mississippi State University. Dr. Marszalek is an assistant professor in the counseling program at Xavier University in Louisiana. Previously, he was an assistant professor at Barry University in Miami, and maintained a full-time mental health counseling practice in Fort Lauderdale. He has also taught elementary school, worked in a psychiatric hospital, and worked as an HIV/AIDS prevention educator and counselor in a community agency. His research interests include applying Ivey's developmental counseling therapy (DCT) to gay and lesbian identity development theory and to dream interpretation in counseling. He has presented his research at regional and national counseling conventions, developed a counselor education video, and published in counseling journals.

Amy L. McLeod, PhD, LPC, NCC, is an assistant professor at Argosy University, Atlanta. Her research interests include multicultural issues in counselor education and supervision, assessment and diagnosis, women's issues, and crisis and trauma counseling.

H. George McMahon, PhD, is an assistant professor in the Department of Counseling and Psychological Services at Georgia State University, where he teaches Group Counseling, Career Counseling, Counseling Theories, Introduction to School Counseling, and School Counseling Practicum and Internship. He received his MEd from the University of Virginia and his PhD from the University of Georgia. Dr. McMahon's research interests include the application of Transforming School Counseling Initiative and the American School Counselor Association national model ideas, school counselor professional identity and professional self-efficacy, group supervision in counseling programs, and the role counselors of privilege play in multiculturalism.

Tammi F. Milliken, PhD, NCC, is assistant professor of human services in the Department of Counseling and Human Services at Old Dominion University in Norfolk, Virginia. She received her doctorate in counselor education with an emphasis in family–school collaboration from the College of William and Mary, and her MS in education from Old Dominion University. Her work experience includes serving as director of Project EMPOWER, a school-based prevention program, as an elementary school counselor in Norfolk Public Schools in Virginia, and as a family counselor for New Horizons at the College of William and Mary. She is an endorsed Harvard Mind/Body Stress Management Education Initiative facilitator and trainer. Dr. Milliken's research interests include critical issues in human services, developmental theory and application, adult development and learning, ethics, and multicultural competence in human services.

Rasha H. Mohamed, BA, currently works as a case manager for a private agency in Raleigh, North Carolina. She is currently earning her master's in community counseling at North Carolina State University. Her interests are in working with immigrant families in the areas of domestic violence, parent–child relationships, and other family issues. Ms. Mohamed hopes to pursue a doctoral degree in counselor education, and to develop programs focused on eliminating discrimination among minority groups in the United States.

Bogusia Molina, PhD, is an associate professor of counselor education at Fairfield University in Fairfield, Connecticut. Her research interests include group processes, life span human development, and clinical supervision.

Cheryl Moore-Thomas received her PhD in counselor education from the University of Maryland. She is a National Certified Counselor. She is an associate professor in the Educational Specialties Department, school counseling program at Loyola College in Maryland. Over her professional career, Dr. Moore-Thomas has published and presented in the areas of multicultural counseling competence, racial identity development of children and adolescents, and accountability in school counseling programs.

Sylvia C. Nassar-McMillan, PhD, is an associate professor at North Carolina State University, where she serves as the clinical coordinator for the counselor education program. She earned her PhD in counseling and counselor education from the University of North Carolina at Greensboro in 1994. She has served in a variety of community mental health settings for over 20 years. Her scholarship includes gender and multicultural issues, with a special focus on Arab Americans. She is the current associate editor of Practice and Multicultural Issues for the *Journal of Counseling and Development* and a member of the Census Information Center advisory board to the Arab American Institute and the North Carolina Board for Licensed Professional Counselors.

Kathryn S. Newton, PhD, is an assistant professor at Shippensburg University in Pennsylvania. Her emphasis on social justice issues in counseling has grown out of her clinical practice serving low-income children and families, and individuals mandated to substance abuse treatment. Her publications and presentations include work addressing mental health and poverty, gender and sexual orientation issues, and social advocacy; she is currently developing a social justice curriculum for counselors-in-training and supervision. Dr. Newton was extensively involved as a founding member of the first university-based chapter of the Association for Lesbian, Gay, Bisexual and Transgender Issues in Counseling and served as a graduate student representative for the Association for Counselor Education and Supervision.

Jonathan J. Orr, PhD, is an assistant professor in the Department of Counseling and Psychological Services at Georgia State University. He received a bachelor's degree in English and classical history from Tulane University, a master's degree in counseling from the University of New Orleans, and a PhD in counselor education from the University of New Orleans. His counseling and research interests include groups, supervision, multicultural counseling, feminist theory, professional counselor identity, and social justice. He has coauthored or authored several journal articles and conducted workshops and presentations at the local, state, regional, and national levels. Dr. Orr is a Nationally Certified Counselor and a Licensed Professional Counselor in Georgia and Louisiana. He is an active member of the American Counseling Association (ACA), the Association for Specialists in Group Work, and the Association for Counselor Education and Supervision (ACES) and has served as a member on the ACA Committee on Human Rights and the ACES Product Development Committee.

Pamela O. Paisley, PhD, is a professor and the coordinator of the school counseling EdS program at the University of Georgia. She has worked as a teacher and counselor in public schools and as a counselor educator at Appalachian State University. Dr. Paisley has been principal investigator on a national grant to transform school counseling preparation and practice, president of the Association for Counselor Education and Supervision, and a member of the Governing Council of the American Counseling Association. She is currently involved in data-driven program development and evaluation with advanced graduate students in school counseling as well as practicing counselors in Georgia and chairs the Assessment Committee for the College of Education at UGA.

Anneliese A. Singh, PhD, LPC, NCC, is an assistant professor at the University of Georgia. She completed her doctoral program in counselor education and practice at Georgia State University.

She was also the director of Multicultural Affairs at Agnes Scott College. Her research interests include resilience and coping of marginalized populations (e.g., LGBT, South Asian imigrants and refugees, people of color), traumatology, and child sexual abuse. She is Past-President and the multicultural consultant for the Association for Lesbian, Gay, Bisexual and Transgender Issues in Counseling (ALGBTIC), and is active in numerous local, regional, and national organizations serving LGBTQI Asians. She is the recipient of the first graduate student award from ALGBTIC.

José A. Villalba, PhD, received his doctorate in counselor education from the University of Florida. He is an assistant professor in the Department of Counseling and Educational Development at the University of North Carolina at Greensboro. Dr. Villalba's teaching interests include multicultural counseling, counseling in school settings, career development and counseling, and group counseling. His research interests include addressing the academic success of Latina/o students through school counseling interventions, as well as establishing relevant school counseling interventions specifically aimed at Latina/o schoolchildren living in rural and nonrural burgeoning Latina/o communities. He has published several articles and book chapters, presented at several scholarly conferences, and served as keynote speaker for a conference on skills for school counselors working with Latina/o children and adolescents. He is of Cuban and Colombian descent.

The Foundations of Multicultural Counseling

CHAPTER 1

The Culturally Competent Counselor

DANICA G. HAYS AND AMY L. MCLEOD

PREVIEW

This initial chapter provides essential context for the development of culturally competent counseling, including trends in demographic projections for the United States and explanations of the complexities and key concepts of multicultural counseling. This discussion concludes with an introduction to multicultural counseling competence from a systems approach.

THE CULTURALLY COMPETENT COUNSELOR

> If we are to achieve a richer culture, rich in contrasting values, we must recognize the whole gamut of human potentialities, and so weave a less arbitrary social fabric, one in which each diverse gift will find a fitting place.
>
> —MARGARET MEAD *(1901–1978)*

> Every view of the world that becomes extinct, every culture that disappears, diminishes a possibility of life.
>
> —OCTAVIO PAZ *(1914–1998)*

Since the inception of helping professions in the time of Freud, counseling and psychotherapy typically involved one-to-one interventions whereas a client, who was primarily White and middle to upper class, would receive treatment for several years. Approaches and interventions in counseling throughout most of the 20th century assumed that clients were similar in demographics (e.g., White, middle to upper class, heterosexual) and thus techniques could be applied universally. The first three forces of counseling (i.e., psychodynamic, behaviorism, and existentialism/humanism) reflected this assumption and described counseling theories to work with clients in a more general manner. As the U.S. population has become increasingly diverse, the counseling profession has shifted its focus to attend to the changing faces of the American client. These dynamics within counseling theory, practice, and scholarship have sparked two additional forces. Multiculturalism and social advocacy have been described as the fourth and fifth forces of counseling, respectively (Pedersen, 1991; Ratts, D'Andrea, & Arredondo, 2004). We as a profession are attending more to the complexities of both counselors and clients in their cultural makeup, the systems by which they are surrounded, and the impact these two components have on what earlier counselors and psychotherapists viewed as "universal" expressions of mental health. In addition, we are challenging each other to address biases and assumptions we have that prevent us from forming an affirming, therapeutic alliance with clients we counsel. These more recent forces of counseling—multiculturalism and social advocacy—are creating space for counselors to focus on cultural diversity and privilege and oppression, and the resilience strategies that clients have. Before discussing how we can develop our multicultural competence while focusing on systemic influences, current and projected demographics of the U.S. population—particularly across race, ethnicity, age, and socioeconomic status—are presented.

UNITED STATES DEMOGRAPHICS

The portrait of the typical U.S. citizen has changed significantly since the 1970s. Reasons for the increased diversity include aging trends, higher birthrates for some racial and ethnic minority groups, and immigration trends that lead to an increase in non-English-speaking individuals (U.S. Census Bureau, 2000b). Statistics for population growth provide evidence that counselors will have to make adjustments to serve varying client needs. The counseling relationship thus becomes more complex as client diversity increases. Clients and counselors bring to the counseling relationship unique cultural identities coupled with contemporary and historical experiences of oppression and other forms of discrimination. Counselors are charged with becoming familiar with current and projected demographic trends within the United States and become culturally competent to work with a changing clientele.

The overall U.S. population is approximately 282 million (U.S. Census Bureau, 2004c) and is made up of several racial and ethnic groups. The predominate racial group in 2000 was White (81.0%; 69.4% non-Hispanic) followed by Black/African American (12.7%), Asian American (3.8%), and all other races (e.g., Native American, Alaska Native, Native Hawaiian) constituting 2.5% of the total U.S. population. However, the percentage of those identifying as White are projected to decrease over the next 50 years (see Table 1.1). The overall foreign-born population in 2003 was 33.5 million, making up

TABLE 1.1 Projected Population Growth for 2010 to 2050 by Race and Hispanic Origin (Percentage of Total U.S. Population)

	2000	2010	2020	2030	2040	2050
White (Hispanic and Non-Hispanic)	81.0%	79.3%	77.6%	75.8%	73.9%	72.1%
Black/African American	12.7	13.1	13.5	13.9	14.3	14.6
Asian American	3.8	4.6	5.4	6.2	7.1	8.0
Other*	2.5	3.0	3.5	4.1	4.7	5.3
Hispanic (any race)	12.6	15.5	17.8	20.1	22.3	24.4
White (non-Hispanic)	69.4	65.1	61.3	57.5	53.7	50.1

*American Indian and Alaska Native alone, Native Hawaiian and Other Pacific Islander alone, and multiracial individuals.

Source: U.S. Census Bureau (2004c).

TABLE 1.2 Projected Age Trends (Percentage of Total U.S. Population)

Age Cohort	2000	2010	2020	2030	2040	2050
0–4 yrs	6.8%	6.9%	6.8%	6.7%	6.7%	6.7%
5–19 yrs	21.7	20.0	19.6	19.5	19.2	19.3
20–44 yrs	36.9	33.8	32.3	31.6	31.0	31.2
45–64 yrs	22.1	26.2	24.9	22.6	22.6	22.2
65–84 yrs	10.9	11.0	14.1	17.0	16.5	15.7
85+ yrs	1.5	2.0	2.2	2.6	3.9	5.0

Source: U.S. Census Bureau (2004c).

approximately 11% of the U.S. population (U.S. Census Bureau, 2004a). Foreign-born individuals are those in this country not originating from the United States, Puerto Rico, Guam, American Samoa, the U.S. Virgin Islands, or the Northern Mariana Islands. Examining the foreign-born population, individuals from Latin America (e.g., the Caribbean, Central America, South America) represent the largest number of foreign-born individuals presently in the United States (i.e., 53.3%) with individuals originating from Asia (25.0%), Europe (13.7%), and other regions (e.g., North America, Africa, Oceania) accounting for the remaining numbers of foreign-born individuals. This is a marked change since 1970 when a majority of foreign-born individuals were from Europe. More specifically, from 1970 to 2000, the percentage of foreign-born individuals from Europe decreased from approximately 62% to 15%, whereas during the same period, foreign-born individuals from Asia increased from 9% to 25% and Latin America grew from 19% to 51% (U.S. Census Bureau, 2000a).

In addition, the U.S. population is living longer (see Table 1.2). In 2000, the median age was 35.3 years, the highest in U.S. history (U.S. Census Bureau, 2000a). Age trends vary by racial and ethnic group membership (see Figure 1.1). Further, White non-Hispanics are increasingly represented in older age

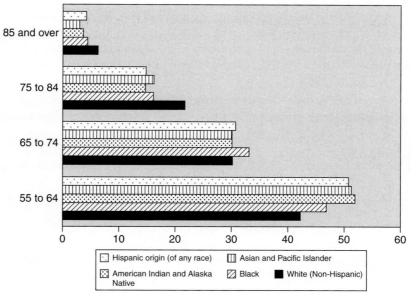

FIGURE 1.1   Age trends by racial/ethnic group membership.
Source: U.S. Census Bureau (2000b).

cohorts (i.e., individuals 65 years and older) accounting for approximately 81% of this cohort, followed by Blacks/African Americans (8%), Latin Americans/ Hispanics (6%), Asian Americans (3%), and other races (2%) (U.S. Census Bureau, 2004a).

Females outnumber males and experience disproportionate poverty rates. Female heads of households represent approximately 50% of poor families, although they constitute only 17% of all types of families. Further, median household income varies significantly by racial and ethnic group: The group with the highest median household income is Asian Americans/Pacific Islanders ($55,521), followed by Whites, non-Hispanics ($45,856), Latin Americans/Hispanics ($33,447), and Blacks/African Americans ($40,409). Disparities in earnings are further indicated by poverty rates; that is, while the poverty rate for White non-Hispanics was approximately 8%, the poverty rates for Native Americans, Latin Americans/Hispanics, and Blacks/African Americans were 11%, 23%, and 24%, respectively (U.S. Census Bureau, 2000b).

WHAT IS MULTICULTURAL COUNSELING?

Multicultural counseling may be defined as the integration of cultural identities within the counseling process. **Cultural identity** refers to the degree to which individuals identify belonging to subgroups of various cultural groups or categories. These cultural groups may include race, ethnicity, gender, sexual identity, socioeconomic status, disability, age, and spirituality, to name a few. Within each of these cultural categories, we can most likely articulate subgroup memberships in which we align. For example, one individual might identify as a Latina, heterosexual, able-bodied, young female from a middle-class background. Another individual might select salient personal cultural group memberships such as being European American, gay, male, and poor. Every individual, counselors and clients alike, has a unique combination of cultural group memberships that bring forth different social, political, biological, and historical experiences to the counseling process. Thus, most counselors view all counseling relationships as cross-cultural in some manner.

In addition to the cultural identities counselors and clients bring to the counseling relationship, "U.S." or "American" culture is also important to attend to, as American values may not always be congruent with values we hold pertaining to various cultural identities. Activity 1.1 presents some questions to reflect upon with respect to U.S. culture and multicultural counseling.

ACTIVITY 1.1

Discuss in pairs the following questions about U.S. culture and multicultural counseling:

- What does being an American mean to you?
- What values are associated with being an American?
- What values are associated with not being an American?
- How would you describe U.S. culture to a newcomer to the United States?
- What images come to your mind about U.S. culture as you reflect on media images?
- How might images and descriptions of U.S. culture be beneficial to counseling diverse populations? How might they be a challenge?

Culture's role in mental health was first discussed in the 1960s and 1970s when scholars stated that the cultural identities of clients should be acknowledged because they impact clients' experiences in counseling. Additionally, several wrote about the negative ways by which counselors inhibit clients' well-being when not addressing clients' cultural experiences in counseling sessions. Each chapter in this text addresses the role cultural identity plays in clients' lives, including the counseling experience. Additionally, these chapters attend to the forms of resilience as well as negative experiences clients of diverse backgrounds may have in society in general and the counseling relationship more specifically. Before describing variations in cultural expression of values and communication, it is important to review several key terms related to multicultural counseling. The following terms do not represent an exhaustive list, nor do the definitions portray a comprehensive discussion of the term; additional terms related to multicultural counseling and more information on the terms presented here will be introduced throughout the text. After reviewing these terms, complete the activity in Build Your Knowledge 1.1.

Culture

Culture is defined as the totality of the human experience for social contexts. This human experience is mediated by biological, psychological, historical, and political events. Culture includes behaviors, attitudes, feelings, and cognitions related to our identities living within the world. It organizes how groups as a whole, individuals within a particular group, and individuals as a human race behave, think, and feel. The definition of culture incorporates a majority of the key terms that follow, including *worldview, individualism–collectivism, race, ethnicity, nationality, generational status, gender, sexual orientation, socioeconomic status, ability status,* and *spirituality.* The extent to which a group membership is labeled as "cultural" depends on how broadly individuals define culture. For example, a broad definition might include variables such as race, ethnicity, gender, sexual orientation, educational status, language, and geographical origin. A more narrow definition might label culture as race and gender only. For example, consider a multiracial male who presents for counseling. A counselor using a broader definition of culture may attend to how characteristics such as his race, gender, age, education level, nationality, degree of spirituality, family characteristics, and sexual orientation influence his presenting symptoms as well as the counseling relationship. A counselor viewing this client through a narrower definition of culture may attend only to how his being multiracial and male impacts his well-being and the counseling relationship.

Culture may be broadly defined by three, overlapping dimensions: universal, group, and individual. **Universal culture** refers to commonalities shared by all cultures and humankind. Some of these might include use of language as a method of communication, establishment of social norms, bodily functions, or physiological fear responses. **Group culture** is the characteristics shared by a particular group such as Asian Americans, females, individuals raised in the southern United States, and those living in poverty. While individuals are guided by both universal and group culture, they possess behaviors, attitudes, and cognitions unique to them (i.e., **individual culture**). These may include behaviors that are outside the norms of the groups to which they belong, such as making decisions that promote autonomy within a more collectivistic cultural group. Counselors are encouraged to attend to all of these dimensions of culture.

Cultural Encapsulation

Unfortunately, counselors do not always consider the client from the *client's* perspective of the world. **Cultural encapsulation** refers to a narrow and rigid view of the world and other cultural groups using one's own cultural groups as a reference. It involves evaluating other cultures using one's own culture as a standard of normality. This is also known as **ethnocentricism**. Cultural encapsulation is a danger to the counseling profession because counselors may be so entrenched in their cultural values and worldviews that they ignore their influence on clients who may differ from them. For example, a counselor may adhere to a counseling theory that indicates independence and more "rational" thinking as signs of mental health. This theory might be congruent with the counselor's worldview and value systems, yet the client may value making decisions that are best suited for the general welfare of the client's family. This disconnect could impair the client's well-being, lead to early termination of counseling services, or both. It has been argued that traditional counseling theories and views of mental health are reflective of White, middle-class worldviews and valuesystems (i.e., a monocultural view of counseling and mental health). Thus, counselors are encouraged to be open to various cultural perspectives to avoid harming their clients.

Individualism and Collectivism

Individuals tend to guide their decisions by how it benefits and reflects upon themselves or others, or a combination of both. Depending on our cultural identities, we belong at some point to an individualism–collectivism continuum. **Individualism** is the notion that our behaviors and attitudes are guided by incentives that promote self-determination or independence. Some concepts related to individualism include competitiveness, self-disclosure, agency, independence, and self-promotion. That is, individuals may focus on how their actions benefit themselves and how they are responsible for expressing their feelings and beliefs and creating change in their lives. Traditional counseling values are primarily individualistic in that the counselor promotes self-disclosure, emotional expression, and client autonomy.

Collectivism refers to the idea that decisions and thus what is deemed important is based upon the betterment of others. Others might include community or family members. Collectivistic values might include cooperation, "saving face," and interdependence. Individuals from more collectivistic cultures may avoid counseling altogether because they may perceive discussing their personal problems with a counselor as a poor reflection on the community or family. Because individuals may have a combination of individualistic and collectivistic values, it is important to reflect upon the origins of particular values. Reflection 1.1 presents an exercise on values to begin this journey.

REFLECTION 1.1

Create a list of, and describe, at least three principles you feel you received from members of your family, school, peers, and community that reflect your cultural values. How do these values continue to affect your life? Do they impact how you express your emotions and beliefs? Do they guide your decision making?

Race and Ethnicity

Race and ethnicity are two of the major cultural group classifications discussed in multicultural counseling scholarship. **Race** or racial group membership is the arbitrary, socially constructed classification of individuals often based on physical distinctions such as skin color, hair texture, face form, and eye shape. Throughout history, as described in Chapter 4, race as a classification system has divided and perpetuated exploitation of individuals resulting in racism and lowered social, political, and psychological well-being. Examples of current racial categories include White, African American, Asian American, and Native American. **Ethnicity** is a related term that refers to shared characteristics of culture, religion, and language, to name a few. Examples of ethnic groups include Latin Americans and Arab Americans. **Nationality**, a common component of ethnicity, refers to one's nation of origin, such as France, Kenya, China, or Native America. Because of the historical experiences of different races that create unique physiological and social characteristics, particular lifestyles and value systems have formed to promote ethnicity. Several racial groups may share the same ethnicity, such as Whites and Africans sharing South African heritage. Some racial groups, such as Whites, may be unaware of their ethnic group membership.

Generational Status

Generational status refers to clusters of particular age groups within a particular social and historical context. Generations typically span a range of 15 to 20 years and represent individuals who share common characteristics due to their particular experiences in history based on their cohort. Some of the living generations include the GI generation ("government issue," 1901–1924), silent generation (1925–1942), baby boomer generation (1943–1960), Generation X (1961–1981), Generation Y (1982–2000), and Generation Z (those born after 2000). The particular aging of the baby boomer generation has become an increased focus for counselors and other public health professionals. Generational status is an important identity for those who acculturate to the United States, given younger generations may have an easier time navigating U.S. culture.

Gender

Whereas sex refers to the biological distinctions between males and females (e.g., hormonal differences, physical differences in anatomical structures), **gender** is the expression of social categories. These social categories are also known as **gender roles** and describe behaviors deemed appropriate by a particular culture for males and females. For example, in U.S. culture it is socially appropriate for females to demonstrate nurturance and emotionality while males are valued for their expression of rationality and physical strength.

Three terms are useful for thinking about gender and gender role expression: masculinity, femininity, and androgyny. **Masculinity** and **femininity** are the normative expressions of stereotypical and socially accepted behaviors for males and females, respectively. **Androgyny** is the blending of masculinity and femininity for both males and females. As described in Chapter 5, individuals' adherence to socially accepted gender roles has both benefits and challenges. In the United States, the more "masculine" men are (e.g., competitive, aggressive) and the more "feminine" women are (e.g., affectionate, cooperative), the greater each gender fits into social norms. However, as will be discussed in later chapters, compliance to social norms may create psychological, political, and physical consequences for both sexes.

Sexual Orientation

Sexual orientation refers to the sexual or affectional attraction to the same or opposite gender, or both. **Sexual identity** describes the degree of identification with a particular sexual orientation. Thus, individuals may identify as heterosexual, gay, lesbian, bisexual, or questioning, to name a few. Gender and sexual orientation overlap in that sexual orientation falls on a continuum: at one end an individual of one gender may be attracted solely to another of the opposite gender (i.e., heterosexual) and at another end an individual of one gender may be attracted to another of the same gender (i.e., homosexual). Between these points falls various other sexual identities, including bisexual and questioning.

Socioeconomic Status

Socioeconomic status (SES) is typically indicated by household income, education level, occupational status, use of public assistance, and access to health care. The amount of social, educational, and financial resources individuals have determines their SES, although the amount of financial resources is used as the primary measure of SES. SES is most commonly categorized in four ways: upper, middle, working, and under class. Those who belong to lower socioeconomic statuses (i.e., working class, under class) often have negative mental health outcomes as a result of detrimental social, educational, and economic experiences. Racial/ethnic minorities and women as heads of household disproportionately represent the majority of cases of lower SES, making the intersection of SES, race, ethnicity, and gender an important component of multicultural counseling.

Disability

Disability, discussed more thoroughly in Chapter 8, refers to mental or physical impairment that affects at least one of an individual's daily activities. Physical disabilities represent the majority of disabilities. Individuals with disabilities often face negative consequences referred to as **ableism**. For example, others may assume that individuals with physical disabilities have cognitive limitations as well. This may create social, cultural and economic barriers to them, further limiting their ability to integrate and feel as they belong. Several types of legislation, including the *Rehabilitation Act* (1973), *Americans with Disabilities Act* (1990), and the *Individuals with Disabilities Education Improvement Act* (2004), have allowed for increased protection and appropriate treatment of individuals with disabilities.

Spirituality

Spirituality is an important cultural variable for many individuals and refers to the connections individuals have with themselves and the universe as a whole. It provides direction, meaning, and purpose and guides other components for individuals. Witmer, Sweeney, and Myers (1994) proposed that the spiritual dimension of individuals serves as the core of wellness and thus optimal mental functioning. A related term to spirituality is **religion**, which represents the behaviors and practices of individuals' faith. Thus, religion is the organizing construct of spirituality. There are several Western and Eastern religions of the world; some of these include Buddhism, Christianity, Confucianism, Hinduism, Islam, Judaism, and Taoism.

BUILD YOUR KNOWLEDGE 1.1

On a separate sheet of paper, match the definition in the left column with the most appropriate term from the right column.

1. Socially normative behaviors for males and females	a. Privilege
2. Totality of human experience as mediated by biological, psychological, social, and historical events	b. Generation
	c. Oppression
	d. Culture
3. Interdependence as a primary value	e. Religion
4. Using one's own cultural group as a standard to evaluate others	f. Gender roles
5. Age cohorts that share similar characteristics	g. Cultural identity
6. Self-determination as a primary value	h. Locus of responsibility
7. Blending of masculine and feminine characteristics	i. Collectivism
8. Empowering others and changing the status quo	j. Locus of control
9. Typical characteristics include nurturance, emotionality, and cooperation	k. Individualism
10. Having power, access, advantage, and social status	l. Ethnocentrism
	m. Femininity
11. Organized practices of faith	n. Racism
12. Indicated by household income, education level, occupational status, use of public assistance, and access to health care	o. Androgyny
	p. Race
13. Discrimination toward persons with disabilities	q. Ethnicity
	r. Ableism
14. Identification with cultural groups	s. Sexual identity
15. Individuals' relationship to the world	t. Sexual orientation
16. Shared culture, religion, and language	u. Worldview
17. Individual versus external system as cause of particular consequences	

Advocacy, Privilege, and Oppression

Advocacy or **social justice** has become an increasingly important term to counselors as the attention to cultural issues expands. Advocacy refers to promoting an idea, policy, or cause that betters the lives of those who may have less power, access, advantage, or social status. As the practice of multicultural counseling has increased, counselors have noted that many cultural "differences" in value expression, social standing, as well as mental health functioning are the result of social injustice or disenfranchisement. To this end, it is insufficient to be only tolerant and sensitive to individuals and understand their cultural values and differences. Advocacy assumes a sense of responsibility on the part of counselors to change the status quo for individuals with less power and status. Advocacy counseling thus refers to individual and systemic interventions with marginalized clients that seek to empower them and improve social, political, and physical conditions to maximize their well-being.

Counselors who engage in advocacy efforts assume that there is a power differential among U.S. individuals for any particular cultural group. For example, within the dimension of gender, males have more power than females. The amount of power individuals have is complicated by the fact that we are made up of a combination of cultural group memberships, some of which have more advantage than others. For example, an African American male is more at a disadvantage in U.S. society in general than a White male, even though both belong to the higher statused gender. The idea that power is dispersed within a cultural group is embedded in the constructs of privilege and oppression. **Privilege** refers to the often unconscious and unearned power, access to resources, advantage, and social position based on cultural group memberships. Privileged cultural groups in U.S. society include being White, male, heterosexual, higher SES, able-bodied, and Christian. Because certain individuals have privilege, others within various cultural groups experience oppression. **Oppression** is the lack of power, inaccessibility, disadvantage, and minority social status. Oppressed cultural groups include racial and ethnic minority groups, females, sexual minorities, less able-bodied, lower SES statuses, and religious minorities. Section Three of the text discusses advocacy, privilege and oppression for the various cultural identities of race, ethnicity, gender, sexual orientation, SES, age, and disability.

Worldview

Worldview is defined as individuals' conceptualization of their relationship with the world. Sue (1978) described individuals' worldview as embedded within two intersecting dimensions: locus of responsibility and locus of control. Cultural groups use these dimensions to guide their behavior and motivation. **Locus of responsibility** refers to what system is accountable for things that happen to individuals. An internal locus of responsibility (IR) refers to the idea that success (or failure) is viewed as an individuals' own doings and thus the result of individual systems. An external locus of responsibility (ER) refers to notion that the social environment or external system is responsible for what happens to individuals. The second dimension, **locus of control**, is the degree of control individuals perceive they have over their environment. An internal locus of control (IC) is the belief that consequences are dependent upon an individual's actions. An external locus of control (EC) refers to the notion that consequences result by chance, outside individuals' control. Thus, locus of responsibility involves what system is held accountable for actions that happen to individuals, while locus of control refers to who has initial control over behaviors. Individuals' worldviews may be conceptualized according to Sue (1978) as one of four combinations: (a) IR-IC is a common combination among those who hold White middle-class values where individuals control and are responsible for their own actions in the world; (b) IR-EC describes individuals who believe they cannot control actions that occur to them but may blame themselves for any negative consequences; (c) ER-IC includes those who view individual ability to be possible if given an opportunity by those in their environment; and (d) ER-EC involves those who believe they have little control over their actions due to oppression and other systemic pressures and thus see addressing the consequences of this outside of their responsibility. Complete Build Your Knowledge 1.2 to develop examples of each of these combinations.

BUILD YOUR KNOWLEDGE 1.2

Based on Sue's (1978) four types of worldviews, list at least two situations where clients may present in counseling with each of these combinations.

EXAMPLE: IR-IC: *A client visits a career counselor to seek assistance for selecting a college major. The client reports difficulty in the decision-making process. He is interested in a prestigious career that will allow him to be successful, and he wants to select the best college major to obtain this goal. He states that he holds himself accountable for any decision he makes.*

IR-IC:

_____

_____

_____

_____

IR-EC:

_____

_____

_____

_____

ER-IC:

_____

_____

_____

_____

ER-EC:

_____

_____

_____

_____

Kluckhohn and Strodtbeck's (1961) theoretical model creates a different definition of worldview. The five components of the model include (a) human nature, (b) relationship to nature, (c) sense of time, (d) activity, and (e) social relationships. Each of these five dimensions combine in various ways to manifest particular cultural value systems and thus worldviews. **Human nature** involves the continuum that humans are basically good, bad, or a combination of both. **Relationship to nature** refers to how powerful individuals view nature: harmony with nature, power over nature, or power of nature. **Sense of**

time relates to what aspect of time individuals focus upon past, present, or future. **Activity** is how self-expression occurs for individuals. These may include being (i.e., present-oriented with an internal focus on self), being-in-becoming (i.e., present- and future-oriented goal development to create an integrated self), and doing (i.e., actively engaging in activities that are deemed important by external standards). **Social relationships** involve three categories that relate to the degree of hierarchy and group focus within a culture: lineal–hierarchal (i.e., traditional cultures with hierarchal positions, typically patriarchal structures), collateral–mutual (i.e., collectivistic focus), and individualistic (i.e., the needs of groups are secondary to those of individuals).

Integrating and Contextualizing Multicultural Counseling Concepts

These terms introduce some of the complexities of multicultural counseling. Clients will present for counseling with unique experiences and attitudes related to each of these concepts. In addition, you have a unique "story" involving these key multicultural concepts you bring to the counseling relationship. Complete Reflection 1.2 to begin creating your cultural narrative.

REFLECTION 1.2

Construct a narrative or story of your cultural background. Discuss group memberships with respect to race, ethnicity, gender, sexual orientation, socioeconomic status, spirituality, age, ability status, and any others that seem significant to you. In your narrative, articulate how you or your family immigrated to the United States (if applicable), your acculturation experiences, and how your family and community shape your cultural identity. In addition, discuss both positive and negative events that have shaped who you are culturally. Outline how values you hold and communication patterns are influenced by your cultural group memberships.

THE ROLE OF COMMUNICATION IN MULTICULTURAL COUNSELING

Communication is central to the therapeutic process. Clients communicate their self-concepts, emotions, perspectives, and realities through both verbal and nonverbal communication. Through communication relationships are built, trust is established, and understanding and empathy are expressed. In the context of multicultural counseling, differences in language and styles of communication can create a significant barrier to establishing a therapeutic relationship and working toward change.

Verbal Communication

Most of the major counseling theories rely on spoken words as a primary tool for promoting growth and change. Freud referred to psychoanalysis as "the talking cure" and many people still refer to counseling as "talk therapy" (Laungani, 2004). For this reason, language differences between the counselor and client create tremendous challenges. In the United States, English is the dominant language; however, as the population becomes increasingly diverse, counselors are likely to encounter clients who are not fluent in English, speak English as a second or third language, or speak a dialect of standard English (Brown & Srebalus, 2003). Unfortunately, the ethnocentric belief that everyone who lives in the United States should speak English only is still prevalent. Power is embedded in language and clients who do not speak the dominant language are routinely marginalized and experience discrimination (Abreu & Giordano, 1996). Individuals who are not fluent in the dominant language may be viewed as unintelligent or childlike and are blocked from accessing resources and opportunities that are available to individuals who are fluent in standard English. Thus, language differences create barriers that may create lowered self-esteem in clients who speak little to no English (Westwood & Ishiyama, 1990).

Feelings of frustration and invalidation are likely to occur when counselors are not able to convey understanding to culturally and linguistically different clients. Research indicates that within the multicultural counseling setting, clients in the initial stages of therapy identify preoccupation with making themselves understood (Westwood & Ishiyama, 1990). One way to deepen the level of understanding shared by a counselor and client is to incorporate the use of traditional **metaphors** from the client's culture into the therapy session (Parham, 2002a). Metaphors are rich in cultural meaning and may be related to religious teachings or cultural values. Santiago-Rivera, Arredondo, and Gallardo-Cooper (2002a) describe the use of metaphor with Latina clients. The metaphor "Camina la milla" (p. 138), which translates to "walk the mile," can be meaningful when discussing life's struggles and hardships. The metaphor "El oro billa hasta en el basurero" (p. 139), which translates to "Gold shines even in the garbage can," may be used to describe perseverance in spite of discrimination and oppression. As metaphors are passed among generations, they become internalized (Laungani, 2004). Alternate forms of communication such as music, poetry, art, and dance can be used to enhance counselor and client understanding as well (Westwood & Ishiyama, 1990).

Many clients who speak English as a second language may prefer to express themselves in their native language during the counseling process. Often culture-specific phrases, or subtle nuances of words in one's native language, are best able to articulate emotions. Counselors should encourage clients to use the language with which they feel most comfortable expressing themselves (Westwood & Ishiyama, 1990). At a minimum, counselors are to be aware of resources in the community for clients whose primary language is not standard English. Counselors may employ specially trained interpreters to assist in communicating with clients when a language barrier exists. In addition, English-speaking counselors are encouraged to learn a second language.

Nonverbal Communication

Understanding a person's nonverbal behavior is essential in the counseling process. Many people believe that approximately 85% of communication is nonverbal (Ivey & Ivey, 2007). Nonverbal communication includes facial expressions; **proxemics**, the use of personal physical distance; **kinesics**, body movements, positions, and postures; and **paralanguage**, verbal cues other than words (Herring, 1990). Nonverbal communication may relate to or provide additional information about verbal communication. In addition, nonverbal communication often operates outside of conscious awareness and is difficult to falsify (Herring, 1990), therefore making it key to understanding a client's genuine experience. Herring noted that nonverbal behavior is often ambiguous and culturally bound. In other words, the same nonverbal expressions can have drastically different meanings in different cultures. For example, interpersonal distance varies according to culture. "Arm's length" is a comfortable distance from which to communicate for most European Americans. However, in some Arabic cultures for example, communicating at arm's length may be perceived as cold or unfriendly, since approximately 18 inches is typically considered a comfortable interpersonal distance (Ivey & Ivey, 2007). The meaning of engaging in direct eye contact also varies considerably by culture. In traditional Western cultures, a lack of direct eye contact may indicate shame or depression. In some Eastern cultures, lack of direct eye contact indicates respect.

It is imperative that counselors interpret client presentation based on norms from within the client's culture. Imposing Western norms may lead to misdiagnosis and pathologizing of a client when no pathology exists (Sue, Ivey, & Pedersen, 1996). Counselors should also be aware of how their own nonverbal behavior may be interpreted by clients and make an effort to communicate respect through their nonverbal behaviors. To increase your awareness of your nonverbal and verbal communication patterns, complete Activity 1.2.

ACTIVITY 1.2

Increase your awareness of your own verbal and nonverbal communication patterns. Work in triads in which two students conduct a role-play, conversing about a topic of their choice, and the other student observes and records notes about the communication patterns of the other two students. Switch roles until each student has had an opportunity to observe a conversation.

Share your observations with the other students. In receiving feedback about your nonverbal and verbal communications, reflect on the following: What patterns do you observe? What messages are you conveying through verbal and nonverbal communication? How might you modify your verbal and nonverbal communication patterns when working with clients from other cultural groups?

Emotional Expression

All human beings experience emotions. Feelings of sadness, anger, gladness, fright, surprise, and disgust are thought to be universal emotional experiences (Ivey & Ivey, 2007). However, the ways in which emotions are expressed and the beliefs about the causes of emotions vary widely among and within cultural groups. Emotions are usually considered reactions to external events or the result of chemical processes in the brain. In the dominant culture, expression of emotions is typically viewed as a component of mental health. In non-Western cultures, emotions may be experienced somatically and viewed as a component of physical health. Negative emotions may be attributed to an imbalance of fluids in the body, possession by a spirit, or violation of a moral or religious principle (Young, 1997).

Socialization influences the way emotions are expressed. For example, within European American culture, females are typically socialized to be more outwardly emotionally expressive than males. In Asian and Latino cultures, individuals may be guarded in the display of emotions due to social stigma associated with mental health issues (Young, 1997). Reflection 1.3 can assist you with considering the origins of your emotional expressions.

When responding to a client's emotional expressions, counselors should use norms from within the client's culture to determine if the expression is indicative of pathology. The client's beliefs regarding the origin of emotions should also be considered and incorporated into the counseling process.

REFLECTION 1.3

Think about the following questions to increase your awareness regarding ways in which you experience and express emotions.

• What messages did you receive about emotional expression as a child?
• What messages are present in society about emotional expression for cultural groups you identify with personally?
• Which emotions are you most and least comfortable expressing?
• How do you typically experience and express feeling sad, mad, glad, scared, surprised, or disgusted?
• Which emotions are you most comfortable with others expressing in your presence? Least comfortable with?

Communication Patterns of Clients and Counselors

Patterns of communication between a counselor and client are ideally characterized by openness and honesty. To increase open communication, counselors should consistently check with clients to ensure they are accurately interpreting and understanding clients' verbal and nonverbal messages. Clients engaged in multicultural counseling report that feeling accurately understood by the counselor leads to increased trust and a reduced level of defensiveness (Westwood & Ishiyama, 1990).

In addition, counselors should engage in a **self-reflective process** to evaluate how the counselor inadvertently communicates personal biases, values, and assumptions to a client. For example, the aspects of a client's story a counselor chooses to respond to indicates what the counselor considers important. A counselor's response should be based on the client's frame of reference (Freeman, 1993).

Minority clients are often reluctant to utilize formal counseling services due to a distrust of the mental health profession which has historically pathologized and discriminated against individuals who are not White, middle- and upper-class, heterosexual males (Pack-Brown, 1999). Shame and stigma about discussing personal problems with a person outside one's culture or family may also be a barrier to open and honest communication. To build a therapeutic relationship with minority clients increased level of counselor self-disclosure is often necessary. In addition, research indicates that many minority clients prefer a practical, directive, didactic style of communication from counselors.

CULTURE AND CONTEXT

As the U.S. population becomes more diverse, counselors are becoming more aware of the role culturally based contextual factors play in the counseling process. Some of these factors include prejudice and discrimination, immigration, acculturation, and violence and trauma. In addition, there are factors that relate specifically to experiences within the counseling process. These include the incongruence between traditional counseling practices and culturally diverse clients' mental health needs and general attitudes toward counseling. Contextual factors may influence culturally diverse clients' attitudes and behaviors, and increase their risk of mental health problems given that they may have limited resources and support in U.S. society (Ancis, 2004).

Prejudice and Discrimination

Clients with minority statuses (e.g., non-White, female, lower SES, gay, lesbian, bisexual) often deal with prejudice and discrimination in their daily lives. **Prejudice** is defined as prematurely holding a belief or attitude without appropriate examination or consideration of actual data. A prejudice may be either positive or negative and is based on stereotyped views and accompanying emotions. For example, someone might prejudge Asian Americans to be high achievers or females to be too emotional. A prejudice differs from **discrimination**, which refers to covert and overt behaviors based on generalizations held about individuals based on their cultural group memberships. Examples of discrimination include hiring or firing someone based on his or her sexual orientation or supporting laws that may be oppressive to certain racial groups. Forms of prejudice and discrimination are largely based on **stereotypes** we hold about various cultural groups.

Examples of prejudice and discrimination include various forms of oppression, such as racism, sexism, heterosexism, and classism. Depending on their cultural makeup or their perceived cultural makeup, culturally diverse clients will have unique experiences with prejudice and discrimination. Clients have these experiences within several settings, including schools, neighborhoods, churches, temples, and mental health settings. Forms and manifestations of various oppressions will be discussed throughout the remainder of the text.

Prejudice and discrimination may pervade individual, cultural, and institutional practices, and clients may suffer social, economic, political, and mental and physical costs. It affects their amount of social support, occupational status, and socioeconomic status; encourages maladaptive coping responses; serves as a catalyst for depression, suicide, substance abuse, violence, anxiety disorders, and chronic and acute stress; and may fuel medical complications such as hypertension, low birth weight, heart disease, and cancer (Ancis, 2004; Clark, Anderson, Clark, & Williams, 1999). Additionally, experiences of homophobia and heterosexism potentially foster self-deprecation; developmental issues for adolescents; lack of family and peer support; and Posttraumatic Stress Disorder symptoms of somatization, denial, guilt, and numbing of emotions (Dworkin & Yi, 2003; Harper & Schneider, 2003).

As counselors work with clients who may experience daily prejudice and discrimination, it is important that they examine clients' environmental stressors associated with stereotyping. Counselors are encouraged to explore with the clients any attitudes and behaviors they perceive are in response to their cultural group memberships. In addition, culturally sensitive counselors need to identify various stereotypes they hold of various cultural groups. Reflection 1.4 offers space to reflect on stereotypes you possess.

REFLECTION 1.4

Stereotypes are generalizations we hold about individuals based on their cultural group memberships. Describe the following groups honestly and thoroughly with the first thoughts that come to your mind:

Males: _____

Catholics: _____

Native Americans: _____

Gay males: _____

Homeless individuals: _____

Asian Americans: _____

Females: _____

Lesbians: _____

Latin Americans: _____

Jews: _____

Protestants: _____

Whites: _____

Wealthy individuals: _____

African Americans: _____

Middle-class individuals: _____

Muslims: _____

Transgender individuals: _____

Bisexual individuals: _____

Arab Americans: _____

Buddhists: _____

Review the sentences you created. How and from whom did you learn these generalizations? Have any of these stereotypes changed for you throughout your life so far?

Immigration

Immigration is another consideration in multicultural counseling. Immigration refers to the process in which foreign-born individuals settle in a new country. Most racial/ethnic groups were immigrants at some point, with the exception of some groups such as Native Americans, Aleuts, and Native Hawaiians. Immigration can be either voluntary or involuntary. Many individuals select to enter the United States to flee political and religious persecution and poverty or to improve their economic conditions. However, African immigrants arrived in this country involuntarily and were enslaved upon arrival. Other immigrants were indentured servants upon entry with many able to obtain their freedom eventually. In either case of voluntary or involuntary immigration, individuals often are separated from family and their homelands, creating several mental health considerations.

There are different immigration patterns throughout U.S. history as a result of changing immigration policies. Oftentimes, these policies are shaped by current economic needs. However, some may argue that policy is often guided by a desire to keep the United States largely White, as evidenced by the differential numbers of immigrants based on countries of origin (Takaki, 2002b). For example, between 1820 and 1930 many immigrants (about 38 million) came to the United States from Europe, with few arriving from Asia or Africa due to existing policies. This influx was largely in response to the melting pot concept where Europeans were especially encouraged to immigrate to the "land of opportunity." However, the U.S. government needed cheap labor in the mid-1800s to construct the Central Pacific Railroad, a commercial opportunity to conduct business with Asia. Thus, the Chinese were encouraged to immigrate to California for improved economic conditions. However, borders were closed to the Chinese in 1892 after they were viewed as an economic threat. Since 1950, European immigration has declined from about 60% to only about 20%, while 75% of legal immigrants settling into the United States came from Latin America or Asia (Banks, 2003). Recently, the estimated 12 million illegal Latino/a immigrants working and living in the United States have created discussions about criminalizing illegal immigration while legalizing those who are willing to pay fines and wait a period of time before receiving a green card (Campo-Flores, 2006).

Thus, culturally diverse clients will have different immigration histories that impact their sense of belonging. When assessing the role immigration plays in multicultural counseling, understanding the reasons for entry into the United States, length of time in this country, information about the cultural climate of the country of origin, and the degree of prejudice and discrimination faced by a client's family historically and currently become especially important. For example, the historical oppression experienced by southern and eastern Europeans living in urban ghettos is quite different from that experienced by Africans in the South or Asians in the western United States. Further, the experiences of, and thus mental health impact on, Latin Americans seeking political refuge in the United States within the past few years is quite different than someone whose family arrived seeking educational and career opportunities several generations ago.

Acculturation

Acculturation is highly related to immigration. Acculturation refers to the degree to which immigrants identify with and conform to a new culture of a host society, or the degree to which they integrate new cultural values into their current value system. Acculturation may involve individuals identifying with both the homeland and host cultures, embracing one culture over another, or rejecting both cultures (Phinney, 1990). There are four main models of acculturation with which counselors should be familiar. These include the (a) *assimilation* model, whereas highly acculturated individuals identify solely with the new culture, so one group (typically a racial/ethnic minority group) adopts values and customs of another, more dominant group (i.e., European Americans); (b) *separation* model, where individuals refuse to adapt to cultural values outside of their own cultural values; (c) *integration* model, which refers to **biculturalism**—a process where individuals identify with both their own culture and that of the host culture; and (d) *marginalization* model, where individuals reject cultural values and customs of both cultures (Paniagua, 2005). There may be unique counseling considerations pertaining to each of these four models of acculturation. Review Case Study 1.1 and apply each of the acculturation models.

CASE STUDY 1.1

You are a school counselor in a middle school in a small, close-knit community in the Midwest. Lian, a 14-year-old Asian female, was referred to you for social and academic issues. Specifically, her teachers are concerned about her failing grades and isolative behaviors. During your initial session with Lian, you discover that she has been in the United States since age 7 and has lived in your community since age 13. How might you conceptualize her acculturation experience based on the four models of acculturation: assimilation, separation, integration, and marginalization?

Acculturation level is largely determined by the number of years a client has been involved in the acculturation process, the client's country of origin, and the age at which the client began the acculturation process (Paniagua, 2005). It may be assumed that the longer a client is in the United States, particularly if he or she enters the country at a young age, the easier the acculturation process will be. Also, if a client originates from a country that is similar to the United States in some way (e.g., English speaking, shared customs and values), the easier the transition will be. Acculturation is also largely affected by immigrants' ethnic identity. The more immigrants identify with and belong to a particular ethnic group, particularly if their ethnic values contrast with general U.S. cultural values, the more difficult the process of acculturation becomes.

Even when the acculturation process seems easier for some culturally diverse clients, there are many stressors associated with it. The process of acculturation can be a significant stressor for racial/ethnic minorities because they must give up, limit, or deny part or all of their cultural values and customs and become more like the dominant group in order to increase their chances of social and economic mobility. Some responses to these stressors include depression, anxiety, isolation, substance abuse, physical health concerns, and identity confusion (Ancis, 2004). For many groups, acculturation coupled with prejudice and discrimination experiences do little to help them "succeed" in the United States. Many racial/ethnic minorities continue to experience oppression regardless of how long they have lived in this country and how much they compromised their cultural identities to increase their sense of belonging in the general U.S. culture. In fact, research indicates that the more acculturated some racial/ethnic minorities are (e.g., Latino Americans, Asian Americans), and thus the longer they have lived in the United States and have been exposed to oppression, the more mental and physical health problems they report (United States Department of Health and Human Services [USDHHS], 2001b).

Violence and Trauma

Violence and trauma are stressors that relate across cultural identities, including race/ethnicity, gender, socioeconomic status, and sexual orientation. Some immigrants were refugees and fled countries involved in war, killings, starvation, and sexual trauma. Research has linked repeated exposure to these forms of violence and trauma to mental health problems, such as Posttraumatic Stress Disorder and depression. These experiences, coupled with prejudicial attitudes and discriminatory practices in the United States, often make the immigration and acculturation processes more difficult (Ancis, 2004).

For those who have been in the United States for some time, there are daily experiences of violence and trauma. Many lower SES neighborhoods, with a disproportionate number of racial/ ethnic minorities and women as head of household (U.S. Census Bureau, 2001c), experience high levels of unemployment, crime, and violence. In addition, sexism (i.e., negative beliefs and behaviors about the ways in which women should be treated based on the notion that femininity is devalued and "less healthy") often has negative consequences for women by exposing them to potential sexual victimization and other forms of domestic violence. Individuals who identify as gay, lesbian, or bisexual also experience both violence and trauma as they seek safe, gay-affirmative environments and experience homophobic reactions from many in their schools and communities (Dworkin & Yi, 2003; Harper & Schneider, 2003). Thus, with each client, culturally competent counselors are encouraged to explore any incidents of violence or trauma in the client's daily experiences within school, work, and community. Violence and trauma are especially significant for clients with many oppressive experiences.

Culture and the Counseling Process

Many scholars (e.g., Ancis, 2004; Arredondo, 1999; Constantine, 2002a; Sue, Arredondo, & McDavis, 1992) have cited that culturally diverse clients, particularly racial and ethnic minorities, underuse counseling services and terminate counseling prematurely. Several factors may relate to these trends. First, the values of counseling may not be congruent with the values of various cultural groups. For example, counseling values mirror those of dominant U.S. values of individualism and autonomy, a preference for increased self-awareness, self-disclosure, and emotional expression, and an emphasis on a linear time orientation and goal-directedness. Many cultural groups often have different values such as collectivism and interdependence, limited disclosure out of respect for family and community members, and a circular time orientation. In addition, traditional counseling theories tend to minimize a systems approach, often pathologizing close connections among family members with terms such as *enmeshment* and *codependency* and minimizing community and historical factors.

Second, culturally diverse clients may perceive counseling to be a stigmatizing process because some cultures may view mental illness as something to be discussed only within a specific community. Many cultural groups rely on family members, community leaders, and spiritual healers to provide assistance with mental and physical health problems. In addition, kinship networks describe culturally normative behaviors based on age and gender roles (Lee, 1994). Thus, a client's informal support network may perceive traditional counseling to be a threat to community practices.

While reliance on informal support networks may be important for culturally diverse clients, another reason for the stigma view of counseling may be the way normality and abnormality have been defined in counseling. What constitutes normal behavior and thus optimal mental health? A common assumption in traditional counseling practice is that normality is a universal and consistent construct across social, cultural, historical, and political contexts. The role of culture is often ignored. Culture defines expression and attribution of mental health symptoms and thus what is considered normal and socially acceptable. This may make conceptualizing client issues difficult as Western ideas of normality and abnormality are used to make diagnostic decisions for all clients (Ancis, 2004). Thus, the underuse of services by culturally diverse clients may be related to inaccurate problem conceptualizations and thus misdiagnosis.

Third, culturally diverse clients are often mistrustful of counselors, who tend to be predominantly White (Pack-Brown, 1999), because of historical racist, sexist, classist, and heterosexist undertones in counseling practice. Counselors and counselor trainees have varying levels of awareness of the role cultural privilege and oppression play in both the counseling relationship and clients' daily lives (Ancis & Szymanski, 2001; Hays, Chang, & Dean, 2004; Hays, Dean, & Chang, 2007). There is also evidence that counselors may underdiagnose, overdiagnose, or misdiagnose culturally diverse clients' problems because of prejudice (Eriksen & Kress, 2004). This is typically done when the role of culture and sociopolitical issues are inappropriately applied in understanding clients' presenting concerns. A more detailed discussion of diagnosis and culture may be found in Chapter 17.

Finally, mental health services tend to be inaccessible to culturally diverse clients. For instance, there is a lack of mental health services in several communities where people of color and/or lower SES groups reside. Also, counseling is often unavailable for clients who are non-English speaking. The traditional practice of counseling lends itself to face-to-face, 50-minute sessions that only a small percentage of individuals can afford. Thus, counseling services are disproportionately available to clients.

There is a similar prevalence of mental health disorders across cultural groups (USDHHS, 2001a), yet underuse of services due to stigma or inaccessibility means that a higher proportion of individuals of minority statuses may have significant unmet mental health needs (Ancis, 2004). Given culturally specific stressors (e.g., prejudice, discrimination, immigration and acculturative stress, violence and trauma), it is imperative that counselors engage in multicultural counseling practices that better serve the needs of a diverse population. Counselors must continue to evaluate the current methods by which mental health services are delivered, the disproportionate distribution of mental health services, counselors' own biases about the values of counseling as well as those of culturally diverse clients, and ways by which the counseling profession may connect with other social, interpersonal, economic, and political institutions within communities. These goals are part of a call in the counseling profession to develop **multicultural counseling competence**.

DEVELOPING MULTICULTURAL COUNSELING COMPETENCE

Shifts in the demographic makeup of the United States in conjunction with the existence of current and historical experiences of oppression and other contextual factors for culturally diverse clients influence the quality of relationships among majority and minority groups (Arredondo, 1999; Sue et al., 1992; USDHHS, 2001a). Further, sociopolitical realities of minorities (i.e., oppression experiences) are often reflected and perpetuated within the counseling relationship. This has led to an increased focus on multicultural issues in general, and multicultural competencies more specifically, in counselor training, research, and practice. There is a growing consensus that multicultural competence is a necessary precursor to general competence for counselors, suggesting a strong relationship between general and multicultural competence (Constantine, 2002b; Fuertes & Brobst, 2002).

In response to the potential impact of increased diversity on the counseling profession, Sue and colleagues (Sue et al., 1982; Sue et al., 1992) constructed 31 multicultural counseling competencies (MCC) to introduce counselors to more effective ways to serve clients of color. Further, these competencies were designed to ensure a counselor's ability to attend to cultural factors in the clients' lives and in counseling (Fuertes, Bartholomeo, & Nichols, 2001). Sue et al. (1992) in the MCC standards argued that counselors should be self-aware, examine their beliefs and attitudes regarding other cultures, understand how various forms of oppression influence counseling, appreciate other cultural norms and value systems, and skillfully employ culturally appropriate assessments and interventions (Arredondo, 1999; Sue et al., 1992). Thus, a culturally competent counselor is defined as one who has self-awareness of values and biases, understands client worldviews, and intervenes in a culturally appropriate manner. While these standards were developed to primarily address racial and ethnic factors, the intersection with other cultural identities, such as gender, sexual orientation, socioeconomic status, and spirituality, are increasingly being addressed.

There are three overarching MCC dimensions with corresponding competencies and objectives related to counselor attitudes and beliefs, knowledge, and skills. You are encouraged to review the full description of MCC Standards and Guidelines (Sue et al., 1992; see also the appendix). The MCC may be summarized as follows:

I. Counselor Awareness of Own Cultural Values and Biases

Attitudes and Beliefs: Counselors are aware of themselves and their clients as cultural beings and appreciate these cultural differences. They also understand how their cultural backgrounds affect the counseling process.

Knowledge: Culturally sensitive counselors understand how their cultural backgrounds and values impact their definitions of optimal mental health, understand how oppression affects them personally and professionally, and understand the impact these two knowledge competencies have on their clients.

Skills: Counselors recognize limitations to their MCC and seek out continuing education and personal growth experiences to increase their competencies, which include developing a nonoppressive identity.

II. Counselor Awareness of Client's Worldview

Attitudes and Beliefs: Counselors are aware of how stereotypes and other negative reactions they hold about minority clients affect the counseling relationship, process, and outcome.

Knowledge: Counselors have knowledge of the cultural backgrounds, sociopolitical influences (e.g., acculturative stress, poverty, racism), help-seeking behaviors, within-group variation, identity development, and culturally relevant approaches specific to a particular cultural group with which they are working.

Skills: Counselors engage in personal and professional immersion experiences and research in which they can gain an understanding of unique mental health concerns and daily experiences for minority groups.

III. Culturally Appropriate Intervention Strategies

Attitudes and Beliefs: Counselors identify and respect community-specific values (e.g., spiritual beliefs, indigenous healing practices, language preferences) and actively integrate them into counseling interventions.

Knowledge: Counselors have knowledge of the culture and current practice of counseling, its limitations for work with minorities including existing bias in assessment and diagnostic procedures, limited accessibility for some communities, and restricted use of culturally specific and community resources.

Skills: Counselors engage in both verbal and nonverbal helping responses that are congruent with the helping style of their clients. During helping, counselors understand and articulate expectations and limitations of counseling assessments and interventions. In addition, counselors seek support and consultation from those in clients' communities in cases where healers and practitioners (e.g., language match, spiritual leadership) are appropriate and engage in social justice efforts to improve their clients' lives.

Throughout the text we will present information and activities that allow you to facilitate attitudes and beliefs, knowledge, and skills in a positive manner for working with culturally diverse populations. With respect to attitudes and beliefs, the text highlights ways in which cultural identities and socialization may lead to stereotyping those who are culturally different from ourselves. Several chapters illuminate common misperceptions of various cultural groups to change counselor attitudes and beliefs. In addition, examples of resilience strategies—including system-specific helping strategies—will be provided to challenge beliefs that marginalized groups lack internal strength to fight oppressive experiences. With respect to building knowledge, we offer information about the role that oppression and social advocacy plays in the lives of our clients and how the "culture" of counseling may at times not be appropriate for culturally diverse clients. There are several Test Your Knowledge activities, case studies, advocacy activities, classroom activities, tables, and figures that assist in developing counselors' attitudes and beliefs and knowledge base. For skill development, several personal growth and immersion activities are included to help counselors increase their toolbox of skills for working with all clients.

A Systems Approach to Multicultural Counseling Competence

Developing multicultural counseling competence involves taking a systems approach to working with culturally diverse clients. We cannot become multiculturally competent without considering the influence of family, community, and other environmental factors (e.g., social injustice) on clients' and our own lives, as well as how these systems intersect to create unique cultural experiences. As such, each of the components of a systems approach shown in Figure 1.2 and described below applies both to clients and counselors.

INDIVIDUAL   Culturally sensitive and thus multiculturally competent counselors have awareness, knowledge, and skills of individual-level cultural factors for clients. These include cultural group memberships (e.g., race, ethnicity, gender, sexual orientation, SES, spirituality, disability) and identity development statuses (e.g., racial identity development, level of acculturation, spiritual identity development) that accompany these various memberships. An individual's identity is influenced by and influences other systems. For example, how a gay male views his sexuality and gender are impacted by experiences within his family and surrounding community as well as historical events related to sexuality and gender.

FAMILY   For many culturally diverse clients, family plays a significant role in their cultural identities. Thus, it is imperative that multiculturally competent counselors understand how family as a system impacts clients' worldviews and behaviors. For example, families often affect clients' views of gender role socialization, culturally appropriate behavior, career and educational aspirations, and intimate relationships. In addition, violence and trauma within families could affect how clients perceive various cultural group memberships. To develop multicultural counseling competence, counselors acknowledge how families influence aspects of clients' cultural identities. In addition, they include clients' families in a culturally sensitive manner in counseling interventions as appropriate.

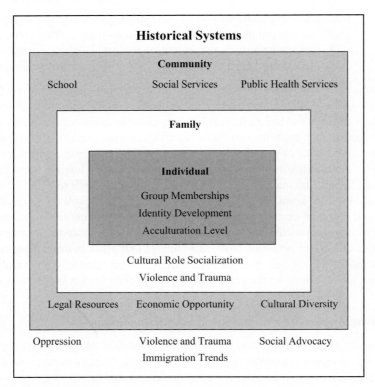

FIGURE 1.2   Systems approach to multicultural counseling competency.

COMMUNITY   Community systems include schools, mental health and other social services, spiritual institutions, public health systems, legal and economic resources, and within-group and between-group cultural diversity. Thus, the client and family experience is embedded with community values, resources, and practices. In developing multicultural counseling competence, counselors are encouraged to increase their awareness, knowledge, and skills in a manner that connects individual and family to community. This may involve connecting clients and their families to available resources, working to change community practices so that clients and their families may have positive mental and physical health outcomes, and increasing community awareness and resources to better serve culturally diverse clientele. Many of these tasks are congruent with the social advocacy movement described later in the text.

In addition to integrating systems, counselors are encouraged to understand how community as a system, and current events that take place in that community, influences clients' worldviews and behaviors. It is important that counselors have an awareness of how a client defines community because community may be defined in various ways. Counselors should explore within-group and between-group cultural diversity within a community along dimensions such as race, ethnicity, sexual orientation, and SES. In addition, counselors understand how current violence and trauma and prejudice and discrimination affect a client's view of community.

HISTORICAL   Historical systems are culturally based events for a community that impact a client. Some of these include racist acts against a particular racial group, the economy of a community, immigration patterns, civil rights events, and historic discrimination based on gender or sexual orientation. Particularly, historical experiences of oppression can create problems for many culturally diverse clients within a community, affecting access to resources, sense of belonging, and thus mental health status. Reflection 1.5 highlights a passage by Marilyn Frye (1983) that likens some historical systems to birdcages.

REFLECTION 1.5

Marilyn Frye (1983) writes:

> Consider a birdcage. If you look very closely at just one wire in the cage, you cannot see the other wires. If your conception of what is before you is determined by this myopic focus, you could look at that one wire, up and down the length of it, and be unable to see why a bird would not just fly around the wire any time it wanted to go somewhere. Furthermore, even if, one day at a time, you myopically inspected each wire, you still could not see why a bird would have trouble going past the wires to get anywhere. There is no physical property of any one wire, nothing that the closest scrutiny could discover, that will reveal how a bird could be inhibited or harmed by it except in the most accidental way. It is only when you step back, stop looking at the wires one by one, microscopically, and take a macroscopic view of the whole cage, that you can see why the bird does not go anywhere; and then you will see it in a moment. It will require no great subtlety of mental powers. It is perfectly obvious that the bird is surrounded by a network of systematically related barriers, no one of which would be the least hindrance to its flight, but which, by their relations to each other, are as confining as the solid walls of a dungeon.
>
> It is now possible to grasp one of the reasons why oppression can be hard to see and recognize: one can study the elements of an oppressive structure with great care and some good will without seeing the structure as a whole, and hence without seeing or being able to understand that one is looking at a cage and that there are people there who are caged, whose motion and mobility are restricted, whose lives are shaped and reduced. (p. 6)

- What are your reactions to this passage?
- Describe how various forms of prejudice, discrimination, and other contextual factors described earlier in this chapter may be conceptualized as a birdcage for clients of minority statuses.

In sum, counselors are charged with understanding how various systems intersect in their clients and their own lives to create unique cultural identities. This mutual understanding may allow counselors to have more developed competencies for multicultural counseling practice.

CONSIDERATIONS IN MULTICULTURAL COUNSELING

The field of counseling has made tremendous progress toward becoming more effective and accessible for members of diverse cultural groups. However, challenges in multicultural counseling still exist. This section highlights some of the major accomplishments of the multicultural counseling movement as well as potential barriers to competent cross-cultural counseling.

Social Justice and Advocacy Issues

The multicultural counseling competencies (Sue et al., 1992) call for counselors to examine their own biases and ways in which they may inadvertently oppress and discriminate against multicultural clients. In addition, counselors are challenged to increase their knowledge regarding the history and current status of privilege, oppression, and marginalization of minority groups on a societal level. This increased level of awareness and knowledge has led to a focus on social justice and advocacy in the counseling profession. Social justice refers to the commitment to ensuring change locally, nationally, and internationally based on the valuing of

> fairness and equity in resources, rights, and treatment for marginalized individuals and groups of people who do not share equal power in society because of their immigration, racial, ethnic, age, socioeconomic, religious heritage, physical ability, or sexual orientation status groups. (Constantine, Hage, Kindaichi, & Bryant, 2007, p. 24)

The social justice movement requires that the counselor expand his or her role to include advocate for social change. In other words, counselors for social justice walk the walk instead of just talking the talk with regard to multicultural competence and advocacy issues. Social justice efforts may include empowering a client, advocating for fair and equal treatment of clients within a counselor's workplace, conducting preventive psychoeducational workshops, working with community organizations, and advocating for policy change at the institutional and societal level.

Constantine et al. (2007) have defined nine social justice competencies:

1. Become knowledgeable about the various ways oppression and social inequities can be manifested at the individual, cultural, and societal levels, along with the various ways such inequities might be experienced by various individuals, groups, organizations, and macrosystems.
2. Participate in ongoing critical reflection on issues of race, ethnicity, oppression, power, and privilege in your own life.
3. Maintain an ongoing awareness of how your own positions of power or privilege might inadvertently replicate experiences of injustice and oppression in interacting with stakeholding groups (e.g., clients, community organizations, and research participants).
4. Question and challenge therapeutic or other intervention practices that appear inappropriate or exploitative and intervene preemptively, or as early as feasible, to promote the positive well-being of individuals or groups who might be affected.
5. Possess knowledge about indigenous models of health and healing and actively collaborate with such entities, when appropriate, in order to conceptualize and implement culturally relevant and holistic interventions.
6. Cultivate an ongoing awareness of the various types of social injustices that occur within international contexts; such injustices frequently have global implications.
7. Conceptualize, implement, and evaluate comprehensive preventative and remedial mental health intervention programs aimed at addressing the needs of marginalized populations.
8. Collaborate with community organizations in democratic partnerships to promote trust, minimize perceived power differentials, and provide culturally relevant services to identified groups.

9. Develop system intervention and advocacy skills to promote social change processes within institutional settings, neighborhoods, and communities. (pp. 25–26)

Improved Practice

Increased awareness of the need for competent multicultural counseling has led to numerous improvements in practice to better meet the needs of the communities in which we live. For example, counselor training programs have increased their emphasis on preparing culturally competent counselors. The Council for Accreditation of Counseling and Related Educational Programs (CACREP) requires that all counselor training programs provide students with educational experiences and exposure to multicultural issues. The multicultural counseling competencies (Sue et al., 1992) have, in fact, led to an increase in the knowledge, attitudes, and skills of many counselors. For example, many counselors may engage in self-reflection to identify and overcome biases. More counselors are aware of the need to work in collaboration with traditional healers or religious leaders from the client's community. School counselors are increasingly likely to create a "safe zone" for gay, lesbian, and bisexual students by decorating their offices with affirming posters or rainbow ribbons. Although tremendous strides have been made, numerous challenges still exist.

Etic Versus Emic Debate

Within the multicultural counseling literature, a debate over how broadly to conceptualize cultural differences exists. The **etic** approach focuses on universal qualities common to all cultures and aspects of counseling that are generalizable across cultures. The **emic** approach emphasizes "divergent attitudes, values, and behaviors arising out of specific cultures" (Ridley, Li, & Hill, 1998, p. 835) and calls for culturally specific counseling interventions. A limitation of the etic approach is a failure to account for legitimate cultural variations. The emic approach is sometimes criticized for overemphasizing specific counseling techniques as tools for change in multicultural counseling. The majority of multicultural counseling literature recommends the emic approach when working with clients from diverse cultural backgrounds. Viewing each client as an individual and evaluating the client using norms from within the client's culture helps reduce stereotyping, prejudice, and the tendency to impose cultural bias.

Within-Group Differences Versus Between-Group Differences

When working with culturally diverse clients, it is essential to remember that there are more within-group differences than between-group differences. Counselors should consider a client's cultural identity and context as well as individual attributes that may distinguish the client from the traditional norms associated with the client's cultural group. In addition, all clients possess multiple levels of cultural identity. The salience of different identities changes across time and context. The counselor should strive to validate and relate to which identity is most salient for the client at a given time (Sue et al., 1996). By viewing clients as unique individuals counselors may avoid stereotyping clients.

Underutilization of Services

Many scholars (e.g., Ancis, 2004; Arredondo, 1999; Constantine, 2002a; Sue et al., 1992) have noted that culturally diverse clients, particularly racial and ethnic minorities, underuse counseling services and terminate counseling prematurely. Several factors may relate to these trends. For example, the values inherent in most counseling approaches may not be congruent with the values of various cultural groups; culturally diverse clients may perceive counseling to be a stigmatizing process; culturally diverse clients are often mistrustful of counselors, who tend to be predominantly White; and mental health services tend to be inaccessible to culturally diverse clients.

Conflicting Cultural Values

Counseling values mirror those of the dominant U.S. values of individualism and autonomy, a preference for increased self-awareness, self-disclosure, and emotional expression, and an emphasis on a linear time orientation and goal-directedness. Many cultural groups often have different values such as collectivism and interdependence, limited disclosure out of respect for family and community members, and a circular time orientation. In addition, traditional counseling theories tend to minimize a systems approach, often pathologizing close connections among family members with terms such as *enmeshment* and *codependency* and minimizing community and historical factors.

Social Stigma

Culturally diverse clients may perceive counseling to be a stigmatizing process because some cultures may view mental illness as something to be discussed only within a specific community. Many cultural groups rely on family members, community leaders, and spiritual healers to provide assistance with mental and physical health problems. In addition, kinship networks describe culturally normative behaviors based on age and gender roles (Lee, 2005). Thus, a client's informal support network may perceive traditional counseling to be a threat to community practices. Reflection 1.6 presents process questions for you to think about your views on help-seeking behaviors.

REFLECTION 1.6

Respond to the following questions:
- How does your family of origin view seeking formal mental health services?
- What messages have you received about seeking formal mental health services from religious or spiritual organizations?
- What cultural groups you are a member of?
- How does the media portray "appropriate" help-seeking behaviors?
- When do you think it is necessary for someone to seek formal mental health services?
- How may your beliefs impact your work as a counselor?

While reliance on informal support networks may be important for culturally diverse clients, another reason for the stigma view of counseling may be the way normality and abnormality have been defined in counseling. What constitutes normal behavior and thus optimal mental health? A common assumption in traditional counseling practice is that normality is a universal and consistent construct across social, cultural, historical, and political contexts. The role of culture is often ignored. Culture defines expression and attribution of mental health symptoms and thus what is considered normal and socially acceptable. This may make conceptualizing client issues difficult as Western ideas of normality and abnormality are used to make diagnostic decisions for all clients (Ancis, 2004). Thus, the underuse of services by culturally diverse clients may be related to inaccurate problem conceptualizations and thus misdiagnosis.

Mistrust of the Counseling Profession

Culturally diverse clients are often mistrustful of counselors, who tend to be predominantly White (Pack-Brown, 1999), because of historical racist, sexist, classist, and heterosexist undertones in counseling practice. Counselors and counselor trainees have varying levels of awareness of the roles cultural privilege and oppression play in both the counseling relationship and clients' daily lives (Ancis & Szymanski, 2001; Hays, Chang, & Dean, 2004; Hays, Dean, & Chang, 2007).

Misdiagnosis

There is also evidence that counselors may underdiagnose, overdiagnose, or misdiagnose culturally diverse clients' problems because of prejudice (Eriksen & Kress, 2004). This is typically done when the role of culture and sociopolitical issues are inappropriately applied in understanding clients' presenting concerns. A more detailed discussion of diagnosis and culture may be found in Chapter 17.

Inaccessibility of Services

Mental health services tend to be inaccessible to culturally diverse clients. For instance, there is a lack of mental health services in several communities where people of color and/or lower SES groups reside. Also, counseling is often unavailable for clients who are non-English speaking. The traditional practice of counseling lends itself to face-to-face, 50-minute sessions that only a small number of individuals can afford. Thus, counseling services are disproportionately available to clients.

Resistance to Multiculturalism

Resistance to the multicultural movement in the field of counseling is still present today. Racism, sexism, ethnocentricism, heterosexism, and ageism are evident within the counseling profession and create barriers to change. In addition, multicultural counseling approaches call for counselors to exercise creativity and try new techniques. Competent multicultural practice requires additional effort on the part of the counselor and may not look like the empirically supported treatments that many counselors are comfortable with. In addition, while multiculturally competent counselors strive for collaborative relationships with clients and the community, some counselors may be unwilling to relinquish the power associated with the expert role.

Addressing Key Multicultural Considerations

We have presented several key multicultural counseling considerations—some of which highlight the benefits of developing MCC and some that emphasize the potential challenges to effective multicultural counseling. To minimize the social stigma attached to counseling, increase use of counseling services, and dismantle resistance to multiculturalism, it is imperative that we begin to build a resource list to introduce to clients the benefits of counseling, create social networks within our communities to make counseling more applicable and accessible to various individuals, and expand our own knowledge of available resources for our diverse clientele. Whereas other chapters in the text present more national resources for various client populations, Activity 1.3 offers an opportunity for counselors to develop a local resource list.

ACTIVITY 1.3

Investigate resources in your local community that help serve culturally diverse clients (e.g., race, ethnicity, gender, sexual orientation, socioeconomic status, spirituality, age, disability, and other cultural identities). Compile a referral list with contact information and a brief description of services provided.

Summary

Becoming a culturally sensitive counselor is a journey that lasts an entire professional career, and the journey is essential to undertake because of the diverse and changing U.S. population. Multicultural counseling recognizes the need for integration of cultural identities within the counseling process. Counselors sensitive to the needs of diverse clients understand and integrate numerous terms within the context of multiple cultural identities. Culture is the totality of human experience for social contexts and can be discussed within three dimensions: universal culture (common to all humankind), group culture (shared by a particular group), and individual culture (unique behaviors, attitudes, and cognitions). Cultural encapsulation (ethnocentrism) occurs when individuals adhere to a narrow and rigid view of the world and other cultures. Cultures are sometimes described as being on the individualism–collectivism continuum. Individualism values self-determination and independence, while collectivism involves decisions and important issues focusing on the betterment of others.

Race, ethnicity, and nationality are frequently discussed as major group classifications, but there are numerous other ways to describe cultural status, including generational status, gender, sexual orientation, socioeconomic status, disability, and spirituality. Further, it is essential to understand that all clients present with multiple cultural identifications and these identities come with privileges and oppressions. Privilege refers to the often unconscious and unearned power and advantages based upon social group membership. Oppression is the lack of power derived from certain social group memberships.

Thus, an individual may be a White, poorly educated, gay male who experiences privileges associated with White and male identities, and concomitant oppressions associated with being gay and of a lower socioeconomic status.

Worldview is conceptualized as one's relationship with the world and has been discussed using the dimensions of locus of responsibility and locus of control. Another way of discussing worldview involves the dimensions of view of human nature (e.g., humans are good, bad), relationship to nature (e.g., harmony, power over nature), sense of time (i.e., past, present, or future orientations), activity (i.e., individual self-expression), and social relationships (i.e., lineal–hierarchical, collateral–mutual, individualistic).

Multiculturally sensitive counselors engage in advocacy and social justice counseling to address the needs of diverse clients. Multiculturally sensitive approaches to counseling consider the intricacies of cross-cultural communication, particularly the differential cultural importance of verbal communication (e.g., use of metaphors), nonverbal communication (e.g., proxemics, kinesics, paralanguage), and emotional expression. Counselors need to understand the context of culture, both their clients' and their own, to help clients with diverse needs, particularly those experiencing prejudice (i.e., beliefs or attitudes without appropriate consideration of actual data) and discrimination (i.e., covert or overt behaviors based on generalizations about cultural group members).

Historically, many foreign-born individuals have come to settle in the United States through a process known as immigration. Acculturation refers to the degree to which immigrants identify with and conform to the new culture of a host society. Four models of acculturation include assimilation, separation, integration, and marginalization. Ordinarily, clients who are younger, have been in the host country longer, or are originally from countries with similar culture acculturate more quickly and easily. Some immigrants have experienced violence and trauma in their country of origin prior to immigrating. Counselors must be sensitive to the diverse, specialized needs of immigrants, remembering that (a) the values of counseling may not be congruent with the values of various cultural groups; (b) culturally diverse clients may perceive counseling to be stigmatizing; (c) culturally diverse clients are often mistrustful of counselors; and (d) mental health services tend to be inaccessible to culturally diverse clients.

To appropriately address the diverse needs of clients, counselors must strive to continuously develop multicultural counseling competence. The multicultural counseling competencies propose that counselors must become aware of their own cultural values and biases, the client's worldview, and culturally appropriate intervention strategies. As such, the systems approach to multicultural counseling competence proposed throughout this book must provide for the influences of individual, family, community, and other environmental factors on clients' and our own lives. We accomplish this through advocacy and social justice counseling approaches.

CHAPTER 2

Cultural Identity Development

CHERYL MOORE-THOMAS

PREVIEW

Cultural constructs significantly contribute to identity and personality development (Pedersen, 2000). "In fact, reality is a perceptual field that is constructed and deconstructed by individuals depending, in part, on their cultural group memberships" (Constantine, 2002a, p. 210). Racial and cultural identities, therefore, are important to consider in the movement toward multicultural counseling competence (see Arredondo et al., 1996; Mobley & Cheatham, 1999). Culturally competent counselors must not only consider issues of cultural identity as they relate to their clients, but also as they relate to themselves. Self-awareness of one's racial and ethnic identity development is undeniably reflected in the counseling relationship and client–counselor interaction processes. While this is true for counselors working in all cases, this may be of particular concern for counselors working with clients who do not share their racial, cultural, or ethnic heritage. Given the importance of identity development theory and related interventions and strategies to multiculturally competent counseling, this chapter begins with a review of key concepts that underlie the understanding of cultural identity development theory and models. The chapter continues with a discussion of several specific models of cultural identity development and factors that may affect that development. Finally, the chapter includes reflection activities and case studies to provide additional opportunities for readers to consider and apply concepts and theories in relation to self and the continuing development of multicultural counseling competence in work with clients.

KEY CONCEPTS

Although this chapter focuses on cultural identity development, a review and clarification of related vocabulary and key concepts is imperative. Broad discussions of culture, race, ethnicity, enculturation, and acculturation in particular provide the reader with a knowledge baseline aimed to enhance the understanding of and set a context for the cultural identity development text that follows.

Culture, Race, and Ethnicity

Within discussions of multicultural counseling the terms *culture, race,* and *ethnicity* are often used interchangeably and with little clarity. These terms include important distinctions. **Culture** is the set of "values, beliefs, expectations, worldviews, symbols, and appropriate behaviors of a group that provide its members with norms, plans, and rules for social living" (Gladding, 2001, p. 34). Relatedly, **cultural identity** is a process developed within the context of both formal and informal connections that leads not only to knowledge of values, beliefs, expectations, worldviews, symbols, and behaviors but also acceptance of those in personally meaningful ways (Pedersen, 2000). Cultural identity may refer to any cultural group classification including race, ethnicity, gender, sexual orientation, and spirituality. As the definitions suggest, culture and cultural identity are complex, multidimensional, and integrated. Understanding and appreciating the multidimensionality of culture and cultural identity gives counselors valuable insight regarding their own and their clients' sense of self, including language and communication patterns; values and beliefs; use of time and space; relationships with family and significant others; and ideas about play, work, and use of knowledge (Whitefield, McGrath, & Coleman, 1992). Activity 2.1 provides an opportunity to begin to explore this concept by reflecting on our silent but telling nonverbal markers of cultural identity.

ACTIVITY 2.1

Sometimes the most significant markers of our cultural identity are nonverbal. In groups of two or three people, take a few moments to think about your clothing, personal belongings, and home and work environments. Then discuss the following questions:

- What symbols of your cultural identity are present?
- Which are most congruent/salient for you?
- What do these symbols say about you?
- How might clients respond to these symbols?
- What surprised you about this reflection?
- In what ways were the findings surprising?

Race is a powerful political and socioeconomic construct that is correlated with artificial categorical differences in physical appearance (Brace, 1995; Yee, Fairchild, Weizmann, & Wyatt, 1993). This correlation can impact an individual's psychological functioning, including the identity development process. Understanding the complexity of race and its political, social, and economic implications allows counselors to more appropriately and fully address clients' concerns and their own issues of **racial identity development** (see Benedetto & Olisky, 2001; Bradley & Kiselica, 1998; Helms, 1995; Kwan, 2001; Tatum, 2003).

Ethnicity is related to race but moves beyond visible group membership and includes cultural and sociohistorical experiences (Holcomb-McCoy, 2005). Ethnicity is a "group classification in which members believe they share a common origin and a unique social and cultural heritage such as language or religious belief" (Gladding, 2001, p. 45) that is often passed from generation to generation. Ethnic classifications may help shape clients' sense of identity, appropriate behavior, and opportunity (Blum, 1998). While client-centered understandings of issues of race and ethnicity are important, counselors must also be aware of ascribed categorization and stereotyping that some clients experience. This may be a particular concern for clients who are members of **visible racial or ethnic groups**. These clients oftentimes negotiate not only internal developmental processes but also those placed on them by society or significant individuals in their lives. For example, a multiracial child, because of the color of her skin or texture of her hair, may be labeled by peers or teachers in a way that is inconsistent with her self-identity. Thus, **ethnic identity development** is a complex process in which individuals negotiate the degree that particular ethnicities belong to them. This negotiation is influenced in part by external evaluation.

Orthogonal cultural identity recognizes the multiplicity of coexisting identities in individuals. Orthogonal identity suggests that adaptation to cultures can be independent, and that true societal pluralism is possible. Simply stated, orthogonal cultural identity recognizes that individuals can belong to several cultures at the same time: It recognizes the possibility of multiethnic identity. This allows cultural groups to exist without isolation, remain appropriately distinct from the dominant culture, and maintain the kind of identity and preservation of culture that promotes physical and mental well-being (Pedersen, 2000).

Enculturation and Acculturation

Enculturation is the socialization process through which individuals learn and acquire the cultural and psychological qualities of their own group (Delgado-Romero, 2001). This cultural transmission process can take place through interactions with parents or caretakers (vertical cultural transmission), peers (horizontal cultural transmission), or from other adults and culturally based institutions or affiliations (oblique cultural transmission) (Berry, 1993). In contrast, acculturation involves changes in behavior, cognitions, values, language, cultural activities, personal relational styles, and beliefs as a cultural minority group comes in contact with the dominant culture. Models of biculturalism that reflect simultaneous adherence to both indigenous and host cultures explain this more complex process (Kim & Aberu, 2001). The process of bicultural identity development is discussed more fully later in this chapter.

Cultural Identity Development

Cultural identity development is the process of making one's cultural group membership salient. Most models of cultural identity development begin with stages of low salience or noncritical evaluation and acceptance of societal views and values regarding culture, and then move to high levels of involvement with the given culture and increased cultural knowledge and pride. This stage later resolves in definitions of self as a cultural being that integrate complex, multidimensional personality factors. It is important that information processing and behavioral responses oftentimes mediate these various stages of development (Mobley & Cheatham, 1999).

Some theorists refer to identity development statuses rather than stages. This language recognizes the dynamic, cyclical, and interactive nature of the construct. Human development rarely, if ever, occurs in discrete stages. Often developmental trajectories spiral rather than move in linear paths. Such is the case with cultural identity. Although clients may display characteristics of multiple or overlapping statuses, it is possible and at times helpful to be able to assess a client's primary ego status. The *White Racial Identity Attitude Scale* (Helms & Carter 1990), *Self-Identity Inventory* (Sevig, Highlen, & Adams, 2000), the *Cross Racial Identity Scale* (CRIS; Vandiver, Fhagen-Smith, Cokley, Cross, & Worrell, 2001) and the *Multigroup Ethnic Identity Measure* (Phinney, 1992) are but a few of the instruments based on theoretical models of cultural identity that are used to assess identity.

In summary, cultural identity is of great importance to counselors because it provides a framework that assists in the understanding of client identification within social and cultural contexts and the effects of culture, ethnicity, race, and acculturation and enculturation processes in counseling. Culturally competent counselors can use this knowledge to facilitate clients' understanding of self, individuals, communities, and social interactions, as well as determine nonstereotyped counseling interventions that are based on clients' needs, worldviews, and significant contextual factors (Sevig et al., 2000; Tse, 1999).

RACIAL AND ETHNIC IDENTITY DEVELOPMENT

The previous section explored terminology and general concepts related to cultural identity. With these understandings in place, major principles and specific models of racial and ethnic identity development theory will now be reviewed.

Racial Identity Models

When considering the vast literature base on cultural identity development, discussions often begin with theory and models of racial identity. Cross's (1971, 1995) groundbreaking work on the process through which African Americans came to understand their Black identity gave birth to other significant models of racial identity development most notably including Helms's (1995) people of color and White racial identity models, and Ponterotto's (1988) model of cultural identity for White counselor trainees. Reviews of the Cross, Helms, and Ponterotto models follow.

CROSS'S NIGRESCENCE MODEL   In the early 1970s Cross began reflecting on the psychology of nigrescence, or the psychology of becoming Black. Cross's model (1971b, 1995), which he developed and continued to shape over the years, identified stages people go through as they affirm and come to understand their own Black identity. These stages begin with *Pre-Encounter,* which includes a preexisting identity or an identity to be changed. Individuals navigating this stage may hold low salience for race or anti-Black attitudes. The *Encounter* stage, the second stage of the model, induces identity change. During this stage, individuals experience a personalized encounter that challenges or gives credence to their personal experience of blackness. During the *Immersion–Emersion* stage, individuals immerse themselves in the symbols and signs of Black culture. This oversimplified cultural identification resolves as individuals emerge with a more sophisticated and nuanced understanding of Black identity. Cross's fourth stage, *Internalization,* is marked by self-acceptance and a proactive Black pride that infuses everyday life while leaving room for appreciation of other dimensions of diversity. *Internalization–Commitment,* the fifth and final stage, challenges individuals to integrate their personal sense of Black identity into a way of being and/or long-lasting commitment to the Black community and issues.

More recently Cross's model has been expanded to include a focus on attitudes and social identities (Cross & Vandiver, 2001) that are shaped by events and contexts of group identity across the life span. Rather than developmental stages, the expanded model is marked by three thematic categories—preencounter, immersion–emersion, and internalization, that suggest multiple identities rather than one type of Black identity. Thus, the expanded model of nigrescence allows for negotiation of various levels of multiple attitudes simultaneously. Each of these thematic categories describes frames of reference or ways of understanding the world (Worrell, Cross, & Vandiver, 2001). *Preencounter* attitudes of the expanded model include assimilation to White culture that may reflect low race salience or self-hatred. *Immersion–emersion* attitudes are marked by changing and intense themes of pro-Black and anti-White involvements that move toward more complex understandings of race and identity. *Internalization* themes can be recognized by a positive adherence to a Black cultural identity that acknowledges the salience of other racial and cultural identities of self and others (Worrell, Vandiver, Schaefer, Cross, & Fhagen-Smith, 2006). Cross's work on racial identity development theory influenced the development of many other models including Helms's people of color and White identity models. These two models are briefly reviewed in the following section.

HELMS'S PEOPLE OF COLOR IDENTITY MODEL   Helms's (1995) people of color identity model includes the ego statuses of Conformity (Pre-Encounter), Dissonance, Immersion/Emersion, Internalization, and Integrative Awareness. The *Conformity* status includes acceptance of racial characteristics and external self-definition. Individuals negotiating this status may feel uncomfortable around other people of color or blame the group for societal challenges or social ills. During this status, information is processed selectively and with no awareness of racism or socioracial concerns.

Characteristic of the *Dissonance* status is confusion about one's connection to groups of people of color and Whites. This confusion may result from cross-racial interactions that elucidate personal or one's reference group's experiences with racism. One may also experience guilt and anxiety about personal feelings or beliefs about people of color. As a result, information related to race is often repressed.

During the *Immersion/Emersion* status, people of color idealize their own racial group while devaluing what is perceived to be White and expressing resistance to oppressive external forces. Individuals in this stage tend to process information in a dichotomous manner that expresses hypervigilance toward racial stimuli.

The *Internalization* status is characterized by the capacity to use internal criteria for self-definition as well as the ability to objectively respond to Whites. Flexible and analytic information processing are aligned with this status.

The final status, *Integrative Awareness*, includes a valuing of one's collective identities and the recognition and appreciation of the similarities between oppressed people. This results in a universal and inclusive resistance to oppression and commitment to social and political activism and abilities to process information using flexible and complex strategies.

HELMS'S WHITE IDENTITY MODEL   Helms's (1995) White identity model includes six statuses that describe how Whites interpret and respond to racial cues. Each ego status is a multifaceted expression of an individual's identity and is accompanied by specific information processing strategies which reflect certain race-related attitudes, behaviors, and feelings. The model's first status is the *Contact* ego status. This status is characterized by satisfaction with the status quo and acceptance of socially imposed racial characterizations and rules. The associated information processing strategy is rooted in nonawareness of race and its associated issues.

The *Disintegration* status is marked by confusion regarding one's commitment to one's own group and racial moral dilemmas. A way of processing information in this stage includes ambivalence, suppression, or movement between feelings of comfort and discomfort about race. Individuals may respond to this ambivalence and confusion in two ways, as described in the following two statuses.

The *Reintegration* status involves idealization and championing of one's own group and group entitlement. External standards are used to define self and others. During this status, individuals express out-group distortions or a lack of empathy for others.

In the fourth ego status, *Pseudo-Independence*, individuals rationalize commitment to their own group and tolerance of others. Tolerance of others, however, is based on the acceptance of White standards. The information processing strategy for this status involves selective perception or paternalistic attitudes that reshape reality.

The *Immersion/Emersion* status challenges Whites to understand how they have benefited and contributed to racism. It requires questioning, self-reflection, and critical analysis that may result in an information processing strategy that yields hypervigilant responses to racism.

TABLE 2.1 Helms's Models of Racial Identity Development	
People of Color Racial Identity Model	**White Racial Identity Model**
Conformity (Pre-Encounter) Status	Contact Status
Example: "We would be better off if we would stop talking about race. Focusing on race is keeping us from moving forward."	*Example:* "I don't know what Black people complain about. I work hard, too. That is what you have to do in life. You have to work hard to get ahead. It is as simple as that."
Dissonance (Encounter) Status	Disintegration Status
Example: "I am the only person of color in my class. I don't fit in with the White students, but in high school I never really fit in with the students of color. I thought this college was a good choice for me. Now, I am not so sure."	*Example:* "My college is wonderful, but I am concerned that no students of color are in leadership positions. I didn't even notice it until Helen mentioned it to me. I guess it is true. I wonder what is going on."
Immersion/Emersion Status	Reintegration Status
Example: "When I moved into the dorm I made sure I put Black art on the walls and I only played music by Black artists. I know who I am and I am proud of it."	*Example:* "I work hard just like my parents and grandparents did. If Whites are willing to work hard to get ahead and others are not, whose fault is that?"
Internalization Status	Pseudoindependence Status
Example: "I am not defined by what I choose to wear or what kind of music I like. To me, being Black is so much more than that. I haven't figured it all out yet, but I do know my race is bigger than some particular kind of dress or item."	*Example:* "I think people of color can learn from what White people and others have done right in this country. If we all work together we can make this world a better place. I think I am going to volunteer at the after-school program down the street. I have a lot I can offer those children."
Integrative Awareness Status	Immersion/Emersion
Example: "I enjoy the diversity in my class. I am the only person of color in the class, but through interacting with others I learn more about them and more about me. It is sort of unexpected, but I think I now appreciate who I am and who others are in a more complete way. I like what I bring to the class as a person of color. I also like what others bring to the class."	*Example:* "I did not have anything to do with the fact that no people of color were elected to positions in student government. It isn't even my fault that no people of color were selected to head any of the subcommittees. I have to ask myself some hard questions. An even tougher job will be trying to figure out what I am willing to do about all of this. But, I can't do nothing. I have to do something."
	Autonomy Status
	Example: "I chose this college because I wanted to learn from diverse people and points of view. I think that is really valuable. I can't continue to grow only seeing the world from one point of view. I want true change for the world. That can't happen if we as people don't get to know each other in real ways."

The final status of the model is *Autonomy*. Whites operating in this ego status use internally derived definitions of self, demonstrate positive racial group commitment, and possess the capacity to relinquish racial privilege. Flexibility of thoughts and attitudes is the hallmark of the processing strategy for this status (Daniels, 2001; Helms, 1995). Table 2.1 summarizes Helms's models.

Racial identity for people of color and Whites may mediate relationships, including counseling interactions. Helms's (1995) work on **racial interaction theory** discusses the interaction effects of expressed racial identity development strata between client and counselor and the effects of those interactions on therapeutic change. Specifically, Helms describes **parallel interactions**, which emphasize congruent race-based communications that deny or avoid tension. In this type of interaction harmony is obtainable because the participants share similar or analogous ego statuses that ascribe to similar racial attitudes and assumptions. For example, counselors and clients working at preawareness statuses of racial identity development may be able to establish comfortable counseling environments, but because of the developmental status of each, meaningful exploration of issues of race and culture may not occur.

Regressive interactions are marked by differentiated social status of the participants with the participant of higher social power exhibiting a less complex ego status. A client working with a counselor operating at a regressive status of interaction may be frustrated because the counselor may be unable to recognize or acknowledge the issues of race as related to the client's concerns.

Progressive interactions are also marked by differentiated status. In these interactions, however, the participant of higher social power also possesses a more cognitively complex ego status and may therefore be able to respond to racial events in a more complete and growth-engendering manner. Counselors operating from progressive interaction statuses may be able to assist clients to recognize broader issues of race and culture and work toward possibilities and solutions that facilitate client integration and development.

PONTEROTTO'S MODEL OF CULTURAL IDENTITY DEVELOPMENT   Ponterotto (1988) suggested a model to be used specifically with White counselor trainees. In the *Preexposure* stage, White counselor trainees unfamiliar with multicultural issues are comfortable with the status quo. During the *Exposure* stage, trainees become aware of racism and other issues of diversity. This awareness is often initiated by coursework in multicultural counseling and may lead to feelings of anger, guilt, and motivation for change. In the *Zealot-Defensive* stage, White counselor trainees may become pro-minority and anti-White. In the *Integration* stage, a balanced perspective is achieved as White counselors in training are able to process their emotions and make meaning of their learning and growing levels of cultural awareness. Awareness of this model may help White counselor trainees reflect on their cultural identity development and the manner in which associated information processing strategies affect values, beliefs, worldviews and interactions with clients.

Counselors are encouraged to use cultural identity theory and models to better understand clients. The importance of using cultural identity theory and models to better understand oneself, however, is equally important. Activity 2.2 encourages reflection on several questions that may prove helpful in your exploration of your own cultural identity. The activity highlights and reinforces some of the themes discussed in the preceding review of many of the field's most significant models of cultural identity development.

ACTIVITY 2.2

In small groups, reflect on your cultural identity. How would you describe your cultural heritage? How has that heritage affected your worldview, behaviors, attitudes, beliefs, and values? List three specific ways your cultural heritage is shaping your emerging professional identity:

1. _____

   _____

2. _____

   _____

3. _____

   _____

What implications do these manifestations of your cultural heritage have with your work with clients who are culturally similar? What implications do these manifestations of your cultural heritage have with your work with clients who are culturally dissimilar?

Research suggests that individuals' cultural identities take shape around the age of 10 years and are necessary for the development of a healthy self-concept and intercultural perspectives (Holcomb-McCoy, 2005). Early examination of cultural identity is therefore crucial. Phinney (1996) proposed a model of ethnic identity that explores this important issue in early adolescents.

Phinney's Model of Ethnic Identity

Phinney (1996) described ethnic identity as self-perceived significance of ethnic group membership that includes a sense of membership in an ethnic group and the attitudes and feelings that are associated with that membership. Phinney's model of ethnic identity suggests that young adolescents, due to a lack of need, interest, or relevance, may experience a status of identity development that is ill-defined. This first stage of *unexamined or diffused ethnic identity* leads adolescents to either accept or take on ethnic identities of significant family members without exploration, or accept and internalize stereotyped identities that pervade the media and popular culture. Phinney's second stage is marked by *exploration of identity and differentiation* of the culture of origin and the dominant culture. This stage, which is called *moratorium,* involves emotional experiences and a rapid sense of personal and cultural awareness as adolescents begin to shape a personal understanding of who they are as cultural beings. During the final stage of the model, individuals gain increased *acceptance* of their identity in ways that are healthy and allow for full appreciation of multiculturalism.

Some research is available that explores the relationship between ethnic identity and academic achievement for adolescents. Phinney (1992) found that high school students with more developed levels of ethnic identity were more likely to report grades of A or B, than those with lower levels of developed ethnic identity, while Guzman, Santiago-Rivera, and Haase (2005) found no significant relationship between levels of developed ethnic identity and self-reported grades of Mexican American students. Looking specifically at African American students, Sandoval, Gutkin, and Naumann (1997) found that adolescents' racial identity attitudes were significantly related to their academic achievement. Examining the same population, Chappell and Overton (2002) found that African American adolescents' reasoning performance was positively associated with stronger ethnic identity. While the research in this area is still developing, it appears that these initial findings could have important implications for counselors who work with young adolescent populations. In far-reaching and perhaps unexpected ways, who adolescents are as cultural beings could have connections with who they are and how they see themselves in other aspects of development. Reflection 2.1 will help you think about Phinney's model in a more personally relevant way. Use the activity to think about how the major concepts of Phinney's model apply to your own early cultural identity development.

REFLECTION 2.1

Phinney (1996) conceptualized ethnic identity as having three statuses. In what ways does her model resonate with your personal experiences of ethnic identity development? Recognizing that ethnic identity development is ongoing, what was one of your earliest memories of movement through the following ethnic identity statuses:

1. Unexamined or diffused identity:

_____

_____

_____

2. Search/Moratorium:

_____

_____

_____

3. Identity achievement:

_____

_____

_____

One of the benefits of Phinney's (1996) model is that it can be applied to all racial and ethnic groups (i.e., it is a multigroup model). It does not, however, address multiracial or multiethnic identity development. The following section introduces models that explore multiracial and multiethnic identity development.

Biracial and Multiracial Identity Development

In recent years the population of multiracial individuals in the United States has increased dramatically. According to the 2000 U.S. Census, 2.4% of the population, or approximately 7 million people, self-identified as multiracial—that is, belonging to many racial or ethnic groups (Miville,

Constantine, Baysden, & So-Lloyd, 2005). Given the complex history of race, culture, and identity in America, it is important that specific attention be given to the cultural and racial identity development of the biracial and multiracial communities.

BIRACIAL IDENTITY DEVELOPMENT   Poston (1990) developed one of the first models of biracial identity development after recognizing the inability of race specific models to adequately describe the developmental trajectory of biracial individuals or individuals whose parents come from two different races. Poston's five-stage model includes Personal Identity, Choice Group Categorization, Enmeshment/Denial, Appreciation, and Integration. *Personal Identity* occurs when a child or young person's sense of self is primarily based on personality constructs that develop within the family context rather than a race or culturally specific group context. As a result of this development, individuals in this stage may not be aware of their biracial heritage. In the second stage of the model, *Choice Group Categorization*, individuals are forced to choose an ethnic or racial identity because of peer, situational, community, or physical appearance factors. During *Enmeshment/Denial*, individuals may feel guilt, disloyalty, and self-hatred rooted in choices made during the previous stage of development. During the fourth stage, *Appreciation*, multiple heritages are explored as individuals engage in activities and traditions, and learn about the histories and worldviews of their previously ignored racial or cultural group. During the final stage of Poston's model (*Integration*), individuals experience a sense of wholeness as they learn to integrate their multiple cultural identities in personally meaningful ways. While many move through this stage gaining a biracial identity, others may maintain a single race identity that values multiculturalism.

The research base in biracial identity is in its infancy. However, Kerwin and Ponterotto (1995) attempted to integrate existing empirical data in an age-based model that acknowledges variance in identity influenced by personal, social, and environmental factors. In the Kerwin and Ponterotto model, children from birth through 5 years of age recognize similarities and differences in skin color and hair texture. This awareness that is characteristic of the *Preschool* stage may be due to parents' heightened sensitivity or by contrast, parents' denial of the tangible differences in biracial families. In the *Entry to School* stage, biracial children may be forced to classify themselves. This is often done with a monoracial label, or a descriptive term that identifies skin color. During Kerwin and Ponterotto's third stage, *Preadolescence*, youth become increasingly aware of group membership and the social meanings ascribed to skin color, race, hair texture, language, and culture. Increased social interactions and other environmental factors may trigger this heightened level of awareness. In the *Adolescence* stage, developmental (e.g., the need to belong, intolerance for difference) and societal factors pressure biracial youth to choose a specific cultural group identity. Biracial individuals may enter the *College/Young Adulthood* stage continuing to embrace a single culture identity; however, the expanding sense of self that is experienced during this period of growth often results in the capacity and desire to integrate one's multiple heritages. Finally, the *Adulthood* stage is characterized by further exploration of one's race and culture and increased flexibility in one's interpersonal relations and understanding of self.

MULTIRACIAL IDENTITY DEVELOPMENT   In contrast to these stage models, Root (1998) offered an ecological model of multiracial identity development that recognizes gender, politics, socioeconomic status, inherited influences (e.g., language, phenotype, sexual orientation, nativity, name), traits and skills, social interactions, and racial and ethnic groupings as contributors to identity development. As a result of these ecological factors, Root concluded multiracial identity can be situational, simultaneous, flexible, and variant in private and public domains. Furthermore, Root's study of multiracial siblings found that multiracial identity development is significantly influenced by family dynamics, sociopolitical histories, hazing (i.e., a demeaning process of racial or ethnic authenticity testing), and other group affiliations including those with religious and career/professional groups.

The racial and ethnic identity development models discussed in this chapter are but a few of the many models currently being examined in the research literature. There are several race and ethnicity specific models that due to space limitations could not be discussed. These include Ruiz's (1990) Chicano/Latino ethnic identity model; Choney, Berryhill-Paapke, and Robbins's (1995) health model for American Indians; and Sodowsky, Kwan, and Pannu's (1995) nonlinear model of Asian ethnic identity development.

In the interim, counselors are encouraged to learn more about the models reviewed in this chapter and others. Furthermore, counselors may find it helpful to use theories and models of racial and ethnic identity development to form initial client case conceptualizations. These important first steps may provide insight and clinical direction for counselors' work with diverse clients. Case Study 2.1 applies cultural identity theory to illustrate this point.

CASE STUDY 2.1

Quang, a Vietnamese student, is new to Oakdale High School. Quang is 14 years old. He has attended school in the northern part of Vietnam since he was a little boy. Quang was sent to America to live with his cousin and to continue his education. Unfortunately, Quang and his cousin do not know each other well. They met only one week ago. Quang and his cousin visit the school counselor's office to register for high school. They do not have any school records; however, Quang has been cleared by the school district's international student office to start high school.

After meeting with Quang and his cousin, the counselor recognized that Quang's transition to Oakdale High School would likely be uniquely affected by several multicultural counseling issues including acculturation and cultural identity development processes. He also realized that although Quang was his student, Quang's cousin was significant to Quang's academic achievement. For that reason, the school counselor reflected on the role of family support in mediating possible feelings of marginalization. Furthermore, the counselor realized that in his efforts to establish a productive counseling relationship with Quang, he would need to examine his own biases, values, and worldview. Given the school counselor's lack of familiarity with Vietnamese culture, he decided to consult with a colleague and school counseling literature on issues of identity development in the Vietnamese culture. He also understood that to blindly apply any acquired knowledge to Quang would be unethical. He decided that as he continued to meet with Quang on a biweekly basis, he would gain insight on the salience of cultural identity development and other diversity factors to Quang's transition to high school.

Addressing Racial and Ethnic Identity in Counseling

Understanding and integrating appropriate principles of racial and ethnic identity may help counselors understand within-group differences (Liu, Pope-Davis, Nevitt, & Toporek, 1999) and normalize and process clients' cognitive, emotional, and behavioral responses (Hargrow, 2001). While allowing clients the opportunity to appreciate the universality of their emotional and behavioral responses and experiences, using the discussed racial and ethnic identity models and other similar models may provide counselors with opportunities to validate clients' unique experiences and feelings. Counselors do not force movement through developmental statuses. However, counselors can and should assist clients in thinking and responding in more productive ways. This broadening of perspective can lead to beneficial, self-realized cultural identity development (Tse, 1999). Furthermore, understanding these developmental models in client-specific cultural contexts can assist counselors in providing counseling interventions that not only address clients' presenting concerns, but also foster continued identity development. This can be done by identifying and utilizing systems of support for clients and providing opportunities for clients to tell their own stories regarding their identity development. Moreover, counselors should consider integrating activities such as journaling, creative writing, drawing/painting, art and music projects, and constructing genograms to help clients explore their cultural heritage, beliefs, and values (Delgado-Romero, 2001). Questions related to self-definition of culture and cultural identity; clarification of value systems, religious and cultural expectations, family experiences, experiences with racism, oppression, discrimination, and marginalization; and exploration of confusion and dissonance regarding cultural identity are also helpful (Daniels, 2001; Delgado-Romero, 2001).

Practicing counselors and counselor trainees must also seek to increase self-awareness and historical competence regarding issues of multiculturalism through continued study, training, and clinical supervision. This stance demands a willingness to confront and challenge negative or distorted culturally based perceptions. Furthermore, counselors must engage in advocacy and social justice issues that address discrimination against individuals of diverse cultures. More specific discussion of these implications can be found in later chapters.

GENDER AND SEXUAL IDENTITY DEVELOPMENT

The identity development models discussed thus far have provided a framework for understanding how individuals come to understand themselves as racial and ethnic beings. In reality, people navigate multiple, intersecting cultural and social identities throughout life. Important intersecting identities yet to be discussed in this text include gender and sexual identity development. Gender identity development or male and female awareness and acceptance, and sexual identity or sexual orientation awareness and acceptance are theorized to move through statuses and processes in ways similar to those of race and ethnicity. As individuals navigate these important aspects of self-identity, the movement is never completely linear or straightforward. Development intersects with and responds to biological, psychological, and social influences. Beginning with a discussion of three major gender identity models, the following section reviews gender identity and concludes with a discussion of several sexual identity models in relation to important contextual influences and counseling considerations.

Gender Identity Models

The identity development models discussed thus far provide a framework for understanding how individuals come to understand themselves as racial and ethnic beings, but fail to address the convergence of race and gender. The dominant and dynamic statuses of race and gender, however, may have significant implications for individual development and therefore cannot be overlooked (Davenport & Yurich, 1991). To fill the void, gender-specific models have been developed. Discussions of the key model (Scott & Robinson, 2001), the Downing and Roush (1985) feminist identity development model, and the Hoffman (2006) model of feminist identity follow.

While it is important to note that males and females may develop gender identities that do not conform to traditional notions, data do suggest that males are exposed to stereotyped gender information and norms at an early age. These include encouragement to be assertive, powerful, strong, independent, and courageous. Furthermore, males are encouraged to restrict display of their emotions that suggest vulnerability (e.g., sadness, fear). These implicit and explicit messages often converge into a more specific, and perhaps more dangerous, stereotyped notion of manhood that largely conforms to White, middle-class, Christian, heterosexual images (Scott & Robinson, 2001). Driving this classification is the culturally pervasive and competitive desire for power and control of economic and social structures. This poses an interesting challenge for White men. Given their position in American society as privileged due to their race and gender, it is understandable that the theory to describe the cultural development of White men would involve those factors. The key model of White male development recognizes the primary developmental task for men to be the abandonment of entitlement that leads to a greater sense of self that is neither defined nor restricted by debilitating socialized notions of male identity.

THE KEY MODEL   The key model (Scott & Robinson, 2001) describes types of gender identity attitudes for White males that are flexible and responsive to situations and experiences. The *Noncontact* type describes attitudes which have little awareness of race, where race is ignored, denied, or minimized. Traditional gender roles are valued. In general, the status quo is reverenced with no recognition of the ways in which current conditions may not meet the needs of diverse people. The second type, the *Claustrophobic* type, holds attitudes that blame women and people of color for any personal discomfort related to lack of accomplishment, progress, or privilege. Men in this stage of development believe "others"—namely women, immigrants, and people of color—prevent them from acquiring what rightfully belongs to them. The *Conscious* type reevaluates his belief system due to a precipitating event that creates internal dissonance. He begins to recognize the role of racism and sexism in sociopolitical events. The *Empirical* type more fully recognizes the implications of sexism and racism and his role in their perpetuation. Furthermore, he becomes aware of his own unearned power and privilege. Finally, the *Optimal* type has an understanding of diversity and the rewards of interacting with others in a holistic way. He is committed to the elimination of oppression in all of its forms and measures himself based on internal measures rather than stereotyped ideas of maleness.

DOWNING AND ROUSH'S MODEL OF FEMINIST IDENTITY   Like the key model (Scott & Robinson, 2001), the Downing and Roush (1985) model of feminist identity describes progression from unawareness of inequity and discrimination to commitment to meaningful action aimed to eliminate discrimination and sexism. The *Passive Acceptance* stage involves acceptance of traditional sex roles with denial or unawareness of prejudice and discrimination against women. The *Revelation* stage involves a crisis or series of crises that lead to self-examination of roles and ideas and dualistic thinking that affirms women and denigrates men. *Embeddedness–Emanation* leads to involvements with women that are supportive and affirming and over time lead to more relativistic thinking regarding men. The fourth stage, *Synthesis*, is characterized by positive identity that integrates personal and feminist identities. The *Active Commitment* stage focuses on action toward meaningful societal change and identification of personal goals of empowerment.

HOFFMAN'S MODEL OF FEMINIST IDENTITY   More recently Hoffman (2006) proposed a theoretically inclusive model of female identity that identifies statuses of Unexamined Female Identity, Crisis, Moratorium/Exploration, and Achieved Female Identity. The model moves from women's endorsement of a passive acceptance stance to one of revelation. These endorsements are embodied in Hoffman's *Unexamined Female Identity* and *Crisis* statuses, respectively. The *Moratorium/Exploration* and *Achieved Female Identity* statuses of her model are characterized by women's commitments to active identity search and identity synthesis. Integral to this model is an understanding of gender self-confidence. Gender self-confidence is the degree of alignment with one's personal standards of femininity or masculinity. In essence, gender self-confidence is the degree to which one accepts and values himself or herself as a male or female. Furthermore, in Hoffman's model gender self-confidence encompasses gender self-definition and gender self-acceptance, offering a new understanding to gender identity development theory. Table 2.2 presents a comparison of this model with the Downing and Roush (1985) model.

ADDRESSING GENDER IDENTITY IN COUNSELING   Although gender is an important identity construct, counselors must be mindful of the varying degrees of salience it holds for individual clients. In therapeutic environments, it is important for clients to have the opportunity to share their personal stories and sexual scripts and ideologies (i.e., images, perceptions, messages, thoughts, and behaviors that guide and shape identity development) in safe, nonjudgmental environments so that counselors may acknowledge feelings and discern the ways in which gender identity intersects with the clients' presenting problems (see Stephens & Phillips, 2003; Striepe & Tolman, 2003). Counselors must also recognize that gender identity statuses are not hierarchical; one status is not higher or better than another. Each represents a worldview that describes values, perspectives, and aims. It is the counselor's responsibility to help clients clarify their worldview and understand the benefits and costs of particular ways of interacting in the world. This may require the use of didactic, cognitive, affective, or behavioral counseling interventions including the facilitation of culturally relevant decision-making processes. Furthermore, counselors must be cognizant of personal gender identity statuses and the implications of their own development on their work with clients. Clinical supervision, training, and self-reflection may provide opportunities to carefully monitor these implications.

TABLE 2.2 Feminist Identity Models

Downing and Roush Model	Hoffman Model
Passive Acceptance	Unexamined Female Identity
Acceptance of traditional women's roles	*Acceptance of traditional women's roles*
Revelation	Crisis
Consciousness-raising experiences that affirm women and denigrate men	*Awareness of societal discrimination of women*
Embeddedness–Emanation	Moratorium/Exploration
Involvement in supportive relationships with women and selected men	*Commitment to active identity search*
Synthesis	Achieved Female Identity
Integration of personal and feminist identities	*Synthesis of female identity*
Active Commitment	
Movement toward empowerment, societal change, and activism	

Sources: Adapted from Downing and Roush (1985); Hoffman (2006).

Sexual Identity Models

Several identity development models describe the cultural identity process for sexual minorities (e.g., gay, lesbian, bisexual, questioning). In general, sexual identity is conceptualized as a continuous, developmental process that begins with awareness of same sex attraction and exploration, and culminates in self-acceptance, disclosure, and identity integration. These processes are more fully described in the following descriptions of Cass's (1990) model of sexual identity, Troiden's model of sexual identity (1989), McCarn and Fassinger's (1996) model of lesbian/gay identity formation, and Weinberg, Williams, and Pryor's (1996) model of bisexual identity. Table 2.3 summarizes the models of sexual identity development discussed in this chapter.

CASS' MODEL OF SEXUAL IDENTITY   Cass's (1979) work on sexual identity formation is among the earliest. Beginning in the late 1970s, Cass proposed a six-stage model of development that affirmed homosexual identity. *Conscious Awareness*, the first stage of the model, is marked by a realization that gay, lesbian, or bisexual identity is possible. Individuals in this stage may feel alienated as they wrestle with this inner realization. *Identity Comparison* begins as individuals leave the first stage of development and start to tentatively commit to a homosexual identity. Here, awareness of the

TABLE 2.3 Sexual Identity Development Models

	Cass	Troiden	McCarn & Fassinger	Weinberg et al.
Stage 1	Conscious Awareness	Sensitization	Awareness	Initial Confusion
Key Traits	*Realization*	*Awareness*	*Awareness at individual and group levels*	*Unsettled feelings*
Stage 2	Identity Comparison	Identity Confusion	Exploration	Finding and Applying Labels
Key Traits	*Tentative commitment*	*Incongruence*	*Exploration of feelings at individual level; assessment of feelings at group level*	*Assignment of meaning*
Stage 3	Identity Tolerance	Identity Assumption	Deepening Commitment	Settling into Identity
Key Traits	*Informative and supportive relationships*	*Acceptance*	*Commitment to same-sex intimacy at the individual level; commitment to the gay and lesbian community at the group level*	*Emerging sense of self*
Stage 4	Identity Acceptance	Commitment	Internalization and Synthesis	Continued Uncertainty
Key Traits	*Normalcy*	*Positive identity development*	*Internalization of same-sex love at individual level; synthesis of lesbian culture at group level*	*Recognition of social intolerance*
Stage 5	Identity Pride			
Key Traits	*Strong Commitment*			
Stage 6	Identity Synthesis			
Key Traits	*Full self-integration*			

Note: The McCarn and Fassinger (1996) model of lesbian/gay identity formation describes phases of development as opposed to stages. This differentiation acknowledges the flexibility and fluidity inherent in sexual identity development.

Sources: Based on Cass (1979, 1990); Troiden (1989); McCarn and Fassinger (1996); Weinberg et al. (1994).

difference between self and those with a heterosexual identity is realized. Individuals negotiating this stage may begin to accept their homosexual identity, reject their homosexual identity due to perceived undesirability of homosexuality, or partially accept their homosexual identity with a rationalization of homosexual behavior as a "one-time" or "special case" experience. During stage three, *Identity Tolerance*, individuals seek out sexual minorities to help alleviate feelings of alienation and enhance self-awareness. In the *Identity Acceptance* stage individuals begin to establish a sense of normalcy as issues of incongruence between one's view of self and others' views (or perceptions of other's views) are resolved. The fifth stage, *Identity Pride,* is characterized by a strong commitment to homosexual identity and activism that may not yet be fully integrated with an individual's total self-identity. In the *Identity Synthesis* stage, however, one's homosexual identity is fully integrated with other dimensions of self-identity. As a result, meaningful and supportive relationships are sought and maintained with individuals with diverse sexual orientations and identities.

TROIDEN'S MODEL OF SEXUAL IDENTITY   Troiden (1989) suggested a four-stage model, which includes *Sensitization* or awareness of same-sex attraction; *Identity Confusion*, which is defined by a growing awareness of same-sex attraction coupled with incongruence between assumed heterosexual and homosexual orientations; *Identity Assumption*, or acceptance and same-sex sexual experiences; and *Commitment*, which involves a positive homosexual identity and committed same-sex relationships.

INCLUSIVE MODEL OF LESBIAN/GAY IDENTITY FORMATION   McCarn and Fassinger (1996) argue that many existing sexual identity models do not sufficiently account for environmental context and subtly presume a discriminatory stance against nonpublic acceptance of homosexual identity. To address this limitation, they proposed a four-phase model of sexual minority identity formation. Their model includes an individual sexual identity process and a parallel and reciprocal process of group membership identity (see Fassinger & Miller, 1996). These dual processes recognize that an individual's sense of self can be separate from identity with or participation in lesbian or gay culture (Fassinger, 1995). The model begins with an *Awareness* phase which is marked by an awareness of feeling different at the individual level and the awareness of different sexual orientations at the group level. The *Exploration* phase yields strong, often erotic same-sex feelings at the individual level and assessment about feelings and attitudes at the group level. The third phase of the model involves *Deepening Commitment* at the individual and group levels. During this phase individuals commit to personal choices regarding intimacy and sexuality while committing to the lesbian and gay community at the group level. Finally, the dual processes of model conclude with an *Internalization and Synthesis* phase. During this phase the individual process moves toward internalization of same-sex love. The group process of the Internalization and Synthesis phase moves toward synthesis of membership within the same-sex culture into one's total self-identity. Important to note that while the two phases of the model are in fact parallel and reciprocal, they may not necessarily be experienced simultaneously.

BISEXUAL IDENTITY DEVELOPMENT   Models of bisexual identity development are few in comparison to those of gay or lesbian identity development (Yarhouse, 2001). This may be due in part to the tendency to view sexuality as a dichotomous variable and uncertainty regarding the possible relationship between homosexual and bisexual identities. Weinberg and colleagues (1994), however, developed a model that describes bisexual identity as a distinct developmental trajectory. The Weinberg et al. model of bisexual identity development begins with initial confusion and a finding and applying label stages. These first two stages involve unsettled feelings regarding attraction to both sexes and assignment of meaning to those unsettled feelings.

The third stage of the model, settling into identity stage, is marked by an emerging sense of self-acceptance. This is followed by the last stage of the model, continued uncertainty. The continued uncertainty stage results from the lack of closure that stems from society's lack of tolerance of bisexual identity.

ADDRESSING SEXUAL IDENTITY IN COUNSELING   Unfortunately, gay and lesbian identity formation is often stigmatized by issues of discrimination, marginalization, and prejudice. These painful and unjust realities demand individual and systemic interventions from culturally competent counselors. First, counselors must work to create inclusive and supportive therapeutic environments that provide safety, acceptance, and freedom from heterosexist assumptions. This process begins with thorough self-examination of biases and attitudes regarding sexual orientation and identities, and includes the use of counseling skills that encourage client disclosure and provide opportunities for validation and normalization of feelings. Second, counselors must recognize that although some clients may follow models of sexual identity development, others may follow a very individualized, nonlinear path of identity development. Third, counselors should coordinate and facilitate client awareness of community resources that support lesbian, gay, and bisexual (LGB) individuals. Fourth, counselors must continue to enhance their awareness, knowledge, and skills regarding appropriate counseling interventions for LGB clients through coursework, consultation, training, and other professional development opportunities (Pearson, 2003). And fifth, counselors should support and engage in research that furthers understanding of sexual identity formation and the intersection of multiple identities. Case Study 2.2 demonstrates how sexual identity development may involve the counseling practices we offer.

CASE STUDY 2.2

Todd, a first-year college student, is meeting with a counselor at the university counseling center to discuss his transition to college. Academically, Todd is doing well. Socially, he is unsure of how he fits in with his peers. In particular, Todd is confused by his relationship with his friend, Michael. Todd is concerned because he is sexually attracted to Michael. Todd does not know what his feelings mean and has been too afraid to share them with anyone, even Michael.

   During their first session the counselor asked Todd what brought him to the office. Todd shared his concerns regarding adjustment to college and being away from home. After sensing there was something more on Todd's mind, the counselor asked him about his social adjustment. Todd shared a little about his feelings for Michael. Through the use of reflection, the counselor learned of Todd's uncertainty about his sexual orientation and fear of others' perceptions.

   The counselor recognized that Todd's presenting problem could not be adequately approached without consideration of the implications of his sexual identity development. Given Todd's seeming position in the beginning stages of sexual identity development, over the next several sessions the counselor provided safe and comfortable opportunities for Todd to explore who he is in terms of his multiple, intersecting identities. Todd began to more clearly define himself as a man, a student, a son, a friend, and a sexual being. Also as time passed, the counselor gave Todd access to materials and knowledge designed to dispel myths and stereotypes about same-sex sexual orientation. While the center offers counseling and support groups for LGB students, the counselor recognized that these interventions would not be appropriate for Todd given his current stage of development. As Todd gains a clearer level of awareness and comfort with his identity, these interventions may become more appropriate.

Counselors should also be cognizant of available research on sexual identity development. While most research has been conducted with White, middle-class, gay men, there is evidence that suggests gender, race, ethnicity, religious affiliation, cultural context, and historical factors can all influence the sexual identity development process (see Fassinger & Miller, 1996). Thus, the intersection of multiple identities must be considered. For example, emerging research suggests that the experiences, perceptions, and developmental processes of gay and lesbian people of color may be different than the experiences, perceptions, and developmental processes of White, gay men particularly for Helms's (1995) *Integration* status (Barry & Motoni, 1998; Parks, Hughes, & Matthews, 2004). Specifically these differences may include level of involvement with same-sex related social activities or the LGB community, and comfort with disclosure and the coming-out process (Rosario, Schrimshaw, & Hunter, 2004). Case Study 2.3 offers an opportunity to consider these counseling implications through discussion and reflection.

CASE STUDY 2.3

Martina, a 52-year-old, recently divorced woman and mother of one grown son, has made an appointment to meet with a career counselor in a neighboring city 25 miles from her home town. Facing this time of personal transition, Martina is excited yet fearful and uncertain of the life choices ahead of her. Martina has not worked outside the home since she was in her 20s. Everyone in her town knows about her divorce and her recent decision to move in with her lifelong friend, Gloria. Martina is aware that some of her friends and family do not approve of her decision to live with Gloria. Martina's sister refuses to call or visit since Martina moved in with Gloria. Martina is very upset about her strained relationship with her sister. She often feels she spends all of her time simply trying to figure out how to repair her relationship with her sister and how to make enough money to make ends meet. Martina is not sure where her life will take her, but she is sure of three things: she must reenter the work force; she needs to earn enough money to support herself; and she wants Gloria to be a significant part of whatever her future holds.

1. What counseling issues may present in this case?
2. What specific cultural identity issues should be explored? How would you approach these issues?
3. What important considerations should the career counselor keep in mind while working with Martina?

SPIRITUAL IDENTITY DEVELOPMENT

Spirituality involves the acknowledgment of and relationship building with a supernatural force that infuses existence (Griffith & Griggs, 2001; Marris & Jagers, 2001). Furthermore, one's spirituality informs values, perspectives, and judgments and provides meaning, mission, and purpose to life (Doswell, Kouyate, & Taylor, 2003; Newlin, Knafl, & Melkus, 2002). Spirituality need not evolve within the context of an organized religion (Chandler, Holden, & Kolander, 1992). Counselors may, therefore, encounter clients who believe in God or a supreme being, but have no religious institution affiliation. Chapter 15 provides additional information regarding the relationship between spirituality and religion.

The terms *spiritual development* and *faith development* are sometimes used interchangeably. The constructs are related yet not synonymous. As previously defined, spirituality involves a search for meaning, transcendence, and purpose. Faith is the process of making meaning (Love, 2001). Since development is understood as a process, it is appropriate to think of one's spiritual development as the process of faith development. The questions in Reflection 2.2 may be used to further your consideration of your own spirituality and faith development.

REFLECTION 2.2

What are your beliefs about spirituality? How, if at all, have these beliefs changed over time? How have these beliefs affected your personal and professional development? How may these beliefs affect your work with clients?

Fowler's Model of Spiritual Identity

Fowler's (1981) theory of faith development has six stages: *Intuitive–Projective Faith*, a stage in which young children become aware of cultural faith taboos; *Mythic–Literal Faith*, a stage of late childhood that focuses on religious systems and symbols; *Synthetic–Conventional Faith*, an adolescent stage of noncritical evaluation of faith and faith traditions; *Individuative–Reflective Faith*, a stage that challenges older adolescents and adults to demythologize spirituality and critically evaluate spiritual paths; *Conjunctive Faith*, a stage reached by adults who are able to appreciate the cultural and traditional faith systems without being bound by them; and *Universalizing Faith*, a stage of spirituality characterized by transcendent moral and religious actions, words, and quality of life.

Parks's Model of Spiritual Identity

Parks (2000) suggested a four-stage model of spiritual development that moves from reliance on external authorities to a position of self-valuing and self-understanding. The stages include *Adolescent/Conventional*, a stage of growing self-awareness and openness to multiple perspectives; *Young Adult*, a stage of probing commitment and the critical choosing of beliefs and values; *Tested Adult*, a stage of further commitment and the "testing" of spiritual choices that is generally reached by individuals in their early 20s or older; and *Mature Adult*, a stage of demonstrated interdependence and interconnectedness that is comfortable within the context of strong, personal conviction.

Furthermore, Parks suggests that imagination, an important concept underlying her theory, allows individuals to put together insights, ideas, and images in a way that makes meaning and approximates Truth. Unlike fantasy, which moves toward that which is not real, imagination moves toward that which is ultimately real in the most personally significant ways; it moves toward authenticity and wholeness. Imagination, or the meaning-making process, must be viewed in light of individuals' socially constructed experiences (Tisdell, 2007). Therefore, in broad terms, the ability for counseling clients to use imagination and see and create meaningful options for themselves and their lives may be related to their spiritual development.

Poll and Smith's Model of Spiritual Identity

In contrast to the models discussed, Poll and Smith (2003) offer a model of spiritual development that is based on a sense of self in relation to God. It is important to note that movement through this model is not linear, but may in fact involve doubling back or spiraling through various stages again and again from late childhood throughout the life span. During the *Pre-Awareness* stage individuals do not recognize themselves as spiritual beings or have low salience for spiritual experiences.

Generally, due to a crisis, challenge, or series of personally meaningful events, individuals enter the *Awakening* stage. This emotionally charged period leads to an awareness of God that is fragmented and specific to the crisis at hand. *Recognition*, the third stage, involves a cognitive and emotional understanding of God that permeates all life existence and experiences. It is during this stage that individuals begin to develop spiritual themes that shape faith practices, behaviors, and beliefs. The final stage, *Integration*, is marked by internalized notions of God that order perceptions, interactions, relationships, and behaviors. Due to individual factors such as personality, faith traditions, and spiritual experiences, the manifestation of spirituality may vary. What is constant, however, is that each stage of the model leads to a developing understanding and relationship with God that is personal and internally derived. Case Study 2.4 explores some important elements of the previously reviewed models of spiritual identity development.

CASE STUDY 2.4

John's 2-year-old son was recently diagnosed with autism. John is trying to process what this means for his son and his family, but he cannot get over his anger with God. John believes God has taken away the little boy he once had and given him a stranger to rear. John is hurt, angry, and scared. In his despair, John meets with the pastoral counselor at his church. The counselor recognizes that while John once possessed a fairly integrated sense of spiritual development, his relationship with God now is fragmented and confrontational. This is to be expected during periods of crisis. The counselor explained this to John and committed to helping him negotiate his current, spiritual relationship. The counselor and John spent time exploring John's value system and worldview. They were later able to connect these to John's understanding of God. Given these learnings, over time, John and the counselor were able to identify some spiritual practices and faith-based behaviors that John could incorporate into his daily life. Although John still faces challenges in processing his emotions and learning about and providing for his son's needs, he is able to take comfort in his developing spiritual identity.

- How would you characterize John using the three spiritual identity models presented in this chapter?
- What types of questions would be useful to further explore spiritual identity with John?

Addressing Spiritual Identity in Counseling

This discussion has provided the beginning of a fundamental knowledge base needed to move toward the provision of culturally competent counseling services to clients who express and/or value spiritual orientations. However, in order to enhance spiritual and religious cultural competence, additional steps must be taken. As part of the ethically mandated process of continual education in areas of diversity, counselors should increase awareness of their own spiritual and religious development through articles, books, conversations, activities, reflection, and experiential activities (see American Counseling Association [ACA], 2005). As an extension of this process, counselors can work to understand clients' faith histories, possible stressors (e.g., social isolation, prejudice, discrimination, oppression), and implications for counseling through collaboration, outreach to community religious leaders, worship service attendance, continuing education courses, and clinical consultation. This kind of work may lead to a much needed awareness of, and respect for, the indigenous support (e.g., pastors, deacons, ministers) and healing systems of various faith traditions. With heightened awareness and sensitivity, counselors may be well suited to apply applicable spiritual development theory and principles, and use multiple helping roles (e.g., advisor, advocate, facilitator, consultant, change agent) (Atkinson, Thompson, & Grant, 1993) to aid clients' efforts to meet counseling goals. Specifically, this may include:

- Helping clients identify and talk about personal spiritual experiences
- Providing a safe therapeutic environment that normalizes and provides language for the discussion of spirituality
- Asking nonthreatening, open questions related to meaning and philosophy of life to assess spiritual identity status (Griffith & Griggs, 2001)
- Referring clients for further spiritual guidance and direction
- Incorporating spirituality and the reliance on God in work toward counseling goals
- Assigning homework that includes spiritual reflection, attendance at worship services, spiritual reading, meditation, and prayer (Griffith & Griggs, 2001)
- Facilitating client alignment with values and personal images of God

Importantly, counselors are to consider spirituality and religiosity throughout their work with clients. Further, true counseling competence requires counselors' ongoing commitment to continuous learning and counseling skill acquisition regarding religiosity, spirituality, and all other issues of client diversity. These issues are addressed in greater detail in Chapter 15.

Summary

Cultural identity constructs extend beyond the typical categories of race and ethnicity to include among others, considerations of gender, sexual orientation, and spirituality. This chapter explored some of the dominant theories of cultural identity development as specifically applied to these areas of diversity. While empirical research in the field is in its infancy, these constructs, models, and theories hold promise for counselors as frameworks to better facilitate understanding of self and client.

This important work begins, of course, with counselor reflection, self-evaluation, and continuing professional development. In all areas of identity development culturally competent counselors willingly and repeatedly ask themselves the tough questions as they work to better understand who they are as cultural beings and how their cultural identity shapes their counseling. Although this may best be accomplished through supervision and consultation, this chapter illustrated how self-awareness can also be gleaned through becoming familiar with current research on cultural identity, participating in experiential activities, reading broadly on culture and identity, and developing partnerships with culturally relevant community-based resources.

Moreover, this chapter discussed the ways in which counselors can use an understanding of cultural identity theory and models to develop more accurate case conceptualizations and more fully understand and address clients' needs. While counseling interventions must never be stereotypically applied to clients, this chapter discussed assessments, interview protocol, and counseling strategies and interventions that may prove helpful in assessing and addressing client issues which significantly involve cultural identity. These included recognizing and discussing relevant cultural constructs and within-group differences along multiple cultural dimensions; using cultural identity models to help clients normalize and process cognitive, behavioral, and emotional responses; using cultural identity models to help clients understand and broaden worldview in culturally appropriate ways; using creative arts to help clients explore multiple aspects of cultural identity; and implementing systemic interventions as appropriate. Given the importance of cultural identity to healthy human development, culturally competent counselors must stay ever committed to exploring, processing, and successfully navigating self and client evolving narratives of cultural identity.

Social Advocacy

CHAPTER 3

Social Justice Counseling

CATHERINE Y. CHANG AND PHILIP B. GNILKA

PREVIEW

Social justice and social advocacy have been and will for the foreseeable future remain fundamental to the practice of counseling. Due to the convergence of certain economic and societal issues, the roles of social justice and social advocacy have gained more prominence in recent years. Based on the momentum from this focus, some have argued that social justice in counseling should be considered the "fifth force" following the psychodynamic, behavioral, humanistic, and multicultural counseling forces that exist in the profession (Ratts et al., 2004). We begin this chapter discussing some key constructs related to understanding social justice and social advocacy, explore the historical context of social justice and social advocacy in counseling, and then discuss the relationship between social injustice and mental health issues. Strategies and challenges of being agents of change are infused throughout these topics. This chapter ends with a call for professional counselors to be social change agents.

KEY CONSTRUCTS TO UNDERSTANDING SOCIAL ADVOCACY

> We must be bold enough to challenge inequality, brave enough to speak out against social injustice, and visionary enough to believe we can change our condition as a people if we put our collective energies forward. (Parham, 2001, p. 881)

Do you believe that every individual in the world has the same worth? Do you believe some people are more valuable than others? Should everyone receive equal benefits of society? Do you believe all people should have equitable rights? Do you believe all people have the right to a "good life"? The counseling profession has moved more toward addressing social inequities and their impact on clients' psychological and physical health within the counseling session as well as throughout the systems they experience—from their families, to schools, to local communities, to historical institutions that continue to marginalize them.

Social justice counseling and *social advocacy counseling* are used interchangeably in the counseling literature. **Social advocacy** refers to the act of arguing on behalf of an individual, group, idea, or issue in the pursuit of influencing outcomes, whereas **social justice** refers to a belief in a just world (i.e., a world with fair treatment and equal distribution of the benefits of society) that respects and protects human rights. One can argue that the goal of social advocacy counseling leads to social justice. For example, supporting the rights of gay men and lesbians to adopt children (social advocacy) could assist in giving them equitable opportunities to be parents (social justice). For consistency we will use *social justice counseling* throughout this chapter to denote both the act toward and belief in a just world.

   Social justice counseling refers to counseling that recognizes the impact of oppression, privilege, and discrimination on the mental health of individuals. According to Hays, Chang, and Chaney (2007), the majority of counselors and counselor trainees defined social justice as equitable treatment (e.g., equity among groups, nondiscrimination and equitable distribution of advantages and disadvantages). Some defined social justice in terms of **social injustice**, such as punishment for not following norms and the unequal assignment of privilege. Thus, social injustice refers to the unequal distribution of rewards and burdens. Examples of social injustice include discrimination across cultural identities, limited housing, and educational achievement gaps in schools, poverty, classism, sexism, child exploitation, racial profiling, homophobia, and violence toward racial and ethnic and sexual minorities (Hays, Chang, & Chaney, 2007). The goal of social justice counseling is to promote access and equity to all persons, focusing particularly on those groups that have been disenfranchised based on their cultural/ethnic background (e.g., race/ethnicity, gender, age, socioeconomic status, sexual identity). Based on the belief that all people have a right to equitable treatment and fair allocation of societal resources, the goal of social justice counseling is to establish equal distribution of power and resources through advocacy to ensure that all people have the tools and resources for a "good life" (Lee, 2007; Ratts et al., 2004; Rawls, 1971; Speight & Vera, 2004).

   As such, one of the goals of social justice counseling is the eradication of oppression. **Oppression** refers to "a state of asymmetric power relations characterized by domination, subordination, and resistance, where the dominating person or groups exercise their power by restricting access to material resources and by implanting in the subordinated persons or groups fear or self-deprecating views about themselves" (Prilleltensky & Gonick, 1996, pp. 129–130). Oppression is pervasive and exists across multiple groups (e.g., people of color, the poor, gay men, persons with disabilities) and at varying levels (e.g., individual, institutional, cultural).

   Oppression also can be described as an intersection of two modalities (i.e., oppression by force and oppression by deprivation) and three types (i.e., primary, secondary, and tertiary). **Oppression by force** involves the act of imposing on an individual or groups an object, label, role, experience, or living condition that is unwanted and causes physical and psychological pain. Examples include sexual assault and negative media images of women. **Oppression by deprivation** includes the act of depriving an individual or groups an object, label, role, experience, or living condition and hinders the physical and psychological well-being. Examples include neglect and depriving individuals of certain job promotions due to their minority status as well as certain groups based on their skin color and socioeconomic status a rich educational experience.

   Primary oppression includes overt acts of oppression including oppression by force and oppression by deprivation, while **secondary oppression** involves individuals benefiting from overt oppressive acts against others. Although individuals involved in secondary oppression do not actively engage in oppressive acts, they do not object to others who do engage in overt oppressive acts and do benefit from the aggression. For example, one might overhear a racial slur by a family member yet not call direct attention to the oppressive nature of the comment. To this end, he or she perpetuates that it is "okay" if others use racial slurs. **Tertiary oppression**, also referred to as **internalized oppression**, refers to the identification of the dominant message by members of the minority group often to seek acceptance by the dominant group. Like secondary oppression, tertiary oppression can be passive in nature (Hanna, Talley, & Guindon, 2000). A female who internalizes messages of sexism may buy into the message that males are more superior and that women should be subjugated. This internalization process is likely to lead to lowered self-esteem, psychological issues such as depression and anxiety, and increased risk for physical or sexual violence.

   Oppression is complex and multidimensional in that an individual can be a member of both oppressive and oppressed groups and experience oppression at various levels. By virtue of our race, sex and gender, sexual identity, class, religious/spiritual affiliation, age, and physical and emotional abilities, we are all potentially victims and perpetuators of oppression to some degree. For example, a White gay man, who is majority by race and gender, but minority by sexual identity, can be oppressed by individuals (e.g., victim of hate crimes), and institutions (e.g., institution that does not recognize same-sex marriages) as well as experience cultural oppression (e.g., living in a culture that does not acknowledge his sexual identity) while being an oppressor (e.g., having sexist attitudes). The result of oppression is an imbalance of **power** (i.e., having control, choice, autonomy, and authority or influence over others), with one group having more power, access, and advantage than the other group (i.e., oppressed vs. privileged). Specific forms of oppression (i.e., racism, sexism, heterosexism, classism, ableism, and ageism) will be discussed more thoroughly in other chapters.

Privilege is defined as having power, access, advantage, and a majority status. Power refers to having control, choice, autonomy, and authority or influence over others. Access relates to not only monetary and material possessions, but also to opportunities (e.g., opportunities for higher education). Having connections, favorable treatment, entitlement, and social support all relate to having advantage, while majority status refers not only to being the majority in number but also the majority in social standing and having the power to define who is who. Therefore, oppression and privilege can be viewed as inversely related (Hays et al., 2004).

Privilege, like oppression, is complex and multidimensional. Privilege manifests itself differently based on multiple identities, personal experiences, desire for status, and level of self-awareness. One can have privilege based on race (White privilege), gender (male privilege), class (socioeconomic privilege), sexual orientation (heterosexual privilege), and religious affiliation (Christian privilege). It is imperative as we understand the concepts of oppression and privilege to reflect on our own experiences with power. Activity 3.1 and Reflection 3.1 provide ways to explore personal experiences with privilege and oppression.

ACTIVITY 3.1

Consider the definitions of oppression and privilege presented in this chapter. In the first column, make a list of privileges that you have personally experienced or witnessed over the past week. In the second column, make a list of oppressive acts that you have experienced or witnessed over the past week. In the third column, indicate whether the acts are examples of power/lack of power, access/lack of access, advantage/lack of advantage, and majority status/minority status.

Privileges	Oppressive Acts	Power/Access/ Advantage/Status

Discuss your listings in a small group. Are there any acts that you did not include in your list that were in others' lists? Are there any acts that others included that you found surprising?

Based on qualitative data, Hays et al. (2004) developed a model that defined privilege and oppression as well as described how an individual's conceptualization of privilege and oppression is developed and what factors impact one's level of awareness of privilege and oppression. A person's conceptualization and awareness of privilege and oppression is cyclical and develops in response to his or her perception and internalization of various external factors (i.e., government, religion, media, family, industry, and education). That is, the way a person becomes aware of privileges and oppressive acts changes as he or she interacts more with surrounding systems. The internalization and awareness processes of privilege and oppression are further influenced by visibility (i.e., visible evidence of privileged or oppressed status) and perception. Perception is related to self-perception as well as a perception of how others react to a person based on the visibility of that person's status. In most cases the more visible a status is as privileged (e.g., being male) or oppressed (e.g., Arab American)- as well as the degree to which these statuses receive overt privileges and oppression (e.g., males being paid more, Arab Americans receiving more airport security checks), the more self- and others' perceptions are influenced. Hays et al.'s model is presented in Figure 3.1.

Take, for example, an Asian American, heterosexual, Christian female. How did she become aware of the various cultural groups both privileged and oppressed in which she holds membership?

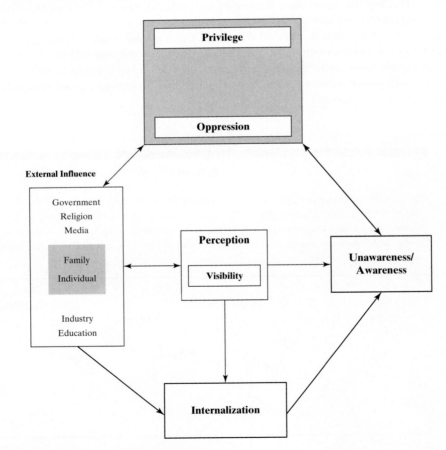

FIGURE 3.1 Developing awareness of privilege and oppression.
Source: Hays et al. (2004).

According to the Hays et al.'s (2004) model, her level of awareness of privilege (Christian and heterosexual) and oppression (Asian American and female) is based on external influences that include the government, religion, media, industry, and education. Her sexual identity is validated through the governmental laws, which provide her the rights of marriage, and through industry practices, which provide her spousal insurance coverage. They are further validated through images of her own parents and images of the "traditional" family espoused by media. However, her image of being an Asian American female can be invalidated through negative images of Asians and women in the media as well as validated through pride in her Asian heritage that is promoted in her family. These messages are internalized throughout her life and further validated or invalidated through the visibility or invisibility of her cultural group (sexual identity can be considered an invisible cultural group and Asian and female are visible) as well as self- and others' perception of that group. This individual's level of awareness related to her group membership in this privileged group (heterosexual) and oppressed group (Asian and female) is based on the internalization process that filters the external influences and the visibility of the group as well as the self- and others' perception. This process can be continuous and cyclical as the individual encounters additional external influences or perceptions of others.

It is important to consider our own awareness of privilege and awareness and how it has changed over time based on our interactions with systems. Reflection 3.1 provides a forum for considering your experiences with power.

REFLECTION 3.1

Membership has its privileges! Memberships in various "cultural" groups can be associated with certain "privileges." Name two cultural groups you identify yourself with and list "privileges" associated with that group. How might these privileges you experience affect others who do not belong to your group?

Cultural Group: _____

Privileges:

1. _____

2. _____

3. _____

4. _____

5. _____

Cultural Group: _____

Privileges:

1. _____

2. _____

3. _____

4. _____

5. _____

REFLECTION 3.2

Consider your cultural identity. Use a broad definition of culture to identify aspects of your identity, such as race, ethnicity, socioeconomic status, and ability status. Construct a narrative using the components of the model presented in Figure 3.1. How does this model either support or not support the development of your various cultural identities?

Empowerment is another important construct in social justice counseling. The goal of social justice counseling involves equitable distribution of power, which means empowering disenfranchised groups. McWhirter (1994) defines empowerment as

> the process by which people, organizations, or groups who are powerless and marginalized (a) become aware of the power dynamics at work in their life context, (b) develop the skills and capacity for gaining reasonable control over their lives, (c) which they exercise, (d) without infringing on the rights of others, and (e) which coincides with actively supporting the empowerment of others in their community. (p. 12)

As evident in this definition, empowerment is a complex process involving self-reflection and action from both the client and the counselor at both the individual and community levels and thus forms the foundation for social justice counseling (Lee, 2007). Some examples of empowerment include validating a client's anxiety with coming out to his or her parents, normalizing a trauma survivor's symptomology, supporting clients as they search for positive coping strategies to deal with acculturating to the United States, and collaborating with others to address lack of resources in a local school.

A key aspect of empowerment involves building upon clients' sources of resilience. **Resilience** is defined as behaviors and attitudes that clients identify as beneficial in coping with stressful situations (Singh, Hays, & Watson, 2008). These stressful situations may involve experiencing violence and trauma based on being a member of an oppressed group or acculturative stress in clients who have migrated to the United States recently, and living in a substandard neighborhood that lacks sufficient community, school, and medical resources, to name a few. Professional counselors working in mental health, school, rehabilitation, and college counseling settings are encouraged to identify these stressful situations and the coping resources clients use to combat them. To this end, identifying and building upon client resources fosters resilience (Singh et al., 2008).

HISTORICAL CONTEXT

Although social justice issues have contributed to the positive evolution of the counseling profession, recent developments have magnified and reinforced their historical and future role as fundamental to modern counseling. Evidence of such includes, but is not limited to, (a) Loretta Bradley (ACA president, 1999–2000) selecting social justice and advocacy as the thematic focus of her presidential year; (b) chartering of Counselors for Social Justice as a division of ACA in 2001 (www.counselorsfor socialjustice.org); and (c) endorsement of the advocacy competencies by the ACA Governing Council in 2003 (Lewis, Arnold, House, & Toporek, 2003).

However, in order to appreciate this professional shift, we must first refine our perceptions to acknowledge the lineage of social justice's integral impact to the counseling profession. At its inception the counseling profession began with individuals responding to social injustice and advocating for changes in social policy (e.g., Clifford Beers spearheaded the mental hygiene movement, Carl Rogers believed that the principles of psychology should be used to address social problems, Clement Vontress advocated for students in urban schools) (see Hartung & Blustein, 2002; Kiselica, 2004; McWhirter, 1997). Frank Parsons held the belief that wealth and power were unequally distributed throughout society, and he was committed to empowering immigrant and poor children in their employment and social roles in the United States during the early part of the 19th century. Parsons did this by founding the Boston's Vocational Bureau to provide vocational guidance to the people in society who were the least powerful and had the fewest resources. From this genesis flowed a developing dialogue of social injustice that directly molded the counseling profession:

1. 1971: "Counseling and the Social Revolution," a special issue of the *Personnel and Guidance Journal* (currently the *Journal of Counseling and Development*), is published. This edition advocates for counselors to actively engage in the social change process and address issues related to racism, sexism, destruction of the environment, and ending warfare.
2. 1987: The American Association for Counseling and Development (currently the American Counseling Association [ACA]) publishes a position paper on human rights that urges counselors to advocate for social change through personal, professional, and political activities.
3. 1992: Sue et al. (1992) publish the multicultural counseling competencies and standards.
4. 1998: *Social Action: A Mandate for Counselors* is published, edited by Courtland Lee and Garry Walz.
5. 1999: A special issue of the *Journal of Counseling and Development*, edited by Robinson and Ginter, is dedicated to racism.
6. 2005: The revised *ACA Code of Ethics* (ACA, 2005) places an increased emphasis on multiculturalism and social justice issues in counseling. Particularly, the new standard E.5.c., directs counselors to "recognize historical and social prejudices in the misdiagnosis and pathologizing of certain individuals and groups and the role of mental health professionals in perpetuating these prejudices through diagnosis and treatment."
7. 2007: The Association for Counselor Education and Supervision adopts the theme "Vanguards for Change: ACES and Social Justice" and sponsors a Social Justice Summit as part of the conference.

As an evolving tenet of the counseling profession, social justice issues will continue to serve as a primary force in the maturation of the counseling profession.

SOCIAL INJUSTICE AND MENTAL HEALTH ISSUES

Social justice counseling becomes clear when one considers the relationship between social injustice (i.e., oppression, discrimination, and prejudice) and the mental health of marginalized groups. The U.S. Surgeon General's report titled "Mental Health: Culture, Race, and Ethnicity: A Supplement to Mental Health" (USDHHS, 2001a) helped illustrate potential consequences of social injustice and predictors of mental illness for various racial/ethnic minority groups and move the field of multicultural counseling forward. This report was seminal in that it expanded counselors' and other mental health professionals' thinking of what culturally competent (and culturally incompetent) practice focuses upon. More specifically, findings served as an impetus for conceptualizing multicultural counseling competence as more than cultural sensitivity and tolerance of difference. It called for mental health professionals to examine how cultural "difference" and poor conditions for certain groups may be based on negative social conditions and other oppression experiences. In addition, it demonstrated how various minority statuses for an individual intersect to create additional adverse conditions. Similar research discusses the need for social justice in school counseling (Bemak & Chung, 2008), rehabilitation counseling (Harley, Alston, & Middleton, 2007), and career counseling (Hartung & Blustein, 2002).

Although racial, ethnic, and cultural minorities (e.g., people of color; women; and lesbian, gay, bisexual, and transgender [LGBT] individuals) are exposed to greater levels of discrimination and poverty than the majority culture, they have limited access to mental health care due to socioeconomic and language factors (Harper & Schneider, 2003; Travis & Compton, 2001; USDHHS, 2001a). Experiences of oppression can leave a person exposed to chronic stressors and challenges that threaten well-being (Greene, 2005), making them more susceptible to depression, suicide, substance abuse, violence, anxiety, chronic stress, and acute stress, which in turn may lead to medical complications including hypertension, low birthrate, heart disease, and cancer (USDHHS, 2001a).

Stress has been identified as the primary cause of emotional disturbances and the principle sources of stress are poverty, sexism, and being born unwanted (Albee, 2006). According to Evans (2004), poor children, compared with more economically advantaged children, experience greater family turmoil, and more violence, instability, and lower social support. Poor children also more frequently attend inferior schools and live in crowded, noisy, and dangerous neighborhoods. The following statements about poverty were presented at the 1993 Bi-Annual Congress of the World Federation for Mental Health (WFMH):

> Poverty dampens the human spirit creating despair and hopelessness. Poverty underlies multiple problems facing families, infants, children, adolescents, adults, and the elderly. Poverty directly affects infant mortality, mental retardation, learning disabilities, and drug and alcohol abuse. Poverty is the major factor in homelessness. Poverty increases the incidence of racial, ethnic, and religious hatred. Poverty increases abuse against women and children. Poverty results in suicide, depression, and severe mental illness. Poverty is directly linked to violence. (as cited in Albee, 2006, pp 451–452)

Clearly, marginalized groups are at a greater risk for psychological, physical, interpersonal, and financial risks. The remaining chapters of this book provide a more in-depth discussion of the costs of White privilege, racism, sexism, heterosexism, classism, ableism, and ageism.

COUNSELORS AS SOCIAL ADVOCATES

Lee (2007) calls for a paradigm shift in order for counselors to engage in social justice counseling. If counselors are to be agents of social justice, then they need to look beyond the traditional role and scope of the counselor and reject the notion of neutrality. Counselors must reconceptualize the theory and practice of counseling. Social justice counseling calls for counselors to broaden their scope of practice intervene not only at the client level but the societal level as well. It also calls for counselors to reject the notion of value neutrality in counseling. The assumption of value neutrality supports the status quo of inequity in society. Counselors following traditional counseling theories are at risk of leaving societal issues unaddressed by prescribing interventions that assist clients in adapting to an unjust or inequitable social system (McClure & Russo, 1996). If counselors want to work for social justice, then they must work for a just and equitable social system.

As a first step toward a just and equitable social system, Lee (2007) calls for action at the personal level with self-exploration. He proposes five personal action steps that include (a) exploring your personal life's meaning and commitment, (b) exploring personal privilege, (c) exploring the nature of oppression, (d) working to become multiculturally literate, and (e) establishing a "personal social justice compass" (p. 260). Based on these action steps, Reflection 3.3 offers an opportunity for professional counselors to develop their own social justice plan.

REFLECTION 3.3

Develop your own personal social justice plan based on Lee's five personal action steps.

Social Justice Plan	Process Questions/Tasks
1. Explore life's meaning and commitment	"What do I do and why do I do it? How do I do it? Who do I do it for? What do I believe about my clients? Am I committed to fostering and supporting a society that is more enlightened, just and humane through my life and work?" (p. 260)
2. Explore personal privilege	Explore the privileged cultural groups that you are a member of and challenge yourself to utilize your privilege to promote social justice. See Reflection 3.2.
3. Explore the nature of oppression	Consider how you have oppressed others in the past as well as how you have been oppressed by others by virtue of your group membership.
4. Become multiculturally literate	• Experience various ethnic groups by traveling locally, nationally, and internationally. • Read newspapers and literature from other ethnic groups. • Be open to new cultural experiences.
5. Establish a personal social justice compass	Develop your own personal agenda for social justice based on your personal principles and ideals.

Advocacy Competencies

Due to the development and subsequent application of the multicultural counseling competencies (MCC; Sue et al., 1992), the multicultural counseling movement has evolved to the social justice movement with a greater emphasis on the influence of environmental factors (i.e., oppression and social problems) that affect the well-being of clients. The emphasis on social justice issues is further heightened by the growing awareness of the relationship between oppression and mental illness; thus social advocacy increasingly is becoming a part of counselors' roles and responsibilities. In accordance with the MCC, "Culturally skilled counselors possess knowledge and understanding about how oppression, racism, discrimination, and stereotyping affect them personally and in their work" (Sue et al., 1992, p. 482). The **CSJ advocacy competencies** and the ACA Governing Council's adoption of these competencies answer this call for increased knowledge of social justice in counseling. Additionally, in response to an increased awareness of the role of advocacy in counseling, the revised ACA *Code of Ethics* (ACA, 2005) included the following statements in reference advocacy:

A.6.a. Advocacy: When appropriate, counselors advocate at individual, group, institutional, and societal levels to examine potential barriers and obstacles that inhibit access and/or the growth and development of clients.

A.6.b. Confidentiality and Advocacy: Counselors obtain client consent prior to engaging in advocacy efforts on behalf of an identifiable client to improve the provision of services and to work toward removal of systemic barriers or obstacles that inhibit client access, growth, and development. (p. 5)

TABLE 3.1 CSJ Advocacy Competencies Examples
___

1. Client/student empowerment
   a. Identify strengths and resources of clients and students.
   b. At an appropriate development level, help the individual identify the external barriers that affect his or her development.
   c. Help students and clients develop self-advocacy action plans.
2. Client/student advocacy
   a. Negotiate relevant services and education systems on behalf of clients and students.
   b. Help clients and students gain access to needed resources.
   c. Identify potential allies for confronting the barriers.
3. Community collaboration
   a. Identify environmental factors that impinge upon students' and clients' development.
   b. Alert community or school groups with common concerns related to the issue.
   c. Develop alliances with groups working for change.
4. Systems advocacy
   a. Identify environmental factors impinging on students' or clients' development.
   b. Analyze the sources of political power and social influence within the system.
   c. Assess the effect of counselor's advocacy efforts on the system and constituents.
5. Public information
   a. Recognize the impact of oppression and other barriers to healthy development.
   b. Identify environmental factors that are protective of healthy development.
   c. Assess the influence of public information efforts undertaken by the counselor.
6. Social/political advocacy
   a. Distinguish those problems that can best be resolved through social/political action.
   b. With allies, prepare convincing data and rationales for change.
   c. With allies, lobby legislators and other policy makers.

___

Source: From "Advocacy Competencies [Electronic version]," by J. Lewis, M.S. Arnold, R. House, and R.L. Toporek, 2003. Retrieved June 21, 2008, from http://counselorsforsocialjustice.com/advocacycompetencies.html. Copyright 2003 by the American Counseling Association. Reprinted with permission. No further reproduction authorized without written permission from the American Counseling Association.

The advocacy competencies for counseling professionals span levels of advocacy from the microlevel of clients and students to the macrolevel of interventions in the public arena and across six domains: (a) client/student empowerment, (b) client/student advocacy, (c) community collaboration, (d) systems advocacy, (e) public information, and (f) social/political advocacy. These advocacy competencies assert that advocacy requires social action in partnership with the client as well as on behalf of the client/student. See Table 3.1 for a sample listing of the advocacy competencies (Lewis, Arnold, House & Toporek, 2003). Activity 3.2 is designed for professional counselors to operationalize some of the CSJ competencies in a manner that is relevant to the setting in which they will be working.

ACTIVITY 3.2

This activity will help you become familiar with the advocacy competencies.

Review the CSJ advocacy competencies (Lewis, Arnold, et al., 2003) outlined in Table 3.1, mark the ones that you have already participated in, and then develop a plan of action in dyads for engaging in some of the other competencies.

THREE-TIER MODEL OF SOCIAL ADVOCACY

Based on the belief that social justice is necessary for optimal psychosocial health (Lee & Walz, 1998) and that counselors can more effectively advocate for their clients if our profession is recognized by other mental health professionals, legislators, and policy makers (Myers, Sweeney, & White, 2002), Chang, Hays, and Milliken (in press) developed a three-tier model of advocacy using a social constructivist framework. According to social constructivism, reality is constructed through human interaction and is a reflection of socially constructed concepts. Our sense of reality is flexible and changeable according to the social, cultural, and historical contexts. Social constructivism stresses the importance of culture and context in understanding what occurs in society and constructing knowledge based on this understanding (D'Andrea, 2000; Vygotsky, 1978). This model urges counselors and counselor educators to consider social justice issues relative to two fronts (i.e., client advocacy and professional advocacy) and across three tiers (i.e., self-awareness, client services, and community collaboration).

Myers et al. (2002) call for a comprehensive national plan for advocacy that includes advocacy for client well-being and for the profession of counseling. "Counselors can be more effective advocates for clients when our profession is recognized by other mental health professions as well as legislators and policy makers" (p. 401). Social change is necessary for optimal psychosocial health of both counselors and clients (Lee & Walz, 1998). For counselors to promote psychosocial health for themselves and their clients, we believe they must work toward self-awareness, consider their clients from a social justice perspective, and work toward social justice with others who share their vision. Activity 3.3 allows students to practice advocating for others.

ACTIVITY 3.3

Write down a hypothetical personally challenging scenario that involves advocating for a client or oppressed group with someone in a decision-making capacity (e.g., clinical director, politician, school administrator).

Create triads in which students are assigned the roles of Counselor, Decision Maker, and Coach. Each member of the group should have the opportunity to play each of the three roles at least once. The Coach provides a scenario that calls for social advocacy. The Counselor and Decision Maker converse for several minutes about a scenario. Once the conversation has ended, the Coach provides feedback and offers suggestions. Then, the roles should be rotated and the new Coach will provide a different scenario. As you role-play, be sure to practice what you would say rather than simply discussing social justice advocacy.

Once you have completed the activity, discuss the following as a class:

- What are some thoughts you have in advocating for your client or oppressed group?
- Was the experience easier or more difficult than you expected?
- Did any approaches work better than others?
- What else could you do to help make it easier for you to advocate in the future?

Self-awareness includes an awareness of one's own cultural values and biases (Sue et al., 1992). Relative to social justice counseling, counselors need to be able to identify and discuss the privileges that they personally hold in society by virtue of race, socioeconomic status, religious affiliation, sexual identity, sex, or physical ability. Other scholars echo the importance of self-awareness in conducting social justice counseling (Lee, 2007; Lee & Walz, 1998) and developing professional pride and professional advocacy (Myers et al., 2002). One method for developing self-awareness is constructing a cultural genogram (see Reflection 3.4). Figure 3.2 provides a sample cultural genogram.

REFLECTION 3.4

Construct a "cultural" genogram. A cultural genogram is a graphic depiction of your family tree that highlights the various cultural group memberships of your family members. Next to each cultural group membership mark whether it is a privileged group (P) or an oppressed group (O) and outline some of the messages that come from being a member of that group. In the margin of the genogram, include information related to resources (e.g., family, friends, religious affiliation, employment, housing assistance) and stressors (e.g., financial strain, legal difficulties, employment difficulties, day care issues). There are many genogram software programs available online as well as many Web sites that publish common symbols used in genograms. Additionally, McGoldrick, Gerson, and Shellenberger (1999) have published *Genogram: Assessments and Intervention* which provides instructions for constructing a standard genogram, conducting a genogram interview, and interpreting the results.

Consider the following:

- How does your membership to privileged and oppressed groups either support or not support the development of your various cultural identities?
- Which memberships come from earlier generations, and have changed over time?
- Are there memberships that do not come from earlier generations?
- Which memberships exert the strongest influence on your cultural identity?
- Which memberships exert the least influence?

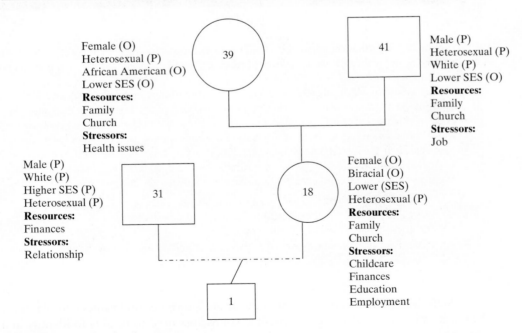

FIGURE 3.2   Sample cultural genogram.

Client services in social justice counseling involves the empowerment of disenfranchised clients. According to this model, the counselor must first have a clear understanding of the client's worldview before the counselor and the client can move toward empowerment. Counselors working from a constructivist framework consider the social factors as well as the developmental, emotional, and cognitive processes of the individual client. These factors and processes influence and are influenced by various aspects of the client's system (see Chapter 1). Additionally, counselors recognize the interaction of these systems over time. Working from this model, counselors formulate questions that expose the conditions that promote social, political, and educational advantages and disadvantages (Griffin, 1993). Quality of client services is influenced by the development of a clear professional identity. As such, it is essential that counselors develop their professional identity and professional pride (see Reflection 3.5).

REFLECTION 3.5

Questions to Facilitate Professional Identity and Professional Pride

- Describe your role as a professional counselor.
- What qualities make professional counseling unique?
- What role does advocacy play in counseling?
- You are a counselor working in a battered women's shelter and one of your clients has recently secured a job and housing? What role did you play in assisting your client with her situation?

Community collaboration involves working toward social change at the organizational and institutional levels. Because counselors work with a diverse group of people, they may be the first to become aware of difficulties within agencies, external organizations, and the community. As counselors become aware of external factors influencing their clients, they must look beyond direct clinical work and be willing to intervene at the organizational and institutional levels to promote client and professional advocacy. Dinsmore, Chapman, and McCollum (2000) suggest the following organizational interventions: (a) challenge institutions to provide clients with easier access to critical information that may impact their well-being; (b) serve as a mediator when a client and an institution reach an impasse; (c) negotiate with external agencies and institutions to provide better services for clients; (d) participate in lobbying efforts related to social justice issues; and (e) inform funding agencies of inadequate or damaging practices. Additionally, counselors can work toward educating the community about the relationship between oppression and mental health issues through the development of programs for different organizations and the community related to multicultural and social justice issues.

There are several ways to integrate the three-tier model of social advocacy in professional counseling. Social justice issues may be addressed in supervision (Case Study 3.1), mental health counseling (Case Study 3.2), school counseling (Case Study 3.3), and rehabilitation counseling (Case Study 3.4), to name a few.

CASE STUDY 3.1

Case of the Three-Tier Model: Supervision

Consider the following case study and how the three-tier model can be applied to this case.

You are a supervisor who is supervising the following intern. The intern is at a community agency that includes a battered women's shelter and provides crisis counseling for survivors of domestic violence. The majority of the clients in this agency are women who are poor and women of color. The intern is White from a middle-class background. During the intern's first week of internship, her first client is a woman who is so severely beaten that her face is completely bruised and she has a difficult time speaking because of the swelling. In addition to this case, the intern is asked to see a woman who has brought along her 2-year-old daughter because she cannot afford child care. The intern informs you that she did not receive any training on site prior to seeing her first client.

- What issues related to self-awareness might come up for this intern? Consider cultural identities such as race/ethnicity, socioeconomic status, and education level, to name a few.
- What questions do you have about the quality of client care? Keeping in mind the context of the client, what would you want to consider in working with these women? How would you deal with the presence of a child during the session?
- As the university supervisor, how can you work with your intern to educate the site about appropriate training (advocacy for the intern and counseling profession) as well as client care (client advocacy)?

CASE STUDY 3.2

Case of the Three-Tier Model: Mental Health Counseling

Consider the following case study and how the three-tier model can be applied to this case.

You are a White counselor working at a child advocacy center. You have been assigned a new client, Mia, who is a 14-year-old Latina who is 6 months pregnant with her biological father's child. She has been sexually abused by her biological father for the past 4 years. She reports that she loves her father and that they have a "loving" relationship. Her father is currently in prison. Mia's mother is developmentally challenged and considered incompetent to take care of her children; therefore, Mia, along with her three younger siblings, is living with her maternal aunt and uncle and their two children. Her aunt speaks very limited English and requires a translator during the counseling sessions. In addition to your concerns about this client, you have been informed that a major source of funding has been cut from the child advocacy center, which may result in some counseling positions being terminated thus increasing the caseload for the counselors who already have a heavy caseload.

- What issues related to self-awareness might come up for this professional counselor? Consider cultural identities such as race/ethnicity, socioeconomic status, and education level, to name a few. What potential biases might be an issue for this counselor?

- What questions do you have about the quality of client care? Keeping in mind the context of the client, what would you want to consider in working with the client and her aunt?
- As the professional counselor how would you balance concern for this client with concern for your job?

CASE STUDY 3.3

Case of the Three-Tier Model: School Counseling

Consider the following case study and how the three-tier model can be applied to this case. You are a school counselor currently working at a suburban high school in a conservative part of the country. Several students during the course of the school year individually confide in you their struggles at school due to their sexual orientation. All of them described being called names such as "faggot" by other students and several teachers. Several of the students asserted they had been physically assaulted by other students and nothing was done by the school. When you review the grades and attendance records of the students, all of them show performance below their abilities and increasing number of absences.

- What issues related to self-awareness might come up for this school counselor? Consider sexual orientation identities, cultural identities such as race/ethnicity, and socioeconomic status. What potential biases might be an issue for this counselor?
- What concerns do you have about the quality of education being provided for these students?
- What are some community resources and schoolwide resources or programs you could assist in forming?
- What are some of the benefits and risks you might encounter for advocating on a systems or community level?

CASE STUDY 3.4

Case of the Three-Tier Model: Rehabilitation Counseling

Consider the following case study and how the three-tier model can be applied to this case. You are a rehabilitation counselor working in an outpatient clinic. One of your new clients has come due to feelings of hopelessness and despair. Your client is a married, middle-aged Latina who has two children and has never been in trouble before. When you usher her into your office, she is accompanied by her service dog. After brief introductions, you inquire what brought her to your office. She stated that she was in the public library attending a public forum with her service dog when a librarian stated her dog would have to leave the building. After explaining that she was blind and it was perfectly legal to have a service dog with her, the librarian contacted the police. When the police responded, they would not listen to her side of the story, so she refused to leave

(continued)

the building, forcing the police to place her under arrest. She states that no one will listen to her, and she is unsure what to do.

- What issues related to self-awareness might come up for this rehabilitation counselor? Consider cultural identities such as race/ethnicity, socioeconomic status, disability status, and gender among others. What potential biases might be an issue for this counselor?
- Keeping in mind the context of the client, what would you want to consider in working with this client?
- What are some community resources and communitywide resources or programs you could assist the client in either finding or establishing? What other interventions would you consider when working with this client?

CHALLENGES AND BENEFITS OF SOCIAL JUSTICE COUNSELING

Despite the importance of social justice work, there are several factors that may prevent counselors from engaging is social justice activities. Hays, Chang, and Chaney (2007) identify three reasons that may prevent counselor trainees from engaging in social justice counseling. These include (a) the high intrapersonal and interpersonal costs for counselors (e.g., burnout, job loss, harassment); (b) social justice initiatives that may be incongruent with traditional counseling theories and interventions and traditional ethical standards; and (c) lack of appropriate training in dealing with oppression issues on behalf of the client. Counselor trainees further identified the following challenges in implementing social justice initiatives: (a) the dominant groups (e.g., close-mindedness of others, minimal support system); (b) counseling process (e.g., communication difficulties, counselors, and clients with differing levels of awareness of social justice); (c) logistics (e.g., administrative and time constraints); (d) ethics (e.g., imposition of values); and (e) counselor emotions (e.g., feelings of isolation, helplessness). Additionally, reasons that counselor trainees gave for not engaging in social advocacy activities included counselor emotions (e.g., powerlessness), multicultural competence (e.g., lack of advocacy skills), and dominant groups (e.g., fear of conflict and rejection). Reflection 3.6 is designed to assist counselors in identifying resources to offset the danger of burnout.

REFLECTION 3.6

Consider the following statement: "Enjoying the pleasures of life can help sustain us in advocating for change." What does that mean to you? What are some of the "pleasures of life" that sustain you? How does this statement fit with the burnout many counselors face?

Despite the challenges and costs of social justice counseling, it can also be rewarding. Social justice work can lead to personal satisfaction and growth from empowering others and learning from that experience (Kiselica & Robinson, 2000). Additional perceived benefits of social justice initiatives in counseling include general benefits for society (e.g., promoting equal rights), general benefits for clients (e.g., culturally appropriate counseling for all), an improved counseling process (e.g., increasing client self-advocacy), general benefits for the counselor (e.g., increased awareness of self), and an imparting of knowledge to clients and communities (Hays, Chang, and Chaney 2007).

It is important for professional counselors to identify their own personal challenges and benefits of social justice work (see Reflection 3.7). In doing so, they are more inclined to locate activities that they can engage in to help end oppressive acts as they attend to the resilience in clients' lives. Table 3.2 offers several activities in which professional counselors may get involved.

REFLECTION 3.7

Have you engaged in any social justice initiatives? If so, what were some of the challenges and benefits of those experiences? If not, were there any situations where you would like to have engaged in social justice work but did not? What kept you from intervening?

TABLE 3.2 Additional Social Justice Activities

1. Become a member of professional counseling organizations such as the American Counseling Association (ACA) or the American Mental Health Counselors Association (AMHCA). Our professional organizations lobby on behalf of our profession and clients. The larger our organizations, the more clout we have in Washington, DC, and state capitals across the country. You can also find a list of ACA state branches on ACA's Web site under the divisions/regions/branches icon.
2. Join and get involved in ACA divisions that advocate for social justice causes such as Counselors for Social Justice (CSJ), the Association for Lesbian, Gay, Bisexual and Transgender Issues in Counseling (ALGBTIC), or the Association for Multicultural Counseling and Development (AMCD). By getting involved in divisions within our profession, you can help institute change within our profession on social justice issues.
3. Join the ACA Government Relations listserv to stay updated on events affecting our profession and how you can make a difference. Send an e-mail to CLum@counseling.org with the subject line "GR Listserv Sign Up" to subscribe.
4. Have your voice heard by sending a fax or e-mail to your legislators through the ACA Legislative Action Center located at www.counseling.org/PublicPolicy. Through this center, you will be able to send personal emails to your U.S. senators and representatives about important legislation that impacts our profession. It takes only a few minutes to set up and under a minute for each fax or e-mail.
5. Organize a lobby day at your state capital with other counselors. When you find a group of counselors who want to join you on the lobby day, find out when your state legislature is in session. Second, figure out who your representatives are and contact them to set up an in-person meeting. Once you have appointments set up with your state legislators, prepare a brief presentation that explains who counselors are, what we do, and why counseling is needed. The ACA Public Policy Web page, www.counseling.org/PublicPolicy, has excellent resources that summarize the effectiveness and cost benefits of counseling services both in school and community settings.
6. Start a letter-writing campaign at your office or school. First, obtain a list of people who are interested in participating and get their names, phone numbers, and home addresses. Next, find out who their legislators are in Congress and at the state level. You can enter all this information into an excel spreadsheet. Next, join the ACA Government Relations listserv to keep abreast of current activities in Washington, DC, that impact the counseling profession or your state counseling association for state issues. When you receive an alert, prepare a form letter using a mail merge function in a word processor for each individual to send. Some individuals may want to personalize the letter or even compose handwritten letters, so you may need to provide them with talking points. Keep in mind that legislators put much more emphasis on handwritten letters than form letters. This is an excellent way to get people in an organization to be active in public policy matters.

(continued)

TABLE 3.2 Additional Social Justice Activities (Continued)

7. Volunteer for a political campaign. By volunteering for a politician, you will be much more influential in that particular politician's eyes. You can do many things such as work a phone bank, campaign for them in your neighborhood and among friends, or simply make a cash contribution. If they are elected, you will have more access and influence in having them support your issues.

8. Support or volunteer time with other local service organizations that work for social justice issues you are interested in. For example, you could volunteer time for the local domestic violence shelter or HIV/AIDS service organization. Some of these organizations also have public policy directors and lobbyists who may need help in finding and summarizing counseling research and literature about their particular issues. This is an excellent opportunity to use your skills of interpreting research for politicians and the general public.

9. Create a giving circle. Giving circles are a popular way for individuals to leverage the power of their contributions by pooling their contributions with others to achieve a greater inpact. Giving circles can be small and informal with a few people pooling their money and giving it to a chosen charity, or they can be highly organized, requiring multiple contributions and a commitment of many years. Most giving circles are democratically arranged, meaning donors have equal voice in deciding where their contributions go. To obtain more information on what a giving circle is and how to start one, check out the Giving Forum at www.givingforum.org.

Summary

If counselors are going to be agents of change in society for the prevention of emotional disorders, then they must jettison the notion of neutrality in counseling and begin to intervene on all levels for change. Social justice counseling focuses on the fact that both social and economic forces are powerful influences on how people and our society develop. The differences in power are a result of oppression that exists across multiple groups and different levels of society. This in turn gives some groups privilege over others, resulting in an inverse relationship between oppression and privilege. A person's awareness of privilege and oppression is a complex cyclical process that develops not only in response to external factors but also in response to one's perception and internalization of external factors. Visibility of various external factors also influences the internalization and awareness processes.

One key goal of social justice counseling is the empowerment of clients on all levels (e.g., individual, community). Empowerment is the process by which people or organizations who are oppressed become aware of the power differential in their life, and then learn and exercise the skills necessary to control their lives without oppressing other groups.

The relationship between oppression and the mental health of marginalized groups was identified through the U.S. Department of Health and Human Services 2001 report on mental health. The report linked discrimination and oppression experienced by marginalized groups to a greater risk of emotional disturbances and illness. This report helped the counseling profession's viewpoint of multiculturalism evolve from just promoting cultural sensitivity and understanding to exploring how oppression creates poor conditions for certain groups. Counselors must actively promote change in power dynamics in addition to promoting multicultural awareness, tolerance, and understanding.

Counselors should be aware of the social justice advocacy competencies for counseling professionals that span multiple levels of advocacy across six domains. These 43 advocacy competencies require social action by the counselor on behalf of the client in addition to personal counselor participation in social action. A three-tier model of advocacy was created for counselors to view social justice issues on two fronts, client advocacy and professional advocacy, and across three tiers: self-awareness, client services, and community collaboration. Self-aware counselors should be able to identify and discuss the privileged and oppressed groups they belong to as well as have a sense of profession pride and identity. Client services involves the process of empowering oppressed clients and providing privileged clients an ability to become more self-aware. Community collaboration involves counselors engaging at the institutional and societal levels for change that would affect oppressed clients.

While multiple challenges exist for counselors engaged in social justice counseling (e.g., harassment, burnout, isolation, difficulty integrating traditional theoretical counseling models), many benefits can be gained from such activities (e.g., personal satisfaction from empowering oppressed clients, personal growth, a more just society).

If the counseling profession wants to create meaningful change in the prevention of mental disorders, the disequilibrium of power that causes oppression and privilege must be confronted. Counselors are the leaders of the fourth wave—the multicultural movement that is sweeping the helping professions—and are once again positioned to bring about a fifth wave in the profession: social advocacy counseling. If social and economic power that breeds oppression is directly challenged and altered, emotional disorders across our society and world will be significantly reduced. Counselors have the opportunity to make a serious impact on the mental health of people across the world.

CHAPTER 4

Racism and White Privilege

DANICA G. HAYS AND MARC GRIMMETT

PREVIEW

Racism and associated racial privilege is one of the prominent social justice issues in the counseling profession today. In this chapter, we define racism and White privilege and provide examples of how they have been perpetuated throughout history and continue to pervade society in general health and mental health more specifically. Costs for both people of color and Whites are discussed, and strategies for eradicating racism are provided.

HISTORICAL FOUNDATIONS OF RACE AND RACISM

Individuals are routinely asked to identify their race on school and employment applications, state and federal documents, and even church and local advocacy group membership forms. The complexity of **race** is often simplified and masked by everyday social tasks and perceived physical and human differences. Race can appear to be innate and concrete, rather than an ascribed human characteristic used to categorize human beings into subgroups (Smedley & Smedley, 2005; Zuckerman, 1990). Racial "differences" are largely a result of genetic drift, isolation, the interaction between geography and biology (e.g., production of melanin as a biological adaptation with lighter skin tones in latitudes that receive less sunlight, development of sickle cell disease as an adaptive response to living in malaria-prone regions), and the effect of temperature on mean body size (Cameron & Wycoff, 1998). However, these physical distinctions among individuals have served as a method for classifying them and mistakenly assigning complex traits such as musical ability, intelligence, or athleticism to a few biological markers. These racial classifications are so ingrained in our psyche that we believe physical differences are a natural justification and evidence that racial differences exist.

When two people who have lived in a society with an institutionalized racial classification system (e.g., United States) meet for the first time, visual cues such as skin color, apparent hair texture, and eye color initiate an automatic cognitive process that results in their perceived racial identification of each other (Tatum, 2003). Auditory cues are used similarly to place people in particular racial groups using dialectical and vernacular information. Have you ever called a customer service phone line and almost immediately assumed the race of the customer service representative based on his or her accent or manner of speech? Because race can be defined as the subjective interpretation of individual physical characteristics or human differences, there are almost automatic beliefs we hold about our own race as well as others'. Reflection 4.1 offers some considerations related to our positive and negative beliefs concerning our own racial membership or memberships.

REFLECTION 4.1

What are some things you like about being a member of your race or races? What are some things you dislike about it? How do you think your life would be different if you were a member of other races?

Although it is confused with the term *ethnicity*, *race* implies a "common descent of heredity" (Cameron & Wycoff, 1998, p. 278) while **ethnicity** refers to cultural characteristics (e.g., rituals, work ethic, social mores and values). These concepts often overlap and are used synonymously in discussions of culture, and individuals group (often erroneously) various ethnicities into the same racial category even though an ethnicity can contain several "races." Additionally, some individuals fail to acknowledge their ethnicity due to the salient, privileged status of their racial category (i.e., Whites). Reflection 4.2 provides space for thinking about ethnicity, particularly how it relates to race.

REFLECTION 4.2

With which ethnicity or ethnicities do you identify? How does this relate to your racial group membership or memberships? What values and traditions do you associate with your combined racial and ethnic heritages? List these below.

_____

_____

_____

_____

Review your list of values and traditions associated with being a member of your race and ethnicity. How might your racial and ethnic heritage influence your work with clients?

For the U.S. federal government, racial categories are not biologically based yet represent social constructs used for collecting data on race and ethnicity (Office of Management and Budget [OMB], 1997). The OMB, within the Executive Office of the President of the United States, provides the *Standards for the Classification of Federal Data on Race and Ethnicity*:

> Development of the data standards stemmed in large measure from new responsibilities to enforce civil rights laws. Data were needed to monitor equal access in housing, education, employment, and other areas, for populations that historically had experienced discrimination and differential treatment because of their race or ethnicity. . . . The standards have been developed to provide a common language for uniformity and comparability in the collection and use of data on race and ethnicity by Federal agencies. (OMB, 1997, p. 2)

This means that the OMB designates five racial categories: (a) American Indian or Alaskan Native, (b) Asian, (c) Black or African American, (d) Native Hawaiian or Other Pacific Islander, and (e) White; and two ethnic categories: (a) Hispanic or Latino and (b) Not Hispanic or Latino, that are to be used as a minimum to collect federal information. The justification and categories provided by the OMB for the current racial classification system acknowledge historical social injustices related to race, without reference to the essential oppressive nature of the system itself (i.e., racism) enabled by the social construction of race. You will notice, however, that there is no category for Arab Americans, an ethnic group discussed in Section Three of this text.

Social Construction of Race

In Spanish, Portuguese, Italian, and French folklore prior to the 16th century, race was usually identified with a breeding line or stock of animals (Smedley, 1999). The primary definition of race began to change in the 16th century where it was used by Spanish writers as "one of several ways of referring to new populations discovered in their travels" (p. 39). Later the term race was adopted by other European settlers in the Americas, particularly the English, "where it generally denoted populations of differing origins in the heterogeneous mix of peoples" (p. 37). Smedley asserts that "the term 'race' made possible an easy analogy of inheritable and unchangeable features from breeding animals to human beings" (p. 40).

Throughout history we have seen race classified in various ways. Beginning with Linnaeus, a Swiss scientist and explorer, humans were subdivided into four geographic regions (i.e., Americas, Europe, Asia, Africa) and further labeled individuals' characteristics depending on their predominant "fluid" (i.e., blood, phlegm, choler, and melancholy). In essence, humans from the four regions were described as obstinate, happy, and free (the Americas); white, optimistic, muscular, active, intelligent (Europe); melancholy, stiff, severe (Asia); and black, slow, foolish, negligent (Africa). In 1777, Johann Blumenbach expanded Linnaeus's classification system and coined the term *Caucasian* to describe White (European) as ideal beauty based on his belief that humans originated from the Caucasus Mountains in Russia, created from "God's vision." He also labeled other racial groups as the "Mongolian variety" (East Asian inhabitants), "Ethiopian variety" (Africans), "American variety" (Native Americans), and the "Malay variety" (Melanesians, Polynesians, and Australian Aboriginals) (Cameron & Wycoff, 1998). Thus, early racial categorizations were quite Eurocentric and hinted at a rank order of races, with Whites or Europeans at the top, Asians and Americans in the middle, and Africans at the bottom. Other "scientific" methods for distinguishing races include measuring skulls to indicate degree of intelligence (to attempt to demonstrate that European Americans had "superior intellect" and African Americans' brains were most inferior) and examining blood quantum where "one drop" of African American or Native American blood was predictive of lower intelligence (McDonald & Chaney, 2003; Turner & Collinson, 2003). Early racial classification systems based on physical characteristics paved the way for later forms of racism discussed in later sections of this chapter.

As described earlier, individual physical characteristics (e.g., the shape of one's nose) and human differences (e.g., how one talks) are often used as social criteria for race. These criteria are seemingly consistent with a genetic or biological foundation for race, in accordance with the origin of the word. Physical characteristics alone, however, are insufficient to make distinctions among people for several reasons (Littlefield, Lieberman, & Reynolds, 1982; Smedley & Smedley, 2005). First, with early exploration and colonization people of different ethnic backgrounds (i.e., geographic regions, national origins, and cultures) reproduced multiethnic offspring that varied in their physical appearance. Individual ancestry, therefore, is responsible in part for the diversity that exists in the physical characteristics of individuals who identify with the same racial group. Alternatively, these same individuals may be perceived by others as either being within the same racial group or not based on their subjective interpretation of the physical characteristics of the individual. The use of physical characteristics to define race, then, is relatively arbitrary. Second, genetic information is also contrary to biological or physical definitions of race (Marks, 1995). The genetic makeup of all human beings in the world is nearly 100% identical, with more genetic variation occurring within so-called racial groups than between them. Only 0.1% of all human genes are responsible for individual differences such as physical appearance and disease risk. Finally, anthropological and genetic evidence indicate that Africa was the earliest home of modern humans (i.e., all racial classifications): (a) the earliest modern human fossils were found in Omo Kibish, Ethiopia; (b) the diversity of genetic markers is greatest within the African continent; and (c) the genetic makeup of all human beings is a subset of Africa's gene pool (Shreeve, 2006). Such evidence indicates that Africa was the earliest home of modern humans. The physical, biological, or genetic definition of race is, therefore, unfounded. It is important to note that it was also the scientific community—including anthropologists, psychologists, and others—that played perhaps the most prominent role in the justification of the concept of race and its associated ideologies of White superiority and the inferiority of all other "races" through self-serving theories and research motivated by social and political agendas (Guthrie, 1998; Smedley, 1999, 2006; Smedley & Smedley, 2005).

Human differences in behavior are also better explained through social learning than inherent genetic or biophysical differences. While it is evident that race functions in the identification of others within a society that uses a formal racial classification system, self-racial identification (i.e., racial identity) is essentially learned from the family (or primary caregivers) and the immediate social and cultural environment of the individual (Helms, 1990). The process of learning to identify oneself with a particular racial group and to make distinctions and associations among people based on race is the result of indirect and direct racial socialization enabled and sustained by an institutionalized racial classification system known as racism.

Defining Racism

Physical buildings are designed and constructed for particular functions. A grocery store requires storage space and refrigeration. The concept of race, similarly, was created or constructed to serve a particular social function. Race and the original racial classification system were instituted by English colonists to ensure that the demand for agricultural labor was met as transatlantic entrepreneurial markets emerged (Bennett, 2003; Smedley, 1999; Zinn 1999). This was accomplished by the establishment of a hierarchical system of oppression that exclusively granted basic human rights, social privileges, and prestige to individuals of European descent (Allen, 1994, 1997). In the late 17th century,

> Colonists used the physical differences among various populations interacting in the New World to establish categories that were economically, socially, and politically unequal. The ideology homogenized a diverse assemblage of Europeans into a "White" category; subsumed peoples of varying cultures, religions, and languages from Africa into a "Negro" category; and meshed all indigenous peoples together as "Indians." (Smedley, 2006, p. 181)

Native Americans, or American Indians, the original inhabitants and cultivators of the land and society in North America, had their land, resources, and tribes people stolen, destroyed, or killed in the violent conquests and wars that were employed by the English colonists to dominate and control the land. American Indians and Africans captured and transported to the first American colony in Jamestown, Virginia, were the most disenfranchised in terms of their access and participation in the emerging English civilization and had the least resources to protect themselves or to appeal for protection of the government. Without legislative representation or economic power, American Indians and Africans had no voice in the establishment of this new government that created laws making them slaves for life based on the "new" concept of race. Africans were particularly vulnerable given their absence of political power and easily identifiable brown skin, in addition to the chronic traumatization of being captured, held hostage, brutalized, enslaved, and forcibly acculturated into an unfamiliar social system (Franklin & Moss, 2002).

Racism is an ongoing, multidimensional, and dynamic process inherent to the development and maintenance of an institutionalized, hierarchical racial classification system (Jones, 2000). It operates simultaneously on individual, group, and system levels and involves intentional and unintentional negative, erroneous, or stereotypical beliefs about race and the consequences of actions (e.g., interpersonal behavior, public policy decisions). The use of racial classifications in all institutions of society (i.e., family, schools, employment, government) results in the socialization of a racial worldview for all its members. **Racial worldview** is a defining cultural characteristic in that individuals and groups perceive and understand each other through this socially constructed prism that will be transmitted to succeeding generations. The process of racism engineers a racial worldview that is securely fastened to the cognitions of all members of a society initially without their detection or protest. Like other process-defined systems, racism is built to maintain itself (Feagin, 2006). The components of this system are individuals actively (e.g., lobbying to eliminate affirmative action policies) and passively (e.g., ignoring racist comments by a colleague) complicit in the reinforcement of racial worldview structures (e.g., prejudices, discrimination, racial inequities) through intentional (e.g., voting, gentrification, employment practices) and unintentional (e.g., obliviousness to absence of workplace diversity) actions. Preservation and perpetuation of racism enabled by a racial worldview and institutionalized racial classification system continues to serve its initial purpose, to give unmerited social power to European descendants and to thwart meaningful human connections between diverse peoples based in trust, understanding, and solidarity. Hope lies in the parallel process of racial identity development, ironically driven by both racism and a racial worldview, which matures with a commitment to dismantle the structures, internal and external, of racism and to develop relationships with like-minded allies.

Jones (1997) identified three levels of racism: individual, institutional, and cultural. These levels intersect and influence one another and may be covert or overt, unintentional or intentional. Reflection 4.3 provides space to consider how these levels of racism may impact professional counselors' work with clients. **Individual racism** refers to personal attitudes and beliefs in White superiority and the inferiority of people of color, with physical differences among individuals used as an explanation of social, moral, and intellectual behavior. It involves adverse behavior of one individual or small group of people. Examples are racial slurs and stereotyping. **Institutional racism** is characterized as customs and practices within social systems that lead to racial inequalities. Examples include disproportionate numbers of racial minorities underemployed, undereducated, incarcerated, and underresourced (D'Andrea & Daniels, 1999). **Cultural racism** refers to the belief that cultural values and practices of White, European descent individuals are superior to those of other racial groups. These values may be evident in things such as art, economics, religions, and language. A few examples of institutional and cultural forms of racism throughout U.S. history are listed in Table 4.1. These levels of racism have several negative cognitive, affective, interpersonal, and physical costs for people of color.

REFLECTION 4.3

Identify overt and covert and intentional and unintentional forms of racism that may impact your work with clients of color.

Individual: _____

_____

_____

_____

Institutional: _____

_____

_____

Cultural: _____

_____

_____

TABLE 4.1 Examples of Institutional and Cultural Forms of Racism in U.S. History

Naturalization Law (1790)	Excluded Asians and Native Americans from gaining citizenship.
Manifest Destiny (mid- to late 1800s)	Belief that the United States was destined to expand to the Pacific Ocean. Right of discovery of Western lands outweighed Native Americans' right of occupancy of their lands. This led to the concept of "White Man's Burden" in that Whites viewed themselves as a world power to "civilize" others.
Jim Crow Laws (1876–1965)	Enacted in U.S. southern and border states a "separate but equal" status for African Americans. These laws required separate facilities (e.g., public schools, public transportation) for Whites and African Americans, limiting civil liberties for African Americans.
Dred Scott Decision (1857)	African slaves could not become free citizens. Dred Scott, a freed slave of a U.S. Army officer, had sued for his freedom. The decision stated that U.S. citizenship could not be granted to any African descendent, freed or enslaved. The decision was a major catalyst for the Civil War because it also declared the Missouri Compromise unconstitutional, a law stating slavery could not spread north past a particular boundary of lands gained in the Louisiana Compromise.
Dawes Act (1887)	Driven by those who believed that reservations limited integration and progress, Congress allowed the president to allot Native Americans heads of families 160 acres of certain reservation, although many tribes were excluded from this act. "Excess" lands were designated for Whites to build schools for "education and civilization" (Takaki, 2002a, p. 234). The federal government was to hold title to the land in trust for 25 years. The Dawes Act was one of several Congress passed to assimilate Native Americans and expand Western territory.

(continued)

TABLE 4.1 Examples of Institutional and Cultural Forms of Racism in U.S. History (Continued)	
Indian Removal Act (1830)	This congressional act mandated the removal of American Indians from east of the Mississippi River to territory west of the Mississippi.
People v. Hall (1854)	Supreme Court Decision: George W. Hall was acquitted of murder of a Chinese man because it was ruled that three of the witnesses who were Chinese could not by law testify against Whites.
Boarding School Movement (1870s)	Method used to assimilate Native American children into the mainstream educational system. The program isolated them from their families, subjected them to emotional and physical abuse when they tried to retain their culture, forced them to work in underfunded schools, and mandated they change their names and appearance to conform to Western or White culture.
Indian Appropriation Act (1871)	Congress specified that no tribe thereafter would be recognized as an independent nation with which the federal government could make a treaty. All future Indian policies would not be negotiated with Indian tribes through treaties, but rather would be determined by passing congressional statutes or executive orders.
Chinese Exclusion Act (1882)	This law limited Chinese immigration after many were fearful of Chinese Americans hurting the U.S. economy.
Eugenics Movement (1883)	Concept coined by Francis Galton that asserted scientific progress could only be sustained by racial purification and that the "superior" race (i.e., White) was endangered and selective breeding was necessary (Turner & Collinson, 2003).
Indian Reorganization Act (1934)	This act encouraged Indians to "recover" their culture and sought to promote tribal self-government by encouraging tribes to adopt U.S. style constitutions and form federally chartered corporations. Many tribes rejected the IRA, most fearing the consequences of more government control.
California Proposition 227 (1998)	Sought to establish English as the only legitimate language in schools and workplace.

COSTS OF RACISM FOR PEOPLE OF COLOR

Imagine, just as a part of your day, wondering if you were overlooked in a store; people were staring at you in a restaurant; someone discounted a comment that you made; you did not get a job, appropriate medical or legal advice, a bank loan, an apartment lease, a reasonable interest rate on a car loan, all because of your race. Experiences like these cause anxiety and guardedness because discriminatory social rules are not explicit, nor are individuals who participate in discrimination against people of color typically able to recognize their prejudicial behavior, as systemic injustices validate and normalize their actions (Tatum, 2003).

Racism is an inescapable reality for people of color in the United States. The imprint of racism is historically rooted in the social structure (i.e., laws, traditions, customs) of the United States and lives within its social systems (e.g., occupational, educational, judicial) (Jones, 2000). Racism, therefore, is a complex and dynamic form of social oppression that fundamentally affects the daily lives of people of color. The effects of racism essentially amount to quality of life costs, both charges and expenditures, imposed on people of color within an oppressive system. Consequently, racism has associated cognitive, affective, interpersonal, and physical costs for people of color. After reviewing each of these costs, complete Activity 4.1 to identify unique expressions or consequences for racial and ethnic minorities.

ACTIVITY 4.1

List below in dyads as many costs of racism for people of color as you can. Consider costs as they relate to daily lived experiences in families, schools, workplace, communities, and society in general. After you create the list of costs, consider how these costs may differ for various racial minorities. Why do you think these differences might exist?

Cognitive Costs:

_____

_____

_____

Affective Costs:

_____

_____

_____

Interpersonal Costs:

_____

_____

_____

Physical Costs:

_____

_____

_____

Cognitive Costs

Cognitive costs of racism include the mental energy and psychological processes (e.g., assessing, reflecting, questioning, interpreting) used to evaluate life incidents and experiences where racism is potentially involved. An individual's perception and understanding of racism is related to his or her racial identity development (Helms, 1995). People of color at earlier statuses of racial identity development assess, interpret, and cope differently with racism-implicated life events (e.g., racial profiling) than those in later stages.

During the process of racial identity development, an inevitable question emerges in the minds of people of color that effectively sums up the cognitive costs of racism: Did this happen to me (or others who share my racial classification) because of my (or their) race? This question usually comes to life as a result of an ambiguous cross-racial incident, or potentially racism-related life experiences, where people of color think or feel they may have been treated differentially, unfairly, or disrespectfully, conceivably because of their race (Cross, 1995; Helms, 1995). The question develops into a cognitive filter that is used to assess subsequent cross-racial situations as well as social experiences in general. A person of color, then, is left to reflect on daily interactions, situations, and behaviors, producing a general psychological vigilance in cross-racial interactions that taxes the mind, body, and spirit (Sue, Capodilupo, et al., 2007). Thus, social evaluation is necessary for people of color and contains many cognitive costs. Generalized negative thinking as a result of racism experiences can create additional costs such as chronic anxiety and lowered self-esteem, outlook (hope), and motivation.

A salient cognitive cost for people of color is internalized racism. **Internalized racism** supports the belief in White superiority and White as normative for people of color. In essence, people of color discount the value of their individual, institutional, and cultural contributions to society and engage in self-hatred. This may lead to denying their racial heritage or isolating themselves from their racial group. Internalized racism can create cognitive dissonance in that, as people of color increasingly introject White ideals and ignore the values of their group, they may find that they do not belong in either group.

Affective Costs

Byproducts of psychological vigilance (i.e., cognitive costs) include frustration, irritation, and hostility, which are antecedents for anger and possibly depression. Similarly, emotional responses may be triggered outright by unintentional and intentional racist acts or covert and overt institutionalized forms of racism. Emotional awareness of racism, however, can also be a tool for people of color, where affective cues provide information within social situations that can be used for self-preservation, self-protection, and empowerment.

The emotional costs of racism accompany racism-related stress (Harrell, 2000). Stress, in general, facilitates all negative emotions (Lazarus & Folkman, 1984). As described earlier, the psychological exercise that a structural system of racism produces sets the stage for hypervigilance or psychological stress. When a person of color perceives that vigilance is necessary, it can lead to anger, disappointment, and sadness. Such emotions inevitably develop in persons of color in the process of their racial identity development and understanding of racism.

People of color experience historical and generational emotional costs of racism as well. Within specific families and racially classified groups in the United States, the emotional costs of racism can be transmitted through generations, given their particular histories and experiences with racism. Children of parents who have experienced racial discrimination, for example, potentially sense and take on the emotional resonance of their parents' experiences with racism. This can happen directly or indirectly, even if the parents desire to shield them from their harmful experiences or deliberately try not to impart negative messages to their offspring. Other parents, educators, or adults, conversely, may be very intentional in sharing their experiences with their children, either to help protect, educate, and empower them, or because of their own unresolved racism-related issues and/or diffuse parent–child boundaries. In either case the emotional resonance that accompanies historical experiences of racism, within families or racially classified groups, factor into the individual emotional responses people of color have to racism.

Finally, emotional costs are associated with overt manifestations of racism, such as racial slurs, direct references to skin color, or culturally ubiquitous racial stereotypes (e.g., media portrayals of people of color). Occurrences such as these, expectedly, rouse an emotional response in many people of color. The principle distinction with racial offenses, however, is that these incidents have historical and cultural implications that demean the individual, his or her family, culture, ancestry, history, and all other people who identify with the person's racial classification.

Interpersonal Costs

The interpersonal costs of racism are perhaps the most visible and concrete of all the costs of racism described. Most people in the United States grow up in parts of cities, communities, neighborhoods, schools, and places of worship that are physically as well as functionally segregated. The segregation of people by racial classifications as a result of institutional racism (Jones, 1997) presents a social, even physical, barrier to the establishment of meaningful relationships between people from different racial groups. Social segregation creates an environment for misinformation, misunderstanding, and miscommunication between White people and people of color, as well as between different groups of people of color. It places barriers and limitations to the development of cross-racial relationships, perpetuates racism and discrimination, and maintains social inequities.

Interpersonal costs are, therefore, "fixed" in a social system of racial oppression. Specifically, the social structure that preserves dominant and subordinate groups does not support the development of trust between these groups, different oppressed groups, or members of the same oppressed group (Tatum, 2003). As a result, people of color are often ambivalent about developing relationships with Whites, or members of the "dominant group." At the same time, internalized racism contributes to intergroup and intragroup relational discord among people of color. The interpersonal costs of internalized racism, then, are fear, suspicion, and distrust even between and among people of color, who are similarly oppressed in a racist society.

Physical Costs

Distinctions made among mind, spirit, and body are largely conceptual, in that they are used for identification, explanation, and other functional purposes. It is understood, therefore, that the effects of racism are not only experienced cognitively, affectively, and interpersonally, but physically as well. The physical costs of racism refer specifically to associated physical and physiological symptoms and consequences experienced by people of color, which include hypertension, chronic fatigue, delivery of very-low-birth-weight preterm infants, and physical violence (Clark et al., 1999; Peters, 2004; Thompson & Neville, 1999; USDHHS, 2001a). Physical costs of racism also include outcomes related to health care. An Institute of Medicine (IOM; 2002) report "concluded that minority patients [people of color] are less likely than whites to receive the same quality of healthcare, even when they have similar insurance or the ability to pay for care. To make matters worse, this healthcare gap is linked with higher death rates among minorities" (p. 2).

WHITE PRIVILEGE

Imagine if you never had to think about what it is like to be a member of your race. You go through your day with academic, social, and career opportunities that seem natural to you, surrounded by people who look like you and share similar histories as you. You do not think about racism because you cannot recall significant experiences like those described previously where you were discriminated against because of your race. In fact, there may be instances where you had advantages over others of different races. You may feel comforted by your skin color but may feel guilt and sadness for the access and status your race affords you. This scenario is common for Whites and is known as **White privilege**.

Although many scholars discuss racism as a White problem (Katz, 2003), White privilege is the "other side of the coin" that typically receives little attention in the discussion of racism. White privilege refers to the positive ways that Whites benefit from racism. Oftentimes, these benefits or privileges are unintentional and unconscious. It is related to idea of **White supremacy**, the belief that the superiority of Whites justifies disproportionate access to social and economic resources. It "is the belief that only one's standards and opinions are accurate . . . and that these standards and opinions are defined and supported by Whites in a way to continually reinforce social distance between groups, thereby allowing Whites to dominate, control access to, and escape challenges from racial and ethnic minorities" (Hays & Chang, 2003, p. 135).

Peggy McIntosh (1988) wrote one of the most cited works on White privilege whereby she described 46 conditions of unearned advantages of having White skin color. These advantages include individual experiences (e.g., favorable situations in stores and job interviews, and not experiencing discrimination in daily living), institutional advantages (e.g., positive portrayal in media, adequate housing, and education opportunities), and access to things representative of her culture and the ability to avoid or ignore cultural contributions of other racial/ethnic groups.

Having racial privilege is like having an "invisible weightless knapsack of special provisions, assurances, tools, maps, guides, codebooks, passports, visas, clothes, compass, emergency gear, and blank checks" (McIntosh, 1988, p. 77). It refers to unearned advantages based on being constructed as White. Some of these unearned benefits include having control or authority over another group, possessing material and social resources, receiving favorable treatment, and being a majority status allowed to establish norms (Hays et al., 2004). Thus, White privilege entitles Whites the choice to acknowledge and discuss race and racism. It leads to conferred dominance (McIntosh, 1988), a state of being resulting from historical domination of other racial/ethnic groups. Many of these benefits are derived from a history of Whites implementing individual, institutional, and cultural racism, dating back to when Columbus "discovered" America.

Because race may be invisible to Whites, it is imperative to reflect on early memories of being a member of a particular racial group or racial groups. Consider the questions in Reflection 4.4.

REFLECTION 4.4

Describe a specific memory or critical incident when you first realized you were a member of your race. Who was involved in the experience? What thoughts, feelings, or behaviors do you note from the experience? What thoughts, feelings, or behaviors do you note now as you remember the incident?

TABLE 4.2 Early Memories of Whiteness and White Privilege

The following are quotes from counseling students as they reflected on their earliest memories of being a member of the White race:

"When asked to recall my earliest memory of being a member of my race, I was unable to come up with a specific event. I think that this is because I am White and I have always gone to school in White communities and I always remember being a part of the majority. . . . The fact that I don't have a major event that comes to mind when remembering my race demonstrated that because I am White, I am oblivious to recognizing that I had White privilege." (28-year-old White female)

"My first memory of discovering my race was in third grade. . . . I was not in a complete bubble, and knew that Black people existed. However, I never had contact with a Black person. . . . I made the transition to the public school system. . . . I noticed things were 'different'. There were kids that had a different skin color than mine. I recall being afraid of them and found many of these kids to be rather rambunctious. . . . One time I dreamed that people from the library were painting me black and it would not come off." (39-year-old White female)

"Growing up in the South in the 1940s and 1950s, I knew that I was privileged because I was White. My dad took me with him to pick up farm machinery shipped by train. Our little town's depot had 'colored' restrooms and 'colored' drinking fountains. . . . Even at 8 or 9 years of age, I knew that something was not quite right about the treatment of 'colored' people. My parents never questioned the situation and became disturbed with me in high school when I professed to believe in the civil rights movement." (65-year-old White female)

Additional characteristics of White privilege include:

- *White privilege is often invisible to Whites.* Given the advantages received based on lighter skin tones and other physical features associated with Whiteness, it might seem that White privilege would be more visible to Whites. Whites engage in interracial interactions daily, yet they do not experience prejudice or discrimination from people of color. White privilege also remains invisible to many because addressing racial issues is challenging. For those who become aware of their racial privileges, not only is it difficult to address racism, but also to address how one has benefited personally from racism seems nearly impossible. For example, many counselor trainees have difficulty identifying examples of personal racial privilege (Hays et al., 2004).
- *White privilege contains psychological and intellectual costs to Whites.* Depending on their level of awareness of White privilege, feelings associated with dealing with this awareness include helplessness, frustration/anger, defensiveness, sadness, anxiety, guilt, and shame. In addition, Whites may experience cognitive dissonance between their beliefs in individualism and equality and their overt and covert racist behaviors. Thus, even though White privilege is a benefit, there are many costs associated with being White (Ancis & Szymanski, 2001; Hays et al., 2004; Neville, Worthington, & Spanierman, 2001). These costs are described more fully later in the chapter.
- *There are several myths that Whites hold that can perpetuate White privilege.* Oftentimes, Whites inaccurately perceive their daily experiences and cultural values. These include the myths that Whiteness and White culture are desirable and universal; power affects everyone the same; guilt is a sufficient response to addressing racial privilege; feelings of discomfort can be used to resist change or accept privilege; and those with less power can be truly honest about their feelings regarding racism without consequences (Vodde, 2001).
- *White privilege differentially benefits Whites.* Whites may possess a combination of privileged and oppressed statuses, making their experiences with White privilege unique at times. For example, a White lesbian may experience oppression from her statuses as female and a sexual minority. Because of these forms of oppression, she may find it difficult to note specific advantages attributed to her skin color (Neville et al., 2001).
- *Individuals who do not identify as White may have some degree of White privilege.* White privilege is the valuation of lighter skin tones, particular hair texture, nose shapes, cultural values, and language. The more "White" an individual appears or approximates its value system, the more privileges he receives (Leonardo, 2004). For example, a light-skinned Latino may identify as Latino, yet can be perceived as White if his physical features approximate Whiteness.

COSTS OF RACISM FOR WHITES

Racism has been described as a major mental health problem, a psychological disease beginning as early as age 4 years. It has been considered a form of schizophrenia, creating a gap between how Whites think and behave regarding race and racism (Katz, 2003; Thompson & Neville, 1999). Racism as a disease contributes to a distorted sense of self, reality, and others. The ways in which Whites cope with and respond to racism and racial privilege has cognitive, affective, and interpersonal costs for them, although these costs are minimal compared to those for people of color (Goodman, 2001; Kivel, 1996; Spanierman & Heppner, 2004; Spanierman, Poteat, Beer, & Armstrong, 2004).

Cognitive Costs

Cognitive costs refer to the delusion of White superiority and individuality where Whites cannot see themselves as White and can deny racism because they are "individuals" (Katz, 2003). This delusion is created primarily as a result of an inaccurate portrayal of history and can isolate Whites from fully experiencing their culture and ethnicity. Thus, they lack an accurate awareness as a racial being and experience intellectual deficits because they are unable to develop a full range of knowledge of racial issues and culture in general.

White racial identity development (WRID; see Helms, 1995) is greatly impacted by racism and White privilege (Carter, 1990). The more racial identity statuses one possesses, the more race-complex situations they are able to engage in (Pack-Brown, 1999). White racial identity models assume a component of White guilt and rely on Whites abandoning entitlement to societal resources and privileges (Hays & Chang, 2003; Swim & Miller, 1999). Lower racial identity statuses (i.e., *Contact, Disintegration, Reintegration*) serve to enhance opportunities and cultural preferences for Whites and thus maintain the racial status quo (Jones & Carter, 1996), while higher statuses (i.e., *Pseudo-Independence, Immersion–Emersion, Autonomy*) view race as a complex construct that is often laden with misconceptions of minorities. A challenge of WRID is that it is difficult to promote a nonracist identity when Whites mostly do not think of themselves as racial beings. Whites at varying levels of White racial identity statuses will experience various psychosocial costs (Spanierman & Heppner, 2004). As individuals transition among racial identity statuses, they have emotional responses when confronted with the "White as oppressor" role.

Affective Costs

Emotional costs vary depending on Whites' awareness of racial issues. Fear is one common emotion Whites possess. Whites may have an irrational sense of danger or safety of people of color. They may fear certain neighborhoods because of stereotypes they hold. They may fear supporting racial affirmative laws and policies due to a fear of their impact on White norms. As Whites acknowledge their racial privilege, they may become fearful of losing privileges to which they have become accustomed. Anger is another emotional cost for Whites. Anger may create apathy in Whites, and they may demonstrate a lack of interest in addressing racism. Anger can also result in the use of denial, discussed in the following section.

Awareness of racism and White privilege could create guilt for Whites (Swim & Miller, 1999). This guilt is often associated with a sense of helplessness and sadness, as Whites may feel incapable of ending racism. Whites may feel anxious because of this guilt and experience lowered self-esteem. Guilt can be portrayed individually or collectively (Arminio, 2001). For example, White guilt may result from a race-associated action (or inaction) that an individual engages in or as a result of understanding how Whites have been oppressive to people of color. Whites may not feel personally guilty but may feel guilt for being a member of their racial group. In counseling, a counselor's guilt may manifest as **color consciousness**, which refers to being intentionally cognizant of racial issues and potentially overemphasizing the role race and racism plays in the client's problems (Ridley, 2005).

Interpersonal Costs

Interpersonal costs refer to the loss of relationships with either people of color or other Whites, depending on how aware and committed Whites are to addressing racism and White privilege. The distorted sense of others that accompanies White racism indicates greater reliance on stereotypes and thus a lack of understanding of people of color. This often results in limited interactions with people of color and thus limited social competencies as Whites restrict themselves when learning about other cultures, races, and ethnicities.

The more people connect with people of color, the more they disconnect with racist friends and family and segregated institutions (Arminio, 2001). As Whites address racism and racial privilege, they may lose relationships with other Whites, including family members and friends, who are not engaged in social advocacy and personal growth. This is a particular challenge for Whites that often prevents them from acknowledging racism and White privilege. Consider specific interpersonal costs and complete Reflection 4.5.

REFLECTION 4.5

List potential interpersonal costs that you may experience as you engage in multicultural counseling and social advocacy in your personal and professional roles.

_____

_____

_____

_____

_____

WHITES' PSYCHOLOGICAL RESPONSES TO RACISM AND WHITE PRIVILEGE

There is great cognitive and emotional dissonance associated with racism and White privilege awareness. Racism contradicts what we have been taught about being an American: "Liberty and justice for all"; "Equal opportunity for all"; and "All [humans] are created equal." How do Whites negotiate thoughts and feelings that come with a belief in racial justice and wanting to maintain their sociocultural and economic statuses? According to the fight or flight response to racism (Ponterotto, 1991), the ways in which Whites interact with other racial groups includes avoiding contact or reacting defensively toward them. Examples include White flight into "Whiter" neighborhoods and schools and increased prejudice and stereotyping when threatened. Further, Whites engage in various defense mechanisms as a way to help them reduce the costs of White racism. They may attempt to change their views of reality or assimilate race-related data to fit existing ideas they have about racial groups (Skillings & Dobbins, 1991). Remaining racist impacts the psychological growth of Whites (Utsey, McCarthy, Eubanks, & Adrian, 2002).

Denial is one of Whites' key defense mechanisms that helps maintain White privilege and alleviate dissonance and emotional discomfort. Most Whites do not believe that they are racist and thus the discussion of racism and White privilege dissipates. Three examples of ways Whites deny the existence of racism and White privilege include holding color-blind racial attitudes, believing in the myth of meritocracy, and focusing on exceptions to refute claims of White racism.

Color-Blind Racial Attitudes

Having **color-blind racial attitudes** or being color-blind refers to the distortion or minimization of race and racism. It is helpful in justifying racial discrimination and the current racial status quo. Examples include: "I don't see a person's color. I see her only as a person" and "There is only one race—the human race." When counselors act color-blind, they may have difficulty establishing a trusting, therapeutic alliance, particularly with racial/ethnic minorities (Neville, Spanierman, & Doan, 2006). White counselors may avoid the topic of race in an effort to manage their own anxiety about its impact on the counseling process (Ridley, 2005).

Myth of Meritocracy

The **myth of meritocracy** is the notion that all individuals regardless of racial makeup can succeed if they "work hard." Examples include: "Racial minorities could be more successful if they just tried harder" and "I have things because I worked for them." It is an "addiction to a belief in the American myth that the standard and style of living that is enjoyed by 'successful' Mainstream Americans is due exclusively to their individual efforts" (Skillings & Dobbins, 1991, p. 210).

Focus on Exceptions

Oftentimes, Whites will deflect their role in perpetuating racism by focusing on times when they were discriminated against by people of color, a concept known as **reverse discrimination**. Reverse discrimination may be viewed in several Whites' responses to laws and policies such as affirmative action in universities and the workplace and increased immigration allowances. Examples include: "We are oppressed in that we are required to include everybody" and "People should be compared based on their merit or skills, not their race." Further, they may select instances when they experienced oppression due their cultural makeup. This is a natural defense because many Whites hold both privileged and oppressed statuses and can easily see times where they had been treated unfairly because of their gender, socioeconomic status, religion, and so on. One related mechanism Whites use to deal with increased awareness is projection. **Projection** refers to the preoccupation of racism of others or the intellectualization of the problem (Skillings & Dobbins, 1991). Each of these examples illustrates a way to deny or minimize Whites' personal investment in perpetuating racism and White privilege.

Psychological Dispositions of White Racism

In a 15-year qualitative study involving over 1,200 White individuals across the country, D'Andrea and Daniels (1999) assessed how these individuals thought about and reacted to issues of racism and race relations in the United States today. From this research they identified five psychological dispositions of White racism, each characterized by cognitive, behavioral, and affective responses. They include:

- *Affective–Impulsive Disposition.* Whites demonstrating this disposition engage in limited, stereotypical thinking about non-Whites and deny the existence of racism. These thoughts are often related to aggressive and hostile feelings towards people of color and impulsive actions (e.g., destroying property, racial slurs, physical violence). Whites who predominantly identify with this disposition often exhibit little to no shame or guilt in their interactions with people of color.
- *Rational Disposition.* Whites of this disposition are somewhat aware of how racism exists yet they tend to engage in either-or thinking about race relations. Further, Whites operate from a superficial tolerance of people of color until they encounter them, in which they then exhibit negative (yet often not as hostile and impulsive as those of the Affective–Impulsive disposition) reactions to any policies or practices that encourage racial integration (e.g., affirmative action, integration of neighborhoods, interracial relationships).
- *Liberal Disposition.* This worldview is characterized by a greater understanding of racism and other forms of social injustice, including insight into others' perspectives and experiences. This disposition was dominant for most of the White counselor educators and students in this study, with individuals reporting an interest in multicultural issues in general yet apathetic or

not motivated to explore how White racism influences mental health and social issues of people of color. While there is some sadness demonstrated by these Whites, there is inaction on their parts because they perceive that they will experience negative reactions from others or will have to confront their own White privileges (see McIntosh, 1988).

• *Principled Disposition.* Whites operating from the Principled disposition are very knowledgeable about how White privilege in their personal and professional lives influences racism, can cite specific examples of systemic racism in the United States, and (for those in counselor training programs) can note gaps or flaws in the ways by which multicultural issues are addressed in counselor preparation. Even with a passion and sensitivity to racial issues, these individuals tend to integrate discussions of racism with others in a superficial manner and report that they are cynical that current racial dynamics in the United States will change.

• *Principled Activistic Disposition.* Constituting less than 1% of the sample, Whites in this disposition are similar to earlier dispositions because they have an understanding of racism yet are different in that they are hopeful and active in creating sociopolitical change. Oftentimes, these individuals are not overwhelmed by making systemic changes and cite that other Whites have the potential to have this perspective and facilitate "spiritual connection and moral empathy" to eradicate racism. Whites of this disposition are considered social advocates that seek to eliminate racism in specific ways within their personal and professional lives.

In sum, racial issues, particularly racism and White privilege, greatly impact the counseling process (Ridley, 2005; Thompson & Jenal, 1994). Clients of color may react to a counselor's racial makeup (i.e., White) or race-based discussions (or lack thereof) based on specific racial events they experience within or outside the counseling session. These responses will vary depending on the racial identity statuses of both counselors and clients. When racial issues are not discussed in the counseling relationship, it can be considered a form of racism because it negatively impacts the relationship; clients may become frustrated and feel ignored and distrustful. White counselors who avoid racial discussions or disregard how race plays into client problems may perceive the client to be defensive or resistant, which could in turn lead to labeling client behaviors as pathological. Further, if White counselors have a high need for power or control over a client of color based on the counselor's racial identity status, clients may be oppressed further, impacting their mental well-being. Thus, White counselors who address racism and White privilege are less likely to rely on stereotypes, have more therapeutic relationships with clients of color, are more likely to contextualize problems and thus consider social and other environmental causes of client problems, have increased empathy for clients of color, and will be more in tune to racial dynamics within the counseling session (Neville et al., 2001, 2006).

Acknowledging and addressing racism and White privilege is a challenging process for White counselors. Although it is accompanied by various costs to Whites, the costs are insignificant as compared to those of people of color within and outside the counseling session. When counselors ignore racism, it threatens racial minorities in counseling and the core values of counseling (Ridley, 2005). Therefore, "Whites 'must forgive themselves' of the misteaching they have learned, but they must also become responsible for behaving consistently with new attitudes" (Arminio, 2001 p. 249).

ERADICATING RACISM

Eradicating racism involves a systematic approach that focuses on counselor self-awareness, client services, and changing systems. The following are some intrapersonal and interpersonal recommendations for ways in which counselors may increase their multicultural competence to end racism and redistribute racial privilege.

Counselor Self-Awareness

Self-awareness of one's own attitudes and behaviors regarding racism and racial privilege is the first step toward social change (see Activities 4.2 and 4.3). Ridley (2005) outlines various factors that contribute to counselor racism. Counselors should reflect on these factors and reflect on how they might play into their counseling relationships. While these factors were developed as guidelines for White counselors, counselors of color are also encouraged to reflect on them. They include:

- *"Cultural tunnel vision" or ethnocentrism.* Counselors who maintain cultural tunnel vision view client problems from the perspective of their own cultural socialization. Counselors may fail to view presenting problems from the client's worldview and minimize the role of racism and other forms of oppression in the client's issues.
- *Victim blaming.* Victim blaming refers to labeling clients as solely causing their presenting issues and/or identifying client behaviors in counseling that differ from the counselor's expectations as pathological or a form of resistance. Thus, counselors may exhibit racist attitudes and behaviors and ignore potential effects of racism on client problems.
- *The limitations of consciousness raising.* Consciousness raising often involves increasing knowledge and awareness of racism; however, this is often at a superficial level. For example, counselors may be aware of the definitions and causes of racism and racial privilege yet fail to identify specific overt and covert behaviors associated with each as well as have limited behaviors to address them. Many counselors who are aware of racism and its effects might suggest cultural sensitivity as a sole goal, minimizing the need to end racism.
- *Race-based stereotyping.* Counselors of all races and ethnicities hold various stereotypes of themselves and racially/ethnically different individuals. This may partly be based on thinking of race as a biological construct and viewing racial groups as distinctly superior or inferior. Examining stereotypes could provide important insights for counselors.

ACTIVITY 4.2

Bring in items that symbolize what it means to be a member of your race. As an alternative to concrete items, use indirect representations (e.g., photos, magazine pictures, songs, poems, food). Each student may discuss the following in small groups or as a class:

  a. Describe your cultural identity via props.
  b. What is your definition of mental health? What is your racial/ethnic group's definition of mental health? How is it similar to and different than yours?
  c. When your family and/or friends discuss (or discussed) "other" people in the previous cultural identities, how did they describe them?
  d. What does racially different mean to you? How do you think clients who are racially different from you view you or react to you as their counselor?
  e. What does racially similar mean to you? How do you think clients who are racially similar to you view you or react to you as their counselor?
  f. Articulate one contribution regarding how your race or racial identity influences your counseling style and relationships with clients.

ACTIVITY 4.3

Attend a school or community event that focuses on a racial or ethnic group other than your own. Record your observations of the content and processes within the event. Write a reaction paper that addresses the following questions:

- What were your expectations of the event prior to attending?
- What thoughts and feelings did you have before, during, and after the event?
- How, if at all, did these thoughts and feelings relate to concepts discussed in this chapter?
- To what degree did you participate in the event?
- What factors affected your level of participation?
- What did you learn from the immersion experience?
- How can this learning apply to your work as a counselor?

Client Services

Counselors may address and work to end racism for the client by intervening both within the counseling session and within the client's school and community. These strategies may be helpful for both White clients and clients of color.

ADDRESSING RACISM IN THE COUNSELING SESSION   The first component for eradicating racism within clients' lives involves actions within the counseling session. Race-related stress may manifest itself at varying degrees depending on the client and presenting issues. Exploring each of the following areas as relevant may help build a stronger therapeutic alliance.

- *Assessing the client's racial identity.* Racial identity development models outline statuses that describe racial attitudes toward self and others, attitudes that vary according to which status(es) is (are) most prominent for individuals. (See Chapter 2 for a complete description of models.) Assessing a client's racial identity using available tools can illuminate which attitudes they hold about race, racism, and White privilege. Counselors can present the results, discuss specific items, and process how racial identity development may affect the client's experiences within the counseling relationship and surrounding community.
- *Exploring client problems for race-related stress.* As clients present their concerns in counseling, counselors may want to investigate with them how their concerns may be impacted by their racial makeup and others' racist attitudes. Knowing which racial identity statuses are most salient for each client may assist in this discussion. Counselors are encouraged to assess any examples of racism clients may be experiencing that created, is maintaining, or will hinder psychological healing. Counselors should remain empathic during this exploration and self-disclose their own struggles as appropriate.
- *Investigating intersections of trauma and other forms of oppression with race-related stress.* Because clients come to counseling with multiple cultural identities and life experiences, they may present with issues concerning negative events within their families and communities. These issues may result from violence or trauma and/or being a member of a sexual minority, lower socioeconomic status, or other minority status. Racism experiences intersect with stress

from these other experiences. Counselors are to examine both benefits and challenges clients experience as a result of their cultural identities and life experiences. In addition, counselors are to integrate this information with other aspects of client concerns.

- *Moving a client through race-related guilt.* Ivey (1995) proposed liberation therapy, which helps clients (specifically White clients) move through guilt associated with racial privilege. Steps in this approach include identifying the instance of oppression (e.g., racism), reflecting and redefining the experience, and integrating the experience for increased self-understanding. According to this therapy, counselors may process the following questions with clients dealing with these issues: Who were you with when the instance occurred? What caused the guilt? What did you do with the guilt? Are there any discrepancies between your attitudes and behaviors? What did you learn from the guilt? What can you do with what you have learned about guilt?

ADDRESSING RACISM IN THE CLIENT'S SCHOOL AND COMMUNITY   In addition to addressing and dismantling racism within the counseling session, counselors are encouraged to examine the systems in which clients live and experience racism. Further, counselors should work to build stronger coping mechanisms for clients by strengthening and developing community resources.

- *Cultivating client resources.* As clients present their stories, counselors are encouraged to search for personal, cultural, and community resources that clients may draw upon in counseling. Clients may present their concerns in the form of challenges, and counselors can process with them hidden strengths they have to deal with these challenges and instances when they overcame specific challenges in the past. Additionally, counselors should collaborate with clients and identify existing support systems and personality attributes as well as resources clients would like to integrate into their lives.
- *Assessing the degree and existing forms of racism.* Depending on their cultural makeup, clients will present in counseling with varying degrees of racism experiences. Counselors are to evaluate these experiences by asking clients about specific overt and covert racism they experience in their daily lives and ways it impacts their psychological well-being.
- *Developing new resources.* Counselors as social advocates are responsible for initiating and participating in school and community initiatives that will assist in eradicating racism. To this end, they are charged with collaborating with others to develop and implement programs that educate teachers, administrators, parents, legal and health services professionals, and community leaders about the impact of racism on people of color. As these programs are developed, counselors are encouraged to ensure that clients and their families have knowledge of and access to these programs. Refer to Activity 4.4.

ACTIVITY 4.4

Consider the following in small groups and compile a list for each of the questions:

- What resources are available to clients of color in your local schools and community?
- Where are there opportunities for program development?
- What are the needed economic, legal, and public health services for clients of color?

Changing Systems

Changing existing political, legal, economic, and public health systems is another major component in eradicating racism. Counselors are encouraged to assess each of these systems to better understand how racism and racial privilege are present.

POLITICAL AND LEGAL CONCERNS   In addition to attending to race-related issues within the counseling relationship and the client's immediate environment, counselors need to be familiar with historical and current legislation and court decisions that address racial issues or have implications pertaining to racism. In familiarizing yourself with these, consider both positive and negative consequences. Some of these may be unintended consequences. Have some of these laws and policies made racism and White privilege issues worse? Some examples of historic laws and policies that have attempted to address racial/ethnic issues and oppression include:

- *Treaty of Guadeloupe Hidalgo (1849):* This treaty granted citizenship to Mexicans living within acquired territories.
- *Reconstruction (1865–1877):* This era ended slavery and briefly gave African Americans voting rights and "40 acres and a mule."
- *Indian Reorganization Act (1934):* This act abolished the land allotment program and provided funding for tribes to allow them to redevelop and establish self-governments.
- *Brown v. Board of Education, Topeka, Kansas (1954):* This decision ruled that "separate was inherently unequal" and made racial segregation in schools illegal.
- *Warren-McCarran Act (1962):* This permitted non-White immigrants to be naturalized.
- *Civil Rights Act (1964):* This act prohibited employer discrimination in hiring, placement, and promotion of employees based on race, color, religion, or ethnicity.
- *Immigration Act (1965):* This act set the stage for future immigration laws whereby individuals of various nationalities had an equal chance for immigration, abolishing the national origins quota system in place at that time.
- *Affirmative Action (post–civil rights era):* Legal policies implemented to help level the playing field and create occupational, educational, and business opportunities for racial/ethnic minorities.
- *Public Law 93-638 (1975):* Also referred to as the Indian Self-Determination and Education Assistance Act of 1975, this law provided Native Americans more authority in developing community-specific educational and federal services.
- *Indian Health Care Improvement Act (1976):* This act allocated funds for health care services for Native Americans in tribal communities.
- *No Child Left Behind Act (2002):* This act stated that public schools make adequate yearly progress. One of the main goals of this act was to close the achievement gap among various racial/ethnic groups.

In addition to these laws and policies, counselors should attend to current legislation to ensure that there are no potential negative effects for people of color.

ECONOMIC CONCERNS   Even with affirmative action, people of color receive disproportionate incomes and job opportunities in comparison to their White counterparts. This is often based on individual, institutional, and cultural forms of racism (Jones, 1997) discussed earlier in the chapter. Counselors should remain mindful of how racism impacts economic opportunities for people of color. This is particularly important in career counseling with people of color. Further, Chapter 7 explains how poverty influences people of color.

PUBLIC HEALTH CONCERNS   People of color experience a variety of health-related concerns as a result of racism. The surgeon general's report supplement on race, ethnicity, and mental health (USDHHS, 2001a) has numerous examples of how oppression impacts mental health, specifically related to misdiagnosis, staff, facility and program resources, length of treatment, and dissatisfaction with treatment. Counselors need to be aware of health disparities for people of color and how racism contributes to them. Several chapters throughout this text highlight how racism and other forms of discrimination impact various racial and ethnic groups.

TAKING ACTION   In sum, race-related stress in the forms of racism and/or White privilege has detrimental effects on clients' psychological, physical, and social well-being. Additionally, clients often experience oppression and other forms of trauma from other cultural identities they possess. Taking into account the strategies listed for building counselor self-awareness, advocating for clients within the counseling session and their communities, and examining and creating institutional changes, counselors are encouraged to develop a vision for ending racism and other intersecting oppressions. Activity 4.5 provides a beginning forum for this vision.

ACTIVITY 4.5

Divide the class into small groups and distribute various materials and resources that could be used to develop a model for what a nonracist community would look like. Upon completion of the project, have each group discuss their proposed community and consider the following:

   a. What would nonracist counseling services in schools and communities look like?
   b. What school and community services would be available?
   c. What existing school and community services would be adapted?
   d. How are the various class proposals similar and different?
   e. What is one thing you could do to achieve this community?

Summary

The way race has been defined throughout history has created significant physical, psychological, social, academic, legal, political, and economic consequences, to name a few. Racial classifications have created an oppressive system for both Whites and people of color (i.e., American Indian or Alaskan Native, Asian, Black or African American, Native Hawaiian and Other Pacific Islander) known as racism. Racism exists at three interlocking levels (i.e., individual, institutional, and cultural) that continue to primarily serve the interests of Whites and justify covert and overt exploitation of people of color.

Costs of racism for people of color include cognitive (e.g., internalized racism, challenges in racial identity development), affective (e.g., race-related stress, hypervigilance, anger, sadness), interpersonal (e.g., segregation, relational discord), and physical (e.g., hypertension, physical violence) costs. While people of color have suffered more severe consequences of racism, Whites also experience personal costs from a system in which they benefit. Some include a false sense of cultural identity, feelings of guilt and fear depending on Whites' level of awareness of their privileged status, and diminished relationships with people of color and thus limited social competence. These costs are often associated with a lack of awareness of and motivation to dismantle White privilege.

White privilege refers to benefits Whites or individuals who approximate a whiter skin tone receive based on their skin color. These advantages include favorable treatment in daily activities such as job interviews and store purchases, adequate and positive representation of the White race in media, and assumptions of intelligence, a good work ethic, and success. White privilege is often invisible to Whites, which hinders many of them from understanding their racial and ethnic identities as well as the experiences of people of color who often do not receive racial privilege. Depending on their level of awareness of racism and racial privilege, Whites possess several psychological responses, including color-blind racial attitudes, belief in the myth of meritocracy, and a focus on exceptions to White privilege and White racism.

Eradicating racism for clients involves a systematic approach in which counselors engage in awareness of their own experiences with racial privilege and oppression, integrate discussions of race and racism in counseling sessions and the larger community, and work to change political, legal, financial, and health disparities throughout various systems.

CHAPTER 5

Gender and Sexism

EDWARD CANNON AND ANNELIESE A. SINGH

PREVIEW

Gender and sexism, two interrelated constructs that have important implications for counselors, will be introduced in this chapter to continue the discussion of social justice and its impact on individuals' mental health. In assessing the degree to which gender and sexism affect clients, as well as the counseling relationship, it is crucial for counselors to pay attention to the convergence of multiple identities (e.g., race, sex, gender expression, sexual orientation, ability status, age, socioeconomic status). Multicultural competence with respect to gender and sexism may be addressed through increased counselor awareness of one's own assumptions, values, and biases regarding gender and gender expression; counselor awareness of clients' worldviews regarding gender and gender expression; and culturally appropriate intervention strategies. School counselors, clinical counselors, rehabilitation counselors, pastoral counselors, addictions counselors, and marriage and family counselors must all have a keen understanding of the powerful roles that gender and sexism play in their own lives, as well as the lives of clients. This chapter defines gender and sexism, discusses the concepts of gender identity and gender expression, outlines implications for counseling from a gender-sensitive perspective, and discusses the intersection of gender and gender identity with race, ethnicity, and culture.

DEFINING GENDER AND SEXISM

Gender is a fundamental component of our personality, development, and culture. It is integral to cognitive, psychosocial, and biological development. The concept of gender is complex, evident through its multiple meanings and expressions. It is such a fundamental component of who we are and how we see the world that we rarely question what it means to be male or female: It just is. However, scholars have argued that gender is both biologically determined and socially constructed (Butler, 1990). In other words, how we learn what gender we are, how we learn what gender others are, and how we learn so-called gender-appropriate behavior are a combination of genetics and environment.

Counselors must be sensitive that in a complex world there are many ways to understand and express gender, and that not everyone will conform to a binary system of male/female. In addition, it is important to recognize the critical role gender socialization plays in an individual's (including our own) development. When we are born, we are usually assigned a gender, male or female, based on physical characteristics. As early as age 2 years, we begin to associate certain behaviors with gender. By age 4 years, we understand that certain jobs, toys, and play are associated with boys or with girls. At age 6 years, most children can tell us "what boys do" versus "what girls do" as a demonstration of their understanding of personality characteristics and mannerisms attached to each gender.

Through interaction with others, who we are shapes our definition of gender, and how we make meaning of our own gender significantly affects our view of ourselves. As in other domains, constructions of gender are fluid and are grounded in personal experiences, yet also contain multiple realities and narratives about who we are and how we interact with others. These narratives are woven into racial, ethnic, religious, sexual orientation, and socioeconomic class contexts. Reflection 5.1 provides key considerations for thinking of counselors' personal experiences with gender.

REFLECTION 5.1

- Think about your earliest memories when you realized you were of a member of your gender. Describe the situation and any feelings and behaviors associated with prescribed roles and expectations.
- In general, what messages did you receive about your gender in your family of origin?
- What opportunities have been available to you because of your gender? What barriers have occurred?
- Which gender roles do you still adhere to as an adult?
- How has your gender and related opportunities and barriers affected your physical and psychological well-being?
- How would your life be different if you were another gender?
- How do you think your gender may be helpful as a counselor? How may it present challenges?

Source: Adapted from Hays and Gray (in 2010)

Transgender "is a broad umbrella category used to describe inner experiences of behavioral disparities between biological sex and gender identity" (Ellis & Eriksen, 2002, p. 290). This definition includes cross-dressers (identical to transvestites, usually heterosexual men who dress in women's clothing) and transsexuals (individuals who identify with the opposite gender assigned to them at birth). It is important to remember that gender is not the same as sexuality, and that transgender identity is not synonymous with gay or lesbian identity.

The existence of transgender individuals has been documented throughout history and cultures around the world, from the Hijras of India, to the Eunuchs of Ancient Greek and Egyptian cultures. Joan of Arc has been embraced by the transgender community, as have other famous people like professional tennis player and physician Renee Richards (born Richard Raskind). According to the National Coalition for LGBT Health (2004), the most urgent transgender community needs include preventing violence against transgender people, HIV prevention and treatment, alcohol and other drug abuse prevention and treatment, and crisis counseling for suicidal ideation and depression. Typically, transgender individuals who seek mental health services are classified—according to the *Diagnostic and Statistical Manual of Mental Disorders,* 4th edition, text revision (*DSM–IV–TR;* 2000)—with Gender Identity Disorder, which is a controversial practice because transgender people do not necessarily believe that their condition is pathological. It is often the stigma attached to being transgender that creates much of the distress for this vulnerable community, and it is the most common reason cited for suicide attempts by transgender individuals (Ellis & Eriksen, 2002).

An increasingly used term is **gender queer** because it is a more inclusive term than transgender or transsexual, identifying individuals who transgress boundaries of gender identity and sexual orientation. Gender queer would include individuals who may be **intersexed**, that is, individuals who possess reproductive or sexual anatomy that does not fit into the socially constructed definitions of male and female. According to the Intersex Society of North America (n.d.), it is estimated that approximately 1 in 1,500 to 1 in 2,000 children are born with noticeably atypical genitals.

Sexism is defined as the oppression of individuals based on gender. It has been historically discussed in relation to the exploitation and dominance of women by men (hooks, 1984). Examples of sexism include women being sexualized in popular media solely for the entertainment of heterosexual men, as well as women on average earning less money than their male counterparts. An additional example pertains to an unequal distribution of labor within the family system for women who may work outside the home. These women often are expected to take on double (sometimes triple) duties by managing a home, family, and career. Still, women continue to be bombarded with negative messages. Because women are systematically surrounded by negative messages and frequently receive negative information about being female, many women start to believe these negative messages. This is called **internalized sexism**. Internalized sexism is a manifestation of male privilege. **Male privilege** refers to unearned rights and societal benefits afforded to men solely based on their biological sex. Activity 5.1 explores male privilege and its effects on both men and women. Examples of male privilege include men generally being socialized not to be afraid to walk alone at night in a public place, and men having multiple sex partners without being viewed as promiscuous.

ACTIVITY 5.1

In small groups, identify some forms of male privilege at the individual, interpersonal, community, and institutional levels. What are the negative effects for both men and women? Discuss strategies to minimize the effects of male privilege. How might male privilege manifest itself in a counseling session?

GENDER AND COUNSELING CONSIDERATIONS

Historically, the field of multicultural counseling has focused on the experiences of racial/ethnic minority clients, but more recently the focus has expanded to include the intersection of multiple cultural identities, including gender (Israel, 2003). Considering your own as well as your clients' identities in counseling is complex. The most important first step is an awareness of your own assumptions, values, and biases regarding gender. Additionally, by learning about your client's worldview regarding issues of gender, you will be better able to work effectively with the client. There are certain factors to consider that may lead to more effective counseling processes and outcomes. These include client–counselor matching, exploration of racial and cultural differences, and communication styles (Matthews & Peterman, 1998). But before discussing counseling considerations of gender, existing literature on client–counselor matching is presented.

Although one might assume that same-race or same-gender client–counselor dyads would always provide better outcomes, the literature shows mixed results (Pope-Davis & Coleman, 1997). Sue, Ivey, and Pedersen (1996) found that while clients of some cultural groups did better with ethnically similar therapists of the same gender, overall it was the degree of similarity between the counselor and client in terms of attitudes, beliefs, and values that enhanced treatment outcomes. The willingness of the counselor to broach difficult topics was also deemed an important variable in determining successful treatment outcomes.

Gender-related variables within the context of counseling have been examined more closely in recent years because today the majority of counselors are female (Kingman, 1997). Not surprisingly, due to gender role socialization, male and female counselors tend to invoke different strategies when interacting with clients. According to Carli (1990), men tend to speak more assertively overall with both men and women, whereas women tend to speak more assertively with other women but more tentatively with men. These are manifestations of sexism. Activity 5.2 challenges you to discuss other examples of sexism in popular culture.

ACTIVITY 5.2

Identify something from popular culture that is sexist in nature (e.g., a song, an advertisement, a movie). As a class discuss how popular culture perpetuates sexism. What are the mixed messages portrayed in the item? Discuss how these representations of popular culture affect the mental health of males and females.

Does gender make a difference in counseling dyads? Prior research has shown little evidence of an influence of gender alone, specifically when clients were asked to rate improvement from beginning counseling to termination (Bryan, Dersch, Shumway, & Arredondo, 2004; Zlotnick, Elkin, & Shea, 1998). Regardless of the makeup of gender dyads, clients generally report perceptions of improvement in counseling, meaning they feel they are resolving the problems that brought them to treatment. In terms of race and gender, same-race and same-gender dyads allow for the client and counselor to more quickly establish rapport, but it is debatable whether this makes a difference in treatment outcomes (Thompson, Worthington, & Atkinson, 1994; Zlotnick et al., 1998). Overall, however, clients of color working with White counselors report higher levels of distress and less improvement than White clients (McGoldrick, 1998; Thompson et al., 1994). Although literature on client–counselor matching is in its infancy and provides mixed results, particularly concerning intersecting cultural identities, it is imperative that counselors consider the complex role gender and sexism play in counseling process and outcome. The following sections will discuss gender-specific counseling considerations and strategies.

Assumptions about gender can negatively impact clients by influencing the techniques and treatment strategies you choose. Bartholomew (2003) presents several issues to consider when providing gender-sensitive counseling to clients. For example, if you believe that women should not show anger, you may help only male clients express this emotion. If you have strong beliefs about how men and women should act (e.g., according to culturally approved gender roles), you may send negative signals to clients who do not conform, thus impeding the counseling relationship. The following section discusses these and related issues in more depth.

Counseling Girls and Women

In the past several decades, girls and women have made great strides in the quest for gender equality. To be judged on the basis of intelligence, character, and accomplishments rather than on the basis of gender is an achievable (yet unmet) goal for women, regardless of ethnicity, social class, or sexual orientation. Despite the great societal changes that have led to increased opportunities for half of the world's population, girls and women continue to face particular challenges. According to the American Psychological Association (American Psychological Association, 2006a), females' life stressors include "interpersonal victimization and violence, unrealistic media images of girls and women, limited economic resources, role overload, relationship disruptions, and work inequities" (p. 2). Table 5.1 provides American Psychological Association (2006a) guidelines for psychological practice with girls and women. After reviewing these guidelines, see Reflection 5.2 to consider concrete ways to apply them.

TABLE 5.1 Guidelines for Psychological Practice with Girls and Women

Diversity, Social Context, and Power

Guideline 1: Psychologists strive to be aware of the effects of socialization, stereotyping, and unique life events on the development of girls and women in diverse cultural groups.

Guideline 2: Psychologists are encouraged to recognize and utilize information about oppression, privilege, and identity development as they may affect girls and women.

Guideline 3: Psychologists strive to understand the impact of bias and discrimination upon the physical and mental health of those with whom they work.

Professional Responsibility

Guideline 4: Psychologists strive to use gender and culturally sensitive, affirming practices in providing services to girls and women.

Guideline 5: Psychologists are encouraged to recognize how their socialization, attitudes, and knowledge about gender may affect their practice with girls and women.

Practice Applications

Guideline 6: Psychologists are encouraged to employ interventions and approaches that have been found to be effective in the treatment of issues of concern to girls and women.

Guideline 7: Psychologists strive to foster therapeutic relationships and practices that promote initiative, empowerment, and expanded alternatives and choices for girls and women.

Guideline 8: Psychologists strive to provide appropriate, unbiased assessments and diagnoses in their work with women and girls.

Guideline 9: Psychologists strive to consider the problems of girls and women in their sociopolitical context.

Guideline 10: Psychologists strive to acquaint themselves with and utilize relevant mental health, education, and community resources for girls and women.

Guideline 11: Psychologists are encouraged to understand and work to change institutional and systemic bias that may impact girls and women.

Source: American Psychological Association (2006a).

REFLECTION 5.2

The American Psychological Association (2006a) developed guidelines for working with girls and women (see Table 5.1) with the goal of promoting awareness, education, and prevention. The 11 guidelines are organized into three sections: (a) Diversity, Social Context, and Power, (b) Professional Responsibility, and (c) Practice Applications. The first section presents a framework concerning social identity and gender role socialization issues followed by more applied sections on professional responsibility and actual practice applications. Although developed for psychologists, these guidelines can greatly assist counselors working with girls and women. In dyads, discuss ways these guidelines may be operationalized for more gender-sensitive counseling practice. List concrete ways that you can counsel girls and women more effectively.

Counselors working with women and girls have a responsibility to evaluate their own awareness, knowledge, and skills related to this population. According to government statistics, women are twice as likely as men to be depressed, and girls are seven times more likely than boys to be depressed. Females are roughly nine times more likely to have eating disorders than males. Compared to men, women are two to three times more likely to experience many types of anxiety disorders (U.S. Department of Health and Human Services, Office on Women's Health, 2001). Chapter 17 provides additional information on the prevalence and diagnosis of mental health issues by gender.

One area of particular concern for counselors is women's gender role expectations. Research supports the existence of a sexual double standard regarding women's expression and the limits of sex roles. Young women, in particular, are continuously bombarded with mixed messages of sexual subordination and constraint. Women are encouraged to cast themselves as heterosexual objects of male desire while being admonished never to succumb to that desire or to acknowledge it. Thus, young women are told to be sexual objects but not to have overt sexual desires.

In addition, young females' primary sexual role is culturally defined as bearing the burden of rejecting or accepting male advances. This sexual ideology denies the possibility of sexual negotiation of a more equitable sexual dialogue. It reminds females that they are defined by their bodies and reinforces the belief that male sexuality is uncontrollable while female sexuality must remain restrained (Tolman, 2002). These social forces, coupled with lower economic statuses generally afforded to women and girls, create a context that can be toxic to both females and males, although more harmful for females.

Internalized sexual prejudices resulting from oppression and sexual double standards within cultural, societal, and religious beliefs can inhibit female development (Tiefer, 1995). It can also have detrimental effects on a female's self-concept. For example, Mock (1985) found that if a female adheres to societal sex role and gender socialization expectations, she may repress her sexual expression or experience stunted healthy sexual development. If she responds to her sexual needs and expresses her sexuality, then she may feel guilty and deviant. Consider these findings as you review Case Study 5.1.

CASE STUDY 5.1

Deborah is a 42-year-old, married African American woman who has made an appointment with you because, she states, "I don't know what to do any more. . . . I think I am depressed and I am hoping you can help me sort it out." She reveals during your first session that she has recently reentered the workforce because her two children will soon be heading to college and the family needs a second income. She also explains that she has seen four other counselors, and they were not helpful. As the session begins, Deborah slumps in her chair, exhales loudly, and avoids eye contact. In a muted voice, tearfully, and almost in a whisper, she says, "I don't really think this is going to make any difference. My husband thinks I need to see someone and I think he just wants me off his back."

- From a gender-sensitive perspective, what would you say to Deborah?
- How would you feel about working with her?
- What might be some gender-specific themes that come up during your sessions?
- How might your beliefs about men and women influence your reaction to Deborah's strong emotions?
- How does Deborah's race impact your reactions to her?
- How might things be different if Deborah were a man?
- Sometimes, the counselor and client have conflicting values regarding gender roles and oppression. How does a counselor decide whether or not to challenge a client's beliefs regarding women's oppression?

Counseling Men

Incorporating a gender-sensitive perspective is as important for the counselor working with males as it is working with females. In our culture, males often exhibit a "relative reluctance to seek help that stands in stark contrast to the range and severity of problems that affect them" (Addis & Mahalik, 2003, p. 6). Conformity to masculine norms reflects an important social reality that men and women often do not understand or think about consciously, yet that profoundly shapes our lives. Reflection 5.3 speaks to some messages that counselors might have encountered about males personally.

REFLECTION 5.3

How were you taught "what boys do" or "what men do" when you were growing up? Compile a list of messages you received from your parents, friends, community, and the media about male behavior. How do these messages contribute to your beliefs about what are the right and wrong ways for boys and men to behave? How might messages given to males influence their mental health?

Are men emotionally shut off? Is there something about the way our culture shapes boys into men that makes them emotionally unavailable? While it is impossible to adequately answer these broad questions, it is important for counselors to keep in mind some realities about the ways that men are socialized in Western culture. For example, masculine norms are communicated to males when they are told that "boys don't cry" or that "it isn't manly to be dependent on others." At the same time, society expects males today to also be able to communicate effectively in their interpersonal relationships and to contribute to raising children. These mixed messages can be confusing, and men often err on the "macho" side by repressing their feelings.

This stifling of emotions can take its toll, and researchers have a term for it. Ronald Levant, a former Harvard Medical School professor, described **normative male alexithymia** as an inability to put feelings into words that results from a long socialization process in which boys are taught to suppress and deny their feelings of vulnerability (Levant, 1996). Many behavioral and emotional differences between males and females can be viewed as rooted in early socialization practices. Research on children from infancy through the school years shows how this can happen. Mothers, for instance, expose baby girls to a wider range of emotions than baby boys, and work harder to control their sons' emotional volatility. Fathers often step in to socialize their toddlers along gender lines at around 13 months, verbally rough-housing their sons and talking in more emotional terms with daughters. As children get older, both parents can foster this rift by discouraging sons from expressing vulnerable emotions and encouraging such expression in daughters. Finally, peer group interactions cement boys' unhealthy emotional development by promoting structured group activities that foster toughness, teamwork, stoicism, and competition (Levant, 1996).

Real (1997) argues that problems that we think of as typically male (e.g., difficulty with intimacy, workaholism, alcoholism, abusive behavior, rage) are really attempts to escape depression. According to Real, depression is a silent epidemic in males, a condition that they hide from family, friends, and themselves, to avoid the stigma of unmanliness. Unfortunately, their attempts to escape this pain hurts the people they love the most, and they often pass their condition onto their children.

European American values prescribe what acceptable behavior is for males, and anything that strays from this is met with disapproval by society. According to Badinter (1989), girls become women through relational activities but boys become men through oppositional behaviors, learning to be independent, tough, and emotionally reserved. The demands of the male gender role tend to exclude anything that could be perceived as feminine (Brannon, 1985). In essence, masculinity is defined by what it is not. Boys learn that becoming men means avoiding feminine attitudes and behaviors and not getting too close to other boys due to their learned restrictive emotionality. This **code of masculinity** (Pollack & Levant, 1998, p. 1) inflicts wounds on both males and females. Reflection 5.4 speaks to this code with respect to the counseling profession.

REFLECTION 5.4

According to Real (1997), the price for traditional socialization for girls is oppression, or the "tyranny of the kind and nice" (p. 130), while the price for boys is disconnection—from themselves, from their mothers, from those around them. Discuss how these concepts have related to your own development, and your decision to become a counselor. How many males are there in your counseling classes? What is the connection between the low rate of male counseling students, sexism, and gender stereotypes?

Many men will use shame-based responses, denial, minimization, and silence as their tools to emotionally relate to others. Some men find asking for help to be shameful. One study using the Gender Role Conflict Scale (GRCS; O'Neil, Helms, Gable, Davis, & Wrightsman, 1986) found that higher scores on the Restrictive Emotionality scale and higher scores on the Antifemininity scale were associated with alcohol problems in men (Monk & Ricciardelli, 2003). Another study found that males who scored higher on measures of gender role conflict and traditional masculinity ideology had more negative attitudes toward psychological help seeking (Berger, Levant, McMillan, Kelleher, & Sellers, 2005).

Male gender role conflict (GRC) is a term used to describe a theory of understanding how traditional male gender role socialization can result in negative consequences for men who remain rigid in changing circumstances (O'Neil, Good, & Holmes, 1995). For example, men in traditionally masculine professions, such as law enforcement, may have difficulty switching from being tough, stoic, and independent while on duty to being warm and affectionate while off duty. Wester and Lyubelsky (2005) described four overall patterns of male GRC: (a) success, power, and competition; (b) conflicts between work and family relationships; (c) restricted emotionality; and (d) restricted affectionate behavior between men. A discussion of each of these patterns follows.

Success, power, and competition (SPC) describes the degree to which men are socialized to focus on "personal achievement, obtaining authority, or comparing themselves to others" (O'Neil et al., 1995, p. 174). For example, many men prefer to excel competitively rather than collaboratively. An authoritarian communication style usually exemplifies this pattern, and men with this trait are used to dealing with problems on their own instead of asking for help. These men get into trouble because interpersonal and spousal relationships require a collaborative approach that can be difficult to accommodate.

The second GRC pattern, *conflict between work and family relationships,* concerns the difficulty many men have balancing work, school, and family relationships. Of course, many (if not most) females have experienced this difficulty firsthand, but it is more socially acceptable for females to ask for help than males. Because of increasing competition, and the rising costs of living, some males may inadvertently place their careers ahead of their families.

The last two GRC patterns, *restricted emotionality* and *restricted affectionate behavior between men,* are closely related and refer to the degree to which men are taught to "fear feelings" (O'Neil et al.,

1995, p. 176) both within themselves and expressed toward other men. This emotional disconnect is comparable to the normative male alexithymia proposed by Levant (1996). Many men have a tendency to avoid showing feelings, out of fear of appearing weak or vulnerable. Consider these GRC patterns as you review Case Study 5.2.

Counselors working with male clients should attend to these socialization processes, while engaging in specific behaviors that will enhance the likelihood that their male clients will experience successful outcomes. For example, setting specific goals early in the counseling process is consistent with the way in which many men are socialized. Also, whereas empathy and support are critical attributes, Wester and Lyubelsky (2005) recommend that the gender-sensitive counselor maximize males' socialized preference for overcoming obstacles through overt effort.

Resistance should be anticipated, but once male clients decide that they want to overcome the obstacles that are impeding them, counselors should not be afraid to begin assisting clients in challenging those gender roles that are no longer working for them. One strategy proposed by Brooks (1998) involves the concept of transgenerational focus, referring to the concept that greater understanding of individual men can be gained through revisiting their relationships with their fathers, grandfathers, and other men in their family tree. Of course, the purpose is not to condemn all male behavior, nor is it to change the client's core identity, but it is to assist the client in developing a broader range of cognitive and emotional skills. "Men must be challenged to initiate a major reevaluation of their gender role values and assumptions in an effort to bring themselves into harmony with a changing world" (Brooks, 1998, p. 219).

CASE STUDY 5.2

As John and his wife Sandra present for family counseling, they report they have been constantly fighting about their 10-year-old son, James. John is angry about his son's serious weight problem and reportedly teases James about his weight. Sandra expresses that she wants John to stop putting down their son. During the course of counseling, John shares with his son for the first time his own experience of being a "fat kid," much heavier than James. He shares the story of the humiliation he felt as a 10-year-old boy, being teased and beaten regularly by older boys on his way home from school.

- From a gender-sensitive perspective, how might you see John's preoccupation with his son's weight as a misguided attempt at protection?
- What does John's childhood experience have to do with his son? How might you assist John in showing concern for his son appropriately?

Counseling Transgender Individuals

According to Eltner (1999), all counselors will see at least one transgender client during their careers, yet counseling programs do not adequately train clinicians to work with this population. Transgender-sensitive counselors seek knowledge about this community in order to perform ethical practice, and to begin to reduce stigma. Gender identity is included in the ACA (2005) *Code of Ethics* as a status protected from discrimination, so counselors should seek opportunities to learn about this diverse community. These may include educating yourself via online resources (see Table 5.2), attending a professional workshop, watching films, or inviting a member of the transgender community to speak to your class.

TABLE 5.2 Transgender Resources

www.gender.org

www.transgender.org

www.sexuality.org

www.gendertree.com (Transgender Christians)

www.nctequality.org (National Center for Transgender Equality)

In working with transgender individuals, counselors should have a strong understanding of the differences and similarities between the terms "sex" and "gender." **Sex** refers to one's biological makeup as male or female, whereas **gender** is used to denote an individual's identification as male or female regardless of his or her biological sex characteristics (Carroll & Gilroy, 2002). These terms may be confused easily, especially within systems of sexism and heterosexism that define them along a binary continuum of male and female. The terms are especially important for counselors to understand in order to have awareness, knowledge, and skills when working with transgender individuals. Transgender people face hate crimes at escalating rates and do not have adequate protection in the workplace. The counseling profession is another institution where transgender people face formalized discrimination, as Gender Identity Disorder is included as a mental illness in the *DSM*. Transgender people seeking sex reassignment surgery (SRS) are typically required to see a counselor before their surgery is approved, despite the significant body of research asserting the distinct biological and medical basis of gender identity issues. Categorizing gender identity as a mental disorder creates significant barriers for transgender people, and access to medical procedures that allow their sex and gender identities to be congruent (e.g., chest surgery for a female-to-male) is more difficult because it is viewed primarily as a psychological illness (Chung & Singh, 2008).

HISTORICAL CONTEXT OF SEXISM

It is important for counselors to understand the historical context of sexism in order to have the knowledge to challenge status quo thinking that enforces narrow definitions of gender in our society. "Patriarchy" refers to a system in which males hold the power and responsibility for the welfare of family and community units (Tolman, 2002). Patriarchal systems have existed across time and culture, although scholars such as Lerner (1986) assert that patriarchy has outlasted its initial relevance. According to Lerner, patriarchy originally began as a system that benefited both men and women. In the early development of humankind, because of the high rates of miscarriage, Lerner postulates that strict gender roles were a biological necessity in order to allow humans to reproduce. Aggressive roles for men and domestic roles for women were appropriate for a certain cultural time period. Yet, over time, Lerner asserts that patriarchy became an entrenched system where men not only wielded more power, but also restricted roles for women to remain around domestic matters.

As patriarchy has overstayed its initial purpose to assist in human survival, patriarchy has also become a system of ownership, where women have become property of men in institutions such as marriage (Lerner, 1993). Although a thorough review of the history of sexism is outside the scope of this chapter, we will review significant events in mental health over the past 50 years that provide counselors with an understanding of how females have resisted or succumbed to cultural norms of gender roles in the United States.

World War II and Women's Return "Home"

In preparation for the large draft of men in the United States who entered the military during WWII, women entered the workforce in unprecedented numbers (Kerber & DeHart, 2003). Although U.S. women, particularly African American women, had a long tradition of working both within and outside the home, this gender shift in the workforce provided women with opportunities to become wage earners in ways that had not previously been available to them because of their gender. Working-class women populated factories and were placed in management positions in the absence of a large number of men during WWI. Traditional roles for women as wife, mother, and homemaker naturally expanded during this time and were endorsed by the U.S. government. One can easily recall the "Rosie the Riveter" advertisement, which was laden with the gender and cultural messages of the time. In this governmental propaganda, the image of a White, middle-class woman with the words "We can do it!" was used to recruit over 18 million women into the labor force to help drive the war industry (Colman, 1995).

The "story" of this time period is that women were brought into the workforce and then returned "home" to resume their domestic duties at the end of the war, when men came back to the United States. However, scholars in women's studies highlight another side of this story, documenting the significant numbers of women who worked full time before, during, and even after the war (Colman, 1995; Kerber & DeHart, 2003). They also noted the sexual and racial discrimination these women faced, often in the form of direct harassment, as they performed their "patriotic duty" to the country. For women who did resume a culture of domesticity after men returned from WWII, they disengaged from dreams of academic and career success in order to "fit" back into narrow definitions of women's work. Especially for middle-class women, the consumer culture that followed WWII provided U.S. families with a boom in prosperity (Kerber & De Hart). Massive media campaigns marketed household appliances and women's magazine headlines focused on preparing women to be optimal caregivers to their husbands and children. Societal standards resumed a strict policing of "appropriate" behaviors and thinking for both genders, with women's focus on the work at home and men's focus at work outside the home.

However, it is important to note that the governmental enforcement of narrow definitions of gender roles was not received passively and also did not impact the lives of women of color and working-class women who had long traditions of work exploitation. One particularly important resistance to women's culture of domesticity and discussion of women's mental health that was well publicized was Betty Friedan's 1963 classic, *The Feminine Mystique*. In this book, Friedan documented "the problem that has no name," which asserted that middle-class, White women were in fact receiving little pleasure from domestic chores, and even more so craved connections with their communities and families that would build their sense of worth and support their longing for freedom and pleasure. Friedan's book was a wake-up call for both women and men, and its publication was one of many historical events documenting women's roles in society.

Historical Resistance to Sexism: The Feminist Movement

The history of feminism as a social justice movement in the United States is comprised of three distinct periods, or "waves." The first wave of feminism came to the United States from the "feminisme" movement in France, a term that referred to suffragists such as Hubertine Auclert who organized against male supremacy in Europe (DeLamotte, Meeker, & O'Barr, 1997). Freeman (1995) described this first wave of feminism as lacking unity, but with a common focus: "It was a coalition of different people and organizations that worked together for a few intense years around the common goal of gaining the right to vote" (p. 541). This wave was successful in obtaining the right to vote for women, the Nineteenth Amendment, and proposed the Equal Rights Amendment, which advocated ending all laws that discriminated against women (e.g., property rights, jury service). However, the movement was a predominately White movement, ignoring important issues of racism in the United States, and lesbian, gay, bisexual, transgender, questioning, and intersex (LGBTQI) issues were not included at all.

The second wave of feminism ushered in a time where gay and lesbian issues in particular began to emerge. The major leaders of the second wave (which came to be called the "women's liberation movement"), such as Betty Friedan who wrote *The Feminine Mystique* about women's relegation to the domestic sphere at the expense of their mental and physical well-being, resisted inclusion of gay and lesbian issues. These leaders attempted to focus on equality of the sexes, fearing that including sexual orientation would distract policy makers from acting on behalf of gender parity. In 1966, Friedan founded the National Organization for Women (NOW), which expanded feminism's focus on equal rights to reproductive rights for women (Freeman, 1995). Most famously from the second wave, emerged the phrase "the personal is political," which was used to describe the connections between systemic and individual oppressions of women. Critiques of the second wave of feminism again referred to an absence of women of color in addition to the heteronormative focus of the movement.

The third wave of feminism attempted to correct the absence of these voices, with specifically young people highlighting issues important to women of color and queer people. Baumgardner and Richards (2000) have described the third wave of feminism as focusing on issues of "sexual harassment, domestic abuse, the wage gap . . . and . . . modern problems of . . . equal access to the Internet and technology, HIV/AIDS, child sexual abuse, self-mutilation, globalization, eating disorders, and body image" (p. 21). Although there has been a focus on lobbying and changing laws, third wave feminists use direct action, independently produced periodicals, the Internet, and other media technologies to deliver their message. Critiques have included questions of whether the intersections of gender with other identities, such as race/ethnicity, sexual orientation, class, ability, and socioeconomic status, are addressed.

CULTURAL INTERSECTIONS OF GENDER

The following is a description of how gender interfaces within four racial/ethnic minority groups: African Americans, Asian Americans, Latino Americans, and Arab Americans. Due to the heterogeneity of these groups, gender characteristics are not necessarily similar for all individuals. Additionally, gender role identity expression may be different for individuals depending on level of acculturation, socioeconomic status, degree of spirituality, and other factors.

African Americans

Gender roles are less traditional for African American males and females. This may partly be due to experiences of racism and males' restricted power and social status in society. Thus, females are often in the position of caretaking and working outside the home. Further, African American families have been stereotyped as matriarchal, with the female role described as one of strength and resourcefulness (Davenport & Yurich, 1991). Willie and Reddick (2003) note that one of the greatest gifts of Blacks to the culture of the nation has been the egalitarian family model in which neither the husband nor the wife is always in charge. Chapter 9 provides additional information on gender role expression among African Americans.

Asian Americans

Asian cultural norms, particularly the more traditional ones, have quite strict guidelines about acceptable behavior for and social distance between men and women (Chung & Singh, 2008). In Asian culture, there is a value of family privacy and intimate topics are typically not shared with people outside the immediate family (Frey & Roysircar, 2004). Levels of acculturation for Asian Americans are important to explore in order to ascertain the degree to which individuals ascribe to traditional gender roles (Singh & Hays, 2008). For example, a female client may feel particularly anxious about sharing very personal information to a male counselor (or vice versa). Of course, much depends on the context, but clients who ascribe to more traditional cultural norms may feel more comfortable with a same-sex counselor, especially with matters of sex or marital issues (Hong & Ham, 2001). Further information on Asian American issues in counseling is discussed in Chapter 11.

Latino Americans

The U.S. Census (2000b) defines Latino or Hispanic Americans as "persons of Mexican, Puerto Rican, Cuban, Central or South American, or other Spanish culture or origin, regardless of race" (p. 2). One critical cultural norm regarding gender is the concept of **machismo**. The *Dictionary of Mexican Cultural Code Words* reports that "machismo meant the repudiation of all feminine virtues such as unselfishness, kindness, frankness and truthfulness. It meant being willing to lie without compunction, to be suspicious, envious, jealous, malicious, vindictive, brutal and finally, to be willing to fight and kill without hesitation to protect one's manly image" (de Mente, 1996, p. 137). Of course, this definition is outdated, but it underscores the historical importance of this gender-defining concept that is still central to Latino culture today. There is also another view of machismo. It can be equated with masculine values and behavior that are the epitome of idealized manhood based on level of social status. The truly macho man is one who supports and protects his family in the face of all odds, who disciplines his children to be upright, honest, and hardworking. This style of machismo is a key factor in the molding and sustaining of the family and personal relationships. **Marianismo**, a term derived from Catholicism that translates to "Virgin Mary," describes the gender role expression of Latinas. It refers to extreme femininity and subordination to males. However, the term has a spiritual connotation in that women who bear children hold a higher spiritual status. As a counselor, you should be comfortable broaching the subject of machismo and marianismo with your Latino clients in order to gauge their thoughts on this aspect of their culture and the role it plays in their lives. Additional information about gender role expression may be found in Chapter 12.

Arab Americans

The Arab American Institute reports that approximately 3 million Arab Americans reside in the United States (as cited in Moradi & Hasan, 2004). "Arab American" is defined by the American-Arab Anti-Discrimination Committee as Americans whose ancestors originate from 1 of over 20 countries, ranging from Algeria to Yemen (Moradi & Hasan). In Arab American culture, much like in Asian American culture, it is the family that is seen as the central foundational structure in society. Arab culture emphasizes the importance of behaving in ways that reflect well on others. Men are predominantly the head of the family, and the culture is based primarily on a patriarchal structure. The role of the father is typically strict and authoritative, whereas the role of the mother is nurturing and compassionate (Nobles & Sciarra, 1997). The preference for male children still exists in much of Arab American culture because of the belief that men will contribute to the family. Because of this belief, boys are trained from an early age to eventually be the head of the household and the caretaker for their unmarried sisters.

In Arab American culture, in general, women are expected to remain virgins until married (Nobles & Sciarra, 1997). Furthermore, a woman can lose her family's honor if she violates this sexual code. Naber (2006) investigated Arab American attitudes about sexuality and found that participants agreed that virginity and a heterosexual marriage were expectations of an ideal Arab woman. The study discussed how a daughter rejecting the ideal notion of an Arab woman could cause cultural loss for the whole family. Chapter 10 expands on this discussion of gender among individuals of Arab descent.

MENTAL HEALTH CONSEQUENCES OF SEXISM

The psychological consequences of sexism on the lives of women and girls are numerous and potentially devastating. Though it is beyond the scope of this chapter to address all of the mental health consequences associated with sexism, we explore a couple of prominent issues that future counselors will likely encounter when working with women and/or young girls.

Women and Depression

Distress from sexism on women's lives is immense, with the consequences resting in several dimensions. It is also important to acknowledge that the majority of clients seeking mental health care services are women. In fact, rates of depression are twice as high for women as they are for men. This gender disparity exists across race/ethnicity, age, and nationality (American Psychological Association, 2006a). In terms of age, girls appear as likely as their male counterparts to experience depression. However, by the time these same girls become adolescents, the incidence of depression for this group begins to spike and the gender differences in depression first become apparent (Nolen-Hoeksema & Girgus, 1994). This apparent difference points to the importance of early intervention in girls' lives in terms of supporting their mental health.

Eating Disorders

One of the greatest mental health consequences of sexism is disordered eating and negative body image. Early exposure that girls have to media images and messages about an ideal of beauty that is thin, White, and Western may have indelible effects on girls' functioning in their lives and self-image (Tiggeman & Pinkering, 1996). In fact, the rates of eating disorders such as Anorexia Nervosa and Bulimia Nervosa have increased exponentially over time, with 3% to 10 % of females between 15 and 29 years old (age of most risk) meeting diagnostic criteria (Bemporad, 1997; Polivy & Herman, 2002) and having differential impacts for females and males (10 to 1) (McGilley & Pryor, 1998; Striegel-Moore, 1997). Eating disorders first gained attention in the helping profession in the late 1960s in the United States, as clinicians noticed women literally starving themselves or using a binge-and-purge cycle in response to negative body image (Polivy & Herman, 2002). Myths continue to exist that eating disorders are a White, upper-class women's issue. Although precise statistics for women of color do not currently exist, several studies have identified eating disorders, body dissatisfaction, and attempts to lose weight across all racial/ethnic groups (Kilpatrick, Ohannessian, & Bartholomew, 1999; Robinson et al., 1996; Story et al., 1997).

These disordered eating patterns are now thought to be coping strategies for many women who struggle with identity issues and managing a sense of control over their environment. Johnston (1996) asserts that disordered eating is on the rise due to the disempowerment of women by a system of sexism that undervalues females, resulting in a literal emotional and physical malnourishment. In their review of the literature on eating disorders, Polivy and Herman (2002) identify the following influences as pertinent to the development of eating disorders in women: sociocultural factors (e.g., media, peers), negative affect, body dissatisfaction, and family factors (e.g., criticism). Treatment of eating disorders is challenging, with one third of females still meeting the diagnostic criteria for eating disorders 5 years after entering treatment (Fairburn, Cooper, Doll, Norman, & O'Connor, 2000). Because of the large numbers of women living with disordered eating and negative body image, counselors should assess for negative body esteem and eating disorders with every female client and be informed of the best practices of treatment for these issues.

PHYSICAL CONSEQUENCES OF SEXISM

The gender depression disparity hints at more serious physical problems left by sexism. If sexism is the undervaluation of women and girls, then it is this undervaluation that allows females in our society to be treated as objects. When women and girls are objectified in this manner, they are more easily made to be targets of violence. Indeed, women and girls do face higher rates of sexual trauma, increased exposure to occupational and environmental hazards, and disordered eating related to negative body image and poor self-esteem. Counselors should be aware of the physical repercussions of sexism and be prepared to openly discuss such issues.

Women are at increased risk for experiencing interpersonal violence, such as sexual assault, child sexual abuse, and intimate partner violence (Kessler, Sonnega, Bromet, Hughes, & Nelson, 1995). Briere (2002) asserts that these events place women at increased risk for developing Post-Traumatic Stress Disorder (PTSD) and that there are social inequalities that put women of color at special risk for meeting diagnostic criteria for this disorder. Feminist researchers have criticized the diagnosis of PTSD because it does not take into account how women may react to repeated and/or chronic traumas (Worell & Remer, 2003). Attention to repeated or chronic trauma experiences is critical to acknowledge because these events often are related to experiences with sexism and other oppressions. Researchers have proposed a diagnosis of complex PTSD (Herman, 1992a), which would acknowledge the insidious trauma (Root, 1990) involving repeated experiences of oppression that women and people from historically marginalized backgrounds experience.

Child sexual abuse and sexual assault are serious concerns for women and are often reasons that women seek therapy. Rates of child sexual abuse for females are 1.7 per 1,000 (USDHHS, 2002). The National Crime Victimization Survey (U.S. Census Bureau, 1997) shows that women are at risk for sexual assault of 10 to 1 in comparison to men. In addition, the National College Health Risk Behavior Survey (USDHHS, 1995) demonstrates that 1 in 5 college-aged women reported being forced to have sex. One of the landmark works on women's trauma experiences and treatment is Judith Herman's (2002b) *Trauma and Recovery*. Herman outlines three stages vital for women's recovery from sexual abuse. The first stage entails ensuring that survivors are safe from their abusers and free of **stressors** (e.g., alcohol abuse, financial stress) that may make it challenging to heal from sexual violence. The second stage is comprised of making meaning of their trauma by reviewing the details of their experience and acknowledging associated feelings. The final stage consists of clinicians helping trauma survivors reconnect with their sense of self and with important relationships in their lives. Ultimately, because of the high rates of trauma for women, it is imperative that counselors conduct a thorough trauma assessment with every female client to determine what experiences of emotional, physical, and/or sexual abuse they may have experienced and be aware of best practices with female survivors of trauma.

With regard to women's experience of intimate partner violence, Worell and Remer (2003) have proposed a three-part model addressing the abuse of women that includes society at large, the male perpetrator, and the female survivor of intimate partner violence. The importance of this model is that it provides clinicians with a helpful frame to understand the pervasive impact of this violence on women, in addition to how sexism reinforces an undervaluing and abuse of women. Through the model, the authors articulate the pattern of victims returning to their abusers, which is a dangerous reality of intimate partner violence in addition to causing frustration to counselors attempting to advocate for the safety of their female clients. The model posits that the societal system of sexism combines with the male abuser to create a hostile climate for women, which ultimately is disempowering for the female survivor. In this disempowerment, a woman is held "hostage to terror and violence . . . [and] escalates her attempts to placate and please; and in doing so, she increases her powerlessness and becomes psychologically and physically entrapped in a relationship from which she feels unable to extricate herself" (p. 261). One limitation of the model is that it does specifically apply to heterosexual relationships.

SOCIAL CONSEQUENCES OF SEXISM

In addition to the aforementioned mental and physical consequences, sexism causes social health consequences as well. Especially for women of color, undervaluation of females and narrow definitions of gender roles for women restrict career development and opportunities for women. For instance, 26% of African American families live below the poverty line as compared to 8.6% of White families (U.S. Department of Commerce, 1998). African American women are typically funneled into jobs that are defined as traditionally female, such as domestic work and child care (Greene, 1997). These tracking strategies begin early in women's educational experiences and continue into higher educational experiences. For example, female students receive less attention, praise, criticism, and encouragement from instructors than male students (National Coalition for Women and Girls in Education, 2002). Additionally, the same report found that pregnant students are directed toward schools that are less academically rigorous than students who are not pregnant. These discriminatory practices undoubtedly affect the types of careers into which women go and the amount of pay received. This is consistent with data that women earn approximately 76 cents per every dollar earned by men (U.S. Department of Labor, Bureau of Statistics, 2001). The disparity in wage earnings is especially likely to negatively impact single-mom families, which constitute approximately 26% of all U.S. families (approximately 10 million households). This is illustrated by the fact that 34% of single-mother-headed families live below the poverty line (Fields & Casper, 2001).

Another way that sexism manifests in the workplace for women is through internalized doubt in their own abilities. This internalized doubt was identified and coined by Clance (1985) as the **"imposter phenomenon,"** used to describe how high-achieving women fear trusting in their intelligence and work talents, resulting in fears that others will eventually "find out" that they are not as capable as they actually are. Rather than acknowledging their natural abilities, these women were found to attribute their success to interpersonal skills, networking abilities, diligent work, and sheer luck of being in the right place to take advantage of opportunities (Clance & Imes, 1978). The imposter phenomenon may help explain why only 21% of full professors at colleges and universities are women (National Coalition for Women and Girls in Education, 2002). This impostor phenomenon is problematic because Clance and O'Toole (1988) found that such successful women became terrified about making a mistake or failing at a work project, and the terror was centered on a fear of being exposed as an impostor. Holding an impostor frame of mind results in a work cycle where a woman

> face[s] a . . . project . . . [She] experiences great doubt . . . [She] questions whether or not she will succeed *this* time . . . [She] works hard, overprepares . . . or procrastinates and then prepares in a frenzied manner . . . [She] succeeds [in the task] and receives positive feedback. The whole cycle is reinforced . . . [and] doubting is reinforced. (p. 52)

Therefore, in addition to understanding the external barriers confronting women in the workplace from achievement, it is also critical that counselors keep in mind the internal barriers resulting from sexism when working with women who are managing career stressors.

ADDRESSING SEXISM IN COUNSELING

Counselors must be aware of their attitudes and beliefs about women and men as a first step to providing nonsexist mental health services. This includes self-examining general and mental health stereotypes a counselor might have about women clients because these stereotypes could interfere with the type and quality of counseling provided. Traditionally, many educators teach students to refer clients if there is a large discrepancy between the values of the counselor and client, or if a counselor is not competent to work with a particular client. However, this recommendation should not be used as a way to avoid working with clients who are culturally different than the counselor. The American Counseling Association (2005) *Code of Ethics* states that counselors have an ethical responsibility to continually educate themselves and to become culturally competent practitioners. This includes being aware of diverse cultural groups and acquiring knowledge about others' cultures. Counselors also have an ethical responsibility to not partake in discriminatory practices. Discrimination in the guise of referring women clients is unethical.

Counselors must also be aware of how their race, gender, age, class status, ability level, and sexual orientation impact the counseling relationship. Greene (2005) contends that these factors affect what counselors and clients choose to see and what they choose to avoid in sessions. Competent counselors will explore with clients what their gender identities and sexual orientations mean to each other, and what the identities mean in relation to the larger social context. Counselors should also critically examine the counseling process, counseling theories, and counseling format. Greene purports that current models of psychotherapy often perpetuate the social status quo, whereby they become socially unjust tools of oppression, particularly for women clients.

Additional ways counselors can minimize sexism in counseling practice is by not assuming that clients' presenting problems are related to their gender identity or expression. Rather, counselors should collaborate with clients to explore how sexism permeates the contextual environments of clients and how clients are affected. When working with clients of color, counselors should integrate ethnic, gender, and sexual identities to achieve maximum wellness. Szymanski (2005) suggested that counselors assess for experiences of prejudice, harassment, discrimination, and violence in relation to sexual orientation, gender, and gender expression. Once these components are assessed, counselors can implement the ACA's advocacy competencies. Specifically, counselors should integrate the advocacy competencies that empower female and transgender clients. The following are a few recommended strategies adapted from ACA's advocacy competencies:

- Identify strengths and resources of female and transgender clients.
- Identify the social, political, economic, and cultural factors that affect female and transgender clients.
- Help female and transgender clients identify external barriers that affect their development.
- Train female and transgender clients to self-advocate.
- Assist female and transgender clients in carrying out action plans.
  - *Lobbying efforts.* Help clients lobby for reproductive rights, women's health issues, and so on.
  - *Men as feminists.* Some men may think that feminist theory is just for women. Because we live in a male-dominated culture, if more men adopted feminist ideologies, greater social

TABLE 5.3 Women's Web Resources
Centers for Disease Control and Prevention
www.cdc.gov/Women/
National Institute of Mental Health
www.nimh.nih.gov/health/topics/women-and-mental-health/index.shtml
Rape, Abuse, & Incest National Network
www.rainn.org
World Health Organization
www.who.int/mental_health/prevention/genderwomen/en/

change could occur. Palmer (2004) described characteristics of feminist theory as including engaging in ongoing self-examination, sharing of power, giving voice to oppressed individuals, consciousness raising, and providing clients with tools to create social change.

Additional strategies specific to women may be found among the Web resources listed in Table 5.3.

RESILIENCE TO SEXISM AND SOCIAL JUSTICE

Although this chapter has detailed the many consequences of sexism on mental health for men, women, and transgender people, counselors should also maintain a focus on how their clients may be resilient to the negative effects of oppression and how issues of social justice may provide opportunities for counselors to take action to end sexism.

Recently, scholars have examined the resilience strategies of survivors of child sexual abuse. In a study of 177 college-aged survivors of child sexual abuse, family characteristics such as family conflict and cohesion were shown to support the resilience of the women to sexual abuse (McClure, Chavez, Agars, Peacock, & Matosian, 2008). For this study, resilience was defined as the degree of self-acceptance, engagement in positive relationships, and mastery of contextual environments. In a qualitative study of South Asian survivors of child sexual abuse, respondents shared that self-care, connection with community, and social activism were among their resilience strategies (Singh, 2006). Scholars have called for the fields of counseling and psychology to refrain from taking a deficit approach to working with survivors of trauma (Burstow, 2003). As counselors work with clients whose mental health has been compromised by sexism, focusing on areas where clients demonstrate strengths in their lives may help clients expand these competencies and build further resilience to sexism in their lives.

Counselors should also consider ways they may work as social change agents to address the issues of sexism in society. For instance, because the rates of trauma for women, men, and transgender people as a result of sexism are so high, counselors may find ways to work with community and government agencies to provide presentations and/or create support groups for survivors of trauma. Counselors may also work with schools, community colleges, and university centers to identify collaborative opportunities to stage events such as Women Take Back the Night (a typically on-campus event where survivors of sexual assault hold a rally with speakers on women's empowerment) and Transgender Day of Remembrance (an event typically held in November nationwide that recognizes transgender victims of hate crimes and murders). Also important is that counselors should be aware of the opportunities for social activism around issues of sexism so they may educate clients on these events as potential experiences of empowerment and healing (Worell & Remer, 2003).

Summary

In this chapter we have discussed gender and sexism, and how the interwoven constructs affect clients, counselors, and the counseling relationship. Because gender is such a fundamental component of identity, we often take for granted that it is a binary concept, either male or female. However, it is imperative to remember that gender identity and expression exist along a continuum, with multiple identities between the extremes of male and female. Couple this reality with other cultural identities such as race, ethnicity, SES, religious affiliation, and so on and it is easy to see the complexities that counselors face as they strive to become culturally competent. This chapter reviewed the relationship between gender and sexism for women, men, and transgender people. From defining these terms to exploring best practices for counselors to follow in working with clients, the authors identified specific influences gender and sexism have on the mental health of *all* people. Reviewing the history of sexism and how gender norms both differ and are similar across diverse cultural groups was also discussed. Finally, the authors urged counselors to not only address the negative impacts of sexism, but also to examine where they may focus on the clients' resilience in the face of sexism and the opportunities for counselors to advocate on behalf of clients and promote social justice.

CHAPTER 6

Sexual Orientation and Heterosexism

MICHAEL P. CHANEY AND JOHN MARSZALEK

PREVIEW

Multicultural counseling has expanded to include various intersections of identity, including sexual orientation (Lowe & Mascher, 2001). Counseling from this perspective must incorporate an understanding of the complexities inherent in clients, including the fact that many come from multiple minority statuses. Multicultural competence with respect to sexual orientation may be addressed through increased awareness of clients' assumptions, values, and biases regarding sexual orientation, awareness of clients' worldviews regarding sexual orientation, and culturally appropriate intervention strategies. This chapter defines and discusses concepts relevant to sexual orientation, and presents implications for counseling lesbian, gay, and bisexual (LGB) clients. Additionally, we discuss the intersections of sexual orientation with race, gender, ethnicity, and culture. Because the research on sexual orientation and heterosexism is often tied to that related to gender and sexism, some information relates to a broader group of lesbian, gay, bisexual, transgender, questioning, and intersex (LGBTQI) individuals.

DEFINING SEXUAL ORIENTATION AND HETEROSEXISM

Sexual orientation is sometimes difficult to define and distinguish because it is often related to gender under the term *sexual identity*. Sexual identity includes (a) physical identity, (b) gender identity, (c) social sex role identity, and (d) sexual orientation identity (Coleman, 1990; Shively & DeCecco, 1993). Whereas **physical identity** is the biological sex of individuals, **gender identity** is the belief a person has about his or her gender (i.e., the psychological sense of being male, female, both, or neither), and **social sex role identity** is the gender roles people adopt or adhere to based on cultural norms for feminine and masculine behavior. For example, a physical male may have a female gender identity, thus feeling more like a female emotionally and spiritually, and may have a female social sex role identity, thus adopting societal behaviors and appearances of a female. **Sexual orientation identity** is different from gender identity; it involves a person's sexual and emotional attraction to members of the other and/or same sex (Coleman, 1990; Shively & DeCecco, 1993).

Klein (1990) described **sexual orientation** as being a set of seven variables: (a) sexual behaviors; (b) emotions; (c) sexual fantasies; (d) sexual attractions; (e) social preference; (f) heterosexual, bisexual, or homosexual lifestyle; and (g) self-identification. Heterosexuality, homosexuality, and bisexuality are all possible culminations of the process of sexual orientation identity development. Heterosexuality, the most common sexual orientation identity, refers to aesthetic, romantic, or sexual attraction to members of the opposite gender (in a binary male–female system). People may or may not use the term straight to describe someone who is heterosexual, since it can be considered a value-laden term. **Homosexuality**, then, is one type of sexual orientation identity; however, *homosexual* is no longer a preferred term used to refer to an individual or group

113

of people who have same-sex feelings and behaviors and who identify with the gay community. **Gay male** or **lesbian** are acceptable terms because they are associated with positive, nonpathological identities, include individuals' emotional and affectional feelings, and refer to a cultural minority group (i.e., the gay community) (American Psychological Association, 2006b; Blumenfeld & Raymond, 1988). In addition, the term *gay* can be used to refer to both men and women and to a broad community and culture that includes both men and women. **Bisexuality**, another sexual orientation identity, refers to aesthetic, romantic, or sexual attraction to members of either the same or opposite gender. Most bisexual people are not equally attracted to men and women, and many are exclusively attracted to one or the other gender at different points in their lives (Anderson, 1994). **Questioning** is a newer term that refers to an individual who is questioning her or his sexual orientation and/or gender identity. For many younger people the Q represents **queer,** a broad term that includes anyone who does not identify as heterosexual.

Recently, researchers have suggested use of the term **affectional orientation** (Lambert, 2005) to describe sexual minorities (i.e., gay, lesbian, and bisexual individuals) because it broadens the discussion beyond simply sexual attraction. Sexual orientation is seen by some as a societal construct that serves to oppress, marginalize, and reduce lesbian, gay, and bisexual (LGB) individuals' identity to the largely taboo realm of sexual behavior. Since LGB relationships are not based solely on sexual attraction, perhaps affectional orientation may be a more accurate term. Like heterosexual relationships, LGB relationships involve attraction based on intelligence, emotional stability, communication style, and other interpersonal factors and feelings that exist for many couples. The term *affectional orientation* may also be more appropriate because it allows the LGB or questioning client to use a broader spectrum of emotional language to explore or accurately represent his or her experience of attraction. In summary, LGB identity is one component of sexual orientation identity. A gay or lesbian identity includes having same-sex behaviors, but also includes attractions, emotions, and a sense of connection with a gay community (Cass, 1990). Reflection 6.1 provides some questions for consideration with respect to the definitions of sexual orientation and affectional orientation.

REFLECTION 6.1

What are your thoughts about sexual orientation versus affectional orientation? What are the benefits of using one term over another? List them here.

_____

_____

_____

SEXUAL IDENTITY DEVELOPMENT

To better understand sexual orientation, we want to introduce you to developmental models of sexual orientation identity. Identity development issues include those issues that arise during each stage of identity development. To outline how LGB individuals become comfortable with and accept a gay identity, theorists have outlined models of sexual identity development to examine ways LGB individuals first become aware of their same-sex feelings and integrate these feelings into their overall identity (Cass, 1979; Coleman, 1981/1982; Troiden, 1984, 1988).

Sexual identity models have been influenced by other minority identity models (see Atkinson, Morten, & Sue, 1989; Cross, 1971a; McCarn & Fassinger, 1996). A major tenet of these models is that cultural minorities experience internal and external conflict in regard to their identity. They may struggle with acceptance of their identity, and they may experience external conflict with their perception of themselves (Ivey, 1993; McCarn & Fassinger, 1996; Walters & Simoni, 1993). See Reflection 6.2 on page 117 to consider how these models compare with each other.

Gay Identity Development

Gay identity development is directly related to psychological adjustment (Marszalek, Dunn, & Cashwell, 2002; Miranda & Storms, 1989). Gay identity is viewed as a developmental process in which the individual plays an active role in forming an identity and is affected by interactions with the environment. The process can be lifelong and complex and can begin at any age. Although the age in which gay men come out to others has decreased due to increased resources, support, and visibility in the gay community (Ryan & Futterman, 1998), acceptance of self in an often heterosexist environment can be a lifelong process.

Cass's (1979) **homosexual identity formation (HIF) model** set the groundwork for future gay identity development models, and is one of the most comprehensive models because it integrates both psychological and sociological perspectives of gay identity (Levine & Evans, 1991). Also, it applies to both gay men and lesbians. Cass's model is composed of six stages: (a) *Identity Confusion*, (b) *Identity Comparison*, (c) *Identity Tolerance*, (d) *Identity Acceptance*, (e) *Identity Pride*, and (f) *Identity Synthesis*. According to Cass, an individual moves from denial of same-sex feelings to tolerance, acceptance, and finally integration of these feelings into the whole self. Cass acknowledged that it is possible for a person to become stagnated at an early stage without ever reaching identity synthesis. However, she believed that individuals cannot skip stages in development.

Coleman's (1981/1982) five-stage model was influenced by earlier gay identity models, including Cass (1979), Dank (1973), Hencken and O'Dowd (1977), Lee (1977), and Plummer (1975). Like Cass, Coleman believed that individuals are greatly influenced by society and that individuals must progress through developmental tasks at earlier stages before reaching identity integration; however, Coleman viewed development as more intricate than a linear model. Consequently, Coleman believed that individuals progress through the development process at varying rates, and that this process can be both forward and backward. Coleman's (1981/1982) five stages are (a) *Pre-Coming Out*, (b) *Coming Out*, (c) *Exploration*, (d) *First Relationships*, and (e) *Integration*. According to Coleman, individuals move from not being aware of same-sex feelings to acknowledging and disclosing them, exploring the new identity by socializing with other gay men and lesbians, developing relationships, and finally integrating the identity into the entire self by acknowledging it publicly and privately.

Troiden (1979) interviewed 150 gay men to determine how they discovered they were gay and how this realization affected their identity development. Troiden made several conclusions: (a) identity is never stagnant but is always being modified; (b) not all men who engage in homosexual behavior will develop a gay identity; and (c) most gay men do not progress through the development model smoothly but face a long process that is at times confusing. Troiden (1988) later applied his model to lesbians also based on their qualitative experiences.

Troiden's (1979) four-stage model of gay identity development is similar to Cass's model. In stage one, *Sensitization*, the individual may have same-sex feelings or experiences, but he or she is not yet able to label them as gay or lesbian. Individuals realize that feelings or behaviors could be gay or lesbian in stage two, *Identity Confusion*. During stage three, *Identity Assumption*, individuals disclose their identities to others and socialize with other gays and lesbians. Finally, individuals make a *Commitment* to and acceptance of a gay identity.

Although Troiden (1984) acknowledged that Cass (1979) set the groundwork for future gay identity development models, his view of gay identity development differed from Cass's in several ways. First, he viewed identity development as a "horizontal spiral, similar to a spring lying on its side" (Troiden, 1988, p. 105) rather than a linear process. He stated that "progress through developmental stages occurs in a back-and-forth, up-and-down fashion. Characteristics of stages may overlap and recur in different ways for different people" (p. 105). Second, Troiden (1984) disagreed that disclosure of sexual orientation must be a criteria for integration of a gay identity and that individuals may choose not to disclose for many reasons. Third, he preferred to define self-identity, perceived identity, and presented identity from a sociological perspective rather than a cognitive perspective.

Lesbian Identity Development

Several of the gay identity development models have been applied to both gay men and lesbians (e.g., Cass, 1979, Coleman, 1981/1982; Troiden, 1984, 1988). Cass (1990) noted that there may be gender differences within each stage of development. According to Cass:

> In the acquisition of a gay identity it is recognized that different factors operate as a result of different socialization patterns for men and women and different societal expectations for gay men and lesbians. These different variables may result in different paths of development being taken within each stage of identity formation, in different images forming the content of homosexual identity, and in different ways of expressing identity and sexual preference. (p. 261)

Cass (1990) identified several differences between the identity development of gay men and lesbians. These include:

- Gay men are more likely to have a sexually stimulating experience trigger the identity development process, whereas lesbians are more likely to have an emotional experience trigger the process.
- Lesbians are more likely to reject societal female sex roles, and gay men are more likely to accept male sex roles and adapt them to their own identities. Cass hypothesized that society views the male sex role as including power, knowledge, and independence, and society views the female sex role as passive and caring for others. Consequently, there is less incentive for men to reject their male sex role.
- Compared to gay men, lesbians often develop a gay identity later in life.

Some theorists (e.g., Chapman & Brannock, 1987; Sophie, 1986) have proposed identity development models exclusively for lesbians. Further, McCarn and Fassinger (1996) proposed a lesbian identity development model drawn from other gay, lesbian, racial, and gender identity development models. Their model differed from other identity models in that it had "two parallel branches that are reciprocally catalytic but not simultaneous: individual sexual identity and group membership identity" (p. 521). McCarn and Fassinger argued that the identity development process involved both the formation of an identity within the self and the formation of an identity with a minority group. They viewed the identity development process as being comprised of four phases of development, with each phase occurring from an individual perspective and from a group minority perspective. The four phases identified were (a) *Awareness,* (b) *Exploration,* (c) *Deepening/Commitment,* and

(d) *Internalization or Synthesis.* In addition, they criticized other gay models because they "conflate these personal and social developmental trajectories, [and because] the conflation of these two processes in existing models results in an odd tyranny in which political activism and universal disclosure become signs of an integrated lesbian/gay identity" (p. 519). They argued that development cannot proceed without coming out to others and without being politically involved.

Bisexual Identity Development

Kinsey, Pomeroy, and Martin (1948a, 1948b) viewed sexual orientation as an individual's place on a 7-point continuum from exclusively heterosexual to exclusively homosexual. They hypothesized that it is possible for individuals to be primarily heterosexual and have some homosexual behaviors or feelings (and vice versa). In addition, it is possible for individuals to be bisexual and have both heterosexual and homosexual behaviors and feelings. In early identity models, bisexuality was viewed as a component of the progression toward a gay or lesbian identity (Fox, 1995). For example, Cass (1979) stated that bisexuality could be viewed as identity foreclosure in the HIF model; however, Cass (1990) later hypothesized that there was most likely also a separate bisexual identity process.

There has been some attempt to define a bisexual identity development process. For example, Weinberg et al. (1994) proposed a four-stage model similar to other identity development models but without a synthesis or integration stage: (a) *initial confusion,* (b) *finding and applying the label,* (c) *settling into the identity,* and (d) *continued uncertainty.* Fox (1995) stated that bisexual identity development has not been defined as a linear process, because it is a "more complex and open-ended process in light of the necessity of considering patterns of homosexual and heterosexual attractions, fantasies, behaviors, and relationships that occur during any particular period of time and over time" (p. 57).

REFLECTION 6.2

How are the lesbian, gay, and bisexual identity development models similar? How are they different? Which of the models described in this section makes the most sense to you? How do you believe sexual orientation identity development impacts and is impacted by other components of one's identity?

In the previous sections, we defined specific terms related to sexual orientation. Additionally, we examined several models of LGB identity development. A common end point for many of the identity models is the disclosure of sexual orientation to one's self and others. However, a barrier that prevents healthy progression through the identity stages for many LGB individuals is heterosexism.

Heterosexism

Heterosexism is defined as the oppression of LGBTQI individuals involving prejudice and discriminatory behavior (Chernin & Johnson, 2002). Societal norms valuing heterosexual identity and practices (e.g., marriage, laws) are a major component of heterosexism, which in turn may devalue the lives of LGBTQI people. Heterosexism also includes enforcement of heterosexual norms that may be consciously or unconsciously endorsed by individuals and institutions. In this manner, prejudicial and discriminatory acts, policies, and behavior are considered to be heterosexist. Heterosexism in these forms is additionally problematic, as it considers heterosexuality to be the "norm" and model of sexual identity for all people. Because heterosexism is a systematic oppression of LGBTQI identity, counselors will likely work with LGBTQI individuals who have internalized this devaluation of their sexual orientation. **Internalized heterosexism** may emerge in counseling sessions as a comparison to a heterosexual norm and an overriding belief system that heterosexuals are "better than LGBTQI" individuals. Heterosexism originates from and is maintained by stereotypes individuals hold about LGBTQI individuals (see Activity 6.1).

ACTIVITY 6.1

Generate a list of stereotypes you have or have heard about LGBTQI individuals here.

effem.

theatrical

Review your list in small groups. When did you learn or hear these stereotypes? Where did they come from?

A related term that many people often confuse with heterosexism is homophobia. **Homophobia** is defined as fear and hatred of LGBTQI people (Bobbe, 2002), whereas internalized homophobia describes the negative attitudes some LGBTQI people hold about their own sexual orientation (Fassinger, 1991; Szymanski & Chung, 2001). Homophobic acts may include hate crimes against LGBTQI individuals and communities that range from verbal to physical assault, and are therefore a component of the larger system of heterosexist oppression. Indeed, hate crimes are a real concern for the LGBTQI community, especially since the Federal Bureau of Investigation (FBI) ranks anti-LGBTQI violence as the third largest group of hate crimes in the United States (FBI, 2001). In fact, over 7,000 hate crimes motivated by sexual orientation were documented (and many anti-LGBTQI hate crimes go unreported) by the FBI in 2002, and the number of these hate crimes has consistently increased in the United States. Unfortunately, only 29 states in addition to the District of Columbia have passed laws that acknowledge hate crimes based on sexual orientation (National Gay and Lesbian Task Force, 2007). This is particularly troublesome because hate crimes involving sexual orientation involve some of the most brutal and violent hate crimes that have been documented, including dismemberment and stabbings (National Coalition of Anti-Violence Programs, 1994). When thinking about the systemic oppression of LGBTQI people, it is important that counselors keep in mind that social justice advocates have recommended using terms such as *homonegativity* or *homoprejudice* (Logan, 1996) in order to acknowledge the devaluation of LGBTQI individuals. Regardless of terminology used, the systemic oppressions of heterosexism and homophobia contribute to LGBTQI individuals being treated as one of the most denigrated and invisible groups in society, often because they live outside the box of traditional heterosexual norms.

A system of heterosexism confers unearned advantages onto heterosexual people, which is called **heterosexual privilege**. It is important for heterosexual counselors to recognize this privilege and its related impact on the mental health of LGBTQI people (see Activity 6.2). Heterosexual privilege includes the right to marry, access to the information of loved ones in the event of a medical emergency, legal and financial rights to property in the event of the death of a spouse, and adoptive and child rights. Heterosexism also gives heterosexuals the privilege to have their relationships validated by media, and colleagues in the workplace, in addition to being able to arrange to be in the company of other heterosexual people in most environments.

ACTIVITY 6.2

In small groups, make a list of heterosexual privileges that LGBTQI people do not have access to in our society. Then, brainstorm a second list of privileges accorded to males simply based on their gender. Identify the commonalities and differences between the two lists. During your discussion, generate ways that one may use heterosexual and male privilege in order to create LGBTQI -friendly environments in counseling.

INTERSECTIONS OF SEXISM AND HETEROSEXISM   Pharr (1988) asserts that heterosexism is a "weapon" of sexism, in that heterosexism functions to systemically and narrowly define gender roles and enforce compulsory heterosexuality. Certainly, the link between heterosexism and sexism is multi-faceted and complex and goes beyond the mere fact that "sexism" is included in the word *heterosexism.* Feminist activist and academic bell hooks (1984) asserted that "challenging sexist oppression is a crucial step in the struggle to eliminate all forms of oppression" (pp. 35–36). In terms of complexity, the connection between heterosexism and sexism includes enforcement of gender roles through socialization practices. For instance, boys are raised with the goal of "becoming a man," which often includes values of emotional restraint, assertiveness, the role of "protector" of the family, competition, and avoidance of displaying vulnerability. The intersection of sexism and heterosexism becomes clear in the derogatory language ("faggot" and "sissy") that is used when a boy steps out of traditional gender norms for males. Girls are socialized to be caregivers, to be dependent on others, to display emotions, and to avoid being viewed as "too strong." When girls and women cross the boundaries of strict gender roles, epithets can include being called a "bitch" or called "aggressive" when asserting their needs.

Culturally competent counselors should have a firm understanding of the aforementioned definitions because much of the power of heterosexism is rooted in the meanings society gives to nontraditional behaviors, thoughts, and emotions. Additionally, culturally competent counselors should understand how heterosexism may be related to the demography of LGBTQI individuals.

LESBIAN, GAY, AND BISEXUAL DEMOGRAPHY

There is much controversy surrounding the actual number of men and women who identify as LGBTQI. Current statistics do not include individuals who may be uncomfortable disclosing an LGBTQI identity, youth and adults who have not yet realized they are LGBTQI, and heterosexually married individuals who may also identify as LGBTQI. Kinsey, Pomeroy, and Martin's (1948a, 1948b) ground-breaking publications *Sexual Behavior in the Human Male* and *Sexual Behavior in the Human Female* reported that 10% of males and 2% to 6% of females were more or less exclusively gay and lesbian. Some researchers and epidemiologists criticized Kinsey's methodology and analysis and challenged these percentages. Forty-five years later, Janus and Janus (1993) reported that 9% of men and 5% of women are gay and lesbian, respectively. A study for the National Center for Health Statistics (2002) that included 12,571 Americans, aged 15 to 44, found 6% of men and 11% of women had same-sex sexual experiences by age 44. Approximately 2% of males between the ages of 18 and 44 identified as bisexual and 4% as something other than heterosexual or bisexual. In the same study, among women aged 18 to 29, 14% reported at least one sexual experience with a woman. It should be noted that a same-sex intimate encounter does not necessarily constitute an LGBTQI identity, nor does a lack of a same-sex sexual experience mean that someone is heterosexual. These discrepancies illustrate the difficulty in accurately identifying the precise number of LGBTQI individuals. Although the statistics are likely underestimated, it estimated that there are 8.8 million LGB individuals in the United States (Gates, 2006).

HISTORICAL CONTEXT OF HETEROSEXISM

As with other cultural groups, LGBTQI communities also have histories. A large part of this history is related to challenging oppressive heterosexist institutions and policies. One of the most noteworthy historical events for members of the LGBTQI communities was the Stonewall Rebellion. This event is credited as starting gay civil rights.

Resistance to Heterosexism: The Stonewall Rebellion

Duberman (1993) provides an important historical account of the events at Stonewall in 1969. Police officers in New York City routinely raided the Stonewall Inn, a gay establishment. During a typical raid, police officers harassed and arrested patrons. On June 28, 1969, patrons of the bar (primarily transgender people of color) fought back against the police, thus challenging the systematic oppression. The uprising lasted for several days. Their courage ignited the gay and lesbian civil rights movement. The story of Stonewall is especially important for counselors to have knowledge of, because LGBTQI clients may not be aware of the history of the LGBTQI liberation movement. Sharing the knowledge of this movement can help normalize for clients that many LGBTQI people were forced into silence and shame, in addition to sharing the hope for visibility, community, and empowerment that Stonewall represents.

CURRENT ATTITUDES TOWARD LGBTQI INDIVIDUALS

In 1975, the American Psychological Association adopted a resolution stating that "homosexuality per se implies no impairment in judgment, stability, reliability, or general social or vocational capabilities" (Conger, 1975, p. 633) following a rigorous discussion of the 1973 decision of the American Psychiatric Association to remove homosexuality from its list of mental disorders (American Psychiatric Association, 1973b). Although homosexuality is no longer considered a mental illness, societal attitudes and institutional policies toward LGBTQI individuals have been slow to improve. For example, many LGB people are not protected from employment discrimination in most states because sexual orientation is not included in the federal Title VII of the Civil Rights Act of 1964, which prohibits employment discrimination for other minority groups (Yared, 1997). However, 17 states, the District of Columbia, and 167 cities and counties prohibit discrimination based on sexual orientation for both private and public sector employment (Human Rights Campaign Fund, 2006).

Despite the increasing visibility of gays and lesbians in U.S. culture (Pew Research Center, 2003), Americans are divided on issues related to homosexuality. In polls taken during the last 5 years, a large majority of Americans (76%) stated that they are comfortable interacting with gays and lesbians in social settings (Pew Research Center, 2003) and a majority of Americans (60%) believed that gays and lesbians should be allowed to serve openly in the military (Pew Research Center, 2003). However, 50% of Americans had an unfavorable view of gay men and 48% had negative attitudes toward lesbians.

Consequently, LGB individuals are often unsure when and where it is safe to disclose their sexual orientation. Pew's poll also found that 60% of Americans opposed same-sex marriage. This is important information for counselors to have because some LGBTQI clients will present with relationship issues and will need to work with a counselor who has been exposed to information about LGBTQI relationships.

LGBTQI Relationship Status and Family Issues

A common stereotype pertaining to LGBTQI individuals is that they are promiscuous. The contrary appears to be true. Approximately 40% to 60% of gay men and 45% to 80% of lesbians are in committed relationships (Elizur & Mintzer, 2003). Another stereotype ascribed to LGBTQI individuals is the HINK (high income, no kids) label. However, LGBTQI couples are increasingly choosing to expand their families. Among partnered lesbians, about 21.7% have children, and within gay male partnerships about 5.2% have children. Of the children within lesbian and gay households, a high percentage of the children are under the age of 18 years (i.e., 71% of children in lesbian homes and 76% of children in gay households) (Black, Gates, Sanders, & Taylor, 2000). As will be discussed later in the chapter, the effects of institutional heterosexism on lesbian and gay couples and their children are numerous. One area where institutional heterosexism is illustrated is around same-sex parent adoption.

In a national survey of 214 adoption agencies, Brodzinsky, Patterson, and Vaziri (2002) reported that 63% allowed adoptions by gays and lesbians, and 38% had placed a child with LGB parents during the previous 2 years. The ability to adopt children, however, varies from state to state. According to the American Civil Liberties Union (ACLU; 2006), in some states, courts have denied or restricted custody by LGB parents. For example, in Florida, Mississippi, and Utah, LGB individuals are banned from adopting children. Some states additionally prohibit them from being foster parents. However, states such as California and New York prohibit discrimination based on sexual orientation in the adoption process (Human Rights Campaign Fund, 2007).

Arguments typically used against LGBTQI individuals from adopting and/or fostering children include (ACLU, 2006):

1. Children must have a mother and a father for optimal child development.
2. Gays and lesbians cannot provide a stable home environment.
3. Gays and lesbians are more likely to sexually abuse children.
4. Children of gay and lesbian parents are more likely to become gay or lesbian, themselves.
5. Children of gays and lesbians will face social prejudice in schools and the community.
6. Research on gay and lesbian families is flawed.
7. Parenting by lesbians and gay men is a social experiment. (pp. 85–91)

Major national organizations, including the American Psychological Association, the American Medical Association, the American Psychiatric Association, the Children Welfare League of America, and the American Academy of Pediatrics, have rejected these arguments and made statements in support of gay and lesbian parenting. Both the American Psychological Association (2006b) and the ACLU (2006) reported that lesbian and gay parents are at least equal to heterosexual parents in terms of mental health, parenting skills, and quality of family relationships. In addition, they reported that research has consistently shown that children of gay and lesbian parents are no different than other children in terms of gender identity development, gender role behavior, sexual orientation, psychological and cognitive development, social relationships, and familial relationships. Given the increasing attention to gay parenting, it is important for counselors to consider their attitudes toward this issue as well as potential counseling considerations (see Activity 6.3).

ACTIVITY 6.3

In a dyad, discuss the following questions:

- How you feel about LGBTQI individuals adopting children?
- What are some advantages of children being adopted by LGBTQI parents?
- What are some of the struggles a child may encounter with LGBTQI parents?
- What assumptions do you have about potential challenges lesbian parents may experience? How about gay male parents?
- How might these advantages and struggles manifest in counseling families?

Educational Status

In general, lesbian and gay individuals have more formal education than their heterosexual counterparts. Approximately 45% of gay male couples have college degrees, compared to 20% for the general heterosexual population (Black, Gates, Sanders, & Taylor, 2002). Lesbians are also highly educated with an estimated 25% holding a college degree, compared to 16% of heterosexual married women having a college degree. At first glance it appears that the myth of the HINK has some truth to it; more education is likely to lead to higher paying jobs. However, when viewed critically, these statistics show that an estimated 55% of gay male couples and approximately 75% of lesbian couples do not have college degrees. This is important because higher education and higher income have been found to be related to increased odds of an individual identifying oneself as LGBTQI and to living in a predominantly LGBTQI neighborhood (Barrett & Pollack, 2005).

Heterosexism and Classism

Although LGBTQI individuals generally have more education than their heterosexual peers, which potentially leads to higher paying jobs, home ownership is lower for partnered lesbians and gays than for married heterosexual couples. This may be due in part to many states having laws that prohibit unmarried couples from owning a home together. However, Black et al. (2000) report that of those lesbian and gay couples who do own their homes, their houses are more expensive than their heterosexual counterparts. One reason their homes tend to be more expensive is due to the location of the home. Although there are LGBTQI individuals everywhere, many choose to live in large, metropolitan cities where there tends to be greater tolerance. A recent analysis (2006) by Gary Gates and the Williams Institute on Sexual Orientation Law and Public Policy at the University of California, Los Angeles, reported that 10 cities have a concentration of 8.0% to 15.4% of LGB individuals. The cities from highest concentration to lowest include San Francisco (15.4%), Seattle (12.9%), Atlanta (12.8%), Minneapolis (12.5%), Boston (12.3%), Oakland, CA (12.1%), Sacramento (9.8%), Portland (8.8%), Denver (8.2%), and Long Beach, CA (8.1%). Because many LGBTQI individuals choose to live in these more accepting cities, which generally have higher costs of living, members of the LGBTQI community who cannot afford to live in such cities often remain invisible. Barrett and Pollack (2005) found that working-class gay men may not have the resources to move to higher amenity gay neighborhoods. As a result, many working-class gay and bisexual men remain closeted, living in nonaccepting areas, where there is an increased likelihood for experiencing psychological distress and physical violence. Moreover, 61% of men in Barrett and Pollack's study reported living in poverty or experiencing financial difficulties, such as having to borrow money in order to meet basic living needs. Because many helping professionals and researchers discuss LGBTQI people only in terms of sexual identity and sexual behavior, issues of race, class, ability, and gender are either forgotten or ignored. Culturally sensitive, nonheterosexist counselors should assess the multiple identities of their LGBTQI clients. Additionally, culturally competent counselors will examine issues affecting LGB youth.

LGB Youth

Counselors who work with adolescents should be aware of the unique pressures faced by these youth. Because of the pressure to conform in adolescence, many gay and lesbian youth are harassed for being perceived as gay or lesbian (Marinoble, 1998). Many public schools have successfully fought against racism and sexism, but dealing with homophobia has been more challenging. High schools may be reticent to show approval of gay and lesbian youth out of fear of appearing to overstep parental authority or religious doctrine. The general thinking seems to be that the schools are telling students what to think, and they may be teaching them attitudes that are opposite what is being taught at home. According to Anderson (1994), ignorance is a big part of the problem. Some educators may believe that teaching young people about homosexuality will make them gay.

Some gay adolescents exist in social, emotional, and informational isolation. Some teachers ignore antigay taunts, and some counselors who support gay students use terms like "personal matter" to distinguish between official school policies (Marinoble, 1998). In middle school and high school, one of the worst things an individual can be called is "faggot" or "queer" (Smith & Smith, 1998). Many gay students risk losing peer status by letting others know about personal feelings, or they may choose to remain silent and try to "pass."

While many schools often fail to protect and affirm gay students, the federal government, courts, and mass media are taking proactive steps to improve their lives. The Equal Access Act (20 U.S.C. sections 4071–74) states that "it shall be unlawful for any secondary school which receives Federal financial assistance to deny access or a fair opportunity to, or discriminate against, any students who wish to conduct a meeting on the basis of the religious, political, philosophical, or other content of the speech at such meetings." Despite this clear mandate, many local school boards are embroiled in a controversy over the existence of gay–straight alliances. These noncurricular clubs seek to increase understanding, promote respect, and diminish fear around sexual orientation issues. Many school boards are refusing to let these clubs meet, despite protection by the First Amendment and the Equal Access Act. According to Kendra Huard, of People for the American Way (PFAW, a nonprofit civil liberties group), "the school board negatively affects these students because by merely asking for the club they think that they have done something wrong. We just really want the board to understand that if they violate the law, they are opening themselves to litigation" (PFAW, 2003, p. 60).

Another protection for LGB youth is Title IX. **Title IX** is a federal statute that prohibits sex discrimination, including sexual harassment. In 1997, the Office for Civil Rights of the U.S. Department of Education released new Title IX guidelines for schools, which for the first time make explicit reference to gay and lesbian students as also being protected. Though more work needs to be done to advocate for and protect LGB youth, progress is gradually being made (see Build Your Knowledge 6.1 for important resources).

BUILD YOUR KNOWLEDGE 6.1

Dr. Mark Pope is currently professor and chair of the Division of Counseling & Family Therapy in the College of Education at the University of Missouri–St. Louis. He is a past president of the American Counseling Association (ACA). Dr. Pope was the first openly gay president of a national mental health organization in the United States. His Web site has a wealth of resources for working with LGBT youth, and can be found at www.umsl. edu/~pope/index.html.

Here are some simple suggestions to advocate for LGBTQI youth:

- Have a "safe zone" sticker at the entrance to your office or classroom (available from the Bridges Project of the National Youth Advocacy Coalition or at www.glsen.org).
- Have literature available on sexual minority youth concerns (see www.umsl.edu/~pope for a bibliography).
- Post online resources for sexual minority students such as International Lesbian and Gay Youth Association (www.ilgya.org); Parents, Family, and Friends of Lesbians and Gays (www.pflag.org); Gay, Lesbian, and Straight Educators Network (www.glsen.org); Gay and Lesbian Teen Pen Pals (www.chanton.com/gayteens.html); National Resources for GLBT Youth (www.yale.edu/glb/youth.html); *Oasis* (teen magazine) (www.oasismag.com); Outright (www.outright.com); Out Proud, National Coalition for GLBT Youth (www.cybrespaces.com/outproud); The Cool Page for Queer Teens (www.pe.net/~bidstrup/cool.html); and National Gay and Lesbian Task Force (www.ngltf.org).
- Use inclusive, stigma-free language in the classroom and in all communication, such as "partners" instead of "husbands and wives."
- Post pictures of famous sexual minority people (see list at www.umsl.edu/~pope).

Age and Disclosure of Sexual Orientation

Lesbians and gay males in the U.S. population are relatively young, with mean ages in the mid-30s (Black et al., 2002). This might partially contribute to ageism and the value of youth held by many within the LGBTQI communities, at the expense of the "gay and gray" community members. Competent counselors will take into consideration an LGBTQI client's emotional age as well as chronological age when strategizing effective interventions. It is common for individuals who come out as LGBTQI in adulthood to experience a late adolescence that they did have when most heterosexual peers went through adolescence. In relation to the process of disclosing one's sexual orientation to others or the self-realization of a LGBTQI identity (i.e., **coming out**), 25% of lesbian and gay adults in the United States are not out to their mothers and 50% are not out to their fathers (Savin-Williams, 2001). This discrepancy is likely due to stereotypical gender roles. For example, it may be easier to come out to mothers who are supposed to be nurturing and accepting, whereas fathers are supposed to be strong and masculine. There may also be a greater fear of being rejected by a father than by a mother. Of those individuals who choose to come out, 10% to 15% are rejected by their parents. Many LGBTQI youth who have been rejected by their parents end up homeless and struggling on the streets, which will be discussed later in this chapter. Reflection 6.3 provides some coming-out considerations for counselors.

REFLECTION 6.3

Write a simulated coming-out letter to someone who is important to you. You do not have to give the letter to the significant person if you do not want to. What was it like to write the letter? How do you imagine the coming-out process is for LGBTQI individuals?

CULTURAL INTERSECTIONS OF SEXUAL ORIENTATION

Scholars have discussed the phenomenon of double and triple minorities, individuals who have two to three minority statuses based on race, culture, gender, and/or sexual and affectional orientation (Gonsiorek & Weinrich, 1991). For example, an African American lesbian may experience oppression in the form of sexism due to her female status, racism due to her African American heritage, and heterosexism for identifying as a lesbian. A major issue for LGB individuals of color is establishing healthy racial and sexual orientation identities simultaneously. It can become quite complex to disentangle how various forms of oppression (e.g., sexism, racism) impact an individual's sexual orientation identity.

Building on earlier gay identity models, Morales (1989) developed a model that helps explain how some LGB individuals of color establish their identities. This model involves moving through the following states: (a) denying conflicts, (b) labeling self as bisexual rather than gay, (c) being conflicted in allegiances between gay and minority communities, (d) establishing priorities in allegiance, and (e) integrating various identities. According to Morales, LGB people of color may experience several states simultaneously. Because LGB clients of color tend to experience unique challenges while trying to establish identities in different domains of their lives, it will be important for counselors to understand how specific cultural groups view individuals who identify as LGB. What follows is a brief introduction into how specific cultural groups may view LGB people. It is important we do not generalize the results of the following studies to all people who comprise the cultural groups represented. There are many heterosexual allies in the proceeding groups!

African Americans

There has been mixed opinion about the degree to which LGB individuals are accepted within the African American community. Lewis (2003) reported that, although African Americans appeared to be more disapproving of homosexuality as compared to Whites, they tended to be more supportive of civil rights for LGB people. Negy and Eisenman (2005) compared African American and White university students' attitudes toward LGB people and found that although African American students were more disapproving of LGB people than White students, when religiosity was controlled for, there were no differences. In other words, individuals who had stronger religious convictions tended to have stronger negative attitudes toward LGB people. This is not surprising considering the influence churches have historically played in some Black communities. This concurs with Loiacano's (1989) reports that some Black LGB individuals may be afraid to come out due to fear of being ostracized in the Black community.

Asian Americans

Chan (1989) administered surveys to 19 Asian American lesbians and 16 Asian American gay men on issues related to being both gay and Asian American. The majority of respondents stated that they were more comfortable in the gay community than in the Asian American community. Furthermore, the majority of participants identified their primary identity as gay and their secondary identity as Asian American. An additional finding of Chan's study was that a majority of participants stated that it was harder to come out to other Asian Americans for fear of being persecuted. The results of Chan's study demonstrate the complex balancing act experienced by many LGB people of color.

Latino Americans

Specific attributes of Latino American culture contribute to the difficulties many LGB Latinos experience during the coming-out process. For example, traditionally many Latinos have a strong religious identification (e.g., Catholicism), and historically, many denominations have judged LGB people negatively. An additional factor that makes coming out more difficult for some Latinos is the role masculinity plays in some Latino cultures. Religion and the role of masculinity may help explain the results of a study by Díaz, Ayala, Bein, Henne, and Marin (2001) that found 64% of gay Latinos felt they had to pretend to be heterosexual, and 29% reported they had to move away from their families in order to be openly gay.

Native Americans

Native American tribes traditionally used the term "two-spirit people" to describe those whose gender expression or sexuality did not conform to typical behaviors of their assigned sex. Prior to colonization, American Indians respected their two-spirit people, and ascribed to them special powers or ceremonial functions (Brown, 1997). Despite this history, as well as greater overall flexibility of gender roles compared to White culture, today's gay and lesbian American Indians do not necessarily have an easier time with the coming-out process. For example, in one study, Jacobs and Brown (1997) found that most American Indians reported that they felt no special role in their community as a result of being gay or lesbian.

The previous sections briefly touched on the intersections of ethnicity and sexual orientation. The primary purpose was to illustrate that all cultures have specific attitudes, values, and beliefs about LGB individuals. As a result, depending on a client's cultural background, unique challenges during the coming-out process may be encountered. In the next section, we look at some of the specific consequences of heterosexism on the lives of LGB people, starting with mental health consequences.

MENTAL HEALTH CONSEQUENCES OF HETEROSEXISM

The effects of heterosexism and homonegativism on the lives of LGBTQI clients are many. What follows is a brief summary of current research and conceptualizations addressing how LGBTQI individuals are negatively impacted by overt and covert heterosexism, homonegativism, and internalized homophobia.

Historically, many mental health providers have attributed mental health problems to LGBTQI clients without considering environmental factors affecting mental well-being. **Attribution bias is** a cognitive bias that influences how we conclude who or what is responsible for an event. Attribution bias is often unconsciously placed upon LGBTQI clients. Culturally sensitive counselors are starting to realize that mental health problems are not necessarily a product of "broken" individuals; rather they are a function of social inequities that become toxic for the individuals affected (Greene, 2005). One aspect of poisonous social environments that affect LGBTQI mental health is stereotypes we have about LGBTQI individuals. Often not thought about are the stereotypes we have about the LGBTQI community's mental health. Corrigan (2004) purports that the stereotypes we have about the mental health of particular groups foster societal discrimination and prejudice, which then leads to self-persecution, increased psychological distress, and psychiatric symptoms. Though stereotypes at times may help us give meaning to certain situations or groups of people, in general, stereotypes that lead to selective discrimination and prejudice are socially unjust and can cause a lot of psychological pain to the people to whom the stereotypes are being applied. Some researchers have even proposed that individuals who engage in heterosexist acts have their own psychopathology (see Reflection 6.4). Guindon, Green, and Hanna (2003) suggest the following:

> Persons who perpetuate pain and injustice on others through racism, sexism, and homophobia . . . are displaying a type of psychopathology that deserves its own particular category. . . . The common denominator of all the above prejudices seems to be intolerance. . . . This intolerance seems to be descriptive of a personality disorder, "Intolerant Personality Disorder. . . ." Intolerance becomes psychopathological when rigid beliefs lead a person to suppress the quality of life of another person or group, causing pain and suffering through denial of liberty, equal rights, or freedom of expression. (pp. 167–168)

REFLECTION 6.4

What are some ways in which heterosexual individuals are negatively impacted by heterosexism? Brainstorm potential mental health, physical, and social consequences of heterosexism for this population.

Research has clearly demonstrated that LGBTQI individuals seek out counseling more than their heterosexual counterparts (Barret & Logan, 2002). It is not that LGBTQI individuals are innately more mentally unstable; rather, LGBTQI persons experience the ramifications of heterosexism and homonegativism more directly than heterosexuals. Research has consistently demonstrated that heterosexism, sexism, and internalized homophobia are related to psychological distress in lesbians (Szymanski, 2005), and that gay men tend to suffer more than heterosexual men from depression, suicide, panic (Cochran & Mays, 2000a, 2000b), anxiety (Sandfort, de Graaf, Bijl, & Schnabel, 2001), and substance abuse disorders (Gilman et al., 2001). Let us explore in greater detail how some of these conditions are related to heterosexism. Specifically, the relationships between heterosexism and suicide and depression, self-esteem and stress, and LGBTQI youth mental health are discussed.

Suicidal Behavior and Depression

One of the most devastating mental health consequences of heterosexism among many LGBTQI individuals is depression and suicidality (ideation and attempts). LGBTQI individuals report disproportionately higher numbers of suicidal thoughts and past suicide attempts than their heterosexual peers. This is often attributed to growing up hearing negative messages about being LGBTQI, shame, and depressive symptoms related to living in a heterosexist and homophobic society. Borowsky, Ireland, and Resnick (2001) found same-sex romantic attractions were predictive of suicide attempts in all racial and ethnic groups in over 13,000, 7- to 12-year-old boys. Furthermore, it has been estimated that same-sex attracted youth constitute up to 30% of all completed suicides. LGBTQI adolescents also are six to seven times more likely than their heterosexual peers to attempt suicide and constitute 63% of all suicide attempts (Bagley & Tremblay, 1997). Among bisexual females and transgender individuals, suicidal ideation and attempts tend to be more prevalent than among bisexual males. Attributed to heterosexism and sexism, bisexual women and transgender individuals also report prior and current psychotherapy and prior and current administration of psychotropic medications (Mathy, Lehmann, & Kerr, 2003).

Bisexual individuals often experience discrimination and intolerance from both the heterosexual and the gay communities. This lack of a sense of belonging often leads to feelings of isolation and loneliness, which in turn may result in an increased risk of depression and suicidal behavior. This is consistent with research that shows a relationship between internalized heterosexism and depression (Smith & Ingram, 2004; Szymanski & Chung, 2003).

For LGBTQI people of color, the risk for depression and suicidal behavior is exacerbated by their additional oppressed identities. More African American gay and bisexual men report elevated levels of depression and anxiety disorders than White gay and Black heterosexual men (Richardson, Myers, Bing, & Satz, 1997). Similarly, more African American lesbians (36%) attempt suicide prior to age 18 years compared to White lesbians (21%), and 32% of African American gay men attempt suicide before 18 years of age compared to 27% of White gay men (Bell & Weinberg, 1978). Reports such as these are not limited to LGBTQI African Americans. For example, among Hispanic gay men, 80% reported feelings of sadness and depression at least once or twice in a 6-month period (Díaz et al., 2001). Belonging to multiple stigmatized cultural groups contributes to the disparity in reports of depression and suicide. Additionally, greater pressure to conform to cultural values and norms among these populations increases the risk of depressive symptomology and suicidal behavior.

The disproportionately high numbers of suicide attempts and ideation may be attributable to heterosexist and homophobic messages LGBTQI individuals hear in the schools, churches, media, and in society that directly attack an individual's self-perception and self-worth. For example, some common negative messages include direct name-calling (e.g., "faggot," "dyke," "queer"), homosexuality viewed as an abomination in the eyes of God, and being gay perceived as unnatural. More covert negative messages are related to the lack of visible LGBTQI mentors and role models in schools and universities, on television, and in music and other forms of popular culture. When LGBTQI individuals are visible in popular culture, for example in movies or on television, they are often stereotyped (e.g., Jack on *Will and Grace* as stereotypically effeminate), pathologized (e.g., characters on *Queer as Folk* were regularly shown engaging in drug use and unsafe, anonymous sex), and used to entertain heterosexual male audiences (e.g., beautiful, nude, feminine lesbians on *The L-Word* engaged in sex scenes). Visible, positive representations of LGBTQI people of color are nearly nonexistent in popular culture. Thus, these messages increase levels of internalized homophobia and put members of the LGBTQI community at increased risk for depression and suicide. Moreover, the lack of positive, visible LGBTQI role models likely affects one's self-esteem (see Activity 6.4).

ACTIVITY 6.4

Rank the following scenarios from most offensive to least offensive, with "1" being the most offensive and "4" being the least offensive. Compare your responses to those of your peers. Discuss what made you rank the scenarios the way you did.

———————— A televised sexual scene between two women

———————— A televised sexual scene between two men

———————— A televised sexual scene between one man and two women

———————— A televised sexual scene between a man dressed as a woman and a woman

---

Stress and Self-Esteem

Matheny and McCarthy (2000) discuss the term **stress** as an umbrella construct that describes a process of events. They define a **stressor** as an environmental or internal event that fuels a stress response. The stress response is the physical, cognitive, and emotional changes that are created as a result of a stressor. Common effects of stress for LGBTQI individuals include depression, suicidal behavior, sleep disturbance, anxiety, shame, substance abuse, eating disorders, and anger.

Stress associated with being a member of an oppressed group is called **minority stress.** Meyer (2003) defines minority stress as the extreme stress experienced among individuals from stigmatized social groups due to their minority social position. According to Meyer (1995, 2003), there are three general sources of minority stress for LGBTQI people. First, stress might be experienced due to chronic or acute outward events or conditions—for example, antigay slurs, the "Don't Ask, Don't Tell" policy, and bullying of LGBTQI youth. A second source of minority stress is the expectation of discriminatory events and the anticipatory energy this expectation requires. It takes a lot of mental and physical energy out of LGBTQI individuals to constantly be "on guard" in anticipation of possible persecution and discrimination. Finally, internalizing society's negative attitudes and feelings toward LGBTQI individuals (i.e., internalized homophobia) creates a large amount of stress. Thus, heterosexist acts not only increase the risk of an LGBTQI individual experiencing greater levels of stress, but they also have negative effects on a person's self-esteem. Studies have shown that internalized homophobia affects self-esteem in negative ways (Allen & Oleson, 1999). Additionally, internalized negative attitudes predict negative self-perceptions among LGBTQI individuals (Frable, Wortman, & Joseph, 1997). Because self-esteem is related to self-perception, and how we perceive ourselves impacts how we perceive our environments, it is not surprising that LGBTQI individuals' mental well-being is compromised more than their heterosexual peers. At particular risk for diminished self-esteem and psychological distress are LGBTQI youth.

LGBTQI Youth

The mental health consequences of growing up in a heterosexist and homophobic culture are particularly troubling for LGBTQI youth. Many LGBTQI youth do not have coping strategies to deal with trauma and abuse often experienced in the schools. Further, they often do not have support of teachers and staff. It is estimated that 42% of LGBTQI students have been verbally harassed (Kosciw & Cullen, 2001). The abuse and harassment often lead to low self-esteem and depression. Many LGBTQI youth attempt to escape and self-medicate the feelings of worthlessness, depression, and anxiety by abusing substances. Ashman (2004) reported that same-sex attracted youth are more likely than heterosexual peers to use illegal drugs including heroin, marijuana, "designer drugs," alcohol, and tobacco. The abuse and bullying that occurs in schools is not limited to verbal and physical. Many LGBTQI youth report being sexually harassed by peers resulting in mental health consequences such as loss of appetite, loss of interest in usual activities, sleep disturbance isolation, sadness, nervousness, and anger (American Association of University Women Educational Foundation, 1993). LGBTQI students who experience direct and indirect heterosexism and homophobia often report experiencing distress well into adulthood. For example, one study indicated that 17% of LGBTQI students who reported being bullied at school because of their actual or perceived sexual orientation experiences posttraumatic stress in adulthood. Furthermore, many LGBTQI persons who experienced homophobic acts during their youth reported increased levels of internalized homophobia, depressive symptoms, and anxiety symptoms in adulthood (Igartua, Gill, & Montoro, 2003). As a result of occurrences of antigay abuse in the schools, many LGBTQI youth drop out of school, and many end up living on the streets.

PHYSICAL CONSEQUENCES OF HETEROSEXISM

There also are physical consequences of heterosexism on the lives of LGBTQI individuals. Culturally competent counselors are encouraged to pay attention to somatic complaints of LGBTQI clients and how physical illness may be related to heterosexism and homophobia.

Substance Abuse

Although substance abuse is classified as a mental health issue, we include it as a physical consequence of heterosexism because of its physical effects, including its relationship to HIV/AIDS. The U.S. Department of Health and Human Services (2001a) has reported that approximately 20% to 25% of lesbians and gays are heavy alcohol users compared to 3% to 10% of heterosexuals. Research has demonstrated that heterosexism and internalized homophobia are related to alcohol abuse for this population (Barbara, 2002; DiPlacido, 1998). African American gay and bisexual men have higher rates of heavy substance use, specifically alcohol and cocaine in comparison to Black heterosexual men (Richardson et al., 1997). Because heterosexism can lead to internalized homophobia, shame, and poor self-perception, some members of the LGBTQI community resort to substance abuse as a way to mask these negative feelings. Due to limited places in our society where it is safe for LGBTQI people to congregate freely, gay bars continue to be the primary gathering place for many LGBTQI persons, which may explain the high rates of alcohol abuse among this group. Although there are no limits to the drugs used by portions of the LGBTQI community, certain drugs tend to be more prevalent. For example, marijuana, cocaine, psychedelics, methylenedioxymethampheatmine (Ecstasy), nitrate inhalants, and methamphetamine are often abused (USDHHS, 2001a).

In addition to the aforementioned substances, nicotine use (cigarette smoking) is extremely prevalent in the LGBTQI community. Approximately 31.4% of gay men smoke, compared to 24.7% for men in general (Greenwood et al., 2005). The smoking rate for lesbians is approximately 48%, whereas 14.9% of heterosexual women smoke (National Organization for Women [NOW] Foundation, 2001; Tang et al., 2004). One reason the smoking rates are so high among the LGBTQI community could be explained by institutional heterosexism. Washington (2002) explained that cigarette companies intentionally market cigarette advertisements toward the LGBTQI community. The increased rates of smoking put LGBTQI people at risk for various types of cancer and other health problems. Smoking partially explains why the life expectancy of gay men is 8 to 20 years less than other men. Interestingly, LGBTQI youth have 30% to 87% higher rates of cancer than their heterosexual peers.

[handwritten annotations at top of page: "— mom's death ... shame, grief, rage. — mom's neglect — mom's ... Andrew—shame — ... trauma"]

HIV/AIDS

Men who have sex with men continue to represent most new HIV infections. LGBTQI youth are increasingly contracting the virus at astounding rates. In fact, HIV among LGBTQI youth is double that of their heterosexual counterparts (D. Smith, 2001). Transgender individuals are also affected by HIV, with 35% of male-to-female transgender persons found to be HIV-positive (Clements-Nolle, Marx, Guzman, & Katz, 2001). Heterosexism is partly responsible for the high HIV infection rates among LGBTQI individuals. When LGBTQI youth come out to their families, many experience homophobic reactions such as violence and rejection. Some same-sex-attracted youth leave home and others are kicked out of their homes. To survive on the streets, many LGBTQI youth engage in sex for money to meet basic needs. They are also less likely to practice safe sex. Approximately 33% of gay or bisexual street youth are HIV-positive compared to 1% of heterosexual male street youth (Moon, McFarland, Kellogg, & Baxter, 2000). In addition, youth who have been bullied at school for being LGBTQI or because they were perceived to be LGBTQI tend to have more casual sex partners in adulthood than their peers (Rivers, 2004). This in turn puts them at greater risk for contracting HIV and other sexually transmitted infections. Finally, HIV-positive LGBTQI individuals who choose to hide their sexual orientation are at greater risk for developing opportunistic infections. Cole, Kemeny, Taylor, and Visscher (1996) found HIV infection advanced more rapidly among gay men who did not disclose their sexual orientation. HIV-negative men who did not disclose their sexual orientation also reported a greater number of health problems.

SOCIAL CONSEQUENCES OF HETEROSEXISM

The negative stereotypes people have about LGBTQI individuals are a social consequence of heterosexism. Madon (1997) investigated college students' stereotypes of gay men and found students viewed gay men as having feminine characteristics and as rejecting masculine gender roles. Other studies examining mental health trainees' stereotypes of LGBTQI individuals have found that trainees believe that most LGBTQI individuals had anxiety, personality, mood, eating, and sexual and gender identity disorders (Boysen, Vogel, Madon, & Wester, 2006). These stereotypes may contribute to LGBTQI individuals reporting dissatisfaction with counseling experiences.

Socioeconomic Status

The HINK (high income, no kids) stereotype mentioned earlier in the chapter is associated with distorted views of socioeconomic status for this population. Many people believe that LGBTQI individuals live extravagant lives because of a perception that they have excess financial resources. Thus, LGBTQI persons are seen as not needing economic, social and health-related services (Lind, 2004). This stereotype contributes to the invisibility of poverty among LGBTQI individuals.

When the topic of poverty comes up, most people do not think of LGBTQI individuals as affected. However, heterosexism is directly related to financial hardship for several reasons. One reason is due to LGBTQI's earning approximately 28% less money than their heterosexual counterparts (Badgett, 1995). Additional research has reported that same-sex female couples have significantly lower household incomes than their married counterparts. Because earnings contribute to lifestyle, many LGBTQI individuals cannot afford to live in the high-amenity, metropolitan cities that tend to be more accepting and tolerant of the LGBTQI community. This results in many poor LGBTQI people living in areas that might be more homophobic and less tolerant. Some LGBTQI persons who live in smaller, more conservative cities may be less likely to live free from discrimination and violence. Research also has shown that being in a lower social class is related to a decreased likelihood of describing oneself as gay and related to not participating in gay social activities (Barrett & Pollack, 2005). Another factor contributing to poverty among LGBTQI persons, particularly among LGBTQI youth, is homelessness. Because many LGBTQI youth are kicked out of their homes upon coming out or run away from abusive homes, many LGBTQI youth are homeless. It is estimated that between 21% and 36% of homeless youth identify as LGBTQI (Kennedy, 1991; Rew, Taylor-Seehafer, Thomas, & Yockey, 2001). Many of these youth do not attend school and as a result have a difficult time finding employment that would financially sustain them.

Institutional Heterosexism

Another social consequence of heterosexism is legalized discrimination in the form of **institutional heterosexism**. Institutional heterosexism is the institutional enforcement of heterosexuality as superior while denigrating homosexuality as inferior. Antigay marriage laws are an example of institutional heterosexism. As of January 2006, 45 states have some form of antigay marriage law. Interestingly, research has shown that the greater number of reported same-sex couple households, the more likely a state was to pass an anti-same-sex marriage law. In the same study, states with higher numbers of cities with domestic partnership coverage for same-sex couples were also more likely to pass an anti-same-sex marriage law (Barclay & Fisher, 2003). At the national level, the **Defense of Marriage Act (DOMA)** exemplifies legalized discrimination against LGBTQI persons. DOMA defines marriage as being between a man and a woman. As a result, LGBTQI couples and families are denied 1,138 federal protections bestowed to heterosexual couples and families by default (e.g., social security benefits, hospital visitation, access to family insurance policies, domestic violence protections, federal taxes). The most recent version of the **Temporary Assistance for Needy Families (TANF Reauthorization Bill)** further promotes legalized discrimination against the LGBTQI community. TANF provides federal funding to states to promote "healthy marriage" activities. Over $100 million in matching grants are given to states to promote healthy marriages, and two-parent (heterosexual) families, to educate students about the "value" of marriage, and to fund marriage enhancement programs for heterosexually married couples. These are just a few examples of institutional heterosexism (see Activity 6.5).

ACTIVITY 6.5

As a class, generate a list of additional examples of institutional heterosexism. How might various forms of heterosexism impact individuals based on their cultural makeup? What are some small action strategies you can implement to begin to make social change for LGBTQI persons?

Diminished Interpersonal Relationships

How heterosexism diminishes interpersonal relationships is another consequence of heterosexism. Internalized homophobia may prevent LGBTQI individuals from reaching out to and participating in the gay community for fear of being identified as gay. Similarly, heterosexuals who may want to participate in gay-related social events may experience fear of being perceived as LGBTQI by heterosexual peers. Some LGBTQI individuals may isolate themselves from family, particularly if the family is not aware of the LGBTQI identity. Last, heterosexism often prevents meaningful platonic relationships between LGBTQI persons and heterosexuals from being established because of fear, lack of knowledge, and prejudices (see Build Your Knowledge 6.2).

BUILD YOUR KNOWLEDGE 6.2

MEDIA RESOURCES ILLUSTRATING HETEROSEXISM

Choose one of the resources and analyze the media for examples of heterosexism. Come up with your own list of examples of heterosexist media and share them with the class.

Motion Pictures/Films	Books	Music
The Adventures of Priscilla, Queen of the Desert	*Running with Scissors: A Memoir* (Augusten Burroughs)	"Criminal" (Eminem)
The Birdcage	*Mississippi Sissy* (Kevin Sessums)	"Hideaway" (Erasure)
Imagine Me & You	*Alice in Genderland* (Richard J. Novic, M.D.)	"She's My Man" (The Scissor Sisters)
Better Than Chocolate	*I Am Not Myself These Days* (Josh Kilmer-Purcell)	"Real Men" (Joe Jackson)
Boys Don't Cry	*Grief* (Andrew Holleran)	"Leviticus: Faggot" (Me'shell Ndegeocello)
Latter Days	*Turning Point* (Lara Zielinsky)	"Andy, You're a Star" (The Killers)
Sordid Lives	*Invisible Life* (E. Lynn Harris)	"Your Gay Friend" (Robbie Williams)
Party Monster	*35 Cents* (Matty Lee)	"Forbidden Love" (Madonna)
Soldier's Girl	*Fish* (T. J. Parsell)	"Coming Clean" (Green Day)

SOCIALLY JUST, NONHETEROSEXIST TRAINING AND CLINICAL PRACTICE

Clearly, these negative consequences are just glimpses into how heterosexism affects the lives of many LGBTQI clients. Due to heterosexism having such a salient presence in the dominant culture, clients are likely to present with their side effects in session. For mental health providers to advocate for their LGBTQI clients, counselors need to possess knowledge and skills related to nonheterosexist clinical training and practice.

COUNSELING STRATEGIES FOR ADDRESSING HETEROSEXISM

Chernin and Johnson (2002) note some of the significant guidelines for ethical treatment of lesbians and gay males. They cite the resolution passed by the American Psychological Association in 1998, "Appropriate Therapeutic Responses to Sexual Orientation," formulated by the Committee on

Lesbian and Gay Concerns. This resolution recognizes that homosexuality has been long-removed from the *DSM* and is not a mental disorder and thus counseling professionals should not pathologize the sexual orientation of lesbian and gay clients. The American Counseling Association (ACA) passed a similar resolution in 1998, which was proposed by the Human Rights Committee—"Appropriate Counseling Response to Sexual Orientation." This resolution states that ACA opposes conceptions that LGB people have a mental disorder and supports practice and research with LGB people, which is affirmative of their sexual orientation.

Gay affirmative counseling includes counselors being aware of their own strengths and weaknesses in working with LGB clients; being able to use a variety of counseling interventions; countering the negative societal messages often internalized by LGB clients; affirming LGB identities; not pathologizing same-sex behavior and affection; and understanding issues affecting LGB people (Harrison, 2000; Maylon, 1993). Major issues include the impact of negative societal attitudes toward LGB individuals; discrimination in the legal, societal, and religious arenas; same-sex relationship dynamics; the effect of HIV/AIDS on the gay community; and identity development issues (Fassinger, 1991; Hall & Fradkin, 1992; Maylon, 1993; McHenry & Johnson, 1993).

Gay affirmative counseling approaches have been proposed to promote positive identity and psychological adjustment among LGB people (Browning, Reynolds, & Dworkin, 1991; Fassinger, 1991; Gumaer, 1987; Hall & Fradkin, 1992; Kauhlwein, 1992; Marszalek & Cashwell, 1998; Shannon & Woods, 1991). Gay affirmative counseling approaches involve applying specific techniques or specific theories such as self-psychology (Beard & Glickauf-Hughes, 1994) or cognitive therapy (Kauhlwein, 1992) to identity development issues. For example, a counselor might use cognitive therapy to help a client recognize how her or his negative beliefs about being gay can lead to self-hate. Gay affirmative counseling strategies for professional school counselors (American School Counselor Association [ASCA], 2005) include becoming:

- Aware of their own beliefs about sexual orientation and gender identity
- Knowledgeable of the negative effects that result from stereotyping individuals into rigid gender roles
- Committed to the affirmation of youth of all sexual orientations and identities

Professional school counselors help LGB students:

- Promote self-acceptance
- Deal with social acceptance
- Understand issues related to coming out, including issues that families may face when a student goes through this process
- Identify appropriate community resources

Regarding identity development, professional school counselors:

- Assist all students as they clarify feelings about their own sexual orientation and gender identity and the identity of others in a nonjudgmental manner
- Advocate for equitable educational opportunities for all students
- Address inappropriate language from students and adults
- Promote sensitivity and acceptance of diversity among all students and staff
- Provide LGB-inclusive and age-appropriate information on issues such as diverse family structures, dating and relationships, and sexually transmitted diseases
- Model language that is inclusive of sexual orientation or gender identity
- Encourage policies that address discrimination against any student

- Promote violence-prevention activities to create a safe school environment that is free of fear, bullying, and hostility

Gay affirmative professional counselors working in the community can support LGB couples and families (Chen-Hayes, 1997) by asking:

- How are issues of gender dealt with in this relationship with respect to both traditional and nontraditional gender roles?
- Do professional counselors follow the couple's ethnic and/or religious traditions?
- How does society perceive this couple or family? Do they get comments as a couple or as parents in public? If so, what strategies do they use or need to develop?
- What ways have been considered for choosing to parent? How do you feel about adoption and surrogacy?

Gay affirmative counselors can support LGB youth (Chen-Hayes, 1997) by asking:

- How safe or comfortable do you feel disclosing your sexual orientation to friends or family?
- If you don't feel safe, do you have other resources you can use for support (e.g., school counselor, support group)?
- Do you know where to find accurate information about health risks and prevention?
- Do you know where to turn for information about different substances (i.e., drugs and alcohol)?
- Do you know where to turn if you ever feel like hurting yourself?

Remember, LGB youth face the same developmental concerns as their heterosexual counterparts, while also dealing with the health and social effects of stigma. By having accurate information, the counselor can provide appropriate interventions, health information, and referrals. It is up to you!

ALGBTIC Competencies

The Association for Lesbian, Gay, Bisexual, and Transgender Issues in Counseling (ALGBTIC, 2005) has additionally created competencies for working with LGBTQI clients that focus on the Council for Accreditation of Counseling and Related Educational Programs (CACREP) areas: human growth and development, social and cultural foundations, helping relationships, group work, career and lifestyle development, appraisal, research, and professional orientation. The ALGBTIC competencies (2005) include:

Human Growth and Development

Competent Counselors will:

- understand that biological, familial, and psychosocial factors influence the course of development of LGB [lesbian, gay and bisexual] orientations and transgender identities.
- identify the heterosexist assumptions inherent in current lifespan development theories and account for this bias in assessment procedures and counseling practices.
- consider that, due to the coming out process, LGBT [lesbian, gay, bisexual, and transgender] individuals often may experience a lag between their chronological ages and the developmental stages delineated by current theories.
- recognize that identity formation and stigma management are ongoing developmental tasks that span the lives of LGBT persons.

- know that the normative developmental tasks of LGBT adolescents frequently may be complicated or compromised by identity confusion; anxiety and depression; suicidal ideation and behavior; academic failure; substance abuse; physical, sexual, and verbal abuse; homelessness; prostitution; and STD/HIV infection.
- understand that the typical developmental tasks of LGBT seniors often are complicated or compromised by social isolation and invisibility.
- affirm that sexual minority persons have the potential to integrate their LGB orientations and transgender identities into fully functioning and emotionally healthy lives.

Social and Cultural Foundations

Competent counselors will:

- acknowledge that heterosexism is a worldview and value-system that may undermine the healthy functioning of the sexual orientations, gender identities, and behaviors of LGBT persons.
- understand that heterosexism pervades the social and cultural foundations of many institutions and traditions and may foster negative attitudes toward LGBT persons.
- recognize how internalized prejudice, including heterosexism, racism, and sexism, may influence the counselor's own attitudes as well as those of their LGBT clients.
- know that the developmental tasks of LGBT women and people of color include the formation and integration of their gender, racial and sexual identities.
- familiarize themselves with the cultural traditions, rituals, and rites of passage specific to LGBT populations.

Helping Relationships

Competent counselors will:

- acknowledge the societal prejudice and discrimination experienced by LGBT persons and assist them in overcoming internalized negative attitudes toward their sexual orientations and gender identities.
- recognize that their own sexual orientations and gender identities are relevant to the helping relationship and influence the counseling process.
- seek consultation or supervision to ensure that their own biases or knowledge deficits about LGBT persons do not negatively influence the helping relationship.
- understand that attempts to alter or change the sexual orientations or gender identities of LGBT clients may be detrimental or even life-threatening, and, further, are not supported by the research and therefore should not be undertaken.

Group Work

Competent counselors will:

- be sensitive to the dynamics that occur when groups are formed that include only one representative of any minority culture and consider the necessity of including supportive allies for LGBT clients when screening and selecting group members.
- establish group norms and provide interventions that facilitate the safety and inclusion of LGBT group members.
- shape group norms and create a climate that allows for the voluntary self-identification and self-disclosure of LGBT participants.
- intervene actively when either overt or covert disapproval of LGBT members threatens member safety, group cohesion and integrity.

Career and Lifestyle Development

Competent counselors will:

- counter the occupational stereotypes that restrict the career development and decision-making of LGBT clients
- explore with LGBT clients the degree to which government statutes and union contracts do not protect workers against employment discrimination based on sexual orientation and gender identity.
- help LGBT clients make career choices that facilitate both identity formation and job satisfaction.
- acquaint LGBT clients with sexual minority role models that increase their awareness of viable career options.

Appraisal

Competent counselors will:

- understand that homosexuality, bisexuality, and gender nonconformity are neither forms of psychopathology nor necessarily evidence of developmental arrest.
- recognize the multiple ways that societal prejudice and discrimination create problems that LGBT clients may seek to address in counseling.
- consider sexual orientation and gender identity among the core characteristics that influence clients' perceptions of themselves and their worlds.
- assess LGBT clients without presuming that sexual orientation or gender identity is directly related to their presenting problems.
- differentiate between the effects of stigma, reactions to stress, and symptoms of psychopathology when assessing and diagnosing the presenting concerns of LGBT clients.
- recognize the potential for the heterosexist bias in the interpretation of psychological tests and measurements.

Research

Competent counselors will:

- formulate research questions that acknowledge the possible inclusion of LGBT participants yet are not based on stereotypic assumptions regarding these subjects.
- consider the ethical and legal issues involved in research with LGBT participants.
- acknowledge the methodological limitations in regard to research design, confidentiality, sampling, data collection, and measurement involved in research with LGBT participants.
- recognize the potential for heterosexist bias in the interpretation and reporting of research results.

Professional Orientation

Competent counselors will:

- know the history of the helping professions including significant factors and events that have compromised service delivery to LGBT populations.
- familiarize themselves with the needs and counseling issues of LGBT clients and use nonstigmatizing and affirming mental health, educational, and community resources.

- recognize the importance of educating professionals, students, supervisees, and consumers about LGBT issues and challenge misinformation or bias about minority persons.
- use professional development opportunities to enhance their attitudes, knowledge, and skills specific to counseling LGBT persons and their families.

Counselor Training

The field of counseling has not been immune to heterosexual bias, and as a result these biases can be seen in classrooms, textbooks, and research. The lack of consistent and accurate training often leads future helping professionals to feel anxiety and incompetence when sitting across from clients who are victims of heterosexism. An action step students can take to becoming more competent to work with LGB clients is to engage in self-exploration. Because we all are gendered, sexed, raced, classed, sexually oriented, and possess various degrees of ability, we are oppressed and privileged in various ways. Furthermore, we bring these identities into classrooms and counseling sessions. Counselor educators and students might begin to examine how these identities function in classrooms, counseling sessions, and society. Once we become aware of how our privileges by default oppress others, we get closer to the creation of a socially just, nonheterosexist society (see Reflection 6.5 and Activity 6.6).

REFLECTION 6.5

Journal about a real-life personal experience where you intentionally or unintentionally oppressed another individual based on your assigned sexual orientation. What privileges come with your assigned sexual orientation? How are these privileges related to the oppressive event you described? Try to identify how the other person may have felt. How did you feel during the event?

The professional literature has additional recommendations for confronting heterosexism in counselor training (Carroll, 2001):

- Explore resources that deal with queer and feminist theories. Counselor training should access other disciplines (e.g., women's studies, human sexuality, anthropology, public policy, etc.). Integrate readings from these disciplines into counselor training. Students should utilize readings and other resources from these disciplines into assignments and class presentations.
- Use narrative texts and films throughout the curriculum that challenge traditional definitions of sexuality. Rather than viewing sexuality as heterosexist dichotomies (straight or gay), integrating multimedia resources that promote the continuum of sexuality helps provide alternative definitions of these socially constructed terms.
- Emphasize nontraditional approaches to therapy, for example, constructivist and narrative paradigms.
- Choose counseling textbooks that are nonheterosexist. Students need to begin reading texts that are feminist and queer-affirmative. In other words, when examining assigned readings and textbooks, students should pay attention to themes of power and control, particularly as they relate to sexual minorities.
- Familiarize yourself with the constructs of discourse, positioning, and deconstruction (Winslade, Monk, & Drewery, 1997). **Discourse** refers to paying attention to the power dynamics in language.

For example, in a classroom, who is speaking and who is not speaking? During discussions, who is being marginalized and who is in control? **Positioning** pertains to the role we take in a particular dialogue. Are we unintentionally (or intentionally) dominating a conversation causing sexual minorities to be silenced because we believe our opinions are more important? Is your voice being silenced because you are fearful of negative repercussions if you expressed a dissenting view? Last, **deconstruction** means removing the hegemonic discourse that is so prevalent in our culture. In other words, it means taking apart and removing dominant ideologies that perpetuate oppression and prevent equal access to resources for LGB persons.

ACTIVITY 6.6

In pairs, take turns telling each other of a recent trip you have taken or what you did this past weekend. While one person tells the story without rules, the other person must adhere to the following rules: You cannot mention significant others or friends, you cannot use first names, you cannot use pronouns, and you cannot use gender-specific terms. Now switch roles. What made this conversation difficult? Did you feel empowered to speak freely? Who had more power in the conversation? Do you think LGB individuals have conversations like this often?

Clinical Practice

Research shows that LGB individuals seek counseling services more than the general population. However, they also report greater dissatisfaction with the services received. Therefore, it is important for counselors to able to provide nonheterosexist clinical services and to create safe nonheterosexist counseling environments. There are several things counselors can do to provide effective counseling to LGB clients.

Counselors must be aware of their attitudes and beliefs about LGB persons as a first step to providing nonheterosexist mental health services. This includes self-examining general and mental health stereotypes a counselor might have about LGB clients because these stereotypes could interfere with the type and quality of counseling provided. Traditionally, many educators teach students to refer clients if there is a large discrepancy between the values of the counselor and client, or if a counselor is not competent to work with a particular client. However, this recommendation should not be used as a way to avoid working with clients who are culturally different than the counselor. The American Counseling Association (2005) *Code of Ethics* states that counselors have an ethical responsibility to continually educate themselves and to become culturally competent practitioners. This includes being aware of diverse cultural groups and acquiring knowledge about others' cultures. Counselors also have an ethical responsibility to not partake in discriminatory practices. Discrimination in the guise of referring LGB clients is unethical.

Counselors must also be aware of how their race, gender, age, class status, ability level, and sexual orientation impact the counseling relationship. Greene (2005) contends that these factors affect what counselors and clients choose to see and what they choose to avoid in sessions. Competent counselors will explore with clients what their sexual orientations mean to each other, and what the identities mean in relation to the larger social context. Greene purports that current models of psychotherapy often perpetuate the social status quo, whereby they become socially unjust tools of oppression, particularly for LGB clients.

Examining the power behind the language counselors choose to use with clients is another way to minimize heterosexism in clinical practice. For example, queer theory views categories such as "straight" and "gay" as contrivances of the dominant culture. These dichotomous labels dismiss individuals who may not identify as heterosexual or gay, such as bisexuals and asexuals. According to Carroll (2001), viewing LGB persons as a separate species is an ideology of power. Competent counselors will ask clients how they prefer to be addressed and will use language that the client uses. Moreover, use of the term *homosexual* is not necessarily appropriate because of its historical significance as a mental disorder. Most LGB persons do not describe themselves as "homosexuals" and neither should culturally sensitive mental health professionals. Note how a client identifies herself or himself (e.g., gay, lesbian, bisexual, queer); that is the appropriate language to use. Last, counselors need to expand the meaning of the word *family*, particularly when working with LGB clients. For many clients, family does not necessarily pertain to biological families of origin. For many LGB persons, friends and other community members constitute a family. In addition, because many same-sex couples are increasingly choosing to expand their family through adoption, the term *family* is not limited to a mom, dad, and kids.

Additional ways counselors can minimize heterosexism in counseling practice is by not assuming that clients' presenting problems are related to their sexual orientation. Rather, counselors should collaborate with clients to explore how heterosexism permeates the contextual environments of clients and how clients are affected. Szymanski (2005) suggested that counselors assess for experiences of prejudice, harassment, discrimination, and violence in relation to sexual orientation. Once these components are assessed, counselors can implement the American Counseling Association's (ACA) advocacy competencies. Specifically, counselors should integrate the advocacy competencies that empower LGB clients. The following are a few recommended strategies taken from ACA's advocacy competencies:

- Identify strengths and resources of LGB clients.
- Identify the social, political, economic, and cultural factors that affect LGB clients.
- Help LGB clients identify external barriers that affect their development.
- Train LGB clients to self-advocate.
- Assist LGB clients in carrying out action plans.

COUNSELORS' ROLE IN CREATING A SOCIALLY JUST, NONHETEROSEXIST SOCIETY

Historically, one of the goals of counseling has been to make a difference in the community. Over the years, the profession has seemed to lose that focus but is once again returning to discussing ways counselors can become agents of social change. Many leaders in the counseling field believe that counseling and activism should not be separate. Therefore, the following are suggested strategies counselors and students might utilize to help create a more socially just, nonheterosexist society.

1. **Lobbying and Supporting Policy Change.** Counselors should actively work together to influence legislators to vote for laws that advocate for LGB persons, such as:
   - Increased HIV/AIDS funding
   - Same-sex marriage, domestic partnership benefits
   - Stronger hate crime penalities
2. **Giving Back to the Community.** Counselors need to go into oppressed communities of LGB individuals and advocate for change. Rather than assuming what needs to be changed, counselors should give voice to community members to hear what the community needs to be changed. Counselors can use their counseling skills to build bridges between and among LGB persons to

work toward common social justice goals among these populations. Further, counselors should serve as consultants for community service agencies to ensure that LGB clients have equal access to services.

3. **Giving Back to the Schools.** Based on the work of Stone (2003), school counselors can advocate for LGB youth in the following ways:
   - Collaborate with schools to develop action plans to reduce sexual harassment.
   - Involve heterosexual allies in system reform.
   - Include LGB issues in diversity awareness and multicultural initiatives.
   - Use inclusive language in classroom guidance lessons.
   - Acquire continuing education on young LGB issues.
   - Work to bridge families and schools.
   - Support the Gay, Lesbian, Straight Education Network (www.glsen.org).

4. **Collaboration with Other Fields.** Counselors and counseling training programs need to expand their areas of competence to include interdisciplinary education (e.g., medicine, human sexuality, public policy, social work, women's studies). Socially conscious counselors will have dialogues with colleagues in these different disciplines to gain knowledge about LGB persons and to better meet the micro and macro needs of these communities.

These strategies may be helpful in developing advocacy projects within the counseling community. Activity 6.7 describes a class exercise to develop a project regarding this population.

ACTIVITY 6.7

Find a local organization in your community that provides mental health services to LGB individuals. As a class, create a small advocacy project that will allow you to give back to that organization before the end of your quarter or semester. At the completion of your project, give a written or oral presentation to students and faculty within your department.

Summary

As the field of counseling is increasingly stressing the need for competent counselors to work with individuals who identify as lesbian, gay, and bisexual (LGB), it is important to increase counselors' knowledge and awareness regarding sexual orientation. We began this chapter by defining important terms that counselors should know because using appropriate language with LGB clients is important, Additionally, we delineated the construct of heterosexism and presented some of the mental health, physical, and social consequences of heterosexism. When working with LGB clients, competent counselors will assess the effects of heterosexism on the lives of their clients. Once a culturally sensitive assessment has taken place, competent counselors will implement gay affirmative counseling interventions. Therefore, we included specific interventions that mental health and school counselors can utilize on behalf of their clients and students respectively. We concluded this chapter by recommending specific ways counselors can advocate for their LGB clients at a systemic level, thereby creating a more just nonheterosexist society.

CHAPTER 7

Social Class and Classism

KATHRYN S. NEWTON

PREVIEW

Socioeconomic status (SES) plays a significant role in personal identity, relationships, and individual and cultural values. It is also a predictive factor for health and well-being. Given the growing resource and income disparities in the United States, and the high likelihood that counselor trainees and counselors will work in communities and schools across the socioeconomic spectrum, this is an important area of competence.

Although many counseling internship sites serve clients at the lower end of the socioeconomic scale, counselor trainees rarely receive training or supervision that helps them identify, conceptualize, and intervene with issues related to SES and social class identity. This chapter will provide an overview of class and class-based discrimination in the United States, the impact on mental health, and implications for counselors. Developing the ability to identify and work with the influences of class and classism can contribute to more effective counseling. The activities and resources throughout the chapter are intended to deepen counselor self-awareness, increase knowledge and skills, and provide direction for professional and client advocacy. While reading this chapter, keep in mind that self-awareness is a foundational aspect of cultural competence. Pay attention to topics, issues, or activities that introduce thoughts or feelings that may be uncomfortable, confusing, enlightening, or liberating.

CONSIDERING SOCIAL CLASS AND CLASSISM

Social classifications are common, if not universal, to human societies. Classifications may be used to assign social roles such as production, protection, child rearing, or spiritual stewardship. These classifications may be based on gender, age, race, ethnicity, ability, or knowledge/ education. Frequently these classifications become a way of designating rank and power, or **social class** status. In some societies, social class may take a formal structure, such as the caste system in India or the traditional social class structure in England. In these instances people are born into a social class that defines their community, vocation, education, language, and behavior toward others within and outside their own social classification. Although the United States may not have a formal class structure our economic, political, legal, educational, and social institutions effectively group people according to their access to and ability to manipulate socioeconomic resources. (Consider how this compares to the United Nations statement in Reflection 7.1.) Those resources, or **class indicators**, include income, job status, wealth, housing, clothing, education, and peer groups.

REFLECTION 7.1

Article 25 of the United Nations' Universal Declaration of Human Rights, established in 1948, reads as follows:

> Everyone has the right to a standard of living adequate for the health and well-being of himself and of his family, including food, clothing, housing and medical care and necessary social services, and the right to security in the event of unemployment, sickness, disability, widowhood, old age or other lack of livelihood in circumstances beyond his control.

Use the following questions to explore your own beliefs regarding human rights:

a. Do all human beings have a *right* to an adequate standard of living?
b. Do all human beings have a right to resources adequate for health *and* well-being, and not just for survival?
c. Do you believe the universal human right to health and well-being is an *attainable* goal?
d. How do these questions relate to the work of counselors?

There are many different ways of conceptualizing and discussing social class structure. One way is based on comparing quantifiable socioeconomic factors (e.g., educational attainment, type of employment, income level, savings, investments, housing and property ownership). Another way of conceptualizing class is subjectively; in other words, how do individuals perceive and experience their own SES in relation to others? Yet another perspective examines complex interactions between economics, gender, and race. Class can also be defined in terms of access to and ability to wield power and influence. Table 7.1 lists some of the more common terms used to reference the social class status of individuals and groups. Although these terms are generally accepted, many of them are also used to covertly reference and perpetuate negative stereotypes. In considering the terms in Table 7.1, notice images that come to mind. Why do certain "profiles" (e.g., race, gender, occupation) get associated with specific terms? What is the source of those associations? Then, complete Activity 7.1 to consider how labels impact individuals' attitudes regarding SES.

What is Socioeconomic Status?

Socioeconomic status (SES) generally refers to a comparative measure of class standing, or status, based upon a combination of educational attainment, income level, and occupational prestige. Other class indicators may be considering in an assessment of SES, depending on the issue

TABLE 7.1 Terms Frequently Used to Reference Social Class

Lower-Class Status	Middle-Class Status	Upper-Class Status
Low income	Middle income	Upper income
Lower class	Middle class	Upper class
Working poor	Working class	Wealthy
Urban poor/rural poor	Professional	New money/old money
Welfare recipient	Home owner	College graduate
High school dropout	High school graduate	Executive
Manual labor	Skilled labor	Elite

ACTIVITY 7.1

Have a discussion in small groups about words you have heard used to negatively indicate SES. Give special attention to words that indicate the intersection of class, race, and gender. For example, what stereotype is indicated by the term *redneck*? How about the term *welfare mother*? And *trust fund baby*? Where do these terms come from? Who uses them? Do adults and children use different language to indicate class status? What impact might this language have on identity development, peer relationships, and community interactions?

---

being explored (e.g., a counselor may wish to include peer group status when assessing an adolescent client). In the field of counseling, SES is often used as a descriptor for clients or research sample populations. A "low-SES" client is assumed to have no more than a high school diploma, and to be working in a low-skill position, probably for minimum wage. On the other end of the continuum, a "high-SES" client is assumed to have a college degree, to be working in a salaried professional career with benefits, and to have acquired assets (property ownership, investments). An example of a "middle-" or "moderate-SES" individual would be a recent graduate of a master's-level counseling program who may be income poor (especially if graduating with student loans), but education rich (just under 10% of the population has attained a graduate-level degree; U.S. Census Bureau, 2006a).

It is important to understand the interaction between social, educational, and economic factors in perceptions of SES. Low, middle, or high SES does not automatically correlate with income level. **Poverty** is a condition in which a person is unable to meet basic requirements for well-being such as food, shelter, and clothing. **Wealth**, on the other hand, indicates a surplus of resources. A person who is wealthy is able to meet his or her basic needs and also accumulate resources to satisfy wants. While it is possible to move between wealth and poverty (consider the role of gambling, stock market investing, inheritance), most individuals will remain at roughly the same income level as their parents.

The concrete results of inequitable resource distribution are obvious, such as hunger, homelessness, educational limitations, or difficulty obtaining insurance. Less apparent are the ways in which class bias and SES influences you and your client. Prejudice (both positive and negative biases) based on SES influence mental health and the counseling process on multiple levels, including the presenting of concerns, the therapeutic relationship, case conceptualization and intervention choices, and access to services. Consider the following profiles of age, education, employment, and income levels—would each individual be considered low, middle, or high SES? How would others from various SESs perceive these individuals? Think about how each of these individuals might perceive and interact with the typical counselor (master's degree, professional position, middle income):

- Age 38, master's degree in business administration, high-level corporate executive, substantial assets; however, recently unemployed (downsizing) and no income.
- Age 22, vocational degree, unemployed assistant mechanic, annual income of $100,000 (lottery payouts).
- Age 28, doctoral degree, working overseas on a Fulbright scholarship, income falls below federal poverty line.

- Age 10, attending private boarding school, high-achieving student, on scholarship (from single-parent household below federal poverty line).
- Age 62, general education diploma (GED), senior tollbooth operator, annual salary of $55,000.

Class-based prejudices can inhibit the development of the therapeutic alliance, contribute to transference and countertransference issues, and lead to ineffective practices. Thus the following section will look more closely at classism and implications for counseling.

What Is Classism?

In its simplest form, **classism** is having discriminatory beliefs about, and behavior toward, individuals and groups based on their perceived or actual SES. From childhood we are exposed to constant messages from family, friends, teachers, and the media about relative class status. These familial and social biases shape our sense of self, our relationship, and our worldview. When our beliefs, values, decisions, and relationships are based on perceptions of respective class status it is known as **internalized classism**. Looking inward, we may feel shame, accomplishment, or superiority, depending on our perceived social class position. Looking outward, we may resent, blame, or admire others based on their comparative SES. As counselors, we need to understand how internalized and **structural classism** (i.e., social and institutional practices that discriminate based on SES) affect mental health and the counseling process.

Although the counseling profession has made significant progress in addressing issues of gender, race, ethnicity, and sexual identity, classism is rarely addressed. Two factors that may contribute to this relative silence are psychological distancing and poverty attribution. **Psychological distancing** refers to ways of thinking and behaving that are used by privileged groups to justify and distance themselves from their role in socioeconomic injustice (Lott, 2002). One way of distancing is to structure education, work, and spiritual and community activities in a way that maintains the separation between socioeconomic classes. This separation prevents the development of empathy that would naturally follow from open communication and close relationships.

Another factor that interferes with actively addressing the consequences of classism is **poverty attribution** (how individuals explain poverty). Studies of both economically privileged and marginalized groups have found that race, gender, political and religious affiliation influence people's beliefs regarding individual wealth or poverty (Cozzarelli, Wilkinson, & Tagler, 2001; Hunt, 2002). One belief is that resources are gained or lost due to individual causation (e.g., people are poor or wealthy because of their personal values, work ethic, or other personal characteristics; people are personally responsible for their economic status). Another belief is that individual wealth or poverty is best explained by socioeconomic and political factors, or structural causation (e.g., people are poor because of discriminatory social policy, oppression, or other institutional forms of exclusion; Hunt, 2004). Hunt found that most participants attributed wealth to individual accomplishment, and attributed poverty to external factors such as a failing economy, politics, or discrimination. The same study found that racial and ethnic minorities were more likely than Whites to attribute both wealth and poverty to external factors such as privilege and oppression. The way we learn to understand and explain relative wealth and poverty is influenced by our life experience, our acquired values, and the ways in which we relate to others—and they to us. Consider how the values presented in Reflection 7.2 impact interpersonal relationships.

REFLECTION 7.2

Circle five values or expectations from the list that seemed to be the most important in your family of origin. Then underline five that were discouraged or devalued. In a different color, go through the same process for your current personal values.

- getting by
- making a good living
- gaining social status or prominence
- communicating openly among family members
- going to a place of worship
- keeping up with the neighbors
- being physically fit or athletic
- getting therapy to work out issues
- helping others
- getting married and having children
- respecting law and order
- defending your country
- staying out of trouble with the law
- being polite and well-mannered
- being politically or socially aware
- gaining personal recognition
- sticking up for others in your community
- doing community service
- being in control
- being independent
- saving money

- making your money work for you
- enjoying your money
- getting a high school degree
- getting a college degree
- getting an advanced or professional degree
- learning a trade
- being smart
- helping advance your racial, religious, and/or cultural group
- maintaining your physical appearance
- being a professional
- being an entrepreneur
- owning a home
- being patriotic
- going to a good school
- not being wasteful
- being respectful of elders
- achieving your goals
- having character
- other: _____
- other: _____

- Look at the values that you have circled or underlined in both colors. These represent family-of-origin values that have remained the same for you as an adult. Why have you retained these values? How might these values support or inhibit your development as a counselor?
- Look over the values that were held by your family of origin, but not by you as an adult. Do the same for the values that were not your family's but that you have acquired as an adult. What experiences contributed to these changes in values?
- Finally, look at the values that are neither circled nor underlined. What associations do you have with these values? If you had a client for whom these values were primary, would you be able to support, encourage, and empathize with those values?

Source: Adapted from the "Class Background Inventory" created by Class Action: Building Bridges Across the Class Divide. Original version available at www.classism.org/action_self.html.

A "Classless Society"?

Despite historical evidence to the contrary, much of the cultural mythology of the United States is rooted in the belief that this is a "classless society" with equal opportunity for all, the so-called American Dream. The predominant cultural belief is that if you work hard, you will get ahead (and conversely, if you are not getting ahead it's because you are not working hard enough). Failing to examine and challenge this myth serves to maintain the status quo, and perpetuates conditions that continue to undermine the well-being of individuals, families, and communities across class levels.

White Europeans who colonized North America brought class structure with them in the form of indentured servants and enslaved peoples and created a political system that favored the dominant social class (White European Christian male property owners; for a complete history of voting rights in this country visit www.crmvet.org/info/votehist. htm). Remnants of this system of controlling social participation, and thus power, have lingered to this day. The wealthiest in the nation are predominantly White and male; the poorest are disproportionately women, children, and racial and ethnic minorities (U.S. Census Bureau, 2006a). Not only do we have an identifiable class structure, but the income gap between rich and poor in the United States is wider than in most other developed nations. Of the top 20 nations in the world for promoting human development, the United States ranks 16th (World Bank, 2005). Furthermore, among those top 20 nations the United States had one of the lowest life expectancies, was in the bottom 3 for functional literacy rates, and had the highest population percentage with incomes below the national median.

Classism plays a central role in resource distribution and access to power in the United States. The degree to which individuals can move between class levels in a society is referred to as **class mobility**. In the United States, many people continue to believe that there is a high degree of class mobility and that individuals can move freely between socioeconomic levels within one life span or over generations. However, actual statistics on income, employment, education, and health indicate otherwise. The communities we live in, the schools we attend, whether or not we attend and complete college, our career opportunities, and our social networks are largely predicted by the socioeconomic class of our families of origin.

U.S. CLASS STRUCTURE   Two percent of the world's population owns more than half of all global wealth, while half of the world's population owns only 1% of all wealth. One third of the world's wealth is owned by North Americans, home to the richest 1% of the global population. Wealth is concentrated even further within that 1%. According to records of the Internal Revenue Service, in 2001 3.5% of the adult population in this country held an estimated 32.7% of total U.S. net worth. Between 1998 and 2000, Americans with a net worth of $5 million or more saw their holdings increase by over 40% (Johnson & Raub, 2001). Since 1977 the number of tax returns reporting incomes over $200,000 has, on average, increased with 2005 being the largest single year increase since 1978 (Balkovic, 2008). The old sayings "the rich get richer and the poor get poorer" and "it takes money to make money" appear to hold true. In an analysis of U.S. Census data, Albrecht and Albrecht (2007) found that low-SES individuals fared worse living in economically advantaged communities as opposed to economically similar neighborhoods. Stagnating wages and the scarcity of affordable housing are two of the many factors that contribute to entrenched economic injustice. Of people aged 16 or older who are at or below the federal poverty line, almost 12% are full-time year round-workers (U.S. Census Bureau, 2007a). Table 7.2 presents a model of the class structure in the United States based on profession, education, and income.

REFLECTION 7.3

Consider the following quotation by Lemieux and Pratto (2003):

> Poverty does not persist because there is a scarcity of resources, nor does poverty exist because some societies have inefficient economic systems, lack natural resources, or because poor people lack ambition. Poverty is a product of human social relationships because social relationships determine how people distribute resources. (p. 147)

- In what ways does this statement support or challenge your own beliefs about the cause(s) of poverty?
- Based on this statement, what might an objective observer assume about human relationships in this country based on the distribution of resources?
- In what way might counselors and the counseling profession use social relationships to work toward alleviating poverty and correlated mental health issues?

TABLE 7.2 Model of U.S. Class Structure

Class Status	Occupational Description	% U.S. Population	Education	Personal Income[*]
Upper-upper	Inherited wealth: investments, interest	1%		$1,000,000+
Upper	Executives, other upper-level professionals	1		$100,000+
Upper middle	Professionals	10	Graduate	$57,585
Lower middle	Professional support and sales	16	Associate or bachelor's	$43,954
Working	Clerical, service, and blue-collar (skilled)	26	Some college	$31,566
Lower	Full- and part-time unskilled	30	High school	$25,829
Poor[*]	Unskilled, part-time and unemployed	16	Some high school	$18,435

[*]The personal income figures represent an average of salaries across gender; in actuality men earn an average of $10,000 to $20,000 more per year than women in every socioeconomic class.

Sources: Johnson and Raub (2001); Thompson and Hickey (2005).

POVERTY AND MENTAL HEALTH

Our respective class status and corresponding ability to access basic resources interact with mental health on several levels. Poverty has been associated with higher incidence of mental disorders, more severe symptoms, and greater difficulty accessing services. Poverty is also associated with greater incidence of exposure to violence and related trauma, depression, anxiety, and Posttraumatic Stress Disorder (World Health Organization [WHO], 2001). This may be especially true for women and children. One study found that a majority of women receiving welfare had a history of domestic violence and one third experienced ongoing abuse (Josephson, 2005). Children from impoverished families and communities have higher exposure to pollutants in air, water, and food. The day cares and schools in low-income neighborhoods are inferior and often toxic, and children have less access to books and computers and other tools for learning (Evans, 2004).

It has been hypothesized that mental illness may precipitate a downward slide into poverty due to difficulty managing basic life tasks. However, recent evidence indicates that poverty is just as likely to precede the development of mental illness, in part due to pervasive and unrelenting life stressors (Hudson, 2005). Because of these direct negative correlations between poverty and well-being, it is important to know more about who is poor and to understand the risk factors and mental health consequences associated with poverty. It is also important to understand the relationship between poverty, identity, and well-being.

Who Is Poor?

The national poverty rate between 2003 and 2005 averaged 12.6% (U.S. Census Bureau, 2006a) and varied significantly by race, gender, family status, and age. The 2005 federal poverty threshold was designated as $15,720 for a family of three and $19,806 for a family of four. Looking at absolute numbers, people living below the poverty line in the United States included 16.2 million non-Hispanic

Whites, 9.4 million Hispanics, 9.2 million Blacks, and 1.4 million Asians. However, poverty averages for the 3-year period from 2003 to 2005 indicated significant economic disparities for racial and ethnic minorities. Average poverty rates for racial and ethnic minorities were as follows: American Indian/Alaskan Native (25.3%), Blacks (24.7%), Hispanic origin/any race (22%), Native Hawaiian/ Pacific Islander (12.2%), and Asian (10.9%). Among Whites, the 3-year poverty rate average was 8.4%.

Women and children are overrepresented among the poor in this country, and this is especially true for women and children from racial minority groups. U.S. Census data (U.S. Census Bureau, 2007a) showed that 24.1% of women and 28.7% of female-headed households were below federal poverty levels, as compared to 17.9% of men and 13% of male-headed households. Children comprised 25% of the total population, but 35% of those in poverty—one of every three people in poverty. The poverty rate among Black and Latino children is three times that of White children. Among children nationwide, 17% live in households with incomes below the poverty line. Forty-two percent of children living in female-headed households experience poverty as opposed to 9% of those in married-couple households.

Risk Factors and Mental Health Consequences

Many of the risk factors associated with poverty are related to challenges meeting basic resource needs. Basic resources necessary for security and well-being include sufficient and nutritious food, education, employment with living wages, safe and stable housing, health care, and child care. Counselors with a basic working knowledge of inequality and stressors in these areas will be better prepared to discuss and assess these issues with their clients.

SUFFICIENT AND NUTRITIOUS FOOD   The U.S. government uses the term **food insecurity** to refer to limited or uncertain food availability. Eleven percent of all U.S. households experienced food instability in 2005, and 4% also experienced hunger (U.S. Department of Agriculture [USDA], 2007). According to America's Second Harvest (ASH, 2006), a national organization that tracks emergency food distribution and also provides direct service, approximately 1 in 12 Americans will have insufficient food at some point during the year. Of those, 45% are White and European American, 33% African Americans, and 17% Latino. Just over half of the people in this country who experience hunger were found to live in urban areas (57%); the remainder lived in suburban and rural areas (43%). Food insufficiency has been linked with incidence of major depression in female welfare recipients (Heflin, Siefert, & Williams, 2005). Food scarcity has been linked with obesity (due to difficulty accessing fresh, healthy foods) and also with depression (WHO, 2001). Reflection 7.4 provides a case to consider the issue of food insecurity.

REFLECTION 7.4

Imagine the following situation. An 8-year old girl, significantly overweight for her age, is referred for counseling for possible behavioral or learning disorders; her intake form indicates that she is both a perpetrator and target of bullying at her school. During the assessment she has difficulty focusing and seems listless. Assuming the counselor remembers that these symptoms, as well as obesity, may be indications of food scarcity, what knowledge and skills might be necessary to address nutritional intake during assessment? To speak to her parents about access to basic resources? Should the assessment uncover that her family is surviving on fast food and food pantry donation, what impact might this information have on the counselor? What impact might a counselor's intervention choices have on the child and her family?

EDUCATION   A significant factor in public education inequity is the means by which public schools are funded. There are currently no federal standards for funding: States determine allocations, which are generally a combination of local, state, and federal sources. The majority of funding in most states has been generated from local property taxes, which is then allocated locally (i.e., a town's property taxes would fund that town's schools). Properties in middle- and upper-income areas generate significantly higher property taxes than those in low-income and poor areas, contributing to profound inequities in school facilities, teacher salaries, and teaching materials.

One of the first legal challenges to this system of funding, California's *Serrano v. Priest* in 1971, was filed on behalf of poor students and demanded a more equitable system of taxation and allocation. Since then, more than 40 states have been subject to court cases challenging the constitutionality of their system of public school funding. Increasingly, states are being held accountable for ensuring that all children have access to adequate education. Recent data from the U.S. Department of Education (USDOE, 2007) indicates that per-student expenditure for students in districts with high poverty has achieved some equity with low-poverty-level districts. However, expenditures in middle districts (i.e., moderate poverty areas) are frequently anywhere from $1,000 to $2,000 less per student.

Funding disparities in public school are exacerbated by family SES and access to resources. Among students from the wealthiest families, half will attend college and these families will spend an average of 7% of their income on that child's college education. Only 1 out of every 17 students from the poorest families will get into college and their families will spend 25% of household income on that college education (Brooks, 2005). Those that do make it to college face reduced availability of federal grant assistance, higher interest rates on student loans, exorbitant textbook costs, and the challenges of balancing work and academics. Students from poor and low-income backgrounds have significantly lower college graduation rates than those from a higher SES. Oftentimes, a lack of financial resources may impact graduate school or professional degrees (see Activity 7.2).

ACTIVITY 7.2

Discuss the following questions in small groups. In what ways does the structure of your university and of your counselor training program support or discourage students from poor or low-income backgrounds? Is your program structured in a way that would allow students to work while completing their coursework and internship (without compromising their health and well-being)? Is work-study available? Graduate assistantships?

EMPLOYMENT   Educational attainment and employment opportunities are closely linked in perpetuating generational class oppression. The lower the education level, the more likely an individual is to be employed at a minimum wage hourly job. While housing, food, utility, clothing, and transportation costs have steadily increased, wages have remained stagnant. Many in this country are experiencing increasing difficulty maintaining their lifestyle; in the world population, few people have "adequate living conditions" as described in the Universal Declaration of Human Rights earlier in the chapter.

In May of 2007 Congress approved a bill to increase the federal minimum wage for the first time since 1997. The minimum wage was increased from $5.15 to $5.85 per hour, and will gradually increase to $7.25 by 2009 (U.S. Department of Labor [USDOL], 2007). An individual working a 40-hour week, every week of the year at federal minimum wage in 2007 will now earn $12,168 annually—before taxes.

Consider that the federal poverty threshold for one individual is $10,294 (U.S. Census Bureau, 2006a) and it is easy to see why many states have already substantially increased their minimum wage, and why there is a growing movement advocating for the creation of a living wage. The campaign for a **living wage** is grounded in the belief that no one who is working full time should be living in poverty, and that work should be adequately rewarded. Over the last decade, living wage campaigns have succeeded in securing hourly wages as high as $9.50 per hour in cities, towns, and at large employers across the country. (To learn more about living wage campaigns visit the Web site of the Living Wage Resource Center at www.livingwagecampaign.org.)

Employment in general is becoming increasingly unstable. Wages have stagnated, health benefits are declining or disappearing, jobs are being outsourced, and rapidly shifting fields and technologies require constant education and training. The unemployment rate does not include individuals who have already exceeded the benefits period without obtaining work, nor does it include those who became dissatisfied with job programs that funneled them into minimum wage employment, nor those who are working part-time and/or temporary jobs.

It takes only one illness in the family or one job loss to fall from employed, to underemployed, to unemployed to social welfare. Women are especially vulnerable due to continuing gender inequity in wages, limited employment options suitable for mothers who are primary caretakers, and the difficulty of finding safe and affordable child care. Welfare limitations on lifetime enrollment have been successful in reducing the welfare role; however, results indicate that these "reforms" have succeeded by cutting off access and not by reducing poverty. Over the past decade, **Temporary Aid to Needy Families (TANF)** welfare eligibility and work requirements have been revised in such a way that less than half of very poor families receive assistance, and those who access benefits may never fully acquire or regain economic stability (Parrott & Sherman, 2006). This and other aspects of employment instability have been found to contribute to anxiety and depression (WHO, 2001). Conversely, improvements in economic well-being have been found to have positive outcomes for psychological well-being (Dearing, Taylor, & McCartney, 2004).

SAFE AND AFFORDABLE HOUSING   The **Fair Housing Act,** adopted in 1968, prohibits discrimination in housing rentals, sales, and mortgage lending on the basis of race, color, national origin, religion, sex, familial status, or disability. This has not eliminated housing discrimination, but it has provided an avenue for complaint and redress. There is no such protection for class discrimination in housing. Steadily increasing housing costs coupled with stagnating wages have created a serious shortage in safe and affordable housing for many Americans. Across the country, public housing is being demolished and replaced by "mixed-income" housing units that are in fact unaffordable for lower income groups. Homeless shelters are seeing an increase in families seeking assistance (National Law Center on Homelessness and Poverty [NLCHP], 2005). Nationwide, approximately 18.5% of all households are paying half or more of their income in rent (Turk, 2004). The national average for monthly rent and utilities for a two-bedroom apartment is $791.00. To earn sufficient income to cover that cost along with food and other necessities, a household must have at least one wage earner working full time at an hourly wage of $15.00 or more (an annual pretax income of approximately $30,000). Despite the recent increase in the federal minimum wage (to $5.85 per hour) it would be impossible for minimum wage earners to maintain housing at those costs, even with two wage earners working full time.

Housing quality and community safety have been found to have positive correlations with mental health. One study randomly moved families out of public housing in high-poverty neighborhoods and into private housing in near-poor or non-poor neighborhoods. Findings indicate that, among families moved into private housing, parental stress was significantly reduced and male children exhibited less anxious and depressive symptoms and fewer dependency problems (Leventhal & Brooks-Gunn, 2003).

HEALTH INSURANCE   The United States is home to the greatest wealth in the world, yet remains one of the few developed nations without universal health care. U.S. Census data indicate that 16% of the U.S. population had no health insurance coverage in 2005 and that, while the number of people with insurance increased marginally from 2004 to 2005, the percentage of people without insurance also continues to rise (DeNavas-Walt, Proctor, & Lee, 2006). The percentage of uninsured Whites is just under the national average (15%), with Blacks (19.6%) and Asians (17.9%) a few percentage points over the average. The highest uninsured rates are among those of Hispanic origin/any race (32.7%), American Indian/ Alaskan Natives (29.9%), adults aged 18 to 34 (approximately 1 in 3), and households with incomes under $50,000 (approximately 1 in 4). In 2004, 89% of U.S. children had health insurance coverage at some point during the year, of which a third were insured through government sources (Childstats, 2006). The percentage of children covered under private insurance dropped a cumulative 8% between 1987 and 2004.

Classism has fatal consequences for children and adults from lower income levels, particularly racial and ethnic minorities. The United States has one of the highest levels of per capita health expenditures, but the investment is not benefiting the economically marginalized. This country has one of the highest rates of infant mortality among developed/industrialized nations (Central Intelligence Agency [CIA], 2007). Child mortality in the general population has been measured at 6.8 deaths per 1,000 births; among African Americans the child mortality rate is twice the national average, or 14 per 1,000 (Office of Minority Health and Health Disparities [OMHD], 2007). Overall life expectancy varies in direct relationship to income. Individuals of higher SES can expect to gain an average of 3 to 4 years of life over those from the lowest SES (Woolfe, Johnson, Phillips, & Philipsen, 2007). Those born into the lowest economic tier not only have a shorter life expectancy, but also evidence higher rates of mental health issues (Hudson, 2005).

Housing and employment insecurity coupled with lack of access to health care can trigger an irreversible decline in economic, physical, and mental heath. After interviewing individuals and families across the country, and seeing firsthand the fate of the uninsured, Sered and Fernandopulle (2005) referred to this decline as a "death spiral." Without adequate health safeguards, jobs are lost due to illness, homes are lost due to job loss, and illness is aggravated by stress, anxiety, depression, and exhaustion attempting to secure basic needs.

Poverty: Perceptions and Identity

Whereas economic status is clearly a powerful factor in overall wellness, it appears that individual perceptions of SES play a role as well. The degree to which we are satisfied or dissatisfied with our SES, relative to others, has been found to influence health outcomes (Operario, Adler & Williams, 2004). Classism and the stigma attached to lower SES status may contribute to feeling deprived of power, place, and voice (Moreira, 2003). The psychological consequences of feeling devalued and displaced may include humiliation, lowered efficacy, low self-esteem, and higher rates of suicide (WHO, 2001). The ability to externalize classism, identify structural causes, and take effective action contribute to positive stress coping and resiliency.

It is important to understand evolving perceptions of class and the relationship between social class and mental health counseling over time. Table 7.3 highlights historical events related to social class and economic injustice that have influenced the development of professional counseling. Reflection 7.5 offers an opportunity to reflect on these events.

TABLE 7.3 Noteworthy Events

Late 1700s	The first labor strikes occur in the United States. The rallying cry for the striking carpenters, printers, and cabinet makers is "in pursuit of happiness," borrowed from the 20-year-old Declaration of Independence.
1850s–1900	As populations in urban centers increase, state mental hospitals are built and used by the state to commit (mostly involuntarily) persons with mental illness, primarily those from the lower class who cannot afford private care.
Late 1800s	The social reform movement takes hold in the United States. Frank Parsons, now referred to as the founder of counseling, is among many people from across class lines who addressed social inequities in access to education, employment, and housing.
1884	The Federation of Organized Trades and Labor Unions, forerunner of the American Federation of Labor (AFL), passes a resolution stating that a workday should be legally limited to 8 hours (adults, youth, and children commonly work 10- to 12-hour days, 6 days a week).
1884–1937	Hundreds of American and immigrant workers are injured, deported, or killed by police and state militia in a sustained effort by business owners and politicians to suppress worker demands for basic rights and safety in the workplace.
Early 1900s	In Europe, Alfred Adler advocates for the application of psychological principles to working-class concerns. These principles are soon adapted in the United States.
1908	Frank Parsons founds the Bureau of Vocational Guidance in Boston as a means of advocating for employment opportunities for immigrant youth and families.
1938	The Wages and Hours Act (later called the Fair Labor Standards Act) is passed, banning child labor and setting the 40-hour work week.
1940s	Carl Rogers advocates for application of psychological principles to world social issues (this work continues throughout his life).
1950s forward	The civil rights movement draws people from across race and class lines to address social inequity.
Early 1960s	Funding the state mental hospital system becomes increasingly expensive and new treatments are allowing patients to return to community life. Federal funding is allocated for the research and construction of community mental health centers (CMHCs).
1963	Congress passes a law mandating equal pay for women.
1980s	There is growing emphasis on a medical model of mental health (biology, neurology, genetics of mental disorders, and the use of medications) and a backlash against social welfare. Funding for CMHCs is scaled down.
1990s	Family systems theory emerges, drawing attention to the influence of larger social structures on individual and family mental health.
1990s forward	The living wage movement grows and numerous cities and businesses implement a living wage for workers.
1999	Counselors for Social Justice (CSJ) is formed, a division of ACA.
2000	There is a rise in managed care and the use of a business model of mental health.
2002	The American Psychological Association publishes the Resolution on Poverty and Socioeconomic Status.
2005	ACA revises the *Code of Ethics* to include and encourage client, community, and social advocacy.

REFLECTION 7.5

Classism has a direct impact on individual and family well-being, and is also intricately connected with the funding and implementation of mental health services. Select one of the events listed in Table 7.3 to investigate further. Research the impact at the individual, family, community, cultural, and political levels. Consider factors across socioeconomic levels (i.e., how might this event be experienced or viewed by individuals who were poor, working class, and middle and upper class?). Also, consider the impact in various settings including schools, colleges, and community agencies. How did mental health professionals, including counselors, contribute and respond to these events?

ADDRESSING CLASSISM IN COUNSELING

We have known for decades that low-SES clients have some of the highest treatment dropout rates (Reis & Brown, 1999; Smith, 2005; WHO, 2001), yet research has focused primarily on individual client motivation and practical barriers to services. Studies have found that individuals from poor and low-income communities have greater difficulty accessing services, that services are of a lower quality, and that they are more likely to be admitted to a psychiatric hospital on an involuntary basis (Chow, Jaffee, & Snowden, 2003). However, there is now a growing awareness that mental health services, as well as the professionals who deliver those services, have played a role in perpetuating class-based discrimination and bias. There are indications that therapist attitudes and values, and the quality of the therapeutic alliance, may contribute to dropout among low-SES clients. Class bias has been identified among teachers, therapists, and other helping professionals. Teachers and school administrators have been found to have lower expectations of children and parents who are poor (Lott, 2001). Classist perceptions are further moderated by the race of both the perceiver and the perceived, and the context in which the perceptions take place (Morris, 2005).

Smith (2005) outlines ways in which class bias may influence therapeutic interventions. Counselors may assume that people with pressing resource concerns (e.g., shelter, food, clothing, safety) cannot benefit from insight or process therapy until those issues are alleviated. Conversely, counselors may ignore resource stressors and do as they were trained: focus on traditional talk therapy without adequately assessing the most immediate concerns of the client. The pervasiveness of middle-class assumptions and values in counseling affects not only clients, but also counselor trainees and counselors. Current and future counselors who come from poor or lower class backgrounds may feel pressure to "act" middle class, and to adopt values and perspectives that do not match their life experience, nor their reason for entering the profession. A study of occupational therapists who identified as being from the lower class found that many felt stigmatized and shamed by their class background, and that they expended considerable energy attempting to "pass" as middle class (Beagan, 2007).

Figure 7.1 illustrates a helpful way to conceptualize the many ways that class status, perceptions, beliefs, and biases influence the counseling relationship. Not included is the intersection of classism with other forms of oppression, particularly racial and gender discrimination. As counselor trainees and counselors develop greater awareness of the role of oppression in counseling they may feel overwhelmed and uncertain about how to be effective in the face of such multifaceted dynamics, many of which involve their own identity and worldview. The following sections will introduce strategies for developing awareness, knowledge, and skills regarding classism in counseling.

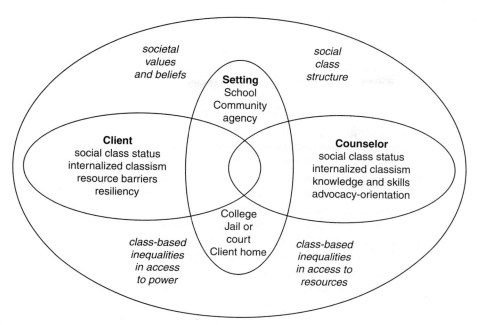

societal values and beliefs

social class structure

Setting
School
Community
agency

Client
social class status
internalized classism
resource barriers
resiliency

Counselor
social class status
internalized classism
knowledge and skills
advocacy-orientation

College
Jail or
court
Client home

class-based inequalities in access to power

class-based inequalities in access to resources

FIGURE 7.1 Classism and the counseling relationship: An illustration of the many external, internal, and contextual social class factors that impact the counseling relationship.

Awareness

Counselor trainees and counselors come from a range of social class backgrounds, as do the clients they serve. Similarities and differences in class backgrounds influence the development of the counseling relationship, yet this aspect of diversity is often overlooked in training and supervision. Before the first words are spoken, counselor and client have often assessed respective class standing and made assumptions, often unconscious, that will impact counseling outcomes. Both differences and similarities in class status can evoke a variety of feelings, including discomfort, resentment, guilt, shame, anger, mistrust, pity, avoidance, pride, or jealousy. Counselors must be prepared to identify and address these feelings in themselves and their clients.

Acquiring awareness is a process that is often accompanied by periods of discomfort. **Cognitive dissonance** describes the state of psychological disequilibrium experienced when we are facing, but have not yet resolved, information that contradicts our worldview. As with any change process, the first step is becoming aware. The move from relative ignorance into a more complex understanding of class issues often fosters a sense of responsibility and interest in social change (Sanchez, Cronick, & Wiesenfeld, 2003).

The following activities provide several opportunities for increasing awareness of class and classism:

- *Write your own class story.* The activity "Exploring Your Class Story" (Reflection 7.6) suggests some possible questions to consider when exploring your own life story in the context of class and SES. Focus your story on the feelings, values, and beliefs you associate with each area.
- *Volunteer.* Find out about volunteer opportunities at local organizations that work with poor and low-income community members. Allow the staff, clients, and community to educate you.

- *Interact with other social classes.* Which social class seems the most "different" to you? Toward which social class do you have the most negative judgment or biases? Challenge your assumptions, fears, and misperceptions by increasing your interactions with other social classes. This may include reading novels, attending social events or community meetings, and talking to peers about relative class experiences.
- *Educate yourself.* Attend a training or workshop that explores social class issues. You will find the resource list helpful in identifying options. If nothing is available in your area, you could create your own workshop by thoroughly exploring the Web sites in the resource list.
- *Interview professionals in your field.* Conduct two informational interviews: one with a counselor who is working with upper-SES clients (private schools and colleges, privately funded mental health agencies or practices) and one with a counselor working with lower-SES clients (public schools, vocational and community colleges, state-funded agencies). Compare their work experiences and environments, and ask them how SES impacts their counseling work.
- *Complete a class privilege inventory.* An interesting version was created by the Women's Theological Center in Boston. "The Invisibility of Upper Class Privilege" is based on Peggy McIntosh's (1988) work on White privilege. You can find the inventory at www.thewtc.org/Invisibility_of_Class_Privilege.pdf.
- *Explore your social class.* Complete a thorough self-inventory of your socialization experiences regarding SES (see Reflection 7.6).

REFLECTION 7.6   EXPLORING YOUR CLASS STORY

Write the story of your upbringing in relation to class and SES. Reflect on memories and stories that have stayed with you, as well as those that have been forgotten. Focus on feelings and relationships. You may choose to touch on all areas or write about only one area in-depth. Following are suggested questions for your reflection.

Work

- When you were growing up, did your parents or guardian:
  - Do paid or unpaid work?
  - Work outside or inside the home? Have a home office?
  - Work for someone else or themselves? Did they supervise or employ others?
  - Do skilled (work requiring special, extended training) or unskilled work?
  - Primarily use their body or their mind during their work?
  - Have the opportunity of advancement and income increases over time?
- Did children living at home have jobs? Did their income go to family expenses?

Education

- What level of education did your parents or the people who raised you complete?
- Did you go to public school or private school? Were you home schooled?
- Were you tracked in school? Were you aware of others being tracked?
- What were the educational goals of the average student in your school? Of your peer group?
- Were you aware of the class status of other students? How?
- Did you engage in organized activities outside the school setting? Whose idea was it to participate? Were there fees? Who paid the fees? How did you get to those activities?
- How does your family of origin feel about your decision to go to graduate school?

Income

- What were the sources of your family's income (e.g., salaried position or hourly wages; family business or farm; stocks and bonds; inheritance; renters or roommates; public assistance/welfare; social security/veteran's benefits; child care services provider; bartering; yard sales; illegal activities; other)?
- Was there sufficient income to put aside money for vacations, savings, college educations, and/or investments?
- Did your parents or the people who raised you discuss income openly?
- Were you aware of the limitations (or absence thereof) of your family's income?

In Your Home

- Growing up, did your family have a home? What type of home was it (i.e., house, apartment, condominium, farm, trailer, mansion, ranch, other)?
- Did you live in one home or move frequently?
- If or when you had a home, did you invite friends over? Why or why not?
- Did your family experience homelessness or transient housing (e.g., shelter, motel)?
- How many people lived in your home growing up? How many generations?
- What type of community did you live in (e.g., urban, suburban, rural, "gated," public housing complex, other)?
- Would you describe your neighborhood as poor; working, middle, or upper class; or mixed? What about the neighborhoods surrounding yours?
- Did your family own or rent a summer home, cabin, recreational vehicle, or other facility aside from your main residence?
- Who cleaned your home and maintained the exterior/landscape?

Space and Environment

- How much private, personal space did you have growing up (your own/shared bedroom, room with other family uses during the day, group sleeping quarters)?
- Were there family photographs in your home? Were they framed? Who took them?
- Was there original art by family members?
- Did the windows have coverings? Were the coverings plastic, wood, or metal blinds? Sheets, curtains, or drapes? Off the rack or custom cut?
- Did your family home have a private yard, porch, deck, or other private outdoor space?
- Were you safe in your home? Outside your home?
- What sounds did you hear most frequently in your home environment (e.g., birds, dogs barking, people mowing lawns, sirens, gunshots, factory or traffic noise)?

Clothing

- Where did you get most of your clothes and footwear (e.g., homemade, hand-me-downs, used clothing/thrift store, discount/grocery/drug store, department store, on sale, high-fashion or specialized clothing/shoe store, custom-tailored)?
- Did you dress the same as, better than, or worse than other children at your school? How about other children in your family (immediate and extended)? In your neighborhood?
- What did you learn from your family about how to dress?

Recreation

- How was your family's leisure time spent (e.g., going camping; visiting family; traveling recreationally; working additional jobs; pursuing educational or creative outlets; watching TV or going to the movies; going to the theater, concerts, or museums; spending social time at home; participating in religious activities; reading; volunteering; other)?
- Where was leisure time spent (e.g., at home, in the community, within the United States, abroad)?
- How did children spend the summer (e.g., going to day or sleep-away camp; taking family vacations; staying with extended family; attending summer school; working (of-age children); staying home alone while adults worked)?

(continued)

Health

- Did your family have health insurance? Did it cover all family members? What kind of insurance was it (privately paid, employment benefit, government assisted)?
- Did you go to private doctors, community clinics, or emergency rooms?
- How frequently did you see doctors and/or dentists (e.g., regular annual visits, emergency care only, not at all)?
- Did you see the same doctor or dentist often enough to build a relationship?
- Were there chronic illnesses or disabilities in your family?
- Were there alcoholism or drug abuse issues?
- What was your family's attitude toward preventive care and wellness?
- Was your family able to access and afford healthy food? Exercise classes? Gym membership? Yoga, tai chi, martial arts, dance, or other wellness-related classes?

Source: Adapted for counselors from the activity "Class Autobiography" created by Class Action: Building Bridges Across the Class Divide. Original version available at www.classism.org/action_self.html.

Knowledge

Once counselors become aware of and are able to identify the impact of class and classism, it is important to have effective tools for addressing these issues in a counseling setting. Professional organizations including the American Psychological Association (2000) and the American Counseling Association (ACA, 2005) have begun to outline standards of behavior that address social inequities. In addition, several theories are being revised, and new theories are emerging, that more fully integrate the role of class identity and classism in mental health. The following theories are drawn from within and outside the field of psychology. Each theory was in some way shaped by or has struggled to include the role of classism in individual and community well-being. Texts, journal articles, and electronic sources are readily available on each of these theories.

- *Feminist Theory.* Originally focused on the social, economic, and political empowerment of women, this theoretical orientation has received criticism for emphasizing the empowerment of middle-class White women. Proponents of feminist theory have strived to improve cultural, economic, racial, and ethnic inclusiveness.
- *Womanist Theory.* This theory emerged as an alternative to feminist theory, which failed to adequately address the needs, concerns, and strengths of African American and other ethnic minority women. Womanist theory directly attends to the concerns of women, men, and children across class levels, and places community and social responsibility in a more central role. It also attends to the intersection of race, gender, and class oppression.
- *Relational-Cultural Theory (RCT).* This theory provides a relational perspective on human development, resiliency, and the practice of therapy (Jordan & Hartling, 2002). The theory has been expanded to address all forms of oppression, including classism.
- ***Social Class Worldview Model (SCWM) and Modern Classism Theory (MCT).*** The SCWM was developed to provide a more psychologically oriented model for understanding social class. It includes three domains: individual perceptions and attitudes; comparison of self to others; and use of material objects as a reflection of self, lifestyle, and learned social behaviors. MCT calls for the exploration of social class context, worldview, and the impact of external

and internalized classism as a means of understanding individual goals and behaviors (Liu, 2004). Refer to Activity 7.3 to consider counseling implications of this model.

ACTIVITY 7.3

Using Liu's (2004) social class worldview model, create several different client profiles (remember to include each of the three domains along with the client's SES). If each of these individuals presented for counseling, what would be necessary to build a safe and trusting alliance? What do you imagine would be the strengths and challenges of each client? How might each of these clients present unique challenges and opportunities for you as their counselor? What theory and intervention might be most effective with each of these clients?

Another area of knowledge important for effective counseling is to be familiar with the needs and concerns of poor and low-income community members of all ages. Any of the following methods can be useful for investigating local issues at the individual, family, community, and political/legislative levels.

- *Informational interviews.* Arrange to visit or conduct an informational interview with schools or agencies serving clients from different socioeconomic levels. What are the concerns of their clients? How do they address socioeconomic issues and resource stressors? What resources do they use and what types of referrals do they commonly make? Do the same with teachers and legislators.
- *Community status reports.* Check local universities, papers, and legislator Web sites for published reports on the status of the community. Know that clients may be directly affected by hospital closings, corporation downsizing, neighborhood and gang violence, changes in property tax rates, and the destruction of public housing.

Finally, it will be very helpful to become more knowledgeable about community resources. This knowledge may be a valuable tool for demonstrating a commitment to clients, and for improving counseling effectiveness by providing a holistic response. The following suggestions and activities provide some direction in building a resource knowledge base.

- *Identify local resources.* United Way provides a helpful resource for finding local services. This is a primary resource for becoming familiar with local services, and is also an excellent contact to provide to clients. Spend some time using both the phone and the Internet locater services. United Way can be contacted by phone at 211, or through its Web site at www.unitedway.org
- *Investigate local resources.* Learn about resource assistance and services in the community before providing direct referrals. Before making referrals research current information on service: hours, location, phone, address; obstacles clients might face in accessing the service (financial, transportation, hours, wait lists, documentation); types of services available; and criteria for accessing those services. Visit the services that clients are most likely to need.

Skills

As with race, ethnicity, age, gender and sexual identity, and ability status, there are patterns but no homogeneity in social class status and identity. Therefore, one of the most critical skills for identifying and intervening in class-related concerns is assessment.

Consider the fact that clients who appear resource-deprived (e.g., utilities have been shut off, wear old and worn clothing, struggle to get by on welfare and food stamps) may perceive themselves to be rich in spiritual, family, and community resources. Despite an apparent lack of resources, they experience wellness. On the other hand, clients who appear to have everything (prominent career, nice home, vacations) may be experiencing significant resource deprivation in relationships and sense of purpose. Objective assessments of SES are inadequate to establish whether SES is a factor in the origin, nature, or severity of a client's presenting concern. Furthermore, class stigma and internalized classism may prevent a client from openly sharing the true nature or extent of resource needs until there is trust and safety in the relationship.

Assessing class and resource-related concerns may provide counselors and their clients an opportunity to openly address obvious differences in their respective SES, and explore any meaning this has for their work together. It is best not to wait for a client to bring up social class issues. Also, it is safe to assume that even if a client is not talking about class and power differences, this does not ensure that these differences are insignificant. Clients will not bring up these differences *because* there is a power and class difference and *because* there is social stigma around having or being "less than." As a counselor it is your job to initiate this discussion in the same way that it is your job to assess other risk and resiliency factors.

There are two significant areas to focus on in assessment: (1) a comprehensive initial assessment of the client, the client's context, and the presenting concern(s); and (2) assessment of counselor values and biases that emerge in response to the client.

- *Comprehensive initial assessment.* Take the time to explore the client's values and beliefs about social class. A competent and socially conscious counselor will routinely assess all clients, regardless of SES, for both stressors and resiliency and will include any concerns or goals, with the client's approval, in the treatment plan. Pay attention to psychological symptoms that may be caused or triggered by aspects of social inequity (either in being subjected to discrimination or in perpetuating inequity). Assess the client's awareness of classism, racism, and gender oppression; internalizing any form of oppression has been found to contribute to mental health issues, in particular depression, low self-esteem, and substance abuse (Curtis-Boles & Jenkins-Monroe, 2000). Refer to Case Studies 7.1 and 7.2.
- *Self-assessment.* Assess your own strengths and limitations in addressing the client's concerns. Do you believe that helping a client locate housing resources is "not part of your job"? Where does that belief come from? How are you defining help? When you notice yourself distancing from your clients or their concerns in any way, or becoming overly involved and "doing for" your clients, it is time for a self-assessment. Use individual, group, and peer supervision to reflect on your internal process, the quality of the relationship, and your case conceptualization and intervention choices.

CASE STUDY 7.1

You are in your first semester of internship, and a fellow intern is sharing his experience working with outpatient clients in a hospital setting. He says that overall things have gone well, but he is feeling stuck with his most recent client. All of his other clients have been able to talk about their feelings and have responded to his empathetic person-centered interventions—until this woman. No matter how much he encourages her to share her feelings, she just won't open up emotionally. He knows she has to be stressed and needing an emotional outlet because of her circumstances: She is due to deliver her fourth child and is living in a shelter after leaving her abusive boyfriend. He also mentions that she is required to come to counseling in order to continue to receive food stamps and housing assistance.

- Why do you think your fellow intern feels stuck?
- What do you imagine the client is experiencing in her interactions with this intern?
- Describe the worldview of this intern and how he is conceptualizing the client's issues.
- Based on what you've learned so far in this chapter, what suggestions might you have?
- What would you identify as the client's short- and long-term counseling needs?
- How might this intern become more effective in helping her meet these needs?
- How could you advocate for this client?

CASE STUDY 7.2

Part I

James is a 36-year-old White male, referred to your agency by the court after a domestic violence incident. The incident involved his wife of 5 years and occurred in front of their two small children, ages 4 and 6 years. The court is requiring anger management classes and individual counseling with duration to be determined by the agency (in other words, you). If James fails to comply and participate fully, or if he commits further violence, he will go to jail. James is assigned to your caseload and you read the intake report prior to your first session. The report indicates that James has another child from a previous marriage, and is also facing charges for failure to pay child support. It states that James is currently unemployed and that he tested positive for alcohol when he was picked up by the police.

- What thoughts and feelings come up for you as you read the report and prepare to meet with James?

Part II

During your first session with James he presents as defiant and tight lipped, but gradually lets down his guard as you discuss the recent local high school football game. You admit your ignorance of game strategy which gives James a chance to reveal his expertise and somewhat diffuses the power differential between you (remember, you and your agency decide how much counseling he has to do to stay out of jail). Eventually James explains that the domestic violence incident happened after he lost his manufacturing job of 15 years due to downsizing.

You remember what you learned about the importance of assessing for class-related issues, and decide to explore his values and beliefs about class and gender roles, and the meaning he assigns to work. He reveals that when his wife went out and got a job without telling him, his shame became unbearable and he lashed out at her, resulting in the domestic violence charge. He states that he has never hit her before and that he is afraid of what this event has done to his relationship with his wife and children. James tells you that unless he secures a regular paycheck soon, his family may become homeless. James handles all the family finances and he has not shared their precarious position with his wife. He is frustrated that the schedule of the anger management classes prevents him from applying for the one job that is immediately available: night shift at another plant. When you ask

(continued)

James how he is coping with these stressors, he tells you that he feels trapped and that the only thing that helps relieve the stress has been spending time at the bar with his buddies.

- What is the presenting concern according to the court? According to James? According to you?
- Is the court-mandated treatment adequate and sufficient to address the presenting concern(s)?
- Do you feel prepared and competent to be effective with this client? Why or why not?
- How might a "traditional" counselor intervene? How might an advocacy-oriented counselor intervene?
- What would you want to accomplish in your next few sessions with James?

ADVOCACY

Advocates are made, not born. The personal stories of social advocates often reveal that their commitment to addressing oppression and injustice grew out of personal experiences, relationships, and challenges (Table 7.3 highlights a small sample of individuals whose advocacy work grew out of their concern about economic and social injustice). Advocacy is a developmental process, moving naturally from awareness to action. Advocacy is a collective response to social injustice: Empowering a client to speak up at a child custody hearing is as necessary as contacting a state senator or leading community education workshops. Advocacy is a normal and necessary element of a counselor's job. The remainder of this section provides ideas for advocacy at several levels of intervention.

Advocacy at the professional level includes:

- *Integrated services.* Pilot studies of programs that employ interagency collaboration and training and that include consumers in program design have demonstrated significant improvements in treatment outcomes (Markoff, Finkelstein, Kammerer, Kreiner, & Prost, 2005). These services advocate for increased communication between the work setting, the client, referring agencies, and community service organizations.
- *Counselor training.* Encourage greater inclusiveness of class issues in counselor training and education. Suggestions include the development of service-learning programs, justice-oriented research, and evaluating the training programs' ability to support poor and working-class students (Lott & Bullock, 2007).
- *Research.* Participate in or initiate research that moves away from defining poverty (overtly or covertly) as an individual problem by examining social perceptions and sociopolitical structures that perpetuate poverty. Learn more about research methods that include participants in identifying research questions, as well as in research design and data interpretation.

Interventions at the individual (client) level include:

- *Attend to basic needs.* The most effective form of prevention for development of major mental illness is attending to the impact of economic stressors such as unemployment, housing instability, and homelessness. This is a consistent finding in social science research (Hudson, 2005). For some individuals in distress, ensuring access to sufficient food may be more effective and cost-efficient than a psychopharmacological intervention (Heflin et al., 2005); reductions in poverty have been found to provide relief for mental health symptoms (Dearing et al., 2004).

Community-level interventions include:

- *Empowerment.* Work with and for economically marginalized communities to promote mental health, assertiveness, and general empowerment as a means of countering deprivation of power, and the pathologizing and medicalization of poverty. It is important that this work be at the invitation of and in collaboration with the community and not imposed "from above by experts." Creating social networks and training peer "counselors" has been shown to increase efficacy, competence, and skills; more cohesive social networks increase the communities relative power and voice (Sanchez et al., 2003).

- *Education and training.* Training areas that may be most relevant to economically marginalized communities include community development, leadership skills, trauma and violence intervention, conflict resolution, and workers' rights (Sloan, 2003).
- *Advocacy in schools.* Suggestions from the World Bank (2005) include increasing teacher incentives and improving basic school infrastructure. Join or start a group that advocates for equitable funding of all public schools. Create a classism or economic injustice awareness program for students in the school.

At the sociopolitical level advocacy includes:

- *Public policy.* Contact local, state, and regional professional organizations for counselors and ask about past, current, and pending advocacy efforts related to class issues. ACA, the National Board for Certified Counselors (NBCC), the American School Counselor Association (ASCA), and other professional counseling organizations provide current information on legislative issues on their Web sites along with suggested actions.
- *Universal health insurance.* Join the effort to ensure access to quality health care for everyone. Educate others about the connection between health care and mental health issues.

Information about these and other activities, resources, and volunteer opportunities are described in Table 7.4 and Activity 7.4. Organizations are grouped by focus areas including (a) social justice; (b) women and children; (c) poverty, hunger, and homelessness; and (d) health care.

ACTIVITY 7.4

Here are some activities for increasing knowledge about social injustices outside the classroom:

- Listen to the podcast on "Race, Schools and Neighborhoods: Reducing Barriers to Achievement." This online audio recording is an extended panel of several experts in educational equity discussing the role of poverty and racial segregation. The podcast includes discussion of the No Child Left Behind Act. You can access this podcast through the Urban Institute Web site at www.urban.org/Pressroom/ thursdayschild/may2007.cfm.
- Read *Savage Inequalities: Children in America's Schools* by Jonathon Kozol (New York: HarperCollins, 1991). Although the book was written years ago, the conditions in many public schools across the country remain the same. What are the social and economic costs we all pay for depriving many of our children of quality education in a safe environment? What are the social beliefs and values that allow these inequalities to continue? What would you do if you were a school counselor assigned to one of the schools Kozol describes?
- Watch the movie *The Pursuit of Happyness* (Columbia Pictures, 2006). If the father were your client, would you have supported his career goal? If you were a school counselor and the son was your client, would you have reported the situation to child and family services? In what ways does this film challenge social beliefs about poverty and homelessness? In what ways does the film perpetuate classist stereotypes?

TABLE 7.4 Resources for Learning and Advocacy

Social Justice Resources

- Counselors for Social Justice (CSJ), http://counselorsforsocialjustice.com/. CSJ members include counselors, counselor educators, graduate students, and school and community leaders who are working to alleviate oppression and injustice in communities, schools, workplaces, governments, and other social and institutional systems. Online resources include information on schools, managed care, classism, corporate media/independent voices, militarism/peace, and globalization/democratic voices. The *CSJ Activist* is a free online newsletter, and CSJ will be publishing a new electronic journal (in English and Spanish) in conjunction with the Psychologists for Social Responsibility (a division of the American Psychological Association), which is also available for free via the Web site.
- Association of Community Organizations for Reform Now (ACORN), www.acorn.org. Founded in 1970, ACORN is a grassroots organization of low- and moderate- income families who are working for social justice and building stronger communities. ACORN advocates for improvements in housing, schools, neighborhood safety, health care, and working conditions.
- Class Action: Building Bridges Across the Class Divide, www.classism.org. Class Action began in 1995 as a cross-class dialogue group, and is now a nonprofit organization offering resources, programs, consultation, professional development, and opportunities for self-awareness and advocacy. Its mission is in its name.
- Highlander Research and Education Center, www.highlandercenter.org. The Highlander Center was started in 1932 to support politically disenfranchised groups with building a progressive labor movement in the south. The center was fully racially integrated by 1942, and became a significant planning, education, and retreat center for civil rights leaders. Today the center provides support and training to address all areas of social oppression.

Resources for Women and Children

- Children's Defense Fund (CDF), www.childrensdefense.org. Founded in 1973 with roots in the civil rights movement, CDF advocates for poor and minority children and those with disabilities. The Web site contains statistics, research, public policy, and advocacy opportunities.
- Institute for Women's Policy Research, www.iwpr.org. The institute conducts research and is involved in women's issues relating to public policy, poverty, employment, family, health, safety, and political participation. The site also lists conferences and events, listservs, public policy action, and advocacy opportunities.

Resources on Poverty, Hunger and Homelessness

- America's Second Harvest, www.secondharvest.org. Second Harvest addresses hunger nationwide through a network of member food banks. The organization collects data and provides reports on hunger. The Web site offers food resources, statistics, and volunteer and advocacy opportunities.
- Living Wage Resource Center, www.livingwagecampaign.org. An offshoot of ACORN, this Web site provides a history of the living wage movement, background information, and resources for those interested in starting a local living wage group. Links are provided to other living wage sites.
- National Law Center on Homelessness and Poverty, www.nlchp.org. Attorneys work to address homelessness and poverty. The site contains information, tools, training, advocacy opportunities, and legislative alerts pertaining to homelessness and poverty.

Health Care Resources

- Access Project, www.accessproject.org. The Access Project provides a policy voice for underserved communities and works to improve health for those who are most vulnerable. The site contains information on medical debt, insurance and hospital billing, and language services.
- Community Catalyst, www.communitycatalyst.org. Community Catalyst works in partnership with consumer and community groups nationwide to increase participation in health system decision making. Its goal is quality, affordable health care for all through community action, legal, and policy advocacy.
- Families USA, www.familiesusa.org. Families USA is a national nonprofit, nonpartisan organization working toward quality, affordable health care. The organization has been in existence for 20 years and functions as a government watchdog and public information clearinghouse. It also provides training and community collaboration.

Summary

Counseling has its roots in the application of psychological principles to community well-being, particularly for groups that are not able to access private psychiatric and psychological services. Counselors have always worked with and within public institutions: schools, hospitals, community mental health centers, substance abuse treatment programs, and trauma centers. As professionals, our history, placement, and training provide a unique position and voice as social advocates. Depending on our personal and professional interests, we may find that our "place" as advocates is at the individual, community, or sociopolitical level.

This chapter opened with introducing important terms and language necessary for discussing classism. It also provided historical context for understanding classism in the United States, and outlined the class structure in this country. Identifying the history, context, structure, and pervasiveness of classism is necessary for understanding the impact on the counseling profession. The chapter provided an overview of poverty in this country. Women, children, and racial and ethnic minorities continue to experience disproportionate rates of poverty. Significant physical and mental health consequences are experienced by individuals, families, and communities that do not have consistent access to basic needs for well-being such as food, education, employment, housing, and health insurance. It is not only the very poor who experience these risk factors and consequences, but also increasingly the working and middle classes.

Classism has played an integral role in the development, implementation, accessibility and effectiveness of mental health services. Although it has been known for some time that clients from lower-SES groups have higher dropout rates, it is only recently that therapists have begun to seriously examine the role of professionals in perpetuating class bias. Counseling is primarily based in middle-class values, which infuse theories, training, and practice. Current counselor trainees are unlikely to receive adequate preparation for working with the impact of classism on their relationships with clients. Furthermore, while counselor trainees are often placed at internship sites that serve poor and low-income clients, the trainees may have little or no preparation for effectively assessing and addressing the concerns of these clients.

Self-awareness is a critical area for counselor trainee development in order to better understand classism in themselves, their practice, and the system(s) within which they will be working. Knowledge of classism, class-related issues, and community resources can support counselors-in-training in improving their competence. Developing effective skills is also critical, and one of the most important areas for new counselors to develop is assessment. Comprehensive initial assessments should include a holistic review of resources, stressors, and client strengths.

Finally, awareness and knowledge of classism, and the ability to choose and implement effective interventions, is not enough. There is growing evidence that social change is the most effective intervention for addressing the psychological consequences of economic, racial, ethnic, and gender oppression. While it is important to alleviate immediate symptoms, true well-being will not take hold without attention to social and political injustices. The chapter concluded by providing suggestions for advocating at the individual, community, and sociopolitical levels, as well as within the counseling profession.

CHAPTER 8

Disability, Ableism, and Ageism

DEBRA E. BERENS

PREVIEW

This chapter will explore the concepts of ableism and ageism with applications to the practice of counseling. For ease of counselor awareness, learning and understanding, this chapter will be divided into two major sections—"Ableism" and "Ageism"—although in clinical practice there may be some overlap or similarities between these concepts within the counseling relationship. The chapter will begin with relevant definitions of disability, including models of disability and an overall systematic view of disability with relevant legislation and advocacy action, then will explore deeper the concepts of ableism and ageism and implications for the counseling process. Because disability and age-related issues can involve not only medical considerations but also social, economic, and cultural considerations, this chapter is designed to help counselors and counselors-in-training become familiar with and aware of ableism and ageism issues to develop a more culturally competent and meaningful level of service to clients. Specific strategies with regard to awareness, advocacy, and activities to build counselor knowledge and skills are included.

DISABILITY DEFINED

Historically, family members and relatives, and to some degree society in general, have demonstrated a certain amount of responsibility in the caring for one another, especially toward people who are aged, young (children/adolescents), ill, or disabled. The extent that family or society has the available economic resources generally defines the amount of support and services that are available to people who belong to these groups (i.e., **economic security**). Although the need for economic security affects people of all ages and classes of society, for individuals who have a disability or are of young or old age, who traditionally have limited voice and resources to access care and services, this form of security is even more important. What does disability refer to? Complete Reflection 8.1 before continuing to read this chapter.

REFLECTION 8.1

What is the first thing that comes to mind when you hear the words *disability* or *disabled?* Write down at least three descriptors and reasons why these descriptors come to mind.

As a precursor to this section on ableism, it is helpful to define the term **disability** and offer some global constructs surrounding disability in the United States to provide a foundation. However, the very definition of disability can and does vary depending on the particular service delivery system, legislative act (law), or individual, entity or agency that is using the term, and disability can have different meanings to different groups. As an example, *Merriam-Webster's Online Dictionary* ("Disability," n.d.) defines disability in two ways: "a disqualification, restriction, or disadvantage," or "an inability to pursue an occupation because of a physical or mental impairment." More specific perhaps to the field of disability and to working within systems designed for people with a disability are four commonly recognized definitions of disability:

- *Social Security Administration:* The definition of disability differs even within the Social Security Administration's (SSA) two national benefits program for eligible persons (children and adults) with a disability: Social Security Disability Insurance (SSDI) or Supplemental Security Income (SSI) programs. Under the SSDI program (for eligible individuals who have a previous work history and have "paid into the system" through FICA taxes usually withheld from each paycheck or through self-employment taxes if self-employed), disability is defined as due to any medically determined physical or mental impairment specifically diagnosed by a qualified medical provider and must constitute a "total disability," meaning not a partial disability or temporary or short-term disability. Examples of such impairments are provided by the SSA within various diagnostic categories (see www.ssa.gov/disability/professionals/bluebook/listing-impairments .htm for specific listings of impairments for adults and children). Further, under SSDI, disability is defined as the individual's inability to work in a job he or she previously held or an inability to "adjust to work" in another job within the national labor market given the person's disability, age, education, and work experience. The disability must have lasted or be expected to last a minimum of 12 months or to result in death. In contrast, although the SSI program essentially uses the same disability criteria as SSDI, it does not define disability by its effect on one's ability to perform work, but rather by the individual's income, assets, and net worth. Given this definition under SSI, children with a significant disability may be eligible for the SSI program but not for the SSDI program.
- *Americans with Disabilities Act (ADA) and other federal nondiscrimination laws:* The definition of disability under the ADA includes three critical elements: (1) a physical or mental impairment that (2) substantially limits (3) one or more major life activities. As defined by the ADA, physical or mental impairment includes any physiological disorder or condition, cosmetic disfigurement, or anatomical loss affecting one or more body systems, or any mental or psychological disorder. Major life activity includes those necessary daily activities, such as caring for oneself, performing manual tasks, seeing, hearing, speaking, breathing, learning and working, sitting, standing, walking, lifting and reaching, that an individual without a significant impairment generally can perform with little or no difficulty.
- *Individuals with Disabilities Education Improvement Act (IDEIA):* For school-age children who have a disability, the federal law under the IDEIA defines disability as a physical or mental impairment that adversely affects a child's educational performance. Specific disability categories are defined in the legislation and specialized educational services can be provided by the public school system.
- *State Vocational Rehabilitation (VR) Programs:* Disability as defined under the federal–state vocational rehabilitation program includes a physical or mental impairment that cannot be acute or of an emergency nature and that must be stable or slowly progressive. The impairment must constitute or result in a substantial impediment to employment such that there is an expectation the individual will benefit from rehabilitation services to achieve successful employment [work] outcomes.

In addition to the previous definitions, the definition of disability often varies depending on the social system or agency providing services to the individual. Another unique challenge is that the overall concept of "disability" generally is not considered universal and many cultures and languages do not have a single word or definition for "disability." In actuality, different societies from around the world seemingly tend to group together individuals with specific types of disabilities (e.g., blindness, paralysis), and respond to these groups differently depending on the cultural and social interpretations associated with the disability (Groce, 2005). It is important for counselors to be aware of various types of disabilities and their meanings across cultures (see Activity 8.1).

ACTIVITY 8.1

Awareness of disabilities and cultural meanings attached to them is a step in developing multicultural counseling competence for counselors working with clients with disabilities. With your classmates, create a list of various disabilities or disabling conditions. Beside each one, list some of the common cultural meanings attached to the particular disability. Give special attention to classmates from cultures other than the dominant culture and the meanings regarding each disability that may come from those cultures. Are there certain disabilities that are more accepted or less feared than other disabilities? If the answer is yes, think about why that might be. Does it vary depending on the culture? Why or why not?

Types of Disability

Given the previous definitions of disability, it can be confusing to know what are some specific types of disability for which these definitions apply, and whether or not one of your clients may fall into one of the disability categories. Following is a list of some types of disabilities or disabling conditions that counselors may encounter with clients. It is provided as an overview and is not intended to be all-inclusive:

- Blindness or vision impairment
- Deafness or hearing impairment
- Developmental delay in one or more areas of physical development, cognitive development, communication/language development, social/emotional development, and/or adaptive development that constitute an impairment or impediment
- Medical conditions severe enough to fit a definition of disability, including heart/cardiovascular disease, diabetes, sickle cell anemia, HIV/AIDS or other immune system disorders, gastrointestinal difficulties, respiratory/pulmonary disease, and other conditions significantly affecting one or more body systems or functions
- Mental retardation
- Neurologic impairment such as uncontrolled epilepsy (seizures) and severe peripheral neuropathy (damage to nerves usually leading to the upper and lower extremities and includes significant numbness, tingling, burning or weakness)
- Orthopedic or musculoskeletal (motor) impairment caused by congenital problems, traumatic events (spinal cord injury), disease (bone cancer), or conditions such as cerebral palsy and amputation or limb loss
- Psychiatric or mental health impairment or mental illness
- Traumatic brain injury that causes cognitive and learning/memory disability

Disability Statistics

Have you ever taken the time to notice how many people you pass in your daily life who have a disability? If you notice them, it is because these individuals generally have a "visible" disability and are noticeable by something external or observed with the eye, typically use of a wheelchair, cane, walker, walking stick or guide dog, dark glasses, hearing aid, personal attendant, prosthetic/artificial limb, obvious burn scars, supplemental oxygen, unusual or atypical behaviors, and the list goes on. In addition, there are those in our community who have an "invisible" disability such as traumatic brain injury or any number of medical conditions that constitute a disability and are not obvious to the casual observer. The U.S. Census Bureau (2006b) suggests there are approximately 51.2 million people (18.1%) living in the United States who have a disability, with 32.5 million (11.5%) of them living with a severe disability. In this context, the definition of disability includes a person who has difficulty performing a specific task or activity such as seeing, hearing, bathing and/or doing light housework, or has a specified medically diagnosed condition. The disability is defined as severe if the individual is completely unable to perform one or more of these tasks or activities, needs personal assistance to perform them, or has a severe condition as defined by the Census Bureau.

Of those people with a disability, over 30 million of them are reported to be between the ages of 16 and 64 years, the age range considered by the Census Bureau to be "of working age" (U.S. Census Bureau, 2003), and the age range when people generally are considered reaching and in the "prime" of their life in terms of educational achievement, career attainment, social status, partner relationships, and family life. However, it should be no surprise that disability occurs across the life span and touches people of all ages, including the approximately 4 million children, aged 6 to 14 years, who have a disability. Also, approximately 72% of people aged 80 and older have a disability. A further analysis of age and gender differences among individuals with a disability shows that older people are more likely than younger people to have a disability, with a disability rate of 8.4% for people under 15 years of age, 19.4% for people aged 45 to 54 years, and 38.4% of people between 65 to 69 years of age. With regard to gender differences, the majority of people with disabilities, including severe disabilities, living in the United States are female (19.5%) compared to males (16.7%).

Given these numbers, it is clear to see that counselors will likely see clients, young and old and across the life span, who have some type of disability. It is important to note, however, that these statistics do not include soldiers injured while serving in the military (veterans) or people with a disability who live in institutionalized settings (e.g., nursing homes, mental health facilities, psychiatric hospitals), thus making the number of individuals living with some type of disability in the United States higher than these statistics suggest. This can only increase the odds that you will have a client with a disability seek out your professional counseling services. Activity 8.2 provides an opportunity to reflect on current images of people with disabilities that are important to consider with an increasing number of those seeking counseling.

ACTIVITY 8.2

Cultural stereotypes regarding people with disabilities are created and/or perpetuated by how individuals are portrayed in the media. As you read this chapter, think about the periodicals you read (e.g., newspapers, journals, magazines) and the television shows you watch (e.g., news reports, sitcoms, documentaries, movies) to become aware of how people with disabilities are portrayed in the media. A common example is a statement like, "he is *confined* to a wheelchair," or "she suffered a tragic condition that left her mentally

(continued)

retarded." Cut out articles that include reference to people with disabilities or are written specifically on people with disabilities. Also, write down the name of the television show, movie, or news report (and date) that mentions someone with or something about a disability. Present the information to the class to identify how often and in what ways people with disabilities are depicted in the media, even in the 21st century.

MODELS OF DISABILITY

Over the past several years, there has been a gradual paradigm shift in the conceptualization of health and disability with a focus away from a purely medical model. Historically, disability and rehabilitation models have relied on the medical model that uses the individual's medical diagnosis as the basis for counseling and determining the needs and functional abilities of the individual with a disability. More recently, however, is inclusion of a social model that considers the consequences of a health condition or disability (i.e., diagnosis) that are experienced not only by the individual with the diagnosis but also the overall social context in which the individual lives. With this comes a need to understand the full experience of health that also includes functioning, disability, quality of life, and well-being (Ustun et al., 2001).

Models of disability have long existed as a way to categorize or understand disability both in practice and in the professional literature. Most recently, Smart and Smart (2006) described four broad models of disability: biomedical, functional, environmental, and sociopolitical. However, for purposes of this chapter, two of the more well-known models of disability, medical model and social model, will be presented, with a discussion of each and a description of some variations of the social model of disability.

A **medical model** of disability can be defined as a model in which disability or illness occurs as the result of a physical or mental condition. Because something is identified as "wrong" with the individual, curing or managing or controlling the disability or illness becomes important. In the United States, one way to cure or manage disability is to invest resources in health care and related services that not only focus on the medical aspects of the disability or illness, but also promote the person's maximum level of functioning and restore the person to as near normal a life as possible. The medical model focuses on medical procedures, surgeries, diagnostic tests, therapies (physical and/or psychotherapeutic), and assistive or adaptive devices that can be used to help "normalize" the individual with a disability.

Over the past several decades, some disability rights groups and advocates have criticized the medical model for focusing on what is wrong with the person with a disability and the resultant need to "fix" the person. In partial response to this criticism, the **social model** of disability has gained recognition in recent years. The focus of this model is on societal barriers and biases against people with disabilities, not on the person, the disability, or the medical condition itself. The social model recognizes that although some people may have a physical, mental, social, psychological, or other condition that is considered different from what is "normal" in that society, the disability is created from society's failure or perceived inability to embrace and accommodate the person and incorporate him or her into society to the fullest extent. Smart and Smart (2006) suggest that in this model, the limitations and disadvantages experienced by people with disabilities in our society are what define the disability, not the actual condition or difference itself. In this model, disability is not viewed as a personal fault based on a medical diagnosis or limitation, but as a public concern. The counseling perspective, therefore, falls nicely in line with this view in that the focus of the helping process is on the strengths, interests, abilities, and capacities of each person, not on the person's diagnosis, weaknesses, or deficits.

The origins of the social model of disability in the United States can be traced to the civil rights movement of the 1960s and the belief in equal rights for all people. The emphasis on equality for people with disabilities can be compared to other socially marginalized groups in our country in that equal rights for all individuals lead to empowerment and the ability to have choice and make informed decisions. This, in turn, leads people with disabilities (and other marginalized groups) to have the ability to fully and freely participate in society.

In comparison with the medical model of disability, which focuses on what is wrong with the person that makes one different from others (and creates a need to fix him or her), the social model of disability focuses on what is wrong with society that makes us view the person as being "different." The social model of disability suggests that attempts to change, fix, or cure someone with a disability, rather than look at society's contributions that perhaps make the person disabled, can be discriminating and prejudiced. Examples of society's contributions to the disability process may include attitudinal barriers, physical or architectural barriers, and/or communication or language barriers.

Variations on the Social Model of Disability

The social model of disability described previously attempts to explore the effect society and the environment has on determining whether someone with a physical, mental, or psychological difference is disabled. The social model implies that disability is more than the individual's difference and includes attributes that are outside the individual (i.e., socially or culturally based). According to LaPlante (2002), disability is highly correlated with low education, poverty, community setting, environment, and with low resources. To support this, the U.S. Census Bureau (2006b) reveals that people with a severe disability have an increased likelihood of living below the poverty level, having "fair to poor" health status, receiving public assistance, having Medicare or Medicaid coverage, and having an annual household income of less than $20,000. By comparison, the poverty rate for people 25 to 64 years of age with no defined disability was 8%; 11% for individuals with a "nonsevere" disability, and 26% for individuals with a severe disability (U.S. Census Bureau, 2006b). Yet it has not sufficiently been shown whether low education and low socioeconomic status (SES) are risk factors for the development of disability, or whether disability is a risk factor for poverty (Lollar, 2002).

In considering models of disability, one model of the disability process espoused by Verbrugge and Jette (1994) and partially adapted by the World Health Organization (WHO) in 1980, the U.S. Academy of Science Institute of Medicine (Pope & Tarlov, 1991), and based on the work by sociologist Saad Nagi (1965, 1991), consists of four main parts that emphasize the relationship between pathology, impairments, functional limitations, and disability (see Figure 8.1.)

In this model, **pathology** refers to the individual's diagnosis, disease, injury, condition, or illness; **impairments** refer to the individual's dysfunction or structural abnormalities in a specific body system (e.g., neurologic, cardiovascular, or respiratory); **functional limitations** refer to the individual's ability to perform daily or life activities such as walking, reading, or speaking; and **disability** refers to the individual's difficulty in doing basic activities such as work, household management, hobbies, leisure/recreation, and social interactions (Verbrugge & Jette, 1994).

This model is helpful for counselors to gain a greater understanding of the disability process not only because the model includes an explanation of a main pathway to disability starting with a specific pathology or diagnosis, but also because it considers potential risk factors that may influence

Pathology → Impairments → Functional limitations → Disability

FIGURE 8.1   One Model of the Disability Process.

the onset of pathology which then leads to the disability. Examples of these risk factors include low SES, chronic health conditions, poor health habits, and poor access to health care. Further, the model considers **extraindividual intervention** strategies such as effective medical and rehabilitative care, caregiver support, adaptive/assistive devices, social service programs, and structural or architectural modifications. In addition, it considers **intraindividual intervention** strategies such as lifestyle and behavior changes, psychological attributes, coping strategies, and activity accommodations that help the person maintain independence for as long as possible (Verbrugge & Jette, 1994).

COUNSELING INDIVIDUALS WITH A DISABILITY

Considering the social model of disability, the counselor can begin to understand that different societies view and present people with disabilities with different challenges based on the beliefs and biases of that particular society (see Case Study 8.1). Within and among societies and cultures, individuals, families, and communities perceive and respond to disabilities differently. One example might be that some Southeast Asian cultures view a person with blindness in a favorable way and believe that a blind person possesses a specific and valued insight rather than as someone who has a vision disability and cannot see (Sotnik & Jezewski, 2005). In counseling individuals with various disabilities as well as various cultural backgrounds, it is important to be aware of these factors. Following is a discussion of the various roles that may intersect when counseling individuals with a disability, based on Groce (2005).

Role of the Individual   The role that a person with a disability is expected to have in the community helps shape the willingness of the community to integrate the person with a disability into the culture, including the willingness to spend financial or other resources for the person. For an adult, the person's contribution to the family income, full integration into society, and ability to contribute to society are all considerations that must be explored both intrinsically (within the person) and extrinsically (within the culture or society). It is the potential tension that exists between the person with a disability's views and the views of the greater society that may create conflict. This occurs particularly when trying to balance the person's needs, expectations, and the concerns of family and community against the person's plans and aspirations for life both now and in the future.

Role of the Family   In approximately 94% of the world's societies, the extended family, not the nuclear family, is the norm and influences where a person lives, works, marries, and even seeks health care (Groce, 2005). This is in contrast to the United States and most Western societies, which emphasize individualism and agency. The Western view of rehabilitation and counseling tends to foster independence and individuality and maintain an already existing view of economic self-sufficiency and productivity that seems to pervade U.S. culture. It can be seen that this view may be at odds with individuals from other cultures or societies with regard to the very basics of rights of individuals with disabilities and what their specific cultural beliefs are.

Role of the Community   In the United States, the right and ability of a person with a disability to obtain and maintain employment is a primary goal of rehabilitation and rehabilitation counseling, and is a key outcome in rehabilitation service delivery. Conversely, in many other cultures, which typically have a more communal society and recognize the influence and importance of extended families, involvement by family, friends, and neighbors can have a significant impact on an individual with a disability. More specifically, in many cultures, having an individual with a disability engage in the workforce can be considered a sign of neglect and abuse by the family and a "shirking" of the family's role and responsibility toward caring for the individual.

CASE STUDY 8.1

Alex is a 27-year-old first-generation Mexican American who immigrated to the United States when he was 17 years old. He graduated from high school and attended technical school to become a welder. He currently works full time as a welder. Three years ago, he married Elaine and they have a 2-year-old child. Elaine is pregnant with their second child. Together they had planned to work and raise their family, living the American Dream. But Alex became injured on the job and is no longer able to work. Alex and Elaine wonder what the future holds for them being that he is permanently disabled and of a different ethnicity and cultural background.

- Based on what you have read so far in this chapter, does Alex have a disability? Why or why not?
- Given the previous scenario, what cultural implications can the counselor consider when working with Alex, a Hispanic male with a disability living in the United States?
- In providing counseling services to Alex, what strategies can the counselor use to focus on his strengths, interests, abilities, and capacities?
- Under the social model of disability, what disabilities may be imposed on Alex based on what you know about American society's view of an individual with a physical injury?

ABLEISM

With a good foundation of the various definitions of disability and a description of some models of disability, it is important now to turn to the concept of ableism. **Ableism** refers to social attitudes, rehabilitation and counseling practices, and policies that favor individuals who have or are perceived as having full physical and mental health abilities. In contrast, individuals who have or are perceived as having physical and mental health limitations (i.e., disabilities) typically are excluded from having social power and full access to the same services and resources as individuals without health limitations. In defining ableism, there must be a focus on not only the individual's functional abilities but also the role of the larger society. Included in the larger context also are cultural attitudes, beliefs, and perceptions regarding a person's abilities (or disabilities). Language is also an important component of ableism (see Table 8.1).

It is perhaps no surprise that different cultures may have different expectations surrounding an individual's ability or function based on age, gender, socioeconomic status, education level, geographic location, and other factors. It is important to note, however, that in all societies, ableism exists to some extent in that individuals with disabilities are not only recognized as different from the general population but many times a specific value and meaning is attached to their condition (Groce, 2005). An example of this that occurs frequently in our culture is the level of inclusion and acceptance of individuals who are blind or visually impaired over the inclusion and acceptance of individuals with mental health disabilities who may, in fact, be ignored, shunned, or even ridiculed.

DISABILITY, ABLEISM, AND THE COUNSELING PROCESS

The preceding sections of this chapter have provided an overview of the concepts of disability and ableism as demonstrated in the current culture of the United States. Understanding the complexity, sensitivity, and variability of how these concepts are portrayed in our diverse culture

TABLE 8.1 Words That Empower	
Language is a powerful tool and can be used in either a positive or negative way. In the media and elsewhere, people with disabilities are frequently referred to in ways that promote stereotypes. Following is a chart of words and phrases commonly used to describe individuals with disabilities.	
Positive Attributes	**Negative Attributes**
Brave	Weak
Courageous	Unfortunate
Inspirational	Pitied
Superhuman	Burdened
Defeated a terrible fate	Infirm
Survived against all odds	Suffering
Differently abled	Challenged

What other words or phrases can you add to either list? What words/phrases have you used in the past when referring to someone with a disability?

Remember:

- People with disabilities are people first who happen to have a disability. They prefer to be called just that: a person with a disability.
- Having a disability is the only "culture" or minority group that any one of us can join at any time.

can give counselors and counselors-in-training a greater appreciation of the importance of providing multiculturally competent counseling services. Especially with regard to having a disability, few counselors themselves have a disability and they may be perceived as not being able to fully understand the client with a disability or as being "superior" to the client. Further, as cited by Sotnik and Jezewski (2005), different definitions or interpretations of disability can create conflict or disconnect between the client and counselor. For this reason, counselors must be attuned not only to the basic tenets and philosophies of the counseling process, most notably the tenet to do no harm to the client, but also to the individual client's beliefs and value system. To be sensitive to the unique beliefs, needs, and abilities of clients who are physically, mentally, cognitively, and/or socially different from you, as a counselor, means that you have reached a certain level of awareness and competence to work with clients with differing abilities (and potentially their family) to facilitate their understanding of the counseling process as a tool to reach their goals.

Awareness

According to Stone (2005), the counselors who become more aware of ableism and its effects on individuals with disabilities are better able to deliver effective counseling services. The importance of counselors becoming social advocates and more directly involved in helping clients overcome barriers to full inclusion in society, rather than maintaining a professional objectivity and neutrality, is becoming more important and more impactful on the lives of the clients whom we serve. In this way, the counselor's role takes on more of an advocacy role in addition to a counselor role, and counselors are now seen as taking a more proactive and less passive role when working with clients who are confronted by oppression and injustice (Stone, 2005). Miles (1999) suggests that in order for culturally competent counselors to be fully attentive and have an understanding of and appreciation for their clients' needs, the counselor should have a general awareness of the range of human beliefs with regard to ableism, disability, and functional impairment that crosses cultures, societies, and even individual beliefs. Activities 8.3 and 8.4 provide methods for increasing counselor self-awareness.

ACTIVITY 8.3

Obtain enough loaner wheelchairs for each dyad in the class. Wheelchairs can be arranged through local rehabilitation hospitals, local wheelchair equipment vendors, local wheelchair repair shops, or local facilities or programs for people with disabilities, such as Goodwill Industries.

Have one person from each dyad use the wheelchair to navigate through campus to a preselected site (e.g., library, student union, campus dormitory). The other person serves as a recorder and safety monitor and accompanies the classmate in the wheelchair with a pad and pen. As the classmate in the wheelchair navigates through campus, the other classmate ensures his or her safety (and that of others) as well as writes down campus areas that are inaccessible (or difficult to maneuver using a wheelchair), bumps along the way (both literally and figuratively), and time in transit to get to the desired location. Please keep safety and courtesy at the forefront at all times. Once at the preselected location, the classmates switch places and the recorder now uses the wheelchair with the other classmate serving as the new recorder and safety monitor. The same information is recorded for the ride back to class.

Once back in class, allow time for each dyad to debrief about the experience and the information recorded during their travels. Were the experiences similar or dissimilar? Were there common challenges or difficulties? Were some classmates better able to navigate the campus in a wheelchair than others? If so, what may be some reasons? What were the experiences of the classmates from other students on campus? How might this activity be in line with our views of a person with a disability whom we see in public on campus, at the mall, in the grocery store, or airport?

ACTIVITY 8.4

Bring enough clean bandanas or scarves to blindfold one student in each dyad in the class. Have one student wear the blindfold and the other student serve as the guide and safety monitor to navigate through campus to a preselected site such as a library, student union, campus dorm, and so on. (If both awareness activities are done, you should select a different site for the blindfold activity than the wheelchair activity.) Please keep safety and courtesy at the forefront at all times. The guide is responsible to get the blindfolded classmate to the preselected site safely and without incident. Once at the preselected location, the classmates switch places and the guide is blindfolded with the other classmate serving as the new guide and safety monitor. The same task is done for the students to walk back to class. Once back in class, allow time for each dyad to debrief about the experience. Consider the questions listed in Activity 8.3 for discussion purposes. Additional questions might include: How did it feel to be dependent on another person for getting you where you needed to be, and safely too? Was it difficult to give up your control to someone else? What amount of control did you feel you kept during this exercise? What would have been helpful from your classmate as you walked through campus wearing a blindfold?

Knowledge

Despite best intentions, advocacy efforts, and well-meaning legislation, the rehabilitation service delivery system and laws that govern the system in the United States are not "culture-free" (Groce, 2005). The population of individuals with a disability is probably one of our country's largest minority groups with a long history of disability policy and legislation. Although a detailed account of U.S. disability legislation is beyond the scope of this chapter, an overview of key disability policy and legislation is included for historical context. In a very broad context, social policy can be considered to both follow and lead public opinion about relevant social issues. Overall, the view of disability in the United States has evolved from initially viewing disability as a military manner and the "unfortunate outcome" of patriotic service to our country, to a view of disability as an unintended consequence of the Industrial Revolution, to a societal cause for charitable treatment, and, finally, as an indication of membership in a minority group with a push for empowerment and equal rights of individuals with disabilities (Schriner & Batavia, 1995, p. 261).

Dating back to 1776, the U.S. government established a support program for individuals with disabilities through a system of monetary compensation for soldiers wounded or disabled in the Revolutionary War. Current-day programs administered through the U.S. Department of Veterans Affairs continue to administer to soldiers and veterans. These programs are perhaps receiving more notice and recognition during the present conflicts in Iraq and Afghanistan and the large numbers of service men and women returning from the war with injuries and lifelong disabilities.

Although modern-day society is more familiar with current programs administered by the Social Security Administration, Social Security did not really arrive in America with the passage of the Social Security Act in 1935. And it was not until the Social Security Act was amended in 1960 that the federal government included benefits to individuals who were of working age who were disabled and to their dependents. In the 1970s, the Social Security Act was again amended to offer benefits to individuals who were not of working age and did not have a history of working (i.e., children).

However, not until 1918 did the U.S. government establish a formal program of training *and* counseling (i.e., vocational rehabilitation) for U.S. veterans with passage of the **Soldier Rehabilitation Act**. Almost simultaneous with the desire to support the country's soldiers with disabilities was a growing awareness of the needs of individuals who had received industrial or occupational-related injuries as a result of our growing and advancing country. By the 19th century, improved societal attitudes toward people with disabilities began, in large part, as a result of improved technology and machines, improved economics as a result of the Industrial Revolution, greater societal understanding, compassion, and optimism, and better science and medicine that influence individuals and families (Neulicht & Berens, 2004) (see Reflection 8.2 and Reflection 8.3).

REFLECTION 8.2

Did you know that two important demographic changes happened in our society beginning in the middle 19th century that changed social programs for individuals with a disability and individuals who are aging: the disappearance of the "extended" family and the increase in life expectancy.

Today's society in the United States generally considers "family" to include parents and children, or what is commonly known as the "nuclear family." This is in contrast to our society for most of our history, which generally was comprised of "extended families" that included children, parents, grandparents, and other relatives. The advantage of the extended family was that when a family member became ill, disabled, or old, other family members were available and commonly assumed responsibility for their care and support. In the present day, however, our society is more mobile with children commonly moving away from their family of origin once they become adults. As a result, with the more transient nature of society today, the role of the nuclear family becomes more important.

Similar to a change in the role of the nuclear family in present times is an increase in life expectancy of people in our society. It is difficult these days not to hear about the aging of the baby boomer generation. But, did you also know that as life expectancy has been increasing, the birthrate in our country has been decreasing (Atkinson & Hackett, 2004), thus creating more of an increased emphasis on the older population? With the increase in life expectancy comes a concurrent need for increased services for the older and aging population. This is true in the mental health and counseling professions as well, where practitioners are and will be expected to provide services to a population of clients who are living to an old age and experiencing life as an older adult. What are some of the needs and issues of the older and aging population? What are some of the life transitions as an older adult? With women generally living longer than men, what is the impact of gender differences among older adults? What impact does health have on older and aging clients? The ageism section in the second part of this chapter attempts to address some of these questions and other effects of increased life expectancy.

REFLECTION 8.3

Take a moment to define your nuclear family and extended family. Note the individuals you place into each category. Also include the geographic location of each family member. As you list family members, think about the frequency with which you communicate with each of them. Think, too, about the health status and age of the family members. Consider a plan of action in the event one or another of your family may become injured, ill, disabled, or approaching advanced age. Be sure to "customize" the plan to each family member's unique traits and personality in order to be most effective. Now consider how would you wish to be taken care of and by whom if you should experience chronic illness, disability, or advanced age.

As an important social issue, the rise of occupational injuries and disabilities as a result of the injuries contributed not only to the formation of labor unions, but also to state-based workers' compensation systems designed to compensate workers injured on the job. In general, state workers' compensation programs, both then and now, provide for health care costs related to the employee's work injury as well as provide a percentage of the employee's average weekly wages for the time in which the employee is out of work due to the injury. As early as 1921, 45 states and territories in the United States had some form of workers' compensation law. Today, all U.S. states and territories have workers' compensation laws that provide some form of renumeration for medical care and treatment related to the injury and compensation for lost wages as a result of the injury. Some states also provide vocational rehabilitation of injured workers if within a certain disability category or level of severity of disability (Berens, 1994).

To expand the trend toward disability policy in the United States, the **Civilian Rehabilitation Act** was passed in 1920 and provided grants to states to implement programs that addressed the needs of "ordinary citizens with disabilities" (Schriner & Batavia, 1995, p. 261). Numerous other laws have been passed over the last almost 90 years designed to protect the rights of individuals with disabilities, provide for their care, and prevent discrimination of them as a minority group. The first half of the 20th century saw a proliferation of federal programs, initiatives, and disability legislation with the goals of repaying a societal debt to those who had served and became injured or disabled in the military or in the workforce, and providing care for those who were not involved in military or work injuries (and therefore not covered under their respective compensation systems), but were seen by society and public policy as a population of people "deserving of assistance" (Schriner & Batavia, 1995, p. 267).

Disability laws, while presumably well intended, generally reflect the values of society at each point in time and, therefore, appear to favor some social roles over others. For example, the laws appear to have a gender bias while favoring men over women, as well as a disability-specific bias by appearing to favor individuals who are blind over individuals who are deaf, individuals who are physically impaired over individuals who are mentally impaired, and so on. Further, although many years later, disability legislation spilled into the education arena with the passage of the **Elementary and Secondary Education Act of 1965** that authorized federal monies to states to educate "deprived" children, including children with disabilities. Subsequent amendments have led to the **Education for All Handicapped Children Act of 1975** with the goal of helping children with disabilities receive a free and appropriate public education in the least restrictive environment, as well as providing early intervention programs for children with disabilities from birth to age 3 years, and special education preschool programs for children with disabilities aged 3 to 5 years. Formerly known as the **Individuals with Disabilities Education Act (IDEA),** disability legislation for the education of children with disabilities was recently re-authorized (amended) and signed into law in December 2004 under the revised title **Individuals with Disabilities Education Improvement Act of 2004**. However, the legislation continues to be commonly referred to as IDEA.

Consistent with the historical path of legislation regarding children with disabilities in a public school setting is legislation regarding people with disabilities in a general public setting. The passage of the **Americans with Disabilities Act (ADA)** in 1990 is regarded by some as the culmination of a quarter-century trend toward the establishment of legal protections for people with disabilities and is considered a major victory in the disability rights movement (Schriner & Batavia, 1995). The ADA protects the rights of people with disabilities and prohibits discrimination in employment, public accommodations, government services, some communication services, and public and private transportation systems. Although quoted by then-president George Herbert Walker Bush, on July 26, 1990, at the signing of the ADA, "let the shameful wall of exclusion finally come tumbling down," approximately two decades after passage of the ADA, individuals with disabilities in the United States continue to experience discrimination and exclusion in the very areas to which the law was designed to prohibit, particularly employment.

Throughout time, disability policy in our country, while proud of a long history of change and proactive legislation, has created boundaries that separate people with disabilities from people without disabilities. By allowing "positive discrimination" in the implementation of services, programs, and benefits designed specifically for people with disabilities, we also strive to eliminate "negative discrimination" against people with disabilities (Schriner & Batavia, 1995, p. 269). Martha Minow perhaps sums up this situation best by describing it as "the dilemma of difference" (Minow, 1990, p. 20), which risks creating or perpetuating further disadvantages for members of an oppressed group by either focusing on the differences (in this chapter either ability or age or a combination of them), or by glossing over the very differences that make each person unique and individual in his or her own right. Reflection 8.4 provides an opportunity to consider this dilemma with your future work with clients with disabilities.

REFLECTION 8.4

In discussing counselor awareness, knowledge, and skills for working with individuals with a disability, relating to clients in a way that emphasizes ability differences may reinforce the stigma and social isolation they receive in the broader social context (i.e., they are different from what is considered normal). On the other hand, treating all clients the same despite differences in ability may be perceived as being insensitive, ignorant, and privileged. How would you resolve this dilemma if working with a client with a significant physical, intellectual, or emotional disability?

It is important to note that there is no expectation for multiculturally competent counselors to have a thorough knowledge or deep understanding of all cultures, but rather to understand some of the basic principles and common themes of a culture. Included in that is a better sense of how individuals with a disability perceive disability within that culture and what goals and methods of rehabilitation are commonly accepted. Understanding the challenges associated with different cultures and different disabilities or abilities is crucial in providing counseling services that help eliminate the concept of ableism (or dis-ableism as discussed in this chapter). To assist in this process, a culturally competent counselor will use counseling and advocacy strategies that involve not only the individual client, but also family, peers, and community, as appropriate, to assist with and inform the individual with a disability (and potentially family) of the possibilities that exist to reach their fullest potential and inclusion in our society. Table 8.3 at the end of this chapter provides resources for advocacy for ableism that may be helpful as counselors build their knowledge and awareness for working with this population.

Skills

As counselors and counselors-in-training, it may be helpful to reinforce that the strength of the counseling profession is defined by the skills of the practitioners who practice counseling. As counselors, we are trained and qualified to provide counseling services to a diverse population of clients. The following list compiled by Smart and Smart (2006) may be helpful for counselors to consider when working with clients with a disability.

1. Fully and continually assess the client's feelings about experiences of having a disability and the counselor's understanding of their experience and how it interplays with the counselor's own identity.
2. Recognize that, depending on where they are in their adjustment to disability, most clients with a disability may view their disability as a basic and valued part of their identity and that, in actuality, they discern positive aspects of the disability rather than negative. Counselors must be comfortable asking a client about the client's identity as an individual with a disability and what the client's expectations are as related to the counseling process. It is important for counselors to understand that offering sympathy and lowered expectations for a client just because of the client's disability may be viewed as stigmatizing and prejudicial and may serve to further negative attitudes toward people with a disability.
3. Believe that the client with a disability is a person first, who happens to also have a disability. As with all human beings, clients with a disability have multiple identities and multiple roles that they serve in their lives, and the competent counselor will acknowledge and facilitate an understanding of the client's multiple identities, functions, and social contexts.
4. Collaborate with the client in identifying and promoting full participation and integration into society based on identities and roles.
5. Avoid imposing the counselor's values onto the client with a disability, or avoid the potential tendency to put a client into a "disabled role" just because the client has a disability.
6. Allow the full development of rapport and trust between counselor and client by minimizing the power differential between the counselor, who oftentimes does not have a disability, and the client who has a disability. Not only is this power differential counterproductive to the counseling relationship, it also may be a continuation of the views of the larger society in which the client lives.
7. Listen and hear what the client's experiences are as a person with a disability to fully understand what the client may share about experiences of discrimination, oppression, and prejudice.
8. Be competent in working with clients with disabilities and obtain appropriate training to advance your skills.

9. Be knowledgeable about various topics that relate to disability issues to be better informed in ways to serve clients with a disability.

10. Establish professional relationships and partnerships with agencies that typically serve people with disabilities to broaden your knowledge of the disability experiences of others with similar challenges.

11. Create effective change within local, regional, state, and national policies and systems that affect individuals with disabilities.

12. Contribute to research efforts by ensuring that the assumptions made about the various models of disability and the values about people with disabilities are made clear.

Further, in counseling individuals with a disability, the counselor must serve as an advocate for the client and the client's needs. With regard to social advocacy, the advocate's role is to promote the rights of the client and/or change the system on behalf of the client's needs. In this way, social advocacy involves the counselor initiating and/or participating in activities that are aimed at redistributing power and resources away from those individuals or groups that are considered the most "able" to those individuals or groups who demonstrate the need. Another component of social advocacy on the part of being a counselor is the ability to inform, empower, encourage, and support clients so that they are better able to make informed decisions that meet their own needs (Jezewski & Sotnik, 2005).

With the long history of individuals with a disability, disability legislation, and rehabilitation policy in the United States comes a long list of social advocates who have made their mark on improving social systems and societal attitudes toward individuals with a disability. Table 8.2

TABLE 8.2 Social Advocates in Disability and Rehabilitation

This list features some of the more prominent and contemporary advocates for disability and rehabilitation in the United States.

- **Billy Barner**—first African American student at the University of California at Berkeley's Cowell Residence Program for Physically Disabled Students, 1969–1973.
- **Henry Betts, MD**—pioneer in the field of rehabilitation medicine. Strong advocate and leader for people with physical disabilities.
- **Mary Lou Breslin**—Cofounder and director of the Disability Rights Education and Defense Fund.
- **Justin Dart Jr.**— Strong disability rights activist. Cofounder of the American Association of People with Disabilities (AAPD) with Paul Hearne, I. King Jordan, John Kemp, and Dr. Sylvia Walker. Sat on stage with President George H. Bush at the signing of the ADA in July 1990.
- **Senator Bob Dole**—Republican senator from Kansas who is partially disabled from war injuries and was an original cowriter of the ADA with Senator Tom Harkin.
- **Isabelle Goldenson**—Cofounder of the United Cerebral Palsy organization. Strong lobbyist of U.S. Congress to pass legislation to assist individuals with a disability.
- **Judy Huemann**—Cofounder of Disabled in Action. Also, cofounder (with Joan Leon and Ed Roberts) and codirector of the World Institute on Disability. Deputy director of the Center for Independent Living (CIL).
- **Mark Johnson**—Grassroots leader and strong advocate for individuals with disabilities. Helped create the Americans Disabled for Accessible Transportation (ADAPT) in 1984 that has been an effective force for change in the national disability rights movement. Current director of advocacy at Shepherd Center in Atlanta, GA.
- **Douglas Martin**—National leader in Social Security health benefits reform. Helped pass the ADA. First executive director of the Westside Center for Independent Living (CIL).
- **Mary Switzer**—Commissioner of Vocational Rehabilitation. Helped shape the Vocational Rehabilitation Act of 1954.

provides a compilation of some individuals who have contributed to our understanding of ableism and social advocacy. The list is not intended to be all-inclusive.

AGE DEMOGRAPHICS

Estimates are that, by the year 2030, 20% of the population will be comprised of older adults (Atkinson & Hackett, 2004). The U.S. Department of Health and Human Services (USDHHS) Administration on Aging (2003a), reports that nearly 35 million Americans are aged 65 years and over and that three in five people in this age group are female. Over the next 40 to 50 years, the number of people aged 65 years and older is expected to double and the number of people aged 85 years and older is expected to triple. Along with general trends for America's population, minority populations, too, are living longer, getting older, and becoming more racially diverse (USDHHS, 2003b).

The growth of the older population is in contrast to historical trends. For example, in the year 2000, there were many more people between their mid-30s and 40s than any other age group in this country. By the year 2025, when nearly all **baby boomers** (i.e., individuals who were born between the years 1946 and 1964) will have reached the age of 65, the distribution will increase accordingly such that by 2050, people are projected to continue to live into their 80s, 90s, and even 100s. The biggest change by the turn of the 22nd century is expected to be in the number of older men (Cavanaugh & Blanchard-Fields, 2006).

Data from the USDHHS Administration on Aging (2003a) show that the number of older adults among ethnic groups in the United States is increasing faster than among European Americans in the United States, with larger increases in the numbers of Asian/ Pacific Islander and Latino American older adults as compared with African American older adults. The advancing age of the baby boomers, combined with increased life expectancy of older adults, and the increased racial and ethnic diversity of older adults will put more emphasis on social policies that directly benefit older adults.

As medicine, science, and technology improve, and the life expectancy of people in the United States is lengthened to where people are now living and working longer into old age, it is inevitable that counselors will find themselves working with an older and aging population. According to the USDHHS Administration on Aging (2004), national demographic estimates predict that by the year 2020 there will be 53.7 million people aged 65 years and over, as compared to 34.8 million people aged 65 years and over who were alive in 2000. Whereas in the 1900s an average person could be expected to live to 47 years of age, data now published by the Centers for Disease Control and Prevention's National Center for Health Statistics (NCHS) show that the life expectancy of the average person born in the United States has reached a record high of 77.8 years for all races and genders (USDHHS, CDC, NCHS, 2006). This means that aging-related issues that previously have not been experienced by society in general and counselors in specific will now begin to surface. To address this need, counselors must be ready to assess and treat these issues in an effective and competent way (see Case Study 8.2).

CASE STUDY 8.2

Agnes is a second-generation Greek American, divorced, and recently referred to counseling by her adult daughter. Agnes is 60 years old and has been working for over 2 years as the maintenance manager at a large Greek Orthodox church. The pay is not great, but it has full health benefits and she

(continued)

enjoys the work and the people. With her daughter's help she recently bought a small house. Last month, she lost her job when the church realized it needed to reduce its operating budget. Although church members took up a collection that is helping Agnes pay for food and utilities, she has enough in her account for only one more mortgage payment and no savings. She is afraid and ashamed to ask her daughter for help, knowing that her daughter's household is on a tight budget with three young children and a single income. Agnes is afraid that she will not be able to get a job with benefits due to her advanced age. Although her physical health is good, she also is afraid she cannot continue much longer doing physically demanding work. Her anxiety and fear have triggered acute depression, and she is finding it difficult to get out of bed, which exacerbates her anxiety about her ability to find work. If she does not find a job soon, she will lose her home, which she loves. Agnes has been willing to try counseling, yet she doubts her "20-something" counselor can really understand her experiences of being an aging adult and what it is like to face these issues as an older adult.

- What feelings and thoughts did you notice in yourself as you read this scenario?
- As a counselor, do you feel adequately prepared to address Agnes's concerns?
- What role (or roles) could a counselor take in working with Agnes?
- What would Agnes's counselor need in order to be effective? (knowledge, skills, resources, supervision)

AGEISM

Ageism is defined as the assumption that chronological age is the main determinant of human characteristics and that one age is better than another. In this context, ageism generally refers to a form of discrimination against those age groups with higher vulnerability and less access to resources and power (i.e., the chronologically youngest and oldest of a population). Children, youth, seniors, and elders are all subject to ageism as a form of discrimination and, as a result, are among the most marginalized populations in our society. Similar to disability and ableism stereotypes, cultural attitudes toward aging are evidenced in media, social policy, and legislation, and, similar to ableism, ageism in the media seems to promote stereotypes that our society places on remaining young, healthy, beautiful, and successful.

Another form of discrimination distinct from ageism yet related because of an awareness of one's age is adultism. **Adultism** refers to discrimination against young people (youth) and children. In a very broad sense, adultism occurs when adults form beliefs about youth and children and behave toward them in ways that generally do not show respect for who they are. Some commonly held beliefs are that youth and young people are ignorant, untrustworthy, and unpredictable, and have nothing to contribute to their own well-being or to society as a whole. Along with these negative beliefs about young people comes a power differential in which adults believe they can and should exert control over young people and orchestrate their lives. This form of discrimination creates a sense of oppression and disempowerment among young people that can be carried on and perpetuated once they become an adult. Specific child and youth advocacy organizations, such as the Child Welfare League of America and others, have been formed to protect children, youth, and their families from adultism (Child Welfare League of America, 2003). It is important to note that the remainder of this section on ageism will focus on issues specific to the population of older and aging adults given the expected increase of older Americans over the next several years with whom counselors will likely be providing services.

Ageism and Older Americans

BUILD YOUR KNOWLEDGE 8.1

Read the following statements and answer True or False.

1. People naturally know when they are old.
2. Most adults over age 65 years face a steady decline in physical and mental wellbeing.
3. Older people are similar in their habits, beliefs, and ideas.
4. As people age, they are less able to adjust to changes in the world around them.
5. Older people tend to become more irritable, critical, and demanding as they age.
6. Most older adults (men and women) have little or no interest in sex or sexual activity.
7. Older adults typically are lonely and would like to live with their adult children.
8. Older adults ultimately become a financial burden to their adult children or to society.

Responses to all of these statements are false based on what we know about older adults today!

Older Americans have distinct psychological and physical issues associated with aging that may result in experiences with ageism (see Build Your Knowledge 8.1). From a physical standpoint, some of the more obvious changes for older adults that may present themselves during a counseling session include changes in skin (wrinkles and less elasticity), hair (thinner and grayer), and voice (softer and weaker). Other obvious changes are changes in height (shorter) and changes in mobility (slower gait, off-balance). Age-related medical or health conditions common among older adults that may impact the therapeutic relationship include cancer, cardiovascular disease, arthritis, and, especially among women, osteoporosis (Cavanaugh & Blanchard-Fields, 2006). The CDC reports that although 88% of people over age 65 years have at least one chronic health condition, the majority of older Americans are able to successfully cope with the physical and cognitive changes associated with aging (USDHHS, CDC, 2007). For those unable to cope with age-related changes associated with advanced age, an awareness of these issues is imperative for the competent counselor.

Psychological concerns common among older adults can be related to the physical changes already described and can affect older adults' self-concept, as well as reduce their independence and ability to take care of themselves or perform their normal daily routines. Further, onset of age-related dementia is "probably the worst stereotype about aging" (Cavanaugh & Blanchard-Fields, 2006, p. 67), and affects how society views older adults and the fear adults have of living to an old age. Although dementia is not a specific disease and can be described as a "family of diseases that are characterized by cognitive and behavioral deficits" (p. 132), with Alzheimer's disease the most common form, data show that roughly 6% to 10% of people older than age 65 years develop dementia, with the risk doubling about every 5 years (Qualls, 1999; USDHHS, CDC, 2007). Some characteristics of dementia include significant memory problems as opposed to the occasional memory lapse, difficulty with abstract thinking, reduced decision making that may affect safety and judgment, lack of insight, and personality changes. Alzheimer's disease has received much media attention in recent years and it is easy for a counselor to realize that the impact of age-related dementia can be severe and progressive and, at its most significant level, alter the persons' total daily functioning as well as the lives of their families and caregivers.

Coupled with the loss of memory common in dementia as well as the loss of thinking and functioning that can occur in advanced stages of dementia are various other losses that are experienced by older adults, such as the loss of a spouse, family members, and aging friends. Probably each of us has experienced loss in some way and has an appreciation of the grieving process as being complex and individualized to the person grieving. There is no right or wrong way to grieve. In fact, what works for one person grieving may and probably will not work for another person. Further, the length of time needed for the grieving process will vary by person as well. Cross-cultural differences in grieving also vary and the astute counselor must be sensitive to these issues. In older adults, the experience of loss and grief may be prolonged and frequent and may have greater impact as they realize the finality of their own life.

In addition to psychological and physical issues among older adults, socioeconomic issues also are relevant for older adults. In the United States and most of Western society, views of older people generally have been based on a function of their role in the economy. The economics of older people living in the United States seem to have greatest impact on individuals who are single, especially single older women; from ethnic minorities; seriously ill; and are considered "old-old" (generally over age 85 years). A U.S. Census Bureau report based on 1992 census data shows a bimodal distribution of income levels for older adults and reveals how being single and over age 75 years affects income (Atkinson & Hackett, 2004). Based on data, 53% of White married couples with one spouse over age 65 years had annual income >$25,000 and 17% had annual income >$50,000. Conversely, 44% of white married couples with one spouse aged 75 or over had annual income <$20,000 while 54% of single adults aged 75 years or older had income <$10,000 and 86% of single adults aged 75 years or older had income <20,000. Black married couples with at least one spouse aged 75 years or older were economically worse off than their White peers.

It is interesting to note that, as a group, 13% of older adults live below the poverty level as compared to 15% of younger people. However, federal figures on older people and poverty are misleading in that figures to compute poverty level are adjusted by age, such that older people aged 65 years and older have a lower poverty level than people in the age range of 15 to 64 years (Atkinson & Hackett, 2004).

Related to socioeconomic concerns, employment perhaps is one area where ageism or age discrimination may occur for older individuals. Even the Social Security Administration's definition of retirement age has been extended in recent years from the traditional or "normal" age of retirement, age 62 years, to the current age of retirement, age 67 years, for all people born after 1959 (U.S. Social Security Administration, 1983; Social Security Online, 2007). Counselors should strive to eliminate age discrimination as well as increase their own awareness and sensitivity to ageism when working with an older client. Due care must be given to ensure that myths and stereotypes regarding older clients do not bias judgment in working with an older client (Linkowski & Sherman, 2006). As defined, **age discrimination** is illegal in the United States and involves denying a job or promotion to an individual solely on the basis of age (Cavanaugh & Blanchard-Fields, 2006). Although passed into legislation over 20 years ago, the **U.S. Age Discrimination in Employment Act of 1986**, which protects workers over age 40 years, has done seemingly little to reduce age discrimination at work. Reports of age discrimination in employment have risen over the past 10 to 15 years and continue to exist.

In more recent legislation, the **Older Americans Act Amendments of 2006** protect the rights of older people who, under this act, are entitled to:

> (1) An adequate retirement income in retirement in accordance with the American standard of living, (2) The best possible physical and mental health which science can make available and without regard to economic status, (3) Obtaining and maintaining suitable housing, independently selected, designed and located with reference to special needs and available at costs which older citizens can afford, (4) Full restorative services

for those who require institutional care, and a comprehensive array of community-based, long-term care services adequate to appropriately sustain older people in their communities and in their homes, including support to family members and other persons providing voluntary care to older individuals needing long-term care services, (5) Opportunity for employment with no discriminatory personnel practices because of age, (6) Retirement in health, honor, dignity—after years of contribution to the economy, (7) Participating in and contributing to meaningful activity within the widest range of civic, cultural, educational and training and recreational opportunities, (8) Efficient community services, including access to low cost transportation, which provide a choice in supported living arrangements and social assistance in a coordinated manner and which are readily available when needed, with emphasis on maintaining a continuum of care for vulnerable older individuals, (9) Immediate benefit from proven research knowledge which can sustain and improve health and happiness, (10) Freedom, independence, and the free exercise of individual initiative in planning and managing their own lives, full participation in the planning and operation of community based services and programs provided for their benefit, and protection against abuse, neglect, and exploitation. (Older Americans Act, n.d.)

AGE, AGEISM, AND THE COUNSELING PROCESS

Aging and older individuals are accustomed to being independent and living their life being able to make their own decisions, much as they have throughout their lifetime. The counselor's role, therefore, is to facilitate guiding the older client in making informed decisions and showing respect for the client's years of life experiences, knowledge, and expectations that form the client's individual decisions. As with disability issues discussed in the previous section, counselors need to be aware of discrimination against persons because of age. Ageism can affect how the counselor views the client as well as how society views older adults in general, and people of all ages and abilities need to be viewed in terms of their strengths and abilities. Thus, counselors are encouraged to increase their awareness, knowledge, and skills for working with an aging and older population.

Counselors who specialize in working with aging and older clients are known within the counseling profession as gerontological counselors. By definition, a **gerontological counselor** is a counselor who provides counseling services to elderly clients and their families when faced with changing lifestyles as they grow older (U.S. Bureau of Labor Statistics, n.d.). Recognizing the lack of formal training in gerontological issues and in an effort to enhance training opportunities for counselors in working with older clients, the American Counseling Association (ACA) conducted five national projects on aging between 1977 and 1991 that focused on developing models and resources for preparing counselors to work with older adults. Myers (1992) wrote about efforts taken by ACA to propose and approve standards for training in gerontological counseling that were adopted by the Council for Accreditation of Counseling and Related Educational Programs (CACREP). These standards were designed to infuse gerontological counseling into the common core areas of accredited counselor training programs so that all graduates from accredited programs would have at least some knowledge of issues unique to counseling older adults (Myers, 1992). To read about the gerontological competencies for counselors and human development specialists adopted by the American Counseling Association (then known as the American Association for Counseling and Development) in 1990, see www. uncg.edu/~jemyers/jem_info/docs/competencies.htm. For a more recent article on gerontological counseling, see Maples and Abney's (2006) article on the maturation of the baby boomer generation and the development of gerontological counseling.

Awareness

It is important that counselors are aware of their attitudes toward individuals of various age groups, including commonly held myths (see Reflection 8.5). Myths and stereotypes about aging and older adults can often be found in the media, for example (see Activity 8.5). In the counseling process, ageism may be manifested in the following ways:

- Assumptions of limitations on behavior due to youth *or* aging
- Positive or negative stereotypes about younger *or* older persons
- The belief that children and youth are not competent and must be directed (adultism)
- The belief that older people have been socialized to handle their own problems
- The belief that mental health needs decrease with age

REFLECTION 8.5

Following are some common myths held by mental health professionals about the counseling needs of older people. What myths can you add to the list?

- Mental health issues disappear after midlife.
- Depression, anxiety, and other problems in old age are to be expected (by the mere act of getting old), and they are not worth treating.
- Older people are "developmentally static" and coping mechanisms learned in their youth and young adulthood should work for them into old age.
- Older people lack resources to seek counseling.
- Older adults are "too old" to change.

The sheer number of older individuals living in the United States and elsewhere are making society increasingly aware of the mental health needs of older adults. How can you respond to their needs?

ACTIVITY 8.5

In our society, there are many misconceptions about aging and older adults. Look for examples of myths and stereotypes about aging in cartoons, magazines, and newspapers, on television, and in movies and other forms of media. Select three of your examples and discuss the possible origins of these stereotypes. Use the information and resources on aging provided in this chapter to refute each stereotype.

Knowledge

The **ACA gerontological competencies** (American Association for Counseling and Development [AACD], 1990) include competence statements that were prepared to assist counselor educators in developing curricula and other training experiences to ensure adequate preparation of counselors in gerontological issues. The competencies provide a listing of minimum essential competencies that give an overview of the competencies required of effective generic and specialty counselors to work with older persons. In addition, they provide extensive statements of competencies for generic and specialty training based in the core areas of counselor preparation as defined in CACREP standards.

CACREP is the national accrediting body for training in the counseling and human development professions. According to the standards (AACD, 1990), a gerontological counselor

- Exhibits positive, wellness-enhancing attitudes toward older persons, including respect for the intellectual, emotional, social, vocational, physical, and spiritual needs of older individuals and the older population as a whole.
- Exhibits sensitivity to sensory and physical limitations of older persons through appropriate environmental modifications to facilitate helping relationships.
- Demonstrates knowledge of the unique considerations in establishing and maintaining helping relationships with older persons. Demonstrates knowledge of human development for older persons, including major psychological theories of aging, physiological aspects of "normal" aging, and dysfunctional behaviors of older persons.
- Demonstrates knowledge of social and cultural foundations for older persons, including common positive and negative societal attitudes, major causes of stress, needs of family caregivers and the implications of major demographic characteristics of the older population (e.g., numbers of women, widows, increasing numbers of older minorities).
- Demonstrates knowledge of special considerations and techniques for group work with older persons.
- Demonstrates knowledge of lifestyle and career development concerns of older persons, including the effects of age-related physical, psychological, and social changes on vocational development, factors affecting the retirement transition, and alternative careers and lifestyles for later life.
- Demonstrates knowledge of the unique aspects of appraisal with older persons, including psychological, social, and physical factors which may affect assessment, and ethical implications of using assessment techniques.
- Demonstrates knowledge of sources of literature reporting research about older persons and ethical issues in research with older subjects.
- Demonstrates knowledge of formal and informal referral networks for helping older persons and ethical behavior in working with other professionals to assist older persons.

In addition to the competencies for gerontological counselors, counselors interested in working with this population may want to investigate available professional and community resources presented in Table 8.4 at the end of this chapter.

Skills

Like disability, aging can be viewed as negative or positive, as loss or gain (Linkowski & Sherman, 2006). As counselors, it is more helpful to facilitate our clients to build upon the positive aspects of aging, such as lessons learned from a lifetime of experiences, knowledge, and skills that have been developed over time, rather than focus on the client's losses or perceived losses due to old age. In this way, clients can understand that aging is inevitable and we can be successful in the outcome. But how is "successful" defined when applied to the aging process, and who determines if it is successful? More than four decades ago, Havighurst (1961) defined successful aging as the process of adding life to one's years (rather than years to one's life) and getting satisfaction out of life. More recently, Rowe and Kahn, in their book titled *Successful Aging* (1998), define **successful aging** as the avoidance of disease and disability, the maintenance of cognitive and physical function, and sustained engagement with life. While this three-part definition of successful aging has become a central theoretical paradigm in the study of gerontology and geriatrics, Holstein and Minkler (2003) assert that it appears to assume certain things must be true in order to be successful with aging; most importantly that people have the resources to live a healthy life, adequate access to health care, a safe living environment, and the ability for individual decision making. This may be aspirational for most, if not all, of us as we age, but the reality is that not all older adults experience lives that support this definition of successful aging. Does this mean that older people who have physical or psychological or emotional health problems have not successfully aged? Just as "beauty is in the eye of the beholder," successful aging is defined by the person living the process. In other words, as a counselor, it will be helpful to understand (and even facilitate) our client's definition of successful aging in their own terms. Refer to Reflection 8.6 to process your ideas of successful aging.

REFLECTION 8.6

Is there a problem associating successful aging with having good physical and psychological health and the resources to maintain that into old age? Why or why not? Given what you have read on aging and ageism, how do you think older adults will define successful aging in the future? What is a counselor's role in helping their clients assess their own definition of successful aging and facilitate their personal growth into old age?

TABLE 8.3 Resources for Learning and Advocacy Related to Ableism

ACA Division

American Rehabilitation Counseling Association (ARCA)
Web site: www.arcaweb.org/
Mission: To enhance the development of people with disabilities throughout their life span and to promote excellence in the rehabilitation counseling profession.
Journal: *Rehabilitation Counseling Bulletin*, quarterly publication. Free online access for members of ARCA.
Newsletter: Free online access via ARCA Web site.
Resources: Go to www.rehabjobs.org for information on careers in rehabilitation counseling; www.crccertification.com for information on the Commission on Rehabilitation Counselor Certification (CRC credential).
Links:
- **www.crccertification.com**—The site provides links to the Code of Professional Ethics for Rehabilitation Counselors and Scope of Practice for Rehabilitation Counseling.
- **www.core-rehab.org**—The Council on Rehabilitation Education is the accrediting body for graduate programs in Rehabilitation Counselor Education (RCE) whose purpose is to promote, through accreditation, the effective delivery of rehabilitation services to individuals with disabilities by promoting and fostering continuing review and improvement of master's degree level RCE programs.
- **www.rehabeducators.org**—The National Council on Rehabilitation Education is a professional organization dedicated to quality services for persons with disabilities through education and research.
- **http://nrca-net.org/**—The National Rehabilitation Counseling Association is a professional association that is a division of the National Rehabilitation Association and represents professionals in the field of rehabilitation counseling in a wide variety of work settings.
- **www.rehabpro.org**—The International Association of Rehabilitation Professionals is a professional association that serves a diverse membership practicing in the fields of long-term disability management consulting, case management and managed care, forensics and expert testimony, life care planning, and Americans with Disabilities Act (ADA) consulting.

Art and Advocacy
- *DisThis!* Film Series, www.disthis.org/
- AXIS Dance Company, www.axisdance.org/
- Theater by the Blind, http://tbtb.org

- Visible Theater, www.visibletheatre.org
- Nicu's Spoon Theater Company, www.spoontheater.org/

Legislative/Policy Resources
- Federal legislation, http://thomas.loc.gov/home/thomas2.html
- National Council on Disability, www.ncd.gov
- Americans with Disabilities Act, www.ada.gov/pubs/ada.htm
- Individuals with Disabilities Education Improvement Act (IDEIA) of 2004, www.ed.gov/offices/OSERS/Policy/IDEA/the_law.html
- Rehabilitation Act of 1973, www.ed.gov/policy/speced/reg/narrative.html
- Developmental Disabilities Assistance and Bill of Rights Act of 2000, http://frwebgate.access.gpo.gov/cgi-bin/getdoc.cgi?dbname=106_cong_public_laws&docid=f:publ402.106

Advocacy and Issue-Specific Resources
- National Institute on Disability and Rehabilitation Research (NIDRR), www.ed.gov/about/offices/list/osers/nidrr/about.html
- Online Resource for Americans with Disabilities, www.disability.gov
- Brain Injury Association of America, www.biausa.org

TABLE 8.4 Resources for Learning and Advocacy Related to Ageism (Continued)

ACA Division

Association for Adult Development and Aging (AADA)
Web site: www.aadaweb.org/
Mission: "Chartered in 1986, the Association for Adult Development and Aging, serves as a focal point for sharing, professional development, and advocacy related to adult development and aging issues and addresses counseling concerns across the lifespan. The AADA seeks to improve the standards of professional service to adults of all ages by (a) improving the skills and competence of American Counseling Association members, (b) expanding professional work opportunities in adult development and aging, (c) promoting the lifelong development and well-being of adults, and (d) promoting standards for professional preparation for counselors of adults across the lifespan. The AADA also develops partnerships with other organizations that hope to improve the standards for care of adults and older adults."
Journal: ADULTSPAN Journal (with AADA membership or by subscription).
Newsletter: ADULTSPAN Newsletter (with AADA membership or by subscription).
Guidelines: Gerontological competencies.
Resources: Information for caregivers; topical information covers benefits, health, medical and legal resources, housing information, physician referrals, web resources on aging issues

Legislative/Policy Resources
- Administration on Aging, www.aoa.gov
- American Association of Homes and Services for the Aging, www.aahsa.org
- American Association for Geriatric Psychiatry, www.aagpgpa.org
- National Institute of Aging, www.nia.nih.gov/
- National Council on Aging, www.ncoa.org
- Combined Health Information Database, http://chid.nih.gov/

Resources and Organizations for Clients
- American Association for Retired Persons (AARP), www.aarp.org
- Eldercare, www.eldercare.com
- Senior Citizen/Elderly/Aged Resources, www.at-la.com/@la-senior.htm#gerlab

(continued)

TABLE 8.4 Resources for Learning and Advocacy Related to Ageism (Continued)

Professional Resources
- American Geriatrics Society, www.americangeriatrics.org
- American Psychological Association, Division 12, Section II, Clinical Geropsychology, http://geropsych.org/membership.html
- American Psychological Association, Division 20, Committee on Aging (CONA), www.apa.org/pi/aging/cona01.html
- American Society on Aging, www.asaging.org
- Gerontological Society of America, www.geron.org
- International Longevity Center, www.ilcusa.org
- National Association of Area Agencies on Aging, www.N4A.org
- National CDC Report on Older Adults, www.cdc.gov/nccdphp/sgr/olderad.htm

Alzheimer's Information and Support
- Alzheimer's Association, www.alz.org
- National Institute of Aging, www.alzheimers.org

Elder Abuse
- Elder Abuse Prevention, www.oaktrees.org/elder

Children and Youth
- Advocates for Youth, www.advocatesforyouth.org/
- Americans for a Society Free from Age Restrictions (ASFAR), www.asfar.org/
- Children's Defense Fund, www.childrensdefense.org/site/PageServer
- Child Welfare League of America, http://cwla.org
- National Youth Rights Association, www.youthrights.org/
- Youth for Human Rights International, www.youthforhumanrights.org/index.htm

Issue-Specific Resources
Center for Successful Aging (CSA), http://hhd.fullerton.edu/csa/
California State University, Fullerton
800 N. State College Blvd., KHS-241
Fullerton, CA 92831-3599
(714) 278-7317

Published Goals of the CSA (partial list):
- Conduct interdisciplinary research on issues related to healthy aging.
- Provide training to prepare practitioners to work with older adults.
- Collaborate and partnership with community agencies and facilities to provide services to improve quality of life in later years.
- Serve as advocate for affecting public policy related to healthy aging.

Gray Panthers, Age and Youth in Action, www.graypanthers.org/: An intergenerational, multiissue organization working to create a society that puts the needs of people over profit, responsibility over power and democracy over institutions.

National Youth Rights Association (NYRA), www.youthrights.org/: A national youth-led organization that defends the civil and human rights of young people in the United States through educating people about youth rights, working with public officials and empowering young people to work on their own behalf. Holds the belief that certain basic rights are intrinsic parts of American citizenship and transcend age or status limits.

Americans for a Society Free from Age Restrictions (ASFAR), www.asfar.org/: An organization dedicated to protecting and advancing the legal civil rights of youth.

American Association for Retired Persons (AARP), www.aarp.org: A nonprofit membership organization of people aged 50 years and older dedicated to addressing their needs and interests.

Summary

This chapter was designed to give counselors and counselors-in-training an understanding of the concepts of ableism and ageism, both which continue to exist in our society today. Given the large and growing minority group of individuals with disabilities in our society, it is likely that counselors, regardless of their specialty area or theoretical orientation, will be providing services to clients with disabilities and/or chronic medical or physical challenges at some time in their career. When working with clients who are "differently able," it is crucial for counselors to view the client with a disability as an individual first and to acknowledge that the client has multiple roles and functions within the family, community, culture, and society, all of which may impact the counseling process.

Similarly, the growing population of individuals in our society who are older (typically aged 55 years and older) forms the basis for the section on ageism and older adults. While ageism as a concept refers to any form of discrimination based on age (young or old), older adults was the population on which most of the chapter focused since older adults represent the largest growing segment of our population projected over the coming years. It is clear based on the projected numbers alone that there is a growing need for counselors and counselors-in-training to specialize in addressing the needs and concerns of older adults and to advocate for effective services. In this way, counselors who are competent and interested in working with older adults may be considered on the "cutting edge" of the counseling profession and are poised to fill a great need both now and in the future. By recognizing that ability and age are diversity issue within our society, the multiculturally competent counselor can facilitate the counseling process and help clients of all ages and abilities achieve their goals.

Counseling Multicultural Populations

CHAPTER 9

Individuals and Families of African Descent

KATHERINE M. HELM AND LAWRENCE JAMES JR.

PREVIEW

This chapter will explore the past and present experiences, cultural values, and common presenting issues for individuals, families, and couples, as well as other subpopulations of people of African descent in the United States. It will review common past and present experiences of African Americans, racial identity development, acculturation and racial identity as mental health indicators, African American culture and values, common support systems for African Americans, and the efficacy of traditional psychotherapies and assessments with this population and multiculturally sensitive interventions.

INDIVIDUALS AND FAMILIES OF AFRICAN DESCENT

Individuals of African descent have a rich and varied history of survival in the United States despite disparaging odds. Although the United States was a country founded on principles of religious and ethnic freedom, discriminatory laws and historically poor treatment of individuals of African descent contradicted these principles. One must understand the history of this group in the United States to truly understand and provide a context for how African American culture developed and is maintained; how the psyche, racial identity, and worldview of individuals of African descent formed over time; the common presenting treatment issues of African Americans in therapy; and the deeply ingrained racism and discrimination that many individuals of African descent face on a daily basis. This includes a discussion of enslavement. The impact of one group of people being the legal property of another group of people on the collective psyche and mental health of individuals of African descent cannot be underestimated. The historical and current effects of this physical enslavement and psychological degradation can be seen on African Americans. This impact also underlies many of the common presenting treatment issues among African Americans in seeking counseling.

You may ask yourself: How is counseling a person of African descent different than counseling individuals of other backgrounds? The answer is that it is very different in some ways and not so different in other ways. Effective counselors recognize that to fully understand clients and client issues, counselors have to recognize that each of us walks in a different world. We are all treated and judged differently based on perceived race, ethnicity, gender, perceived sexual orientation, religious background, height, weight, disability, level of attractiveness, as well as other statused variables in our society. Because skin color is readily seen, it is often the variable by which we are judged most quickly. In working with clients of African descent, multiculturally competent counselors are able to combine their academic knowledge, practical and personal experiences, and common sense to understand and be sensitive to clients' varied experiences in their individual worlds. Reflection 9.1 offers counselors an opportunity to explore their own assumptions and biases about this population.

REFLECTION 9.1

Compile a list of initial thoughts that come to mind about individuals of African descent. Examine your assumptions and beliefs about this population. Explore how these views could positively and negatively affect your work with these clients.

_____

_____

_____

_____

_____

Terminology

This chapter is titled "Individuals and Families of African Descent" because that is the most inclusive title of this population at this time. The chapter does not include individuals of North African descent (e.g., Egyptians, Libyans, Moroccans); however, this information is discussed in the following chapter on individuals and families of Arab descent.

Throughout time Black Americans have been referred to as Negroes, Colored, Blacks, Afro-Americans, and African Americans. Historically, Black Americans began labeling themselves publicly as a group, most especially in the 1960s with the slogan "Black is beautiful" (Boyd-Franklin, 1989). This represented the idea that as a people, Blacks could celebrate their own diversity of skin tones and that Black people had a proud heritage to celebrate. Prior to this movement, African Americans in the United States were named by those in power. The term *African American* came about in the 1980s coined by Reverend Jesse Jackson and it emphasized Black Americans' ties to Africa as well as the country of their citizenship, the United States. Not all African Americans wish to be called "African American" or "Black." Therefore, multiculturally competent counselors should ask their clients of African descent what they prefer to be called. This chapter will use the terms *Black, African American,* and *individuals of African descent* interchangeably to reflect the ways in which many Blacks in the United States refer to themselves; however, each term is different and can represent for an individual a sense of his or her own identity and pride.

DEMOGRAPHICS   According to 2001 U.S. Census data, African Americans comprise approximately 12.3% (34.7 million) of the U.S. population. An analysis of immigration patterns finds that they come from diverse places including Africa, the Caribbean, the West Indies, Latin American, central Europe, and South America (Kent, 2007). According to Neville and Walters (2004), the Black population is expected to grow only marginally in the next decade. The Black population is roughly distributed evenly between males (48%) and females (52%); nearly one third of the population is under 18 years (31%) and only 8% are over 65 years (Neville & Walters, 2004). The number of Blacks immigrating from Africa and the Caribbean (although outnumbered by non–Black Hispanic and Asian immigrants) is growing at a remarkable rate. From 1980 to 2005 Black immigration rates have increased from 1% to 8% (Kent, 2007). African descent people disproportionally face many issues including struggles with poverty and unemployment at three times the rates of Whites (Sue & Sue, 2003). Physical and mental health disparities, such as lack of health insurance and a lower life span than Whites by 7 years, are also issues facing the Black community. In their work, Neville and Walters (2004) review educational, economic, employment, and mental and physical health issues of African Americans. These include the following: 15.5% of Blacks are college graduates compared to 27.7% of Whites; urban school districts (in which many school attendees are Black) receive about 12% less funding for each child compared to predominantly White school districts. Poor urban schools often lack important resources such as computers, current textbooks, after-school activities, and Advance Placement courses. Nearly 22.7% of Blacks live at or below the poverty line and, according to Cable News Network (CNN) 2007 data, Blacks make up 41% of the nation's 2 million prison population compared to 37% of Whites and 19% of Hispanics (CNN, 2007). So many of these struggles are reflective of the oppression Blacks face in American society based on historic and current racial discrimination. Despite these serious issues facing individuals of African descent, African Americans' history of resilience and survival in an often hostile and highly racialized climate cannot be denied.

AFRICAN AMERICAN HISTORY

Throughout their tenure in the United States, people of African descent have been labeled in many different ways. Historically, race was considered a biological construct (Axelson, 1999; Nagayama-Hall & Barongan, 2002). Individuals were categorized based on phenotypic characteristics (Robinson & Howard-Hamilton, 2000). Because Europeans were responsible for the categorical system based on race, the darker one's skin and the farther an individual's features were from the European standard, the lower the status of the individual in society. Racial categories were always hierarchical where the darkest individuals were compared to animals and the lightest individuals were considered to be made in "God's image" (Kambon, 1998). This hierarchical system is evident in the **one drop rule,** which states that having one drop of Black blood makes one Black (Kambon, 1998; Nagayama-Hall & Barongan, 2002). Slave owners and subsequent laws obsessively classified individuals of African descent based on how much White blood one had. For example, mulattoes were half Black and half White, quadroons were one fourth Black, and octroons were one eighth Black (Axelson, 1999). Often the more White blood slaves had, the more privileges they had over their darker counterparts. Lighter skinned slaves were able to work in the slave owner's house while darker skinned slaves had to work outdoors all day. Slaves with lighter skin were also considered more attractive by White slave owners because they were closer to the White beauty ideal. Lighter skinned slaves were often the result of the slave owners sexually assaulting darker slaves. This is why many slaves were actually related to their slave owners for generations.

Colorism still exists in the Black community today where African Americans with lighter skin are often perceived as having an easier time than African Americans with darker skin (Animifu, 1995). There is some basis to this perception both currently and historically. It is a form of internalized racism whereas lighter skin is sometimes more valued than darker skin in the African American community. Occasionally in Black families, parents or grandparents may knowingly or unknowingly prefer children based on skin tone. This can often be a very painful issue (Boyd-Franklin, 1989) that may not be openly discussed or acknowledged. In working with African American women especially, this may often be a hidden treatment issue because skin color can be related to self-esteem, body image issues, and feelings of attractiveness. A multiculturally competent counselor might therefore explore the salience of clients' self-perceptions related to skin tone that might be relevant to their self-concept or presenting issue (Anminifu, 1995).

Race no longer exists as a solely biological construct. We cannot always look at someone and know what race he or she is. Today, race is a social, economic, psychological, and ideological construct. In other words, what race someone is has economic and social consequences for living in the United States. It also shapes one's worldview and oftentimes how he or she is perceived and treated by others in society. In the United States, race and social class are often confounded. For example, it is often assumed that most Blacks are poor. The media frequently enhances this perception by depicting news stories, movies, and television programs that support this idea. This perception does not allow for heterogeneity among African Americans. It is true that a disproportionate number of African Americans are poor relative to their numbers in the population; however, it is also true that most African Americans are not poor (Neville & Walters, 2004).

Individuals of African descent have a distinct culture that is influenced by geographic region, origins (e.g., Haitian American vs. Dominican American), ideology, social class, and many other variables. Without understanding the diversity within African American culture, a counselor cannot work effectively with clients of these backgrounds. Those with "black skin" do not all have the same culture. Afro-Cubans, Black Americans, individuals from Ghana, and individuals from the Caribbean may all have similar skin tones, but their cultures, values, experiences, and worldviews may be vastly different. Multiculturally sensitive counselors educate themselves about their client's personal (individual) and collective (group) culture. This is why it is extremely important in working with clients of African descent to assess their level of acculturation and to understand some of their cultural values. Assessment of acculturation level will be discussed later in this chapter.

DISCRIMINATION EXPERIENCES

The first Africans arrived in the United States in 1619 as indentured servants, similar to how many White settlers came. Within 20 years there were laws against racial mixing and interracial marriage (Nagayama-Hall & Barongan, 2002). Very soon after that, Africans began arriving upon the shores of the United States as slaves. From the mid-1600s through 1965, laws were used to justify the physical, mental, and spiritual abuse of African Americans. Early models of mental health pathologized Africans (Guthrie, 1998; Kambon, 1998). For example, **drapetomania** was a noted mental illness of slaves who tried to escape from their owners (Kambon, 1998). White Americans at the time justified slavery by assuming that Blacks were not human beings and that they could not feel pain to the same extent as Whites. Laws considered slaves to be one tenth of a human being.

During the years of the slave trade, Africans from different tribes were ripped from their families and culture and forced onto severely overcrowded ships where over half of them died before coming to the shores of the United States. Upon arrival, they were sold away from other family members to White slave owners. They were beaten, starved, and forced to work 18 hours a day.

Africans were forced to give up their African names and culture and were given European names. Even their reproductive lives were not their own as men were often used as "studs" to make more slaves and women were seen as breeders. All children born were considered the property of slave owners and many were promptly sold away from their families. Thus, the nuclear family unit was seldom allowed to form among slaves. Often slave children were raised by whatever adults and older children were left on the plantation. Rarely were these the children's actual relatives. Thus, slaves made family where they found it. Although more traditional mental health models and models of family therapy have pathologized Black families because many of them are not "nuclear," this clearly has a historical basis and is not pathological (Boyd-Franklin, 1989). It is still true that Black families are not strictly nuclear and Black children are often raised by their close biological relatives and extended family. Although the dehumanization and denigration of Blacks and Black culture began in times of slavery, current society often continues this pattern. These practices can be seen in racial profiling, the criminalization of Blacks, and the view that Blacks are undesirable people and a group to be feared.

Shortly after slavery ended in 1865, the **Jim Crow** era began. Briefly, Jim Crow laws maintained and supported segregationst policies that governed the lives of Blacks in America (Nagayama-Hall & Barongan, 2002). These racist policies were enforced by legal institutions such as the police and courthouses through the 1960s. Thus, throughout their history in the United States, Blacks have been made to feel unwelcome, undesirable, and pathologized. Blacks have been seen as a "problem people," a people to be hated and feared, and a threat. It is upon this backdrop that African values with American influences were maintained in the traumatic war zone of slavery, the Jim Crow era, and continued racism and discrimination. Although racism and discrimination are rarely openly tolerated in today's times, they still exist. Today's racism is often passive, hidden, unconscious, and systemic but it is still extremely damaging and hurtful.

For example, recent research on health care disparities and medical treatment document well that African Americans often receive poorer health care, and are often diagnosed with life threatening illnesses and mental illnesses later than their White counterparts (Neville & Walters, 2004; Thompson & Isaac, 2004; Wicker & Brodie, 2004). Thus, passive and unconscious racism can have devastating life-threatening consequences for the lives of African descent individuals. As a result, many African Americans are distrustful of medical and mental health professionals because in the not-so-distant past Blacks were victims of medical experiments done without their permission (e.g., Tuskegee syphilis experiment) and involuntary sterilization in which they were harmed and even died as a result. The *New York Press* (Bergman, 2005) reported that the New York City foster care system (most of the children in foster care across the country are Black) gave HIV-positive children toxic experimental drugs for treatment without the children's or guardians' permission. Foster parents who refused to give children these drugs were removed from these parents' care. It is also true that often the only contact some members of the Black community have with mental health professionals is when social workers come in to remove children from their homes or through the welfare system (Boyd-Franklin, 1989).

In the U.S. school system of the mid-to-late 20th century, mental health professionals were also involved with the disproportionate labeling of Black children as mentally retarded. Intelligence tests, which had not at the time been normed on Black children or children of lower socioeconomic status (SES), were used as the sole measure for placing children into special education programs. Historically, these children were often placed in a special education curriculum without their parents' knowledge or consent. This past negative history has contributed to the general cultural mistrust that some African Americans have of government, medical, and mental health professionals and institutions (Whaley, 2001). Whaley stresses the importance of assessing and addressing cultural mistrust early in the therapeutic relationship.

BLACK RACIAL IDENTITY

Understanding racial identity among African Americans is essential to effectively counseling members of this group. Counselors must also understand Black cultural variables and their clients' level of acculturation. The Cross (1971b) model of Black racial identity development is a prominent framework for understanding Black racial identity. It has been modified, researched extensively, and applied to counseling settings with cross-racial dyads of clients and counselors (Parham, 1989; Parham & Helms, 1981), client racial preferences for counselors (Helms & Carter, 1991; Morten & Atkinson, 1983; Parham & Helms, 1981; Ponterotto, Anderson, & Grieger, 1986), and supervisor–supervisee cross-racial pairings; and used to explore how racial identity can change over the life span (Parham, 1989, 2002a). The Cross model has been updated (Cross & Vandiver, 2001); however, the basic core of the model has remained the same. The model describes a process by which most African Americans come to embrace and internalize a positive Black identity despite instances of racial discrimination and negative societal messages about being Black. Some individuals of Black descent do not embrace a positive Black identity and do not consider their Black heritage to be an important aspect of their identities, whereas others see being Black as a central part of their identities (Cross & Vandiver, 2001). Chapter 2 reviews racial identity models in more detail. It is therefore essential in working with clients of African descent that therapists assess how central clients' racial awareness and identity is to who they say they are as individuals.

Other literature finds that a client's Black identity (especially if excessively negative) can have negative implications for mental health issues and self-esteem (Neville & Walters, 2004; Wicker & Brodie, 2004). This can present as the internalization of the White beauty ideal, the rejection of a Black identity and high negative feelings about being Black, the disparagement of other Blacks, and other forms of internalized racism. So, "if the client's racial identity or view of himself or herself is in contradiction with the culture in which he or she exists, the client may have potential issues that need to be addressed" (Wicker & Brodie, 2004, p. 116).

Research demonstrates that for individuals of African descent, a positive racial identity serves a protective function (Barker-Hackett, 2003; Cross, 1991; Neville & Walters, 2004) against negative societal messages about being Black. Specifically, Neville and Walters (2004) state, "there is now mounting documentation of the link between racial identity attitudes and mental health, generally suggesting that greater internalization of a positive racial identity is related to increased psychological well-being and more effective coping skills among African Americans" (p. 93). Assessment of racial identity is useful for a counselor to hypothesize the types of conflict a client deals with and how the client views the world. In addition to assessing and understanding clients' racial identities, level of acculturation must also be explored.

ACCULTURATION

Parham (2002a, 2002b) believes that solely focusing on racial identity as opposed to cultural identity is too limiting because it forces a homogenic experience onto a whole group of people. Landrine and Klonoff (1996) echo these concerns in their studies of **acculturation**. They assert that the use of race and not culture obstructs a counselor's ability to understand human behavior. Briefly, the difference between racial identity and acculturation is this: Racial identity has to do with how one identifies oneself and if race is a key component of one's identity, whereas acculturation refers to specific socialization influences and how one's racial identity is practiced. Acculturation speaks more to culture than race.

"Acculturation loosely refers to the extent to which ethnic and cultural minorities participate in the cultural values, beliefs, and practices of their own culture versus those of the dominant 'white' society" (Landrine & Klonoff, 1996, p. 1). In addition to the acculturation model presented in Chapter 1, acculturation can be viewed on a continuum from *traditional* to *acculturated*. Landrine and Klonoff describe the following groupings:

> **Traditional** an individual who is immersed in many of the beliefs, practices, and values of their own culture.
>
> **Bicultural** an individual who is in the middle of the continuum, has retained beliefs and practices of his or her own culture but also has assimilated some beliefs and practices of the dominant White society, and, thus, participates in two very different cultural traditions simultaneously.
>
> **Highly acculturated** an individual who rejects the beliefs and practices of his or her culture of origin in favor of those of the dominant society or never learned his or her own cultural traditions.
>
> **Marginal** an individual who either rejects or never acquires beliefs and practices of his or her own culture or of White culture.

Thus, a multiculturally competent counselor should assess how invested a Black client is in traditional African American religious beliefs and practices, traditional African American socialization experiences and values, and preferences for African American things that will give the counselor an indication of the client's level of acculturation.

Understanding a client's racial identity and level of acculturation will guide the counselor in recommending or acknowledging appropriate support systems for clients. Highly acculturated clients may wish to use Black organizations (e.g., churches, fraternities and sororities, Black-run charities, Black-owned businesses) as a source of emotional, financial, and social support. Referring a Black client who does not consider being Black an important part of her identity to traditional Black support systems in the community would be contraindicated and the client could be offended.

AFRICAN AMERICAN CULTURE AND VALUES

Sue and Sue (2003) state that "an American cultural orientation or worldview promotes individualism, competition, material accumulation, nuclear families, religion as distinct from other parts of culture and mastery over nature" (p. 306). This differs from African-centered values in the following ways: the significance of the collective over the individual; kinship and affiliation; extended family; spirituality, connectedness, and harmony with nature; and holistic thinking (Asante, 1987; Parham, 2002a, 2002b).

Many individuals of African descent in America feel kinship or a connection to other African Americans because of a shared history of oppression and discrimination. However, counselors should not assume that all African Americans feel connected to one another. In addition to natural feelings of being linked together for this shared history, there is also a forced collectivism that exists for individuals of African descent in America that comes from the way society as a whole views African Americans. For example, most African Americans understand that if one African American does something negative (e.g., a criminal act) the collective (i.e., African Americans as a group) are judged by this act, especially if the negative act of the Black individual reinforces a stereotype about Black people. Most individuals of African descent understand, even though it is unfair and oppressive, that for racial ethnic minorities in America, the whole group is often judged poorly by the negative acts of a few. This forced collectivistic view impacts the way African Americans are seen as a group in society and does not acknowledge the heterogeneity among African Americans. A summary of general values for individuals of African descent is included in Table 9.1. These values will be expounded upon throughout the chapter.

TABLE 9.1 General Values Associated With Individuals of African Descent

- Collectivism and group consciousness (a group identity)
- Communalism—person-centered versus object-centered
- Care for elderly at home
- Flexible time orientation
- Racial socialization of children (helping children deal with the realities of racism)
- Kinship bonds (relationship bonds with family, extended family, and nonrelatives)
- Spiritual and/or religious orientation
- Harmony and interrelatedness with nature
- Extended family relationships
- Collective child-raising practices (multiple adult and adolescent caregivers may be involved with raising young children)
- Nonrelative familial relationships
- Educational attainment
- Gender egalitarian romantic relationships
- Respect of adult figures by children
- Assertiveness
- Expressiveness in communication style
- The "family business" stays in the family

Families of African Descent

In Boyd-Franklin's extensive work with Black families (Boyd-Franklin, 1989; Boyd-Franklin & Hafer-Bry, 2000) she states that there is no such thing as the typical Black family. As stated previously, from slave times Black families have not been strictly nuclear. Obviously in Africa, children were raised in tribal cultures that did not emphasize the nuclear family as the primary unit. Early models of mental health and family therapy pathologized Black families characterizing them as "disorganized, deprived, disadvantaged kids coming from broken homes" (Boyd-Franklin, 1989, p. 14) and "fatherless homes promoting a matriarchal culture which is abnormal" (Peters, 2007, p. 207). Deficient views of Black families were perpetuated by applying Eurocentric models of family therapy to Black families.

Many Black families are female-led. However, this does not automatically mean that there is no male involved in raising the children (Boyd-Franklin, 1989). Thus, counselors need to be sensitive to the role of many Black women as single parents and Black men who may be involved with their children but not living in the same household. Both roles involve multiple stressors.

Boyd-Franklin (1989) and Boyd-Franklin and Hafer-Bry (2000) suggest a strengths-based approach when working with Black families. This involves assessing a family's strengths and utilizing these strengths in therapy to empower clients. Hill (1972) cites that some of the strengths of Black families include strong kinship bonds, strong work orientation, adaptability, high achievement orientation, and versatility. These represent African-centered values (Boyd-Franklin, 1989) and are coping strategies African decent people have used to survive societal oppression. For example, versatility of family roles grew out of necessity. It is often true that in Black families, older siblings are responsible for helping raise other siblings. Additionally, Peters (2007) states that these roles are not restricted to gender (e.g., an older brother would be as responsible for helping raise younger siblings as an older sister would). In Black families, many of these roles are determined by age and not gender.

Black families often keep generational secrets that are never talked about inside or outside the family. Boyd-Franklin (1989) reports that common family secrets include informal adoptions of children, true parentage of children, unwed pregnancies, a parent who had "trouble" early in life, substance abuse, HIV status, an ancestor who was mentally ill, domestic violence, White relatives, and skin color issues.

Black parents and other adult caregivers often racially socialize Black children whereby they foster a sense of racial pride, teach children about their African American heritage, help the child develop a positive racial identity, and discuss ways in which to deal with racism (Boyd-Franklin, 1989; Cross, 1991; Nagayama-Hall & Barongan, 2002; Peters, 2007). This socialization often serves as a protective function against lowered self-esteem when children face racism. For example, when an African American child comes home and tells his mother of a racist incident at school, the child is less likely to believe that something is wrong with him personally because of this racial socialization.

Black families come in all different skin tones within the same family. As mentioned previously, given that light skin was historically, and continues to be, valued over dark skin in our society, some Black families may have internalized this form of racism. Therefore, caregivers may deliberately or inadvertently choose favorites or scapegoat children based on the darkness or lightness of skin color (Boyd-Franklin, 1989). This may present as a treatment issue in counseling or may be simply related to other treatment issues such as self-esteem or family conflict.

African American parents, especially working-class parents, are more likely than Whites to use physical punishment to discipline their children (Pinderhughes, Dodge, Bates, Pettit, & Zelli, 2000). Unlike with White children, physical punishment has not been found to be associated with more acting out among Black children (Deater-Deckard, Dodge, Bates, & Pettit, 1996). In some Black families, obedience is valued and seen from parent to child as a sign of respect and as an eventual survival skill to be successful in school and future employment (Peters, 2007). Obviously, as with other racial/ethnic groups, level of education and SES influence how families discipline their children. African American families are not an exception. In the clinical realm, physical punishment should be separated from physical abuse and one should not be confused with the other.

In working with Black families, Boyd-Franklin (1989) and Sanders (2007) recommend that counselors be flexible. Because religion and spirituality often play a part in African American family life and child rearing, counselors are encouraged to be aware of and involve community resources in treatment, especially the Black church if the family is religious or spiritual (McAdoo, 2007).

Additionally, counselors should be flexible in their conceptualization of Black families. An assessment of involved extended family and fictive kin (i.e., nonrelatives who are as close and involved in the family as blood relatives) is common (McAdoo, 2007) and should be included in the picture of who a family is. Counselors need to ask who lives in the home and who helps take care of the children, and understand how the multigenerational role of racism, oppression, poverty and victimization, both past and present, impact Black families (Boyd-Franklin, 1989; McAdoo, 2007).

In using a strengths-based approach with Black families, a counselor should emphasize the positive values, support systems, and strengths of that family (Boyd-Franklin, 1989). Counselors should focus on empowering the family to function effectively. This can include restructuring the family so that power is appropriately used to mobilize the family's ability to successfully interact with external systems (Boyd-Franklin, 1989; Boyd-Franklin & Hafer-Bry, 2000).

Common presenting issues of Black families may include finances; blended families; missing father figures; siblings in the same family who have different fathers and different levels of involvement with these fathers; violence; multigenerational role conflict; the negative impact of colorism; and unemployment. Obviously, understanding the social and cultural context of each family is essential to working effectively with individual Black families. Once again, socioeconomic status impacts presenting issues of Black families and their access to community and other resources. The multiculturally competent counselor readily understands issues common to most Black families, is connected to important community resources, uses a strengths-based approach, and views the family through the family's cultural lens. Case Study 9.1 offers an example of how family dynamics may be considered in counseling.

Couples of African Descent

Couples of African descent often have unique challenges to face in addition to the common issues couples of all ethnic backgrounds face. According to Chapman (2007), in 1970, couples headed more than 68% of African American families. Currently, the proportion of African American families headed by couples is 41%. The divorce rate for Black couples is also higher than it is for Whites. For example, Black couples' divorce rate is 23 couples per 100 each year (Chapman, 2007). With Black couples, many predictors of marital dissatisfaction are similar to other groups (e.g., conflicts, affairs, feelings of marital unhappiness). The number of unmarried women has increased across all groups but especially among African American women. According to Wicker and Brodie (2004), this is in part due to the disproportionate number of incarcerated African American men, the growing educational attainment disparities between African American men and women, a high mortality rate of African American men due to homicide, African American men who marry non–African American women, and those African American men who are gay. Marriage trends demonstrate that African American women are less likely to marry than their counterparts of other ethnic groups (Kelly, 2003). Kelly reports that compared to Whites, African Americans report significantly less happiness in their marriages and are less likely to remarry after divorce.

Some issues that are often unique to Black couples include economic problems; unemployment due to the decreasing number of blue-collar jobs available; women making more money than their male partners which may cause conflict between spouses; substance abuse; blended families involving multiple children in the same household with different biological parents; the sex ratio that favors men over women so fewer marriageable men are available (often contributing to a power imbalance in the marital relationship and/or an increased incidence of affairs on the part of the male); internalized racism of one or both partners; and the realities and pressures of daily racism faced by Black couples (Kelly, 2003). These issues can significantly contribute to marital dissatisfaction. On the other hand, strengths of Black couples include the support system often provided by the couples' extended families, the Black church and other Black organizations, the gender egalitarian nature of Black couples, a cultural connectedness often shared by Black couples, and a flexible role orientation within the relationship. Black couples (and individuals) are more likely to seek support from religious leaders than counselors when they begin to experience relationship problems. Therefore, multiculturally sensitive counselors need to consider collaborating with clients' community resources (e.g., church leaders) when working with couples. Additionally, sensitive counselors integrate couples' spiritual belief systems in psychotherapy as this is a strengths-based approach.

CASE STUDY 9.1

Bernadine is a 42-year-old woman of African descent. She has been heavily encouraged to go to counseling by her supervisor at work who maintains that she has an anger problem. Bernadine has been short-tempered and highly irritable at work. She has repeatedly gotten into tense disagreements with colleagues when she feels like they are not showing her respect. Bernadine is one of two African Americans in her office. She works for a Fortune 500 company as a middle-level manager.

She has threatened to sue the company for discrimination because several younger White employees whom she trained have succeeded her into top-level management positions while her ascent to the top has been stalled for several years now. When she has brought this up at work, she was accused of playing the "race card." Bernadine has an MBA from a prestigious university and was recruited 12 years ago directly out of graduate school.

Bernadine's husband of 17 years filed for divorce 6 months ago. The couple has two children aged 10 and 12. Her husband left her for a woman who is not African American.

In your first intake session with Bernadine you find her to be angry at being forced into treatment and hostile toward you, the counselor. Reflect on the following questions:

- How might the history of discrimination of individuals of African descent in the United States be impacting the way this client views her situation? How might this history impact the way others see this client?
- How would you cultivate therapeutic rapport with this client given that she may not be receptive to receiving treatment?
- Pretend you are ethnically different from this client. How would you address this in counseling? When would you address this in counseling?
- What would you hypothesize this client's underlying treatment issue(s) to be?
- What are some possible diagnoses for this client?
- How would you assess this client's racial identity? Level of acculturation?
- What are other things you need to know before beginning treatment with this client?
- How would you assess whether this client's claims of discrimination on her job are accurate?
- How would you go about validating this client's perception of her experiences at work?
- How might there be evidence of resilience for this client?

irrational
↓
Chaos, going to hell,

Interracial Couples

Since the last of the miscegenation laws were repealed in 1967, there has been an increase in the number of interracial and intercultural couples in the United States. Interracial and intercultural couples face unique challenges as well, including lack of support by one or both members' families; the social stigma that continues to exist for those dating or marrying a partner of a different ethnic background; criticism within their own same-race communities; fears about their children's adjustment to a biracial identity; and social pressure from being stared at in public or being socially rejected solely on the basis of their being an interracial couple. Multiculturally competent counselors understand the common issues most couples deal with as well as the unique issues faced by Black couples and interracial couples. These unique issues can have a significant impact on the quality of the couple's relationship.

Children of African Descent

Children of African descent will often face different issues depending on whether they come from middle- or working-class backgrounds and where they reside (e.g., urban, suburban, rural areas). Inner-city children often face issues of poverty, disparity of educational resources, poorer mental and physical health care, temptations of drugs and violence, teen pregnancy, growing up in predominately female-supported households, and fewer community support resources. Middle-class children of African descent, particularly those living in suburban areas, may face difficulty with issues regarding fitting into predominately White environments, feeling isolated from other children of color, being the only person of color in a classroom, having to develop bicultural skills enabling them to fit into all-Black and all-White environments, parental divorce, growing up in predominately female-supported households, and feelings of not being "Black enough" or "White enough" depending on their social environments (Day-Vines, Patton, & Baytops, 2003). When working with children of African descent, multiculturally competent counselors are aware of several issues, including racial identity; problems children might face given their school, home, and social environments; and how racism impacts normal developmental challenges children face. Effective counselors are aware of available culturally appropriate community resources for children and their families. Counselors also are open to including significant community members (e.g., one's minister) in a child's treatment if therapeutically indicated and if parental permission is given.

Black Middle-Class Persons and Mental Health

Sue and Sue (2003) report that more than one third of the African American population is middle class. Middle-class African Americans often face different issues than working-class African Americans (Day-Vines et al., 2003). For example, middle-class African Americans are more likely to have to operate biculturally, that is, in both all-Black and all-White environments. This can be very stressful, especially for children and adolescents who are just learning the implications for being Black in predominately White environments. Middle-class Blacks who are isolated from the Black community may experience symptoms of depression and guilt for "making it" (i.e., "survivor guilt") when others in the Black community have not (Boyd-Franklin, 1989; Conner-Edwards & Spurlock, 1988; Day-Vines et al., 2003). This conflict can be stressful and it has an impact on mental health. Thus, social class can obviously have a distinct impact on the presenting treatment issues of clients of African descent. Counselors need to assess and understand how social class interacts with and affects Black clients' treatment issues and experiences with discrimination.

Across all socioeconomic levels, institutionalized racism increases psychological distress for African Americans. Klonoff, Landrine, and Ullman (1999) report that racial discrimination is a strong predictor of psychological symptoms, in general, and somatization and anxiety, in particular, while Williams and Williams-Morris (2000) found a relationship between internalized racism and alcohol consumption, psychological distress, depression, and lower self-esteem. In sum, Wicker and Brodie (2004) state that Blacks experience mental illness proportional to that of Whites, but the contributing factors may be different. Clearly, regardless of SES, the psychological and physical effects of racial discrimination are damaging. Counselors should assess the impact of discrimination on their African decent clients' lives.

Gender

African American men and women often bring different treatment issues into the therapeutic realm. Obviously, environmental influences impact these issues. In the authors' individual therapy practice settings, some presenting issues of Black women include single parenthood, weight, skin color, self-esteem, depression, anxiety, parenting issues, economic struggles, perceived lack of available same-race romantic male partners, childhood sexual abuse, domestic violence, inappropriate use of anger as a defense, relational mistrust, and emotional intimacy issues. Presenting issues for men of African descent may include formation of a Black male identity in a society that fears and rejects Black men as "problem people," absent or distant relationships with father figures, self-esteem, economic struggles, domestic and other violence, relational mistrust, emotional intimacy issues, depression, anxiety, and substance abuse.

These issues are negatively influenced by Black men being perceived as threatening or dangerous in our society, and Black women being perceived as angry and unapproachable. These stereotypes of Black men and women can be internalized by Black men and women themselves. Internalization of these stereotypes serves as an impediment to healthy relationships. Additionally, counselors who hold these stereotypic views of Black men and women are ineffective and often harmful in their work with clients of African descent.

Black Elderly Individuals

As a whole, Black elderly people in the United States often face issues of poverty, poor mental and physical health care, illiteracy, gender discrepancies (e.g., Black elderly women far outnumber Black elderly men), employment discrimination, social and physical isolation, disability, and grief and bereavement issues (Rayle & Myers, 2003). Some of these issues are identical to those faced by elderly individuals as a whole in the United States. However, a higher percentage of Black elderly persons than White elderly individuals are poor. Normal developmental aging issues are complicated by the interplay of poverty and racial discrimination. Issues faced by Black elderly Americans will vary as a function of an individual's SES, health, and familial and community support. As with all subgroups within the Black community, multiculturally competent counselors are aware of economic, social, emotional, and spiritual resources in the community that can be helpful to this population. Counselors also attend to any negative stereotypes or assumptions they have about this client population.

Black Gays and Lesbians

Robinson and Howard-Hamilton (2000) state that "African American gay men and lesbians encounter homophobia within their racial communities and racism within the White gay community" (p. 137). Thus, gay and lesbian African Americans often deal with multiple sources of oppression and discrimination. They may feel conflicts in allegiances (i.e., allegiance to the Black community or allegiance to the gay community), struggle to integrate different aspects of their identities (e.g., being an individual of African descent, being a woman, and being a lesbian), and feel the pressure to hide their gay identity from friends and family. Additionally, many African Americans hold a religious orientation and many conservative Black churches do not support gays and lesbians. This is often a painful experience for those gays and lesbians who look to the Black church for social support and spiritual guidance, and may increase the likelihood that they face discrimination in their own communities and families. Dealing with multiple sources of oppression can be extremely stressful. When working with gay and lesbian clients of African descent, it is important to assess whether identity conflict (e.g., issues as a Black person, a gay person, or both) are relevant to the presenting treatment issue in therapy. Finally, as with all other client populations, multiculturally competent counselors are aware of relevant community resources and are aware of their own negative assumptions about the client population in which they are working.

GENERAL MENTAL HEALTH ISSUES OF AFRICAN DESCENT INDIVIDUALS

> In exploring the physical and mental health needs of Blacks counselors must have an understanding of the environment and context in which African Americans exist and how environmental factors can affect their expression, interpretation, and prevalence rates of physical and mental illness. (Wicker & Brodie, 2004, p. 105)

Wicker and Brodie (2004) provide an excellent overview of many of the common physical and mental health issues individuals of African descent in America face. In brief, some common health issues are diabetes, heart disease, HIV/AIDS, prostate cancer, higher infant mortality rates, substance abuse, sickle cell anemia, lead poisoning, and teen pregnancy. As mentioned previously, lower-SES

African Americans are more likely to receive poorer health care and not have health insurance. Many of these physical illnesses have an impact on the development of psychological disorders as well.

Additionally, Wicker and Brodie (2004) find that African Americans are disproportionately represented in the lower-SES group and research indicates that there is a correlation between SES and diagnosed mental health disorders. Among African Americans and Whites, Ostrove, Feldman, and Adler (1999) found more depressive symptoms among individuals from lower SES than among those with higher levels of education, wealth, and income. Higher rates of mental illness often go hand in hand with poverty, rates of violence, and little attention to mental health treatment. Additionally, there remains a negative social stigma within the African American community around mental illness and treatment for mental illnesses (Wicker & Brodie II, 2004). As a result, African Americans may underutilize mental health services, may seek them out only in times of crisis, and may be more severe once attaining treatment. African Americans are more likely to be misdiagnosed and to drop out of treatment earlier than their White counterparts (Cornelius, Fabrega, Cornelius, Mezzich, & Maher, 1996). Additionally, African Americans are more likely to express their psychological symptoms in a physical form. Thus, they may seek medical treatment for physical complaints when they are actually suffering from psychological issues, leaving the psychological issues untreated (Adebimpe, 1981).

Disorders such as depression, anxiety, posttraumatic stress, and schizophrenia are seen in the African American community at similar rates as with Whites, even though misdiagnosis may be common (see Chapter 17 for a detailed discussion). However, it is important to recognize cultural influences on symptom presentation as well as understanding that racism, blatant or institutional, can be a significant contributing factor to feelings of depression and anxiety even if the client does not recognize it. For example, depressed Black women may present with feelings of irritability or physical complaints, opening the door to misdiagnosis.

As discussed at the beginning of this chapter, the Black community faces some uniquely negative environmental influences that impact Blacks' mental health. This might include higher unemployment rates, education and occupation deficits, more grief and bereavement issues, higher rates of incarceration for Black men, higher rates of violence in urban communities, single-parent status and economic hardships, the unavailability of same-race male partners for Black women, poverty, and lower educational attainment (Wicker & Brodie, 2004). These environmental issues most certainly influence the presentation of psychological issues in Black clients, and these factors are heavily influenced by socioeconomic status. For example, middle-class African Americans may not experience poverty but they may be more likely to encounter institutionalized racism in the form of "glass ceilings" at work. Given the relationship between psychological issues and environmental stressors due to race and cultural difference, complete Reflection 9.2 to begin considering how to address these in counseling.

REFLECTION 9.2

How might counselors of non-African descent address issues of racial and cultural differences with clients of African descent? Write some ideas below.

_____

_____

_____

_____

COMMON SUPPORT SYSTEMS FOR INDIVIDUALS OF AFRICAN DESCENT

Taylor, Hardison, and Chatters (1996) write that "almost 85% of African Americans have described themselves as 'fairly religious' or 'very religious' and that prayer is among their most common coping responses" (p. 299). Therefore, a common support system for many clients of African descent will include "spiritually directed activities (e.g., involvement in Black churches or Mosques). Spirituality and religion play an important role in the lives of many Black families and individuals and help combat societal oppression and increase economic support" (p. 299). Participation in religious activities allows for opportunities for self-expression, leadership, and community involvement. Counselors should elicit and encourage use of spiritual resources (Boyd-Frankin, 1989; Boyd-Frankin & Hafer-Bry, 2000).

Other support systems include Black organizations, such as fraternities and sororities, or the National Association for the Advancement of Colored People (NAACP); extended family; Sister Circles, which are social groups for Black women whose sole purpose is to provide one another with emotional and spiritual support; Brotherhood opportunities, which are social experiences for Black men that provide connection to and support of Black men; and activities for children (e.g., sports, music). Activity 9.1 describes a method for accessing these support systems in counseling.

ACTIVITY 9.1

In small groups, develop a list of questions or areas for exploration that could be used when counseling individuals and families of African descent to identify and strengthen support systems.

AN AFROCENTRIC PSYCHOLOGICAL PERSPECTIVE

Earlier in this chapter we discussed and shaped an argument for and about the uniqueness of the life experience of people of African descent in America. Even with these elaborated differences, it is not clear, nor has it been definitively established, that there exists a need to have counseling techniques that are designed specifically for this group of people and its subgroups. However, Afrocentric psychotherapies are supportive and sensitive to the cultural values of African decent peoples. These psychotherapies can be utilized as a primary treatment modality or as an adjunct to other modes of treatment. Therefore, this section of the chapter will briefly explore Afrocentric therapeutic approaches and theory as well as some traditional (Eurocentric) models of counseling with clients of African descent.

Much of the critical thinking in this area has centered on the inadequacies of Western psychological principles and techniques for understanding and treating individuals of African descent (Parham, White, & Ajamu, 2000). Equally, many African descent scholars have focused their attention on or around the concepts underlying the empowerment of African Americans to incorporate positive thoughts of themselves and their communities into their self-concepts—for example, Black is beautiful, I'm Black and I'm proud, the Black 100 (Parham et al., 2000). The goal of these interventions endeavors to bring about individual and collective empowerment, and to support a client's positive self-image, sense of self-respect, client growth, and healthier emotional functioning.

NTU Psychotherapy

An Afrocentric approach to psychotherapy developed by Phillips (1990) is described as "spiritually based and aims to assist people and systems to become authentic and balanced within a shared energy and essence that is in alignment with natural order"(p. 55). Phillips states that NTU (pronounced "in-too") is a Bantu (central African) concept that describes a universal, unifying force that touches upon all aspects of existence including a spiritual force inside an individual and a spiritual force outside the individual. It focuses on the essence of one's life. The basic principles of NTU psychotherapy include harmony, balance, interconnectedness, cultural awareness, and authenticity, which are all Afrocentric values.

Counseling is considered to be a healing process based on a spiritual relationship between the client and counselor (healer). The counselor assists the client to rediscover his or her own natural alignment. Phillips (1990) states that there are five phases of NTU psychotherapy: Harmony, Awareness, Alignment, Actualize, and Synthesis. These phases of treatment are considered in a circular rather than linear time frame such that they may occur simultaneously or even "out of sequence." The goal of treatment is to assist people and systems to become harmonious, balanced, and authentic within a shared energy and essence that is in alignment with the natural order. An additional goal is to help the client function within the guidelines of the Nguzo Saba (the seven principles of Kwanzaa).

Natural order is described as a unity of mind, body, and spirit throughout life. Relationships within one's life are purposeful and orderly and, at their base, spiritual. Further, Phillips (1990) asserts that natural order infers that our lives and our relationships have a purpose and a direction. Consequently, it is our ongoing task in life to be in tune with the natural order.

In NTU counseling, the counselor's role is to assist the client to reestablish harmony. This implies a shared responsibility between the client and the counselor which is generally contrary to the more traditional approaches of doing therapy whereby the client assumes most of the responsibility for his or her own treatment process. While NTU also emphasizes the special nature of the relationship between the counselor and client, it also encourages counselors to more clearly explore their own connections with the client. Counselors (healers) are encouraged to use their intuition and inspiration as a part of the therapeutic experience. This kind of exploration is not pathologized as in the concept of Freudian countertransference, nor is it diminished as in client-centered therapy.

Pros and Cons of Traditional (Eurocentric) Counseling Approaches With Clients of African Descent

The next section of this chapter will briefly review client-centered, psychodynamic, and Adlerian psychotherapy approaches. The utility of using these approaches with African American clients will be explored. Reflection 9.3 challenges the reader to consider how these may be applied in counseling.

REFLECTION 9.3

In reviewing the key characteristics of the three traditional counseling approaches presented here, consider how you could apply concretely techniques and assumptions from these approaches when counseling individuals and families of African descent.

Client-Centered Counseling

The primary characteristic of this treatment modality is its focus on the relationship between the counselor and the client and how client change is facilitated through the development of the therapeutic relationship. These conditions include genuineness, congruence, positive regard, acceptance of the client, and empathic understanding. The therapeutic process moves a client from a place of rigidity, remoteness from feelings and experience and distance from other people, toward fluidity, acceptance of feelings and experiences, and unity and integration of one's self. This approach's ultimate goal of client self-acceptance is consistent with the African worldview (i.e., unity and integration).

With the African descent client, client-centered counseling has utility especially with regard to helping set or create conditions in which the client may feel comfortable and supported within a counseling relationship. All of this is accomplished by developing rapport and being empathic with and understanding and nonjudgmental of clients. By setting these conditions, it is then possible for clients to begin the process of exploring their own problems.

A limitation of this approach is its idea that the intent to promote growth by the counselor seems to suggest a hierarchical relationship that is more consistent with a European rather than an African worldview. Further, this appears to suggest that the client lacks, in some basic way, an understanding of self or the concept of harmony and unity which is inherent in the African worldview. Finally, the focus remains solely on the individual, primarily without any focus upon the connection to others as a part of the concept of self which is rooted in a connection or existence within a community. In an African worldview, the concept of the individual exists within the context of community (unity), and harmony or balance within the larger universe structure. This concept brings to mind the Akan proverb "I am because we are, we are because I am."

Psychodynamic Counseling

Psychodynamic theory focuses on the individual and not the community. The idea of individualism is also expressed in that the change process is dependent upon the work or effort of the individual undergoing treatment. Mental processes are considered to be largely unconscious. Psychoanalysis believes that impulses, which are described as sexual, cause nervous and mental disorders (Freud, 1924). These general principles are inconsistent with an Afrocentric framework.

In Hall's (2004) review of the book *Psychotherapy with African American Women* (Jackson & Greene, 2000) she acknowledges some of the benefits (e.g., capacity to deal with the individual and multiple complexities of their lives, focuses on early childhood experiences and their impact on client functioning in later life) and limitations associated with psychodynamic psychotherapy with an African descent populations. The primary limitation discussed is the lack of attention to cultural factors. In particular, the authors assert that theories and treatment approaches need to be reformulated to acknowledge the effects that racial and class stereotypes— legacies of slavery, present-day racism, African or Caribbean cultural influences, and gender-based maltreatment—have on the psychological life of women and the interplay between these factors and the individual Black woman's intrapsychic world. Exploration of these factors needs to be encouraged and understood in the context of the therapeutic dyad. Other shortcomings of traditional psychodynamic theories include a tendency to pathologize cultural differences, the limited experience of many analysts with African descent women patients, the authoritarian style of the analyst with respect to the client, heterosexism, and the likelihood of racial attitudes of White therapists that have not been addressed in their own therapy (Jackson & Greene, 2000).

Adlerian Counseling

According to Perkins-Dock (2005), the Adlerian approach focuses upon social interest as an organizing principle. This approach explores an individual's social nature during interactions and the influences of the social environment on development. Thus, the Adlerian approach is thought to be respectful of individual and cultural heritage. Inherent in the approach is attention to cultural factors on development and presenting treatment issues. The theoretical principles of this approach appear conducive to therapeutic work with African descent clients. These principles include the concept of collective unity and social interest, importance of family atmosphere, emphasis on collaborative goal setting, influence of multigenerational legacy, and flexibility of intervention strategies. Collective unity and social interest consists of working toward fitting in within the community, contributing to the community, and supporting the cultural value system of many Blacks.

The family atmosphere concept emphasizes harmony in interpersonal relationships, interdependence, and mutual obligation for creating harmony and peace. It focuses on cooperation and the goals of therapy are chosen collaboratively. Finally, Perkins-Dock (2005) asserts that Adlerian counseling is congruent with many traditional beliefs of African descent people and offers flexibility within the range of interventions that it is able to offer.

Clearly, there is some utility in the use of traditional counseling approaches with clients of African descent. However, the treatment outcome research has been somewhat equivocal. For example, according to Friedman, Paradis, and Hatch (1994) cognitive behavioral therapy has been found to be effective for African Americans and Whites in the treatment of anxiety disorders. Lichtenberg, Kimbarow, Morris, and Vangel (1996) found behavioral treatment generally effective for a sample of older Black medical patients. However, Chambless and Williams (1995) found that Blacks were less responsive to cognitive treatment for agoraphobia. Thus, multiculturally competent counselors are aware of the current literature on the effectiveness of treatment approaches for the population for which they are providing therapy and do not assume that "one therapy fits all" when working with clients of African descent.

GUIDELINES FOR WORK WITH CLIENTS OF AFRICAN DESCENT

The ideal or "gold standard" for counselors is to be trained in an African-centered worldview counseling system and to employ the theory and techniques of that system when working with African descent clients. The belief in the values espoused by this worldview system could be employed by African descent and non-African descent therapists alike.

Practitioners who continue to use European worldview counseling systems and techniques with clients of African descent must become aware of the limitations of these systems related to treatment efficacy. Case Study 9.2 provides a clinical example of culturally centered practice with a family of African descent.

Pedersen and Ivey (1993) make the following suggestions to counselors to help facilitate client investment in the therapeutic process.

1. Establish a collaborative working relationship.
   a. Provide the client with a brief explanation of the treatment, how it works, and how you generally interact with clients.
   b. Offer the client the opportunity to express how he or she typically likes to talk or interact with others to help guide your decisions about how to engage the client in the therapeutic relationship.
   c. Communicate openly and honestly to facilitate the client reciprocating the same behavior.
   d. Bring yourself into the therapeutic encounter by exposing and expressing your humanity within the therapeutic encounter. Appropriate self-disclosure on your part can often humanize the therapeutic relationship.

2. Facilitate awareness through the use of clinical skills and techniques.
   a. You must exhibit a desire to work hard to assist the client on the journey.
   b. In particular, you must show a desire to tackle difficult topics including race and gender issues and biases.
   c. Acknowledge and/or use culturally congruent techniques such as prayer, exploration of folk beliefs, and rituals within sessions.
3. Continually assess.
   a. Hypothesize and reconstruct your thoughts and feelings about the client and his or her situation throughout a session and the therapeutic process. The seeds for hypotheses are the thoughts, feelings, and spirit (intuition) of therapy. Formal psychological testing may also be beneficial in this area.
4. Use goal development and planning.
   a. Work with your client to determine what he or she desires to work on in therapy. Work with your client to create a process upon which he or she can rely in order to achieve cognitive, emotional, or spiritual goals.
5. Implement and evaluate strategies.
   a. Assist the client to evaluate the efficacy of his or her coping strategies related to cognitive, emotional, and intuitive factors.
   b. Maintain balance in evaluating the efficacy of coping skill strategies.
   c. Alter or change ineffective coping strategies to meet the need for balance.
   d. Evaluate the coping process and strategies relative to the cognitive or emotional need expressed in goal setting.

CASE STUDY 9.2

The following is a case example taken from one of the authors' professional practice.

Mr. M. called my office to set up an appointment for his son. He admits that no one in his family has ever sought the help of a mental health professional. He seems at a loss on what to do. His son had recently seen a psychiatrist who had prescribed an antidepressant medication the previous week. In communicating with Mr. M., I noted that he spoke English with an accent.

At the first session, I met with the 15-year-old identified client and his parents, Mr. and Mrs. M. The three older female children in the family did not attend the session. While the son waited outside, I spoke with the parents about their concerns. Mrs. M. was an energetic African American female who expressed her concern that her son is depressed and had seemingly been going down hill for several months since entering high school. She noted that he had always been somewhat reserved with few friends, but things had gotten worse since beginning high school even though he had a girlfriend. His grades were dropping at school, he seemed sad, and now he was talking about suicide.

She stated she had a close relationship with her son, tried to talk with him all the time about how he was doing, but she did not really know what was bothering him. Mr. M. stated he was concerned about his son as well. Mr. M. indicated that he was very concerned about his son's grades at school and how poor grades would limit his options in life. Mr. M. stated he was helping his son with his homework and with studying, but that this was not helping at the high school level even though in grade school it had made a positive difference.

Mr. M. noted that he had grown up poor in West Africa and that education had been a way out of that situation for him and to the United States. He did not have any idea why his son might be depressed because he had so much more than what Mr. M. had had as a child. However, he did speculate that his son's relationship with his girlfriend, who was Asian, may be a part of the problem as her father did not like her dating someone Black. Mr. M. did not understand why his son would put himself in such a position knowing that it was against the wishes of the girlfriend's father. He also felt that his wife supported the son remaining in the relationship even though he hoped his son would leave it.

Throughout the conversation, the son (Reginald) sat passively listening to his parents and completing paperwork. He did not interject or overtly disagree with anything that either of his parents stated about him or his situation when they were speaking about him. When asked about these things in their presence, he acknowledged that he had been depressed but he did not know why and that he was having trouble at school.

At this point, I then discussed with Reginald and his parents the limits to confidentiality. Included in this discussion were limits related to suicidal/homicidal ideation. We agreed on issues that his parents wanted to be directly informed of, such as drugs, suicide, or violence. But outside of these stated issues, I allowed Reginald to discuss his concerns with me without having to report everything back to his parents. Both Reginald and his parents acknowledged their understanding of these limitations to confidentiality.

Mr. and Mrs. M. were asked to wait outside while the counselor and Reginald spoke. He was a very quiet, soft-spoken, and reserved young man who was passive in his presentation. His posture, facial expression, and body language suggested a person who was sad, but his verbal responses seemed incongruent with his presentation. Although he said "I don't know" often, intuitively I felt that such statements were inaccurate. Instead, it felt like he was being somewhat evasive. When talking about his girlfriend, he did not appear to have any joy, but he stated she was the only thing good in his life. When asked how he felt about his girlfriend's father disliking him because he is Black without ever having met him, he acknowledged that it was dumb, but did not indicate any strong emotional reaction to this situation. When explored further with him, I introduced emotion-laden words such as *hurt* and *angry*. He stated he "guessed" he felt a little angry about it because the father did not know him personally and just assumed he was dumb and a "thug with baggy pants." He also stated that it bothered him because he could not see or talk to her when her father was in town because of the father's reaction to the relationship. He denied being close to his family and stated he did not care for his eldest sister because she was mean to him. He stated that he and his best male friend were no longer close because the friend would not come over to his house anymore. Reginald stated that his best friend seemed to have made other friends outside their relationship. He denied any plans for suicide, but stated he'd rather be dead if he couldn't be with his girlfriend. He indicated that his goal for therapy was to feel better, but he did not know what that meant to him.

Within this initial session, some of the culture-centered counseling techniques were implemented. However, it should be clear from the case description that the use of these ideas, concepts, and techniques provide for some subtle rather than overt differences in treatment at this initial stage. Examples of culture-centered practices in the session include:

1. Establishing that counseling is a collaborative process involving—in this case, the identified patient, the counselor, and the family. If necessary, others could be brought into the process, including friends, siblings, and school personnel, and other members of the community (e.g., minister).

2. Exploring the problem or issue as existing with the family system (e.g., client and his parents) and not just as a problem of the individual. Probing the parents led to an understanding of the family structure and the fact that the family has a complex primary cultural history (African father, African American mother) that impacts child-rearing practices. For example, Mr. M. is primarily focused on his son's educational development and seems to perceive other issues as secondary. It will be important in future sessions for Mr. M. to understand that he can help his son develop a greater cognitive and emotional balance in his life which involves an emotional focus. In addition, future sessions might explore differences between the parents in child-rearing practices. This might, in part, account for Reginald's imbalanced relationships with his parents. This can be accomplished in a meeting with the parents either together with Reginald or separately. Parental involvement will be maintained in treatment both formally and informally. Often informal involvement occurs before or after sessions via simple acknowledgments of client progress, parental concerns, and so on.

3. Communicating openly and honestly. The discussion of confidentiality especially as it relates to the relationship between myself and Reginald, as well as my relationship with his parents, is respectful and sets the tone for our work together. Speaking with the parents about concerns that Reginald might communicate in counseling exhibits this concept. This kind of openness empowers Reginald to feel free to discuss what he feels he needs to talk about in therapy or limit it as well, but the end result is he actively makes choices for himself and his own treatment.

4. Setting goals collaboratively. Although the responsibility for establishing goals resides with Reginald and what he decides might help him feel better, my role as counselor will assist him to achieve his goals.

5. Assessing "the problem." Assessment is ongoing and is informed by what is said within session, my observation of him, my emotional reactions to him, and my intuition or felt sense. In this session, my intuition or felt sense overtly informed my belief about his level of depression as well as the depth of the problem, even though it appeared that Reginald was minimizing it.

6. Allowing the ebb and flow of the session to be organic. There was no overt time limit imposed on the time spent with the parents, the client, or on discussing a particular topic. The exploration occurred in such a fashion as to be thorough enough that any topic change felt like a natural progression. Topics were explored enough to be satisfactory, but not belabored. The focus of the session was not technique driven. Instead, my approach utilized the skills necessary and appropriate for Reginald's situation and presenting issues.

7. Focusing ongoing treatment on the continued development of the relationship with Reginald and his family. The process of assessing and exploring Reginald in his cultural context will continue and he will be assisted in becoming more aware of his own wants, needs, and desires as well as how they may interact and impact his emotional well-being. The organic flow of this exploration will lead to more concrete examples of when his emotional needs are met, when they are not, and how the choices that he makes in a variety of situations impact that process. Future sessions will help him explore and process "instances of success" (i.e., when he had his emotional needs met and the process that occurred to accomplish this goal). Subsequently, this process will be explored for its utility in how he can make empowering choices for himself. A goal of therapy might be to help Reginald evaluate the efficacy of his own therapeutic process throughout treatment. Ultimately, my hope for this client is that he can accomplish better emotional balance (well-being).

Summary

This chapter has explored historical and current influences of African descent people's experiences in America, cultural values of this diverse group, racial identity and acculturation, and common issues faced by Black children, men, women, and other subpopulations within the Black community. This review has some important implications for counseling practice.

The role of the counselor for African American clients may need to be broader than with White clients. For example, African American clients may need help in dealing with agencies and making connections to the community. Multiculturally competent counselors are to bring up differences in background; explore feelings about coming to counseling and how it will be beneficial to them as clients; explore the clients' worldview; establish egalitarian therapeutic relationships that can be helped with self-disclosure; assess assets of clients, such as support systems, family, community resources, church; explore external factors that might be related to the presenting problem; not dismiss racism as "just an excuse"; and help clients define goals and problem-solving solutions.

Neville and Walters (2004) discuss the harmful effects of counselors employing a color-blind racial ideology, which is a "set of beliefs that serves to minimize, ignore, or distort the existence of race and racism" (p. 95). At its core is the belief that racism is a thing of the past and that race and racism no longer play a significant role in current social and economic realities. This is obviously a harmful worldview in working with this population because it is invalidating and dismissive of clients' experiences. Therefore, in counseling clients of African descent, recognizing, acknowledging, and honoring a client's ethnic and cultural background is an important rapport-building tool for an effective therapeutic relationship.

Multiculturally competent counselors also understand that clients of African descent may display cultural mistrust toward counselors. Effective counselors do not pathologize or personalize this mistrust. Instead they understand where this mistrust comes from and how it develops. They acknowledge it and discuss it openly in therapy.

Boyd-Franklin (1989) discusses the importance of explaining to clients of African descent what counseling is, and what boundaries of relationship are, and

---

TABLE 9.2 Media Resources of the Individual and Family of African Descent

The Color of Fear (1994)
The Way Home (1998)
The Birth of a Nation (1915)
Rosewood (1997)
The Color Purple (1985)
CNN Presents: Blacks in America (2008)
Remember the Titans (2000)
Shaft (1971)
Glory (1989)
American History X (1998)
Higher Learning (1995)
School Daze (1998)
Malcolm X (1992)
Guess Who's Coming to Dinner (1967)
The Great Debaters (2007)
To Kill a Mockingbird (1962)

engaging in thoughtful informed-consent procedures with clients. She states that for Black clients, counseling can be seen as intrusive and cautions counselors not to use first names with older clients as it might be seen as disrespectful. The multiculturally competent counselor asks clients what they would like to be called. Finally, African American clients may prefer African American counselors. Thus, if a client has a racial preference for a counselor and it is possible to meet that client's need, every attempt should be made to do so. Not all clients of African descent will have a same-race counselor preference, but some will.

This chapter has reviewed some of the relevant history and current experiences of African decent people in the United States. Table 9.2 provides examples in popular media that counselors and counselor trainees may want to explore to better understand the experiences of clients of African descent.

CHAPTER 10

Individuals and Families of Arab Descent

Sylvia C. Nassar-McMillan, Laura McLaughlin Gonzalez, and Rasha H. Mohamed

PREVIEW

Who are Arab Americans, anyway? There are many more answers to this question since the New York City Twin Towers tragedy of September 11, 2001, an event that unwittingly seemed to catapult this population into the public eye. This chapter will help you determine the accuracy of your perceptions about Arab Americans. Despite their educational, professional, and economic successes over the past 100+ years, Arab Americans have had a somewhat turbulent immigration history in the United States. Although the population number is estimated by leading advocacy groups at over 3 million, research on mental health and counseling, particularly within the post-9/11 context, has only recently begun to emerge.

In this chapter, key issues about historic and geographic descriptions of the Arab Middle East, as well as immigration history from that region, will be addressed. Sociopolitical aspects of the Arab American experience will be explored next, along with diversity among the population. Cultural characteristics, such as collectivism, religion and faith, socioeconomic demographics, and communication styles will be explored, followed by acculturation and identity development from a current-day perspective. The final sections of this chapter will address mental health issues and guidelines for counseling Arab Americans and include case studies to illustrate the points presented.

ARAB AMERICAN HETEROGENEITY

For many people in the United States, terms like *Arab* or *Middle Eastern* are associated with a complex mix of images and impressions, but few facts. Efforts to clarify the boundaries and contents of these terms are necessary for counseling students who seek to increase their multicultural competence. Although there is not one comprehensive definition of the Middle East or its Arab citizens, the following perspectives should alleviate some of the confusion.

The region centered around the Persian Gulf became known to English-speakers as "the Middle East" or the "Near Orient" in the early 1900s (Said, 1978). Its central position made it a crossroads of strategic importance and thus a coveted geographic region. Centuries of important historical events have occurred in the **Middle East**, one of the earliest cradles of civilization. It is also an area rich in religious history and symbolism, with cities such as Jerusalem and Mecca within its boundaries. Some of the religious groups coexisting in the Middle East include Muslims, Christians, Jews, Bah'ai, and the Druze. Such a confluence of political and spiritual activity has meant that the Middle East holds great diversity in a relatively small area. It encompasses both Arab-speaking and non-Arab-speaking countries; examples of the latter include Iran (where Farsi is spoken), Turkey, and Israel (Hakim-Larson & Nassar-McMillan, 2008; Nassar-McMillan, 2003).

Thus, all citizens of the Middle East are not Arabs. People who trace their ancestry to the Kurds, Berbers, or Chaldeans, for example, are not considered to be Arabs (Nassar-McMillan, in press). Geographically, **Arabs** are persons who have ancestral ties to the Saudi Arabian peninsula and historically have practiced Islam (Abudabbeh & Aseel, 1999).

About 80% of Arabs in the Middle East are **Muslim**, so these categories are not completely overlapping (Nassar-McMillan, 2003). In addition, the majority of the Muslims in the world reside outside the Middle East, so it is inaccurate to consider Arab and Muslim to be synonymous. The common use of the Arabic language has been another way to indicate Arab people; however, this strategy is not without its problems. Arabs can also be described in varying ways in terms of race or skin color, so it is more appropriate to consider Arab an ethnic or cultural category (Hakim-Larson & Nassar-McMillan, 2008). In this chapter, **Arab American** is used to mean any individual who defines himself or herself as part of that ethnic group and has heritage linked to the League of Arab States. Because not all countries in the *geographic* Middle East self-define as "Arab" (e.g., Turkey, Afghanistan), many contemporary scholars, ourselves included, define those as being of Arab descent originating from the **Arab Middle East**.

The **League of Arab States** was founded in 1945 (Haynes, 2002). Currently, these 22 states include Algeria, Bahrain, Comoros, Djibouti, Egypt, Iraq, Jordan, Kuwait, Lebanon, Libya, Mauritania, Morocco, Oman, Palestine, Qatar, Saudi Arabia, Somalia, Sudan, Syria, Tunisia, United Arab Emirates, and Yemen (Nassar-McMillan, 2003). These are sometimes grouped into the Gulf states (such as Kuwait, Saudi Arabia, and Oman), Greater Syria (including Iraq and Lebanon), and the area of North Africa referred to as the Maghreb (Egypt, Libya, and Morocco, among others). There are some Arab-speaking countries that are not part of the Arab League, however. This intercontinental alliance again points to the diversity of the Arab world, with some countries having significant Western influence (e.g., Lebanon) and other countries being fairly isolated from such influence (e.g., Sudan or Yemen). Dialect of spoken Arabic, cultural and religious traditions, political history, and geography are all dimensions along which the Arab League countries may differ.

Subject to colonialism over the past several centuries by multiple Western entities, the Arab Middle East has faced a variety of pressures. Although the United States is currently the most powerful Western country attempting to wield influence in the Arab Middle East, both Britain and France have historically held colonies and swayed policy in the region (Said, 1978). Some of the borders that are disputed today were dictated at the end of World War I when the Ottoman Empire was carved up by the victorious allies. Although this political history can be complex, it takes on increased importance in light of the current struggles among Western powers and various religious, ethnic, and cultural groups that populate the Arab Middle East. Misunderstandings, conflicts, and wars have contributed to the flow of Arab refugees and immigrants that now populate the United States and may seek out counseling services.

Arabs have arrived in the United States in four distinct waves of immigration. Each group had different reasons for immigrating, different characteristics, and different experiences in their host or adopted country. The first group of immigrants came primarily from Lebanon, Syria, Palestine, and Jordan at the end of the 19th century and beginning of the 20th century (Abudabbeh, 1996; Naff, 1994; Orfalea, 1988). Most of them were Christians who wanted to escape the Islamic Ottoman Empire. They tended to be uneducated laborers with little in the way of material resources. Upon arrival, they maintained their communities by settling in ethnic enclaves in various cities in the

United States. Their religion allowed them to settle into Christian-influenced areas with fewer challenges than later Muslim immigrants would face (Faragallah, Schumm, & Webb, 1997).

The second group of Arab immigrants arrived after World War II (Abudabbeh, 1996). These individuals were fleeing their homelands due to political tensions, such as the Palestinians who were escaping civil war in 1948 as the British Mandate in the area expired and territories were seized by Israel. This wave also included Syrians, Jordanians, Egyptians, and Iraqis, and to a lesser extent Yemenis and Lebanese. Some have called this the **Brain Drain** (Orfalea, 1988) because those who left were educated Muslims with the means to escape undesirable situations.

The third wave of immigrants was also comprised predominantly of educated Muslims, this group searching for better lives as part of the American Dream. Immigration restrictions had been eased in the 1960s and thus it was easier to take advantage of the opportunity. Many of the people arriving at this time were Palestinians who wanted to escape the Israeli occupation (Abudabbeh, 1996; Orfalea, 1988).

Finally, the Persian Gulf War created a situation where refugees had very few options left and were compelled to flee. This group included Iraqis, for example, who worked with the United States in their war efforts in the region and were facing harsh consequences for that choice. Renewed conflict in the region is likely to lead more Iraqi refugees to the United States, but this possibility has not been well documented because of its recency (Cainkar, 2002; Nassar-McMillan & Hakim-Larson, 2003).

In sum, Arab Americans have come from a variety of backgrounds and have made their homes in the United States at varying times and for varying reasons. The history, culture, and religion of the country of origin may continue to influence Arabs in their new communities, but it is also possible to meet a fourth-generation Arab American for whom this country is his or her only frame of reference. In terms of U.S. Census categories, the largest group of people of Arab descent are from Lebanon, followed numerically by Syria, Egypt, Palestine, Morocco, and Iraq. Estimates are that there are approximately 3 million Arab Americans, although census data has not always reflected a category to distinguish this group (Arab American Institute, n.d.).

Readers who have spent less time learning about the community of Arab descent in the United States may at times feel surprise (as described in Reflection 10.1) as they uncover individuals and groups that they did not know were Arab American. If this describes you, take advantage of the opportunity presented in Activity 10.1 to discover more of these "hidden" famous people who are Arab American. Readers who are already building from some knowledge base may benefit more from Reflection 10.2, which encourages you to deepen your understanding.

REFLECTION 10.1

Reactions to National Public Radio (NPR) Story (January 31, 2008, Morning Edition)

Kibbe at the Crossroads: A Lebanese Kitchen Story

I am tuned in to NPR and hear the sweet undulations of a southern drawl. I believe the man's name is Pat Davis, and he is the current owner of Abe's BAR-B-Q in Clarksdale, Mississippi. To my surprise, he is talking about his father, the original owner of the restaurant since 1924 and an immigrant from Lebanon. Another Lebanese immigrant to the Delta area, Chafik Chamoun, tells about how he started his business by going door to door peddling goods to his neighbors. No one had very much then (1950's) and sometimes his neighbors would buy from him just to help sustain him for one more week, not because they needed anything or had much to spare themselves. Indeed, when he opened his restaurant in 1960, he had the chance to return the favor. The civil rights era had created enormous tensions between African Americans and European Americans, so the Lebanese immigrants in the southeast were among the few who would serve food to their Black patrons. I was surprised by this history, generations of Arab Americans building the culture of the U.S. in ways I had not suspected. I also was touched by the willingness of people on the margin to help each other, looking past their differences and seeing the commonness of humanity.

Reflect on the following:

- What are your thoughts and feelings related to this reaction?
- How might this influence the way you work with clients of Arab descent?

CONTEMPORARY SOCIAL PERCEPTIONS AND DISCRIMINATION EXPERIENCES

REFLECTION 10.2

Do you know anyone who self-identifies as Arab American? What do you know about this person's culture, family, values, or lifestyle? What have your interactions been with this person? How has this individual or your interactions informed or impacted your view of Arab Americans in general? How has this experience "fit" with stereotypes you may be aware of about Arab Americans?

ACTIVITY 10.1   FAMOUS ARAB AMERICANS

Look up famous Arab Americans at www.aaiusa.org/arab-americans/23/famous-arab-americans. Select an individual or group of individuals of interest. What stereotypes might they represent? Think about how those stereotypes may have originated, and how the current sociopolitical climate either promotes or discourages them. Discuss these issues in dyads.

Various scholars have noted the complexity of existence for early-21st-century Arab Americans (Abu El-Haj, 2002; Ammar, 2000; Arab American Institute, 2002; Sarroub, 2002). The post-9/11 United States has become intent on securing its borders against real or perceived threats and has engaged in preemptive actions in the name of the war on terror. The tragedy of the attacks on the World Trade towers is certainly real, as is the backlash suffered by the Arab American community. Changes in national policy (e.g., the PATRIOT Act, among others) have altered the civil liberties often taken for granted in the United States, including expectations not to be under surveillance or be detained without cause (Elaasar, 2004). Arab Americans, as well as other leading civil rights advocates, have challenged whether these policies are fairly implemented rather than used to target those perceived as "Middle Eastern" or "Arab." Such acts of profiling perpetuate the stereotypes of Arab Americans as Muslims and extremists (Nassar-McMillan, in press).

Hate crimes and profiling against U.S. citizens and immigrants, regardless of how closely they do or do not fit the stereotypical "Middle Eastern" images, have gone up dramatically in recent years. The American-Arab Anti-Discrimination Committee (ADC) listed over 600 attacks against persons who the perpetrators assumed to be Muslim Arabs in the months following September 11, 2001 (Nassar-McMillan, in press). For example, Sikhs, who are often of Indian descent and are not Muslim, have been attacked for their custom of wearing a turban. Certainly, most non-Arab Americans have not participated in overt acts of violence; these actions can be attributed to an extreme element (Elaasar, 2004). In fact, alongside the many Arab American organizations publicly condemning the 9/11 attacks, many non-Arab American counterparts expressed the view, via public opinion polls, that the United States, on the foundation and spirit of tolerance, should extend the benefit of the doubt to citizens of this country who also happened to be Arab.

Stereotypes of Arabs as callous oil barons, desert nomads, religious zealots, and repressive dictators do not help promote intercultural understanding (Shaheen, 1997). These images come to the United States in movies, fictional novels, and even the news media and educational textbooks (Barlow, 1995). There are very few normalized images to counter those exaggerated and falsified images that permeate U.S. culture and consciousness (Zogby, 2000). Most U.S. citizens would have a difficult time envisioning an average Arab or Arab American family sitting down to dinner in the evening, celebrating a wedding or grieving at a funeral, getting ready for work or school in the morning, or making purchases at a store. It is ironic and sad that in the current historical moment, images of roadside bombings in Baghdad may be more familiar than images of neighboring Arab Americans in their daily lives. Activity 10.2 highlights some of the authors' perspectives of the intricacies of these images.

ACTIVITY 10.2

Review the following excerpts and discuss your reactions in small groups:

Media Reflections

What would I learn as a student of counseling and human development if I turned to the media to inform me about Arabs and the Middle East? The women I see on the news might be covered head to toe in dark fabric, their eyes darting toward the camera only briefly. They seem very mysterious, almost impenetrable. They are usually in the home or purchasing food in the market. The men might be grouped together shouting slogans angrily toward the camera, protesting something that is not made entirely clear. We might also be treated to the sight of "terrorist training camps" where men are covering their faces as they learn to operate missile launchers. Children are not in schools but more often shown wandering in the street or staying in their homes.

I recall that there is a family in my neighborhood with women who wear veils, but I don't know what country they originally are from. They seem a little less foreboding than the women on the news. Their head coverings are in bright colors sometimes and they wave when we walk past. I wave back, but I have not had the courage to say more than hello to them, to my embarrassment. Is it possible that the gross misunderstandings generated from what I seen on my television have limited my ability or willingness to interact with people who live right down the street? This family could be less "foreign" than I think, perhaps born and raised in the United States. We could have some things in common as neighbors, parents of children, concerned citizens. There could be much to gain from releasing my misconceptions and interacting with them as individuals and probably very little to lose.

—Laura M. Gonzalez

Thoughts on Belonging

In our city, a young Latino boy who does not speak English well looks to associate with individuals who "have his back," *la familia*. Brown Pride, the Latino gang, offers him the collectivism that he grew up with in his culture. His circumstances create an environment that makes him vulnerable to gang involvement. In Afghanistan, a young boy with the same or even more difficult circumstances becomes involved with a terrorist group. He wants to be honored as being part of a group. I daresay the boy in my hometown and that boy in Afghanistan have a lot in common—poor circumstances and the desire to belong, with the ultimate goal of creating a support system. Collectivism lends itself to what Western societies called a cult.

—Rasha H. Mohamed

Pictures of Human Faces

I recently saw a media exhibit at a gallery in a local college—*Families of Abraham*. It focuses on the three major world religions—Judaism, Christianity, and Islam—all originating from the family of Abraham. Showcasing contemporary families of all faiths through photographs, accompanying narratives explain the religious traditions and each family's and individual's perspective and role in carrying them out. It tells about their lives, their occupations, their hobbies, their lifestyles—it made them all so human! I wish this was the way our news media would portray people—all people.

—Sylvia C. Nassar-McMillan

Against this backdrop of stereotypes and misunderstanding, the personal and political choice of Arab Americans to identify strongly with their ethnicity can be a difficult one (Shain, 1996). Some have responded with fear and embarrassment, perhaps internalizing the negative stereotypes of Arabs and denying their heritage (Ajrouch, 2000; Nassar-McMillan & Hakim-Larson, 2003). Some have experienced discrimination or threats and have had to decide whether to respond or be silenced by their mistreatment (Sarroub, 2002). In addition to hate crimes, the ADC recorded over 800 cases of workplace discrimination, spanning loss of employment to religious or personal harassment (American-Arab Anti-Discrimination Committee, 2005). As well, the federal government itself was noted to become increasingly strict in screening Arab Americans for jobs or other benefits. In the face of such real discrimination, survival instincts may outcompete the desire to express one's ethnic pride.

Others have responded to the post-9/11 environment by realizing the need for solidarity among members of the Arab American community (Elaasar, 2004; Nassar-McMillan, 2003). Muslims in particular were involved in community education efforts, opening local mosques to those who wanted to understand Islam and praying for those who had lost their lives (Elaasar, 2004). Some Arab Americans also started to describe the things that they were proud of in their culture, as a way to counter the negative images generated after 9/11 (Zogby, 2001).

ARAB AMERICAN CULTURE AND VALUES

As is true with any large and varied ethnic group, it is an overgeneralization to say that every Arab American adheres to an equal extent to the cultural values mentioned here. Following are the traditional values that may be moderated over time by exposure to the U.S. culture, but may also be maintained by strong family systems and ethnic enclaves, or communities: collectivism; religion and faith; education, work, and economic status; and communication styles.

Collectivism

Above almost all else, Arab Americans should be understood as holding a collective worldview (Dwairy, 2002; Sayed, 2003). Thus, as opposed to the U.S. system in which individuals are expected to become more independent as they mature, Arab Americans are likely to continue seeing themselves as part of an extended family and community structure. Decisions are made within this context, help is sought from other members of the collective group, appropriate behavior is defined by the shared beliefs of the community, and interdependence is valued as a sign of dedication and loyalty to the group. Career counseling, for example, would have a very different feel in this collective context as opposed to the context of helping clarify the work-related interests of an individual. One would be expected to sacrifice individual goals or needs for the sake of the extended family. As one common proverb emphasizes, "We rise together, we fall together" (Sayed, Collins & Takahashi, 1998 p. 444).

The strength of the collective bonds within the group may promote the tendency toward clannish behavior and cause separation between themselves and others who have different countries of origin, religious preferences, races, and the like. Another common proverb states: "It is my brother and I against our cousin; but it is my cousin and I against a stranger" (Nassar-McMillan & Hakim-Larson, 2003). Collective societies value trust, so outsiders must work to gain favor through sustained demonstrations of knowledge, awareness, and skillful assistance. However, before trust is earned, individualistic U.S. influences may be viewed with some suspicion.

One example is that parenting styles of Arab Americans may be even more authoritarian than parenting styles of Arabs in their home countries, with U.S. cultural values viewed as a potential threat to the structure of the Arab American family and its value system, particularly in the case of Muslims (Nassar-McMillan, in press). Parents may impose social constraints on young girls to prevent them from falling prey to sexual permissiveness or other problematic U.S. influences (Hakim-Larson & Nassar-McMillan, 2008). Counselors in schools may not understand a family's request that their daughter not wear a swim suit or enter a pool, for example, but pushing the family to reconsider may only heighten their sense of a value conflict and cause them to become even more resolved to protect their children.

Extended family systems are common within Arab households (Hakim-Larson & Nassar-McMillan, 2008). That tradition may be carried on in the United States, but if immigration patterns have disrupted the connection among generations, the roles of elders may be picked up by other members of an ethnic enclave. These communities tend to be close-knit and share common places of origin (the same city or area in the old country), if not blood. These relationships with Grandmother or "Auntie" are an important source of stability and very important to assess within the context of counseling (Nydell, 1987). Counselors in any setting should be careful to ask about family or other important relationships in a very broad and inclusive way. Counseling related to family issues should be undertaken with the understanding that relationships will be close and interdependent in a way that might be described as "enmeshed" if one were working with an individualistic family. Care should be taken not to label relationships as unhealthy or inappropriate if they are simply adhering to different cultural standards.

Religion and Faith

The religious diversity of the Arab American community is an aspect that may come as a surprise to those unfamiliar with its traditions (see Figure 10.1). The Islamic heritage of some Arab Americans has received more attention due to its distinctiveness from the dominant religious traditions of the United States. In addition, it is true that the majority of Arabs in the Middle East are Muslim. However, the largest religious group within Arab Americans is Catholic (i.e., 35%) (Arab American Institute, n.d.). Only 24% of Arab Americans practice Islam, while another 20% are Orthodox. Another 11% practice a Protestant religion, whereas the final approximate 13% of Arab Americans describe themselves as not having a religious affiliation (Jackson & Nassar-McMillan, 2006; Nydell, 1987). Recalling the fact that the Arab Middle East is the birthplace for several of these traditions, it makes sense that there would be a range of practices among Arab descendents of the region. In addition, the immigration process may selectively bring more members of one group than another to a host country, so it is also logical that the percentage of Arab Muslims residing in the United States is different than the percentage of Arab Muslims in their region of origin (Camarota, 2002).

Because less may be known about Islam than some of the other, more dominant U.S. faiths mentioned, a fuller description of its tenets is provided in Build Your Knowledge 10.1 as well as in Chapter 15 of this text. **Islam** began between the years of 7 and 10 AD when the Prophet Muhammad began to deliver God's messages in the area of the Arabian Peninsula (Azayem & Hedayat-Diba, 1994). Muhammad did not claim to be divine, but said he received divine revelations from the Archangel Gabriel. These messages from Allah (the Arabic word for God) were written and became known as the Qur'an. In this way, the Qur'an is not drastically different from the Old or New Testaments of the Bible, which were God's revelations delivered through faithful messengers (Nassar-McMillan, in press). Muhammad himself was actually an orphan at a young age and was raised in Mecca by family and community who tended to practice polytheistic traditions.

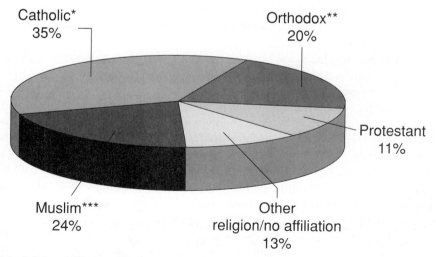

FIGURE 10.1   Religious Affiliations of Arab Americans.
*includes Roman Catholic, Maronite, and Melkite (Greek Catholic); **includes Sunni, Shi'a, and Druze
***includes Antiochian, Syrian, Greek, and Coptic
Source: Arab American Institute Foundation. *Religious affiliations of Arab Americans.* Retrieved April 22, 2008, from www.aaiusa.org/demographics.htm#Religion. Reprinted with permission.

Muhammad made the firm decision to worship only one God, the God of his ancestor, Abraham. Of interest, it is written that the progeny of Abraham's son Isaac became Jews and the progeny of Abraham's son Ishmael became Muslims (Jackson & Nassar-McMillan, 2006).

BUILD YOUR KNOWLEDGE 10.1

TENETS OF ISLAM

Some of the basic beliefs of Islam include that persons are responsible for their own deeds and must always remain accountable to God and aware of his presence (Azayem & Hedayat-Diba, 1994). Muslims also share the Christian belief in Heaven and Hell. Islam emphasizes unity among peoples, even across racial or religious lines. Five important spiritual practices, known as the Pillars of Islam, are (a) *Shahadah*, the declaration of faith to one God, Allah, and in Muhammad as God's prophet; (b) *Salat*, or the formal practice of worshiping by bowing toward Mecca five times daily and praying; (c) *Sawm*, the monthlong fast observed during Ramadan, which serves to build patience and obedience to God as well as to teach compassion for those who go hungry; (d) *Zakat*, or the donation of 2.5% of one's income to the mosques as a form of giving alms; and (e) *Hajj*, or the pilgrimage to Mecca. Those who are not able to make the journey to Mecca are encouraged to sponsor someone else's pilgrimage.

Many Muslims view Islam as not merely their religion, but their guide for everyday life. Indeed, Islamic law is written to help believers lead ethical lives that respect others and promote peace. The very word *Islam* means peace through submission, which would not condone actions taken with the express purpose of hurting or terrorizing another person or group (Azayem & Hedayat-Diba, 1994). The goal of global unity is supported by Islamic ethics, including religious unity and racial and ethnic unity (Nassar-McMillan, in press). For counselors who may not typically include religion as a topic of assessment, the presence of Islamic ethics in all parts of daily life means that an important influence could be otherwise missed.

Another misconception of Islam is that it asks women to be subservient to men (Council on Islamic Education, 1995). In fact, males and females are considered by Islam to be equals before God. Muslim women are allowed to obtain education, own property, make their own decisions about marriage and divorce, and vote. Muslim women also pray in the same way that the men do, but as with many other activities in traditional Arab Muslim households, the genders are separated (Haddad, 2004). Depending on the attitudes of the Imam, or religious leaders, women typically dress modestly, particularly when they go to pray in the mosque, and generally pray in a separate, women-only area. It should also be noted that local customs may interact with Islam in such a way to limit women's rights, although this is typically due to sociopolitical influences of the particular country, rather than to a tenet of Islam (Nassar-McMillan, in press).

Although some of the customs may appear different at first, there is much common ground among Islam, Christianity, and Judaism (Nassar-McMillan, in press). The Catholic tradition that exists in Arab American communities has its roots in the crusades of the 12th century and the Maronites (mostly from Lebanon) and Melkites (Greek Catholic). There were also Orthodox groups that split from Rome and the Catholic Church, including Egyptian Coptics, Syrians, Antiochian, and Greek Orthodox. For these Arab Americans, as well as for their Protestant counterparts, traditions in the United States do not represent a dramatic departure from their customary worship.

Just as with other U.S. groups that associate with a religion, there are Arab Americans who adhere strongly to their faith traditions and maintain a daily or weekly practice, while others spend relatively less time attending religious services or in other spiritual matters. Degree of religiosity is an important aspect to learn about in a counseling relationship, especially with stereotypes about extremist Muslims influencing U.S. opinions about the more typical members of the group (Nassar-McMillan, 2003). Religion for Arab Americans of any faith tradition is often a source of comfort and strength, a valued connection to cultural roots, and a resource in times of difficulty (Faragallah et al., 1997). For Muslims in particular (as a religious minority in the United States), the strain of being misunderstood and perhaps mistreated in everyday life can be counterbalanced by time spent with other Muslims at the mosque. The sense of community that is often generated in the mosque extends beyond religion to the social, psychological, and physical well-being of its members. The Imam (i.e., religious leader) may be sought for counsel in handling daily stressors and the worshipers may assist each other with issues related to family life, work, and education (Nassar-McMillan, in press). Of course, daily transactions with non-Muslims have meant that members of the Islamic faith must integrate themselves with the wider community to an extent. However, in personal matters of values, religion, and family, Muslims may choose to maintain their cultural traits and traditions (Hashem, 1991). For a counselor working with a traditional Arab American of Islamic faith, the option to include an Imam or other important religious figure in the process may be greatly appreciated by the client.

Education, Work, and Economic Status

Contrary to some stereotypes, education is strongly encouraged for boys and girls alike in the Arab American community (Hakim-Larson & Nassar-McMillan, 2008). Although schoolchildren in the Arab Middle East may be segregated by gender, Arab American children follow the norms of schooling in the United States. Some children attend private Islamic schools where they also learn Arabic culture and language, but many are students in the public schools of their communities (Samhan, 2001). Education and professional preparation are both emphasized across the Arab Middle East and therefore carried over into the United States. The community has a laudable record of educational accomplishment, with 85% of Arab Americans having a high school diploma and over 40% having bachelor's degrees (Nassar-McMillan, in press). Arab Americans tend to have career paths similar to other groups in this country, although there are more participating in business and other entrepreneurial activities and fewer participating in government, perhaps for reasons mentioned earlier in this chapter (Zogby, 2001). Some of the most recent immigrants may have professions and educational certifications from their home countries, but may not be able to practice those professions in the United States. The overall rate of employment among Arab Americans is high, as is the mean household income (Camarota, 2002). This does not mean that Arab Americans would not present for career-related counseling, of course. In addition to some of the typical career-related concerns seen with any client (e.g., occupational exploration, workforce transition issues, balancing career and family or other adjustments), Arab Americans may also discuss issues related to workplace discrimination, expectations from a collective cultural viewpoint, or the impact of immigration or cultural adjustment on work.

Communication Styles

Because counseling is an activity highly dependent upon quality of communication, it is important to understand some manners of expression that Arab Americans may use. Some of the characteristics that are different from the average U.S. conversational style include use of nonverbal gestures to express emotion, comfort with touching and standing in close proximity while communicating, and use of high volume or repetition to emphasize a critical point (Faragallah et al., 1997; Hakim-Larson & Nassar-McMillan, 2008; Jackson & Nassar-McMillan, 2006; Via, Callahan, Barry, Jackson, & Gerber, 1997). At the same time, such expressiveness may not extend to the sharing of emotional feelings or issues. On the contrary, Arab Americans may be reluctant to share in that way, particularly with those outside their culture. Moreover, they may be reluctant to say anything negative about another person, particularly within their family or community. Kissing cheeks as a greeting and holding hands (even among adult males) is common in the Middle East, and these customs may or may not be observed in the United States.

There may be a hierarchy in terms of communication among family members, with an emphasis on children speaking respectfully to their elders and women being respectful to men while in public settings. If counseling is being sought for marriage or family-related issues, the counselor may consider one separate meeting before working jointly with the couple, to have the opportunity to hear the woman's concerns when she is not constrained by custom to defer to her husband. If the counselor is seen as an authority figure, the client (in any setting) may expect him or her to provide concrete solutions to problems rather than to ask questions designed to promote insight into the situation (Nassar-McMillan, in press). Arab Americans may initially be reserved with members of other ethnic groups until an initial sense of trust is established, especially in matters with emotional importance. Some clients could feel that they are betraying their families by sharing personal matters with an outsider (the counselor). Another tendency that may impact counseling is the Middle Eastern tradition of gender separation during certain activities. Same-gender pairs, where available, may be more comfortable for Arab American clients. Therefore, both communication style and content of counseling sessions may be impacted by these trends, which would be most relevant with the client who holds fast to cultural traditions. As a counselor, particularly a non-Arab American one, learning a few key Arabic greetings and other phrases, along with cultural traditions, from one's clients could go a long way in building rapport.

INDIVIDUAL DIFFERENCES AND IDENTITIES

Identity is a multilayered construct, one that may operate at a subconscious level for some areas and may be foremost in our minds for other areas. Our identities include our sense of who we are as gendered, ethnic/racial, and religious beings. They are influenced by our age, our abilities, our family constellation, and our country or culture of origin, among a host of other factors. Our identities are shaped by where we work and live, with whom we partner, what we believe to be good and just. All of these interacting streams of identity develop at different rates, continue to change over time, and respond to different influences. Identity development for an Arab American may be complicated for additional reasons. There may be differences between the self that can be presented while at school or working in the community and the self that is nurtured and accepted in the family home or among friends (Hakim-Larson & Nassar-McMillan, 2006). For counselors, it is useful to consider some of the external and internal influences that may be important to the identities of Arab American clients.

Acculturation

Immigration and the resultant process of acculturation (the multidimensional changes that occur when two or more cultural groups come into contact with each other) are never easy. Acculturation is not a simple linear progression to one final solution, but rather, a process that occurs at different rates within individuals, families, and communities (Baker, 1999). For the newest members of the community, the process of encountering an unfamiliar culture can result in a variety of outcomes. Some individuals invest years learning about their new home and become so assimilated to those customs that they leave behind their former cultural values. Others may add the new cultural competencies to the old and become bicultural or integrated in their acculturation status. Other individuals may keep themselves separated from the new culture and cling tightly to their original traditions. Still others may come to feel marginalized in both cultures, not belonging to either one, not feeling comfortable anywhere (Oppedal, Rysamb, & Sam, 2004). It is certainly possible to sustain one's original Arab identity and also take on a U.S. citizen identity over time (Ryder, Alden, & Paulhus, 2000), but this biculturalism is challenging when one identity is being actively disparaged by the main cultural outlets (Keshishian, 2000). Indeed, research is just beginning to identify the long-term impact of trying to build a secure Arab American identity in the context of ongoing U.S. war efforts in the Arab Middle East and the so-called war on terror that has targeted Islamic extremists as the enemy (Hakim-Larson & Nassar-McMillan, 2006).

For some of the Arab immigrants to this country, similarities to the predominant U.S. culture provided initial pathways to connect with their new homeland and perhaps eased part of the acculturation process. For example, Arabs with lighter skin tones and Christian religious heritage would not draw as much attention in the United States as darker skinned Arabs who maintained Islamic religious practices (e.g., veiling, praying five times a day, fasting) (Nassar-McMillan, in press). Some of the factors influencing the ease or difficulty of the adjustment process might include the specific country of origin, the reason for coming to the United States, language used in the home, and proximity to an Arab American enclave. For example, Muslim immigrants often received mistreatment for their notable differences. The negative images of Muslims in the media and common conversation could influence how new immigrants come to see themselves as they consolidate identity in a new place (Keshishian, 2000). Counselors who have worked with new immigrants from other parts of the world already have some basic knowledge about common adjustment issues and how they pervade all aspects of life. This perspective will be helpful when working with new immigrants from the Arab world, although each group still has specific issues that need to be explored as well. Counselors who are not familiar with immigration stress might begin with Reflection 10.3 as a way to sensitize themselves. Clearly, a more positive outcome related to acculturation and adjustment would be associated with better mental health status (Ghaffarian, 1998).

REFLECTION 10.3   ACCULTURATION VISUALIZATION

If you have never traveled outside the country of your birth, take a moment to imagine what it would be like to experience such a profound change. Almost everything you take for granted at this moment could be different. Looking out your window, you may see a geography that is unfamiliar and cause simple acts like getting dressed for the day or choosing a method of transportation to be challenging. If you find a food substance that is to your liking for breakfast, then you might leave your residence and try to navigate your way through a world that includes signs and conversations you do not understand and work or leisure activities that you cannot participate in due to laws, lack of familiarity, or lack of preparation. If you are accustomed to being respected as a woman, as a practitioner of a certain religion or a certain profession, as a member of an approved social class, that respect might not be offered to you now. Support systems that you relied on before (e.g., family, friends, schools, churches) could be partly or completely absent. People whom you pass on the way might or might not look anything like you, and they might be curious about

(continued)

your appearance, your manner of dress, your hair. Depending on the distance between this new place and your home, you may not be able to rely on seeing all of those familiar things again for quite some time. Possibly, you had to leave your home at a very young age or due to a crisis and are still trying to understand what happened. You might have to worry for the first time in your life about how you will find food or shelter and it might not be clear who can help you with those necessities.

Source: Based on research topics identified by H. Portela Myers (2005), written by L. Gonzalez.

Involuntary immigration, or situations in which newcomers seek refuge due to intolerable situations at home, carries unique difficulties and stressors. Refugees from war, violence, occupation, and instability may experience Post Traumatic Stress Disorder and are less capable of attending to the process of establishing themselves in their new communities (Nassar-McMillan & Hakim-Larson, 2003). These individuals often have been forced to leave and may continue to grieve the losses of home, family, and a familiar way of life for some time. It was and is often the case that they have not arrived with many supportive resources, either economic or social. Families may be separated, communities torn apart, and familiar sources of comfort (e.g., mosques, religious leaders, customs, and traditions) are no longer present. To compound these difficulties, refugees might also face a lack of understanding in their new host country, ranging from neglect to hostile discrimination (Leopold & Harrell-Bond, 1994). Iraqis, comprising some of the current wave of Arab American immigration, provide an example of the problems associated with refugee status (Gorst-Unsworth & Goldenberg, 1998; Jamil, Nassar-McMillan, & Lambert, 2007; Takeda, 2000). Many of these individuals were allies to the U.S. military forces in their country, only to find themselves at danger in their homelands and facing discrimination and misunderstanding in the United States as their host country. Refugees who left war, famine, ethnic cleansing, or political turbulence behind them have a distinct set of issues to be addressed. They may not be likely to seek counseling as a primary resource, although they may be referred when they contact agencies for basic needs like food, medicine, or shelter. Counselors living in areas that are receiving groups of refugees have an ethical obligation to educate themselves about posttraumatic stress and be prepared to work with these needy individuals.

Ethnicity

Beyond the Hollywood images of sheiks or the evening news images of women wearing veils, what does a contemporary Arab American look like? Interestingly, even the U.S. government has categorized Middle Easterners with terms as various as *Asiatic, Colored,* and *White* since the late 1800s (Samhan, 2001). Given the many skin tones, hair, and eye colors that are possible, there is no phenotypical look common to all Arabs. In the United States intermarriage also causes new variations in the physical attributes of Arab Americans, which can make cultural identity a more complex issue for the children (Kulczycki & Lobo, 2002). Therefore, some members of the community may go unnoticed or unidentified by their neighbors or associates, especially if their names have changed from the original Arabic surname. One clear exception would be practicing Muslims whose attire or customs may trigger some of the common Middle Eastern stereotypes and thus receive unwanted attention from non-Arab Americans. Other external influences on Arab American ethnic identity could include political discourse of the times, predominant religions in the local communities, absence or presence of other Arab Americans, or any other acculturation-related factors such as length of time in the United States or language spoken at home. Activity 10.3 provides an author's perspectives on Arab ethnic identity with some questions for you to consider.

ACTIVITY 10.3

What Is It Like Being an Arab American Woman?

Being Arab American is wonderful. I have a rich background including ancestors who contributed to the construction of the sphinx and pyramids. Although my heritage is unique I have always struggled with my identity. I struggled with the uneasiness of others' inability to easily categorize me and my family. Internally I have strived to be loyal to my upbringing and my family but many times the things I was taught simply did not seem to match me. My family is Muslim from Cairo, Egypt, where it seems to me people are a little less conservative, relatively speaking, than elsewhere in the Arab Middle East.

Growing up, my behavior was often considered socially unacceptable for a girl. I wanted to be accepted by my fellow Arabs but never could quite fit in. It seemed to be a very conditional relationship. If I followed the traditions of being a girl then I was OK, and even pleasing to God. For me, religion and culture came together in a dominating way.

I was taught that you were born Muslim and you will die a Muslim; the whole idea of predestination. Sometimes I felt extremely trapped by that idea since I viewed the world differently even at an early age. Those feelings led me to think that there was something very wrong with me. If the religion and family was not faulty then it must be me who was corrupt or damaged in some way. That idea was reinforced when I had to make a difficult decision about whether or not to marry outside the Muslim faith.

Outside my family I did not feel totally accepted by any group of peers at school or out in our community. When I was younger I lived in a larger community of Arab Americans, but when I was a little older my family moved to a city in the southeastern United States without an Arab American enclave. At school the White kids did not accept me because I was not White and the Black kids did not accept me because I was not "all the way Black." It was all very confusing.

The Arab girls I did meet in school were traditionally Muslim. They covered their heads, they did not have friends who were boys, and they all ate lunch together. I did not cover my head and I played sports and loved to be social. I just did not fit in with any one particular group.

As an adult I began dating outside my faith which caused me to become very isolated from my own family. Also, I had limited interactions with males in my own family because many of them lived overseas. It seemed that being an immigrant to this country was both a blessing and a curse. I felt torn between two worlds: one that was less familiar and very far away and another that I wanted to fit into but didn't know how to without disappointing the people I loved.

As an adult I appreciate and respect the things I was taught as a child. Growing up in a Muslim home taught me about self-control, willpower that came from learning about fasting and prayer. Also, I learned from the teachings to be grateful for things you have and to not be wasteful. My parents instilled in me the ideas of using my gifts and talents to better society, that we are all connected to each other, and that my behavior can affect someone else either positively or negatively. Islam taught me about the mind and body connection

(continued)

and the importance of health and fitness. My father believed in the spirit realm and taught me that there is more to life than the things I can see with my eyes. Those lessons helped me in my career and raising my son as a single parent.

Being in the United States since I was 2 years old, I have not connected with a group of people who share my heritage and are accepting of me and my son. I look forward to finding my path and exposing my son to his heritage as an Arab.

—Rasha H. Mohamed

In dyads, consider the following:

- What are your reactions to Rasha's ethnic identity development?
- What cultural dynamics are mentioned as a part of her development process?
- What are examples of oppression?
- What are examples of resilience?
- How could you connect with Rasha if she presented for counseling?

Jackson and Nassar-McMillan (2006) make the cogent point that ethnicity and religion must be understood together in any attempt to investigate ethnic identity of Arab Americans. This intersection is demonstrated in a more personal way in Reflection 10.1. White Christian Arab Americans would be likely to integrate with ease, while Black Christian Arab Americans and White Muslim Arab Americans would each have some unique challenges to navigate. Black Muslim Arab Americans may be faced with the most difficult road in terms of finding acceptance in mainstream U.S. society. Religion is clearly one of the key determinants of how acculturation proceeds (or doesn't proceed) in this community.

If those with the ability to blend and integrate cause confusion for non-Arab Americans, it can also mean that Arab Americans themselves may have difficulty in defining their ethnic identity. There are already differences among members of the community with respect to country of origin, education, generation of immigration, religion, and social status. Some individuals may identify themselves mostly by their religion or their country of origin (e.g., "I'm Lebanese, you are Yemeni.") and not with the pan-ethnic term *Arab American* (Haddad, 2004). Some Arab Americans may adhere more strongly to traditional value systems, whereas others may be comfortable assimilating to U.S. value norms. Indeed, there can be occasional in-fighting with more traditional Arab Americans referring to the more assimilated as "White," while the more assimilated may think of the others as "Boaters," newly immigrated, and thus too old fashioned (Ajrouch, 2000; Hakim-Larson & Nassar-McMillan, 2008). Some Arab Americans who have successfully integrated into U.S. society do not wish to be associated with an ethnic minority or receive special treatment (Llorente, 2002). Especially if a family does not live near an ethnic enclave and does not have ties to a cultural community, it may be more challenging for some adolescent Arab Americans to identify with their Arab culture or origin (Ajrouch, 2000).

An in-depth focus on some of the identity development tasks of young Arab Americans may be useful for those preparing to become professional counselors. School counselors in particular will want to read Activity 10.4, which provides a multidimensional way to conceptualize Arab American adolescents in the context of a non-Arab-majority school. There are three levels that should be considered when thinking about how an Arab American identity could be constructed (Hakim-Larson & Nassar-McMillan, 2006). On the individual level, all adolescents must navigate gender identity as they approach adulthood, but this process is likely to intersect with religion, social values from the country of origin, and acculturation status for young Arab Americans. Also on the individual level, these adolescents must come to understand their ethnicities, build a sense of self-esteem, and confront the roles that take up most of their time (e.g., student, family member, friend). On the level of family and peers, there may be a difference among Arab American youth in terms of how much they feel their values are similar to or conflicting with those of the parental generation. It is likely that they will have absorbed some emphasis on collectivism from their family life, but this will bump up against the predominant U.S value of individualism in school and other settings. Finally, at the sociocultural level, Arab American children may come to learn that discrimination exists in the United States and that this discrimination is occasionally directed at members of their community. They may learn more about the politics of the Arab Middle East or what types of pressures led their family to immigrate in the first place. If a level of fear accompanies these growing realizations about the difficult place of Arab-heritage individuals in the United States, it could also cause insecurity in their nascent identities. This process is parallel in some ways to the role of internalized oppression in the identity development of other racial minorities in the United States (see Chapter 2 of this text).

In some of their typical developmental tasks, children from collectivistic families are less likely to struggle for independence or have noticeably turbulent relationships with their parents (Hakim-Larson & Nassar-McMillan, 2006). Adolescents of any culture are likely to focus on building competence in schoolwork, finding a group of friends, and preparing themselves for an acceptable future. For children of individualistic families, part of preparing for the future is learning how to be independent of their parents by making their own choices and defining their own roles. In contrast, among children of collectivistic families, preparing for the future is not something that requires moving outside the family influence. Indeed, if the Arab American parents have chosen the culturally preferred authoritative parenting style, then the children may come to understand and expect that someone in the family hierarchy is looking out for their interests and will help them with important decisions. There are benefits and liabilities to each system, but the critical point for Arab American youth who are raised in this way is that they observe the individualistic system by day as they interact with classmates and teachers, and they live the collectivistic system by night at home with their families. The contrast between the two could be confusing for a young person trying to build an identity. Of course, the less difference there is between the school environment and the family environment (e.g., an Islamic school) or the less overlap between the two systems (e.g., the student goes to school only to learn, does not try to make friends, and fulfills all social needs through a mosque, church, or community center), the less friction will result.

ACTIVITY 10.4   SCHOOL COUNSELING CONSIDERATIONS

A school counselor working with Arab American students may wish to maintain awareness of some important influences (Hakim-Larson & Nassar-McMillan, 2006). Is the student different in a way that is obvious to non-Arab peers, perhaps prompting them to express discriminatory attitudes and reject the Arab American child? How can this uniqueness be addressed constructively,

(continued)

given the possibility that the non-Arab students are repeating comments they hear at home? How long has the Arab American family lived in this country or when did they arrive? If they are recent immigrants or refugees, how old was the child upon leaving the country of origin? Was the social and political situation in the home country dangerous and destabilized? Is the family highly traditional; do they seem to keep their social contacts within their ethnic community? Does the student appreciate or resist the type of support offered by his or her family, especially Muslim families who may try to counter the influence of U.S. values? If the student seems to have any conflict about his or her ethnic group membership, school counselors need to be aware that they are not likely to criticize their parents to an outsider and that questions must be asked in a context of respect for collective values.

Gender Identity

Non-Arab U.S. citizens may hold multiple stereotypes about Arab or Arab American women, particularly those who are Muslim. There are movie images of harem girls doing belly dances, contrasted with news images of the oppressed women cloaked in dark fabrics who could not leave the house, drive a car, or have an opinion (Shakir, 1997). As is most often true with stereotypes, these images are not a good portrait of the majority of Arab women, and even less so of Arab American women. The personal perspective provided in Reflection 10.4 helps situate gender as an important aspect of identity, but not the only relevant one. Many Arab American women are quite modern as compared to the stereotypes; they dress as most other Americans do, divide time between work or school and family, hold political opinions, and are active in a variety of communities (Read, 2003). Even historic images of Arab women that are held by Westerners are often one-sided. Evelyn Shakir (1997) shares an interesting story of an 18th-century British woman who was living with her diplomat husband in Turkey. Her view of the "oppressed" Arab woman changed after some Turkish women were helping her change clothes and remarked on the cruel and unusual punishment that she was enduring—the bone corset. Thus, this chapter offers a special focus on understanding "**bint Arabs**," or Arab daughters.

Some of the traditional social customs from the Middle East that encourage separation of the sexes for various activities are particularly hard for Americans to understand (Haddad, 2004; Shakir, 1997). From the U.S. perspective, it is unfair to put girls in separate classrooms, whereas from some Arab Muslim perspectives, this segregation protects them from harassment or inappropriate male behavior. From a traditional Arab perspective, allowing an unmarried and sexually protected young woman to go on a date with a young man would be putting herself and her reputation in danger, whereas from the U.S. perspective it is a necessary ritual for finding a partner. The lack of such restrictions for young men does indicate a double standard, but Arab culture would not be the only one to provide differing social instructions to women and men (Nassar-McMillan, in press). Arab American women may decide to adhere to their Arab culture's gender roles to different extents. Some may pray or worship in a setting apart from men to improve their focus on God, and yet may work and share living space comfortably with men (Haddad, 2004). Indeed, some may be third- or fourth-generation American women who feel less of a connection to a distant country in the Arab Middle East. The important point for counselors is to explore a client's perspectives on gender without preconception or judgment based on stereotypes.

REFLECTION 10.4

Gender

As I think about personal reflections from a woman's perspective, two angles come to my mind: the first being what I, as a woman, think about Arab and Arab American cultures; the second being what my experience has been as a woman of Arab descent. When I think about the culture, images of strong and principled peoples come to mind. Among Arab Americans, I think about some of the most noteworthy individuals who have provided leadership among a diversity of arenas (for more information, see www.aaiusa.org/arab-americans/23/famous-arab-americans). These famous people are both women and men. Likewise, within the Arab Middle East of today, many contemporary leaders are women. But, following the media images and even the work of some scholars, one would believe that women are oppressed within Arab culture, and that their oppressors are men. It is challenging, even for an engaged and critical scholar, to discern the reality of gender issues within Arab culture. The women and girls whom I have known have not considered themselves to be oppressed, or at least not any more than their non-Arab American peers. The gender roles prescribed by Arab culture date back to times when the survival of the culture, originally a nomadic one, depended on each person playing her or his role. This dynamic is parallel to many other world cultures, both historic and contemporary. At the same time, there are many subcultures within the Arab Middle East that do indicate oppression of women. I do not view these oppressive acts as maintained or condoned by Arab culture, or by Islamic principles, but rather by oppressive governments and their respective male leaders. In this sense, again, I find many parallels with historical Judeo-Christian-based cultures that condone the oppression of women through alleged religious or cultural moral justifications.

Personally, as a woman of Arab descent, the developmental and lifelong messages I received have been equally mixed and confusing. On the one hand it seemed as though my education was not valued as much as that of my brother's, although in hindsight that perspective was not just from my Arabic family members' and parent. On the other hand, education for women does seem to be praised, among both my family and my respective communities, as well as nationally. In some situations, both personal and professional, I may have once viewed my prescribed role as subservient or submissive, but with increased understanding have come to perceive my role, in the company of male Arab American friends and colleagues, as one of mutual and culturally acceptable modesty. My own gender role negotiation within the culture has been an interesting one, alongside Muslim sisters as they have navigated dilemmas such as whether to practice "veiling." While I have been valued within my scholarly and professional communities as an Arab American woman, I have been certain to use my "Dr." title, just as my male colleagues use theirs!

—Sylvia C. Nassar-McMillan

Generation of immigration and time spent in the United States can influence acculturation status and, thus, choices about cultural norms and gender roles. Haddad (2004) described an interesting change that occurred in the Arab American enclave in Dearborn, Michigan. The earlier immigrants had adopted some American customs, such as allowing women to take charge of activities outside the home (e.g., raising money for establishing a new mosque, planning weddings and other social events there, helping with family business ventures), but later male immigrants from a more traditional culture in the Arab Middle East found this level of involvement to be unacceptable. They took control of the mosque via court action and told the women they would be allowed to enter only through a back door that led to the basement. They brought a more traditional Imam who supported their perspectives and eliminated all social activity in the mosque, returning it solely to a place of prayer. Thus, the way women's roles are defined in the Arab American community may shift with time and religious traditionalism. Trying to bridge the two cultures at their points of greatest differences could potentially cause frustration and a sense of incongruence for women.

Another example of the variations in Muslim Arab American gender identity is the practice of veiling (Read & Bartkowski, 2000). The use of the veil may be viewed by non-Muslims as oppressive, whereas Muslim women and girls who agree to wear veils may feel that it is a sign of their religious devotion and cultural pride. Some women who veil their faces or dress in very modest attire also indicate that they are free to develop their minds and opinions when attention is taken away from their physical selves. Other Muslim women may have an ambivalent relationship with the practice of veiling, accepting it at certain times and places in their lives and rejecting it at others (Shakir, 1997). As is the case with many things, it is easier to reject and criticize that which we do not understand as outsiders to a community. Women who wear veils have not forfeited their rights; they can study, they can choose professions, they can exercise authority in the family and in the community (Abu-Ali & Reisen, 1999; Adams & Markus, 2001). At times they face discrimination for adhering to the choice in non-Muslim settings like work and school (Shakir, 1997). Some European countries have recently debated laws about not allowing students to veil (seen as a symbol of religion) in public schools, for example.

Thus, whether or not a Muslim woman wears a veil, her religious identity and her gender identity can still take a variety of forms. More often, degree of religiosity has more influence on the content of gender roles for Arab American women than being Christian or Muslim (Frable, 1997; Read, 2003). That is, more fundamental belief systems tend to have more restrictions on how men and women should act, regardless of the actual religion. For example, a Christian Arab American (or Christian non-Arab American) woman may be strongly opposed to the practice of premarital sex. Counselors who meet a client for the first time and observe her wearing a veil would be wise not to make interpretations about that choice until other aspects of the client's personality and values become clear.

It can be complicated to construct a gender identity if one is also influenced by two fairly distinctive cultural and/or religious traditions. A wonderful interview from Shakir's (1997) book sheds light on this question as the subject discusses wearing traditional Muslim attire.

> The more in touch with reality I became through the teachings of Islam, the more of a feminist I became, meaning that yes I wanted to be free, free from all these lies they're telling me, free from cultural influences that tyrannize young people. I wanted to be emancipated from having to wear my skirts up to here or heels this high or being a slave to fashion. (p. 121)

Throughout one's lifetime, the process of constructing and adapting one's gender identity can be viewed as a dialogue between the values of the self and the values of the outer world (Adams & Markus, 2001).

RISKS AND RESILIENCIES: MENTAL HEALTH ISSUES AMONG ARAB AMERICANS

In this section, we detail key potential mental health consequences related to some of the issues presented earlier in the chapter, such as oppression, immigration and acculturation, ethnic identity development, and other psychosocial issues. Mental health–based research within Arab American communities indicates these presenting issues as most relevant to the clients they serve (e.g., Erickson & Al-Timimi, 2001; Nassar-McMillan & Hakim-Larson, 2003). Within each topic section, a brief vignette is provided to illustrate the issue presented. We will frame each in terms of both risks to the client, as well as resiliencies that may be present within the overall context or ones that may be positively facilitated by the counselor. In the next section on counseling considerations, we will revisit the scenarios, along with accompanying probes to facilitate thought and discussion about possible ways to handle each case.

Oppression and Discrimination

As popular media sources portray Arabs and Arab Americans in a manner that reflects the politically tense relations between the United States and various Arab Middle East countries, such portrayals are then internalized by both non-Arab Americans as they "learn" more about individuals of Arab descent, as well as Arab Americans themselves, as they learn more about themselves, particularly those in earlier stages of developing their cultural identities. Both overt and covert discrimination are detrimental to the mental health of individuals to whom those acts are directed. Ethnic pride can either be promoted or discouraged by such oppression. If appropriately developed or supported, it can serve as a strong source of resilience among Arab Americans.

MEET AHMED: A SAUDI ARABIAN MIDDLE SCHOOLER   Ahmed was born in Saudi Arabia. When he was 10 years old, his father, a university administrator, took a position at a midwestern U.S. university to direct the new Middle East studies program there, about an hour outside a large Arab American community, or enclave. His family (i.e., mother, father, three brothers, and one sister) relocated to the United States for an indefinite time period. Ahmed is now in middle school in their urban community school system. There are a number of other Arab American students in the school community. Some of the other students are second- and third-generation Arab Americans from Lebanon, although they still maintain strong ties to their ethnic heritage. Another group is first-generation students from Yemen, a relatively rural country with a lower socioeconomic and educational base. Along with these groups, there is a military base within a few hours of the city, and a large number of students in the school have at least one parent affiliated with the U.S. military, with some currently deployed in Iraq.

Ahmed often feels lonely and sad. He doesn't seem to fit in with either group of Arab American students even though most of them, except for some of the Lebanese students, are Muslim. The Lebanese group calls him a "boater" like they do the Yemeni students because he is less acculturated to U.S. cultural norms and speaks English with an Arabic accent. The Yemeni students also do not accept him because he comes from a more affluent and educated background than they do. Moreover, when there are military and political flare-ups related to the situation in Iraq, some students in the school make anti-Arab remarks to him, along with the others, about "going back where they came from," calling them "camel jockeys" and the like.

Acculturative Stress

More and more attention has been given to researching the various types of stressors encompassed by the acculturation process. Along with learning a new language and cultural customs, immigrants must learn to navigate within an entirely new societal structure of education, employment, and government, among others. These transitions are often very challenging, particularly with "transferring" from former levels of education or employment credentials to new host systems that might not recognize them. For example, it may be difficult to determine student grade levels within a new structure, particularly among postsecondary institutions. It also might be challenging, and at times impossible, for professionals to have their former credentials recognized in a reciprocal way. For example, a pharmacist in the country of origin might have to either undergo an entire training program in the United States in order to achieve the U.S. recognized credentials, or forego that career path altogether. Understandably, these difficulties can sometimes lead to anxiety or depression among recent immigrants. Resilience within this arena can be fostered if immigrants are able to appropriately transfer their former training, if not credentials, to comparable or similar careers in the new host country.

Intergenerational stress, among both recent and later generations of immigrants, may pose additional family stressors. In some cases in which English language acquisition has not been fully achieved, particularly by the parents or older generation, children may be inadvertently placed in a situation of having to translate notes or other directives from school to their parents, thus creating a role reversal in terms of a traditional hierarchy. In addition, rules or expectations from the culture of origin may be stricter or otherwise different from those recognized by their school and community peers, and in this way cause conflicts in the parenting arena. For example, rules about curfews, dating, or other aspects of supervised activities may be imposed that may result in children feeling "different" from their peers with whom they are trying to fit in. Such situations can pose additional stressors for all generations and family members involved. Dialogue among Arab American youth and families around these acculturation issues can yield self-exploration opportunities of both psychoemotional stressors as well as cultural strengths and positive values.

MEET THE AL-DINS: AN ALGERIAN FAMILY   The al-Dins moved to the United States approximately 15 years ago. Mr. al-Din (Abdallah) was a young business professional in his family's business in Algeria. Several of his brothers and sisters are involved in the business. An opportunity arose at that time for him to develop a branch of the business in the United States. He and his new wife (Nafisa), at that time, decided to take the opportunity for economic advancement. She had studied to be a nurse in Algeria, and hoped to practice in the United States.

During the first 15 years of settling into their new life in the United States, Abdallah's business became prosperous. At the same time, Nafisa was unable to pursue nursing because she would have had to complete a new degree program in nursing in the United States in order to obtain the nursing credentials. With English being a third language (after Arabic and French), she decided to indefinitely postpone that idea until after raising a family. Over the years, the al-Dins had four children, the elder two being girls.

Not living in an Arabic enclave, Nafisa had decided early on that she would begin wearing hajib, or veiling. It was not that she felt unsafe in the community, but she felt more comfortable wearing conservative clothing and a headdress that could allow her to feel she was upholding her cultural value of modesty. She came from a family that had not practiced that tradition in the past, but she felt that in this new environment it would be the best thing to do. She decided, several years ago, that her daughters would follow this tradition as they approached their preteen years. In recent years she has had increasing power struggles with her daughters. They want to go out without what she believes is appropriate supervision, even with boys. Nafisa has thought about taking them back to Algeria during the summers so that they can learn more about their culture-of-origin values. Her daughters are worried that she wants to bring them there to "marry them off." Nafisa does not have much cultural support in the community, and no one to discuss these issues with. She has grown increasingly depressed, realizing that their decision to move to the United States 15 years ago has created many stressful situations in terms of keeping her daughters protected. Had she stayed in Algeria, she believed that the environment would be much safer for them.

Ethnic and Gender Identity Development

Historically, "Arabism" and ethnic identity development among Arab Americans has paralleled their immigration history in the United States. As discussed earlier in the chapter, demographic definitions of Arab Americans, especially within the census arena, have evolved significantly over the years. Paralleling such U.S. trends, along with overall global relations and other politics, pride in ethnic heritage, particularly for Arab Americans, did not emerge fully until the 1960s. Over the course of the last 50 or so years, political and other conflicts between the United States and the Arab Middle East, as well as domestic acts of violence either legitimately or falsely attributed to Arabs or Arab Americans, have often served as the catalyst for the ebb and flow of ethnic pride within the Arab American community nationally. Even within Arab American enclaves, where young people, in the midst of their identity development, may have access to role models and peers sharing their heritage, negotiating such an identity development process in the face of sociopolitical challenges has not been easy. Intentional mentoring can support resilience among Arab American youth and young adults as they mature through these stages and processes.

Along with overall identity development, mixed messages about "appropriate" gendered development may cause additional challenges. These messages can emerge from families of origin, communities—either ethnic enclave communities or the community at large, and of course, the media and other sources to which young people are constantly exposed. Questions such as "Should women seek postsecondary and graduate education?", "Which careers are appropriate for women?", or "Should I get married?" are thought about by young women of most ethnic groups, and Arab Americans are no different. This issue often is at the crux of related, sometimes concurrent issues, such as sexual or career identity development. Role modeling and mentoring, here, too, can promote resilience among Arab American youth, particularly those who may be perceived by themselves or others as in the "minority" with regard to sexual orientation, career choice, or other issues.

MEET LAILA: A LEBANESE GRADUATE STUDENT   Laila is a graduate student in engineering at a university in a large Arab American enclave. Her family is of Lebanese descent, with several of her grandparents being the first immigrants from the family. Originally merchants, their family business expanded enough to provide more than adequate financial support for later generations to better themselves economically. Laila is not the first of her siblings and cousins to pursue graduate education. She is, however, the first female to pursue a graduate degree in a male-dominated field. Living in the large Arab American community, she does know numerous other young women in her program, and knows the struggle that some of them have had in terms of negotiating their gender identities within their families, communities, and the university program, the latter being male dominated within student and faculty groups. She also has begun to question her sexuality. She thinks that some of this questioning may be related to her school environment and lack of role models, but she does not feel comfortable talking to any of her peers about it.

Laila loves the academic challenges of her program, and has considered going on to pursue her doctorate in engineering. On the other hand, she has experienced some strain from not having adequate role models or mentoring in her program, and sometimes feels as though she is floundering in her career direction. She has not seen many females go on to the doctoral program, even though they may have initially planned to.

Other Psychosocial Issues

Arab Americans, like their non-Arab American counterparts, experience any number of developmental and crisis issues, along with psychological disorders. Particularly because Arab Americans are not identified as a special population by most governmental or mental health agencies, there are no specific data on the prevalence of issues within this population as compared to the overall population of communities.

For recent immigrants who are refugees, however, there is a high prevalence of Post Traumatic Stress Disorder (PTSD), often accompanied by elevated rates of anxiety and depression, among other psychoemotional and medical complaints, as well. These refugees came from Lebanon in the 1970s and 1980s, and most recently from Iraq, as veterans and other refugees of the 1991 Gulf War, often via refugee camps elsewhere in the world. Accurate diagnosis and treatment of these medical illnesses is prerequisite to effectively tackling any other issues and developing overall resilience within this population.

Psychosocial issues, for Arab Americans, often present as somatic, or physical issues. Depression or anxiety, for example, may become manifest in digestive, sleep, or any number of other physical disorders. This type of pattern is important for all types of health care and mental health care providers to be attuned to in working with Arab American clients or patients in particular. Again, effective identification and treatment better ensure resilience in working through other related psychosocial issues.

MEET SAMIR: AN IRAQI AMERICAN VETERAN'S HOSPITAL PATIENT   Samir is a veteran of the Gulf War. He served on the side of the United States against Saddam Hussein, and therefore was granted amnesty by the United Nations. He and his family spent 5 years living in a refugee camp in Saudi Arabia before being granted entry into the United States. His brother's family was in the same refugee camp but was assigned refugee status in Australia. Samir's parents were allowed to make a choice, and because Samir's brother had a larger family, even though one of the children had died in the refugee camp, Samir's parents chose to go to Australia.

Since being in the United States, Samir has felt extremely depressed. He cannot sleep because of his recurrent nightmares about atrocities witnessed during combat. He also has nightmares about his children dying. He has begun to gamble in the local coffeehouses and casinos, and cannot seem to hold down a job. He was an attorney in Iraq but has been working in a convenience store deli delivering food because he cannot practice law in the United States. His wife has threatened to divorce him so that he cannot gamble away her meager remaining financial resources. Samir sees his wife having to rely on their eldest son for financial and other household support, and yet he cannot seem to mobilize himself to do anything about it.

CONSIDERATIONS FOR COUNSELING ARAB AMERICANS

Within the most recent decade, both scholars and practitioners have focused on "best practices" counseling interventions with clients of Arab descent (e.g., Al-Krenawi & Graham, 2000; Erickson & El-Timimi, 2001; Nassar-McMillan & Hakim-Larson, 2003). Among these best practices, counselors should avoid the tendency to impose Western biases and approaches, engage community and family member involvement as much as possible, understand and identify the nature of stigmas and help-seeking behaviors, and be mindful of standards for cultural competence.

Approach

Many Western approaches to counseling apply insight-based strategies. For Arab American clients who are more acculturated, this may serve as a beneficial approach. However, think for a moment about what you've learned about Arab culture and societal structure. Family and community units are tight-knit, and each person has a role that is critical within those structures. Thus, any goals aimed at building additional client insight run the risk of concurrently creating more internal conflicts. Instead, Arab Americans as a group tend to prefer solution-focused, cognitive behavioral, or other pragmatic or practical interventions. It is important to add, though, that constructivist approaches may be useful in that they allow clients, particularly in a situation in which the counselor is non-Arab American, to tell their own story and be heard, understood, and validated.

Other issues mentioned earlier in this chapter, such as emotional expression or concepts of time, may emerge in counseling as well. For example, clients may be reluctant to express a negative emotion or thought toward a parent or other respected person in the community. Or, conversely, if they are engaging in an emotive process with a counselor with whom they feel comfortable and have established rapport, they may be highly expressive in aspects such as tone, volume, gesticulation, and so on, perhaps more so than a non-Arab American client. Building a positive working alliance with an Arab American client will involve both intellectual skills (e.g., understanding preferred approaches, learning about the individual and the group) and personal skills (e.g., monitoring internal prejudices, becoming empathetic, finding ways to relate). Reflection 10.5 provides a metaphor for considering and combining these skill sets. Going one step further, Activity 10.5 on page 243 addresses specific knowledge, self-awareness, and skills related to working with Arab American clients.

REFLECTION 10.5

As a counseling trainee, you are perhaps like a carpenter learning to use all of the tools assembled in your tool belt. The first few times you hold them, they may seem awkward, but with repeated practice, they become more familiar to you. You are unlike a carpenter, however, in that your most important tool is yourself. We could make the analogy that the tool belt represents your personality, your skills, your life history, your view of the world. Thus, in order to help clients of any culture or background, you should be familiar with the tools of our trade (e.g., theoretical approaches and techniques, methods for assessing and evaluating problems, exercises to improve health or work through those problems, resources for assistance) and the condition of your tool belt.

What is the state of your knowledge, awareness, and skills with respect to Arab American clients? Have you taken an opportunity to broaden your horizons by talking to people from a variety of backgrounds? Do you recognize any stereotypes or limited ideas present in your thinking about Arab Americans? Do you have an emotional response to the information in this chapter?

Think back to the acculturation visualization (Reflection 10.3) that you did earlier in this chapter. Recall some of the feelings that came to you as you imagined yourself in a whole new world with very little that was comforting or familiar. The empathy that you now have as a result of trying to walk in someone else's shoes (while still acknowledging that there can be limits to your understanding) is part of you. To reach out to a client, counselors can use some of what they know as part of the human experience, some of what they have learned about the specific journeys of others, and some tools that may clarify or resolve the physical, mental, emotional, or spiritual stress of the client. Spend some time thinking about how the tools you have acquired so far in your training would be useful with Arab American clients, and how you can polish up your tool belt (yourself) so that you are ready to respond.

Family and Community Involvement

Remember, Arab Americans tend to be collectivistic peoples. Therefore, in order to promote resilience, individual counseling should not only be focused on the collective unit rather than the individual, but also should involve individuals within that unit. Whenever possible and appropriate, it can be beneficial to bring in other family members. Engaging the support of community leaders, such as Imams (Islamic religious leaders), or other trusted individuals can also serve as a powerful intervention or strategy.

Along those lines, whenever attendance at a local community event can be incorporated into the treatment plan, it could be important to do so. For example, inviting a person who is self-conscious about appearance or social skills to a community event, with homework involving the counselor or others, can be beneficial. This approach may appear to run counter to the traditional Western view, but for this population may be far more effective.

It is important to gauge with each client or family whether the level to which the counselor is perceived as being a member of the greater community is a positive or negative attribute to the therapeutic relationship. On the one hand, it may be viewed as a positive in the sense that the counselor may have a better understanding and appreciation of cultural issues. On the other hand, issues of confidentiality and other boundaries may be less clear and may need to be reiterated more as a part of the counseling process.

Stigmas and Help-Seeking Behaviors

In the previous section on mental health issues, the high prevalence of somatization, or the physical manifestation of psychological distress, was mentioned. This presentation is rooted historically within Arab culture, although there have been and still are a wide array of tribal and other indigenous individuals whose holistic treatment of the person includes the psychological as well as physical symptoms and etiology. For counselors, being aware of this tendency toward somatization can help develop an authoritative stance, perhaps more consistent with that of a medical professional, which may be most effective.

In addition, counseling is viewed as a Western concept, therefore more likely to be sought out by later generations of Arab Americans. Individuals more recently immigrating, if seeking help at all, might do so from medical professionals or clergy members. Thus, particularly for counselors living near an Arab American enclave or urban community with a large population of Arab Americans, it is important to collaborate with helping professionals across a variety of arenas to develop client education interventions about counseling services as well as referral networks to promote resilience among individuals and communities. For counselors of Arab descent, counselor ethnicity may serve as an advantage in the sense that prospective clients might feel more culturally understood, or a disadvantage in the sense of confidentiality issues if the client and counselor live in the same community.

Vignettes Revisited

Now that we've explored some of the issues that might be likely to emerge in working within an Arab American community or with Arab American clients, as well as counseling and other treatment considerations, let's review each case again in further detail.

AHMED: A SCHOOL COUNSELING CASE   Recall the case of Ahmed, the middle schooler who recently relocated to the United States. Lonely and sad, not fitting in with the other Arab American kids or the non-Arab American ones, Ahmed has recently gotten involved in several fights at school. The principal has asked the parents to come in and meet with him and one of the school counselors for consultation. Both parents came to discuss the situation. The principal is recommending that Ahmed work with the school counselor and possibly a counselor from the outside community. During that meeting, the parents express their concerns. They have some questions about the counseling process, and share some hesitation about having their son involved in it, but they are assured that it is viewed as academic support. They are less willing to participate in community counseling at this point.

Imagine that you are the school counselor to whom Ahmed is assigned. Think about the following list of questions as you prepare for your work with him. In terms of your approach:

- What are some of the approaches that might be less helpful? More helpful?
- What are some of the strategies/techniques that might be least helpful? Most helpful?

In terms of engaging the family and community:

- How, if at all, should or could the family be involved?
- Which family members should or could be involved, and in what ways?
- To what extent is the family involved with the local community?
- To what extent is the family involved with the nearby Arab American community?
- To what extent is Ahmed interested in connecting with the various communities?
- Are there key individuals or community leaders who could be helpful in providing support to Ahmed or his family?
- How can these or other, additional approaches foster resilience among this individual and family?

In terms of stigmas:

- How do you think Ahmed might feel about seeing the school counselor?
- How do you think Ahmed might feel about having his family involved?
- How do you think Ahmed's family feels about him (and them) needing this extra support?
- Are there other ways in which this psychological distress and other stressors may be manifesting for Ahmed? For other family members?

THE AL-DINS: A FAMILY COUNSELING CASE   Abdallah has grown concerned about the rifts and conflicts within his family, and especially his wife's anxiety and increased isolation. He spoke generally about it with one of his colleagues, who suggested a specific counselor at a local family counseling agency. According to the colleague, this particular counselor has experience with and appreciation of cultural issues. Imagine that you are the family counselor. As you prepare to work with the al-Dins, consider the following issues. In terms of your approach:

- What are some of the approaches that might be less helpful? More helpful?
- What are some of the strategies/techniques that might be least helpful? Most helpful?

In terms of engaging the family and community:

- How, if at all, should or could the family be involved?
- Which family members should or could be involved, and in what ways?
- To what extent is the family involved with the local community?
- To what extent is the family involved with any Arab American community?
- To what extent are the al-Dins (individually or collectively) interested in connecting with the various communities?
- To what extent are the al-Dins connected with their home community and family in Algeria?
- Are there key individuals or community leaders who could be helpful in providing support to the al-Din family?

In terms of stigmas:

- How do you think each family member feels about counseling?
- How do you think each family member might feel about having family members involved?
- What possible consequences (positive or negative) might occur from this scenario?
- Are there other ways in which this psychological distress and other stressors may be manifesting for Nafisa? For other family members?

LAILA: A COLLEGE COUNSELING CASE   Laila's master's program is coming to an end, and she is feeling pressured by her family to make a decision. While they have been supportive of her educational pursuits, they feel it is time for her to focus on finding a marital partner alongside her upcoming career goals. Her brothers tease her about being being in a "men's" program and profession, adding to her self-questioning of gender, sexual, and career identity issues. Feeling confused and isolated, Laila decides to go to the counseling center to talk to someone about her concerns. In terms of your approach:

- What are some of the approaches that might be less helpful? More helpful?
- What are some of the strategies/techniques that might be least helpful? Most helpful? Most likely to foster resilience?

In terms of engaging the family and community:

- How, if at all, should or could the family be involved?
- Which family members should or could be involved, and in what ways?
- To what extent is Laila involved with the local Arab American community?
- To what extent is Laila involved with the local community-at-large?
- Are there key individuals or community leaders (in the Arab American community or the larger community) who could be helpful in providing support to Laila?

In terms of stigmas:

- How do you think Laila might feel about counseling?
- Can you identify any possible cultural stigmas that are involved in Laila's identity development processes (e.g., gender, sexual, career)?

SAMIR: A MEDICAL CASE   You are a counselor in a veteran's hospital. You receive a referral from one of the physicians for Samir. He has been coming to the hospital complaining of severe gastrointestinal distress. Although he has undergone a battery of tests, no medical etiology has been determined. The physician wants you to screen Samir for Post Traumatic Stress Disorder, depression, and anxiety.

Samir is extremely upset about the referral. He insists that his symptoms are medical and does not want to discuss personal issues with a stranger. On the other hand, he knows he needs to be somewhat compliant in order to maintain his Veteran's Administration benefits. As you prepare to work with Samir, consider the following. In terms of your approach:

- What are some of the approaches that might be less helpful? More helpful?
- What are some of the strategies/techniques that might be least helpful? Most helpful? Most likely to promote resilience?

In terms of engaging the family and community:

- How, if at all, should or could the family be involved?
- Which family members should or could be involved, and in what ways?
- To what extent is the family involved with the local community?
- To what extent is the family involved with any Arab American community?
- To what extent are Samir and his family (individually or collectively) interested in connecting with the various communities?
- To what extent are Samir and his family connected with their home community and family in Australia?
- Are there key individuals or community leaders who could be helpful in providing support to Samir and his family?

In terms of stigmas:

- How do you think Samir might feel about needing to seek counseling?
- How do you think Samir might feel about having his family involved?
- How do you think Samir's family feels about him (and them) needing this extra support?
- Are there other ways in which this psychological distress and other stressors may be manifesting for Samir? For other family members?

ACTIVITY 10.5

According to the American Counseling Association, self-awareness, knowledge, and skills are the key components to developing basic multicultural counseling competence (Sue et al., 1992). In counseling Arab Americans, these components can be addressed in the following ways. Feel free to add your own ideas to the list!

  I. **Self Awareness:** Learning about our own personal and cultural biases toward Arab Americans and determining ways to overcome them. In so doing, counselors can gain increased respect for their Arab American clients' culturally different backgrounds, experiences, and values.
 II. **Knowledge:** Learning about how our own culture both personally and professionally affects our attitudes toward Arab Americans; how oppression, racism, discrimination, and stereotyping against Arab Americans may affect our work with Arab American clients, including assessing internalized oppression; how traditional counseling settings may be incongruent with the cultural values of some Arab American clients; how Arab Americans' help seeking behaviors may affect the counseling process; and how testing and assessment may be culturally biased.
III. **Skills:** Learning ways to seek out education, training, and consultation to improve our effectiveness in working with Arab American clients; employing a wider range of verbal and nonverbal communication styles and responses, seek consultation with supporting personnel, and work to eliminate biases, prejudices, and discriminatory practices in their counseling settings and communities.

In small groups, discuss other ways by which you can increase your awareness, knowledge and skills for working with individuals and families of Arab descent.

COUNSELING CONSIDERATIONS ENDNOTE

More than ever before, today's counselors are charged with the task of serving as advocates for their clients, individually, locally, and nationally. Most helping professions have identified this new role as a critical one in today's world, given the vast diversity across culture, religion, sexual orientation, and the like. Working with Arab Americans, in particular, given the global post-9/11 climate, requires a knowledge level of U.S. foreign policy toward the Arab Middle East and neighboring regions, civil liberties issues around profiling and harassment, and laws surrounding immigration and seizure (Nassar-McMillan, 2003). All these in addition to the basic multicultural competencies applied to Arab American clients are requisite for building resilience effectively. (For more information about these multicultural competencies applied to Arab Americans, please see Nassar-McMillan, 2007.)

Living within an ethnic enclave can provide the necessary support to Arab Americans in order to move beyond initial stages of identity development and arrive at a mature and consolidated sense of ethnic identity. Individuals moving into those advanced identity stages could focus on projecting the positive aspects of their culture with pride. In various communities, support organizations have formed to promote employment (e.g., Arab American Chamber of Commerce), expand religious tolerance and understanding (e.g., Center for Muslim-Christian Understanding), provide accurate information about the history and politics of the Middle East (e.g., Middle East Institute), and support members of the community (e.g, ACCESS: Arab Community Center for Economic and Social Services). These resources also are available to counselors at large, interested in working with this population. Even outside ethnic enclaves, these organizations have a national scope and seek to provide information on a national level, and can provide the resources necessary to help counselors further develop their competencies. Table 10.1 provides a preliminary list of resources.

TABLE 10.1 Resources for Counseling Individuals and Families of Arab Descent

General Web Resources

www.aaiusa.org/

www.aaiusa.org/links.htm.

www.aaiusa.org/links.htm#On

www.accesscommunity.org

www.arabamericanbusiness.com

www.adc.org

http://angelfire.com/or/uasa

www.aaiusa.org/links.htm#Religion

www.cie.org

www.mideast.org

www.amideast.org

www.mepc.org

Books

The following selected resources are from *Teaching About Islam & Muslims in the Public School Classroom: A Handbook for Educators*, 3rd ed., produced by the Council on Islamic Education:

Al-Faruqi, L. (1991). *Women, Muslim society, and Islam.* Plainfield, IN: American Trust Publications.

The author of this text discusses a wide range of issues, such as marriage, divorce, gender roles, feminism, legal rights, education, and the family model. (ISBN: 0-89259-068-8)

Haneef, S. (1985). *What everyone should know about Islam and Muslims.* Chicago: Kazi Publications.

This text is a straightforward approach toward explaining the religion of Islam and its adherents. It is particularly useful as it explores life for Muslims in the United States and the challenges that young Muslims face growing up in the American cultural milieu. (ISBN: 0-935782-00-1)

Kahf, M. (1999). *Western representations of the Muslim woman.* Austin: University of Texas Press.

The author has made an intriguing analysis of the ways in which the idea of the Muslim woman has figured in Western literature, plays, songs, and the popular imagination. (ISBN: 0-2927-4336X)

Maqsood, R. (1994). *Teach yourself Islam.* Chicago: NTC Publishing Group.

This text is a clear and refreshing overview of Islam, with emphasis on contemporary issues and lifestyles. (ISBN: 0-86316-155-3)

Peters, F. E. (1990). *Judaism, Christianity, and Islam.* Princeton, NJ: Princeton Paperbacks (ISBN 0691020558)

This text takes the basic texts of the three monotheistic faiths and juxtaposes extensive passages from them to show the similarities and common issues facing the followers of each.

Legal Resources

- The following resources on discrimination and civil liberties are from the Arab American Institute Web site, www.aaiusa.org/discrimination.htm. Two general resources include:
- The U.S. Commission on Civil Rights Hotline, 1-800-552-6843
- The U.S. Department of Justice Civil Rights Division's Initiative to Combat the Post-9/11 Discriminatory Backlash, www.usdoj.gov/crt/nordwg.html
- To file a complaint about an alleged civil rights violation by a U.S. Department of Justice employee, including employees of the FBI, the Drug Enforcement Administration, the INS, the Federal Bureau of Prisons, and the U.S. Marshals Service: www.usdoj.gov/oig/hotline2.htm
- For a brochure on federal protections against national origin discrimination: English: www.usdoj.gov/crt/legalinfo/natlorg-eng.htm Arabic: www.usdoj.gov/crt/legalinfo/natlorg-ar.pdf
- For information on the Civil Liberties Restoration Act of 2004 (pdf): www.immigrationforum.org/documents/TheDebate/DueProcessPost911/CLRAsecbysec.pdf
- For information about the rights of INS detainees: www.immigration.gov/graphics/lawsregs/guidance.htm
- For resources on Workplace Rights of Muslims, Arabs, South Asians, and Sikhs under the Equal Employment Opportunity laws (updated May 2002): www.eeoc.gov/facts/backlash-employee.htm
- To learn about employer responsibilities concerning the employment of Muslims, Arabs, South Asians, and Sikhs (updated July 2002): www.eeoc.gov/facts/backlash-employer.html
- For information on federal laws against religious discrimination (a brochure published by the U.S. Department of Justice's Civil Rights Division, September 2002): www.usdoj.gov/crt/religdisc/religionpamp.htm

Summary

This chapter provided an exploration of the history of the Arab Middle East in terms of geographic and religious roots, along with the diversity of its inhabitants, definitions of Arabs and Arab Americans, and a discussion of the immigration waves to the United States. Working up the present day, some of the key issues comprising the global and domestic climate as they relate to the Arab Middle East were presented, as well as some of the sociopolitical challenges facing Arab Americans today, such as profiling and civil liberties.

The culture and values of many Arab Americans, like the importance of family and collectivism, were explored. Even though the majority of Arab Americans are non-Muslim, a basic understanding of Islam was presented because of the way Islam is interwoven into early and present-day Arab cultures of origin.

Many of today's Arab Americans, like their counterparts becoming more in touch with their own respective cultures of origin, are exploring their personal ethnic identification. For Arab Americans, of course, it is a little more complex given the sociopolitical climate discussed. Other important issues may play into that process, such as gender and acculturation stress.

Finally, and most importantly, this chapter provided a discussion about how some of the history, culture, sociopolitics, and all the background information may translate into potential counseling issues for some Arab Americans. Important considerations for working with this population were presented, especially the need to take on an advocacy role.

CHAPTER 11

Individuals and Families of Asian Descent

Arpana Inman and Alvin Alvarez

PREVIEW

At 4.2% of the population, the 12 million individuals who describe themselves as Asian American (Reeves & Bennett, 2004) have rapidly emerged onto the racial landscape of the United States. With a growth rate of 72% between 1990 and 2000, the Asian American community has been characterized as one of the fastest growing racial and ethnic communities in the United States (Reeves & Bennett, 2004). In particular, Asian Americans represent three broad yet distinct groups: East Asians from China, Taiwan, Japan, Philippines, and Korea; South Asians from India, Pakistan, Bangladesh, Sri Lanka, Nepal, Bhutan, and the Maldives; and Southeast Asians from Vietnam, Laos, Hmong, and Cambodia (Tewari, Inman, & Sandhu, 2003). Despite being categorized under the umbrella of "Asian Americans," there is much ethnic, linguistic, and historical diversity among these communities. Indeed, the U.S. Census Bureau (2004b) estimates that by 2050, this diverse Asian American community will increase by over 200% and constitute 8% of the country's population. Nevertheless, despite the statistical overview that such figures provide, numerous scholars have argued that treatment of this community in strictly aggregate terms obscures the complexities and heterogeneity of the lived experiences of Asian Americans both currently and historically (Hall & Okazaki, 2002). Consequently, to shift away from broad statistics, the first section of this chapter begins with a historical overview of Asian Americans and the role of discrimination in their lives. The second section examines the ethnic, socioeconomic, linguistic, and educational complexities that characterize its heterogeneity. The following three sections provide counselors with a baseline understanding of Asian American culture and values, individual differences, and the prevalence of psychological distress. Last, the final sections of the chapter explore issues related to help-seeking and coping and outline counseling guidelines. Before beginning this chapter, complete Reflection 11.1.

REFLECTION 11.1

Assume you are Asian American. Using the following three lenses, write your thoughts:

1. How do you perceive yourself as a member of this group?

_____

_____

_____

2. How might others perceive you?

_____

_____

_____

3. How would you like to be perceived?

_____

_____

_____

ASIAN AMERICAN HISTORY

Since the large-scale arrival of Chinese laborers on the sugar plantations of Hawaii and the gold mines of California in the mid-1800s, immigration has been a common thread shared by numerous Asian ethnic groups. Whether they were "pushed" from their countries of origin by political strife, economic instability, social persecution, famine, or war, Asian immigrants have been "pulled" to the United States (what the Cantonese called *gam saan* or "Gold Mountain") by the lure of similar factors: economic fortunes, high-paying jobs, and the potential to provide for one's family. Indeed, the same hopes that currently lure Asian immigrants from Taiwan, China, and India to Silicon Valley are reminiscent of what drew Cantonese and Punjabi laborers to the hills and fields of California since the 1850s.

Similar to the pull of immigration, Asian immigrants have also faced similar forms of hostility and discrimination. For instance, Chinatowns began to develop because Chinese Americans were restricted from living among Whites and were not allowed to own land, buy property, intermarry with Whites, or obtain an education (Chan, 1991). Because they were perceived as economic and social threats, anti-Asian violence was also a shared experience of early Asian American immigrants as evidenced by events such as the anti-Chinese riots at Rock Springs, Wyoming, in 1885 with 43 casualties; the armed expulsion of 100 Asian Indian laborers from Live Oak, California, in 1908; the armed expulsion of over 100 Japanese farm workers from Turlock, California, in 1921; and the anti-Filipino riots of 1930 in Watsonville, California (Chan, 1991).

Parallel to the individual treatment of Asian immigrants, institutional and legislative forms of discrimination were also enacted against Asian American communities. From antimiscegenation codes, housing restrictions, and educational limitations to ethnic-specific business taxes, antinaturalization and anti-immigration laws, Asian Americans faced numerous obstacles in their search for Gold Mountain. Examples of exclusionary immigration laws include the **Chinese Exclusion Act of 1882,** the first ethnic-specific ban of its kind; the **Gentleman's Agreement of 1907**, which restricted Japanese immigration; the **Immigration Act of 1917**, which restricted Asian Indian immigration; and the passage of the **Tydings-McDuffie Act of 1934**, which effectively restricted Filipino immigration despite the fact that Filipinos were considered U.S. nationals at the time (Chan, 1991). In effect, despite the variety of Asian ethnic groups that immigrated to the United States, each group faced strikingly similar instances of institutional discrimination. Indeed, the height of institutional discrimination was exemplified by the 1942 incarceration of 120,000 Japanese Americans (62% of whom were U.S. citizens) who were forced to evacuate their homes and sell their businesses as they were imprisoned in remote internment camps without trial, due process, or right to appeal.

Contemporary Asian America emerged with the passage of the Immigration and Nationality Act of 1965. Prior to 1965 existing immigration laws severely restricted Asian immigration, as previously noted, while also favoring European immigration. After 1965, immigration was based on family reunification rather than on national origins quotas. As a result, the number of Asian immigrants has grown dramatically from 800,000 in 1970 to 7.3 million in 2000, an 800% increase (Reeves & Bennett, 2004). In contrast to the influx of voluntary immigrants after 1965, the experience of Southeast Asian refugees after the 1975 fall of South Vietnam is quite distinct. As a result of U.S. military involvement, brutal communist reprisals, as well as class-based cleansing and genocide, over 1 million Southeast Asians have fled Vietnam, Cambodia, and Laos since the mid-1970s. Enduring starvation, overcrowded conditions, disease, and death in both reeducation camps and refugee camps, as well as the involuntary loss of homes and forced resettlement, the psychological and traumatic experience of forced migration under such conditions is quite different than that of voluntary immigrants.

Given the relatively recent influx of both Asian immigrants and refugees, the notion of an "Asian American" community is an equally recent phenomenon. Despite the arrival of Filipinos in the bayous south of New Orleans in the 1760s (Chan, 1991), Asian Americans as a demographic, psychological, and sociocultural community did not emerge until 200 years later. Not until the 1960s did Japanese, Chinese, and Filipino student activists begin to informally use the term *Asian American* in recognition of their commonalities and shared history of oppression. Inspired by the civil rights movement, the nationalism of the Black Panther Party, and the anti–Vietnam War movement, the notion of a pan-ethnic or racial community was intended in a spirit of political unification that was in stark contrast to a 200-year history characterized more by ethnic separation (Chan, 1991).

Yet beyond a simple narration of history and migration, the threads of immigration and discrimination that are woven throughout various Asian ethnic communities also reflect their shared psychological experiences. To leave one's country, family, friends, and all that is familiar for a country where you may not know anyone, may not have a job, may not know the language or customs—and to do so with only the hope of a better life—is a psychological experience that is embedded within Asian American communities both past and present. Similarly, to be faced with laws, regulations, and attitudes rooted in racism and discrimination, and to receive the message both covertly and overtly that one does not belong, has been and continues to be a shared experience of Asian Americans. Consequently, although counselors often place an emphasis on understanding their clients as individuals, it is equally important to recognize that individuals live within a larger community that is shaped by both historical and sociopolitical influences.

CONTEMPORARY FORMS OF DISCRIMINATION AND STEREOTYPES

To better understand the sociopolitical context in which Asian Americans live, it may be helpful to examine how Asian Americans have been perceived and treated within the United States. According to Jones (1997), **institutional racism** is reflected in regulations, laws, policies, and procedures that restrict the lives of individuals on the basis of race. Consistent with the historical examples of institutional racism that were previously discussed, Asian Americans continue to encounter contemporary forms of institutional racism. According to the U.S. Commission on Civil Rights (1992), more current examples of institutional racism against Asian Americans include "English-only" language initiatives; income-to-education disparities, in which Asian Americans earn incomes that are disproportionately lower than Whites with the same level of education; and glass-ceiling effects in career advancement, in which Asian Americans, despite their experience and training, are underrepresented in administrative and managerial positions. Similarly, Asian Americans also continue to experience **individual racism** from those who endorse and act upon the belief in one racial group's superiority over another group (Jones, 1997). Examples of contemporary individual racism range from differential treatment, verbal insults, and racial slurs to physical harassment, vandalism, and in some cases homicide. Indeed, the murder of Vincent Chin in 1982 by ex-autoworkers who regarded him as the reason for losing their jobs and the 1987 murder of Navroze Mody by a Jersey City gang called the Dotbusters (referring to South Asian women's bindis) have become galvanizing rallying points for the Asian American community (Chan, 1991).

The discrimination that Asian Americans face is directly related to stereotypic perceptions and attitudes that people have of them. Beginning with the large scale arrival of Chinese immigrants in the 19th century and the xenophobic portrayal of this immigration wave as the "yellow peril," Asian American stereotypes have cast this community as "other." Images of Asian Americans as "heathens," "dog-eaters," "martial-artists," "exotic," and "dragon ladies" have objectified this community by reducing them to one-dimensional caricatures set apart from and unassimilable into dominant White society. Hence, such stereotypes add fuel to the treatment of this community as economic, labor, cultural, and most recently national security threats to what is deemed "mainstream America." Of particular relevance to contemporary Asian Americans are the stereotypes of the "perpetual foreigner" and the "model minority."

From the seemingly innocuous question "Where are you from?" to a national headline that proclaimed "American Beats Kwan" in reference to native Californian figure skater Michelle Kwan, the perception of Asian Americans as being "perpetual foreigners" has been a persistent theme in the daily experiences of Asian Americans. Despite the repeal of antinaturalization laws that explicitly prohibited them from becoming citizens, Asian Americans continue to be implicitly regarded as being what Tuan (1998) calls "illegitimate Americans," regardless of their nativity or citizenship. Current events—such as campaign finance scandals, the racial profiling of Wen Ho Lee at Los Alamos National Laboratory, and the presumptive treatment of South Asians as terrorists since September 11—have further perpetuated the perception that Asian Americans are not only foreigners, but foreigners who cannot be trusted and are potential threats to national security (National Asian Pacific American Legal Consortium, 2003; Tuan, 1998). As Tuan succinctly states, "Ultimately, being an American is equated with being White" (p. 40) and without the option to cast aside their visible racial differences, Asian Americans, at best, can claim a hyphenated status.

The implicit second-class status of the perpetual foreigner stereotype stands in distinct contrast to the **model minority myth**. Since the 1966 *New York Times Magazine* article titled "Success Story: Japanese-American Style," the model minority stereotype has been used to describe and elevate the status of Asian Americans. According to this stereotype, Asian Americans as a group have become a model community that has "overcome" its minority status despite the barriers presented by racism. Presumably, high academic achievement, high family incomes, low mental health utilization rates, and low delinquency rates of Asian Americans are all indicators of this community's success. However, numerous scholars (Chan, 1991; Tuan, 1998) have noted that the emergence of this stereotype coincided with the racial unrest of the civil rights movement and that the "presumed success" of Asian Americans was used to pit racial groups against one another, while simultaneously minimizing the racial and socioeconomic inequities raised by communities of color. To counter such idyllic portrayals of Asian Americans, scholars (Chan, 1991; Tuan, 1998) further argued that the aggregation of Asian Americans into a seemingly homogeneous and monolithic racial group fails to account for the heterogeneity and diversity of this community and thereby overemphasized

Asian American success while obscuring legitimate racial disparities. Thus, the following section examines both the complexity and heterogeneity within the Asian American community. Reflection 11.2 provides an opportunity to investigate some Asian American communities.

REFLECTION 11.2

Explore various Asian American communities via the Web. For a start, you may want to read the discussion forums on Angry Asian Man (www.angryasianman.com), Mixed Asians (www.mixedasians.com), or the Asian Pacific Islander Blog Network (www.apiablogs.net). What are your reactions to the postings? What resonates with you? Is there anything that is unfamiliar to you? How are these views similar to or different than the perspectives you have been exposed to?

ASIAN AMERICAN HETEROGENEITY

Given the unidimensional portrayals that characterize these aforementioned stereotypes, multicultural competence with Asian Americans is directly related to understanding this community's demographic heterogeneity. Without such an understanding, counselors may inadvertently generalize their knowledge of the Asian American community and assume that what applies for one segment of this community will also apply to other segments. However, the heterogeneity of the Asian American community, along dimensions such as ethnicity, language fluency, educational attainment, and socioeconomic status, may have implications for counseling Asian American clients. Indeed, factors such as language proficiency, immigration history, and educational level may influence the manner in which Asian American clients understand their presenting issues, their attitudes toward counseling, and their expectations of the counselor, their access to resources as well as the effectiveness of counseling itself. Consequently, this section examines the demographic heterogeneity of the Asian American community with the intent of providing a baseline appreciation of this community's within-group diversity.

The aggregation of Asian Americans as a racial group obscures the ethnic heterogeneity of this community and the approximately 43 distinct Asian ethnic groups from 24 different countries of origin (Hall & Okazaki, 2002) that are subsumed under this broader racial category. Although historical dominance has led to an assumption that equates Asian with being East Asian (i.e., Chinese, Japanese, Korean), the 10 largest Asian ethnic groups according to the U.S. Census (i.e., Chinese, Filipino, Asian Indian, Vietnamese, Korean, Japanese, Cambodian, Hmong, Laotian and Pakistani; U.S. Census Bureau, 2000) clearly underscore the inaccuracy of this assumption. Indeed, an examination of the smaller Asian ethnic communities, ranging from Bhutanese to Indonesian to Sri Lankan to Mien, simply corroborates the ethnic diversity of this community. Moreover, given that the five fastest growing Asian ethnicities (i.e., Bangladeshi, Asian Indian, Pakistani, Hmong, and Sri Lankans) are quite distinct (Lai & Arguelles, 2003) from the five largest groups, it stands to reason that the ethnic composition of this community will continue to evolve.

Asian Americans are also diverse in terms of their immigration histories. Although large-scale Asian immigration began in the mid-1800s with the Chinese, the majority of Asian Americans (i.e., 69%) are foreign-born (Reeves & Bennett, 2004). Indeed, 76% of all foreign-born Asian Americans have arrived since 1980 or later. Nevertheless, within-group ethnic differences in immigration should also be noted. For instance, whereas 75% or more of some Asian ethnic groups (i.e., Asian

Indian, Vietnamese, Korean) are foreign-born, only 40% of Japanese Americans are foreign-born. Relatedly, the paths to the United States have been varied across ethnic groups. For example, whereas 88% of Laotians immigrated to the United States as refugees, 36% of Taiwanese have immigrated to the United States through employment preferences. Hence, for counselors working with Asian Americans, it may be important to recognize that they may encounter a continuum of immigration and refugee histories, ranging from a fourth-generation Chinese American to a newly arrived college-educated immigrant from South Korea to a Cambodian refugee with little formal education. More importantly, these immigration patterns may have implications for their clients' understanding of and adaptation to U.S. cultural norms.

Particularly in light of the model minority assumptions about Asian Americans, beliefs about the universal economic and academic success of Asian Americans have rendered issues of poverty and educational inequities in certain Asian ethnic groups nearly invisible. While a high median income of Asian American families has often been interpreted as evidence of their economic well-being, the use of such a statistic fails to account for the larger number of wage-earners in Asian American households, the concentration of Asian Americans in high-cost urban areas, and income-to-education-level disparities (U.S. Commission on Civil Rights, 1992). For instance, statistics show that in California, Korean men make 82%, Chinese men earn 68%, and Filipino men make 62% of the income that White men make (Uy, 2004). Relatedly, the U.S. Census (2000c) showed that only 53.1% of Asian Americans owned homes when compared to 73.2% of Whites. In fact, it has been noted that Asian American men make 10% to 17% less than White men, and Asian American women make 40% less than White women (Uy, 2004). Furthermore, although Asian Indian and Japanese American families have median incomes that are $11,000 higher than the national median, it is also important to recognize that Cambodian and Hmong families have median incomes that are approximately $15,000 lower than the national median. Indeed, although Asian Americans on the whole have higher median family incomes than White Americans, their poverty rates are actually higher than White Americans. For instance, Hmong and Cambodians have poverty rates (38% and 29%, respectively) that are considerably higher than the national average of 12% (Reeves & Bennett, 2004).

Similar trends are also mirrored in occupational status and educational attainment. Whereas 50% or more of Asian Indian, Chinese, and Japanese Americans are in professional or management positions, only 17% or less of Laotian, Hmong, and Cambodian Americans are in similar positions (Reeves & Bennett, 2004). In regard to educational status, Asian Americans as an aggregate have a higher percentage of individuals with a bachelor's degree compared to the national average (i.e., 44% vs. 24%). However, this aggregation masks the fact that while over 50% of Asian Indians and Pakistanis have a bachelor's degree, less than 9% of Laotian, Hmong, and Cambodian Americans do. Indeed, over 49% of Laotian, Hmong, and Cambodian Americans have less than a high school degree compared to the national average of 19% with a similar educational level. Moreover, it is critical to recognize that for many recent Asian immigrants, this educational capital is reflective of the education they received in their countries of origin rather than in the United States. Indeed, many of the college-educated, professional immigrants who immigrate to the United States can be rightfully described as the "elites of their countries of origin" (National Commission on Asian American and Pacific Islander Research in Education, 2008, p. 26). Thus, an understanding of the economic and educational diversity within the Asian American community may provide counselors with insights into the resources that are available to their clients and the resulting academic, sociocultural, and occupational capital that comes with such resources.

Linguistic diversity may also have implications for counselors in working with Asian American communities. As a group, 21% of Asian Americans spoke only English at home and approximately 40% reported that they spoke English less than "very well" (Reeves & Bennett, 2004).

However, as with other demographic characteristics within this community, closer scrutiny of the data yields notable within-group differences. For instance, among all Asian ethnic groups, only Japanese Americans reported that more than 50% of their community spoke only English. In contrast, less than 9% of Vietnamese, Cambodian, Hmong, Laotian, and Pakistani Americans reported that they spoke only English at home. Indeed 62% of Vietnamese reported concerns with English proficiency whereas less than 25% of Asian Indians and Filipinos reported similar fluency concerns. Consequently, in a profession that is highly dependent on verbal expression, counselors may need to recognize that their Asian American clients may enter counseling with a range of linguistic abilities.

Hence, the notion of what constitutes "Asian America" is both complex and continually evolving. As these demographic statistics demonstrate, counselors may encounter a wide range of Asian American clients—many of whom will have immigration experiences and academic and socioeconomic resources that are entirely different from one another. Therefore, multicultural competence will be demonstrated by a continuing and fluid openness to learning the different segments of this community.

ASIAN AMERICAN CULTURE AND VALUES

Cultural values influence our socialization by impacting our psychological and social functioning (Inman, Constantine, & Ladany, 1999). Although there is much diversity, Asian Americans are influenced by some common values, ideologies, and philosophies that guide their lives and perspectives (Inman & Yeh, 2007). This section highlights specific values that provide a baseline foundation to understanding their experience. However, it is important to note that the extent to which Asian Americans adhere to these values is influenced by their generational status, immigration histories, and acculturation levels. Thus, it is our belief that it is the counselor's responsibility to assess the extent to which the particular Asian American client identifies with these values and beliefs. To prevent making generalizations, counselors are encouraged to increase their knowledge of the complexities of and distinctions within the Asian American culture. To help in this process, various forms of media provide numerous examples of Asian American culture (see Table 11.1 at the end of this chapter).

Family

Within the Asian community, family or kinship refers to an extended network of relationships that encompass several households (Das & Kemp, 1997). In many instances, multiple generations and caretakers may reside in the family (Yee, DeBaryshe, Yuen, Kim, & McCubbin, 2007) and influence decisions. For instance, it has been noted that older siblings play an important caretaking role in South Asian communities (Seymour, 1993). Furthermore, significant family members who might reside in the country of origin may also exert psychological pressures and influence decision making in the families in the United States.

The family is considered to be of primary importance and family needs often override individual needs. Relatedly, the notions of a private space or an individualistic identity go against the Asian collectivistic value orientation (Prathikanti, 1997) because one's actions are considered to influence the welfare and integrity of the family. This emphasis on a family identity and interdependence makes filial piety a strongly espoused value in the Asian American family. Within this context, obligation, respect, and a strong sense of duty to the parents and elders is not uncommon. In fact, a strong allegiance to parents can continue after adult offsprings (especially the male child) are married. For instance, it is common for adult children to reside with their parents until and even after marriage and for married sons to take care of their parents in their old age (Tewari et al., 2003). This emphasis on family ties plays an important role in "saving face" and protecting the honor of the family. This is influenced by parenting that tends to be authoritarian and directive. Actions that benefit the family are praised whereas guilt-inducing techniques such as withdrawing familial support are often used as a means of enforcing discipline and maintaining family cohesion (Ina, 1997; Sue, 1997).

Gender Roles

Socialized primarily within a patriarchal society, a well-functioning family is one that prescribes to the specific gender roles and communication rules set by the family (Sue, 1997). Gender roles and responsibilities are clearly prescribed and based in one's authority and status in the family and social hierarchy (Ramisetty-Mikler, 1993). For instance, age is valued and elders are accorded great respect and importance. Respect is implied in obedience, formality, and social restraint in relationships with elders. Men are the primary decision makers in the family whereas women's roles and status primarily evolve from being married and having children (Ibrahim, Oshnishi, & Sandhu, 1997). Education is seen as a marketable tool in marriage for women (Almeida, 1996). However, it is important to note that within-group differences exist. For example, Japanese Americans tend to be more acculturated and hence more egalitarian in their roles due to several generations having lived in this country. Filipino Americans also tend to be more egalitarian whereas Chinese Americans, Koreans, and Southeast Asians tend to be more patriarchal and traditional in orientation (Blair & Qian, 1998). On the other hand, South Asians have been noted to be traditional in their homes but contemporary in relation to education- and achievement-related issues (Dhruvarajan, 1993).

Interpersonal Relationships

Among Asian Americans, maintaining harmony governs interpersonal relationships (Ina, 1997). Thus, being nondirective, nonconfrontational, and silent are considered a virtue. Moderation in behaviors is valued through self-restraint and self-control. Asians tend not to be too emotionally demonstrative in their relationships as displaying strong emotions is often seen as a sign of immaturity. Relatedly, humility in deeds and actions is seen as maintaining respect and dignity in relationships.

Intimacy and Marriage

An important aspect of interpersonal relationships is issues related to intimacy and marriage. Asian American youth are traditionally not encouraged to date. Dating and sexuality are intimately linked and parents often fear negative repercussions related to dating (Dasgupta & Dasgupta, 1996). Often, parents and extended family play an important role in choosing a mate for their children through social networks. For example, arranged or semiarranged marriages are a common practice among South Asian communities with children typically encouraged to marry within their ethnic community. Because marriage is considered a union of two families, the choice of mate involves introducing potential candidates from families with "good educational and financial backgrounds" (Inman, Howard, Beaumont, & Walker, 2007). However, marriage based on love and mutual compatibility has increasingly become a norm for Asian American youth (Yee et al., 2007). Furthermore, although Asian Americans traditionally tend to be modest regarding their sexuality and nondemonstrative in their sexual and physical affection there are generational variations based on levels of acculturation. For instance, the more acculturated the individual, the greater likelihood of being demonstrative and having open discussions regarding sexuality and dating (Inman et al., 1999).

Divorce and interracial marriages have traditionally not been a very common practice among Asian Americans. The U.S. Census indicates that less than 10% (as compared to 19% of the total population) of Asians are likely to be separated, widowed, or divorced (Reeves & Bennett, 2004), with Japanese Americans having the highest rates of divorce. However, recent trends suggest that there are specific gender and ethnic differences among Asians who marry interracially. For instance, compared to 23% of Asian women, only 12% of Asian men marry interracially. In terms of ethnic and gender differences, Japanese Americans (20% men and 41% women) have been known to have a higher percentage of interracial marriages when compared to Filipinos (13% men and 33% women), and Koreans (4% men and 27% women). These trends suggest greater intermarriage among U.S.-born Asians when compared to immigrant Asian Americans (Xie & Goyette, 2004). However, it is interesting to note that among Asian Indians, foreign-born Asian Indians seem to engage in higher interracial marriages than U.S.-born Asians (U.S. Census Bureau, 2000c).

Education

Asian Americans have a high regard for learning. In most Asian American families, academic achievement and a successful career are highly valued and indicative of a good family upbringing. The educational emphasis is seen as going beyond the individual to enhance the whole family (Sue, 1997). Relatedly, there is pressure to spend time studying at the expense of other curricular activities. While the pressure to obtain certain jobs (e.g., science related or technical) over others (e.g., psychologists) has been noted as a cultural expectation, recently, Inman, Howard, et al. (2007) noted that Asian Indian parents believed that these choices went beyond culture to ensure that their children gained occupational and financial security as minority members within the United States. Indeed, Sue and Okazaki (1990) have convincingly argued that in response to perceived restrictions and limitations due to discrimination, Asian Americans place a higher value on education as the most viable means of upward mobility, a concept they refer to as **relative functionalism**.

Religion

Depending on the geographic region, different religious teachings serve as important spiritual philosophies guiding Asian American lives. For instance, East Asian Americans like the Chinese Americans tend to follow Confucianism, Buddhism, and Christianity. Due to a Spanish influence, Filipinos oftentimes tend to be Catholic, whereas Buddhism, Christianity, and Shinotoism are primary religions practiced among Japanese Americans (Lee, 1997). Although Hinduism is the major religion in South Asia, Islam, Sikhism, Jainism, Zoroastrianism (Parsi), the Bahai faith, and Judaism are also practiced in India and other regions of South Asia (Tewari et al., 2003). On the other hand, Southeast Asians such as the Cambodians and Laotians have been strongly influenced by Hinduism and Buddhism, whereas the Vietnamese practice Buddhism and Catholicism. Conversely, the Mien and Hmong tend to believe in supernatural powers and are animistic (Lee, 1997). Either based in a polytheistic or a monotheistic notion of God, a majority of Asian communities believe in fate, rebirth, and an afterlife. Commensurate with this is the belief that pain (or stress) and pleasure are essential to one's existence and a natural part of a lifelong process (Palsane & Lam, 1996). These religious philosophies influence perspectives on life, health, and illness (Inman & Yeh, 2007). In many of these communities, places of worship (e.g., churches, mosques, temples, monasteries) and religious figures such as the priest or minister (Christianity), the mullah/Imam (Islam), pundit (Hinduism), or monk (Buddhism) may be key sources of support during times of difficulties. Alternatively, there may be several Asian Americans who are atheists or agnostics.

Death and Dying

While death is a universal phenomenon, expressions of grief and death rituals vary by ethnicity and religion. However, the basic premise underlying death rituals seems to have a common thread among the different Asian communities. For instance, death is a communal affair among several

Asian groups. Burials and cremation ceremonies are traditionally performed by the males in the family and elders are often consulted in performing rites (Inman, Yeh, Madan-Bahel, & Nath, 2007). Another common theme is that of the impact of the rituals on the family and the deceased. The Hmong believe that proper burial and ancestral worship influence the health, safety, and prosperity of the family (Bliatout, 1993) whereas Buddhists believe that proper burial rituals and state of the mind of the dying person influence the rebirth process (Truitner & Truitner, 1993). Similarly, for Hindus, cremations and other death rituals are designed to assist with rebirth and release the soul from its earthly existence; for Muslims, burials are crucial to the Islamic belief in the physical resurrection of the dead (Rees, 2001).

INDIVIDUAL DIFFERENCES AND IDENTITIES

Because of their diversity, to speak of Asian Americans as a single homogeneous entity is misleading. There are multiple ways in which aspects of diversity (e.g., immigration, ethnicity, race, gender) shape the socialization processes, identity development, and interactions for Asian Americans. Understanding the complexity of Asian Americans involves examining the meaning behind their experiences, situations, and behaviors (Uba, 2002). In this section, we highlight this complexity by addressing issues related to immigration and multiple identities that frame Asian American lives. Although we deconstruct these issues and examine them separately, it is important to note that the multidimensionality of Asian American identities must be examined through the interrelated axes of the different contexts (e.g., race).

Immigration, Enculturation, and Acculturation

The nature and reason for immigration, the age at immigration, language abilities, past and present exposure to Western cultures, immigration status, socioeconomic status, professional status, ethnic pride, and the length of stay in the United States are factors that have been known to mediate Asian American adaptation to the U.S. society (Lee, 1997). In attempting to understand the adaptation experience of Asian Americans, researchers have focused on the constructs of enculturation and acculturation. Enculturation refers to socialization within one's own ethnic cultural values, attitudes, and behaviors, while acculturation occurs within the context of contact with the dominant culture (White culture in the United States) and refers to the extent to which one becomes socialized to the "host culture" thorough involvement in the values, behaviors, and other aspects of the host culture (Berry, 1980). Whereas acculturation is not linear and total assimilation to the host culture is not desirable (Lee, 1997), literature suggests that Asian Americans who are further removed from their immigration experience are likely to be more acculturated to the dominant culture when compared to Asian Americans who are closer to their immigration experience (Kim, Atkinson, & Umemoto, 2001).

To facilitate success, Asian Americans have been noted to selectively adapt to certain U.S. cultural norms (e.g., English proficiency, career goals, dress) while holding onto fundamental ethnic cultural values related to family relations, religion, and intimate relations. In this context, although Asian Americans might engage in U.S.-based activities, they may not fully identify with the American culture. Conversely, it is important to note that Asian Americans who are born in the United States may have a stronger identification with the American culture first and Asian culture second. Alternatively, there may be those who are both strongly acculturated to the American culture and strongly identified with the Asian culture (Liebkind, Jasinskaja-Lathi, & Solheim, 2004).

In highlighting these realities, Uba (2002) challenges us to question the traditional conceptualization of acculturation. By aligning the Asian subcontinent as the "home country" for Asian immigrants as well as U.S.-born Asians, the latter group often gets seen as "guests" in their own homeland.

Although past and recent immigrants have had to acculturate to a predominantly White culture, the current makeup of the United States is multicultural and multigenerational and encompasses values from multiple cultural groups. These individual differences and identities are important issues in contextualizing the complexities of Asian American lives. Attend to Reflection 11.3 to further consider the role of acculturation.

REFLECTION 11.3

Acculturation is a significant clinical consideration. In working with a client, how do you determine a client's level of acculturation? What are some indicators of this? What sorts of questions might you ask to determine this? Write your thoughts below:

Ethnicity and Race

Ethnicity refers to shared but unique cultural values, traditions, norms, and customs within an ethnic community, whereas **race** refers to an arbitrary classification system based in positions of power and privilege. In the United States, ethnicity and race operate as essential frames of reference through which social interactions are interpreted (Outlaw, 1990). Against this backdrop, acquiring an ethnic and racial identity becomes important as one navigates relationships, and maintains visibility within the context of both the culture of origin and the dominant culture (Inman, 2006).

Although the process of ethnic identification begins at a very young age with family playing a significant role in this socialization process, the social construction of ethnic identity within the context of a U.S. society takes on a unique and different meaning for Asian Americans. Growing up in a bicultural setting, a fundamental dilemma that evolves for Asian Americans is the degree to which one's ethnic identity is valued and must be retained (Inman, 2006; Kwan & Sodowsky, 1997; Sodowsky et al., 1995).

While ethnic identity research has revealed that a strong attachment and sense of belonging to one's cultural roots and traditions has positive psychological outcomes for Asian Americans (Phinney & Alipuria, 1990; Yip & Fulgni, 2002), Cheryan and Tsai (2007) believe that the tendency to focus on attachment to one's Asian ancestral country of origin alone tends to obfuscate other identifications that Asian Americans may have. Because ethnic identity may function differently for foreign-born Asians versus U.S.-born Asian Americans, there is a need to understand ethnic identification more broadly to include the attachment one feels to all "cultural heritages, including those not based specifically on one's country of origin" (Cheryan & Tsai, p. 125). For instance, Inman (2006) found that ethnic identification was a greater buffer against stress for foreign-born first-generation South Asians than U.S.-born second-generation South Asians. Similar results were found in Ying, Lee, and Tsai's (2000) study on foreign versus U.S.-born Chinese Americans.

In essence, because of a bicultural influence, Asian Americans internalize two cultures that inform and influence their lives—the Asian identity and the American identity. Although being "American" is not consistent with an ethnic identity (Cheryan & Tsai, 2007), identifying with an American identity and being seen as American provides Asian Americans with a sense of belonging, a sense of legitimacy, and cultural competence that increases their ability to navigate interactions effectively and to access resources (Phinney, Horenczyk, Liebkind, & Vedder, 2001; Ying et al., 2000).

Interestingly, how particular aspects of identity may operate in particular situations is influenced by social cues that Asian Americans experience (LaFromboise, Coleman, & Gerton, 1993) as well as exposure and connection to a cultural context (e.g., visiting Asia or lack of contact with Asia; Cheryan & Tsai, 2007), with some aspects being seen as more salient than others. Thus, different aspects of identity may be activated based on different contexts, a notion termed as **cultural frame switching** (Hong, Morris, Chiu, & Benet-Martinez, 2000). Related to these varying aspects of identity is the role of racial identity in Asian American lives.

The concept of race and racism has been an elusive one for Asian Americans. Despite a long history of racism and discrimination (e.g., denial of land ownership and citizenship, antimiscegenation laws, racial profiling, targets of racial slurs and violence, internment camps) (Alvarez & Helms, 2001; Chan, 1991) there are varying views of acceptance from within and outside this community. The difficulty in recognizing that Asian Americans experience discrimination is a function of several factors: the model minority myth (Wu, 2002), tendency to dichotomize racism as a Black–White issue (Espiritu, 1997; Sue, 1994); the lack of racial socialization and a language to speak to these issues among new immigrants (Demo & Hughes, 1990); and related racial politics of success and economics. These factors tend to mask the negative effects of discrimination on the well-being of Asian Americans. To counter this, Alvarez, Juang, and Liang (2006) find that discussions around race and racism with significant individuals in one's life are critical to enhancing Asian Americans' awareness of racism.

However, there has been a greater attention to and awareness of racism within this community due to discrimination (Kessler, Mickelson, & Williams, 1999; Liang, Li & Kim, 2004; Sue, Bucceri, Lin, Nadal, & Torino, 2007; Ying et al., 2000) and reports of increased anti-Asian sentiment since the terrorist attacks on September 11, 2001 (Inman, Yeh et al., 2007; National Asian Pacific American Legal Consortium, 2002; Yeh, Inman, Kim, & Okubo, 2006). In fact, Sue, Bucceri, et al. (2007) highlight racial microaggressions that can come in the form of microassaults (e.g., racial slurs such as "chinks," "Fresh off the Boats" [FOBs], "American-Born Confused Desis" [ABCDs]), microinsults (e.g., assumption that Asian Americans may not be good managers), and microinvalidations (e.g., Asian American complemented for speaking good English or speaking without an accent). These forms of discriminatory acts relegate Asian Americans to a perpetual foreigner status despite several generations having grown up in this country. Thus, the intersections of ethnic and racial identities must be considered when working with Asian Americans.

Gender Roles

Traditional Asian cultures suggest clear and stringent gender roles for Asian men and women with several religious teachings (e.g., Confucianism, Hinduism) seeing masculine and feminine characteristics intrinsic and complementary to each other. In keeping with this, there is a greater variability in notions of masculinity among Asian men when compared to White men (Chua & Fujino, 1999). Based in Asian cultural values, men are brought up to be group and family focused (Liu & Iwamoto, 2006), fulfilling parental and familial expectations (Lee, 1996) and expected to be the main breadwinner in the family. Furthermore, due to a patriarchal emphasis, men seem to experience less stringent rules and expectations in relation to sexual behaviors and intimacy. Asian women, on the other hand, experience greater community censures related to gender roles and intimacy issues, and bear the disproportionate burden of passing on cultural traditions (Dasgupta, 1998).

Asian men and women have had to deal with long-standing stereotypes and tensions between multiple cultures and gender role expectations (Root, 1995). Although there are some similarities between Asian and White values, the emphasis has often been on the contrasting differences. For instance, there are images of Asian women as being subservient, passive, childlike, innocent, and exotic, and as mail-order brides, dragon ladies, and conscientious hard workers. Asian men are often stereotyped as being nerdy or geeky, feminine, industrious, passive, and asexual (Chan, 1998; Liu, 1997; Liu & Chang, 2007). The stereotypes attributed to Asian women (e.g., mail-order brides, dragon ladies) have in effect led to sexual exploitation and a continued objectification of these women. Conversely, the dominant myth of Asian males as asexual and feminine renders Asian men as less desirable. Within the context of a bicultural socialization, Asian men and women have needed to negotiate competing cultural representations of masculinity or femininity. This has important implications as they manage their gender identity.

Another aspect that has complicated this picture is the shifts in roles and responsibilities. Immigration has created role reversals for some Asian immigrants, significantly influencing their family roles and expectations. The shifts have resulted in greater need for dual-income families and greater struggles on the part of women to achieve equal access to resources. Due to difficulties in occupational mobility for some foreign-born Asian men (Uba, 1994), more women have experienced a need to work outside the family.

Sexuality and Sexual Identity

Although one's sexuality and being attracted to another individual is an integral part of human life and relationship, the meanings attached to sexuality and sexual behaviors are experienced and informed differently based on cultural, religious, familial, and acculturative influences (Suggs & Miracle, 1993). Historically, Asian cultures have depicted their attitudes and openness to sexual issues through the arts, literature, religion, history, and philosophy with sexual themes covering a range of orientations. For instance, the existence of homosexuality, bisexuality, and other forms of sexuality have been noted in erotic art, paintings, and wall carvings as normal subjects in Japanese and Indian artistic ventures (Carson & Sperry, 1999; Pope & Chung, 1999; Ruan, 1991). Yet, through the years, due to political, social, and religious influence, Asian cultural norms have become more restrictive and place a strong emphasis on silence surrounding issues of sexuality (Hirayama & Hirayama, 1986). This negative attitude is not only seen within the context of heterosexual intimacy issues, but takes on great significance within the context of homosexuality. Specifically, Asian Americans perceive homosexuality as a Western concept (Chung & Katayama, 1998). Based in the notion that one becomes homosexual from contact with "foreigners," homosexuality has been seen as a "White disease" and therefore not a natural part of the Asian societies (Leupp, 1995).

Although acculturation and exposure to U.S. values may play an important role in more positive attitudes toward sexuality and sexual identity issues (Pope, 1995), familial and cultural influences may predominate. For instance, there is an expectation in traditional Asian American families that children will marry and have children. As Asian American sexual minorities develop their identity, experience pressures related to marriage and the fear of familial rejection may be major hindrances in the ownership of their identity and the coming-out process (Chan, 1989; Pope & Chung, 1999).

Culturally, religion may also play a significant role. For instance, the majority of the religions (Christianity, Islam, Hinduism, Taoism) seem to have negative and stringent attitudes toward sex and homosexuality (Pope & Chung, 1999). Although some religious teachings (i.e., Confucianism, Hinduism) subscribe to a balance between female (i.e., yin in Confucianism, shakti in Hinduism) and male (i.e., yang in Confucianism, shiva in Hinduism) attributes, the focus is primarily on heterosexual relations. Any leanings toward homosexuality are seen as a sin and thus unacceptable (Pope & Chung, 1999).

According to Chung and Katayama (1998), it is important to recognize that Asian Americans undergo a dual but parallel developmental process in relation to their ethnic and sexual identities. These two processes of identity development may occur simultaneously or one may follow the other and may be complicated by their racial socialization as well. How Asian Americans negotiate these minority identities, what the relative salience of each identity might be for the person, and how the identities intersect or interact at different points in a person's life become important.

GENERAL MENTAL HEALTH ISSUES OF INDIVIDUALS OF ASIAN DESCENT

Understanding Asian American culture and its individualized manifestations creates unique mental health issues for this population. In the following sections, prevalence and expression of common mental health problems and help-seeking behaviors are discussed.

Psychopathology

Questions about the prevalence of psychological disorders among Asian Americans are questions of both clinical and empirical concern. For instance, answers to questions such as how prevalent is depression among Chinese or how common is it for Filipinos to encounter racism are critical in providing researchers and clinicians with a baseline understanding of the psychological status of Asian American communities. However, despite the value of such questions, counselors should be cautious in reviewing the literature for "answers." As a relatively new field, research on counseling Asian Americans is far from definitive and more likely to provide conflicting answers as a function of different samples, surveys, and analytical strategies.

To provide insights rather than answers to these questions, researchers have generally used two approaches: (a) epidemiological studies that attempt to be representative of a particular population at large, and (b) small-scale studies that often use smaller convenience samples. While epidemiological studies are clearly valuable, drawing conclusions from national epidemiological studies has been hampered by relatively small samples of Asian Americans and the aggregation of Asian Americans across ethnic groups (Yang & WonPat-Borja, 2007). Nevertheless, a few studies such as the Chinese American Psychiatric Epidemiological Study (CAPES) and the Filipino American Community Epidemiological Study (FACES) have provided invaluable insights and the recently completed National Latino and Asian American Study—the first nationally representative study—is promising to be a rich source of information. Consequently, in this section we review the existing literature on racism and its relationship to psychological distress and, more specifically, prevalence of depression, Post Traumatic Stress Disorder (PTSD), domestic violence, anxiety, and schizophrenia.

RACISM   Research on prevalence rates for racism is both emerging and far from definitive. Part of the challenge in such studies is in the manner in which a construct such as racism is defined and measured. For instance, Kuo (1995) found that 15% to 39% of Asian Americans reported having experienced a major incident of racial discrimination whereas Alvarez et al. (2006) reported that 98% of Asian Americans experienced at least one instance of racial microaggression (e.g., racial insult, being treated rudely). Hence, counselors may benefit from attending to methodological issues in evaluating such studies.

Nevertheless, there has been consistent empirical evidence to indicate that racism is related to lower levels of psychological well-being for Asian Americans. Racism has been found to have an adverse impact on self-esteem (Greene, Way, & Pahl, 2006), depression (Beiser & Hou, 2006), race-related stress (Liang, Alvarez, Juang, & Liang, 2007), drug use (Gee, Delva, & Takeuchi, 2006), body image (Iyer & Haslam, 2003), HIV risk behaviors (Yoshikawa, Wilson, Chae, & Cheng, 2004), and PTSD (Loo et al., 2001). For example, Loo and colleagues (2001) found that racism within the military put Asian American Vietnam veterans at risk for PTSD more so than exposure to actual combat. Additionally, challenging the belief that seemingly positive stereotypes are not harmful, Cheryan and Bodenhausen (2000) found that when ethnic identity was salient for Asian Americans, their academic performance diminished under what was called a "choke under pressure phenomenon." Presumably this was the result of the pressure to conform to "model minority" expectations of high academic standards. Thus, racism appears to be an experience with considerable and adverse psychological consequences.

DEPRESSION   Studies on depression among Asian Americans have generally suggested that Asian Americans experience major depressive disorders at a rate that is equal to or lower than that of the general population (Yang & WonPat-Borja, 2007). However, there are studies that indicate that depression rates may be higher than that of the general population. In the CAPES study with a sample of 1,747 Chinese American adults in the Los Angeles area, Takeuchi et al. (1998) found a 3.4% rate of depression over the last 12 months, which was lower than the 6.6% rate found in the general population for a replication of the National Comorbidity Study (Kessler et al., 2003). However, using self-report measures, depression rates among Asian American adults have ranged from 12% to 41% (Yang & WonPat-Borja, 2007). Among studies with youth, Yang and WonPat-Borja (2007) found that in seven out of nine major studies, there were no significant differences in depression rates between Asian Americans and other racial groups and that rates ranged from 2.6% to 12.8% using diagnostic interviews. Of the demographic groups that have been examined, elderly Asian Americans appear to be at greatest risk for depression, with rates as high as 40% (Mui, Kang, Chen, & Domanski, 2003). However, in their review of seven studies with elderly Asian Americans, Yang and WonPat-Borja (2007) found three studies with rates lower than that of White Americans, three studies with comparable rates, and one study with higher rates. Consequently, with such a wide range of conclusions, it may be more helpful for counselors to evaluate such studies with some degree of caution.

POST TRAUMATIC STRESS DISORDER (PTSD)   Premigration traumas, particularly among Southeast Asian refugees, have been consistently associated with the incidence of PTSD, suicide, and depression (Chung & Bemak, 2007; Sack, Him, & Dickason, 1999). In the most comprehensive study to date on Cambodian refugees, Marshall, Schell, Elliott, Berthold, and Chun (2005) found that 62% suffered from PTSD and 51% had major depression in the last year. To contextualize these rates, they also described that 99% of the participants reported near-death starvation, 90% had family or friends murdered, and 54% were tortured prior to coming to the United States. The effects of such trauma can also be multigenerational. For instance, in a study of Cambodian American refugees, Sack et al. (1994) found that 58% of mothers, 29% of fathers, and 18% of children demonstrated symptoms of PTSD. Rates for depression were also similarly elevated and ranged from 11% for children, 14% for fathers, to 18% for mothers. As this study also illustrates, it seems that women exhibit higher levels of psychological distress (Chung & Bemak, 2007). More disturbingly, there has been evidence to indicate that the effects of migration trauma can persist over time. Sack et al. (1999) found that after a 12-year follow-up, 35% of Cambodian refugees continued to exhibit PTSD symptoms and 14% exhibited symptoms of depression. Hence, the experiences of Southeast Asian American refugees are significantly different from their immigrant peers.

DOMESTIC VIOLENCE   Efforts at determining the prevalence of domestic violence among Asian Americans have been hampered by limited research, particularly in terms of representative epidemiological samples (Kim, Lau, & Chang, 2007). In the National Survey of Violence Against Women, Tjaden and Thoennes (2000) found that Asian Pacific Islanders were targets of rape and physical assault by their partners at lifetime rates of 3.8% and 12.8%, respectively. These rates were lower than that reported for White Americans (i.e., 7.7% for rape, 21.3% for physical assault). They also reported that 49.6% of Asian American women reported being physically assaulted, and 6.8% were raped by some individual (not necessarily their partner). Additionally, the authors cautioned that rates may be underreported due to cultural values around self-disclosure. Indeed, Kawahara and Fu (2007) observed that silence around domestic violence may be perpetuated by cultural values such as the need to maintain group harmony and save face, as well as by tactics such as social isolation, threats to women's "reputation," and their immigration status.

Given the limited research in this area, studies using nonrepresentative convenience samples may be the best alternative to date. For instance, in a relatively large survey of 336 Asian Americans by the National Asian Women's Health Organization (NAWHO, 2002), 8% of the women reported that they had been raped, 19% were pressured to have sex, and 26% reported that they were the target of physical or emotional abuse by their partners. Additionally, Kim et al. (2007) reported that community-based studies of domestic violence among Asian American women have found rates ranging from 24% to 60%. While the existing evidence in this area is far from definitive, perhaps the most salient finding for counselors to consider is that the overwhelming majority of Asian American women (95% to 97%) have never used preventive or treatment services despite the high incidence of violence in their lives (NAWHO, 2002).

ANXIETY AND SCHIZOPHRENIA   Fewer studies have been conducted on the prevalence of anxiety disorders and schizophrenia. Available research has been relatively consistent in suggesting that these disorders occur at rates lower than or similar to Whites (Sue, Sue, Sue, & Takeuchi, 1995; Zhang & Snowden, 1999). For instance, in Zhang and Snowden's analysis of the Epidemiological Catchment Area data set consisting of over 18,000 participants across the country, they found that Asian Americans reported the lowest lifetime rates of Schizophrenia, Phobias, and Obsessive-Compulsive disorders among all racial groups. Similarly, Sue et al. (1995) found that Chinese Americans reported lower rates of generalized anxiety disorder, agoraphobia, simple phobia, and panic disorder. Nevertheless, Sue et al. cautioned that definitive conclusions about the status of psychopathology among Asian Americans may be premature given the limited range of studies in this area and the failure of existing studies in tapping the heterogeneity of the Asian American communities.

To bridge this methodological issue, Takeuchi et al. (2007) conducted the National Latino and Asian American Study (NLAAS), the most comprehensive study of Latino and Asian American mental health thus far. The NLAAS involved a probability sample of 2,095 Asian Americans consisting of 600 Chinese, 508 Filipinos, 520 Vietnamese, 141 Asian Indian, 107 Japanese, 81 Koreans, and 138 individuals categorized as Other. While much of the NLAAS data have yet to be published, the limited amount that has been published is promising. For instance, they reported that the lifetime prevalence rate for either depression, anxiety, or substance abuse was 17.3% and the 12-month rate was 9.2%. Lifetime rates did not differ by gender or ethnicity. Immigration also appears to be a particularly robust predictor of mental health disorders for Asian American women in particular, with lifetime rates of 24.6% for U.S.-born participants compared to 15.2% for foreign-born Asian Americans. As the NLAAS data continue to be published, counselors may wish to refer to them given the study's methodological rigor.

Help-Seeking and Coping

Help-seeking is a complicated process. Although a need for mental health services exists, only a portion of those who need professional help seek out such services (Leong, Wagner, & Tata, 1995). Although several variables influence help-seeking, researchers have emphasized that coping strategies and their perceived effectiveness must be understood and evaluated against the backdrop of a cultural group's values, norms, and worldviews (Inman & Yeh, 2007; Inman, Yeh et al., 2007; Lee & Lu, 1989; Yeh et al., 2006). For us to understand Asian American help-seeking, we need to understand how help-seeking may be influenced by Asian values and worldviews. The remainder of this section highlights specific issues related to mental health use among Asian Americans.

UTILIZATION RATES   Literature has consistently revealed that Asian Americans underutilize mental health services (Leong, Chang, & Lee, 2007; Narikiyo & Kameoka, 1992). Data from the National Institute of Mental Health (Matsuoka, Breaux, & Ryujin, 1997) on utilization rates for a broad range of mental health services have revealed that Asian American Pacific Islanders (AAPI) were three times less likely than their White counterparts to use mental health services. Interestingly, similar results were found for 16 of the states with the highest AAPI populations (Leong et al., 2007).

The NLAAS (Abe-Kim et al., 2007) reports that only 8.6% of Asian Americans with a psychological problem sought any form of professional help. Of those who received help, only 3.1% of Asian Americans sought help from a mental health provider, and U.S.-born Asian Americans were more likely to see a mental health provider than foreign-born Asian Americans. In fact, Suan and Tyler (1990) found that Asian Americans in general are less likely to seek professional mental health providers as their primary source of help. Conversely, when Asian Americans do seek help, they were noted to prematurely terminate psychotherapy treatment (Zane, Hatanaka, Park, & Akutsu, 1994). Comparisons of help-seeking attitudes between Asian international students and European American students have also yielded similar results. Studies have shown Asian international students have less favorable attitudes toward psychotherapy (e.g., Mau & Jepsen, 1988). Similar trends have been found in large-scale studies analyzing the public mental health system usage. McCabe et al. (1999) explored the patterns of service use among four Asian ethnic groups across five public youth service sectors in San Diego County from 1996 to 1997. Irrespective of socioeconomic status, these groups were found to be significantly underrepresented in services for children with serious emotional problems as well as child welfare and other mental health sectors.

Conversely, there have been some instances when researchers (Maynard, Ehreth, Cox, Peterson, & McGann, 1997) have found a small percentage of Asian Americans to overutilize mental health services. In particular these trends have increased since the 1970s. For instance, Sue, Fujino, Hu, Takeuchi, and Zane (1991) examined data maintained by the Los Angeles County Department of Mental Health for clients entering the system between 1983 and 1988. Although Asian Americans constituted only 3.1% of outpatients and 8.7% of the county populations, these patients seemed to exhibit more severe disorders when compared to their White counterparts, engaged in a greater number of treatment sessions, and received medication-based treatments more frequently (Flaskerud & Hu, 1992). Similar trends were found in Chen, Sullivan, Lu, and Shibusawa's (2003) analysis of public mental health service use in San Diego County between 1991 and 1994. In addition to severity of symptoms and longer lengths of stay, Asian Americans were more likely to use outpatient and day treatment programs when compared to other ethnic groups. Furthermore, there have been several Southeast Asian and East Asian groups that overutilize mental health services (Zane et al., 1994).

Research has also revealed other instances when Asian Americans seem to utilize services at higher rates. For instance, Tracey, Leong, and Glidden (1986) noted that Asian American college students tend to seek counseling when faced with academic and vocational problems. This may be because the emphasis on career issues is consistent with Asian cultural values related to education. Similarly, studies have found that when Asian American communities offer ethnic-specific services, both Asian American children and adults are less likely to drop out of treatment prematurely, stay in treatment for longer periods, and have better treatment outcomes (Flaskerud & Hu, 1994; Takeuchi, Sue, & Yeh, 1995; Zane et al., 1994).

ATTITUDES AND BARRIERS IN HELP-SEEKING   Although Asian Americans experience difficulties with a range of issues including academic, interpersonal, familial, intergenerational issues, substance abuse, health, identity, and racism (Inman & Yeh, 2007; Tewari et al., 2003), they may display less favorable attitudes toward seeking help from a professional mental health provider (Suan & Tyler, 1990; Zhang, Snowden, & Sue, 1998). While the interaction between client and counselor can influence help-seeking, there are several individual, sociocultural, and structural/institutional barriers that have been noted as influencing Asian American help-seeking attitudes and behaviors.

At the individual level, lack of knowledge or exposure to Western mental health treatment and misconceptions about professional counseling may be barriers to seeking professional help (Akutsu, 1997; Kawanga-Singer & Chung, 2002; Loo, Tong, & True, 1989; Mau & Jepsen, 1988; Morrissey, 1997). This may be closely related to immigration history (Takaki, 1998), length of stay in the United States, and levels of acculturation. Further, authors (Akutsu & Chu, 2006; Atkinson & Gim, 1989; Atkinson, Whiteley & Gim, 1990) have noted a significant positive relationship between highly acculturated college students and attitudes toward seeking professional help. Other demographic variables that have been noted to influence help-seeking include gender (Atkinson, Ponterotto, & Sanchez, 1984; Gim, Atkinson, & Whiteley, 1990; Nolen-Hoeksema, 2002), age (Leong & Lau, 2001), and history of previous treatment (Solberg, Ritsma, Davis, Tata, & Jolly, 1994). For example, some authors have found that women and those who have sought previous clinical help have tended to be more open to mental health treatment whereas others (Akutsu, Lin, & Zane, 1990; Leong et al., 1995) have found no gender differences in help-seeking attitudes. Further, older, more traditional and less acculturated Asians tend to hold on to traditional cultural beliefs and are likely to have less favorable attitudes toward mental health services use when compared to younger acculturated clients (Chiu, Ames, Draper, & Snowdon, 1999).

Additionally, limited language proficiency (Kawanga-Singer & Chung, 2002) and client–counselor ethnic matching are other individual-level factors that have been deemed to influence help-seeking among Asian Americans (Uba, 1994). For instance, Sue et al. (1991) found that client–counselor ethnic matching not only increases utilization of services, but also decreases premature termination among Asian Americans. This was particularly true for clients who did not have English as their primary language. Conversely, ethnic matching in the client–counselor dyad was not found to predict increases in services for Southeast Asians (Ying & Hu, 1994). Perhaps as with other groups it is possible that racial/cultural identity (Ladany, Brittan-Powell, & Pannu, 1997) might play a more important role.

At the sociocultural level, cultural values and views of mental health, expression of distress, stigmatization of persons with mentally illness and mental health services use, and availability of alternative healing practices have been noted to contribute to underutilization of mental health services (Inman, Yeh, et al., 2007; Kawanga-Singer & Chung, 2002). This may be especially true of Asian Americans residing in immigrant communities (Sue, 1999). For instance, the notion of shame or loss of face has been identified as a significant barrier in mental health services utilization.

According to Sue (1994), terms like *Haji* among the Japanese, *Hiya* among Filipinos, *Mentz* among the Chinese, and *Chaemyun* among Koreans are often used to highlight the shame that may be incurred in these communities (p. 203). Utilization of mental health services may be seen as a public admission that something is wrong and thus likely to compromise the family and their social status (Sue, 1999); personal problems and weaknesses are not only shared by family members, but the family is also seen as responsible for taking care of the problem (Gomes, 2000; Yeh & Wang, 2000). Seeking professional counseling may be seen as breaking away from familial reliance and going against the privacy of the family (Tewari et al., 2003).

Cultural factors also influence how Asian Americans may perceive the symptoms or causes of a disorder, and in turn the specific intervention that might be effective (Kakar, 1982; Leong, 1986). Within Asian cultures, the mind and body are considered inseparable. Health and well-being are seen holistically and include mental, physical, and spiritual components (Hilton et al., 2001). Due to the interconnectedness between the mind and the body, psychopathology is often conceptualized within physical and spiritual frameworks (Mullatti, 1995). For instance, it is not uncommon to see Asian Americans present with physical symptoms (e.g., headaches, dizziness) when emotionally stressed. Furthermore, due to a spiritual focus, symptoms may also be seen as embedded within a religious context. Studies (Inman, Yeh, et al., 2007; Lee & Lu, 1989; Sue, 1999; Yeh et al., 2006) of South Asians, Southeast Asians, and East Asians have revealed that these immigrant communities believe that problems are preordained, a result of past lives, karmic, caused by supernatural forces or an imbalance between the yin and the yang. Consistent with these beliefs, these communities have been known to seek indigenous forms of healing. Activity 11.1 provides an opportunity to obtain more information on indigenous healers.

ACTIVITY 11.1

Interview an Asian American nontraditional or indigenous healer. How does this method compare to Western perspectives of counseling and treatment? What preconceptions, biases, or beliefs based in your own socialization did you have about this type of healing? What did you learn from this experience?

At the structural level or institutional level, conflict between the values endorsed by the Western mental health systems and Asian values may be a major deterrent to seeking professional help (Atkinson & Gim, 1989). For instance, Western approaches to counseling often focus on self-disclosure of personal, highly intense issues and feelings, insight-oriented intrapsychic approaches, and individual goals (Leong & Lau, 2001; Sue, 1999). Given the focus on self-reliance, emotional management, willpower (Leong & Lau, 2001), keeping personal issues in the family (Leong et al., 1995), and a collectivistic orientation to problems (Yeh et al., 2006), Western approaches tend to be antithetical to Asian values and thus may deter these communities from seeking help (Leong & Lau, 2001).

Akutsu et al. (1990) found that perceived counselor credibility was strongly related to utilization of services among Chinese students. In a related fashion, authors (Gim, Atkinson, & Kim, 1991; Inman, Yeh, et al., 2007) have found that lack of culturally sensitive and competent counselors have been another reason for high dropout rates or reticence in seeking professional help. Inaccurate evaluations or misdiagnoses due to cultural biases, different social norms, or culturally incongruent scales may create significant difficulties in perceived credibility among Asian

Americans (Leong & Lau, 2001; Uba, 1994). Finally, other systemic issues such as ease of access to services either due to transportation or location, familial obligations (e.g., child care), and financial costs are factors that can influence mental health use.

SITES OF RESILIENCY   Sites of resiliency represent those psychological and/or physical spaces that help Asian Americans cope. In keeping with this, several sites of resiliency have been identified for the Asian American community. For instance, use of alternative forms of healing has been noted as an important source of resiliency. This may be particularly true of Asian immigrants whose cultural values and beliefs greatly influence their daily lives and practices toward health and well-being (Inman, Yeh, et al., 2007; Yeh et al., 2006). Alternative forms of healing are not only consistent with Asian cultural values but seem integral to maintaining a sense of self within the communities (Froggett, 2001). For instance, alternative healers tend to treat the illness within a cultural, familial, and communal context (Kakar, 1982).

Because of a holistic emphasis on health (Hilton et al., 2001; Lee, 1997) and a spiritually guided life (Mullatti, 1995), themes of fatalism, karma, and religion play a significant role in coping with daily stressors (Yeh et al., 2006). In light of this, Asian Americans have been known to seek religious/faith healers and religious organizations (e.g., churches, temples) and engage in chants, prayers, religious ceremonies, and lighting of lamps. Other related sources have included palm reading and astrology. Due to the belief in creating mind–body harmony, Asians may engage in activities such as Tai Chi, yoga, Qi-gong, acupuncture, and therapeutic massage. Furthermore, due to the belief in bodily imbalance across several Asian cultures (e.g., Chinese, Indian), nutrition is another popular means of restoring health. This is exemplified in the use of herbal medicine or specific foods.

A central source of alternate support or resiliency is the family and social community. The family as a major source of support has been discussed across several Asian groups. For instance, authors have found that first-generation adults (Inman, Yeh, et al., 2007; Yeh et al., 2006) and second-generation Asian American college students (Yeh, Inose, Kobori, & Chang, 2001; Yeh & Wang, 2000) tend to seek support from family members when faced with personal difficulties. Furthermore, social supports beyond the family can provide important psychological and social support (Ramisetty-Milker, 1993). Because of the emphasis on a collectivistic culture and potential for familial conflicts (Lee & Liu, 2001), social networks with individuals that are ethnically and racially similar may be important in buffering individuals from stressful situations (Yeh & Wang, 2000).

GUIDELINES FOR COUNSELING CLIENTS OF ASIAN DESCENT

Different cultural values, a lack of familiarity with the counseling process, potential language difficulties, discrimination, and other cultural experiences can challenge the therapeutic relationship resulting in miscommunication and premature termination. Given that counseling may be a foreign concept to many Asian Americans, education about counseling and the utility of mental health services is very much needed among Asian Americans who may not be acculturated to Western conceptualizations of health care (Ying & Miller, 1992). In this regard, counselors should be prepared to answer in lay terms seemingly basic, yet critical questions such as "How does talking help me?", "Why do I do all the talking?", or "What do you do?" Whether explicitly asked or not, the client may be wondering about the answers to these questions—answers that may be critical to enhancing their intrinsic motivation to remain in counseling (Alvarez & Chen, 2009). Hence, counselors play an integral role in educating clients about the counseling process. In this section, we highlight some critical areas that counselors should focus on as they work with Asian American clients. Reflection 11.4 may be helpful for you in conceptualizing cross-cultural help-seeking behaviors.

REFLECTION 11.4

Reflect upon what you have been taught in terms of "appropriate" help-seeking and support. Who can you turn to? What can you discuss? How will others react? How does this compare with what you know about Asian American attitudes regarding help-seeking? How might this shape your expectations about seeking help and, more importantly, how might this facilitate and/or inhibit your work with Asian Americans?

Counselor Self-Assessment

Multicultural competence begins before counselors enter the session with a frank assessment of themselves. Specific to Asian Americans, counselors are encouraged to obtain training, attend workshops and presentations, and familiarize themselves with the literature on this community prior to beginning their work with Asian American clients. In effect, counselors should assess the extent to which they are familiar with the information presented in this chapter.

On a personal level, counselors would do well to reflect upon their socialization experiences with Asian Americans, their assumptions and biases about this community, and the extent to which this may all influence their work as counselors. Indeed, Alvarez and Chen (2009) have argued that the need for this self-reflection is mandatory regardless of whether the client and the counselor are similar or different in terms of race, ethnicity, gender, or any other cultural dimension. In effect, despite phenotypic similarities between a counselor and client, the psychological meaning that each attributes to these identities may be entirely different and far more critical. Last, given the significance of issues such as race, gender, and experiences of oppression, counselors may further benefit from an awareness of the extent to which they are comfortable and able to raise such issues in counseling. As relatively "taboo" topics, it is important to recognize that clients are unlikely to raise such issues on their own initiative, despite their potential significance in the counseling relationship. For instance, how often do you think a client will simply say, "I'd like to talk about the fact that you're a White counselor and I'm Asian American." As a result, both the responsibility and the power to do so lies with the counselor (Alvarez & Chen, 2009).

Counseling Process

Counseling process refers to what happens in therapy between the counselor and the client. Specifically, this refers to within-session interactions and factors that influence the dynamics in counseling. In essence, this includes overt and covert contributions from the counselor (e.g., professional training, personalities, interpersonal styles, verbal and nonverbal interventions used, countertransference, intentions), the client (e.g., personalities, worldviews, previous experiences in and outside of therapy, readiness for change, transference), and the interactional dynamics between the counselor and the client (e.g., working alliance, rapport) (Hill & Corbett, 1993). Being attuned to these different aspects is key to effective counseling.

When treating Asian American clients, understanding how counseling and the counseling process may be conceptualized within a cultural context plays a significant role in providing culturally sensitive therapy. For example, the emphasis on equality in counselor–client relationships is an important aspect of some Western psychotherapeutic approaches (e.g., feminist therapy). However, Asian Americans tend to be deferential to people in authority (e.g., the counselor); thus, equality may not be the most effective way of creating a therapeutic alliance (Marsella, 1993). In a related fashion, because of their authoritative roles, counselors are seen as experts. For instance, Asian American clients who work with a college counselor may expect the counselor to tell them what to do in terms of choosing majors or classes. Furthermore, Asian Americans may not understand the need for intrusive questions and the lengthy process a psychological evaluation might take (Uba, 1994). Additionally, because of the use of brief interventions with physicians, shamans, or other elders, where they are evaluated, diagnosed, and given a prescription in one session, there may be a tendency on the part of Asian Americans to expect a quick fix to the problem. As a result, the client who comes in to see a career counselor may be puzzled by a process that involves a lengthy assessment of his or her values and interests and career socialization, as well as the administration of a battery of surveys. Due to a lack of understanding or familiarity with the conceptual underpinnings of Western approaches to counseling, Asian American immigrants may feel frustrated with therapy.

The primary focus in counseling is on verbal communication (Uba, 1994). This expectation that clients talk about their issues goes against some of the Asian cultural values such as the stigma attached to sharing personal information with strangers. Developing a relationship first with your Asian American client is important in creating a trusting environment that will allow conversations to occur. In particular, the use of specific types of counselor self-disclosures (e.g., strategies, intimate disclosures) has been found helpful in the client–counselor relationship (Kim et al., 2003). For instance, disclosing tangible ideas used in personal challenges that might share some similarity with those of the client have been noted to increase trust levels in client–counselor relationships (Inman & Tewari, 2003; Kim et al., 2003). In a related fashion, initiating discussion on potential counselor–client differences can also assist with building a relationship with your Asian client. Discussing differences related to aspects such as race, ethnicity, and gender allows for contextualizing the experience and addressing any potential for miscommunications that may evolve in this emotional and personal relationship. Consider how you would work with the client discussed in Activity 11.2.

ACTIVITY 11.2

Discuss the following in dyads:

Imagine that your Pakistani American client has just decided that she will follow the career path that her family has decided is best. What is your personal reaction to this decision? How does this compare with your own values and assumptions? How will you manage and address these reactions? How might this affect counseling?

Conceptualization of the Problem

When clients present with specific issues in counseling, it becomes important to align the conceptualization of the problem to the multiple contexts in which individuals exist. In capturing the complexity of an individual's life, assessing the relative significance of various relationships (families, friends), systems (school, work), and environments (immigration, discrimination, racism) and the intersection of the three within the lives of Asian Americans becomes very important (Inman,

Rawls, Meza, & Brown, 2002). For instance, due to the emphasis on family and community within the Asian culture, exploring the makeup of the actual household, the influence of the extended family (whether in the United States or in the country of origin), and the different alliances in the community becomes necessary. However, the ethnic social support that goes beyond the family can, on one hand, provide Asian Americans with important psychological, moral, emotional, and physical support (Ramisetty-Mikler, 1993), but on the other hand, also create great stress for the individual (Yee et al., 2007). Thus, some caution should be taken in this regard.

A second major force shaping Asian American identities is their immigration experience. Many families migrate to the United States in order to procure better opportunities for their families. Within this context, preimmigration experiences (e.g., age at immigration, reasons for immigration, immigration status on arrival [voluntary or involuntary], exposure to Western values, educational and skill levels, sacrifices made in leaving their country of origin) and the postimmigrant adjustment (e.g., sacrifices made in taking care of families, level of intergenerational conflict, changes in economic and social status, potential gender role and parent–child role reversals, level of community support, religiosity, and experiences of discrimination and racism) are significant factors that need to be considered in understanding the socialization and adjustment of Asian Americans in the United States. Moreover, it is important to recognize that the psychological significance of immigration is not limited to the first generation alone given that the sense of sacrifice and hardship associated with this period may reverberate across generations. For instance, a school counselor who is working with a young Cambodian American student may need to consider that the importance of school to this student and her family takes on a unique significance in light of the possibility that they may be refugees who have lost a great deal in coming to the United States. These become important influential factors not only in the extent to which families acculturate to the host culture but also in the responsibilities that Asian Americans experience in their families (Almeida, 1996; Inman, Yeh et al., 2007).

Further, because of the diversity within the Asian American groups with regard to educational levels, occupations, socioeconomic status, and experiences of racism, oppression, and privilege, exploring the negotiation between education and class, ethnic and racial identities, and gender and sexual identities is paramount so that counselors can understand potential pressures that Asian Americans experience. For instance, educational and career choices do not occur in a vacuum but are influenced by social systems (e.g., language barriers) and institutional barriers (e.g., access to managerial jobs). Acknowledging and utilizing the different cultural contexts that frame the lives of Asian Americans are important considerations in delivering comprehensive culturally sensitive psychological services to these individuals (Inman et al., 2002).

Intervention

In working with Asian Americans, the literature has identified some general counseling principles based in Asian cultural values. For instance, because of the emphasis on privacy within Asian American families, research suggests that Asian Americans may not openly express strong emotions. They may not also publicly disclose personal and family issues that may bring shame upon their families. Others (Atkinson & Lowe, 1995) have noted that Asian Americans typically prefer an authoritarian, directive, and structured approach to treatment. Yet other researchers have observed that Asian Americans do better when there is both ethnic and gender matching in the therapeutic relationship (Atkinson, Morten, & Sue, 1998; Fujino, Okazaki, & Young, 1994). It has also been identified that Asian Americans expect concrete goals and strategies that are solution focused. Finally, because of the significant role that families play, family therapy might be an appropriate therapeutic intervention. Nevertheless, rather than "comply" with these findings, counselors would do well in exercising some caution in implementing these results.

Although the literature dictates some general guidelines surrounding therapeutic interventions, when working with Asian Americans, it is important to keep in mind that Asian Americans as a group are extremely heterogeneous. Thus, interventions should be responsive to the specifics of your client rather than following what has been found in the literature without question. To prevent stereotyping or overgeneralizations, it is essential to assess individual differences that exist within and across generations and ethnic groups. For example, length of stay in the United States can significantly influence the extent to which Asian Americans may hold onto their traditional cultural values or take on dominant cultural values. Literature suggests that American-born Asians tend to acculturate at a faster pace than first-generation foreign-born Asians. Due to these different rates of acculturation, the specific needs and adjustment issues of American-born Asians can be quite different from those of foreign-born Asians. For instance, because of unfamiliar systems, or limited language proficiency, immigrant parents may not only experience challenges in guiding their American-born children in schoolwork (Shea, Ma, & Yeh, 2007), but also rely on their children for interpretation of social mores and managing daily chores (Leong & Gim, 1995). This reversal in roles can create significant cultural conflicts for these children and their parents as children become cultural brokers for their parents. Relatedly, the relevance of a racial versus an ethnic identity has been noted to be different for these two groups. Inman (2006) noted that race seemed more salient for American-born Asians whereas ethnicity appeared more salient for foreign-born Asians. Even within the foreign-born Asians group, those who have lived in the United States for a considerable amount of time can experience issues quite differently from international students who might live in the United States for short periods. For example, international students are likely to experience greater cultural shock than foreign-born Asians who have lived in the United States for longer periods (Sandhu, 1999). Similarly, voluntary Asian immigrants' needs and adjustments can differ from those of nonvoluntary immigrants or refugees from Asia. For example, Southeast Asian refugees (e.g., from Cambodia, Vietnam) have higher rates of PTSD and depression than other voluntary immigrants (Chun, Eastman, Wang, & Sue, 1998).

Thus, developing a range of treatment modalities would be important in working with the diverse Asian community. Assessing if the problem is individual, systemic (e.g., relational), environmental, or a combination of these is important as well. Similarly, considerations need to be made in terms of application of traditional Western modalities on Asian Americans. The preference for use of alternative healing approaches (e.g., indigenous healers, family, friends, and other social supports) must be factored into treatment. Complete Activity 11.3 and reflect on the common values and assumptions as well as heterogeneous nature of those of Asian descent.

ACTIVITY 11.3

Discuss the following in dyads:
   Imagine that you have been assigned a Vietnamese American client. You may be similar to the client in terms of race and ethnicity or you may be different. As you begin working with this client, how do you raise these racial and ethnic differences and similarities? Or do you? Be specific and develop concrete examples of what you might say.

Outreach and Nonclinical Visibility

For some Asian Americans, use of mental health or counseling services has been related to knowing someone who works or is connected to someone in such a setting (Inman, Yeh, et al., 2007; Salvador, Omizo, & Kim, 1997). In essence, "word of mouth" referrals play a significant role in Asian Americans seeking counseling. This is strongly related to the issue of credibility.

As noted previously, counselor credibility is an important factor in mental health utilization among Asian Americans. Subsumed within the definition of credibility are notions of counselor expertness and trustworthiness. Perceived expertness in a counselor "is typically a function of a) reputation, b) evidence of specialized training, and c) behavioral evidence of proficiency and competency" (Inman, Yeh, et al., 2007, p. 85). For example, a rehabilitation counselor's credibility may be reflected in her familiarity with state and federal legislation on disability issues and how that affects her client's rights. Such a testimony of expertness becomes all the more important when coming from someone within the community. Perceived trustworthiness, on the other hand, "encompasses such factors as sincerity, openness, honesty, or perceived lack of motivation for personal gain" (p. 87). Intrinsic to developing trust is the extent to which a counselor self-discloses personal information. Knowing counselors at a personal level allows Asian American clients to develop a sense of safety and kinship that may be needed to build the therapeutic relationship. In a related fashion, the fact that "actions speak louder than words" is a notion that has been well established in the South Asian community (Inman, Yeh et al., 2007). For instance, these authors noted that when caseworkers and other professionals went beyond the client to address client systems such as engaging in advocacy and facilitating connections between services, the South Asian participants in the study seemed to accord these individuals with more credibility. Thus, the extent to which a counselor is considered credible can manifest itself in the way client issues are conceptualized and the specific interventions that are used in solving problems. Given that Asian Americans are apprehensive of counseling, engaging in outreach and maintaining visibility (clinical or nonclinical) in the community is extremely important to develop credibility.

Social Advocacy and Social Justice

Issues closely related to outreach are social advocacy and social justice. As stated in Chapter 3, **social advocacy** refers to the act of arguing on behalf of an individual, group, idea, or issue in the pursuit of influencing outcomes. **Social justice** refers to a belief in a just world (i.e., a world with fair treatment and equal distribution of the benefits of society) that respects and protects human rights. In essence, it refers to the ethics surrounding equitable access to resources and services.

In examining the ethics codes and guidelines for several mental health organizations (e.g., the American Counseling Association, the American Psychological Association, the National Association of Social Workers, and the American Association for Marriage and Family Therapy), we notice that there are a few recurring themes surrounding the ethical behavior of counselors. The first recurring theme is *respect for the integrity and strength of clients or communities.* Respecting communities involves acquiring adequate knowledge about a community and being respectful of differences. Respect is the foundation for engaging in social justice work because it ensures that "counselors understand and abide by a community's strengths, goals, and determination" (Toporek & Williams, 2006, p. 18). Thus, as you work with Asian American communities, be mindful of the constant shifts and changes in cultural boundaries within different contexts. While it is possible to be informed about the Asian community, it is not possible to know everything. It is important to engage in a constant process of raising your awareness about Asian Americans in different contexts (e.g., media, work), understand how meanings of identity shift through different social locations (e.g., race, gender), and sort through your assumptions and stereotypes (e.g., model minority) about this heterogeneous group. Be conscious that theories cannot be universally applied and that imposing Western modalities without modifications and adaptations is culturally insensitive. Thus, theories that are individually focused (e.g., client-centered therapy, psychodynamic theory) need to be critiqued. For instance, the "size of self" may be smaller among Asian communities. Thus, examining how these theories may need to take on a more collective focus would need to be explored.

A second theme in the ethical guidelines is that of *responsibility*. Responsibility is an assertion that counselors will help clients have access to resources, minimize bias and discrimination, and thus be part of the solution. This involves challenging the model minority myth for Asian Americans. When using interventions, assess its impact not only on the individual but also on the Asian American community. Thus, when engaged in career counseling with an Asian student, consider the implications of encouraging the student to assert his or her independence in vocational choices that may go against familial desires and circumstances. Be conscious about the academic pressures that Asian American youth face. Engage teachers and other school personnel in dialogues about the need to be mindful of imposing or acting on these pressures to the detriment of the child. Examine the role of external forces in Asian American lives. Challenge the oppression and discriminatory behaviors that occur at the individual (e.g., racist jokes, racial profiling), cultural (e.g., representation of Asians as a model minority in the media), and systemic (e.g., glass ceiling) levels. Develop multiple hypotheses about issues and be cognizant about the social and personal costs that Asian Americans may incur as a function of their acculturation and their alliances to their different identities (e.g., race, ethnicity).

Finally, the third theme in ethics is that of *action*. This is an explicit and intentional call to take steps, to contribute professional time to service without compensation or personal advantage. Action can occur through education, advocacy, and lobbying for the betterment of a community (Fouad, Gerstein, & Toporek, 2006). Rather than relegate highlighting Asian American history and experiences during Asian American History month alone, explore how issues salient to Asian Americans are being addressed and integrated in day-to-day curriculum, instruction, and activities. Social justice involves becoming actively involved with the "other" outside the counseling setting— for instance, through community events, social and political functions, celebrations, friendships, and neighborhood groups—to develop a perspective that is beyond academics.

Yet, for counselors accustomed to thinking of their work as strictly involving individual counseling, the question remains: "How do we take action on behalf of Asian American individuals and communities?" To facilitate in this process, it may be helpful to review the Lewis, Arnold, et al. (2003) model of advocacy competencies. According to the authors, counselors can move beyond their individual work with clients by forming collaborations with like-minded individuals or organizations as well as mobilizing these coalitions to address systemic barriers that adversely impact Asian Americans. At a local level, collaboration may mean building alliances with an Asian American professional's association, an Asian American church or temple, or perhaps a local community service agency devoted to Asian American communities. At a national level and outside the field of counseling and psychology, counselors may join with national Asian American civil rights groups such as the Organization of Chinese Americans, the Japanese American Citizens' League, or the Sikh American Legal Defense and Education Fund to address systemic and sociopolitical injustices. Counselors can also use their professional affiliations as a path toward advocacy. For instance, counselors can lend their time and energy by becoming members of the Asian American Psychological

Association—the nation's oldest professional association dedicated to Asian American mental health—as well as becoming involved in groups such as the American Counseling Association's Association for Multicultural Counseling and Development or the American Psychological Association's Division 45—Society for the Psychological Study of Ethnic Minority Issues. In short, counselors have a range of potential coalitions through which they can channel their interests in advocating for Asian American communities.

Through their community and professional collaborations, counselors can be advocates for Asian Americans by identifying barriers as well as developing and implementing action plans that improve the communities and systems in which their clients live (Lewis, Arnold, et al. 2003). A major issue that affects Asian American communities is the cultural competence and diversity of the service providers in their communities. For example, rehabilitation counselors may serve as advocates by developing training programs, workshops, or curricula that underscore the unique cultural dimensions of working with Asian Americans with disabilities and their families. Relatedly, school counselors can advocate for increased representation of Asian Americans in hiring new counselors, teachers, coaches, and principals in their schools and school districts. Additionally, language access and linguistic competence have also been significant barriers to Asian Americans in need of counseling. Thus, counselors can be advocates for Asian Americans by making linguistic fluency in an Asian language as a criteria for hiring a new counselor, or they can urge their respective agencies to translate pamphlets, intake forms, publicity flyers, Web sites, and so forth into the languages of the major Asian American ethnic groups in their area. Indeed, although such steps are specific to enhancing access to counseling services, the issue of resource access in general is of vital importance to Asian American communities. Given the myth of the model minority (Lee, 1996) and the tacit assumption that Asian Americans are successful and have no need for services, Asian American communities may be deprived of and lack access to numerous services. For instance, college counselors may find opportunities for advocacy in a university that provide minimal recruitment, outreach, financial aid, tutoring, mentoring, and advising to Asian Americans under the erroneous presumption that all Asian Americans are academically successful. In effect, counselors can advocate for Asian Americans by identifying systemic policies, procedures, and regulations that serve as barriers to the welfare of Asian Americans.

Yet beyond community, agency, or school, Lewis, Arnold, et al. (2003) argue that counselors also have an advocacy role in the larger public and political arena. As educators and researchers, counselors can advocate for Asian Americans simply by helping disseminate accurate information and research that challenge the myths and stereotypes that the larger community may have about Asian Americans. Thus, counselors can help ensure that accurate, culturally competent information is distributed through staff trainings, workshops, community outreach, conference presentations, and journal publications as well as books and book chapters. Moreover, counselors can be advocates by developing research programs that shed light on the needs, concerns, and effective practices in serving Asian Americans. Last, counselors can be advocates in effecting change in municipal, state, and federal regulations and policies that affect Asian Americans. For instance, by partnering with civil rights groups such as the Asian American Justice Center, counselors can draw attention to legislative issues that directly influence Asian American communities, such as hate crimes monitoring, immigration policies, research funding, and language access. Given that the opportunities for Asian American advocacy are clearly vast, counselors may find this daunting. Thus, it is critical that counselors recognize that the power and expertise to effect change beyond individual counseling is within their grasp and that the first step for doing so may simply begin with an openness to learning and self-examination. One mode of learning is to gain knowledge of the Asian American community (see Activity 11.4).

ACTIVITY 11.4

There are different ways that one can learn about a community—through an indirect/observational approach and through an interactive/direct participatory approach. As part of the indirect/observational approach, watch a movie or film or read a book related to Asian American experiences (see Table 11.1 for examples). As part of the interactive/ direct participatory approach, interview Asian Americans about their experience. Compare the two types of learning. Identify the value or effectiveness of each method of learning. For each, describe and explain whether the learning is cognitive, affective, and/or behavioral.

TABLE 11.1 Media Resources About Asian American Culture

Films About Family Relationships and Identity

- *The Joy Luck Club.* Based on the book by Amy Tan (1989), this film (1993) focuses on mother–daughter relationships.
- *Knowing Her Place.* A film by Indu Krishnan in which an Indian woman looks at her life, her marriage, and her role in contemporary society in both India and the United States.
- *My America (. . . Or Honk If You Love Buddha).* A film by Renee Tajima-Peña as she travels the United States to search for what it means to be Asian American.
- *Letters to Thien.* A documentary detailing the life and murder of a gifted young Vietnamese American, Ly Minh Thien, and how the hate crime affected Thien's community.
- *Desi: South Asians in New York.* This film presents dozens of first- and second-generation New Yorkers who share their insights, reflections, and experiences to illustrate the wide spectrum of Pakistanis, Indians, Bangladeshis, Sri Lankans, Nepalese, and other South Asians who have become an integral part of the city.
- *Silent Sacrifices: Voices of the Filipino American Family.* A film by Patricia Heras about the cultural conflicts Filipino immigrants and their American-born children encounter on a daily basis.
- *Bend It Like Beckham.* A film about an Asian Indian family that deals with coming-of-age, interracial relations, and gender issues.
- *The Namesake.* Based on a book by Jhumpa Lahiri (2003), the film (2007) is about names, identity, and Asian Indian family relations.
- *American Adobo.* A comedy about five Filipino American friends and their lives in New York.

Films About Asian Sexuality

- *Chutney Popcorn.* A film about an Asian Indian lesbian, estranged from her parents, who agrees to carry a child for her infertile sister, much to chagrin of her partner and parents.
- *The Wedding Banquet.* A film that explores what happens when the parents of a Taiwanese gay male visit him in America.
- *Dim Sum Take Out.* Focuses on one woman's difficulties and her personal issues of independence and sexuality.
- *Fated to be Queer.* Four charming, articulate Filipino men illuminate some of their issues and concerns as of people of color in the San Francisco Bay Area.

(continued)

TABLE 11.1 Media Resources About Asian American Culture (Continued)

Films About Asian Sexuality

- *Khush*. Interviews with South Asian lesbians and gay men in Britain, North America, and India concerning the intricacies of being gay and of color.
- *Saving Face*. A young Chinese American lesbian and her traditionalist mother are reluctant to go public with secret loves that clash against cultural expectations.

Films About Race Relations

- *Mistaken Identity: Sikhs in America*. An investigation of attitudes toward Sikhs in the United States following the terrorist events of September 11, 2001. The film also explores the religion, culture, and history of Sikhs in America, highlighting contributions that Sikh Americans have made to the American society and economy for over 100 years.
- *Raising Our Voices: South Asian Americans Address Hate*. A film developed to raise awareness about hate crimes and bias incidents affecting South Asians living in America, with particular reference to their increase since the terrorist attacks of September 11, 2001.
- *Hapa*. Marathon runner Midori Sperandeo talks personally about her biracial heritage and reflects on the phenomenon of being biracial, with interviews from a number of ethnically mixed-raced people with additional viewpoints. Midori, her mother (who is also interviewed), and the others offer an overview of the struggle of racially mixed people to be accepted and understood and how that role has changed as the United States becomes a more multicultural society. In describing her own personal struggles, Midori likens them to the challenges encountered in learning to be a long-distance runner.
- *Rabbit in the Moon*. A very poignant PBS documentary about Japanese and Japanese-American internment during World War II in the United States. The film does a great job exploring the issues these individuals faced via testimonials from survivors.
- *Who's Going to Pay for These Donuts Anyway?* Addresses the profound effect of the Japanese American internment on generations of individuals. Chronicles the director Janice Tanaka's search for her father.
- *Children of the Camps*. In this documentary, six Japanese Americans who were incarcerated as children in the concentration camps during WWII reveal their experiences, cultural and familial issues during incarceration, and the long internalized grief and shame they felt and how this early trauma manifested itself in their adult lives.
- *The Way Home*. A documentary about women (of different racial groups) and race relations.
- *Who Killed Vincent Chin?* A classic about the murder of Vincent Chin in 1982 and its effects on the Asian American community in Detroit and across the nation.
- *American Sons*. A provocative examination of the role of racism and stereotypical gender expectations in the lives of four Asian American men.
- *A.K.A. Don Bonus*. A moving video diary of a young 18-year-old Cambodian man as he struggles against racism and poverty and adjusts to life in San Francisco.
- *Sa-I-Gu*. The post–Rodney King 1992 Los Angeles uprising through the eyes of the Korean American women shopkeepers who were in the midst of the rioting.
- *Carved in Silence*. A documentary about the detainment of Chinese immigrants at Angel Island during the Chinese Exclusion period.
- *Conscience and Constitution*. Documentary of Japanese American internees who refused to be drafted during WWII as a sign of protest.

- *Yuri Kochiyama: Passion for Justice.* The story of the legendary activist from her work with Malcolm X to Japanese American reparations to prisoner rights.
- *Combination Platter.* The story of a Chinese illegal immigrant and his life in New York and his work at a Chinese restaurant.

Films About Religion

- *In the Name of God.* This documentary by a South Asian filmmaker shows the political/religious movement prior to the destruction of the Barbri Mosque in Uttar Pradesh, India.
- *On Common Ground*: *World Religions in America.* Diana L. Eck and the Pluralism Project at Harvard University capture the fundamental beliefs and practices of different faiths and the transformation of old traditions into new settings.

Web Resources

Asian American Justice Center, www.advancingequality.org

Asian American Nation, www.asian-nation.org

Asian American Psychological Association, www.aapaonline.org

Asian Pacific Islander Health Forum, www.apiahf.org

Center for Asian American Media, www.asianamericanmedia.org

National Asian American Pacific Islander Mental Health Association, www.naapimha.org/

National Asian Pacific American Womens' Forum, www.napawf.org/

Books

Asian Women United of California. (1989). (Eds.). *Making waves: An anthology of writings by and about Asian American women.* Boston: Beacon Press.

Dasgupta, S. D. (1998). *A patchwork shawl: Chronicles of South Asian women in America.* New Brunswick, NJ: Rutgers University Press.

Eng. D. L. (1998). *Q & A: Queer and Asian American.* Philadelphia: Temple University Press.

Gupta, S. R. (1999). *Emerging voices: South Asian American women redefine self, family and community.* Walnut Creek, CA: AltaMira Press

Han, A. (2004). *Asian American X: An intersection of twenty-first century Asian American voices.* Ann Arbor: University of Michigan Press.

Kodama, C. M., McEwen, M. K., Alvarez, A. N., Liang, C., & Lee, S. (2002). *Working with Asian American college students: New directions for student services.* San Francisco: Jossey-Bass.

LEAP Asian Pacific American Public Policy Institute and UCLA Asian American Studies Center. (1993). *The state of Asian Pacific America: Policy issues to the year 2020.* Los Angeles: Authors.

Lee, S. J. (1996). *Unraveling the "model minority" stereotype: Listening to Asian American youth.* New York: Teachers College Press.

Okihiro, G. Y. (1994). *Margins and mainstreams: Asians in American history and culture.* Seattle: University of Washington Press.

Prashad, V. (2000). *The karma of brown folks.* Minneapolis: University of Minnesota Press.

Shankar, L. D., & Srikanth, R. (1998). *A part, yet apart: South Asians in Asian America.* Philadelphia: Temple University Press.

Takaki, R. (1998). *Strangers from a different shore: A history of Asian Americans.* New York: Penguin Books.

Wu, F. H. (2001). *Yellow: Race in America beyond Black and White.* New York: Basic Books.

Wu, J. Y., & Song, M. (2000). *Asian American studies: A reader.* New Brunswick, NJ: Rutgers University Press.

Zia, H. (2000). *Asian American dreams: The emergence of an Asian American people.* New York: Farrar, Strauss, and Giroux.

Summary

Asian Americans are one of the fastest growing racial and ethnic minorities, contributing significantly to the overall population growth in the United States. Although the term *Asian American* denotes a common identity with shared cultural values and beliefs, Asian Americans are comprised of distinct and heterogeneous ethnic groups with diverse immigration histories, acculturation levels, discrimination experiences, languages, intergenerational issues, socioeconomic statuses, educational backgrounds, and religious practices. This heterogeneity underscores the need for counselors to conceptualize Asian American client issues against the backdrop of these multiple influences.

In this chapter, we presented literature that highlights help-seeking attitudes, willingness to seek mental health services, and data on particular aspects of psychopathology pertinent to Asian Americans. While this research provides some glimpses into the underutilization of mental health services, the findings are mixed and raise several questions about the applicability of both theories and empirical research in understanding the experience of Asian Americans. In counseling Asian Americans, use Uba's (2002) deconstructionist approach in framing Asian American experiences. Our intention in this chapter has been to encourage you to critique and challenge the assumption and practices that tend to reify and deify traditional and stereotypical notions of Asian Americans and the role of the "model minority"—to reconstruct, redefine, and recognize how global shifts, immigration histories, demographic trends, and external experiences and internal processes related to cultural and personal identification are inextricably tied to Asian American lives. Relatedly, gaining a systemic approach and developing a sense of advocacy and outreach are important elements in working with Asian Americans. In particular, the intent of this chapter has been to provide a cultural framework for working with Asian Americans while highlighting the multiple contexts and intersections within which Asian Americans' identities are embedded.

CHAPTER 12

Individuals and Families of Latin Descent

JOSÉ A. VILLALBA

PREVIEW

Generational differences, language preferences, family, legal status, acculturation to U.S. customs, holding onto native traditions, religion, and geographical location are but a few of the factors that influence how U.S. Latinas/os perceive their environment. In turn, these factors also contribute to how members of the at-large U.S. society view Latinas/os, the nation's largest minority group. As this minority group continues to grow, the likelihood of encountering Latina/o clients in clinical settings (e.g., public schools, community counseling centers, college campuses, private practice, inpatient hospital facilities) increases. Therefore, it is in the best interest of counseling professionals to increase their knowledge of this population in an effort to attain heightened multicultural competence. The information provided in this chapter is not intended to be an "end all, be all" regarding the experiences of Latinas/os living in the United States. Rather, this chapter should serve to stimulate further actions on the part of helping professionals and those training to become helping professionals in their attempt to assist Latina/o clients.

A LATIN AMERICAN HISTORY PRIMER

Terms like *Latina/o* and *Hispanic* are grounded in the history of Latin America. For example, *Hispanic* is derived from the Spanish word "Hispano," which itself is derived from "Hispañola" where Christopher Columbus first made landfall on the American continent (present-day Dominican Republic). Consequently, U.S. Census terminology such as *Hispanic* has an inherent offensive connotation for some as it references Latin America's colonial period and European heritage (from 1492 through the early 1900s), one marred in bloodshed and forced land acquisition from native-born Latin Americans, while minimizing the unique traditions and history of each Latin American country and indigenous civilizations (e.g., Aztecs, Ciboneys, Gauanajatabeys, Incans, Mayans, Taino) on which they were founded (Shorris, 1992). Unfortunately, Latin America's history also includes political and economic struggle with influential protagonists ranging from "liberators" such as Simon Bolivar (recognized in several South American countries) to "dictators" such as Hugo Chavez (Venezuela), and persecuted philosophers such as Paolo Freire (Brazil) and José Marti (Cuba). In essence, Latinas/os from all countries share a set of common bonds and pride grounded in perseverance, respect for one's ancestors, and the acknowledgment of history's influence. There are 20 Latin American countries of which individuals and families descend (see Build Your Knowledge 12.1).

For this reason, the term *Latina/o* is considered most appropriate by the author instead of *Hispanic, Hispanic American,* or *Hispano;* it is a term that honors the indigenous heritage of Spanish-speaking individuals with Latin American ancestry. Furthermore, to differentiate from Latinas/os living outside the United States who may have different experiences and concerns than those living in the United States, the term *U.S. Latinas/os* will be used throughout this chapter. Nevertheless, counselors are encouraged to ask their Latina/o clients how they identify themselves, instead of assuming one term is better than another. (It also should be noted that individuals from Brazil, Guyana, Surinam, and French Guiana are considered to be *Latino*—but not *Hispanic*—since these parts of Latin America were colonized by French and Portuguese conquistadors. *Hispanic* implies a connection to Spain and the Spanish language, and *Latino* alludes to a connection with other popular romance languages—French, Portuguese, Italian, for example—based on the ancient European language: Latin.)

BUILD YOUR KNOWLEDGE 12.1

Write down as many Latin American countries as possible in the next 60 seconds (Spain and the United States do not count):

_____

_____

_____

_____

Have each person share her or his list with the class. Next, explore the types of customs, foods, traditions, dances, religious practices, and so on that may be representative of immigrants from these different countries (and do not be afraid to "be wrong"; it is okay to become aware of our own perceptions and stereotypes). Finally, discuss how the differences within these Latinas/os impact the counseling profession and counseling professionals.

LATIN AMERICAN HETEROGENEITY

U.S. Latinas/os currently account for over 15% of the U.S. population, or roughly 45.5 million residents (U.S. Census Bureau, 2008). However, there are as many, if not more, differences within the demographic grouping as there are similarities (Pew Hispanic Center, 2005; U.S. Census Bureau, 2008). These differences stem from the fact that Latinas/os living in the United States come from 19 different countries in addition to the United States. Several Latinas/os living in the southwestern United States are quite proud of the fact that their ancestors lived in territory that would later become states or parts of states (i.e., Arizona, California, Colorado, Nevada, New Mexico, Texas, Utah, and Wyoming) *before* these states became part of the United States after the Treaty of Guadalupe ended the Mexican-American War in 1848 and ceded Mexican territory to the United States. Aside from nation-specific foods, Spanish dialects, indigenous tongues, folk tales, burial rituals, dances, and religious nuances, U.S. Latinas/os also report a wide variety of educational experiences, immigration statuses, career opportunities, and economic realities. In short, aside from the traditional use of the Spanish language, a general affiliation and tradition with the Catholic Church, and basic family traits with adherence to collectivistic values, U.S. Latinas/os represent many experiences and worldviews (Santiago-Rivera, Arredondo, & Gallardo-Cooper, 2002b).

Apart from cultural factors, Latinas/os generally share certain demographic realities that may stand as obstacles to political, social, educational, and, consequently, emotional stability. For example, 36% of Latinas/os do not have a high school diploma, compared to 9% of non-Latinas/os (Pew Hispanic Center, 2005). The Pew Hispanic Center also reported that 31% of Latinas/os are employed in private domestic services and 21% are construction workers, while only 9% are employed in medical professions or education. The unemployment rate for Latinas/os also is higher (6.8%) than the national average (5.4%), which contributes to 22.5% of Latinas/os living below the poverty line compared to 8.2% for non-Latina/o Whites. One final generalization for U.S. Latinas/os is their relative youth; the median age for Latinas/os in this country is 25 compared to 36 for Whites (Pew Hispanic Center, 2005). Though these statistics may present an inclination to lump together all U.S. Latinas/os, the fact is that there are many aspects that set Latinas/os apart from one another. Therefore it becomes necessary to address some of the differences between Latina/o groups in the United States. The following are basic characteristics of the larger groups of U.S. Latinas/os.

Mexicans

Mexicans comprise the largest group of U.S. Latinas/os. The Pew Hispanic Center (2006a) reported that Latinas/os with Mexican heritage (i.e., those born in Mexico or who were born to Mexican parents) account for 64% of all U.S. Latinas/os. The size of the U.S. Mexican population can be attributed to the shared U.S.–Mexican border, the annexation and ceding of Mexican territories (including Texas, California, and New Mexico) at the conclusion of the Mexican War in 1848, and the sustained and increased immigration of Mexicans particularly during the mid-1970s.

More recently, the U.S. immigration debate has focused on Mexicans due to their large concentration along border states (e.g., Arizona, California, New Mexico, Texas) and the fact that 40% of Mexicans (roughly 15,000,000) living in the United States are not native-born. Unfortunately, some individuals -assume these non-native U.S. residents are in this country illegally, leading to racism and stereotypes. For many Mexicans, issues of discrimination and limited socioeconomic advancement also are compounded by large high school dropout rates (61% for first-generation Mexican immigrants and 40% for second-generation Mexican immigrants) and low 4-year college completion rates (6% for first-generation Mexican immigrants and 11% for second-generation Mexican immigrants) (President's Advisory Commission on Educational Excellence for Hispanic Americans, 2003). In spite of educational barriers, immigration-related stressors, and limited employment opportunities, many Mexicans and those of Mexican heritage have managed to impact society (e.g., Cesar Chavez), have ascended to governorships (e.g., Bill Richardson), and have influenced the performing and visual arts (e.g., Diego Rivera, Edward James Olmos).

As you consider the experiences of Mexicans and Mexican Americans, it is important to consider your values and assumptions related to these experiences as well as characteristics of this population. Reflection 12.1 offers an opportunity to reflect on beliefs you hold about this group collectively.

REFLECTION 12.1

Think of common stereotypes regarding Mexicans and Mexican Americans you may have heard or may believe. List specific media outlets, instances, and experiences that have contributed to these stereotypes:

hard work, catholic, drugs

Now, think about how these stereotypes would impact your work with Latina/o clients of Mexican descent. More importantly, how could you counter these stereotypes? Where would you acquire the knowledge and experiences to minimize the impact of these stereotypes with Latina/o clients of Mexican descent?

Puerto Ricans

The second largest group of Latinas/os in the United States is of Puerto Rican heritage, making up 9% of the U.S. Latina/o population (Pew Hispanic Center, 2005). Unlike Mexicans who tend to cluster in the southern and southwestern parts of the United States, Puerto Ricans tend to live in and around metropolitan centers in the northeastern states. Because Puerto Rico is a U.S. territory, all Puerto Ricans born in Puerto Rico are considered to be U.S. citizens. For this reason, only 1% of Puerto Ricans living in the United States are considered to be "foreign-born" (e.g., a child born to Puerto Rican parents while they were stationed as military personnel in Germany).

As a whole, Puerto Ricans living in the United States have a higher mean income than Mexicans, and attain educational experiences almost as high as Cubans (Pew Hispanic Center, 2002a). However, Puerto Ricans experience higher poverty rates, and unemployment, and receive more public assistance than Mexicans or Cubans. These realities confound many theorists and public policy makers considering this group's automatic U.S. citizenship status. Regardless, Puerto Ricans have influenced the arts (e.g., Tito Puente, Tony Orlando, Tomas Batista) and politics (e.g., José Serrano). Reflection 12.2 offers an opportunity to reflect on stereotypes regarding this population.

REFLECTION 12.2

Think of common stereotypes regarding Puerto Ricans and Puerto Rican Americans you may have heard or may believe. List specific media outlets, instances, and experiences that have contributed to these stereotypes:

_____

_____

_____

Now, think about how these stereotypes would impact your work with Latina/o clients of Puerto Rican descent. More importantly, how could you counter these stereotypes? Where would you acquire the knowledge and experiences to minimize the impact of these stereotypes with Latina/o clients of Puerto Rican descent?

Cubans

The third largest U.S. Latina/o population is Cuban immigrants and those of Cuban heritage, accounting for 4% of all U.S. Latinas/os (Pew Hispanic Center, 2005). What are your attitudes toward this group (see Reflection 12.3)? Unlike other groups of U.S. Latinas/os, which tend to be more dispersed throughout the nation, Cubans are concentrated in South Florida and New York City (including neighboring communities in New Jersey). The immigration pattern for Cubans is different from Mexicans and Puerto Ricans for two reasons: (a) most came to the United States for political reasons, and (b) most Cuban immigration is fairly recent (within the last 50 years). With regard to the political nature of Cuban immigration, the rise of Fidel Castro's communist regime in 1959 accounted for the first sustained wave of Cuban immigration, from the early 1960s through the early 1990s (de las Fuentes, 2003). The earliest Cuban immigrants from that postcommunist wave of immigration were well educated, economically stable, and lost many of their possessions to the Castro government. In 1980 a spike in Cuban immigration to the United States (specifically Miami, Florida) occurred as a result of the Mariel Boatlift, named for the Cuban port of departure for most of these individuals. This wave of 100,000 to 125,000 Cuban immigrants was not as well educated or as economically stable as previous Cuban immigrants. Consequently, some of these individuals, known as Marielitos, were the victims of discrimination by fellow Cubans.

For the most part, Cubans and those of Cuban heritage living in the United States have made large strides in political circles, educational attainment, and economic success. For example, this group of Latinas/os has the highest rate of high school and college graduation (National Center for Education Statistics, 2000). Furthermore, Cubans generally have higher mean earnings than all other U.S. Latinas/os (Pew Hispanic Center, 2002a). Also, considering the relatively small number of Cubans in the United States and their limited presence in this country, they held three congressional seats in the 110th U.S. Congress, and two seats in the 2007 U.S. Senate. However, it should not be assumed that all U.S. Cubans are free of economic hardships, acculturative stress, or educational barriers.

REFLECTION 12.3

Think of common stereotypes regarding Cubans and Cuban Americans you may have heard or may believe. List specific media outlets, instances, and experiences that have contributed to these stereotypes:

_____

_____

_____

_____

Now, think about how these stereotypes would impact your work with Latina/o clients of Cuban descent. More importantly, how could you counter these stereotypes? Where would you acquire the knowledge and experiences to minimize the impact of these stereotypes with Latina/o clients of Cuban descent?

Caribbean Hispanics/Latinas/os, Central and South Americans

The remaining U.S. Latina/o population comes from the Dominican Republic, Central American countries (not including Mexico), and South America. Dominicans, Colombians, Guatemalans, and Salvadorans make up a large percentage of the "other" U.S. Latinas/os, with at least 500,000 individuals from each group residing in the United States (Pew Hispanic Center, 2002b). Immigration patterns for Latinas/os of non-Cuban, non-Mexican, or non–Puerto Rican descent are much more difficult to characterize. For example, while 45% of U.S. Latina/o immigrants arrived in the United States prior to 1990, 50% of Dominican and 51% of Salvadoran immigrants were here prior to 1990, compared to 41% of Guatemalan and 44% of Colombian immigrants (U. S. Census Bureau, 2007b). In contrast, 20% of U.S. Latina/o immigrants came to the United States after 2000; however, the percentage of Dominicans and Salvadorans who immigrated to the United States after 2000 was lower than the average for all U.S. Latinas/os (13% and 17%, respectively), but the percentage of Colombians and Guatemalans immigrating to the United States after 2000 was higher, by 3% for both groups, than the average U.S. Latina/o. It is equally difficult to establish patterns with other U.S. Latinas/os of Central and South American heritage. Caribbean, Central, and South American U.S. Latina/o immigrants also have a plethora of reasons for leaving their native lands, including political persecution, economic hardship, and educational barriers. This heterogeneity is mirrored by the experiences of these immigrants once in the United States.

It is difficult to make generalizations about "other" U.S. Latinas/os due to the inherent nature of their heterogeneity as it relates to education level, unemployment, public assistance, and mean earnings. Therefore, counselors are encouraged to find out more about their U.S. Latina/o client's experiences before drawing quick and potentially incorrect conclusions. Part of this knowledge acquisition has to involve reflecting on perspectives on the Latina/o population as a whole (see Activity 12.1).

ACTIVITY 12.1

Take a few moments individually to write down how you feel about the U.S. Latina/o population expansion, particularly how it has or has not impacted your community. How has the media's representation of Latinas/os, including the coverage on the immigration debate, played a role in your perceptions of U.S. Latinas/os?

I'm scared of being "overrun" at times.

In small groups, develop steps you can take to reframe any negative stereotypes you may have about U.S. Latinas/os and their increasing numbers, especially since it is quite likely you will have Latina/o clients in the near future:

Discuss your ideas with the remainder of the class.

LATIN AMERICAN CULTURE AND VALUES

Because of the aforementioned colonial and indigenous lineage, the shared experiences of being immigrants in the United States, Spanish-language similarities, and the role of religion and spirituality, it is possible to deduce a shared worldview for the majority of the U.S. Latina/o population. This section presents characteristics and experiences that contribute to a general U.S. Latina/o worldview. After reviewing these cultural values, reflect on the Case of Juan presented in Case Study 12.1 on page 285.

"Somos Imigrantes" ("We are Immigrants")

One of the first attributes binding most U.S. Latinas/os is their identification as non-native U.S.-born residents or being descendents of immigrants. This factor allows most U.S. Latinas/os to empathize with each other, even if they trace their roots back to different countries. This is not to say that, for example, Mexicans will have many similarities with Cubans. On the contrary, their reasons for emigrating to the United States and their experiences once here can be starkly different. However, when confronted with U.S. immigration policies that limit access to public education for their children, for example, both Cubans and Mexicans have bonded together to promote public policy initiatives.

In addition, the hardships suffered in coming to this country—whether by land for most Mexicans, Central Americans, and South Americans, or by sea for some Cubans—bring various U.S. Latinas/os together (García Coll & Magnuson, 1997). It is common to hear older generations of U.S. Latinas/os share immigration experiences and related sacrifices with their children and grandchildren. These stories are partially responsible for a shared resiliency displayed by many Latina/o youth living in the United States, regardless of their national heritage or place of birth (Gordon, 1996).

Language

For most U.S. Latinas/os, there is at least a familiarity with Spanish. However, the dominance of Spanish, for written and oral communication, is dependent on the generational status of the individual. According to the Pew Hispanic Center (2005), 72% of first-generation U.S. Latinas/os (those born outside the United States) indicate Spanish as their dominant or preferred language, compared with 7% of second-generation immigrants. Furthermore, 47% of second-generation U.S. Latinas/os reported being bilingual while 46% indicated an English dominance; in comparison, 24% of first-generation U.S. Latinas/os were bilingual and only 4% preferred English to Spanish.

As with the shared immigrant identity, the use of and familiarity with Spanish has helped promote a sense of understanding and community between U.S. Latinas/os from different countries of origin. There is a sense of comfort, for example, when a recently arrived immigrant family can turn on their television in the United States and watch a program, in Spanish, on one of two Spanish-language national networks (i.e., Telemundo, Univision). Most major radio markets now have at least one FM (and several AM) Spanish-language stations, meaning more media choices. In addition, local libraries and national bookseller chains carry Spanish-language books. These types of resources also provide a benefit to counselors and other helping professionals in that it gives them access to some aspects of life for U.S. Latinas/os, even if they are not fluent in Spanish.

Religion and Spirituality

The vast majority of U.S. Latinas/os are Christian, with most identifying as Roman Catholic, though there are Latina/o Jews and Latina/o Muslims (Santiago-Rivera et al., 2002b). This affiliation with Christianity, particularly Roman Catholicism, is related to the colonization of Latin American countries by Spanish and Portuguese conquistadors, who often drew support for their travels from the Catholic Church and regularly included clergy in their crews. Over the centuries, however, Latinas/os from various nations have combined traditional customs with Catholic practices, which has resulted in a rich and dynamic practicing of faith. For example, in Mexico, *El Dia de Los Muertos* (the Day of the Dead) is celebrated annually around November 1 and combines aspects of Catholicism and All Saints' Day with Aztec rituals for honoring and celebrating deceased loved ones. Also, *El Dia de Reyes* (known in English as "Three Kings Day" although its literal translation is "The Day of Kings") recognizes the epiphany of the Three Wise Men and the gifts they gave baby Jesus. It is celebrated with particular vigor in Cuba and Puerto Rico on January 6. In fact, it is *Los Reyes* who bring boys and girls gifts around the winter holidays in these countries, along with Santa Claus. With regard to spirituality, U.S. Latinas/os often use terms such as *gracias a Dios* (thanks be to God), *si Dios quiere* (if God wants), *Ay Bendito* (Oh Holiness), or *hay que tener fe* (you have to have faith) in reaction to stress, happiness, sorrow, or hope—so much so that these expressions are part of the everyday vernacular for many Latinas/os.

Latinas/os who have immigrated to the United States and their U.S.-born offspring have continued their religious traditions. Rites of passage for children are intricately tied to First Communion or Holy Confirmation, the way a Bat Mitzvah might be for a Jewish girl. Religious affiliation is so important to most U.S. Latinas/os that many of their first encounters in the United

States occur in churches and places of worship. U.S. Latina/os also are more likely to turn to a priest, minister, or *curandero* (healing man) in a time of emotional difficulty than a counselor or other mental health expert (Santiago-Rivera et al., 2002b). As a result, it becomes important for counselors to assess the role religion and spirituality play in the lives of their U.S. Latina/o clients, in addition to doing their own research on certain practices with which they may be unfamiliar.

Resiliency

Although resiliency is a personality trait not solely attributed to Latinas/os, it is an additional characteristic that adds to the cultural strengths of Latina/o children and adults. Toro-Morn (1998) and Fennelly, Mulkeen, and Guisti (1998) are just some of the authors who point to resiliency as one of the ways in which Latinas/os manage to cope with common and extraordinary stressors. With newly arrived Puerto Rican women, for example, resiliency helps them come to terms with the expectations of a new city while they long for family, friends, and customs from their native Puerto Rico (Toro-Morn, 1998). In the case of Latina/o teens faced with the trauma of racism and discrimination, Fennelly et al. credit these youngsters' fortitude and inner strengths as examples of their resiliency for dealing with experiences which most of their White peers do not have to struggle. Counselors working with Latina/o clients should be cautious about always pointing to the resiliency of Latinas/os as there may be occasions or circumstances that may not be corrected by resiliency alone. Nevertheless, just as family, faith, and traditional customs can serve to alleviate some of the tension experienced by Latina/o clients, counselors should consider the role of resiliency in their work with Latinas/os.

Gender Roles

Gender roles for individuals of Latin descent are steeped in tradition and religion. To understand the power of gender roles, it is important to become familiar with the concepts of machismo and marianismo (Santiago-Rivera et al., 2002b). **Machismo** represents a strong, virile, omnipotent man who takes care of his family by providing food and shelter. Because of these responsibilities, macho men tend to leave the notions of childrearing and housework to their wives and female daughters. **Marianismo**, in contrast to machismo, is distinctive in that it requires a woman to be pure, make sacrifices for the husband's and children's benefit, not engage in premarital sex, and be a nurturing female role model for her daughters (Lopez-Baez, 1999). The ultimate role model for most Latina women is *La Virgen Maria* (the Virgin Mary), which is where the term *marianismo* is derived.

It may be difficult for non-Latinas/os living in the United States to not characterize machismo as chauvinistic, rude, and hypersexualized, and marianismo as a "step back" in the women's movement, both insulting and demoralizing. Though many first-generation U.S. Latinas/os accept these traditional roles, immigration and generational status may influence their degree of acceptance.

Second-generation and beyond U.S. Latinas/os (and even some first-generation U.S. Latinas/os) begin to question the merit and practice of traditional roles as they acculturate to the United States. This contributes to attempts by older Latina/o generations to emphasize and facilitate adherence to traditional gender roles in younger generations. The devotion to these gender roles and the subsequent rejection by second-generation and beyond U.S. Latinas/os can create dissonance among children, parents, and the rest of the family. As a counselor working with U.S. Latina/o clients and families, the importance and observance of traditional gender roles should be assessed. Moreover, counselors must assess and monitor their own attitudes toward marianismo and machismo.

Families of Latin Descent

The collectivistic nature of Latinas/os in the United States and native lands is directly related to the importance of the family, both immediate and extended. Marín and Triandis (1985) noted that

Latinas/os are more likely to make individual sacrifices for the benefit of their families. This orientation to the family is known as familismo. By definition, **familismo** signifies an individual's consideration of one's parents, siblings, grandparents, aunts, uncles, and even close friends of the family as well as religious godparents when making decisions. Familismo also entails a certain level of automatic respect for older generations, including those older adults who remained in their country of origin while younger generations immigrated to the United States. According to Santiago-Rivera et al. (2002b) familismo can be traced back to the colonization of the Americas by Spain and is a common cultural principle in Latin American countries and U.S. Latina/o communities.

As with gender role orientation, second-generation and beyond U.S. Latinas/os may not be as willing to practice or honor familismo as their parents and grandparents. Younger U.S. Latinas/os may actually resent the notion of sacrificing their own interests for their family's. As a result, counselors working with U.S. Latinas/os should consider the interplay between a client's age, length of time in the United States, family size, presence of older family members, and relevant family members who reside in their native country. If possible, it becomes necessary to gauge how each family member views and defines the immediate and extended family unit. Only by exploring the importance of familismo, and possible resulting conflicts due to generational differences, can counselors demonstrate an understanding of how family systems can influence the individual wellness of U.S. Latina/o clients.

Interpersonal Relationships

Interpersonal relationships with family and friends are held in high regard for most U.S. Latinas/os. This warmth, affection, concern about others, and positive regard for those close to an individual is known as **personalismo** (Santiago-Rivera et al., 2002b). Furthermore, Latinas/os expect these feelings to be reciprocated by their loved ones. So engrained is personalismo in the Latina/o psyche that even strangers and acquaintances are at least afforded the benefit of the doubt, and are often greeted with smiles, hugs, and perhaps an offering of help or even food. In other words, what may be misconstrued by some as intrusive and "lacking of personal space" is simply seen as demonstrating affection and care.

Confianza is another important facet to interpersonal relationships. It translates into trust and confidence, and is the closest counterpart to rapport in the counseling relationship. Confianza, like trust, must be earned and, once earned, must be maintained. However, once confianza is established between two individuals, regardless of nationality, it is a powerful bond. Without personalismo, confianza is difficult to reach in that personalismo helps tear down some of the barriers or obstacles to genuineness and egalitarianism that are crucial to establishing rapport. For this reason, counselors and helping professionals are encouraged to explore the "colder," "more sterile" and "uninviting" nature of clinical relationships and environments, in hopes of reaching some semblance of confianza with U.S. Latina/o clients.

CASE STUDY 12.1

Juan is a 15-year-old, second-generation "Hispanic American." His mother is a 44-year-old Cuban-born U.S. citizen, and his father is a 54-year-old Colombian-born U.S. citizen. Both immigrated separately to the southeastern United States in 1970, and would be considered first-generation immigrants. They still live in the same city they moved to over 30 years ago, an urban center known for its strong Latina/o presence and celebration of Latin American cultures. Unlike their son, they identify themselves as "Cubana" and "Colombiano," respectively, instead of "Hispanic," "Hispanic American," "Hispano," or "Latina/Latino." Juan also has an older brother (mid-20s) who lives outside the home. His brother also is a second-generation American; however, Juan's older brother identifies himself as "Latino" to those who ask, typically coworkers and new acquaintances.

(continued)

Lately, Juan has been having a few misunderstandings with his parents over his adopting of American values, or as his parents put it, "valores Americanos." His parents define these values as "too much freedom," "too much independence," "acting older than you are," "not being responsible for your actions," and "too much focus on friends and being cool, instead of focusing on his family." This has caused strain in Juan's immediate household. On the one hand, Juan would like his parents to understand that some of their customs, traditions, and values just "don't apply to this country, this era." On the other hand, his parents cannot understand why Juan fails to see that adhering to traditional customs and values (e.g., wanting to spend time with family first, seeking the advice and input of family members when making decisions, and having an intrinsic desire to practice and use the Spanish language) have benefited them and their older son and, therefore, should work just fine for Juan.

In an attempt to reconcile issues in the home, Juan's parents seek advice and input from his older brother, his Cuban grandmother, their friends from church, and extended family members. In contrast, Juan seeks support from his school friends, girlfriend, and, on occasion, his older brother. In the end, Juan simply wants his parents to understand him better and "get off my back a bit." His parents, to the contrary, want Juan to start "acting more responsibly" and focus more on his family and studies, and less on his friends and their "bad influences."

- How do you conceptualize the cultural values of both Juan and his parents?
- What individual differences play into conflicting values for Juan and his parents?
- How would you work with this family in counseling?
- What sources of resiliency do you note for Juan?
- How might your cultural values and cultural statuses impact your work with this family?

INDIVIDUAL DIFFERENCES AND IDENTITIES

The core cultural values that shape the U.S. Latinas/os' experiences are mediated by immigration status, generational status, and socioeconomic status. Thus, the degree to which U.S. Latinas/os adhere to a Latina/o worldview depends on their method of entry and current immigration status, length of stay in the United States, and degree of social, educational, and economic barriers and opportunities available to them. Because of the complexities of these three statuses, great variability may exist between Latina/o groups and within Latina/o families and local communities.

Immigration Status

The immigration status of U.S. Latinas/os is crucial to understanding the options, barriers, and opportunities they face living in the United States. Legal residency or U.S. citizenship depends on filing the proper documentation and nation of birth. For those clients who were born in the United States (including Puerto Rico) or have taken the appropriate steps to legalized residency or citizenship, qualifying for student financial aid, medical assistance, social security, in-state tuition rates at state colleges and universities, among other resources is typically not an issue. However, for undocumented U.S. Latinas/os, the doors to economic, educational, and physical wellness tend to be shut, not to mention the stigma that comes with being termed "an illegal" as well as the constant stress from fear of deportation (Bemak & Chung, 2003). The immigration experience is an important consideration for counseling (see Reflection 12.4).

The concepts of forced migration and voluntary migration also play a role in the heterogeneous nature of the American experience for U.S. Latinas/os. According to Murphy (1977) those individuals who were forced to leave their native lands due to political persecution, ethnic violence, war, or religious discrimination may experience more acculturative stress, grief and loss, and feelings of hopelessness than voluntary immigrants who came to the United States for economic opportunities or to improve their lives. As a result, a counselor working with a Cuban client may have to address client experiences involving abruptly leaving family behind, being jailed as a political prisoner in Cuba due to anticommunist activities, and constant worrying for relatives who may suffer repercussions for your client's decision to leave the country. On the contrary, a client from El Salvador who came to the United States with his or her entire nuclear family may want to share issues of frustration with finding resources, adjusting to a new community, or being discriminated at work because colleagues assume he or she is here illegally. These two examples are but glimpses of how immigration status and reasons for coming to the United States can impact the client–counselor relationship.

REFLECTION 12.4

Due to the current contentious immigration debate in the United States, it is quite possible that some Latina/o clients will come into your office to discuss experiences (either directly or vicariously through a family member, friend, or other source) with racism and discrimination. How do you suppose your stance toward the immigration debate might facilitate or hinder your work with clients wanting to talk about immigration-related issues?

Generational Status

Although generational status has been discussed previously in this chapter, the confusing nature of the term as well as the differences between U.S. Latina/o generations justifies additional information. The Pew Hispanic Center (2002a) defines first-generation U.S. immigrants as those who were born in a different country and immigrated to the United States, thereby signifying that their children would be considered second-generation immigrants and their children's children would be third-generation immigrants. However, other authors (e.g., Delgado-Romero, 2001) consider first-generation immigrants to be U.S.-born children of immigrants. Therefore, it becomes essential that counselors find out from their clients what they consider themselves to be in relation to their generational status. This chapter adheres to the Pew Hispanic Center's definition.

The importance of a U.S. Latina/o client's generational status is due to the influence a generation can have on the client's experiences and perspectives. For example, the median age for first-generation U.S. Latinas/os is 34, compared to 11 for second-generation U.S. Latinas/os and 24 for third-generation U.S. Latinas/os (Pew Hispanic Center, 2005). In addition, the rate of second-generation U.S. Latinas/os entering the workforce is growing at two and three times the rate as it is for third-generation and first-generation U.S. Latinas/os, respectively. In addition, the fact that second-generation (and beyond) U.S. Latinas/os have grown up in a hybrid culture composed of U.S. and Latina/o customs may cause tensions with first-generation U.S. Latinas/os. These are but a few examples of how generational status can impact the relationship between intergenerational U.S. Latinas/os as well as counselors with whom they are working. As an illustration, a school counselor could be "caught in the middle" between a U.S.-born Latina/o high school student, who is getting ready to attend an out-of-state university, and her U.S. resident parents and grandparents who wish she would attend a local community college so she can stay close to home.

Socioeconomic Status

An individual's socioeconomic status (SES), or social class, is an amalgamation of income, employment status, educational attainment, experiences with poverty, accumulated wealth, life expectancy, and even number of individuals living within a household. This merging of factors can essentially lead to individuals identifying with peers, not on the basis of race, ethnicity, religion, or even gender, but rather on the basis of being lower class, middle class, or upper class (Liu & Pope-Davis, 2004). Therefore, though some of the economic data suggest that, in general, U.S. Latinas/os earn less, have less desirable jobs, have lower levels of formal education, and are more likely to live below the poverty line than their non-Latina/o peers (Pew Hispanic Center, 2005), counselors should not assume all of their U.S. Latina/o clients will share this description. Furthermore, counselors might have more in common with certain U.S. Latina/o clients based on shared social class than suspected.

MENTAL HEALTH ISSUES OF INDIVIDUALS OF LATIN DESCENT

Systems (e.g., political, economic, religious, educational) play roles in the experiences of U.S. Latinas/os on personal, family, and community levels. Failing to consider the overlapping and influential nature of these systems when working with U.S. Latina/o clients would therefore greatly limit the effectiveness of counseling theories and interventions. Counselors should keep in mind the richness and expansiveness of the U.S. Latina/o experience as they prepare to assess the counseling needs, strengths, and goals of their clients, while they strive to provide the most culturally appropriate and competent mental health assistance possible.

Before detailing some of the principal mental health concerns of U.S. Latina/os, we must explore the types of cultural and societal factors that infringe on the overall well-being of this population. First and foremost is the use of and familiarity with the Spanish language, and consequent limited English fluency, for many U.S. Latinas/os. With roughly a quarter of U.S. Latinas/os considering themselves "English dominant" (Pew Hispanic Center, 2005), there is little doubt that communication barriers contribute to mental health concerns for U.S. Latinas/os (Gopaul-McNicol & Thomas-Presswood, 1998). Whether it is an inability to communicate with coworkers, school peers, members of the justice system, children's teachers, or even understanding traffic signs and laws, many U.S. Latinas/os are bombarded with language-related stressors on a regular basis.

With the exception of organized religion, U.S. Latinas/os also experience barriers and negative experiences in various social systems including the workforce and school settings, which adversely affect and compound mental health. For example, over 80% of U.S. Latinas/os believe job-related discrimination is at least a "minor problem" and interferes with their career advancement (Pew Hispanic Center, 2005). Fox and Stallworth (2005) further explain that racism and on-the-job "bullying" of Latinas/os increases stress and feelings of oppression for these workers.

Although many first-generation U.S. Latinas/os report coming to this country for educational opportunities available to their children, the U.S. educational system is not as equally available or helpful to U.S. Latinas/os as it is to non-Latinas/os. For example, non-Latina/o children are at least 50% more likely to be enrolled in preschool programs, are more likely to graduate from high school by the time they turn 19, and can expect to enter and complete college in greater numbers (Cabrera & Padilla, 2004; Pew Hispanic Center, 2005). In addition, many first-generation U.S. Latina/o parents are unfamiliar with "navigating" the U.S. educational system, which leads to less participation in extracurricular activities, tutoring programs, and free- and reduced-lunch programs. Parent participation in school-related activities also is reduced due to the increased likelihood of working multiple jobs or simply feeling "out-of-place" in their children's schools (Casas, Furlong, & Ruiz de Esparza, 2003; Toro-Morn, 1998).

Lower levels of education, apart from offering fewer opportunities for U.S. Latinas/os and potentially impacting self-efficacy levels, also contribute to higher poverty and limited earnings. In addition, the increased U.S. Latina/o presence in the working-poor and lower-SES class is partially to blame for chronic and infectious illnesses, health disparities, increased reliance on the public health care system, and limited health insurance (Zsembik & Fennell, 2005). A further outcome of lower educational attainment and social class membership is increased homicide rates for U.S. Latinas/os, particularly males living in urban settings (National Center for Health Statistics, 2001).

Struggling to acculturate and get ahead in the United States while managing the obstacles presented by so many social systems is a daunting task for many U.S. Latinas/os. Coupled with a dearth of Spanish-speaking and Latina/o mental health workers, it is easier to understand how mental health issues arise and/or are exacerbated in the U.S. Latina/o population. The following information provides common dilemmas impacting the mental health of many U.S. Latinas/os.

Acculturative Stress

The immigration process for many first-generation U.S. Latinas/os, and the resulting negotiation between native and adopted cultures, can lead to acculturative stress. Johnson (1986) describes **acculturative stress** as the internal psychological reaction to balancing the strains of learning about a new culture while longing for the familiarity of one's previous surroundings. Acculturative stress impacts not only first-generation U.S. Latinas/os as they learn English or figure out hidden rules and agendas at work and in schools, but also future generations of U.S. Latinas/os (Santiago-Rivera et al., 2002b). The impact is a direct byproduct of observing the negative effects acculturative stress may have on their parents and grandparents, such as depression, domestic violence, identity loss, and substance abuse. Most alarming of all, it appears that some U.S. Latinas/os may suffer prolonged mental health concerns as they continue to acculturate (Turner & Gil, 2002). Because acculturative stress can be a lifelong occurrence, and can range from an unpleasant level of pressure to Post Traumatic Stress Disorder (PTSD) (particularly for Latina/o refugees fleeing wartorn lands or political oppression), mental health specialists should regularly assess and monitor their U.S. Latina/o clients' acculturation level (Williams & Berry, 1991).

Grief and Loss

The grieving and loss associated with leaving loved ones behind, sacrificing cultural traits and mores for those of the host culture, or having one or more minority statuses can contribute to feelings of depression and despair. These feelings, which also are connected to a sense of isolation, can lead U.S. Latinas/os to substance abuse, suicidal ideation, acts of domestic violence, and even heart disease (National Council of La Raza, 2005). First-generation U.S. Latinas/os also feel as if they are losing their children and grandchildren to U.S. society whether they were born in their native country or in the United States. These emotions and worries often lead parents and grandparents to generational conflicts and disagreements with younger U.S. Latinas/os, increased levels of strictness and protectiveness for the younger generation, and resentment toward the United States and its perceived more "liberal" child-rearing practices (Santiago-Rivera et al., 2002b). While attending to these emotional responses, counselors working with U.S. Latinas/os are therefore encouraged to ask their clients about family members, friends, and social networks they left behind, as well as their and their families' current experiences and reactions while establishing new roots in the United States.

Additional Concerns

U.S. Latinas/os, like most of the U.S. population, can experience a variety of mental, physical, and social problems. Some of these (e.g., domestic violence, substance abuse, depression) already have been alluded to, and may be directly related to cultural manifestations of grief and acculturative stress. However, divorce, unemployment, teenage pregnancy, physical and sexual abuse victimization, academic struggles, and homelessness are but a few of the factors that may contribute to fear, anxiety, helplessness, hopelessness, or anger in U.S. Latinas/os. The onus is on the counselor working with U.S. Latina/o clients presenting with these issues to augment their services by considering Latina/o cultural customs and preferences, history, and immigration experiences. By practicing the basic tenets of multicultural competence, counselors working with U.S. Latina/o clients increase their likelihood of providing effective interventions to this clientele (see Activity 12.2 for skill development and Activity 12.3 for strategies for increasing knowledge of Latin Americans).

ACTIVITY 12.2

Compile a list of questions or probes that you as a counselor may use with U.S. Latina/o individuals and families to assess the relationship between cultural stressors and counseling concerns. Furthermore, take into account the setting in which you are working (e.g., school, community counseling, college counseling center, vocational rehabilitation services) and how the setting may influence your line of questioning or desired outcomes:

_____

_____

_____

_____

_____

_____

Discuss your list with the class. How could schools and mental and community agencies lessen cultural stressors for Latina/o clients?

GUIDELINES FOR COUNSELING CLIENTS OF LATIN DESCENT

The counseling needs, strengths, goals, and objectives of U.S. Latinas/os vary according to age, immigration status, country of origin, where they live in the United States, economic and socioeconomic status, language preference, and assimilation, to name but a few factors. This section looks at potential considerations and counseling interventions for U.S. Latina/o clients based primarily on age. What is purposefully absent from this discussion is the type of theoretical orientation to use with U.S. Latina/o clients. Counseling theories and techniques that have been demonstrated effective with Latina/o clients include cognitive-behavioral (Pina, Silverman, Fuentes, Kurtines, & Weems, 2003), person-centered (Coatsworth, Maldonado-Molina, Pantin, & Szapocznik, 2005), psychodynamic (Gelman, 2003), and solution-focused therapy (Springer, Lynch, & Allen, 2000). However, though the literature seems to lend more support for using cognitive-behavioral therapy and directive theories with Latina/o clients, counselors and therapists working with U.S. Latina/o clients should not assume a "one-size-fits-all" mentality when deciding on which theories and techniques to use with these individuals. Hence, counselors should explore how the following ideas fit with their theoretical preferences.

Counseling Considerations for Children of Latin Descent

Two key factors must be taken into account when working with U.S. Latina/o children: age and birthplace. Age is rather basic in that counselors must ensure that their interventions are developmentally appropriate, including chronological, cognitive, and social developmental appropriateness. Birthplace, however, is not as commonly deliberated when it comes to working with children.

Latina/o children who were born in the United States are less likely to be Spanish-dominant, bilingual, or have academic difficulty, and are more likely to identify themselves as "Americans" (Pew Hispanic Center, 2005). U.S. Latina/o children who were born in their native country and immigrated to the United States (first-generation U.S. Latinas/os) at a young age are more likely to experience academic difficulty, less likely to attain cognitive fluency in Spanish or English, and face greater risk for acculturative stress (Crawford, 1999; Cummins, 1994). Counselors must therefore become knowledgeable of how long the child and the family have been in the United States if they were born abroad. This information should lead to further inquiry related to experiences in their homeland and possible trauma related to the immigration process (and perhaps current stress due to immigration status). This information may provide the counselor with context for developing counseling interventions, securing interpretative services when necessary, and locating community-based services, as relevant.

Counselors working with U.S. Latina/o children also should be aware of the following issues:

- Child's knowledge of and identification with his or her Latina/o heritage
- Child's family members, both immediate and extended, and where important family members live
- Child's fluency in English and Spanish, and preferred language for communicating in clinical settings
- The role of gender socialization on the child's upbringing (e.g., identification with machismo or marianismo traits)
- Child's reactions to experiences with racism and discrimination
- Child's self-concept and self-efficacy as it relates to academic performance

COUNSELING CHILDREN   Counselors working with U.S. Latina/o children can use individual, group, and family counseling interventions, just as they would with children with non-Latina/o heritages. However, when working with U.S. Latina/o children, counselors should keep in mind the influence of the family and school systems. For example, a counselor working and a 7-year-old, first-generation Latina/o child in a school setting must determine the child's English fluency if working with the child in English, the school's policy for teaching English-language learners, and even the parents' English fluency (Clemente & Collison, 2000). All of these systems will influence how much the child communicates, the level of emotions described, and the details behind the presenting issue.

Group work with young U.S. Latina/o children provides a unique experience to share similar experiences with peers, in addition to enhancing feelings of universality and cohesion (Torres-Rivera, 2004; Villalba, 2003). Group interventions can focus on adjusting to a new school, learning a second language, acquiring study skills, or practicing coping skills for grief and loss. More importantly, group facilitators can help children link the similarities in their experiences while encouraging them to build relationships with each other. In essence, counseling groups and psychoeducational groups can take on some of the characteristics of a "family," particularly for those children who have recently arrived in the United States.

Family counseling and therapy with U.S. Latina/o children also can be an effective counseling intervention (see Build Your Knowledge 12.2 for an example). The strength and influence of the Latina/o family already has been discussed. It is therefore easy to justify the inclusion of family members, either as full participants or resources of information, when providing mental health services to young U.S. Latina/o clients. And, due to the impact of the extended family and friends of the family, children should be afforded the opportunity to share information on as many "relevant" family members and adults as possible.

BUILD YOUR KNOWLEDGE 12.2

COUNSELING ACTIVITY FOR USE WITH U.S. LATINA/O CHILDREN: CUENTO THERAPY

Cuento therapy was first introduced into the counseling literature by Costantino, Malgady, and Rogler (1986). *Cuento* translates into "fairy tale" in Spanish, and Costantino et al. used this counseling modality to model desirable social behaviors for Puerto Rican children. The stories they used were based on Puerto Rican lore, and included Puerto Rican heroes, cultural concepts, and locales. In essence, cuento therapy is similar to bibliotherapy, but instead of reading a book on bullying (like *The Three Little Pigs*) and leading a group or individual discussion with a child, the counselor shares a native folk story with the child(ren) and then processes the events and characters in the story. The stories were unique in that the Puerto Rican children in Costantino et al.'s study felt they could identify with the cuento's characters, situations, and language. In turn, Costantino et al. used the children's identification with characters and themes to facilitate their discussion and use of positive social behaviors inside and outside counseling sessions.

Of course, the biggest hurdle for most counselors who want to use cuento therapy is where to find the cuentos. The best place to start would be to ask parents or guardians for some cuentos, particularly those with strong hero figures and clear notions of right versus wrong, or a problem and its solution or resolution. It may be necessary to consult with a translator if a parent is not fluent or comfortable communicating in English. Children themselves also could teach the counselor about cuentos with which they are familiar. Parents and children are great folks to ask since they will often relay a story unique to their culture and country of origin, thereby decreasing the likelihood of using a cuento that may not be familiar to a child (e.g., a cuento related to Cinco De Mayo (May 5), which is a Mexican holiday, would have little relevance to a child from Argentina).

As counselors accumulate cuentos they can incorporate these stories into their counseling sessions with U.S. Latina/o children. Before using a cuento in a counseling session with children, the counselor should become familiar with the characters, themes, and outcomes of the story, and be able to link these events to the expected counseling goals and objectives. It is not necessary for the counselor to tell the cuento in Spanish, just that they be able to translate the general concepts and characters to the child's needs.

Cuento therapy, therefore, is a great way to demonstrate the counselor's willingness to bring culture into the counseling session while increasing the connection between therapeutic goals and culture. For example, a counselor's eagerness to learn, adapt, and implement a Latin cuento into a counseling session with a young girl who is experiencing acculturative stress shows the child just how important that child's culture, and by association the child herself, is to the counselor. This genuine attempt to bridge cultural traditions and folklore with the counseling process may assuage the child's acculturative stress in that a familiar story is being shared in counseling (which is perhaps a nonfamiliar activity). In the long run, the counselor's efforts to use cuento therapy may help the child understand the counseling process even more, and will contribute to the counseling relationship.

Counseling Considerations for Adolescents of Latin Descent

Due to the important role school plays in the development and socialization of teenagers, counselors should pay close attention to the academic experiences of their adolescent U.S. Latina/o clients. Peer pressure, puberty, adjustments to more rigorous academic material, and the need to "fit in" can be difficult for most middle and high school students. For U.S. Latina/o youth, however, these problems may be aggravated by English proficiency, a need to balance between their home (Latina/o) and school (American) cultures, and limited parental involvement in school and social interests (Casas et al., 2003; Cummins, 1994; Szapocznik, Kurtines, & Fernandez, 1980).

Due to the increased probability that these adolescents' parents attended school outside the United States, were socialized in their native countries, and typically have traditional expectations for their youngsters, conflict tends to arise between first-generation U.S. Latina/o parents and their U.S. Latina/o teenagers, regardless of where their children were born. Consequently, counselors working with them also must assess the type and quality of relationships they have with their parents and other family members. It also would help the counselor to find out what the parents' perspectives are of the relationship, in addition to factors that positively or negatively influence the relationship.

Counselors working with U.S. Latina/o adolescents also should be aware of the following issues:

- Adolescent's difficulty reconciling his or her bicultural status
- Adolescent's feelings toward adhering to gender-related expectations in the face of American values
- Adolescent's sexual orientation development, particularly as it relates to males and the culture's intolerance for homosexuality (Agronick et al., 2004)
- Adolescent's limited exposure to culturally related extracurricular school activities and sports
- Adolescent's potential substance use as a coping mechanism for stress (National Council of La Raza, 2005)
- Adolescent's level of experience and exposure to various career opportunities, as well as determining the client's career models

COUNSELING ADOLESCENTS   Individual counseling interventions are an effective way for helping U.S. Latina/o teens deal with, for example, the pressures associated with being bicultural. Counselors can organize one-on-one sessions so that their adolescent clients can talk about the struggles to fit in at school with peers (Latina/o and non-Latina/o) while adhering to parents' wishes and cultural mores. Individual counseling also can be used to help these teenagers gain insight from their experiences, while helping them frame some of their bicultural skills as assets (Villalba, 2007).

Group counseling, particularly psychoeducational groups, may be an effective method for helping teenage U.S. Latina/o boys and girls deal with gender socialization struggles. Recall that Latina/o gender socialization (i.e., machismo and marianismo) is often at odds with certain U.S. notions of gender socializations. Counselor-led groups organized for high-school-aged youth would provide males and females a medium to discuss issues around "being macho," "being matronly and pure," "having to support the family," or "sacrificing college for being a good wife and mother." Although not all U.S. Latina/o adolescents, particularly third-generation immigrants and beyond, will experience a conflict with gender roles, it would behoove counselors to at least ask these clients if related issues are of concern to them.

Including immediate and extended family members when counseling adolescents can be a tricky event. Some teens are resistant to their parents' suggestions, ideas, and even presence due to normal conflicts that arise between parents and children during adolescence. However, this should not lead counselors to omit the participation of family members when counseling U.S. Latina/o adolescents. For example, brief strategic family therapy (BSFT) has shown to be an effective clinical intervention for helping Latina/o adolescents with substance abuse and behavioral problems (Santisteban et al., 2003). While the success of BSFT with U.S. Latina/o youth can be partially attributed to the overall effectiveness of the technique, it also supports the power of familismo and the family system in Latina/o families. The activity described in Build Your Knowledge 12.3 presents the basic tenets of BSFT with Latina/o families, with the stipulation that further reading and research would be required to fully implement this technique with U.S. Latina/o adolescents.

BUILD YOUR KNOWLEDGE 12.3

COUNSELING ACTIVITY FOR USE WITH U.S. LATINA/O ADOLESCENTS: BRIEF STRATEGIC FAMILY THERAPY

According to Santisteban et al. (2003), brief strategic family therapy (BSFT) is a three-phase counseling technique whereby the professional counselor "joins with," diagnoses, and restructures the family's communication patterns in hopes of making the parents the "primary source of authority and [where] all individuals have equal opportunities to contribute to the family and to voice their issues and concerns" (p. 123). In the joining phase, the counselor helps the family members analyze and process their communication and interaction by summarizing and paraphrasing the family's emotions and behaviors, as well as emphasizing that they interact in their "typical" manner. This process leads to the diagnosing phase wherein the counselor looks for patterns of problems and issues related to power distribution between family members, targeted family members, boundary irregularities, and avenues for conflict resolution. Finally, all of the collected information directs the counselor in developing a restructuring plan to present the family with more effective, realistic, and appropriate communication methods and interactions.

With U.S. Latina/o adolescents involved in generational conflicts—particularly those who are, in the eyes of parents/guardians and older family members, "rebelling against the old ways,"—BSFT can help them and their families take a "time-out" from their culture-centered and generational-centered in-fighting to gauge why their communication patterns are not leading to family cohesion and solutions to discord (see Case Study 12.2). Counselors who join U.S. Latina/o families can help them observe the adaptive and maladaptive communication style and topics of disagreement in order to diagnose where the actual problems are centered. Next, by providing support for the adult's role as authority figure (in line with Latina/o cultural norms) while acknowledging that every family member's voice is valid (though not a commonly held belief in Latina/o culture as it pertains to children, it is a collectivistic concept), the counselor can help each family member develop methods for attaining stronger and healthier relationships. As with most techniques, mental health experts are ethically required to explore and research its merits. Once counselors have become more comfortable with the basic tenets of BSFT, they will most likely find it to be a counseling technique that takes into account many of the cultural norms and customs of U.S. Latina/o adolescents and their families, thereby increasing the likelihood it will be an effective clinical tool.

CASE STUDY 12.2

Sandra is a 14-year-old Mexican American child. Sandra was born in the United States; her parents were born in Mexico. She has been referred to the community counseling center in which you work by her middle school counselor. The middle school counselor, a colleague of yours from graduate school, informs you that Sandra is experiencing family issues at home and that these issues are manifesting themselves in the school, which includes an apathetic attitude toward her schoolwork, aggression toward her classmates, and disrespectful behavior toward school personnel. She elaborates on the issues in the home by saying Sandra is at odds with her parents' child-rearing practices in that her parents are "much more strict" than Sandra's peers' parents. Moreover, Sandra's parents are going back to Mexico this summer for the entire 3 months of summer vacation, and Sandra does not want to go with them. She'd rather be left with an aunt who lives in a nearby town. Finally, your colleague informs you that Sandra has reported "being fed up with all this speaking Spanish stuff in the house, Spanish TV and radio, and tortillas for breakfast, lunch, and dinner. I just wish I was more American like my friends, and not Mexican." The parents have agreed with the school counselor that a community counseling referral would be most beneficial for Sandra. You agree to see Sandra, fully aware of the multiple factors involved in Sandra's presenting school issues as well as the deeper layers of cultural resentment and parental conflict.

- Considering that you will have an intake session with Sandra in the next week, what kind of information would you want to know from this session? Think about what *might not* be on the intake form, that you might want to know anyhow.
- Assuming that you are doing a Mental Status Exam (MSE) as part of the intake, what kinds of formal and informal assessments would you like to include? What cultural considerations would you need to account for as you complete the MSE? What are some of the cultural limitations of the MSE process?
- To what extent would you involve her parents in the intake session? To what extent would you involve her parents in subsequent sessions? How would you deal with generational conflicts in sessions? How would you address generational conflicts outside of session, when they are more likely to occur?
- There are two tiers of circumstances here: (1) the school concerns and (2) the family/home/cultural identity concerns. How do you prioritize these issues, and why? What kind of theoretical orientation and techniques would you use to address these concerns?
- What kinds of goals for Sandra and/or her family would you assist in formulating? How would you achieve this goal formation? And how would you "know" when these goals have been attained?
- What countertransference issues are you experiencing as a result of reading this case study, if any? How do you grapple with these concerns and self-awareness, and how do you address it?

Counseling Considerations for Adults of Latin Descent

When working with U.S. Latina/o adults, it becomes important to consider the impact of immigration status and the practice of cultural and religious customs. Particularly for first-generation adult U.S. Latina/os, their immigration status can be a constant stressor if they do not have the proper documentation to reside in this country. It can also be a source of pride if they have successfully become a U.S. resident or citizen, or guilt if they experience feelings of having to "sacrifice" their affiliation with their country of origin for U.S. citizenship. Even for second-generation U.S. Latinas/os, immigration issues can have an influence on their daily lives. For example, 54% of legal U.S. Latina/o residents and citizens have reported increased discrimination as a direct result of the contentious immigration debate in the United States (Pew Hispanic Center, 2006b). U.S. Latinas/os also worry about the immigration status and visa procedures for loved ones in the United States or those trying to move to the United States. In short, counselors should not assume that immigration is a "nonissue" for U.S. Latinas/os, regardless of status.

The amount of time a U.S. Latina/o adult has lived in the United States also can influence the vigor with which he or she adheres to Latina/o norms, customs, traditions, and even religious practice. The sacrificing or mere fading of one's Latina/o heritage in the name of becoming more "American" can result in feelings of guilt in many adults; almost a feeling of "selling out" the homeland. These circumstances also can be moderated by where the client lives. For example, does the client reside in a community with a historically large and active Latina/o presence (e.g., Los Angeles,

Miami, New York), or has the client settled down in more rural communities with burgeoning, yet small Latina/o populace (e.g., Siler City, North Carolina; Washington County, Arkansas)? In the former case, perhaps the client is more capable of practicing and coming in contact with reminders from home (e.g., ingredients for Latin cooking, Latin restaurants, Catholic services in Spanish); in the latter, there is little likelihood of finding the comforts of their native home. As with other considerations previously outlined, it is the counselor's job to assess if and how the adult client's presenting problems are associated with immigration and a longing for cultural connections.

Counselors working with U.S. Latina/o adults also should be aware of the following issues:

- Adults who struggle with caring for their elderly parents in a society they consider to not be as respectful of the elderly as Latina/o cultures
- Adults who experience discrimination in the workplace or who are underemployed as a result of their educational attainment or immigration status
- Adults finding it difficult to connect with their children because of differences between school culture and home culture
- Adults feeling powerless because they must depend on their children to serve as translators if the child's English fluency is greater than their own (Santiago-Rivera et al., 2002b)
- Adults who feel the need to send remittances to family members, friends, or creditors in their native countries, while struggling to reach economic stability in the United States

COUNSELING ADULTS   Selecting between individual, group work, and family counseling for adult U.S. Latinas/os can be more difficult than it is for children and adolescents. To begin with, U.S. Latina/o adults tend to have stronger Latina/o identities tied to their country of origin, which can often play a role in the type of counseling modality selected. In addition, with the exception of college-aged individuals attending classes or living on a college campus, most U.S. Latinas/os do not have regular access to mental health specialists. Therefore, planning and offering counseling services is more dependent on clients making time for mental health services, in spite of family, work, and life obligations. And it is precisely because of these types of responsibilities that a systems approach to counseling—that is, one that considers all the aspects of a U.S. Latina/o client's environment(s)—is almost as important as selecting between one-on-one counseling, a support group, or family therapy. Reflect on what modalities would be best for Alejandro in Case Study 12.3.

CASE STUDY 12.3

Alejandro is a 54-year-old Honduran man. He came to the United States 24 years ago, and has been a U.S. citizen for 7 years. He recently was laid off from his job as supervisor for a textile company (with 26 garment workers under his management) due to the downturn in the economy. For this reason he was come to you, a vocational counselor, in an effort to find employment in a related field. Typically, you would start off the first session with a new client by asking for some background on his or her past job and assessing interests and skills. However, you realize that Alejandro has a lot more he would like to discuss finding a new job. In this first session he also shares how "lost" he feels now that he can't provide for his family, and that he knows his age is not going to help him get a new job since "any employer would just as soon hire a younger person with less experience and not have to pay him a living wage." You may realize that there are more pressing concerns for this gentleman than finding a new job, and you know that many cultural aspects will need to be considered as you proceed to offer him vocational guidance. Therefore, consider the following questions:

- How do you prioritize his presenting goals of "obtaining a new job" with his anxiety, and stigma, over not being able to "provide for his family"?
- To what extent does machismo factor into this client's perceptions, if at all? Furthermore, how would you raise these issues (if at all) considering your own gender?
- What about his notion of confianza? What role does it play in goal setting, challenging statements, and even reflections with this client considering this is the first session?
- What about the cultural appropriateness of commonly used career assessments? Would they be appropriate for this client based on his age and ethnicity?
- Finally, how comfortable would you feel providing services that went beyond "vocational guidance" to this client? Think about your setting (i.e., the specific role of your agency) and how that may facilitate or hinder your desire to go beyond "vocational guidance" to address Alejandro's many concerns.

If individual counseling is used with adult clients, attention should be paid to the different culturally related factors that may be impacting the presenting issue. For example, if a client is seeking anger management skills, the counselor should help the client explore how his or her experiences as a U.S. Latina/o are connected to antecedents and behaviors associated with anger. In one case, for example, a client from the Dominican Republic may need to consider how the discrimination she experiences at work, delays in getting a U.S. work visa renewed, and feelings about her daughter "becoming less Dominican and more American by the minute" are contributing to her anger at home and on the job. With this client, a counselor would be remiss if he or she focused only on helping her learn anger management skills without at least helping her consider the influence of social, political, and family systems on her feelings and reactions. Processing these circumstances becomes crucial to the overall counseling relationship and related goals, particularly because clients are not solely in control of these systems.

The benefits of cohesion and universality attributable to group work make it a "modality of choice" when working with members of any race, age, or ethnicity. However, because of the strong identification most U.S. Latinas/os have with their country of origin, counselors should proceed with caution before "lumping" U.S. Latina/o clients into any type of counseling group, psychoeducational group, or self-help/support group. Furthermore, counselors should not assume that they could place South Americans (e.g., Peruvians and Colombians and Brazilians) or Caribbeans (e.g., Cubans and Puerto Ricans) together, expecting mutual empathy from the group members based on geographic proximity. In essence, counselors working with group modalities to assist U.S. Latina/o clients process and cope with a variety of issues (e.g., grief and loss, substance use, domestic violence, adjusting to life in the United States) must at least be cognizant of the influence that cultural systems attributed to country of origin can have, even if the client is a second- or third-generation U.S. Latina/o, since customs, dialects, worshiping nuances, and role models can be very different.

Family therapy would seem to be an effective counseling modality for U.S. Latina/o adults, considering the importance placed on the family system. And, though family counseling is most likely a viable option, counselors must keep in mind the resistance by some U.S. Latina/o adults to seek mental health help from someone other than a fellow family member or clergy member (Santiago-Rivera et al., 2002a). For this reason, counselors working with U.S. Latinas/os should ask how clients would feel about involving immediate and extended family members. It may be that a particular adult client has not told any family members that he or she is seeking counseling. Clients may feel that family members would be critical of them going outside the family and church and telling a stranger about their problems. And, because the family system is oftentimes partially responsible or impacted by an individual's reasons for seeking mental health assistance, involving family members can become a precarious experience. The culture-centered genogram, developed by Martiza Gallardo-Cooper, is one method to establish family background, determine relevant family members, and discuss family bonds and relationships for individual and family clients (Santiago-Rivera et al., 2002a). This information could then be used to enhance family therapy objectives, exercises, and goals. Build Your Knowledge 12.4 presents another technique for counseling adults.

BUILD YOUR KNOWLEDGE 12.4

COUNSELING ACTIVITY FOR USE WITH U.S. LATINA/O ADULTS: CULTURALLY SENSITIVE ECO-MAP

The **eco-map**, formally known as an ecological genogram, was developed by Hartman (1995). Eco-maps are visual depictions of the systems that influence an individual's world. Unlike genograms that focus on someone's family history, the eco-map takes into account microsystems (e.g., the individual and his or her family), mesosystems (i.e., relationship between systems), exosystems (i.e., systems indirectly connected to the individual or his or her family such as place of work, school, or church), and macrosystems (e.g., such as religion/spirituality or political systems). Basically, a counselor using an eco-map with a client would ask the client to draw a circle in the middle of a page, which represents the client (i.e., "self"). Then, the client can draw family members in separate circles, his or her place of work and worship, and greater themes such as spirituality and the power of government on his or her life. The client is instructed to draw these systems as circles, too. More importantly, the client is then instructed to carefully consider where he or she "places" each circle in relation to the "self" circle because distance from himself or herself to other individuals and systems indicates importance (closeness) or inconsequence (remoteness). Finally, the counselor instructs the client to "say a bit more" about the relationship between the "self" and the system, using different types of lines to indicate the type of relationship (e.g., a straight line might indicate a positive relationship, a dotted line may signify an indifferent relationship, and a jagged line would indicate a strained or negative relationship—what the lines represent is up to the counselor). The final part of this activity would be to discuss the client's reactions to the eco-map, and perhaps develop future clinical goals or focus.

What makes an eco-map particularly useful with U.S. Latina/o adult clients is how it can open up discussions into, for example, extended family members, the influence of the church, or even the strain of an uncertain U.S. residency. In fact, counselors using eco-maps with U.S. Latina/o clients should stress the importance of placing as many relevant "systems" as possible, while having the client focus on what makes the mesosystems take on the characteristics that they do. If the client is intent on altering mesosystems (e.g., "bringing" a family member closer or redefining the importance of school or church), then the eco-map provides a visual cue for how things look now and how the client would like them to look in the future. Eco-maps do not have to be culturally sensitive by definition, but when used by a culturally competent mental health specialist, they can be very useful in helping U.S. Latina/o clients realize the importance of all the systems that impact their daily lives.

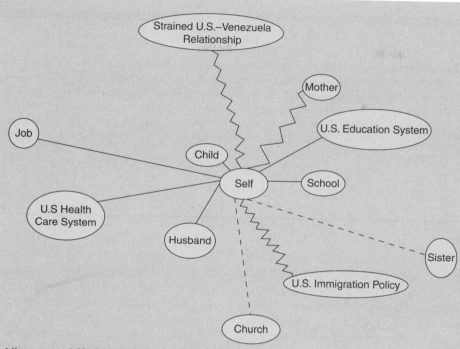

Microsystems: Self, Child, Husband, Sister, Mother
Mesosystems: Straight Line = A Positive Relationship; Broken Line = A Distant, Indifferent Relationship;
    Jagged Line = A Negative, Strained Relationship
Exosystems: School, Church, Job
Macrosystems: Strained U.S.–Venezuela Relationship; U.S. Education System; U.S. Health Care System;
    U.S. Immigration Policy

This hypothetical eco-map was completed by your client ("Self"), a 27-year-old legal U.S. resident who came to the United States from Venezuela when she was 10 years old. She indicates her child (6-year-old son) and husband are her most positive and strongest relationships. However, she does not have much contact with her sister back in Venezuela, and is estranged from her mother who lives in the same city as your client. Relevant exosystems include the community college where she's pursuing studies to become a licensed practicing nurse (as indicated by "School"), and her job. Although she indicates an indifferent relationship between the local Catholic church (as indicated by "Church"), she mentions that she would like to increase her family's participation in church activities. Finally, she mentions that her husband's pending immigration status (his worker visa has expired and he is waiting for an update on if and when it will be renewed) and the current state of U.S. immigration policy, coupled with the strained relationship between the United States and Venezuela, has her worried if he will be deported back to Venezuela before the paperwork is completed. However, she does not want to sound "anti-American," for she is grateful for the U.S. Education and Health Care Systems.

ACTIVITY 12.3

Immerse yourself in a Latina/o cultural experience in your community, one with which you do not have experience. For example, find a Spanish religious service, eat at a new (perhaps non-Mexican) Latin restaurant, or visit a community center serving Latina/o residents. Before you do any of these, write down a list of 10 expectations and/or assumptions about your forthcoming cultural immersion. After you have engaged in the activity, revisit your list and (a) see which of your expectations and/or assumptions were "upheld" and which ones were negated, and (b) compare your level of comfort and/or anxiety prior to and after the cultural immersion exercise.

Summary

U.S. Latina/o clients span all races and religions, reside in all parts of the United States, and possess a multitude of strengths. These clients, however, also are exposed to a variety of stressors, compounded by the very systems set up to support them: family, culture, government, work setting, and local communities. U.S. Latina/o clients seeking assistance from counselors should, at the very least, be able to expect to work with a professional who has knowledge about the unique and expansive U.S. Latina/o experience.

The intent of this chapter was to provide initial information as it relates to potential U.S. Latina/o clients. How a counselor decides to incorporate this information into his or her professional skills and repertoire, however, is up to the individual. Counseling U.S. Latinas/os is a complex yet necessary endeavor. Unless counselors are comfortable enough with their own shortcomings to ask their U.S. Latina/o clients for information on their family, country of origin, immigration, and cultural experience, the counseling relationship will suffer from too many cultural assumptions and misconceptions. Therefore, take the information provided here on the richness that is the U.S. Latina/o experience as a mere *sabor* (taste) and use these ideas, concepts, and activities as a foundation for future exploration into the lives of U.S. Latina/o children, adolescents, and adults.

Acknowledgment: It would have been impossible for me to write this chapter without the continued teachings and help of my parents, José and Tania Villalba. From them I learned not only the basic foundations of being a good person, but also the importance of honoring and respecting my culture, and the sacrifices of my grandparents and ancestors in hopes of making a better life for future generations of our family. ¡*Gracias Mami y Papi*!

CHAPTER 13

Native Americans

MICHAEL TLANUSTA GARRETT

PREVIEW

The purpose of this chapter is to facilitate culturally sensitive and competent counseling practice with Native people by offering a comprehensive overview and understanding of this population through discussion of terminology, historical context, current social and political issues, acculturation, traditional Native values and worldview, spirituality and wellness, symbolism of the eagle feather, communication style, and implications and recommendations for practice related to counseling Native American clients. To better understand how to provide Native clients with culturally sensitive and competent services in the counseling process, we must seek to enter, or at minimum, understand the complexities of the psychological, spiritual, and physical worlds in which our Native clients exist.

UNDERSTANDING NATIVE AMERICANS: REFLECTIONS DOWN BY THE RIVERSIDE

Some of my fondest memories of when I was still a little one go back to times spent with my grandfather, Oscar Rogers, who was Eastern Cherokee. We would spend time sitting on the rocks by the Oconaluftee River in Cherokee, North Carolina. "What do you see when you look into the water?" he would inquire, as he sat on a rock enjoying the afternoon sun. I would look closely to see the water rushing quickly downstream. My eyes would catch the glimpse of a fish, water beetles, flies touching the water, soaked wood floating along at the will of the water, rocks, and green plants.

"I see the water," I said. "What else do you see?" he asked. "Well, I see the fish," I answered, because there were little minnows swimming around in the water. "What else do you see?" he asked. "I see the rocks," I said. "What else do you see?" he asked again. My eyes began to water themselves as I stared intently, wanting so much to please my grandfather by seeing everything he saw.

"Ah, I see my reflection," I responded proudly. "That's good," he replied confidently. "What you see is your whole life ahead of you. Know that the Great One has a plan for you to be the keeper of everything you see with your eyes, 'cause every living thing is your brother and sister." "Even the rocks?" I questioned. "Yes, even the rocks," he answered, "because they have elements of Mother Earth and Father Sky, just as we do."

"Remember to give thanks every day for all things that make up the Universe," said my grandfather. "Always remember to walk the path of Good Medicine and see the good reflected in everything that occurs in life. Life is a lesson, and you must learn the lesson well to see your true reflection in the water." (J. T Garrett, Eastern Band of Cherokee, in Garrett [1996a], p. 12)

As we take the journey into gaining awareness, knowledge and skills about Native people, test your knowledge about Native Americans by completing Activity 13.1.

ACTIVITY 13.1

Indicate the correct response by circling True (T) or False (F).

T F 1. There is a difference socially and legally between people who self-identify as Native versus those who are enrolled tribal members.

T F 2. Columbus was not the first to explore "the new world" or to have contact with the Native peoples of this continent.

T F 3. From 1778 to 1871, there were 370 documented treaties negotiated between the U.S. government and Indian tribes.

T F 4. Indian people were granted U.S. citizenship as soon as they were put on reservations.

T F 5. All of the major tribes in the United States are located west of the Mississippi River.

T F 6. Suicide rates are higher for Native Americans than any other group in the United States.

T F 7. Approximately 50% of the Native American population resides in urban areas.

T F 8. Native traditionalists worship multiple deities in their tribal spiritual traditions.

T F 9. In many Native traditions, the eagle feather serves as a sacred reminder that many things in this world are separate and opposite, and need to be kept that way.

T F 10. Indian people are stoic and seldom laugh.

T F 11. In the traditional style of Native communication, silence means that you lack confidence or that you are hiding something.

T F 12. In many Native traditions, speaking loudly and drawing a lot of attention to yourself is considered arrogant and boastful.

T F 13. The one word that encompasses the essence of a traditional Native worldview is *relation.*

Answer key: 1. T, 2. T, 3. T, 4. F, 5. F, 6. T, 7. T, 8. F, 9. F, 10. F, 11. F, 12. T, 13. T.

Native Americans, a general term referring to American Indian and Alaska Native peoples of this continent, consist of approximately 2.4 million self-identified people with a population that is steadily growing. Although this number represents only 1% of the total population of the United States (U.S. Census Bureau, 2001a), Native people have been described as representing "fifty percent of the diversity" in our country (Hodgkinson, 1990, p. 1). Of those 2.4 million self-identified persons, 1.7 million are enrolled tribal members, and thus at least 770,000 nonenrolled people who consider themselves Native. Across the United States, there are more than 563 federally recognized tribes or nations, 228 of which are located in Alaska, and several hundred state-recognized tribes (Russell, 2004). In addition, there are approximately 245 tribes in various stages of petitioning for federal recognition. Furthermore, there are more than 200 tribes that have become extinct. Tribes that have survived exist in urban areas and rural areas, as well as on 314 federally recognized reservations and 46 state-recognized reservations. Given the diversity of this population, it is important to understand that the term *Native American* encompasses the vastness and essence of tribal traditions represented by hundreds of sovereign nations. Navajo, Catawba, Shoshone, Lumbee, Cheyenne, Cherokee, Apache, Lakota, Seminole, Comanche, Pequot, Cree, Tuscarora, Paiute, Creek, Pueblo, Shawnee, Hopi, Osage, Mohawk, Nez Perce, Seneca—these are but a handful of the hundreds of Indian nations that exist across the United States.

Since approximately 78% of the Native American population resides in urban areas while only 22% of the total population of Native people live on reservations or in rural areas, the degree of traditionalism versus the degree of acculturation to mainstream American values and cultural standards for behavior is an important consideration in counseling Native people (Garrett & Garrett, 1994; Heinrich, Corbine, & Thomas, 1990; Russell, 1997; Thomason, 1991). Native Americans come from different tribal groups with different customs, traditions, and beliefs; they live in a variety of settings (Garrett & Pichette, 2000). For instance, Cherokees and Navajos are both Native Americans, but their regional cultures, climatic adaptations, and languages differ greatly. However, part of what they share in common is a strong sense of traditionalism based on basic cultural values and worldview.

Among some of the terms used historically or currently to refer to Native people are *American Indian, Alaskan Native, Native people, Indian, First American, Amerindian, Amerind, First Nations people, Aboriginal people,* and *Indigenous people.* The terms *Native American* or *Native people* (and sometimes, *Indian*) will be used throughout this chapter to refer generally to those Native people indigenous to the United States, who self-identify as Native American, and who maintain cultural identification as Native persons through membership in a Native American tribe recognized by the state or federal government or through other tribal affiliation and community recognition.

Group Membership

It is not uncommon for a Native person to be asked the question by non-Natives, "How much are you?" referring to blood quantum as the universally accepted sign of what it means to be Indian. As such, it is critical that we begin our discussion of what it means to be Native American by clarifying some definitions and concepts around group membership.

The term *Native American* is often used to describe indigenous peoples of the Western Hemisphere in an effort to provide recognition—viewed by many as long overdue—of the unique history and status of these people as the first inhabitants of the American continent. The U.S. Bureau of Indian Affairs (1988) legally defines *Native American* as a person who is an enrolled or registered member of a tribe or whose blood quantum is 1/4 or more, genealogically derived from Native American ancestry. Native nations across the country set differing criteria for blood quantum from the Cherokee Nation of Oklahoma, which enrolls members with blood quantum as little as 1/512, to the Ute Nation of Utah, which requires a minimum blood quantum of 5/8 for tribal membership; most tribes/nations require 1/4 blood quantum (Russell, 1997). Meanwhile, the U.S. Census Bureau (2001a) relies on self-identification to determine who is a Native person. Oswalt (1988) points out, however, that "if a person is considered an Indian by other individuals in the community, he or she is legally an Indian . . . [in other words], if an individual is on the roll of a federally recognized Indian group, then he or she is an Indian; the degree of Indian blood is of no real consequence, although usually he or she has at least some Indian blood" (p. 5).

However, Native people are the only ethnic minority group members who actually have to prove their cultural identity through blood quantum, and carry an "Indian card" to prove they are what they say they are. For some Native people this is yet another form of oppression, while for others it is just a normal part of everyday life, and for some, a source of pride in tribal membership. According to Russell (1997), it has been estimated that at least 98% of the Native population is tribally mixed, whereas approximately 75% are also racially mixed. These days, the term *full blood* is used to refer to those Native people who consider themselves to be 100% of one tribe. In reality, more often than not the term probably has more to do with spiritual and traditional lifestyle than physiological heritage, per se. Among some of the long-term ramifications for Native people on this issue is the continuing dilution of blood quantum and the survival of urban Indians. Blood quantum causes much division and controversy in Indian communities, and in some cases leads to social and economic inequities. Although some tribes have modified their enrollment criteria to incorporate members who possess heritage from more than one tribe, no tribe allows enrollment in more than one tribe. The reality is that some people are going to be excluded who should be included, and some people will be included who should be excluded.

CASE STUDY 13.1

Case of J. T.: It's Not the Medicine That Does the Work

J. T. is a 65-year-old enrolled member of the Eastern Band of Cherokee who currently works as a county health director in a large coastal area. He is the oldest of three siblings, and though he currently lives with his family about 8 hours away from the reservation on which he grew up, he still travels there frequently where he spends time with family including his mother who still resides there. J. T. was the first member of his nation to receive a doctorate. His first dream was to pursue a career as a high school biology teacher, but he has made a stellar career in public health through both the private and public sectors. At age 51, he had a heart attack (which he still refers to as a "heart opportunity") that forced his retirement from many years of service in the Indian Health Service. As a Vietnam veteran who struggled for years with recurring, restless, and sometimes violent dreams, these days he spends time reflecting more on his life and on the people he loves and has loved the most. One person whom he describes as having the strongest influence on his life was his grandfather, Oscar. His grandfather's death, however, came at an early age, something J. T. still wrestles with, especially now that he has recently become a grandfather as well and worries about leaving this world too soon as so many of the men in his family have done, including his father.

> Well, my grandfather passed on, matter of fact, he died of cancer. And that's something that really bothered me because I couldn't understand, if he was such a powerful Medicine Man, such a powerful spiritual man, why'd he have to die? Why didn't he have Medicine to cure him? 'Cause he told me, and I do remember this, he said, "There's a plant, there's Medicine for everything. Anything that ever happens to you in your life, there's always a special plant out there for it, all you have to do is go out and seek it, go out and find it." So I kept thinking, you know, I was so angry when my grandfather died, why didn't he seek it? You know, he always told me there was. And I guess that's one of the first times that I suddenly realized that people die anyway. That was a concept that I couldn't understand. If we've got Medicine, why were people dying? If we got cures, why would people die? Why would so many people die of influenza, 'cause see, keep in mind, that was a period of time when a lot of people would die every year because of influenza—flu. Also, for me, that was a period of time when there was diseases like polio, and I had a good friend of mine, matter of fact, that got polio. And I couldn't

understand, if we've got all this Medicine . . . . So I remember, one of the first things I was thinking was why wouldn't people share more? And I remember, I asked one of my uncles, "Why didn't he find his own Medicine?," 'cause I know they had cancer cures, 'cause I remember something about curing everything, and I didn't know what "cancer" was. Matter of fact, back then, they used to call it "consumption," and people died of "consumption" or some other name for a disease. My uncle, oh and by the way this was Tingaling Rogers, and Tingaling went through the Baton Death March during WWII, a decorated soldier like many of my uncles who were in the war at that time. But Tingaling had pretty much survived on what he could find, and he knew plants, he knew how to prepare plants, knew how fix them, knew how to cook them, he knew how to use them for Medicine. And he told me a number of times that's what helped him to survive. He'd always volunteer for details to go out and work in the hardest, hottest, worst work you'd do, working with digging up plants and cutting up logs, 'cause what he'd do is he'd scrape part of the bark off the tree for Medicine. And he'd know what kind of plant it was by something that he called "similars." Even to this day, Cherokees feel that there's a similar plant for everything that ails you. If it's your heart, it'll be shaped like a heart leaf, if it's your liver, it'll be shaped like a spade, things like that. He told me, he said, "you know, one thing you have to learn is that when it's somebody's time, and everybody has their own time, it's not the Medicine that does the work, it's the person who has to do the work . . . and even with the Medicine, you have to seek your own Medicine."

NATIVE AMERICAN HISTORY

With the case scenario in Case Study 13.1 in mind, let us reflect on the story it offers as we explore what it means to be Native in this day and age. To do this, we must begin with the influence of the historical context from which Native individuals and their families come. As such, it is important to consider the powerful influence of what many Native people refer to as generational grief and trauma, and the effect it has had on Native worldview.

Many authors have described the deliberate attempts throughout U.S. history by mainstream American institutions such as government agencies, schools, and churches to destroy the Native American institutions of family, clan, and tribal structure, religious belief systems and practices, customs, and traditional way of life (Deloria, 1988; Heinrich et al., 1990; Locust, 1988; Reyhner & Eder, 1992). Deloria (1988) commented, "When questioned by an anthropologist about what the Indians called America before the White man came, an Indian said simply, Ours" (p. 166). Characterized by institutional racism and discrimination, dominant culture has a long history of opposition to Native cultures and the attempts to assimilate Native people, having a long-lasting effect on the cultures and Native people's way of life (Deloria, 1988; Locust, 1988).

It was not until 1924 that the U.S. government recognized the citizenship of Native Americans, no longer a threat to national expansion, through passage of the Citizenship Act (Deloria, 1988). In addition, Native Americans were not granted religious freedom until 1978 when the American Indian Religious Freedom Act was passed, overturning the Indian Religious Crimes Code of 1889, and guaranteeing Native people the constitutional right to exercise their traditional religious practices for the first time in a century (Deloria, 1988; Loftin, 1989). On a more personal note, every time I see a twenty-dollar bill, I am reminded of the betrayal of my tribe by the government back in the 1838 when Andrew Jackson (depicted in all his glory on the twenty-dollar bill) signed off on an illegal act forcing the removal of over 16,000 Cherokees from parts of North Carolina, South Carolina, Tennessee, and Georgia to the Oklahoma territory (Garrett, 1998). In more recent times, massive efforts to "civilize" Native people through government-supported, religiously run boarding schools and the relocation programs of the 1950s have created a historical context of generational trauma and cultural discontinuity (Hirschfelder & Kreipe de Montano, 1993). These events have affected Native Americans psychologically, economically, and socially for generations. From both a historical and contemporary perspective, oppression is and continues to be a very real experience for Native people.

As counselors, we are trained professionals who encourage clients to tell their story, make sense of their story, and actively create their story through intentional living. In working with minority clients, it is important to understand the influence of oppression on their experience, and to assess the extent to which the process of acculturation has affected the clients' cultural identity (Lee, 2001b, 2006; Robinson & Howard-Hamilton, 2000). In the following quotation, a Navajo elder describes her first experience at age 7 in boarding school over 40 years ago, unable to speak any English, and having never left the reservation:

> It was the first time I've seen a brick building that was not a trading post. The ceilings were so high, and the rooms so big and empty. It was so cold. There was no warmth. Not as far as "brrr, I'm cold," but in a sense of emotional cold. Kind of an emptiness, when you're hanging onto your mom's skirt and trying hard not to cry. Then when you get up to your turn, she thumbprints the paper and she leaves and you watch her go out the big metal doors. The whole thing was cold. The doors were metal and they even had this big window with wires running through it. You watch your mama go down the sidewalk, actually it's the first time I seen a sidewalk, and you see her get into the truck and the truck starts moving and all the home smell goes with it. You see it all leaving.
>
> Then the woman takes you by the hand and takes you inside and the first thing they do is take down your bun. The first thing they do is cut off your hair, and you been told your whole life that you never cut your hair recklessly because that is your life. And that's the first thing them women does is cut off your hair. And you see that long, black hair drop, and it's like they take out your heart and they give you this cold thing that beats inside. And now you're gonna be just like them. You're gonna be cold. You're never gonna be happy or have that warm feeling and attitude toward life anymore. That's what it feels like, like taking your heart out and putting in a cold river pebble.
>
> When you go into the shower, you leave your squaw skirt and blouse right there at the shower door. When you come out, it's gone. You don't see it again. They cut your hair, now they take your squaw skirt. They take from the beginning. When you first walk in there, they take everything that you're about. They jerk it away from you. They don't ask how you feel about it. They never tell you anything. They never say what they're gonna do, why they're doing it. They barely speak to you. They take everything away from you. Then you think, mama must be whackers. She wants me to be like them? Every time you don't know what they're doing, they laugh at you. They yell at you. They jerk you around. It was never what I wanted to be. I never wanted to be like them. But my mom wanted me to be like them. As I got older, I found out that you don't have to be like them. You can have a nice world and have everything that mama wanted, but you don't have to be cold. (McLaughlin, 1994, pp. 47–48).

CURRENT SOCIAL AND POLITICAL ISSUES

Effective multicultural counselors know the importance of understanding diverse cultures from the culture's perspective within the context of oppressive structures, and seeking to work from a strength-based, culturally sensitive approach. Native Americans, however, have been continually described in the literature as a group of persons facing enormous problems, as illustrated by demographic information (Heinrich et al., 1990; Russell, 2004) related to issues around health, education, and economic disparity:

Health

- Alcohol mortality is 770% greater than for all other races combined.
- The rate of alcoholism is two times that of the general population.
- Fetal alcohol syndrome (FAS) is 33 times higher than for other Americans.
- Tuberculosis is 750% greater than for all other Americans.
- Diabetes is 6.8 times greater than for all other Americans.
- Pneumonia and influenza are 61% greater than for all other Americans.
- Homicide is 210% greater than for all other Americans.
- Accidental deaths are 280% higher than for all other Americans.
- Suicides are 190% higher than for all other Americans.
- One in six adolescents has attempted suicide, which is four times more often than for all other teenagers.

Education

- 52% finish high school
- 17% attend college
- 4% graduate from college
- 2% attend graduate school

Economic Disparity

- 75% of the Native workforce earns less than $7,000 per year.
- Native people show a median income half that of the majority population.
- 45% of Native people live below the poverty level.
- The average unemployment rate among Native people is 45%, a rate that is 3 to 11 times greater than that of the general population.
- Unemployment on some reservations is as high as 90%.
- In many areas, arrest rates for Native Americans are three times those for African Americans.
- Most housing is inadequate and substandard; on the Navajo reservation, for example:
  - 46% have no electricity
  - 54% have no indoor plumbing
  - 82% live without a telephone

Some of the possible challenges that Native people bring with them to the counseling process are evident when one absorbs the implications of the statistics described above. Keeping this information in mind to help provide a specific context for the struggles that many Native people face in day-to-day living, it is also important to understand the incredible diversity of Native people in general.

In addition to the reality of the many difficulties facing Native people in this day and age, there are social and political issues that create both problems and opportunities for Native people. These issues of blood quantum, resources, treaty rights, religious freedom, mascots, gaming, and cultural preservation will be discussed.

Tribal Resources

There are 314 federally recognized reservations in the United States totaling approximately 55 million acres; 11 million acres (20%) within reservation boundaries are owned by non-Indians. Needless to say, this land base provides many Native nations with an array of resources from which to benefit the people, and also with a number of challenges in how to maintain, protect, or expand that land base. According to Russell (1997) there are 44 million acres in range and grazing; 5.3 million acres of commercial forest; 2.5 million acres of crop area; 4% of the U.S. oil and gas reserves; 40% of the U.S. uranium deposits; 30% of western coal reserves; and $2 billion in trust royalty payments. It is an interesting irony that some of the most desolate reservations have become valuable resources as a result of minerals, environmental resources, and locale.

Treaty Rights

Another issue faced by many tribes/nations is that of treaty rights. Two controversial examples include the fishing rights of Native people in both the Pacific Northwest and the Great Lakes area of Michigan, Minnesota, and Wisconsin. In both instances, tribes have resorted to "fish-ins" that defy state law, but are in accordance with Indian treaty rights with the U.S. government. One of the most controversial topics to hit the media in recent times is the whaling rights of tribes in the Pacific Northwest. Strong opposition has come from state agencies, non-Native fisherman, conservationists and environmentalists, and has only added to the strain already placed upon tribes by an increased influx of people, more industry, and more recreation in many of those areas.

Religious Freedom

As mentioned earlier, passage of the **American Indian Religious Freedom Act of 1978** guaranteed religious freedom for Native people in this country for the first time in a century. However, two U.S. Supreme Court rulings severely limited the religious rights that the law was enacted to protect. First, in the 1988 *Lying, Secretary of Agriculture, et al. v. Northwest Indian Cemetary Protective Association, et al.* decision, the Supreme Court ruled in favor of allowing the U.S. Forest Service to pave a stretch of road through an area that was held as sacred by the Karok, Yurok, and Tolowa tribes of northern California. This decision was made in spite of the U.S. Forest's expert witness who concluded that the road would destroy the religion of those three tribes. Second, in the 1990 *Employment Division of Oregon v. Smith*, the Supreme Court denied Alfred Smith, a Native drug rehabilitation counselor, unemployment benefits because he had been discharged from his position for "misconduct." Smith had attended a meeting of the Native American Church where he used peyote during prayer. Peyote, a sacred, hallucinogenic cactus "button," is used in the Native American Church as a sacrament in much the same way that the Catholic Church uses wine during Holy Communion. However, the Court failed to recognize and uphold the use of peyote as an integral part of that Native spiritual tradition. So alarmed were both the Native and Judeo-Christian communities that coalitions were formed to restore religious freedom through legislative means, and those efforts continue to this day.

Sacred Sites

Traditional Native practices are inseparably bound to the land and natural formations that exist in whatever geographic location that tribe occupies. Native people have sacred places, and go to these sacred places to pray, fast, seek visions, conduct ceremonies, receive guidance from spirit guides, and teach youth the traditional ways. Many physical conditions such as the spraying and logging of trees; the building of dams, fences, and roads; the operation of mines and hydroelectric plants; the growth of urban housing and tourism; and the increase in vandalism inextricably affect sacred sites. Unfortunately, many of the sacred sites revered by Native people do not exist under their control, but instead under the control of federal agencies intent on using the land for tourism development, clear-cutting, and uranium mining. Examples of sacred sites include:

- Blue Lake, New Mexico (preserved), sacred to the Taos Pueblo
- Kootenai Falls, Montana (preserved), sacred to the Kootanai Indians of Montana, Idaho, and British Columbia
- Mount Adams, Washington (preserved), sacred to the Yakima
- Badger-Two Medicine, Montana (endangered), sacred to the Blackfeet, threatened by companies wanting to drill for oil and gas
- Canyon Mine, Arizona (endangered), sacred to the Havasupai, threatened by uranium mining that is permitted by the U.S. Forest Service
- Medicine Wheel, Wyoming (endangered), sacred to the Arapaho, Blackfeet, Crow, Cheyenne, Lakota, and Shoshone, threatened by proposed measures by the U.S. Forest Service to develop the area as a tourist attraction and promote logging activities in the vicinity
- Mount Graham, Arizona (endangered), sacred to the San Carlos Apache, threatened by construction of a seven-telescope observatory
- Celilo Falls, Oregon (desecrated), sacred to the Umatilla, Nez Perce, Yakima, and Warm Springs Indians, flooded by the Dalles Dam which was completed in 1957
- Rainbow Natural Bridge, Utah (desecrated), sacred to the Navajo, Paiute, and Pueblos, destroyed by completion of the Glen Canyon Dam on the Colorado River in 1963 and the rising of Lake Powell
- San Francisco Peaks, Arizona (desecrated), sacred to the Apaches, Hopis, Navajos, and Zunis, destroyed by the development of the Snow Bowl, a portion of the peaks used for downhill skiing

Many of these sites are the cornerstone of Native religious traditions and cannot be substituted. Therefore, legal efforts are being undertaken by tribes across the country to protect and preserve not only the sacred sites on which their culture is based, but to protect and preserve their very way of life from generations past.

Repatriation and Reburial

Many ancient graves of Native people have been disturbed or destroyed by such things as erosion and flooding, plowing, urban development, road building, land clearing, logging, and vandalism. Perhaps worst of all has been the desecration of Native graves by pothunters and vandals seeking to loot for objects that are valued in national and international markets. It has been estimated that grave desecration and looting of Native graves reached its peak in the 1980s. Outraged by such disregard and violations of sacred areas, Native American nations demanded the immediate return of all that was rightfully theirs, including skeletal remains, burial goods, and sacred objects. In the end, Native people have persevered through the passage of critical legislation that now protects

Native gravesites from looting, and provides Native people with legal means for reclaiming both remains and sacred objects. Many of these remains and objects have been ceremonially returned to their original sites when possible under the careful guidance and blessing of tribal elders and Medicine people.

Mascot Issues

As many tribes/nations continue to move toward increased sovereignty, land and natural resources are only part of the issue. A constant source of controversy between Native and non-Native people has been the mascot issue. Sports teams across the country have been challenged to do away with stereotypical, racist images of Native people as mascots. A few examples include the Atlanta Braves, the Washington Redskins, the Cleveland Indians, and the Florida State University Seminoles. For the most part, these images tend to fall into one of two categories: the hostile, warlike Indian, or the dopey, clownlike figure with headdress, a big nose, red skin, big lips, and other stereotypical features. Native people in many places have become increasingly outspoken, demanding the same respect both socially and legally that is paid to other cultural groups in the United States.

Gaming

When it comes to cultural perceptions, one of the biggest issues that comes to mind when most people think of Indians these days is gaming. Casinos and bingo halls are almost everywhere in Indian country, and in most cases, what that means for Native nations is increased capital in a short period of time, and the challenges that accompany it. Northrup (1997) jokingly replies to the question, "why do you call it a Rez instead of a reservation? Because the White man owns most of it" (p. 226). The popular perception by non-Native people is that Indians are getting filthy rich off per-capita checks, the varying amounts of money that are distributed to tribal members as corporate partners, more or less, with tribally owned casinos and bingo halls. The fact is, these per-capita amounts for many tribes are small, are typically distributed maybe once or twice per year, and in most cases have done little to alleviate already high rates of unemployment for Native people across the country. When asked "what is the unemployment rate on the reservation?" Northup (1997) replies, "I don't know, that's not my job" (p. 215). He goes on to comment, "Gambling has done a lot for us in the last decade . . . . [I]t has brought our Rez unemployment rate from 80 percent all the way down to 50% (p. 215)." Although the gaming industry has become a major source of income and economic development for many Native nations, the challenge at this point is how to maintain that investment, and plan for the future so that the growth continues, and continues to benefit the people.

Cultural Preservation

Increased sovereignty for many Native nations also means increased control over the way cultural resources are maintained and preserved. In many Native nations and communities across the country, huge efforts are being made to preserve culture by developing programs both in and outside the schools to teach their youth such things as traditional arts and crafts, the language, ceremonies and prayers, songs and chants, as well as dance. Many of these programs began as remedial efforts in such programs as residential youth treatment centers and sobriety programs for all ages. As the efficacy of such programs has become evident, the popularity of such efforts has grown. This is a far cry from the efforts of the mainstream only one or two generations ago to "civilize Indians" through mandated religious-run, government-supported Indian boarding schools whose primary objective was to strip Native youth of any cultural foundation. Although it is evident that Native people still face many difficulties whose origins lie in the cultural genocide of the past and the resulting cycle of oppression and poverty faced by Native people now for hundreds of years, winds of change have crossed the land. With the surge in cultural pride, one of the biggest challenges for Native people today is to eliminate in-fighting, and find a common vision that will carry the people safely and successfully into the future generations.

ACCULTURATION

Although many of the core traditional values permeate the lives of Native Americans across tribal groups, Native Americans differ greatly in their level of acceptance of and commitment to specific tribal values, beliefs, and practices (Garrett & Garrett, 1996). Native individuals differ in terms of their level of acculturation, geographic setting (urban, rural, or reservation), and socioeconomic status (Choney et al., 1995; Garrett & Pichette, 2000; Herring, 1999). The following levels of acculturation, defined as "the cultural change that occurs when two or more cultures are in persistent contact" (Garcia & Ahler, 1992, p. 24), have been identified for Native Americans:

- *Traditional*—May or may not speak English, but generally speak and think in their native language; hold only traditional values and beliefs and practice only traditional tribal customs and methods of worship.
- *Marginal*—May speak both the native language and English; may not, however, fully accept the cultural heritage and practices of their tribal group nor fully identify with mainstream cultural values and behaviors.
- *Bicultural*—Generally accepted by dominant society and tribal society/nation; simultaneously able to know, accept, and practice both mainstream values/behaviors and the traditional values and beliefs of their cultural heritage.
- *Assimilated*—Accepted by dominant society; embrace only mainstream cultural values, behaviors, and expectations.
- *Pantraditional*—Assimilated Native Americans who have made a conscious choice to return to the "old ways." They are generally accepted by dominant society, but seek to embrace previously lost traditional cultural values, beliefs, and practices of their tribal heritage. Therefore, they may speak both English and their native tribal language. (Garrett & Pichette, 2000)

These five levels represent a continuum along which any given Native American individual may fall. Regardless of blood quantum, the most popular and most deceiving means of determining a person's "Indianness" and degree of traditionalism comes not only from ethnic heritage, but also from his or her life experiences and life choices (Garrett & Garrett, 1994).

NATIVE AMERICAN CULTURE AND VALUES

Native Americans represent a diversity illustrated, for example, by approximately 252 different languages (Thomason, 1991). At the same time, a prevailing sense of "Indianness" based on common worldview and many similar experiences in history seems to bind Native Americans together as a people of many peoples (Herring, 1999; Thomason, 1991). Although acculturation plays a major factor in Native American worldview, there tends to be a high degree of psychological homogeneity, a certain degree of shared cultural standards and meanings, based on common core values that exist for traditional Native Americans across tribal groups (Garrett, 1999b).

Several authors have described common core values that characterize Native traditionalism across tribal nations. Some of these Native traditional values (see Table 13.1) include the importance of community contribution, sharing, acceptance, cooperation, harmony and balance, noninterference, extended family, attention to nature, immediacy of time, awareness of the relationship, and a deep respect for elders (Dufrene, 1990; Garrett 1996a, 1998, 1999b, 2001; Garrett & Garrett, 1996a, 2003; Heinrich et al., 1990; Herring, 1999; Little Soldier, 1992; Plank, 1994; Red Horse, 1997). All in all, these traditional values show the importance of honoring, through harmony and balance, what Native people believe to be a very sacred connection with the energy of life; this is the basis for a traditional Native worldview and spirituality across tribal nations.

Harmony and Balance

Different tribal languages have different words or ways of referring to the idea of honoring one's sense of connection, but the meaning is similar across nations in referring to the belief that human beings exist on Mother Earth to be helpers and protectors of life. In Native communities, it is not

TABLE 13.1 Comparison of Cultural Values and Expectations

Traditional Native American	Contemporary Mainstream American
Harmony with nature	Power over nature
Cooperation	Competition
Group needs more important	Personal goals considered important
Privacy and noninterference; try to control self, not others	Need to control and affect others
Self-discipline both in body and mind	Self-expression and self-disclosure
Participation after observation (only when certain of ability)	Trial-and-error learning, new skills practiced until mastery
Explanation according to nature	Scientific explanation for everything
Reliance on extended family	Reliance on experts
Emotional relationships valued	Concerned mostly with facts
Patience encouraged (allow others to go first)	Aggressiveness and competitiveness encouraged
Humility	Fame and recognition; winning
Win once, let others win also	Win first prize all of the time
Follow the old ways	Climb the ladder of success; importance of progress
Discipline distributed among many; no one person takes blame	Blame one person at cost to others
Physical punishment rare	Physical punishment accepted
Present-time focus	Future-time focus
Time is always with us	Clock-watching
Present goals considered important; future accepted as it comes	Plan for future and how to get ahead
Encourage sharing freely and keeping only enough to satisfy present needs	Private property; encourage acquisition of material comfort and saving for the future
Speak softly, at a slower rate	Speak louder and faster
Avoid singling out the listener	Address listener directly (by name)
Interject less	Interrupt frequently
Use less "encouraging signs" (uh-huh, head nodding)	Use verbal encouragement
Delay response to auditory messages	Use immediate response
Nonverbal communication	Verbal skills highly prized

Source: Adapted from Garrett and Pichette (2000).

uncommon, as an example, to hear people use the term *caretaker*. Therefore, from the perspective of a traditionalist, to see one's purpose as that of caretaker is to accept responsibility for the gift of life by taking good care of that gift, the gift of life that others have received, and the surrounding beauty of the world in which we live (Garrett, 2001).

More or less, the essence of Native American spirituality is about "feeling" (Wilbur, 1999a, 1999b). The feeling of connection is something that is available to all of us, though experienced in differing ways. It is important to note that the spiritual beliefs of Native Americans depends on a number of factors including level of acculturation, geographic region, family structure, religious influences, and tribally specific traditions (Garrett & Pichette, 2000; LaFromboise, Coleman, & Gerton, 1993). However, it is possible to generalize, to some extent, about a number of basic beliefs characterizing Native American traditionalism and spirituality across tribal nations. The following, adapted from Locust (1988), elaborates on a number of basic Native American spiritual and traditional beliefs:

- There is a single higher power known as Creator, Great Creator, Great Spirit, or Great One, among other names (this being is sometimes referred to in gender form, but does not necessarily exist as one particular gender or another). There are also lesser beings known as spirit beings or spirit helpers.
- Plants and animals, like humans, are part of the spirit world. The spirit world exists side by side with, and intermingles with, the physical world. Moreover, the spirit existed in the spirit world before it came into a physical body and will exist after the body dies.
- Human beings are made up of a mind, body, and spirit. They are all interconnected; therefore, illness affects the mind and spirit as well as the body.
- Wellness is harmony in mind, body, and spirit; unwellness is disharmony in mind, body, and spirit.
- Natural unwellness is caused by the violation of a sacred social or natural law of Creation (e.g., participating in a sacred ceremony while under the influence of alcohol, drugs, or having had sex within 4 days of the ceremony).
- Unnatural unwellness is caused by conjuring (witchcraft) from those with destructive intentions.
- Each of us is responsible for our own wellness by keeping ourselves attuned to self, relations, environment, and universe. (pp. 317–318).

This list of beliefs in Native American spirituality crosses tribal boundaries but is, by no means, a comprehensive list. It does, however, provide a great deal of insight into some of the assumptions that may be held by a "traditional" Native client. To better understand more generally what it means to "walk in step" according to Native American spirituality, it is important to discuss four basic cultural elements: medicine, relation, harmony, and vision (Garrett & Wilbur, 1999).

MEDICINE *Everything is alive.* In many Native American tribal languages (e.g., Cherokee, etc.) there is no word for religion because spiritual practices are an integral part of every aspect of daily life, which is necessary for the harmony and balance, or wellness of individual, family, clan, and community (Garrett & Garrett, 2002; Garrett, Garrett, & Brotherton, 2001). Healing and worship are considered as one and the same. For Native American people, the concept of health and wellness is not only a physical state, but a spiritual one as well. **Medicine**, as a Native concept, implies the very essence of our being, or life force that exists in all creatures on Mother Earth (Garrett & Garrett, 1996). In the traditional way, medicine can consist of physical remedies such as herbs, teas, poultices, for physical ailments, but medicine is simultaneously something much more than a pill you take to cure illness, get rid of pain, or correct a physiological malfunction. Medicine is everywhere. It is the very essence of our inner being; it is that which gives us inner power.

HARMONY *Everything has purpose.* Every living being has a reason for being. **Harmony** refers to the interconnectedness among mind, body and spirit. Traditional Native Americans look upon life as a gift from the Creator. As a gift, it is to be treated with the utmost care out of respect for the giver. This means living in a humble way and giving thanks for all of the gifts that one receives every day, no matter how big or small. Native American spirituality often places great emphasis on the numbers four and seven. The number four represents the spirit of each of the directions, east, south, west, and north, usually depicted in a circle. The number seven represents the same four directions as well as the upper world (Sky), lower world (Earth), and center (often referring to the heart, or sacred fire) to symbolize universal harmony and balance (visualized as a sphere). In the traditional way, you seek to understand what lessons are offered to you by giving thanks to each of the four directions for the wisdom, guidance, strength, and clarity that you receive. Not every tribe practices the directions in this way, but almost all tribes have some representation of the four directions as a circular symbol of the harmony and balance of mind, body, and spirit with the natural environment (and spirit world). This is referred to as the Medicine Circle (Garrett, 1998).

RELATION *All things are connected.* Central to Native American spiritual traditions is the importance of **relation** as a total way of existing in the world. The concept of family extends to brothers and sisters in the animal world, the plant world, the mineral world, Mother Earth, Father Sky, and so on. Respect for medicine also means practicing respect for the interconnection that we share. Across tribal nations, there are certain natural or social laws that must be observed out of respect for relation. These often point to restrictions on personal conduct regarding such things as death, incest, the female menstrual cycle, witchcraft, certain animals, certain natural phenomena, certain foods, marrying into one's own clan, and strict observance of ceremonial protocol (Locust, 1988). In general, a rule of thumb in Native tradition is that you:

- never take more than you need,
- give thanks for what you have or what you receive,
- take great care to use all of what you do have, and
- "give away" what you do not need (or what someone else may need more than you).

VISION *Embrace the medicine of every living being.* Across tribal nations, there are many different ceremonies used for healing, giving thanks, celebrating, clearing the way, and blessing (Lake, 1991). Among the various traditions, a few examples of ceremonies include sweatlodge, vision quest, clearing-way ceremony, blessing-way ceremony, pipe ceremony, sunrise ceremony, sundance, and many others (Heinrich et al., 1990; Lake, 1991). One of the functions of ceremonial practice is to reaffirm one's sense of connection with that which is sacred. In American mainstream ideology, the purpose of life consists of "life, liberty, and the pursuit of happiness." From a traditional Native perspective, a corollary would be "life, love, and the pursuit of harmony." Understanding one's **vision** is understanding the direction of one's path as a caretaker moving to the rhythm of the sacred heartbeat. As Black Elk, Oglala Lakota medicine Man, put it, "the good road and the road of difficulties, you have made me cross; and where they cross, the place is holy" (cited in Garrett, 1998, p. 85).

Tribe/Nation

Traditional Native people experience a unique relationship between themselves and the tribe. In a very real sense, Native American individuals are extensions of their tribal nation—socially, emotionally, historically, and politically. For many Indian people, cultural identity is rooted in tribal membership, community, and heritage. Many Native nations are matriarchal/matrilineal or matriarchal/patrilineal, but there are those that follow patriarchal/ patrilineal ways too (or other variations of gender dominance and tracing of family heritage). This, in turn, affects not only communal and social structure and functioning but also family/clan structure and functioning. The extended family (at least three generations) and tribal group take precedence over all else. The tribe is an interdependent system of people who perceive themselves as parts of the greater whole rather than a whole consisting of individual parts. Likewise, traditional Native people judge themselves and their actions according to whether or not they are benefiting the tribal community and its continued harmonious functioning.

In mainstream American society, worth and status are based on "what you do" or "what you have achieved." For Native Americans, "who you are is where you come from." Native Americans essentially believe that "If you know my family, clan, tribe, then you know me." As a result, traditional Native people might be likely to describe some aspect of their family or tribal heritage when asked to talk about themselves.

Family

It has been said that "about the most unfavorable moral judgment an Indian can pass on another person is to say 'he acts as if he didn't have any relatives'" (DuBray, 1985, p. 36). Upon meeting for the first time, many Indian people ask, "Where do you come from? Who's your family? Whom do you belong to? Who are your people?" The intent is to find out where they stand in relation to this new person, and what commonality exists. In fact, this is a simple way of building bridges, or recognizing bridges that already exist but are as yet unknown. Family may or may not consist of blood relatives. It is common practice in the Indian way, for instance, to claim another as a relative, thereby welcoming him or her as real family. From that point on, that person is a relative, and that is that. After all, family is a matter of blood and of spirit.

Wisdom Keepers

Native elders are the keepers of the sacred ways. They are protectors, mentors, teachers, and support-givers, regardless of their "social status." Native communities honor their Indian elders, the "Keepers of the Wisdom," for their lifetime's worth of knowledge and experience. Elders have always played an important part in the continuance of the tribal community by functioning in the role of parent, teacher, community leader, and spiritual guide (Garrett & Garrett, 1997). To refer to an elder as "Grandmother," "Grandfather," "Uncle," "Aunt," "old woman," or "old man" is to refer to a very special relationship that exists with that elder characterized by deep respect and admiration.

In the traditional way, the prevalence of cooperation and sharing in the spirit of community is essential for harmony and balance. It is not unusual for a Native child to be raised in several different households over time. This is generally not due to a lack of caring or responsibility, but because it is both an obligation and a pleasure to share in raising and caring for the children in one's family. Grandparents, aunts, uncles, and other members of the community are all responsible for the raising of children, and they take this responsibility very seriously.

There is a special kind of relationship based on mutual respect and caring between Indian elders and Indian children as one moves through the Circle of Life from "being cared for" to "caring for," as Red Horse (1997) puts it. With increase in age comes an increase in the sacred obligation to family, clan, and tribe. Native American elders pass down to the children the tradition that their life force carries the spirits of their ancestors. With such an emphasis on connectedness, Native traditions revere children, not only as those who will carry on the wisdom and traditions, but also as "little people" who are still very close to the spirit world and from whom we have much to learn. Brendtro, Brokenleg, and Van Bockern (1990) relate a story shared with them by Eddie Belleroe, a Cree elder from Alberta, Canada. In a conversation with his aging grandfather, a young Indian man asked, "Grandfather, what is the purpose of life?" After a long time in thought, the old man looked up and said, "Grandson, children are the purpose of life. We were once children and someone cared for us, and now it is our time to care" (p. 45).

Humility

Boasting of one's accomplishments and loud behavior that attracts attention to oneself are discouraged in the traditional way, where self-absorption and self-importance brings disharmony upon oneself and one's family. In the Circle, the group must take precedence over the individual, and the wisdom of age takes precedence over youth, though it does not make anyone better or more worthy than anyone else. Many times, a traditional Native person may drop his or her head and eyes or at least be careful not to look into the eyes of another as a sign of respect for any elder or other honored person. No one is worthy of staring into the eyes of an elder, or looking into the spirit of that honored person. This is also an act that signifies that a person does not view himself or herself as better than anyone else.

Generosity

Traditional Native views concerning property accentuate the underlying belief that "whatever belongs to the individual also belongs to the group," and vice versa. It should come as no surprise to see Indian people sharing or giving "their possessions" away to others in certain circumstances. Generosity is considered a sign of wisdom and humility.

Patience

Everything has its place. Very often, it is simply a matter of time before one recognizes where and how things fit together. In Native traditions, there is a sacred design to the world in which we live, to the process of life itself. And very often, it is not a matter of whether "things" fall into place, but whether our capacity for awareness and understanding of "things" falls into place. It is important to be able to learn through careful observing, listening, and practicing patience, as well as by asking questions or thinking things through. Everything offers us a valuable lesson, from all of our surroundings to each of our experiences. It takes time and a special kind of willingness or openness to receive all of the lessons that are offered to us throughout life.

Time

Life offers us opportunities to think in terms of what is happening now, and to be aware of what is taking place all around us, by focusing on current thoughts, ideas, feelings, and experiences. Where you are *is* where you have come from and where you are going. We do not always have to live by the clock. Mother Earth has her own unique rhythms that signal the beginnings and endings of things.

Again, one need only observe and listen quietly to know when it is time. So-called Indian time says that things begin when they are ready, and things end when they are finished.

Being

Native tradition ("the Medicine Way") emphasizes a unique sense of "being" that allows one to live in accord with the natural flow of life energy. Being says, "It's enough just to be; our purpose in life is to develop the inner self in relation to everything around us." Being receives much of its power from connectedness. Belonging and connectedness lie at the very heart of where we came from, who we are, and to whom we belong. True being requires that we know and experience our connections, and that we honor our relations with all our heart.

LESSONS OF THE EAGLE FEATHER

Eagle feathers are considered to be infinitely sacred among Native Americans who make use of the feathers for a variety of purposes, including ceremonial healing and purification. Eagle Medicine represents a state of presence achieved through diligence, understanding, awareness, and a completion of "tests of initiation" such as the Vision Quest or other demanding life experiences (Garrett & Osborne, 1995). Highly respected elder status is associated with Eagle Medicine and the power of connectedness and truth. It is through experience and patience that this medicine is earned over a lifetime. And, it is through understanding and choice that it is honored. There is an old anecdote that probably best illustrates the lessons of the eagle feather: Once while acting as a guide for a hunting expedition, an Indian had lost the way home. One of the men with him said, "You're lost, chief." The Indian guy replied, "I'm not lost, my tipi is lost."

The eagle feather, which represents duality, tells the story of life. It tells of the many dualities or opposites that exist in the Circle of Life, such as light and dark, male and female, substance and shadow, summer and winter, life and death, peace and war (Garrett & Myers, 1996). The eagle feather has both light and dark colors, dualities and opposites. Although one can make a choice to argue which of the colors is most beautiful or most valuable, the truth is that both colors come from the same feather, both are true, both are connected, and it takes both to fly (Garrett & Garrett, 1996). The colors are opposite, but they are part of the same truth. The importance of the feather lies not in which color is most beautiful, but in finding out and accepting what the purpose of the feather as a whole may be. In other words, there is no such thing as keeping the mountains and getting rid of the valleys; they are one and the same, and they exist because of one another. As one elder puts it:

> The Eagle feather teaches about the Rule of Opposites, about everything being divided into two ways. The more one is caught up in the physical, or the West, then the more one has to go in the opposite direction, the East, or the spiritual, to get balance. And it works the other way too—you can't just focus on the spiritual to the exclusion of the physical. You need harmony in all Four Directions. (Garrett, 1998, pp. 103–104)

GUIDELINES FOR COUNSELING NATIVE AMERICAN CLIENTS

A key component of culturally competent practice with Native American clients involves consciously integrating their culture and values into each counseling session. This section reviews salient notions of Native American culture that should be addressed and provides practical counseling recommendations based on Native American values discussed earlier in the chapter.

Being Indian

As a counselor, Native or non-Native, respect for individual Native clients means finding out from which tribe the client comes, and possibly whether the person is directly affiliated with the tribe (federal, state, and/or community recognition). It is not our job as counselors to pass judgment on who is Indian and who is not. More specifically, do not ask a Native client how much Indian they are, or relate personal stories of Indian heritage in your family as a way of connecting with the client. That is a quick way to lose a Native person's receptivity and trust. If a client says he or she is Indian, then we must assume it is true. It is another way of better understanding the client without having to get into the painful (and sometimes irrelevant) politics of categorization. More importantly, it gives us insight into that person's perception of his or her experience and place in the world.

Learning From History

Given the historical and political context, the underlying issue in terms of counseling Native clients is: trust versus mistrust. The question to ask yourself as a counselor is, "What can I do to create and maintain trust with a Native client?" By educating yourself about the history of tribes from which clients come, you can better understand the impact of institutional racism and acculturation, as well as the meaning of the Native American experience for any given client.

Assessing Acculturation

When working with a Native client, it is important to get a sense of that person's level of acculturation by informally assessing (a) values (traditional, marginal, bicultural, assimilated, pan-traditional); (b) geographic origin/residence (reservation, rural, urban); and (c) tribal affiliation (tribal structure, customs, beliefs). (For further discussion of formal and informal assessment of Native American acculturation, see Garrett & Pichette, 2000.) Both verbal and nonverbal cues will give counselors a good sense of a Native American client's level of acculturation (Garrett & Garrett, 1994). If questions remain, it is important to pose them in a respectful, unobtrusive way. Following are some examples of general leads intended to respectfully elicit important culturally relevant information:

- Where do you come from?
- Tell me about your family.
- What tribe/nation are you? Tell me a little bit about that.
- Tell me about you as a person, culturally and spiritually.
- Tell me how you identify yourself culturally.
- Tell me how your culture/spirituality plays into how you live your life.
- Tell me about your life as you see it, past, present, or future.

Counselors must avoid making assumptions about the cultural identity of Native American clients without gathering further information. For example, one cannot assume because a person "looks Indian" that he or she is traditional in his or her cultural and spiritual ways, or that because a person "does not look Indian" that he or she is not traditional. To better understand the essence of traditional Native culture, though, it is important to explore the meaning of the core values and beliefs that characterize what it means to be Native for any given client.

Recognizing Traditions

In contrast to many of the traditional Native values and beliefs previously discussed, mainstream American values tend to emphasize self-promotion, saving for the future, domination of others, accomplishment, competition and aggression, individualism and the nuclear family, mastery over nature, a time orientation toward living for the future, a preference for scientific explanations, time-consciousness, winning, and reverence of youth (Garrett, 1995, 1999a, 1999b). For Native people, there is great potential for cultural conflicts due to differing values within the context of the larger society. Therefore, exploration of cultural conflicts may be a viable goal for counseling. Native clients can be encouraged to talk about the meaning of family, clan, or tribe to them as a way of exploring worldview, especially in light of intergenerational differences or the effects of oppression or presenting issues.

Respecting Spirituality

Having a general understanding of Native American spirituality does not prepare a person to participate in or conduct Native ceremonies as part of the counseling process (Matheson, 1996). That is the responsibility of those who are trained as Native Medicine persons, and who also can serve as an important resource to counselors working with Native clients. Native spirituality manifests in many different forms, such as traditional tribal ways, Christian traditions, or Native American Church. With a client who seems to have more traditional values and beliefs, it may be particularly helpful to suggest that family or a Medicine person participate in the process to support the client as he or she moves through important personal transitions and subsequent personal cleansing.

Remembering Lessons of the Eagle Feather

For many Native clients, the understanding and reconciliation of discordant opposites is an essential therapeutic goal in achieving harmony and balance among the four directions—mind, body, spirit, and natural environment. An understanding of the Rule of Opposites is essential for working with Native American clients who may be experiencing dissonance in their lives, but perceive this in a much different way than might be expected within the majority culture. Asking the right questions and being open to what we do not readily perceive bridges the gap between what we see and what really exists. Understanding that everything has meaning and purpose, our goal in counseling becomes one of helping Native clients discover their purpose, examine their assumptions, seek an awareness of universal and personal truths, and make choices that allow them to exist in a state of harmony and balance within the Circle of Life.

Communication Style

Native interaction style emphasizes nonverbal communication over verbal communication. Moderation in speech and avoidance of direct eye contact are nonverbal communicators of respect for the listener, especially if it is a respected elder or anyone in a position of authority (Garrett, 1996a). Careful listening and observation are exercised in order to understand more of what is meant and less of what is actually said. Storytelling is commonly used to communicate feelings, beliefs, and the importance of experience (Garrett & Garrett, 1997). The use of oral recitation emphasizes the need for listeners to be silent, patient, and reflective. In an attempt to be respectful of harmony, traditional Indian people practice self-discipline through silence, modesty, and patience. Direct confrontation is avoided as it disrupts the harmony and balance that are essential in keeping good relations. There are believed to be more effective ways to deal with discrepancies and dissatisfaction. Cooperation and sharing, as a reflection of harmony, are an important part of interacting with others. Individuals in mainstream culture are rewarded for being outgoing and "assertive." Such behaviors as asking questions, interrupting, speaking for others, telling others what to do, or arguing are fairly common in mainstream society. These behaviors severely contradict what traditional Native people have been taught are respectful and appropriate ways of interacting with others (Garrett, 1995).

Once the counselor has some general information concerning the client's cultural background and spiritual ways, he or she has a better understanding of what may or may not be considered appropriate with and for the client. The following recommendations (Garrett, 1999b; Garrett & Pichette, 2000) are intended as culturally responsive ways for working with a traditional Native client:

- *Greeting.* For traditional Native Americans, a gentle handshake is the proper way of greeting. Sometimes, just a word of greeting or head nod is sufficient. To use a firm handshake can be interpreted as an aggressive show of power and a personal insult. It may be important to follow, rather than lead, the client.
- *Hospitality.* Given the traditional emphasis on generosity, kindness, and "gifting" as a way of honoring the relation, hospitality is an important part of Native American life. Therefore, it is helpful to be able to offer the Native client a beverage or snack as a sign of good relation. In the traditional way, to not offer hospitality to a visitor or guest is to bring shame on oneself and one's family.
- *Silence.* In the traditional way, when two people meet, very little may be said between them during the initial moments of the encounter. Quiet time at the beginning of a session is an appropriate way of transitioning into the therapeutic process by giving both counselor and client a chance to orient themselves to the situation, get in touch with themselves, and experience the presence of the other person. This brief time (perhaps a couple of minutes or so) can be nonverbal, noninteractive time that allows the client to be at ease. This is an important show of respect, understanding, and patience.
- *Space.* Taking care to respect physical space is an extension of the principle that one need not always fill relational space with words. In Native tradition, both the physical form and the space between the physical is sacred. In counseling, it is important to respect the physical space of the client by not sitting too close, and not sitting directly across from the client, which allows scrutiny of the other. A more comfortable arrangement, traditionally, is sitting together either more side by side in two different chairs at an off angle. The burning of sage, cedar, or sweetgrass (a method of spatial cleansing known as "smudging") should be done only at the request or with permission of the Native client.
- *Eye Contact.* Native American clients with traditional values (and possibly those who are marginal or bicultural) may tend to avert their eyes as a sign of respect. To subtly match this level of eye contact is respectful and shows an understanding of the client's way of being. The eyes are considered to be the pathway to the spirit; therefore to consistently look someone in the eye is to show a level of entitlement or aggression. It is good to glance at someone every once in a while, but listening, in the traditional way, is something that happens with the ears and the heart.
- *Intention.* One of the biggest issues with many Indian clients in the counseling relationship is trust. This should come as no surprise given the history of broken promises and exploitation survived by many tribal nations. Typically, an Indian client will "read" the counselor's

nonverbals fairly quickly in order to determine whether the counselor is someone to be trusted. Therefore, counselors can focus on honoring the mental space between counselor and client by seeking to offer respect and humility in the counseling process. Acceptance by the counselor means not trying to control or influence the client. This is considered "bad medicine."

• *Collaboration.* In counseling, more traditional clients may welcome (or even expect) the counselor to offer helpful suggestions or alternatives. From a traditional perspective, respect for choice is important, but healing is a collaborative process. Therefore, offer suggestions without offering directions. There is a difference between encouraging and pushing. With traditional Native American clients, actions will always speak louder than words.

Humor

Contrary to the stereotypical belief that Indian people are solemn, stoic figures poised against a backdrop of tepees, tomahawks, and headdresses, the fact is, Indian people love to laugh (Garrett & Garrett, 1994; Garrett, Garrett, Wilbur, Roberts-Wilbur, & Torres-Rivera, 2005; Maples et al., 2001). It is a critical part of the culture, especially around mealtime. It is amazing to watch the transformation that occurs when people come together around food and really begin to open up. In Indian country, mealtime is sometimes the worst time to try to eat because everyone is laughing, cutting up, sharing stories, and teasing each other. Many tribal oral traditions emphasize important life lessons through the subtle humor expressed in the stories. Often, it is the arrogant, manipulative, vain, clownlike figure of Rabbit, Possum, Coyote, or Raven that learns a hard lesson in humility, much to the amusement of others (Garrett, 1998; Garrett & Garrett, 1996; Herring, 1994). Laughter plays a very important role in the continued survival of the tribal communities. After all, laughter relieves stress and creates an atmosphere of sharing and connectedness. As George Good Striker, Blackfoot elder, puts it, "Humor is the WD-40 of healing" (cited in Garrett, 1998, p. 137).

Humor is one of the important Native coping mechanisms. Humor should be used only if the client invites it, meaning that the client trusts the counselor enough to connect on that level. What in one situation can be humoring between two people, in another can be interpreted as ridiculing or wearing a mask. Counselors working with Native clients should exercise caution using humor, but definitely should not overlook it as a powerful therapeutic technique. Indian humor serves the purpose of reaffirming and enhancing the sense of connectedness as part of family, clan, and tribe. Any way that it can serve that purpose in the counseling relationship will be all the better.

Practical Counseling Recommendations

In addition to contemporary counseling interventions and treatment modalities, counselors can incorporate tribally specific interventions as appropriate to meet the cultural/spiritual/ personal/career needs of specific Native clients. It might be useful to examine national organizations (see Activity 13.2) and media resources (see Table 13.2) in developing practical counseling strategies. As a major part of collaboration with Native clients in the counseling process, the following (Garrett & Carroll, 2000) are offered as practical recommendations:

• *Sociodemographics:* Native clients can reconnect with a sense of purpose by finding ways to combat the high rates of unemployment, inadequate housing, low educational levels, poverty-level incomes, and isolated living conditions. Participation in community-wide volunteer programs to help those in need has proved to be a successful part of healing for many Indian people.

- **Physiology:** Native people should be encouraged to get regular physical checkups and blood tests (e.g., blood sugar).
- **Historical context:** A critical component of counseling could include a psychoeducational piece or dialogue. This could provide systemic insight for some Native clients concerning many of the historical factors such as exploitation of Native people through discrimination, assimilation through boarding schools and relocation programs, as well as disruption of traditional cultural and familial patterns. Discussions of this nature might be helpful to Native clients in exploring their own level of cultural identity development.
- **Acculturation/Identity:** Native clients can be assisted with exploration of personal cultural identity and career issues by focusing on the cultural themes of belonging, mastery, independence, and generosity, utilizing the following general questions for each of the four respective areas: (a) Where do you belong? (b) What are you good at; what do you enjoy doing? (c) What are your sources of strength; what limits you? (d) What do you have to offer/contribute?
- **Isolation/Social connections:** Participation in other social events such as family gatherings and powwows allows Native clients to experience social cohesion and social interaction in their communities. Some Native clients can benefit from a sense of reconnection with community and traditional roles. This has been accomplished through the revival of tribal ceremonies and practices (e.g., talking circles, sweat lodges, powwows, peyote meetings), reestablishing a sense of belonging and communal meaningfulness for Native people "returning to the old ways" as an integral part of modern life.
- **Generational splits:** Native clients of all ages can benefit from acting as or learning from elders serving as role models and teachers for young people. This, too, has become more commonly practiced by tribal nations across the country in therapeutic programs and schools.
- **Coping mechanisms:** Native clients can learn better methods of dealing with stress, boredom, powerlessness, and the sense of emptiness associated with acculturation and identity confusion. Consultation with or participation of a Medicine person (i.e., traditional Native healer) may prove very helpful.
- **Noninterference:** Avoidance behavior of family and community members can be addressed with Native clients as well as with family and community members to the extent that it may be destructive. Carol Attneave's (1969, 1985) network therapy has been very effective with Indian clients as a way of working with an individual in family and community context.

ACTIVITY 13.2

Investigate Native social, economic, educational, and political organizations such as the American Indian Movement, First Nations Development Institute, Morningstar Institute, American Indian College Fund, American Indian Science and Engineering Society, Native American Public Broadcasting Consortium, or Native American Rights Fund.

- What are their primary characteristics?
- How do they compare with one another?
- How might they be useful when working with clients in schools? Communities?

TABLE 13.2   Media Resources About Native American Culture

Articles and Papers

- www.counseling.org/Content/NavigationMenu/PUBLICATIONS/JOURNALS/ JOURNALOFCOUNSELINGDEVELOPMENTJCD/jcd_winter00.pdf
- www.counseling.org/Content/NavigationMenu/PUBLICATIONS/JOURNALS/ JOURNALOFCOUNSELINGDEVELOPMENTJCD/jcd_fall00.pdf
- www.apa.org/monitor/mar00/listening.html
- www.apa.org/monitor/jun03/indian.html
- www.apa.org/ppo/funding/ihsbriefingsheet.html
- www.apa.org/monitor/jan04/indian.html
- www.apa.org/monitor/oct04/services.html
- www.uphs.upenn.edu/cmhpsr/PDF/NativeAmericanLitReview.PDF
- www.aisc.ucla.edu/rsrch/uaichildren.htm
- www.mentalhealth.samhsa.gov/publications/allpubs/SMA00-3457/intro.asp

Educational Programs Targeting Counseling to American Indian Populations

- www.uark.edu/depts/rehabres/AmIndian/AImain.htm
- www.uchsc.edu/ai/ncaianmhr/
- www.cvc.edu/catalog/program_detail.asp?SchoolID=24&ProgramID=236
- www.stanford.edu/~lafrom/interventions.html

Agency Resource Pages

- www.doi.gov/bureau-indian-affairs.html
- www.ihs.gov/
- www.nicoa.org/
- www.codetalk.fed.us/UrbanIndianHome.html
- http://native-alliance.org/programs.htm
- http://nativenewsonline.org/resources/
- www.aoa.gov/press/fact/alpha/fact_oaa.asp
- www.nationalhomeless.org/local/minnesota.html
- www.ncptsd.org/facts/veterans/fs_native_vets.html
- www.itcaonline.com/program_hiv.html
- www.aisc.ucla.edu/rsrch/uaichildren.htm
- http://aidtac.ruralinstitute.umt.edu/Health.htm#American
- www.elemnation.com/health_care.htm
- www.wfaa.com/s/dws/spe/2003/familyfirst/counseling.html
- http://members.tripod.com/naicco/
- www.sihb.org/about.html
- http://prod031.sandi.net/parent/programs/indian.html
- www.mcnaa.org/programs.html
- www.ehealers.com/index.html
- www.umass.edu/native/nasss/proginf.html

(continued)

TABLE 13.2   Media Resources About Native American Culture (Continued)

Educational Materials

- www.emicrotraining.com/race4.html#325
- www.emicrotraining.com/race5.html#453
- www.emicrotraining.com/race9.html#532

North American Indian and Indigenous People's Organizations and Associations

- www.yvwiiusdinvnohii.net/assoc.html

Native American Journals

- *Akwe:kon Journal* (American Indian Program at Cornell University): www.oyate.org/catalog/magazines.html
- *American Anthropologist* (American Anthropological Association): www.jstor.org/journals/00027294.html
- *American Antiquity* (Published by Society for American Archaeology): www.saa.org/publications/AmAntiq/amantiq.html
- *American Ethnologist*: www.music.columbia.edu/%7Ececenter/AES/amereth.html
- *American Indian Culture & Resource Journal* (Published by UCLA American Indian Studies Center Publications Unit): www.books.aisc.ucla.edu/aicrj.html
- *American Indian Law Review* (Published by University of Oklahoma): www.law.ou.edu/lawrevs/ailr/
- *American Indian Quarterly* (Published by University of Nebraska Press): www.jstor.org/journals/0095182X.html or www.jstor.org/journals/0095182X.html or www.nebraskapress.unl.edu/journalinfo/1.html
- *American Indian Report*: www.falmouthinst.com/publications.asp
- *American Indian Review*: www.american-indian-review.co.uk
- *American Journal of Archaeology*: www.ajaonline.org/
- *Anthropology and Education Quarterly* (Published by American Anthropological Association, March 2005; Theme Issue: Indigenous Epistemologies and Education: Self Determination, Anthropology, and Human Rights): www.aaanet.org/cae/aeq/#3
- *Archaeology of Eastern North America* (Published by Eastern States Archaeological Federation): http://esaf-archeology.org/
- *Arctic Anthropology* (Published by University of Wisconsin Press): www.wisc.edu/wisconsinpress/journals/journals/aa.html
- *Arctic: Journal of the Arctic Institute of North America* (Published by University of Calgary, Calgary, Alberta, Canada): www.ucalgary.ca/UofC/Others/AINA/pubs/arctic.html
- *Ayaangwaamizin: The International Journal of Indigenous Philosophy*: www.lights.com/sifc/ijip.htm
- *Canadian Journal of Native Education* (Spring/summer issue compiled at First Nations House of Learning at the University of British Columbia; fall/winter edition compiled by First Nations Graduate Education Program at the University of Alberta): www.lights.com/sifc/cjne.htm
- *The Canadian Journal of Native Studies* (Published by Canadian Indian/Native Studies Association): www.brandonu.ca/Library/CJNS/
- *Cultural Survival Quarterly*: http://209.200.101.189/home.cfm
- *Estudios de Cultura Nahuatl*: www.public.iastate.edu/~rjsalvad/scmfaq/ecnindex.html
- *Ethnohistory*: www.dukeupress.edu/ethnohistory/
- *Etudes Inuit Studies* (Published by Université Laval, Québec, Qc [Canada]): www.fss.ulaval.ca/etudes-inuit-studies/

- *European Review of Native American Studies*: http://umlibr.library.umass.edu/search/i?SEARCH=0238-1486
- *HONOR* (Honor Our Neighbors' Origins and Rights): http://honoradvocacy.org
- *Indigenous Policy Journal* (Published by American Indian Studies Program Michigan State University): www.indigenouspolicy.org/
- *International Indigenous Youth Conference*: http://iiyc.resist.ca/
- *International Journal of Cultural Property* (Published by Cambridge University Press): www.cambridge.org/uk/journals/journal_catalogue.asp?historylinks=ALPHA&mnemonic=JCP
- *Journal of American Indian Education* (Published by Center for Indian Education of the College of Education at Arizona State University): http://jaie.asu.edu/
- *Journal of Indigenous Nations Studies* (Published by University of Kansas): www.ku.edu/%7Einsp/insjournal.html
- *The Journal of Indigenous Studies*: www.lights.com/sifc/jois.htm
- *Journal of Native Health*: www.brandonu.ca/Native/JNH.html
- *Journal of World Anthropology* (Published by University at Buffalo): http://anthropology.buffalo.edu/JWA/
- *Latin American Antiquity* (Published by Society for American Archaeology) www.saa.org/Publications/LatAmAnt/latamant.html
- *Midcontinental Journal of Archaeology* (Published by Midwest Archaeological Conference): www.uwm.edu/Dept/ArchLab/MAC/MAC-MCJA.htm
- *Native American Rights Fund*: www.narf.org/pubs/index.html
- *Native Americas*: www.oyate.org/catalog/magazines.html
- *Native Peoples*: www.nativepeoples.com/
- *NativeShare* (Focus educational opportunities for Natives): http://groups.yahoo.com/group/NativeShare
- *Native Studies Review* (Published by Native Studies Department, University of Saskatchewan): http://publications.usask.ca/nativestudiesreview/
- *Native Voter* (Nonpartisan political information for Native community: AZ Native Voter, NM Native Voter, WI Native Voter, MN Native Voter. To sign up, visit): www.ccp.org/resources/lists.html
- *New Directions in Student Services* (Published by Serving Native American Students, Spring 2005, no. 109): www.wiley.com/WileyCDA/WileyTitle/productCd-0787979716.html
- *News from Native California*: www.heydaybooks.com/news/
- *North American Archaeologist* (Published by Baywood Publishing): www.baywood.com/journals/previewjournals.asp?id=0197-6931
- *Pacific Health Dialog*: www.resourcebooks.co.nz/phd/phdback.htm
- *Pacific Northwest Quarterly* (CSPN; published by University of Washington): www.washington.edu/uwired/outreach/cspn/html/pnq.html
- *Peabody Museum of Archaeology and Ethnology*: www.peabody.harvard.edu/title.html
- *Plains Anthropologist*: www.ou.edu/cas/archsur/plainsanth/pa/pa.htm
- *Red Ink Online* (Published by American Indian Studies Program at the University of Arizona): www.redinkmagazine.com/
- *Southeastern Archaeology* (Published by Southeastern Archaeological Conference): www.southeasternarchaeology.org/
- *STANDARDS: An International Journal of Multicultural Studies* (Published by University of Colorado, Boulder): www.colorado.edu/journals/standards/

(continued)

TABLE 13.2   Media Resources About Native American Culture (Continued)

- *Studies in American Indian Literature*: http://oncampus.richmond.edu/faculty/ASAIL/
- *Tribal Arts Review*: www.tribalarts.com/index.html
- *Tribal College Journal*: www.tribalcollegejournal.org/
- *Urban Circle of Voices Newspaper*: http://urbancircleofvoices.org/
- *Wicazo Sa Review* (Published by University of Minnesota Press): http://muse.jhu.edu/journals/wic/ or www.upress.umn.edu/journals/wsr/default.html
- *Winds of Change* (Published by AISES Publishing): www.wocmag.org/
- *Worlds Indigenous People*: http://groups.yahoo.com/group/worlds-indigenous-people

Online Journals

- *American Indian and Alaska Native Mental Health Research: The Journal of the National Center:* www2.uchsc.edu/ai/ncaianmhr/journal_home.asp
- *Gohweli: A Journal of American Indian Literature:* www.uwm.edu/~michael/journal/
- *Native Circle*: http://mayoresearch.mayo.edu/mayo/research/cancercenter/native.cfm
- *The Raven Chronicles:* www.ravenchronicles.org/
- *Redwire:* www.redwiremag.com/
- *Seventh Native American Generation (SNAG)* magazine: www.snagmagazine.com/
- *Studies in American Indian Literature:* http://oncampus.richmond.edu/faculty/ASAIL/
- *Turning Point:* www.turning-point.ca/
- *Wordcraft Circle:* www.wordcraftcircle.org/

Indigenous Listservs

- Indian_education@yahoogroups.com
- indigenousmedia@yahoogroups.com
- redwire@lists.resist.ca
- iiyc2@lists.resist.ca
- indigenousyouth@lists.resist.ca
- urbanvoice@mac.com

Native American History and Culture Books

- *Atlas of the North American Indian:* Excellent, detailed maps showing the pre-Columbian, colonial, and current locations of hundreds of Native tribes and nations. A great classroom reference.
- *Black Hawk:* Autobiography of 19th-century Sauk Chief Black Hawk. This was narrated through a string of translators, so it's not 100% authentic as an autobiography, but Black Hawk's story is still compelling.
- *Bury My Heart at Wounded Knee: An Indian History of the American West*: Western historian Dee Brown's seminal 1971 book, famous for presenting the Native American side of the "Indian Wars" to the general public for the first time. Carefully researched, compellingly written, still important 30 years later.
- *Charcoal's World:* Interesting historical examination of a Blackfoot man's clash with White culture and the law.
- *Cheyenne Again; My Name Is Sepeetza; Out of the Depths:* Books about the Indian residential schools. The first one is a lovely illustrated book for children, capturing the trauma of the boarding school experience without getting into the more adult issues (such as child molestation). The second is a harsher autobiography still suitable for kids. The third one, also autobiographical, is the most powerful, most difficult reading. This is not an easy subject, and these three books treat it well.

- *Encyclopedia of American Indian Costume:* A good overview of the different clothing styles and regalia in hundreds of tribes and nations. Disappointingly few pictures, but the ones that are there are interesting.
- *Encyclopedia of Native American Tribes:* Past and present information about the culture groups of Native North America. Outstanding presentation. This reference book is easy enough to read that it works as a children's resource, but it doesn't "dumb down" or get lost in silly romanticizing. Recommended to anyone with an interest.
- *Encyclopedia of North American Indians: Native American History, Culture, and Life:* Another good resource book presenting different ancient and modern Indian cultures respectfully and fairly. Sometimes it rambles a little—*Encyclopedia of Native American Tribes* is more clearly and uniformly written, but *Encyclopedia of North American Indians* has more pieces by Native authors. Having both volumes together would be ideal.
- *500 Nations: An Illustrated History of North American Indians:* This history of Native America reads a little like a textbook, but is very thorough. Recommended for history buffs, but maybe not for casual or younger readers.
- *Grey Owl: The Mystery of Archie Belaney:* Poetic biography of the Canadian environmentalist married to a Cree woman, by Ojibwe author Armand Garnet Ruffo.
- *Indian Metropolis: Native Americans in Chicago, 1945–75:* An interesting book about Indian urbanization.
- *Keepers of the Children:* An interesting book by the wife of a Pascua Yaqui man about applying Native American parenting techniques to non-Indian life.
- *Killing Custer: The Battle of the Little Bighorn and the Fate of the Plains Indians:* Book about the Battle of Little Bighorn and its aftermath
- *Lakota Woman:* Mary Brave Bird's (Crow Dog) autobiographical history of the American Indian Movement. A civil rights must-read.
- *Life and Death of Anna Mae Acquash:* Book about slain AIM activist Anna Mae Aquash.
- *Massacre at Sand Creek; Sand Creek Massacre; From Sand Creek:* Books about the Sand Creek Massacre.
- *A Native American Encyclopedia:* Another good resource book offering specific historical and demographic information about each tribal group of North America, explaining the differences between the diverse cultures clearly and precisely. This would make a good classroom reference for older kids.
- *The Native American Sweat Lodge:* History of the sweatlodge by Abenaki author Joseph Bruchac.
- *Of Earth and Elders: Visions and Voices from Native America:* Fascinating mosaic of interviews, essays, poems, and other musings from dozens of contemporary Indians.
- *Powwow:* Beautiful photography of contemporary Indian powwow regalia, interspersed with interesting interviews about the powwow.
- *Prison Writings: My Life Is My Sun Dance; In the Spirit of Crazy Horse; Trial of Leonard Peltier:* Books about AIM activist and political prisoner Leonard Peltier. *Prison Writings* is by Leonard himself, and he makes his own case eloquently. *In the Spirit of Crazy Horse* is famous for the FBI's bizarre attempts to stop its publication (the courts didn't let them).
- *Strange Empire: Narrative of the Northwest; Loyal Till Death:* Books about the Cree and Metis people and Canada's Northwest Rebellion.
- *The Vinland Sagas:* Vikings account of their early attempts to colonize America and their interactions with the Native people.
- *War Under Heaven; Pontiac and the Indian Uprising; Haughty Conquerors; The Conspiracy of Pontiac:* Books about Chief Pontiac and the Pontiac Rebellion.

(continued)

TABLE 13.2   Media Resources About Native American Culture (Continued)

- *Where White Men Fear To Tread:* Controversial Lakota activist Russell Means's autobiography and history of the American Indian Movement.
- *Wolf That I Am:* This is an interesting book about how not to do anthropological studies of indigenous people.

Native American Dictionaries and Language Books

- *Abnaki-Penobscot Dictionary; Apache Dictionary; Blackfoot Dictionary; Cree Dictionary: Creek/Muskogee Dictionary; Delaware Dictionary; Hopi Dictionary; Lakota Sioux Dictionary; Maliseet-Passamaquoddy Dictionary; Micmac Dictionary; Mohawk Dictionary; Ojibwe Dictionary; Nahuatl (Aztec) Dictionary; Salish Dictionary; Tsimshian Dictionary:* Native American language dictionaries for sale.
- *Abnaki-Penobscot Language; Algonquin Language; Arapaho/Gros Ventre Language; Atikamekw Language; Blackfoot Language; Cheyenne Language; Cree Language; Innu Language; Kickapoo Language; Lenape Language; Maliseet-Passamaquoddy Language; -Menominee Language; Miami-Illinois Language; Michif Language; Mi'kmaq Language; Ojibway Language; Wiyot Language:* More materials about individual Indian languages; Native American literature.
- *Absentee Indians and Other Poems; Trailing You:* Poems by White Earth Ojibwe writer Kimberly Blaeser.
- *Apache Lessons; Cherokee Lessons; Cheyenne Lessons; Chickasaw Lessons; Cree Lessons; Maliseet-Passamaquoddy Lessons; Mohawk Lessons; Ojibwe Lessons; Shoshoni Lessons:* Native American language learning books and audiotapes for sale.
- *Black Eagle Child; The Facepaint Narratives; Remnants of the First Earth; The Invisible Musician; The Rock Island Hiking Club; Winter of the Salamander:* Poetry and stories by Meskwaki author Ray A. Young Bear.
- *Briefcase Warriors; Survivor's Medicine:* Stories and plays by Fond du Lac Ojibwe writer E. Donald Two-Rivers.
- *Custer Died for Your Sins; Spirit and Reason; Red Earth, White Lies; Behind the Trail of Broken Treaties:* Essays and criticism by Standing Rock Lakota thinker Vine Deloria Jr.
- *Dirt Road Home:* Poems by Abenaki writer Cheryl Savageau.
- *Fools Crow; The Heartsong of Charging Elk; Winter in the Blood; The Indian Lawyer; The Death of Jim Loney; Riding the Earthboy 40:* Novels and poems by Blackfoot/Gros Ventre writer James Welch.
- *Fugitive Colors; Not Vanishing; Dream On; Fire Power:* Mixed-blood lesbian poet Chrystos.
- *Halfbreed:* Wrenching autobiography of Metis writer Maria Campbell.
- *The Hiawatha; Little:* Novels by Leech Lake Ojibwe writer David Treuer.
- *House Made of Dawn; Way to Rainy Mountain; The Ancient Child; In the Presence of the Sun; The Man Made of Words; The Names; Conversations With N. Scott Momaday:* Novels, stories, poems, and memoirs by Pulitzer Prize–winning Kiowa author N. Scott Momaday.
- *In Search of April Raintree; Spirit of the White Bison; Unusual Friendships; In the Shadow of Evil:* Novels and stories by Canadian Metis author Beatrice Mosionier.
- *Indian Singing:* Poems by Onondaga-Micmac writer Gail Tremblay.
- *The Languages of Native North America:* Comprehensive linguistic reference by Marianne Mithun. If you're interested in more than one Indian language, this is your first stop. Brief profiles of each and every language, linguistic information about unusual features of some of the languages, and the bibliography is priceless.
- *Love Medicine; Last Report on the Miracles at Little No Horse; Original Fire; Baptism of Desire; The Blue Jay's Dance; A Birth Year; The Birchbark House; Tracks; The Beet Queen; The Bingo Palace; Tales of*

Burning Love; The Antelope Wife: Novels, poetry, and stories by Turtle Mountain Chippewa writer Louise Erdrich.

- *Molly Molasses and Me:* Stories by Penobscot author Ssipsis.
- *Only Drunks and Children Tell the Truth; The Baby Blues; Bootlegger Blues; Buz'Gem Blues:* Curve Lake Ojibwe playwright/essayist Drew Hayden Taylor.
- *The Rez Sisters; Dry Lips Oughta Move to Kapuskasing; Kiss of the Fur Queen:* Contemporary plays and a novel by Cree author Tomson Highway.
- *Smoke Signals; The Lone Ranger and Tonto Fistfight in Heaven; Reservation Blues; Ten Little Indians; First Indian on the Moon; The Business of Fancydancing; Indian Killer; Toughest Indian in the World:* Screenplay, stories, and poems by acclaimed Spokane/Coeur d'Alene writer Sherman Alexie.
- *Sojourners and Sundogs; Bent Box; Daughters Are Forever; Ravensong:* Stories, poems, and novels by Metis author Lee Maracle.
- *The Surrounded; Wind From an Enemy Sky; Runner in the Sun; The Hawk Is Hungry:* Books on Indian life by prominent Cree author D'Arcy McNickle.
- *Walking the Rez Road; Rez Road Follies:* Stories by Fond du Lac Ojibwe writer Jim Northrup.
- *We Are the Dreamers:* Recent and early poetry by Mi'kmaq poet Rita Joe.

American Indian Legends and Folklore

- *American Indian Genesis:* Creation myths explored by a Blackfoot author.
- *American Indian Myths and Legends:* Well-attributed collection of many diverse traditional stories of Native America. Like any other body of mythology, some of the stories involve adultery, rape, or sexual situations, so be sensible about which ones you share with young children.
- *Full Moon Stories:* Thirteen Arapaho legends from an Arapaho writer/illustrator.
- *On the Trail of Elder Brother: Glous'gap Stories of the Micmac Indians:* Collection of traditional stories retold by a Mi'kmaq author and illustrator.
- *Sacred Stories of the Sweet Grass Cree:* Collection of Cree traditional stories and legends.
- *The Manitous: Spiritual World of the Ojibways; Ojibway Ceremonies; Tales the Elders Told; Mermaids and Medicine Women; Native Myths and Legends; Ojibway Heritage; Ojibway Tales; The Star-Man and Other Tales; Tales of the Anishinaubaek; The Bear-Walker; Dancing with a Ghost:* Books on Ojibway mythology, folklore, and spirituality by Ojibway writer Basil Johnston.

Native American Genealogy Books

- *Cherokee Proud:* How-to book about Cherokee genealogy.
- *Student's Guide to Native American Genealogy:* Step-by-step guide through beginner's genealogy and the process of tracing your American Indian ancestry.

Native American Art Books

- *Beauty, Honor, and Tradition: The Legacy of Plains Indian Shirts:* Showcasing Plains Indian beadwork, quillwork, clothing, and culture.
- *Inuit Art:* Photographs and history of Inuit carving and other traditional arts.
- *Looking at Indian Art of the Northwest Coast:* An overview of northwestern Indian art, designs, and symbolism.
- *Native North American Art:* American Indian art history from ancient times to today.
- *North American Indian Art:* Book by a Cree scholar on contemporary First Nations art.
- *Southwestern Pottery:* Overview of Southwest Indian pottery, with photographs and advice for collectors.
- *The Fetish Carvers of Zuni:* Overview of fetish carvings, their forms and meaning.

(continued)

TABLE 13.2   Media Resources About Native American Culture (Continued)

Native American Children's Books

- *Children's Literature by Bruchac:* Children's books by Abenaki author Joseph Bruchac.
- *Crossing the Starlight Bridge:* A 9-year-old Penobscot girl struggles to keep her culture after her parents' divorce forces her to leave the reservation.
- *Dreamcatcher; Powwow Summer; Jingle Dancer; Coyote in Love with the Moon; Sky Dogs; Star Boy; Cheyenne Again; Death of the Iron Horse; Shingebiss; An Ojibwe Legend; Northwoods Cradle Song*: Picture books for young children about American Indian life.
- *Forest Warrior:* Kids' biography of Ottawa Chief Pontiac.
- *Jim Thorpe: 20th-Century Jock:* Good biography of the celebrated athlete; deals with the complexity of his racial status as well as his athletics.
- *Maria Tallchief:* Biography of Maria Tallchief, the Osage ballerina.
- *Night of the Full Moon:* Historical fiction about two girls (one Potawatomi, one White) trying to escape from a forced relocation westward.
- *People of the Buffalo:* Book about the Plains Indians, written by a Metis (mixed-blood Cree) author.
- *Weaving a California Tradition (Mono); Ininatig's Gift of Sugar (Chippewa); Clambake (Wampanoag); Songs From the Loom (Navajo); A Story to Tell (Tlingit); Fort Chipewyan Homecoming (Dene/Metis); Four Seasons of Corn (Winnebago); Kinaalda (Navajo); The Sacred Harvest (Ojibway); Shannon, Ojibway Dancer (Ojibway); Children of Clay (Pueblo); Drumbeat, Heartbeat (Assiniboine):* The charming "We Are Still Here" photoessays on Indian life, featuring contemporary young protagonists and their families.

American Indian Music and Other Audio

- *Band of Wild Indians; Fingermonkey; Circle:* CDs by Ojibwe musician Keith Secola.
- *Black Lodge Singers; Tribute to the Elders; People Dance; Powwow People; Kids' Pow-Wow Songs:* Music by the popular Blackfoot drum group Black Lodge Singers.
- *Dance Hard; Showtime; Here to Stay; Honor Eagle Feather; Come & Dance; Songs of Caddo:* Music from popular powwow band Northern Cree Singers.
- *Echoes of the Night:* Audio recordings of Abenaki storyteller Tsonakwa.
- *Gluskabe Stories:* Audiocassette of Abenaki storytelling by Joseph Bruchac.
- *Mawio'mi; Tomegan Gospem*: Music from Indian fusion-rock band Medicine Dream.
- *My Ojibway Experience:* Music by Ojibway blues guitarist Billy Joe Green.
- *Up Where We Belong; Illuminations; Moonshot; She Used to Wanna Be a Ballerina*: Music by Cree folksinger Buffy Sainte-Marie.

American Indian Films and Other DVDs

- *The Business of Fancydancing* (Wellspring).
- *Dance Me Outside* (A-Pix). Canadian movie tells a coming-of-age story set on an Ontario reserve. Native cast.
- *Dreamkeeper* (Hallmark).
- *Grand Avenue* (HBO).
- *How the West Was Lost I & II* (Discovery).
- *Incident at Oglala: The Leonard Peltier Story.* Robert Redford documentary about AIM activist and political prisoner Leonard Peltier.
- *Lakota Woman* (New Line). The story of the American Indian Movement, based on Mary Crow Dog's autobiography.

- *Medicine River* (UAV).
- *Pow Wow Highway* (Anchor Bay).
- *Running Brave* (Tapeworm).
- *Skins* (First Look).
- *Skinwalkers* (Warner).
- *Smoke Signals* (Miramax). Sundance feature about a friendship between two Couer d'Alene men, written by Sherman Alexie. Native cast, director, and writer, shot on site at the Coeur d'Alene reservation.
- *Thunderheart* (Columbia Tristar).
- *We're Still Here: Native Americans in America* (PBS).
- *Windtalkers* (MGM). War movie revolving around the Navajo code-talkers of World War II.

Summary

Through culturally sensitive counseling, as we turn to an approach that is more congruent with traditional Native worldviews, we listen to the life stories of Native elders, adults, and youngsters alike, and begin to understand where power moves. With this, we discover a better sense of where Native people have come from and where they are going. We see the powerful influences of history, social and political issues, acculturation, values and beliefs, spirituality, cultural symbolism and practices, and communication style. We see the continuity of the Circle in stories of images and experiences that flow from the heart, and we begin to arrive at a better understanding of where we stand in relation to everything around us, and in relation to our clients. We begin to understand the importance of attending to the stories—the meanings, language, experiences, images, and themes—of our Native clients. And we begin to learn, as it has traditionally been taught by so many Native elders, that true learning is a lifelong process, just as a story unfolds and offers the gift of its life to us. Stories carry the words, ghosts, dreams, and spirit of Native life. The following quote from a Native elder illustrates the power of tradition and community to many American Indians. He was asked to describe who he was as a Native person:

Well, I think the stories probably gave me a sense of connection with the Indian side more than anything else. What I remember most of all is everything that my grandfather ever said because to me, he must have been the tallest man in the world. I was such a little boy, and I'd look up at him, and he was tall, tall and slender. Boy, I thought he was such a fine man. The first thing he'd say every time I'd see him was "Ceo Tsayoga," in other words, hello there little bird, how you doing. The first thing he would always do is he'd put me up on his shoulders, I remember that, and take me down to the creek bank. He'd say, "Come on, let's go to the creek bank . . . gonna do some fishin.'" I never fished. I never got a chance to fish. I don't know that he ever fished. It's like if he had a chance to take me fishing, that was a chance to tell me stories, teach me values. And one that I do remember very much was when we'd look in the water because I really enjoyed as a little kid just looking at the little minnows, seeing the fish in the water. And he'd let me look for hours, and I don't know whether he was fishing or not, I think he was. We never brought home any fish. I think he would always put the fish back, even if he caught one. (J. T. Garrett, Eastern Band of Cherokee, in Garrett, 1996b)

Somewhere even now, a young child sits by the riverside with a grandfather or grandmother, looking at the water and at himself or herself, one and the same. The elder and the child sit together, honoring Mother Earth and all that she has to offer us, honoring life and its constant motion. The elder and the child sit together, one and the same. Stories will be told, and many generations will hear their words flow alongside the trickling of the river's water. Someday, the little boy or girl may earn their first eagle feather, and in doing so, he or she may earn the responsibility and the joy of looking to the surface of the river's water and seeing the true reflection of his or her own grandchild looking back. And so, the Circle continues to move and shift with the all the gifts of life and mysteries of what it means to live.

CHAPTER 14

Individuals and Families of European Descent

H. George McMahon, Pamela O. Paisley, and Bogusia Molina

PREVIEW

Multicultural counseling is often understood as an approach a counselor might take with clients of color, yet it is also important to understand the cultural factors that lead to identity construction of Americans of European descent. Perhaps, when clients of European descent clarify their identity, they will be able to clearly understand the source of their distress and challenges. In addition, it is equally important for counselors of European descent to understand their own cultural perspective in order to better understand their clients. In this chapter, cultural values and traditions from several European ethnicities, including White American ethnicity, are discussed. In addition, implications for multicultural counseling with recent European immigrants as well as individuals and families who identify as "White Americans" are addressed.

EUROPEAN AMERICAN HISTORY

> Martin was, like most inhabitants of Elk Mills before the Slavo-Italian immigration, a Typical Pure-bred Anglo-Saxon American, which means that he was a union of German, French, Scotch, Irish, perhaps a little Spanish, conceivably a little of the strains lumped together as "Jewish," and a great deal of English, which is itself a combination of primitive Briton, Celt, Phoenician, Roman, German, Dane, and Swede. (Lewis, 1925)

To better understand the cultural worldview of European Americans, it is worthwhile to gain an understanding of Europe and the people who settled there. One of the most significant developments of European history is the creation of the idea that "Europe" exists as a distinct region (Baum, 2006). Throughout the first millennium, various nomadic tribes traveled across the Eurasian landmass. The Roman Empire helped create an infrastructure for stable living environments throughout the areas now defined as Europe, and after the fall of the Empire, the region slowly gelled. This new region consisted of many of the same nomadic tribes that had wandered throughout the region for generations, including the Anglos, the Celts, the Gauls, the Saxons, and the Slavs.

The tribes that formed the region of Europe were very different from one another, and had experienced internal conflicts for centuries. The Roman Empire and extensive trading routes, however, had exposed these tribes to cultures from far away. As Bartlett (1993) reports, "When compared to other culture areas of the globe, such as the Middle East, the Indian Subcontinent, or China, western or central Europe exhibited distinct characteristics" (p. 1). Thus, perhaps in large part due to the rather vague boundaries of the region, these early tribes that collectively formed

Europe separated themselves from others along physical and cultural characteristics as much as physical geography (Baum, 2006).

Although the physical features shared by the early European tribes were certainly important in their self-determination of who was and who was not European, cultural practices were also very important. Perhaps no sociocultural factor was more important, however, than the adoption of the Christian religion (Baum, 2006). The rise of Islam in the 7th and 8th centuries helped define "boundaries" between Christian Europe and "infidel" (as Muslims were described by European Christians at the time) areas (Davies, 1996). This Christian–Islamic border was not merely one of physical territory, but became an important social distinction as well. Laws were passed in Europe in order to maintain strict Christian bloodlines within the community (Poliakov, 1974), and active participation in the Latin Christian Church and obedience to the pope were seen as essential criteria (although not sufficient by themselves) to be considered a part of the proper European societies of the Middle Ages (Baum, 2006). This pattern of European peoples categorizing themselves (and others) based on physical features and sociocultural practices was to be repeated throughout their history, and certainly continues today as "Western" people, culture, and ideas.

The Early Colonial Period

> I'm so proud of you, Mom. You're like Christopher Columbus. You discovered something millions of people did before you. (Lisa Simpson, *The Simpsons*, in Burns and Andersen [2007])

The colonization of North America beginning in the late 15th century brought an influx of European settlers to the North American continent (see Table 14.1). American history texts, written most often with a European American bias (Loewen, 1995), provide a description of the "discovery of the new world" while minimizing the reality that tribes of Native Americans had lived, farmed, and worked in this part of the world for centuries. This Eurocentric view of experience within the United States has had and continues to have a powerful influence on the cultural conditioning of all citizens.

Similarly, American history texts often perpetuate the myth of colonization of North America by freedom-loving individuals who sought an open and free society for all. Most early immigrants came for economic reasons, and for those who did come for religious freedom, they typically did not seek religious freedom for others but only to be able to practice their particular set of beliefs without interference (Banks, 2003). In spite of the reasons for their departure, the very power dynamics that

TABLE 14.1 Early European Settlements in What Is Now the United States

Year	Ethnic Group	Area of Settlement	Primary Reason
1607	Anglos, Germans, and Poles	Jamestown, VA	Financial opportunities
1609	Dutch	New Netherland (Manhattan Island)	Financial (East India Trading Co.)
1638	Swedes	Delaware Bay	Fur and tobacco trading
1664	Quakers (Anglos and German)	Philadelphia, PA, and Germantown, PA	"Holy Experiment" (for people to live in peace)
1718	French	Mississippi River (New Orleans to St. Louis to Detroit)	Farming and plantations

Source: www.spartacus.schoolnet.co.uk.

many were escaping (e.g., oppression, class structure) quickly began to appear within the colonies themselves.

The early settlements were very diverse including colonists from England, Scotland, Germany, France, and Africa, as well as Jews and Christians (Banks, 2003; see Table 14.1). These diverse communities were not without conflict, however. The English, who accounted for approximately 60% of the European immigrants, were clearly dominant during this period and had the greatest influence over the creation of both the political and social systems developing in the colonies. This social and political dominance led to the colonies using English as the primary language as well as a notion of supremacy of their cultural values. As Banks notes, "the Anglo-Saxon culture became the ideal by which all subsequent ethnic groups were judged. Becoming acculturated became associated with acquiring Anglo-Saxon Protestant lifestyles, values, and language" (p. 247).

There were a variety of similarities and differences among the cultural values of the different European ethnicities, but the major differences setting the English value system apart included the focus on individuality, a strong work ethic, and the value of external signs of success. Many scholars relate the English work ethic and external signs of success of the Protestant/Calvinist to the belief that success on earth (which was achieved through hard work and individual responsibility) was evidence of predestination for salvation (McGill & Pearce, 2005). Thus, the external rewards of success were proof that one had lived a proper and worthy life in the eyes of God. Consider other values of "American" culture by completing Activity 14.1.

During this early colonial period, many of the European ethnic groups intermarried, with the English culture and values remaining dominant while individuals of other ethnic backgrounds assimilated to the English American culture (McGill & Pearce, 2005). By the time of the American Revolution, the population of the colonies was largely seen as English Protestants, although a great deal of German and Scotch/Irish heritage, along with smaller numbers of French, Dutch, Swede, Polish, and Swiss heritage, had been absorbed into the dominant culture. This cultural mix, in addition to the norm of assimilating into the dominant culture, set the foundation for what would become the dominant social system and worldview, as well as the process immigrants were expected to go through upon arrival in the United States for years to come.

ACTIVITY 14.1   WHERE IS IT FROM?

Nothing is more American than a hamburger . . . except that it's German. The popular American sandwich is named for the German city of Hamburg, where it is believed to have originated. Even hotdogs are European, based on popular sausages such as the German frankfurter and the Polish kielbasa.

Identify some other staples of "American culture" and see if you can identify the cultures from which they originate. Brainstorm in small groups different foods, games, traditions, holidays, art, education, and so forth associated with American culture. Identify rituals that were created to honor relationships and connection with each other and nature.

European Immigration

Although many people associate European settlers with the 1600s, immigration from Europe was by no means limited to the colonial period, and in fact continues today. Between 1820 and 1998, approximately 61% of the over 64,000,000 legal immigrants to the United States came from Europe (Banks, 2003). The period of European immigration in the 19th century was particularly strong,

TABLE 14.2 Major European Immigration Periods

Approximate Dates	Country of Origin	Reason for Immigration	Areas Settled
1845–1854	Ireland	Potato famine and typhus outbreak	Cities along the East Coast, Chicago, Ohio
1848–1858	Germany	Political turmoil (failed revolution)	New York and midwestern cities (e.g., Chicago, Milwaukee, Detroit)
1851	France	Political turmoil	New York, Chicago, New Orleans
1890–1900	Italy	Financial concerns (low wages and high taxes)	Industrial cities (e.g., New York, Philadelphia, Chicago, Detroit)

Source: www.spartacus.schoolnet.co.uk.

due in large part to the political and economic turmoil in Europe throughout the mid 1800s. Table 14.2 lists some of these significant periods of European immigration. The number of immigrant children and families continues to increase today, with the foreign-born population in the United States reaching 33.5 million in 2003. Currently, immigrants of European descent represent approximately 30% of documented immigrants.

Immigrant children and families represent a broad range of diverse and intercultural groups, and the experience of immigrants varies greatly by the time period in which they immigrated, their reasons for leaving, the regions to which they came, and the political climate of the time as well as their own personal circumstances. Table 14.2 identifies other European ethnic immigration periods and reasons behind the immigration.

Although contemporary American media and political debates about immigration rarely refer to European immigrants, this was not always the case. Arbitrary hierarchies that distinguished old immigrants from new ones, or more specifically, that distinguished ethnic groups of northern and western Europe from those of southern and eastern European countries, have been in place throughout much of U.S. history (Banks, 2003). This form of discrimination against ethnic groups was particularly prevalent during periodic mass migrations from certain European countries, particularly southern and eastern European countries.

It seems necessary for counselors to take time and help clients of European descent to reflect on their cultural identity construction. What does being a White European mean to them? What are the underlying perceptions regarding self and others? While individuals of European descent attempted to run from financial hardships, even religious persecution, and lack of freedom, sometimes the oppressed may become the oppressors when their identity construction is based on viewing differences as deficiencies (Banks, 2003). First, counselors may want to visit Reflection 14.1 to consider their thoughts of what it means to be "American."

REFLECTION 14.1

The vast majority of Americans can trace their ancestry to another country, and thus other ethnic backgrounds and culture. Consider these questions:

• What do you think it means to be "American"?
• Who can be American?

- Think about your family specifically. When did individuals in your family become American? What was the process of becoming American like for them?
- What are and/or were the names of your ancestors? How were the names given to them? Did their names change over time?
- To what extent did your ancestors and family members maintain awareness of their previous cultural and spiritual practices that fostered a sense of cultural belonging and well-being?

Dominant American culture reacted strongly whenever the perception was that there were too many immigrants coming at one time period to disperse effectively (i.e., assimilate) into the population (Sacks, 1998; see Reflection 14.2). These periods were pockmarked by warnings from policy makers, the media, and even scientists that true American stock (i.e., primarily Anglo-Saxon Americans) were being polluted by inferior European (and non-European) people. These statements not only led to discrimination and oppression of the immigrants themselves, but at times included admonishing Anglo-American women for allowing inferior immigrants to outbreed them (Banks, 2003). These arbitrary hierarchies provided a convenient scapegoat for urban, economic, and political problems in the persons of recent European immigrants who were "vulnerable and convenient targets ... [and] judged intellectually and culturally inferior to the old immigrants and declared unassimilable" (Banks, 2003, p. 249).

REFLECTION 14.2

In the 19th century, many immigrants who are now considered White were not viewed that way, and were systematically and sometimes violently discriminated against (Rubin, 1998). For instance, records reveal instances of Italians being lynched in the South, and media publications referring to Irish immigrants as "low-browed and savage, groveling and bestial, lazy and wild, simian and sensual" (Roediger, 1991 p. 133). Although the target groups may have changed, what similarities do you see in the way non-White immigrants are characterized in the United States today? What emotions, dispositions, or cultural worldviews do you think underlie the fears White Americans have about immigrants?

TERMINOLOGY

Many different terms have been used at different times and in different settings to describe Americans of European descent. Even within the professional multicultural literature, scholars have used terms including *White, White American, Euro-American, Anglo-American, Anglo,* and *European American* to describe the dominant cultural-racial group in the United States (D'Andrea & Daniels, 2001). Members of this group are also identified as being part of the Caucasian or White racial group. For many Americans, these terms are used interchangeably or the preferred term may vary depending on generation or geographic region.

Although it may seem as though the terms are somewhat arbitrary, there are important differences in the terms and in the ways in which they have been used. Some terms refer specifically to a racial category. Others may refer to ethnicity comprised mostly of the dominant American culture or may involve more specific cultural views of the European ethnicity of origin. In addition, it is important to remember that these terms have been used not only to describe the majority culture, but also to maintain political power by separating the majority culture from non-White ethnic groups (Baum, 2006; Olson, 2004).

In this chapter, the term **White** will be used to describe the larger racial group. Moreover, the authors acknowledge the ongoing debate about the significance of race, and that race as a biological difference has largely been disproved (Baum, 2006). Nevertheless, as a social construct, race is very significant in that those persons and/or groups that have been "racialized" as White have gained advantages over non-White racialized categories in terms of material goods, social status, psychological benefits, and access to resources among other advantages. Moreover, the term **Caucasian**, although commonly used to describe the privileged racialized group, will not be used because Caucasian is, in fact, an ethnic group of people traditionally from the isthmus between the Black and Caspian Seas, and because these groups, ironically, have not been considered European by their neighbors. (In fact, many Russian ethnics have referred to the Caucasian ethnic groups as "Black.") It is important to reflect on how you conceptualize race (Reflection 14.3).

The term **European American** will be used generally to refer to individuals living in the United States who are recent immigrants from or identify closely with their European heritage in terms of values, traditions, and worldview. When talking about specific examples, the specific ethnic label will be used when it is known (e.g., German American). Finally, the term **White American ethnic** will be used to describe individuals of European descent who identify themselves as American ethnically, and who have adopted the culture, traditions, and values of the dominant culture in the United States. The next section will discuss key concepts that contribute to the development of White American ethnics or ethnicity.

REFLECTION 14.3

Race as a biological construct has been largely discredited within the science community, yet the term is still used widely and the *concept* of race is something that many Americans understand (at least in their own way). Currently, there is debate over use of the term *race*. While some argue that using terms like *race* and *racial differences* perpetuates the myth that racial differences exist on a biological level, others argue that the social construction of the concept of race is, from a postmodernist view, very real and must be dealt with as a "real" concept (Baum, 2006). What are your thoughts on the concept of "race," and how should we address the issue, if at all, in order to promote a more accurate understanding of race?

DEVELOPMENT OF A WHITE AMERICAN ETHNIC IDENTITY

My grandmother came from Russia, a satchel on her knee,
My grandfather had his father's cap he brought from Italy.
They'd heard about a country where life might let them win,
They paid the fare to America and there they melted in.

(Ahrens and Warburton [1977])

The multicultural literature in America has long talked about individuals of color being acculturated to the mainstream culture, but little explicit attention is given to the meaning of mainstream culture. Historically, this is reasonable—multiculturalism developed as a reaction against mainstream culture or an alternative to mainstream culture (Sue et al., 1992), so it follows that those pioneers would not want to spend time writing about it. Furthermore, it may have been that assumption that mainstream culture was so apparent to the readers that there was no need to spend time describing it. Although this may have been the consensus among Americans of color, we also know that

White Americans' understanding of their own culture is lacking (Sue, Capodilupo, et al., 2007). It is important to explicitly describe, therefore, the basic tenets of White American culture, which many people may be aware of only implicitly, in order to promote a deeper and more accurate understanding of the context in which the White American culture was constructed.

There are many diverse factors that merged and interacted as the worldview, belief systems, behavioral norms, and traditions of the White Americans began to emerge. Certainly, the philosophical base of the White American ethnicity was the English system that dominated the social and political systems of the early colonies, although other (primarily European, initially) ethnicities added characteristics as well. In addition, the wide expanse of the North American continent, which was seen as unsettled by the new White Americans, combined with the Calvinist understanding of predestination to lead to a "pioneer spirit" that valued exploration and "conquering" the land as a way to prove one's worth. This adventurous spirit and the belief that it was White Americans' "manifest destiny" to dominate over the land is a clear example of how cultural and religious beliefs interacted. Although countless factors contributed to the development of the White American ethnicity, three specific contributions will be discussed briefly: the emergence of the American "melting pot," the development of the American Dream, and the creation of a national heritage.

The Melting Pot

As the newly founded nation of the United States matured, and individuals of different European ethnicities intermarried, a new and distinct culturally homogeneous society began to emerge. Although grounded in the cultural values and worldview of the English settlers, other European ethnicities contributed a great deal to the development of this new and unique sociocultural perspective, traditions, and beliefs. The term **melting pot** was commonly used as a metaphor to describe the process of combining a variety of cultural backgrounds and beliefs to create a new, virtuous (i.e., White American) culture. Although the vision of the melting pot was an idealized notion used to demonstrate the United States as a utopia, non-Europeans, and in some cases non-English-speaking Europeans, were largely excluded from adding their contribution or flavor to the cultural pot, leading to both marginalization of and discrimination against non-White or non-English-speaking Americans.

The popular notion of the United States as a melting pot began to dissolve during the civil rights movement of the 1960s, when people of color demanded that their identity be recognized and respected separate from the White mainstream culture (McGoldrick, Giordano, & Garcia-Preto, 2005). The melting pot idea has largely fallen out of favor, and has been replaced with a new sense of multiculturalism focusing on inclusion and ethnic pride. Several metaphors have been suggested to replace the melting pot, such as viewing the United States as a **salad bowl**, where several different ethnic flavors coexist and add to the overall culinary gestalt while maintaining their own distinct characteristics as well (Lee, 2001b).

This sense of pluralism helped many people of color take pride in their own cultural heritage and develop their ethnic identities, but it also proved confusing for many White ethnic Americans. Many European Americans who have been in the United States for several generations have fully assimilated into American culture to the point that their cultural connection to their European heritage has been lost (McGill & Pearce, 2005). Instead, many of them, in particular those of Anglo heritage, find it uncomfortable and confusing to discuss ethnicity because they consider themselves "plain, regular Americans" (p. 460). This confusion over the meaning of ethnicity in the United States may be responsible for many White Americans' resistance to the concept of multiculturalism, as their concept of "culture" is not well defined and not personalized.

The American Dream

Another important development in the evolution of the White American ethnicity is commonly known as the American Dream. In many ways, the **American Dream** is the manifestation of White American ethnic cultural values, and reinforces the notion of the United States as a utopia. It explains the country's political and social structure, incorporates the nation's stated ideals of liberty, equality, and the pursuit of happiness, and provides an explanation for the success of the American people, as well as a justification for allowing others not to succeed (Johnson, 2006). It is a philosophical position of the United States as a meritocracy with the necessary social and political structures that include equality, freedom, and individual agency (Hochschild, 1995).

One of the common beliefs perpetuated in the United States is that anyone can grow up to be a star, to own a business, even to be president of the country if he or she works hard enough. This is the prime example of the idea of a meritocracy, where individual success is based on personal skills, abilities, and work ethic rather than on external factors. Meritocracies, therefore, rely on an egalitarian society that promises a level playing field where individual merit is the basis for advancement. Legends of folks who have "pulled themselves up by the bootstraps" and have risen to success in spite of humble beginnings are commonly used to reinforce the myth of an American meritocracy. These stories are told and retold to emphasize the principles of a meritocracy, and thus it is hardly surprising that many people within the dominant culture believe the ideology is a reality (Johnson, 2006).

Meritocracy, even as a myth, does provide benefits to those who believe in it. The idea that anyone can be successful provides a great deal of hope and inspiration to many people, encouraging individuals who are struggling to see beyond immediate barriers and believe that success is possible in the long run. In addition to providing a hope for success and explaining the achievement of those who are already successful, however, a meritocracy also provides an explanation for those who are not successful. Specifically, if those who obtained status in society are assumed to have earned their position through natural ability and hard work, than it follows that those without status have earned their fate as well. The implication is that those who struggle in society have brought it on themselves, which provides the middle and upper class with a reason for their success and a rationalization for withholding help from those who are less fortunate (e.g., help will be a wasted effort).

The problem, of course, is that the meritocracy, if it exists at all, exists for a very narrow range of the White American population. For the rest of the country, everyone does not have equal access to resources, the playing field is decidedly not level, and although some are born into privilege, many others are born into oppression. This is exactly where the conflict for White American ethnics emerges. For White American ethnics to acknowledge that social factors inhibit the success of some groups is to acknowledge that the meritocracy, which is at the very core of many White American ethnics' identity, is an illusion. It also means that the privilege they enjoy (relatively guilt free) was not earned after all, a difficult notion for many who are privileged to accept.

Creation of an American Heritage

One of the common factors that help define ethnic groups is a common heritage, yet for more than a century of its existence, the United States was largely without a well-defined national heritage (Shackel, 2001). As part of a rise in nationalism in the early 1900s, the U.S. Department of Defense began funding the preservation of war monuments, which began the process of creating a collective memory and the beginning of a national heritage. The fact that the national heritage movement started with the Department of Defense may not have been coincidental, and was certainly vital to the shaping of the national heritage. To further promote the dominance of the White American ethnicity within the social structure of the United States, the national heritage and collective memory must demonstrate the superiority of the dominant group (D'Andrea & Daniels, 2001). What better way to instill a sense of superiority into the collective consciousness of a nation than to highlight the military conquests, led by White American ethnics (D'Andrea & Daniels).

For a national heritage to fully take hold, however, it must be institutionalized across a broad swath of educational, political, and economic practices (D'Andrea & Daniels, 2001). The educational system in the United States has provided a vital link in the promotion of national heritage and collective memory created by the dominant culture. Not only do American students learn a decidedly Eurocentric and White American ethnic perspective of the brief history of the United States (Loewen, 1995), but the school systems teach a history of the country that is in accordance with the American heritage, continuing to promote the myth of the American Dream and the values associated with the dominant culture (McGill & Pearce, 2005), including hard work, individual responsibility, and external success as proof of personal virtue. Other groups have worked to promote a dominant history (see Reflection 14.4).

REFLECTION 14.4

While serving as chairs for the National Endowment for the Humanities from the early 1980s through 1992, William Bennett and Lynne Cheney discouraged funding for projects that conflicted with the national collective memory, including projects that highlighted labor groups', women's groups, or racial groups' contributions to U.S. history in order to curb the development of alternative or "revisionist" histories (Shackel, 2001). What are your thoughts on some groups' efforts to maintain a consistent understanding of history and other groups' efforts to continue to add pieces to historical understanding? What are the potential benefits and drawbacks of each perspective?

Privilege, Oppression, and Ethnocentric Monoculturalism

I have come to realize that most of my colleagues are well-intentioned and truly believe in equal access and opportunity for all but have great difficulty freeing themselves from their cultural conditioning. They are, in essence, trapped in a Euro American worldview that only allows them to see the world from one perspective. To challenge that worldview as being only partially accurate, to entertain the notion that it represents a false illusion, and to realize that it may have resulted in injustice to others make seeing an alternative reality frightening and difficult. Although using the terms Whiteness and Whites may perpetuate the inaccurate notion that these terms describe a racial group, little doubt exists that skin color in this society exposes people to different experiences. Being a White person means something quite different from being a person of color. (Sue, 2004, p. 762)

An attempt to describe the history of European Americans and of the development of the White American ethnic cannot be conducted without a discussion of privilege, oppression, and ethnocentric monoculturalism. Although not identified as "values" of the European or the White American ethnic, they are among the most widely recognized expressions of White culture worldwide (Baum, 2006). The concepts of privilege and oppression are discussed in more detail elsewhere in the text, yet it is important to cover these topics briefly here in terms of how they contribute to the White American ethnic identity.

Because many members of the White American ethnicity do not see themselves as having an ethnicity, they are often oblivious to their racialized identity (Baum, 2006; McIntosh, 1989).

Embedded within privilege is the privilege to be oblivious to culture, and many White people become aware of their Whiteness only when they are outnumbered by persons of color.

White members of American society are given significant social and economic advantages that have nothing to do with the meritocracy that is supposed to exist in the United States. Instead, these advantages are based on a pattern of social and political practices in the United States to keep power in the hands of those who already have it (Baum, 2006). Just as the advantages that privilege provides are real, so is the obliviousness of that privilege among those who have it. This lack of awareness of advantage is not simply about White Americans choosing not to see it; instead, Whites in America are taught not to see their own privilege (McIntosh, 1989). For a true meritocracy to exist, privilege must be denied. Therefore, the teaching of a national heritage and an American Dream based on a meritocracy go hand in glove with the denial of privilege.

A closely related concept to privilege is **ethnocentric monoculturalism**, described by Sue (2004) as "the invisible veil of a worldview that keeps White European-Americans from recognizing the ethno-centric basis of their beliefs, values, and assumptions" (p. 764). Sue (2004) argues that ethno-centric monoculturalism is conditioned into individuals from birth, and gains its power from its invisibility. Ethnocentric monoculturalism instills in members of a dominant group a belief in the superiority of the values and practices of that group, without making the individuals aware that their beliefs are culturally based. This is an important distinction, because it allows members of the dominant culture to believe that do not discriminate against others based on the color of the skin (a visible difference), even as they reject those who do not hold their same values. The impact is a far more subtle and often invisible (to the majority culture) form of racism in which members of the dominant group are conditioned and reinforced to accept their cultural values as universal truths, and thus view individuals and groups who have differing values and practices as unprincipled (Sue, 2004). Although Sue (2001, 2004) argues that all groups are ethnocentric by nature, the difference is the ethnocentric monoculturalism of the White American Ethnic is in the ability to impose the White American reality onto other groups.

Whereas the myth of meritocracy would suggest that social stratification in the United States is primarily due to ability and effort, it is far more realistic to say that those in power have abused their power in order to remain so, and to marginalize all others who are not (Loewen, 1995). This type of systemic oppression has long been a staple of European Americans, but in many ways it too remains out of the awareness of many White Americans (Sue, 2004). The combination of the myth of meritocracy, religious or virtuous rationalizations for civilizing communities deemed godless or uncivil, and common teachings that racism occurs through "individual acts of meanness" (McIntosh, 1989, p. 12) facilitates the invisibility of the systemic and systematic oppression that European Americans and White American Ethnics have subjected other groups of people. Instead, a collective memory that describes liberty and equality is ingrained, at the expense of all subordinate groups (Shackel, 2001).

In spite of a history suggesting otherwise, it is important to note that being oppressive need not be synonymous with White culture. There may be certain aspects of European American culture that are utilized in the oppression process—such as the ontology of absolutism which designates a "right" and "wrong," and the democratic practice of "majority rule." However, many of the values that are at the core of the American ideal (e.g., liberty, equality, responsibility, the Christian "Golden Rule" of treating others the way you want to be treated) can also lay the foundations for a far more socially just society if the American people, in particular those in power, can begin to live up to the stated values and afford *all* citizens those rights.

Just as the multiculturalism movement has asked that non-White cultures not be seen as "deficient," it is just as important than those of us who strive to hold a multicultural view of the world not see White American culture as deficient. White Americans, and the European-based values they hold, present in their most positive form a determined and self-reliant group of individuals who value courage and adventure, who honor personal achievement and independence, and who possess a strong work ethic and an optimistic belief in the ability of the individual to conquer problems. The challenge for White American ethnics and other Europeans, then, becomes honoring their traditions, beliefs, customs, and values without imposing them on others or using them as a yardstick by which all other cultures and peoples are judged. The gift of pluralism comes as an opportunity for White Americans to explore, perhaps for the first time, the full complexity of their cultural identities, choose the values they wish to honor, and be intentional about living with others in accordance with the values we proclaim (see Activity 14.2).

ACTIVITY 14.2   WHAT DOES IT MEAN TO BE WHITE?

For students who identify themselves as White, identify some salient characteristics about what it means to you to be White and write them down on a piece of paper. Next, identify some characteristics of being White that you think may be most salient to people of color.

For students of color, identify some characteristics of what it means to be White that are most salient to you and write them down. Next, identify characteristics that you think may be most salient to White Americans.

Process the activity either by having students share their thoughts, or by the instructor collecting the papers and writing some thoughts on a board or flipchart. What characteristics are salient to White Americans that are not as salient to people of color? What characteristics are salient to people of color but not to White Americans? What might be some reasons for these differences?

WHO GETS TO BE WHITE?

Previous sections have discussed the evolution of a White American ethnicity, but how did immigrants become part of this American ethnicity? Certainly some members, such as Anglo-Americans, were the forerunners to the new ethnicity, but when and how did the Irish, Italians, Polish, and other ethnicities become "White" Americans? What is the cost to the individual, family, and community?

Although members of White America now enjoy a great deal of privilege, including the privilege of not having to reflect on their privilege, every White family was, at some point, an immigrant family. The transition from European ethnic to White American ethnic is, first of all, dependent upon the individual or family being identified as racially "White" (Baum, 2006). Although this sounds obvious, the prerequisites for being included in this category have altered dramatically over the years (Shackel, 2001). The nation has a long history of setting up a system of stratification, and access to the most exclusive levels of society were contingent upon not only physical characteristics, but also language, religious beliefs and practices, political affiliations, and economic stability.

The idea of "race" as a physical reality began to emerge in the 17th century, when the Anglican settlers in the colonies used the idea that "Black" Africans were a separate race from "White" Europeans, thereby justifying their enslaving of the Africans (Baum, 2006). The White race, then, became synonymous with the dominant culture in the Western Hemisphere, and the idea of race influenced not only social interactions but also political decisions, scientific inquiry, and theological positions for decades (Baum, 2006; Shackel, 2001). Initially, the upper socioeconomic class in the United States was largely limited to wealthy, educated Protestants of English descent (Foner, 1998). Over time, and largely in response to new immigrants coming to the United States from more distant areas with more visible differences to the Anglo-Americans, the parameters for defining who was White became more inclusive. Learning to speak English, adopting "American" names, receiving an American education, and even marrying into a White family were all effective strategies for immigrants to assimilate into the Anglo-based White American culture (Sacks, 1998). Slowly, dominant culture expanded from only English heritage to include other English-speaking or Western and Northern European ethnicities such as German, French, and Scotch-Irish, although for an extensive period European descendants from the Mediterranean and Slavic areas were not as likely to be seen as White.

The world wars in Europe also had a profound effect on the development of the White American ethnicity. The atrocities of those wars, and particularly World War II, and the genocide based on ethnicity prompted many Americans to take a far more accepting view of others (Winawer & Wetzel, 2005). In addition, Americans of German descent, and to a lesser extent Italian descent, would often go "underground" and hide or deny their ethnic heritage by assimilating into the White American ethnicity (Winawer & Wetzel, 2005). In addition, a new, vast middle class was created when soldiers from families who were largely uneducated came home and attended college under the GI Bill (Sacks, 1998). Because the belief that the United States was a middle-class nation holding middle-class values played such a strong role in the national heritage (Loewen, 1995), access to a college education and subsequent middle-class wages provided the opportunity for previously excluded groups to enter the White American ethnicity, if they so chose. As with many interrelated issues, it is often difficult to tell how much becoming middle class helped families be accepted as White, or how much being accepted as White helped families earn middle-class wages (Sacks, 1998).

The Process of Becoming White

Today, we talk about acculturation as the process that non-White individuals learn about majority culture values and learn how to adapt to and work within White cultural settings. In spite of the degree to which an individual of color may acculturate, however, non-European individuals are rarely able to fully "become White." Although, European immigrants (and other immigrants who can trace their family histories back to Europe, such as many South Africans or Australians) can become White. There is strong debate over the process of becoming White, particularly around to what degree non-English and/or non-Christians who appear White choose to become or are coerced into becoming White (e.g., Kaye-Kantrowitz, 2000). That discussion, although a worthy one, is beyond the scope of this text. Instead, this section will focus on describing the process of becoming White, and its implications on individuals and families who make that transition. We hope that you will consider reflecting on your own family's process of becoming White as relevant (see Reflection 14.5), and we have provided our stories of becoming White (see Reflection 14.6).

When individuals become White, the privileges associated with being in the majority culture come along with it. However, the process also has its clear disadvantages. Most importantly, individuals must give up a degree of their original cultural identity in order to fully become White. This process is problematic in that much of what is most meaningful about the culture of origin is lost. No doubt, this is at least partly why so many White Americans have difficulty understanding the concept of culture generally and their own culture specifically. At some point, cultural identity was worked out of the equation. People may know that they have Scottish, Italian, Czech, or Russian background, but those identities may not be very salient or meaningful to the individual. In addition, this process can cause conflict and tension between members of a family, or between families and the larger community. A family who is "upwardly mobile" may be discounted by their own cultural/ethnic groups for striving to be White. Similarly, members of a family may be seen as "too

White," even when family members encouraged the acculturation process. Individuals might be experiencing internal struggles, feeling pressures from the dominant culture to just be "normal," like everyone else and it the process they might lose their source of wellness, stemming from cultural practices that were repressed by those in position of power, without ever feeling fully accepted by the dominant culture.

REFLECTION 14.5

When did your family become White? For readers who identify as White American or European American, identify your European heritage. What does that heritage mean to you? What cultural values and/or traditions are most salient to you? How does your heritage affect who you are today?

Think back on your family history and try to identify when you believe your family became White? Although becoming White is a process, there are often significant events we can identify that signal significant shifts. If you are not sure, ask family members about events that may have indicated steps toward becoming fully White.

EUROPEAN AMERICAN HETEROGENEITY

REFLECTION 14.6   ETHNIC IDENTITY STATEMENTS OF THE THREE AUTHORS

H. George McMahon

My most prominent, perhaps pervasive, cultural identity comes from what I consider a culture of privilege. Having grown up a White male from a well-educated, professional family provided me with numerous opportunities and a degree of freedom that most people do not have. Part of the reason I believe this privilege plays such a prominent role in my perspective on the world is because privilege is, by its very nature, invisible to the privileged. The assumptions that I began to construct about the world and about people were perceived through glasses I was not aware I was wearing. In my professional career I have worked diligently at understanding my own culture and how my cultural perspective influences how I perceive the world. Becoming aware of my culture and my privilege has not meant that they no longer play a part in my worldview; rather, it is the awareness that I do indeed see the world through such a cultural lens that now plays a prominent role as I construct my worldview. I still see the world how I see it, for I can see it no other way; but I now understand that my view, while accurate for me, is quite a limited perspective. While I could talk about specific cultural frameworks, such as my being White American, being male, or being from an upper-middle socioeconomic status (SES), I believe the implications of each of these cultural views is absorbed in the overall culture of privilege, and I cannot separate them from each other.

Although the nature of privilege is that it is invisible to the privileged, it does not mean that the privileged are not aware, at least on some level, of the implications of race, ethnicity, gender, and other socioeconomic variables. I remember, for instance, a dream I had when I was a young boy, probably about third or fourth grade. I remember walking into the lobby of the office building where my father worked, a grand marble covered lobby in a 50-story building. I walked up to the security guard (who was African American in my dream) at the desk in front of the elevator bank and announced, "I'm Daddy's son." The guard smiled and said "go ahead" as he quickly waved me through. Even at such a young age, I was aware on some level that my lineage would grant me access to places and people that were off limits to so many others.

Regarding my specific ethnicity, I am, like many White Americans, of mixed ancestry. My ethnic background as I understand it is primarily British and Irish, with some French, French Canadian, and Choctaw. However, these identities mean little to me as far as my values and outlook on life. This is likely because for the most part, I was raised to be White American, not Irish American or Choctaw. One aspect of my identity that is very salient to me, however, is

(continued)

that I identify as a New Orleanian. This aspect of my identity means far more to me than ethnicity, and I am very aware of the influence the culture of my home city has on my outlook and my values. I believe that this is partly because the history of New Orleans is influenced by French, Spanish, Caribbean, and Indian values, which makes it quite unique among American cities. The pace of the city, therefore, is slow, with less value on a strong work ethic and achievement and more value placed on enjoying the moment and living life to its fullest. Although I usually identify myself as a White male, and I know that those aspects of my identity are very important, I believe that others must understand my New Orleans heritage in order to truly know me.

I am also aware that this part of my identity has become more meaningful after the tragedies surrounding Hurricanes Katrina and Rita. Although I was not directly involved in the storms or their aftermath, many friends and family were, and my city was. Like so many other New Orleanians, the tragedy brought a stronger sense of solidarity and kinship among its citizens, a process I imagine other non-White groups have experienced throughout American history.

Pamela O. Paisley

As a European American, my ethnic heritage is somewhat mixed. While predominately Scottish and English, I also have a bit of background from Germany and Italy. I grew up in a community that was heavily Scottish, where the Highland Games are still observed each October and the small college located there was named for the woman, Flora MacDonald, who helped Bonnie Prince Charles escape. We were taught the Highland Fling in elementary school and were aware of an array of tartans appropriate for kilts based on a variety of family names or clans.

My own awareness of cultural difference was also impacted by context and several critical incidents. I grew up in a county in North Carolina that, in addition to European Americans, also had significant populations of African Americans and Native Americans. All three groups had their own school systems. My first year in high school was the first year of a freedom of choice policy in which students from any high school could optionally request to attend another school. One African American male and two Native American (Lumbee) females opted to join our class. At the beginning of my senior year, the Black and White high schools were merged. A few more Native Americans had joined our class across the years, but the county Lumbee schools were not at that time required to merge. In May of 1969, I graduated with the first integrated class in my community. I am not sure how others in my class internalized that experience then or reflect upon it now, but I have always been so grateful to have been a part of that group. It was not always easy and we had to work through a great deal, but that experience introduced me to a set of conversations that I continue to be engaged in and committed to today.

At this point in my own development related to issues of diversity and social justice, I am committed to continuing my journey of self-discovery and staying fully engaged in the conversation—even when those discussions are very difficult. I am interested in understanding my own heritage and cultural values and am also committed to systemic social change. This journey requires awareness of my own privilege as well as challenging stereotypes, oppression, and injustice on a variety of dimensions of difference. To understand myself and the privileged society in which I have been sometime invisibly advantaged, I have to be in honest, authentic relationships with others who are different from me. I am very fortunate to have graduate students, colleagues, and friends who challenge me daily to be a better version of myself and to question what I think I know. I am trying to make peace internally with embracing my English, Scottish, German, and Italian heritage while also owning the historical and current injustices that are perpetuated by using a European American (particularly Anglo) cultural standard to the disservice of other groups. I have accepted that privilege is not something that I can "get over." Instead, commitment to social justice means a certain vigilance regarding awareness. In this process, I also try to avoid "White guilt" about these issues as I don't find that very helpful or productive. There is not anything inherently wrong with my being White or being European American. My energy is better spent in challenging oppression and social injustice.

Bogusia Molina

I am a great-granddaughter of the people of the land, Polanie, in Polish. My ancestors come from Polish, Hungarian, Austrian, and German backgrounds. My maternal grandmother, one of my best teachers of lessons for living, used to say: "I never left my town or moved, and yet I got to live in three different countries." My ancestors lived in the same geographic location as I did until I was 14—I come from a town called Cieszyn—which means, more or less, a place of joy. Like any place on Mother Earth, it is a beautiful place where creeks rumble through the valleys, winds dance through the mountains and some fields are still filled with hay, and children and even adults still often dance, dance to the rhythm of life and yearning for love and acceptance, despite numerous systemic pressures. Singing, dancing, creating crafts together, and finding a way to honor relationships and life was deeply valued in my family, community, and society. As a child, in many ways my life was still privileged because my family was lucky to live in a home on a small piece of farm land, while others around us were stuck waiting for a small apartment, for over 10 years, as after World War II Poland and its life was destroyed. I was also privileged as in my family and school systems, the word *culture* or being cultured meant knowing and understanding other cultures through literature, arts, and accomplishments.

I was and I am very proud of being Polish and that does not mean I devalue others. I was surprised and did not know until my family moved to the United States that being Polish sometimes for those in positions of power (whether real or perceived) implies that we are the "stupid ones"—I was shocked by the jokes and lack of understanding that are even perpetuated by the textbooks from which young generations learn. I was saddened that people even in the '80s were encouraged to change their names and to give up their identity just to be superficially accepted by the "in crowd." I was surprised to read in textbooks that Marie Curie was listed as a Frenchwoman, although her premarried name was Sklodowski—she was Polish and happened to marry a Frenchman. Copernicus is studied in Western Civilization with no mention that he was Polish, and Chopin's name was spelled in an "American" way, while it really is Szopen. I was surprised when I was encouraged by an American, a government official, to change my first name when I chose to be an American. He said there would be no fee and I told him, "sir, I am keeping my name which was given to me by my family. My grandmother chose it and I am keeping it. Aren't we free in this country to be who we are?" And still today, I wonder who is free to be who they are? Although my ancestors and family members, and to certain extent I, have encountered experiences with difficult, oppressive messages, I still have the privilege of looking "White." I recognize that the privilege of being White can be misused and at the same time is an opportunity to join the walk on a path that strives for finding ways to truly give voice to suffering that still surrounds us, and to care for each other through mutuality where differences are valued, acknowledged, and not viewed as deficiencies.

As a woman I am very aware of the cultural identity construction, including cultural camouflaging, that can enter any culture and justify mistreatment of women, children, or anyone who might be viewed as the vulnerable ones and in the process restrict opportunities for men and women to form and foster relationships based on acceptance and caring for each other without rigid roles being assigned to either gender.

I am aware that I have lived in the United States much longer than I have in Poland and that being an American is also important to me. To me that means always remembering that I am a granddaughter of the people of the land, a daughter of brave people who gave up their motherland and moved to the United States in the hopes of a better future for their children—but a better future never at the cost of hurting others. Most importantly to me, I believe that just like my children, and everyone's children, we are children of the universe, global visitors passing in time and place. I am lucky that others took time to care for me, and perhaps now more than ever I need to be mindful and search for ways through which caring for others can remain the rhythm of the dance of living.

As with other ethnic groups, European Americans have a myriad of intragroup differences, and understanding these differences is vital to understanding an individual. Several within-group variables can vastly affect the cultural views and the behavioral manifestations of those views, including specific European ethnic identity, socioeconomic class and educational level, geographic variables, religious views, generational differences, and nonethnic marginalized group identity (such as ability status or relationship orientation). One of the most prominent variables accounting for intragroup differences, however, among European Americans and White American ethnics is the degree to which individuals identify with their European heritage. There is great diversity among European ethnicities along several lines including focus on achievement, individual or group focus, gender roles, conceptualizations of family, and treatment of elderly people. This is particularly true of recent European immigrants, who may be more likely to identify with the ethnic identities and values of their home culture. Even over long periods of time, some European groups have assimilated into the White American ethnicity to a greater degree while others have been more intentional about holding on to their heritage (McGoldrick, Giordano, & Garcia-Preto, 2005). For instance, German Americans actually make up the largest percentage of European American ancestry among White Americans, although the German influence is often muted (Winawer & Wetzel, 2005). Italian Americans (particularly from southern Italy), on the other hand, maintain strong familial and ethnic allegiances and often value *la via vecchia*, or the traditional way of living (Giordano, McGoldrick, & Klages 2005). Differences among European groups that make up the White American ethnicity are described further in Table 14.3.

TABLE 14.3 Common European Group Values

European Ethnicity	Common Cultural Values and/or Characteristics
Anglo-American	Freedom of the individual, psychological individualism, self-reliance, hard work, insight and reason, autonomy, strong future orientation, prize individual achievement, value external signs of success, see themselves as dominant in structure of the natural world
Dutch American	Self-reliance, individualism, strong sense of faith (Calvinism), ambitious, hardworking, frugal, peace-loving, strong sense of community, internally principled, private, open-minded, receptive, tolerant
French Canadian Franco American	Self-reliance, resourcefulness, persistence, tenacity, duty, self-preservation, centrality of family life, traditional gender roles, appreciation for life's simple pleasures, emotional self-control; values shaped by Catholicism, the French language, family, work, and conservatism
German American	Self-reliance, emotional restraint, industriousness, hard work, loyalty, reliability, structure and hierarchy, family life, well-defined boundaries, privacy; work ethic grounded in thoroughness, craftsmanship, and attention to detail; interest in books, learning, and education
Greek American	Strong family connections and religious traditions/rituals (Greek Orthodox), patriarchal family structure, strong gender roles
Irish American	Emotional restraint, strong sense of faith (Catholic), personal responsibility, a sense of human powerlessness, paradoxes: dreamers, yet hard workers; good humored, hospitable, gregarious, yet avoid intimacy; conformity, compliance, respectability, yet eccentric
Italian American	Strong familial affiliation, unique and culturally specific practice of Catholicism, dependence within family and independence from outsiders, code of obligations regulating relationships, adaptability, pragmatism, resilience; capacity for savoring the present through family gatherings, music, food
Jewish American	Emotional expression, strong sense of history and tradition, closeness and shared suffering, value intellectual achievement and financial success
Polish American	Collectivist; sense of belonging and connection with family, community, region; strong work ethic and commitment to raising children; sentimental and emotionally expressive
Scotch-Irish American	Family, clan, and warrior ethic; frontier spirit matching cultural history of danger, importance of extended family
Scandinavian American	Egalitarian relationships with suspicion of authority, determination, industriousness, stoic, pragmatic, independent and self-reliant yet believe in collective or civic responsibility, solution-focused

Source: McGoldrick, Giordano, and Garcia-Preto (2005).

In *Ethnicity & Family Therapy* (McGoldrick et al., 2005), the authors clearly take the position that, although there is a potential for "fusion of people and cultures" through intermarriage and inter-mingling of groups, "ethnicity will continue to be a distinguishing characteristic even for European Americans for a long time to come" (p. 503). They further acknowledge the complexity and elusiveness of ethnicity as a concept in part due to its basis in both conscious and unconscious processes. They note that "shared ethnic heritage hardly produces homogeneity of thought, emotions, or group loyalty" (p. 503) and in reality can be mitigated by class, gender, region, or personal circumstance. Nonetheless, there are certain values or characteristics that are, if not culture specific at least culture associated, for a variety of groups including those falling under the larger umbrella of European American. With these qualifiers in mind, differences among European groups that make up the White American ethnicity are described further in Table 14.3. (For more detailed descriptions of cultural histories, values, characteristics, and contexts, see Chapters 36 to 48 in *Ethnicity & Family Therapy.*)

Certainly, socioeconomic class also plays a key role in the variance among White American ethnics. The process of becoming middle class or upper class assumes, at least to some extent, the adoption of values, styles, and behaviors that are more typical of the general White American ethnicity. In addition, many of the prerequisites for becoming middle or upper class are connected to ethnic identity. For instance, the more education a student has and the more work experience a person has, particularly white-collar or professional work, the more he or she has been indoctrinated into the White American ethnic values system. In addition, many ethnic enclaves, which help perpetuate ethnic identity, are lower- or lower-middle-class areas.

Geography can also have a significant effect upon variance within the White American ethnic. Part of this difference is historical, going back to the initial British immigrations. Anglos immigrated to the United States in four distinct waves, with each wave coming from a different area of England and bringing with them different values. These four waves also settled in different parts of the United States, setting the tones for regional differences. The Puritans, who largely settled in New England, valued an ordered world whereas the Cavaliers, who settled largely in the southern colonies, believed that freedom meant the right to choose how to live and to conduct business without the interference of others. The Quakers, who largely settled in the Mid-Atlantic and the Midwest, valued privacy and respected the privacy of others while the Appalachian and southwestern immigrants from Scotland and northern England, whose history was strongly affected by unceasing violence, valued self-preservation and protection over a formal education, which may be seen as an invasion. These initial value systems can be seen as influential in many ways today, including voting patterns, approaches to state and local governments, and even the disproportionate numbers of individuals from Appalachia and the Southwest volunteering for military service (and militias) (McGill & Pearce, 2005).

Other geographic variables such as climate and terrain can certainly have an effect, from the northern midwestern U.S. values of hard work, planning, and saving (to manage tough winters) to the more laid-back approaches of Southern California where goods are available year-round. Density of population can also affect how one approaches social life, as can the multiple options for entertainment that large cities can provide, versus the simpler approach to country living. Many larger cities develop their own cultures as well (think New York, Chicago, San Francisco, or New Orleans). These individual differences may develop for a variety of reasons, such as differing immigration patterns (New Orleans is more influenced by French, Spanish, and Caribbean immigrants than by British), or by the nature of the variety of influences (e.g., New York being the port of entry for so many European immigrants).

Other variables influence within-group heterogeneity as well. Religious affiliations, and differing views within those affiliations, can have profound effects on values. Although the original

Anglo-Americans were virtually all Protestant, many Catholics, Jews, and Eastern Orthodox are often included in the White American ethnic (Langman, 2000; Sacks, 1998). Even within the Protestant group, there are multiple variations, from strict fundamentalist to liberal approaches. Generational differences are also apparent, as younger generations of White American ethnics have far more exposure to people from a variety of backgrounds and may be more comfortable with and accepting of differences than previous generations.

Many White American ethnics may also be part of marginalized groups that are not based on ethnicity. People of varying levels of ability may experience discrimination, which may provide a different perspective on the role of privilege in our culture. Similarly, LGBTQI (lesbian, gay, bisexual, transgender, questioning [queer], and intersex) individuals may be White Americans, yet their orientation may play a central role in their identity, and will thus identify with the more open and liberal values and lifestyle common to LGBTQI culture than mainstream White America. Both ability and sexual orientation can vary on the degree to which these identities are visible, which may also affect how one identifies herself or himself. As is the case when understanding an individual from any cultural background, it should be clear that individuals must be understood and appreciated among a variety of identities rather than simply understood as a representative of their ethnic background.

RECENT EUROPEAN AMERICAN IMMIGRANTS

Although in the contemporary media and government the term *immigrants* is often used to refer to non-European immigrants, it is important to remember that the families of all White American ethnics were, at some time, immigrants. Currently, 53 nationalities have been identified within the larger European American umbrella, ranging in number from German American descendents (approximately 43 million) to Cypriot Americans (approximately 7,600) (McGoldrick et al., 2005). European immigration continues, and in 2003 immigrants of European descent represented approximately 30% of documented immigrants. Current European immigrant children and families continue to represent a very broad range of diverse and intercultural groups. The following section will describe the experiences of recent European Immigrants. In particular, stressors related to immigration, conflicts with majority culture, and the acculturation process of recent European immigrants will be discussed.

Immigration Stressors

Like immigrants from any culture, the path of life for many European immigrants has been filled with a variety of stressors, often paired with a loss of previously utilized coping resources. Although in many ways European immigrants face similar challenges as other immigrant groups, the fact that European immigrants may share physical and cultural features with the dominant culture in the United States can lead to acculturation issues and pressures that are quite unique to European immigrant populations. Immigrants might experience a process similar to grieving when adjusting to living in a new country. Navigating through these complexities can be very challenging, especially when isolation and shame become part of daily life experiences. Losses associated with a sense of disconnect from one's community, family, and friends along with experiences of being devalued and silenced frequently penetrate the lives of immigrant families and children. Having to relearn or rediscover conveniences previously taken for granted, such as the layout of a new city, becoming aware of the resources available in the community, and having to find new stores, doctors, and the like can make the transition even more stressful.

For immigrants coming from non-English-speaking countries, the difficulties those immigrants may face when trying to communicate with people in their new community can also cause problems. These problems are particularly severe with first- and second-generation immigrants. Not only are the communication difficulties stressful, but the pressure to learn a new language, particularly at an advanced age, adds additional stress, primarily because the subtle microaggressions that non-English-speakers or people learning the English language often encounter can greatly add to the level of discomfort (Sue, Capodilupo, et al., 2007).

Acculturation

The process of acculturation is often described as adapting to White American ethnic (based in Anglo Protestant) lifestyles, values, and language (McGoldrick et al., 2005). The process of acculturation of several different racialized and ethnic groups has been examined and their ability to adapt, accept, and be accepted by the dominant group. The process is similar for immigrants of European descent, but with some significant differences as well. For instance, simply by the nature of looking "White," immigrants from European countries might not be viewed as foreigners, or may have an easier time assimilating (or being assumed to have assimilated) into the White American ethnic culture. Their physical "Whiteness" can lead to unexamined patterns of privilege and quicker opportunities for receiving the benefits of being seen as White. This often presents an opportunity, if not pressure, for immigrants to assimilate into mainstream American culture, but sometimes at the expense of their cultural heritage.

Just as non-White individuals are often assumed to be rather unacculturated to dominant culture in America (e.g., Sue, Capodilupo, et al., 2007), it may be that recent European immigrants, in particular those with good English skills, may be assumed to be more acculturated than they are. Several factors can affect the process of English-language acquisition, including whether families live in ethnic enclaves, the usage of English in the home, access to native-language media, and school support for English as a second language (ESL) programs while showing appreciation for native languages.

Moreover, because communication plays such an important role in adolescent socialization, children and adolescents are often more motivated to learn English in order to establish relationships with their peers. Although it is developmentally appropriate for children and adolescents to want to connect with and be like their peers, it is also important to consider that immigrant children might experience rejection and isolation within their family and community system when forming unions with individuals from diverse backgrounds. This is true not only in childhood, but as second-generation European Americans become adults and seek intimate relationships with people outside their Ethnic group.

Cultural conflicts can also come into play around family structure and gender roles with recent European immigrants. Many European immigrant families may hold onto traditional roles for the family, including father as primary authority and mother as primary nurturer and caretaker of the family. If mothers do hold jobs outside the home, it is often done without relieving any domestic duties or giving "room" to taking care of herself as that would be viewed as selfish. Furthermore, sons are often given more freedom than daughters (who are expected to stay close to home), and the welfare of the elderly family members is a high priority. This can lead to difficulties within immigrants families in the United States, where it is more common for men and women to share responsibility for the home and family (at least to a greater degree) and daughters have more freedom to pursue careers than in some European countries.

The difference in family structure can also lead to intrafamily stressors, particularly as children and adolescents are exposed to the majority culture within the United States. Adolescents may feel conflicted as they begin to adopt the values and lifestyle of the majority culture in school and with their friends, yet are expected to keep their European ethnic values and traditions at home. Furthermore, the focus on youth in American culture can increase feelings of isolation and even worthlessness in elderly immigrants, who were often treated with more respect in their homelands.

Oppression and Discrimination

Like most other U.S. immigrants, immigrants from Europe have faced and continue to face discrimination in a variety of ways when arriving in the United States. Many European cultural groups have been negatively stereotyped in mainstream U.S. culture by other cultural groups. Overt discrimination is more likely to exist when the immigrants have more visible or more dramatic differences from the majority culture. For instance, immigrants who do not speak English or who have strong accents, those who have ethnic names, and those who have less Anglo-Nordic physical attributes, such as Mediterranean or Easter European immigrants, are more likely to face active discrimination.

In addition to more overt forms of discrimination, European immigrants may face more subtle, but just as damaging, systemic oppression. For instance, immigrants who have poor English-language skills are far more likely to be employed or underemployed, often regardless of their skill level or education. Similarly, because many European countries' education systems are very different from the U.S. education system, immigrants may be much better educated than they are given credit for by U.S. employers.

COUNSELING CONSIDERATIONS FOR EUROPEAN DESCENT INDIVIDUALS

An important factor to consider when understanding mental health concerns of Americans of European descent is that mental well-being and pathology are largely Western European constructs. Like the concept of psychopathology and diagnosis, "traditional" approaches to counseling have long been considered White European male constructs (Sue et al., 1992). Many of the early theorists were White males of European or European American descent, and thus their approaches were developed within their cultural context. Evidence for this can be seen in the individual focus of many early therapy styles, the focus on individual responsibility, and the use of the medical model to describe diagnoses among others. In fact, disruption of autonomous functioning is a major consideration for diagnosis of just about any mental health issue as defined by the most recent edition of the *Diagnostic and Statistical Manual of Mental Disorders (DSM–IV–TR)*. Thus, the "culture" of counseling and what is deemed mental health mirrors the cultural values of White American ethnicity. However, adherence to White American ethnic cultural values can create mental health concerns that should not be minimized. Risks for mental illness are even greater for newly immigrated Europeans given immigration and acculturative stress and oppression experiences.

Mental Health Issues of White American Ethnic Clients

HANK:	Luanne, sometimes life throws you a curve ball. Now there's two ways you can deal with it. You can cry—and that's the path you've chosen—or you can *not* cry.
LUANNE:	How do you not cry?
HANK:	Well, instead of letting it out, try holding it in. Every time you have a feeling, just stick it into a little pit inside your stomach and never let it out.
LUANNE *(TRYING IT)*:	Are you supposed to have a pain under your rib?

HANK: Yes. That's natural. The body doesn't want to swallow its emotions. But now you go ahead and put that pain inside your stomach too.

LUANNE: I think it's workin', Uncle Hank. I feel sick, but not sad.

(Hank Hill and Luanne Platter, King of the Hill,
in Lieberstein, Fino, and Shinagawa [1997])

Understanding the role that cultural values such as meritocracy and individualism/independence, conflicts resulting from changing values within the culture, and conflicts between personal and cultural values may play in the mental health of White American ethnics can be important. The cultural belief in a meritocracy where all individuals start from a roughly even playing field may provide some people with hope, but it can also lead to feelings of inferiority and shame over perceived failures. If poor White American ethnics believe that the United States is a true meritocracy, then they risk carrying the double burden of feeling oppressed by the upper classes as well as guilt and shame for not having been more successful. Middle-class White Americans are not protected from feelings of inadequacy either, as the forward and upward moving society puts pressure on them to constantly do better. Even the wealthy individuals may suffer from a fear of inadequacy, believing that they must continue to perform or risk slipping to lower class (McGill & Pearce, 2005).

As mistakes are inevitable in life, and shame is a common side effect of the perceived "failures" of White American ethnics, many Americans develop coping strategies for dealing with such negative emotions. Scapegoating, often in the form of oppression of and discrimination against a particular ethnic, racial, or other cultural group, is a common way the White American ethnics deal with their feelings of inadequacy and inferiority. These feelings or frustration and fear of inadequacy can be rechanneled into work or hobbies, or can come out as anger toward others, particularly family members (McGill & Pearce, 2005).

The Calvinist idea that good fortune is evidence of righteousness and predestined salvation leads to not only feelings of inadequacy but also to problems when tragedies strike. Without any sense of adaptive fatalism in the White American ethnic, people are often confused over tragedy and believe it to be "unfair" when bad things happen to "good people" (McGill & Pearce, 2005). This adds an additional component to tragedy, where individuals are struck with dealing with loss, and also ask the existential question "why me?" and deal with feelings of victimization by an unfair situation.

The White American ethnic value placed upon independence and individualism, particularly when taken in conjunction with the notions of meritocracy and the Calvinist work ethic, can lead to difficulties as well. As most White American ethnics believe that struggles in life should be overcome by individual effort, it follows that a failure to overcome an obstacle is seen as being due to personal weakness. Furthermore, because asking for help is often seen as an admission of failure, people and families commonly build rigid boundaries and adopt a "no-help necessary" policy. These boundaries protect individuals and families from being pitied by others, but they further isolate themselves from the help they need in the process (McGill & Pearce, 2005). As individuals and families retreat further from help, they may mask painful feelings with alcohol and other substances, or may develop patterns of abusive behavior (Fall, Howard, & Ford, 1999).

Many of the cultural beliefs cited have also contributed to feelings of inadequacy among many White American ethnic women. The White American ethnicity, like many of the European cultural systems from which it has developed, has traditionally been patriarchal. Many women whose role was to manage the house and family felt inadequate or depressed because their contributions were "devalued," and earned no material benefits to demonstrate their worth. As the role of women has changed in recent years in response to the feminist movement, many women now work outside the home (for unequal pay, and thus, unequal value) while maintaining many of the domestic responsibilities they held previously (McGill & Pearce, 2005).

There are also inconsistencies within the larger culture that contribute to stress and frustration for White American ethnics. Perhaps most obviously, Americans have always stated their belief in individual liberty, yet have an ongoing history of denying liberty to others. Religious and cultural values held by most White American ethnics encourage individuals to feel guilty for transgressions, but being accountable is often viewed as admitting fault, which indicates weakness and often leads to feelings of guilt. Moreover, the future orientation of the culture leads many people to prefer "moving ahead" rather than "dwelling on the past" (McGill & Pearce, 2005).

Cultural values also play a role in many family struggles within the White American ethnicity. Certainly, the focus on the individual can mean that the family good is often sacrificed for the good of the individual within the family, particularly when that individual is in a power position. Likewise, because problems are seen as individual problems, they are less likely to be discussed within the family in order to protect both the family member who is struggling (from shame) and the other members (from the burden of being asked to help).

The individual focus can also lead to problems during childrearing. Historically, White American ethnic children have been expected to be rather self-sufficient early, and in many communities were expected to work as soon as they were able. Individuation from the family is widely valued, but the timing of the individuation can have profound effects on the future development of the child (McGill & Pearce, 2005). Children who are given too much responsibility too quickly are at risk for entering a "false adulthood with premature identity foreclosure" (p. 456), and may feel ignored and powerless to get their developmental needs met. Those who are protected longer than the norm are termed "enmeshed," and are often ridiculed for their dependence on their families.

Individualism may play a role in marriage problems as well. In spite of the romantic notion of marriage popularly portrayed through American media, many approach marriage among the majority culture in the United States as little more than a contractual arrangement that is designed to meet each person's individual needs (McGill & Pearce, 2005). When one partner is no longer getting what he or she needs from the relationship, divorce is an acceptable alternative. Even with the high divorce rate, however, divorce can still be a very traumatic experience, at least in part because it is commonly viewed as a personal failure on the part of one or both spouses, leading once again to feelings of anger and/or guilt.

The value on youth and the characteristics commonly associated with youth (e.g., beauty, athleticism, freedom) within the White American ethnic also contributes to emotional difficulties, particularly with older White Americans and those who have disabilities. While other cultures place a great deal of respect on elder members of society for their wisdom, White American ethnics are more likely to complain about what they "lose" as they get older than the wisdom or respect they accumulate. As many White Americans reach old age and begin to lose independence, this loss of freedom is exacerbated by the feelings of guilt of being a "burden" to the family members who take responsibility for caring for them (or paying for their care).

What makes all of these issues even more difficult to identify is the common cultural norm that discourages expression of emotion, and in particular difficult emotions. It is important to keep in mind that many European Americans and White Americans grew up in cultures that valued self-control and self-sufficiency, which meant that suffering was often expected to be borne in silence so that others would not be burdened with problems that were seen as the individual's responsibility (Giordano et al., 2005). This is particularly true in the mental health field, where talking about personal problems with strangers is seen as a sign of weakness, but is also apparent in the medical fields, where studies show that Anglo males often visit the doctor only after long periods of suffering, and would continue seeing a doctor only if they believed they could be healed (McGoldrick et al., 2005). Even more drastic, studies have shown that Irish males and their descendents are particularly poor at seeking help to address physical pain, to the point where they have difficulty articulating the type of pain and even identifying where pain is located in their own bodies (McGoldrick et al.). In fact, many European and White Americans, in particular males, are not likely to seek help for emotional issues (such as sadness or worry) at all; instead, they will seek help only when they see their problems as a threat to their autonomous functioning (McGill & Pearce, 2005). Although many White Americans are willing to suffer in isolation, the thought of being dependent on others or risk having something affect their ability to work or be successful is more likely to bring them to counseling.

Counseling White American Ethnic Clients

Multicultural counseling was developed largely in response to a concern that traditional counseling methods may not be appropriate or as effective for non-White or non-Western clients (Sue et al., 1992). The argument was never that traditional counseling methods were not effective when the counselors and clientele were European or European American. In fact, there is a solid body of research indicating that traditional counseling methods are effective (e.g., Beutler, 2000; Lambert & Bergin, 1994), but the assumption is that these studies were largely completed with European or European American (and often male) counselors and European or European American clientele.

Although these traditional counseling methods (i.e., the recurring theories that take up the first 8 to 12 chapters of a standard theories book) are not considered multicultural theories or approaches, a closer look reveals that culture, particularly European and White American culture, plays a big role in the theoretical approaches. Specifically, many of these approaches simultaneously utilize and challenge the European cultural norms in order to affect change in the clients. For example, person-centered and other humanist approaches rely on the therapeutic relationship as the primary (and in some cases, sole) instrument of change. The therapeutic relationship valued by humanists, based on mutual respect, unconditional positive regard, nonjudgment, free expression, and accurate empathic understanding of another, is very different from the relationship many White Americans are used to, and it may be uncomfortable initially for White Americans who have been socialized to be guarded to enter into relationships where they are asked to and expected to share freely. Relationships that do not conform with White American cultural norms are also utilized in group counseling and therapy, where the group leaders intentionally create a climate within the group that is markedly different from the world outside, where group members are free to express themselves and ask for feedback without fear of reprimand or burdening others with their troubles. In these instances, the healing of counseling comes, at least in part, from helping clients step outside the limits their cultural norms may pose regarding their self-expression and the manner in which they relate to others.

Although many humanist approaches attempt to create relationships that are not in line with cultural norms in order to promote therapeutic change, other traditional theories utilize therapeutic relationships based on culturally appropriate aspects for Europeans Americans in order to build a solid working relationship. Psychodynamic, behaviorist, and some cognitive approaches place the therapist, the one who has external evidence of his status (e.g., degrees), in an expert role, directing the experience. Other approaches, such as Adlerian or reality therapy, suggest the relationship be democratic, which is different than an expert role, but no less Western. Moreover, many of these theories stress the importance of European and White American values in the healing process, such as accepting individual responsibility, committing to "work hard" (the client), valuing the client's right to privacy, and focusing on objective, measurable goals to indicate success. Additionally, the processes of change these approaches use often challenge thoughts or behavior patterns that are seen as maladaptive, but may be culturally appropriate. For instance, cognitive therapies attempt to identify maladaptive thoughts and change them to healthier, more adaptive ones, yet the maladaptive thoughts (e.g., "shoulding," self-reference, blaming) can be seen as grounded in the European or Anglo culture that says each individual is responsible for his or her life and where personal achievement (and the rewards of such achievement) is highly valued.

Adlerian counseling takes this notion further by attempting to understand each client's style of life, or way of understanding the world and one's place in it. The style of life is certainly influenced by one's culture, and embedded within each person's style of life are the roots of the struggles clients encounter. The personality priorities described by Adlerians to describe the patterns in which common styles of life often manifest, including pleasing, superiority, control, and comfort, can be seen as being grounded in European cultural expectations and the values of achievement, and self-reliance. At the same time, however, Adler emphasized the importance of belonging, and he valued a collectivist view where being a contributing part of the whole was healthier than holding power over others, a view that was somewhat of a departure from traditional Western European values. Furthermore, by helping clients bring their style of life into their awareness, a process that parallels the development of an understanding of one's worldview, Adlerian counselors can help their clients become more aware of the (cultural) principles that were guiding their lives, albeit out of the clients' awareness, and choose whether to change their behaviors or adopt a different set of values and view of the world at that point. Although many traditional approaches to counseling and therapy were grounded in Western values and the evidence shows these approaches are effective with European and White American populations, the feminist and multicultural movements have provided a great gift to counseling European Americans by adding the awareness of the role that culture plays in both the presentation of issues and in the helping process, and the realization that all counseling can be viewed as multicultural counseling (Sciarra, 1999). As counselors becoming aware of the cultural and power dynamics in society as well as within the counseling relationship, it becomes imperative that they attend to these dynamics in all situations, including White American counselors working with White American clients.

Although many counselors and counselors-in-training have been exposed to multicultural counseling practices, there is virtually no professional literature on the effective use of multicultural counseling approaches with White American clients. Following are ideas on how to conceptualize White American clients and facilitate the helping process with White American clients from a multicultural perspective. Implications for counselors of color working with White American clients will also be discussed.

When conceptualizing White American clients from a multicultural perspective, a primary consideration for counselors is to be aware of their own worldview they bring into the session, which includes not only their own cultural values but also the theoretical perspective from which they operate (Sue, Ivey, & Pedersen, 1996b). Inherent in all theories is a set of beliefs and techniques that are value-based, so understanding the values under the techniques and beliefs is critical. Second, counselors must understand the major cultural values underlying the White American ethnicity. Although it is true that many counselors of color may understand the White American culture from their own perspective by observing it (and often having it thrust upon them), it is important that they develop an understanding of the true cultural values underneath the practices and appreciate the worth those values hold in order to develop an accurate empathic understanding of those who are raised in the culture.

Counselors can then enter into counseling with an understanding of both their own worldview and the cultural base of the White American client. But as is true with multicultural counseling with other populations, it is not enough to know the general culture. Time must be spent in the counseling session to begin to understand the unique worldview of the White American client, which may be based in White American values but may also differ in significant ways due to a variety of social, geographic, generational, or personal factors and intersecting identities. D'Andrea and Daniels (1997) developed the RESPECTFUL counseling and development model as a guide to help identify and be mindful of several important dimensions of identity that may affect an individual's worldview within the larger culture. The term **RESPECTFUL** represents the following components:

R Religious/Spiritual identity

E Economic class background

S Sexual identity

P Psychological maturity

E Ethnic/Racial identity

C Chronological/Developmental challenges

T Trauma and other threats to one's well-being

F Family background and history

U Unique physical characteristics

L Location of residence and language differences

This model, developed to be used with clients from all backgrounds, may be particularly helpful in understanding White American clients who are often assumed to be culture-free, and thus these sorts of intentional cultural conceptualizations are commonly withheld.

It is important to remember that many White Americans, in particular older White Americans, may not be comfortable discussing their culture and in fact may be unclear about their cultural values, or even that their values are culturally based (Sue, 2004). Therefore, this discussion may begin as a more general discussion about beliefs, approaches to life, and so on. Discussing family traditions and legends, heroes and role models, and the like can also be ways to informally gather information about a client's worldview and values. It is also important to note that the term *values* is often used as an absolute rather than a relative term for some White Americans, particularly by politicians and in the media. This can be seen in the commonly used but vague term *family values,* which is often used to indicate that the speaker has the values that everyone recognizes as "family values" and that others do not. If values are described as an absolute within a counseling situation, it will be important for the counselor to help clients specifically identify what values they are talking about. This is not only a point of clarification for both counselor and client, but can help clients start the process of understanding values as relative rather than absolute entities.

Finally, as a counselor begins to develop a comprehensive conceptualization of the client's general cultural perspective and specific values and beliefs, the counselor can conceptualize the role that cultural conflicts may play in the presenting problem and/or in any underlying issues. These cultural conflicts may be understood as intracultural conflicts, where values and/or beliefs within the White American cultural framework are in conflict with one another or conflict with the reality of the situation. An example may include a client's feelings of guilt arising from his perception of himself as a failure, which may be based in a belief in the meritocracy and an absolute devotion to the principle of individual responsibility. Another example could be a mother's inner conflicting messages to nurture and protect her children without "babying" them, thereby frustrating their ability to be independent.

Conflicts can also arise between cultural beliefs and the client's personal beliefs, and in this way multicultural counseling with White Americans can be very similar to multicultural counseling with clients of color and other recent immigrants. The major difference is that non-White American clients may be more likely to understand the conflict as a cultural conflict (i.e., between "my culture and the dominant culture"). Because White Americans are less likely to be aware of "the dominant culture" in those terms, they may be more likely to personalize these differences, resulting in feelings like "I just don't fit in" or "No one understands me." Furthermore, White Americans whose personal beliefs are not consistent with the White American ethnic, risk labeling from the majority group, ranging from rather benign (but no less marginalizing) terms such as *liberal, creative,* or *marching to the beat of a different drummer,* to more indicting terms such as *traitor, freak,* or *deviant.*

As with all counseling relationships, establishing a relationship with the White American client is a crucial part of the helping process. Although the counselors' chosen theoretical perspective will suggest the style of therapeutic relationship that is seen as most helpful and outline a way of being with the client, there are some important relationship variables to consider when working with White American clients. Because many White Americans, in particular males, are taught to withhold expression of emotion, this may be particularly difficult at first. Instead, clients will often present their problems in terms of disruption of their autonomous functioning, and will want to set specific goals to work toward to combat fears of "wasting time." The White American value of hard work can actually be used to get clients to commit to the process of counseling, and even suggesting that the work will be difficult can present a challenge that many White American clients will want to rise to meet. In addition, many White American clients will appreciate the autonomy to do the work, but may also expect the counselor to provide some sense of guidance early in the counseling process and some feedback regarding progress. This style of relationship fits with different counseling approaches to varying degrees, but it is important to understand it is likely what White American clients will expect. If the counselor values a relationship that will look different, it would behoove the counselor to have an explicit discussion about his or her expectations for what the counseling relationship will look like.

Regarding the specific helping processes, there are several ways to take advantage of common counseling interventions in order to help White American clients from a multicultural perspective. As with most multicultural therapies, consciousness-raising will likely play an important part in the counseling process. Consciousness-raising, or helping clients develop insight or deepen awareness, has long been a staple of many modes of counseling and therapy (Prochaska & Norcross, 2007). In addition to whatever consciousness-raising activities a counselor's theoretical position may suggest, a multicultural counselor working with White Americans will also want to help build the client's cultural awareness in several different ways. First, helping clients fully understand their own culture and making the values of their culture explicit can be an important growth experience for many clients, helping to form a fuller and more accurate self-concept. In addition, counselors can help their clients better understand the power dynamics and the privilege that play out in their lives as a result of being White in America. As mentioned previously, many White Americans are unaware of their own culture and cultural values (McIntosh, 1989), and helping them become fully aware of the extent to which their Whiteness affects their lives can be a difficult process (Sue, 2004). However, this process can also be an important aspect of developing a full understanding of self, and a way to help clients live more authentically.

Finally, counselors can help their clients identify the cultural values and facilitate the process of examining the congruence between White American cultural values and the values of the individual within the culture. When clients have a better understanding of themselves as cultural beings, and a more accurate perception of self within a cultural context, they should be able to conceptualize their difficulties, thus being better able to get the help they need.

One of the more powerful gifts that effective consciousness-raising gives to clients is the ability to choose, something commonly valued by White American culture. When clients are unaware of their difficulties or the personal and systemic factors that affect their lives, their ability to choose how to help themselves remains limited as well. However, when clients become more aware of their surroundings and of choices they never knew they had, the act of choosing can become a form of self-liberation (Prochaska & Norcross, 2007). For instance, as a White American becomes more aware of and examines the cultural values inherent in the White American ethnicity, perhaps for the first time, she can choose whether and to what degree to hold those values on a personal level. Thus, when experiencing guilt or shame due to cultural expectations placed upon the individual, or struggling with isolation related to the White American culture's value of independence and self-reliance, clients can choose whether they want to accept these values or choose a new way of looking at their world and a new way of behaving. Likewise, if clients experience a conflict between a cultural value for achievement and a personal passion for spending time with the family, what may have previously felt like an impossible situation suddenly becomes a choice for the client.

Choosing can also play an important role in helping White American clients to live more according to the cultural values of freedom and equality for all people. As they become more aware of the role privilege plays in their lives, they can choose to continue accepting the privilege, choose not to accept privilege when it is not appropriate, or even work to promote a social justice agenda in which some "privileges," such as not having to worry about being ignored or maltreated in public, are extended to all people rather than just the privileged (McIntosh, 1989). This form of choosing is consistent with social advocacy and social justice, and can help White Americans live in ways that are more consistent with the values of the culture.

Although the need for multicultural counseling may be viewed in terms of White American counselors working with clients of color, it is important to remember that counselors of color need to work multiculturally as well. Regardless of the ethnicity, multicultural counselors need to have an awareness of both their own cultural values and the cultural background of their clients (Sue et al., 1992). Cross-cultural counseling is sometimes approached with trepidation regarding the ability to establish a therapeutic relationship, but the reality may be that cross-cultural relationships may be particularly therapeutic *because* they are cross cultural. In an instance of a counselor of color working with White American clients, the counselor's perspective of White American culture can add a new perspective to the client's exploration of her culture. Moreover, through the client's self-disclosure of her own cultural perspective, White American clients can begin to see their own values as relative rather than absolute truths. The same process can be used to help White American clients increase their awareness of privilege, in which culturally aware counselors of colors should be able to identify quite readily.

It is also important for counselors of color to fully develop the therapeutic relationship with their clients and to use this relationship to further develop therapeutic insight and encourage the therapeutic process for the White American client. Although counselors of color may be nervous about how White American clients would view them, most White Americans prefer to assume worth and respect on individuals (if not always groups of people), in particular people with whom they establish personal relationships (McGill & Pearce, 2005). Thus, whatever biases White American clients may have about ethnicities, they are likely to treat their counselor with respect. This tendency can be used to help build relationships, but can also be used during the working stage of therapy to build awareness of and critically examine the clients' biases. Finally, it is important that counselors of color working with White American clients remember that they have a great opportunity to model an appropriate process for cross-cultural understanding and respect for different cultural values and practices. It may be a strange position for White Americans to be in a position where they are asked to explain their culture to someone else (particularly someone seen in somewhat of a power position), but this experience can be very eye opening and growth producing by itself.

Mental Health Issues of European Immigrants

There seems to be a greater effort in understanding the losses and challenges associated with immigration through media exposure, scholarly works, and community-based interventions, but the challenges facing immigrants remain. Numerous researchers have identified experiences and challenges associated with immigration (e.g., Chun & Akutsu, 2003; Santisteban & Mitrani, 2003). These challenges, particularly when paired with a loss of connectedness and feelings of being misunderstood or not accepted, can lead to feelings of guilt, fear, anger, sadness, and depression to immigrant children and families. A lack of harmony and balance might become part of the fabric of living while experiences of lack of acceptance and respect further give voice to sorrow, pain, isolation, and fear.

One of the primary strains European immigrants will encounter is the cultural conflict between the dominant culture in America and the culture of their home countries. Learning a new culture and having to adapt to new expectations, particularly in the workplace and in school, is a strain in and of itself. This process is particularly difficult for older immigrants, who are likely to more closely identify with their home country culture and more likely to resist acculturation to U.S. cultural norms. In addition, generational differences in identification with home country culture and American culture can lead to further conflict within the family.

The stress of the transition and the financial problems often associated with immigration put a severe strain on many immigrants, and can lead to conflicts within the marriage as well. These stressors can be exacerbated when couples feel pressure to change their spousal roles, particularly when coming from a more formal patriarchal system and moving to a community in the United States where marriages are viewed from a more egalitarian perspective. Couples who are not married, single parents, GLBTQI couples, and other non-male–female married couples may face further discrimination depending on the community in which they settle.

European immigrant adults may initially seek counseling services due to employment and/or financial concerns as a result of their transition, often through employee assistance programs. European immigrants face a variety of the same stressors other immigrants face, including being discriminated against, being underemployed, feeling undervalued, and lacking a social support network. Loss of self-esteem at work can occur when language barriers prevent adults from working in previous careers, and from being perceived as being less educated and/or skilled due to language difficulties. In addition, the loss of financial resources and increased stress that comes from being unemployed or underemployed can result in family stress, particularly for males from patriarchal cultures, who may feel they cannot provide for their families.

In such cases where European immigrants are facing self-esteem and/or self-efficacy threat, one way to encourage individuals to clarify their identity, both within the context of their home culture and American culture, is to explore their source of wellness. For example, Garrett and Garrett (2002) describe Native American perspectives relevant to wellness and healing, leading to centering and feeling grounded. Reflective questions such as "Where do I belong? What do I do well? What is my source of independence—what do I stand for? What can I offer others? " are examples of questions that invite reflection and tapping into one's inner wisdom (Garrett, 1998). Various other models relevant to wellness are available as well, but counselors using a wellness model not based on White American values could both model multicultural respect and help their clients conceptualize wellness beyond the potentially restrictive boundaries of White American values. When the family has children, further stressors can occur over identity development. Conflicts often occur over how the different generations identify with and value the majority culture. Parents may have mixed feelings about wanting their children to acculturate in some ways (e.g., being successful in school) but may feel comfortable with some acculturation (e.g., American social norms, dating behavior, independence) and may not want their children to lose their original ethnic identity. This process of becoming bicultural can be difficult for children and adolescents to understand and to navigate, and can lead to confusion, frustration, and guilt on both the part of the parents and the children.

European immigrant children and adolescents seeking counseling or psychological services will often be first identified within the school system, and are often first identified for academic concerns. Language differences, the pace of the academic learning environment, and the individualistic structure of many classrooms may lead to students feeling overwhelmed with the new demands of the school. In addition, the relationship between teacher and student may be different from what the child is used to, and many immigrant children are unaware of whom or how to ask for help. Furthermore, the cultural foundations of many schools may be confusing to the students, leading to academic confusion or withdrawal and isolation. As classes become more difficult in middle and high schools, and students must rely more heavily on English-language skills to communicate abstract ideas, immigrant students may experience increased frustration over not being able to communicate effectively. These academic difficulties are problems in and of themselves, but can also contribute to emotional issues and conflicts within the family over performance.

Children and adolescents from recent European immigrant families may also be referred for social issues, often related to the child's feeling like an outsider due to differences in dress, in language, interests, and the like. Communication difficulties can also add to barriers to a child's social development. In addition, many children may feel conflicted over the peer pressure to engage in "typical" American behaviors that may be seen as inappropriate within the child's cultural norms. Many children of European immigrants may not feel comfortable going outside the family for help, which can further exacerbate the feelings of isolation and a sense of disconnectedness.

In addition to the academic and social difficulties, children and adolescents may feel a sense of isolation or a lack of connectedness caused by feeling different from other children. These feelings can affect self-esteem, and may lead to feelings of shame about their family or culture when in a majority culture setting such as school. These feelings of shame for one's family and/or country can lead to further feelings of guilt, initiating an emotional cycle. These feelings of social isolation may increase during adolescence, when many immigrants may become frustrated over difficulty fitting into peer groups, and experience isolation and rejection at the hands of their peers. Adolescent immigrants may also have to deal with negative stereotypes other students may hold about their cultural background. In addition, many adolescent immigrants may be expected to spend nonschool hours helping out, which may leave them feeling "left out" when their American peers enjoy great freedom to socialize outside school. This may be particularly true of immigrants living in cultural enclaves, who may have difficulty spending time with friends outside the enclave or even participating in extracurricular activities such as sports teams or academic clubs.

Although many adolescents in America experience a decrease in self-esteem during adolescence, immigrant populations may be particularly prone to self-esteem issues. At a time when adolescents often want to be like their peers, immigrant adolescents may be hyperconscious of their differences. During this developmental stage, it is also common for adolescents to lose respect and even reject their ethnicity, and may experience guilt over decisions made that reject family or cultural values in order to fit in with the peer group.

Counseling European Immigrants

Forced and "voluntary" immigrants are faced with creation of a new lifestyle in a new land, and frequently must focus on survival while immigrant children hope for the restoration of harmony and a semblance of normalcy in their lives. Whereas the cultural, political, economic, and geographic experiences of migrants are different, some unifying elements exist as well. These elements could be conceptualized as the search for protection from trauma, oppression, and isolation for many, while for others it might be a search for better standards of living and experiencing a new lifestyle. Yet, for most immigrants, numerous layers of stressors tend to become a typical part of life. Focusing on survival for many immigrant families might become a pattern for living generations. For many immigrant families, a sense of belonging is replaced with isolation, a sense of harmony replaced with a sense of disruption, a sense of mastery replaced with being devalued, and a sense of independence replaced with dependence. Without understanding and healing, immigrants can become discouraged and might partake in the process of excluding, devaluing, and rejecting themselves and others. The experiences of shame and disconnect may lead to unhealthy patterns of behavior and/or self-medication through the use of alcohol or other substances.

In addition to helping immigrant families rediscover meaningful rituals, counselors can help immigrant individuals and families rebuild a sense of identity and self-efficacy through sharing their stories from their home countries, and helping them construct new narratives of their lives in the United States that are filled with hope and meaning. The narrative approach to counseling—which focuses on allowing the client to narrate life story while the counselor strives to understand, encourage, and convey empathy through mutuality leading to the generation of new possibilities and meanings—can help counselors and their clients toward this end. The narrative approach may be particularly helpful for European immigrants because of its wellness orientation that emphasizes the human potential to continually learn instead of focusing on remediation of problems, which often perpetuates feelings of shame and guilt common in European ethnicities, thus hindering growth.

NARRATIVE APPROACH IN COUNSELING   The narrative approach consists of three core phases: deconstructing the dominant culture narrative, externalizing the problem, and reauthoring the story. The deconstruction process focuses on examination of one's experiences relevant to inferiority and superiority. This can be the most challenging process, as clients feel reluctant and resistant to trusting the process of self-exploration and accepting self and others fully. Counselors may find the process of deconstructing the dominant narrative particularly helpful in working with European immigrants by enabling the clients to gain greater awareness of how their life has been influenced by experiences of inferiority, superiority, and how these experiences help them in finding mutuality and authenticity in relationships.

In the second phase of narrative approach, clients begin to externalize the problems. This may be a particularly helpful process for European American immigrants from cultures who have a tendency toward self-blame and feelings of guilt and shame. In this stage, it is important to distinguish problems as being ecological in nature, rather than pathological tendencies that exist within clients. For example, clients might be asked to identify how negative stereotyping in the majority culture affected their views of themselves, or how the feelings of isolation they felt as a result of their immigration status affected their views of themselves and their lives.

Finally, when clients are able to engage in honest reflections and attend to what may otherwise be hidden due to shame and isolation, the counselors can help clients focus on the final phase of the narrative approach: the reauthoring of the story. In this stage, clients and counselors can collaboratively reflect on being successful in life in spite of, or perhaps in some ways in concert with, the American culture. Counselors can prompt their European clients to reflect on personal strengths used in the past and how these strengths might be utilized to work through present challenges.

While storytelling and retelling seems to be conducive to healing and identifying new possibilities, the storytelling does not have to involve only verbal exchanges. Multicultural creative expressions can be utilized to give voice to those whose thoughts, feelings, and ideas might have been silenced, and may be particularly effective when working across language barriers. Multicultural creative arts as therapeutic interventions focus on the importance of connectedness and provide opportunities for non-threatening ways of communication. Various scholars and practitioners have noted the role of creative arts and interventions in counseling (Gladding, 2005a; Jacobs, Masson, & Harvill, 2006; Molina, Brigman, & Rhone, 2003; Oaklander, 1988). Furthermore, several theories and scholars emphasize the importance of supporting clients in their quest for connecting and searching for meaningful living (Adler, 1964; Frankl, 1959; Jordan & Hartling, 2002). Sharing of life stories, through multicultural creative expressions and practices, further supports the process of relational connectedness.

CREATIVE ARTS   Creative arts can help European immigrant clients find a means of identifying sources of disconnect and frustration, which can be particularly effective with clients who have difficulty expressing such concerns verbally due to language difficulties or cultural norms. In addition, creative techniques can yield opportunities for clients to gain awareness of the healthy source of the power of genuine care which brings energy to living lives fully and enjoying the human experience. Frankl (1959) described several ways of finding meaning in living, such as truly and fully experiencing nature, culture, and through experiencing other human beings through genuine, caring relationships. Perhaps by helping clients gain awareness of what has given energy to their paths of life, counselors and clients might discover anew the healing power of cultural wisdom, strength, and perspectives that multicultural rituals bring to living.

One of the things that immigrant families lose in the transition to the United States is the traditions and rituals of their family and culture. These rituals and ceremonies serve several essential purposes, including maintaining and restoring wellness for individuals, families, and communities. The process of carrying out the rituals and ceremonies focuses on conveying respect, interdependence, reciprocity, emotionality, intimacy, and modesty (Jakubowska, 2003; Lubecka, 2000). It follows, then, that individuals and families across cultures could find healing and wellness by reconnecting with time-honored practices that derive from their culture of origin as well as other cultural groups as each culture has their unique rhythm for meaningful living. Counselors who can provide safe environments for immigrant clients to describe and partake in cultural traditions and practices that are meaningful and relevant to them can help the families begin to reground themselves and begin the healing process (see Resource 14.1).

Resource 14.1   Polish Wreath Exercise

In the Polish tradition, wreaths signify deep relational connections to people, nature, and life events. Wreaths are made for many reasons: to convey or express respect, honor, love, connection, new beginnings, and new endings. The sense of connectedness that the circle offers in essence is deeply embedded

(continued)

in the creation of the Polish wreath making. Specific flowers, herbs, and times of the year are selected for the creation of wreaths. "As much as the Polish wreath can be used in celebration of joy and in times of sadness and grief, it is the spiritual element of the human mind that allows a person to face mortality through the aspiration to live life in its plenitude. Life and death, living and dying are interwoven aspects of all human beings' life stories" (Molina, Monteiro-Leitner, Garrett, & Gladding, 2005 p. 13).

Wreaths can be created as part of an honoring ceremony so that the participants can reflect on their meaning making of living, and dying, while focusing on their cultural, community, and family strengths, their ability to remain generous and share their talents and skills, along with reflection on how they are presently experiencing their lives. Branches, leaves, and flowers are the basic elements needed to create a wreath. Although ideally participants would be asked to go to nature and select parts for the wreaths, in modern society artificial branches, leaves, and flowers might need to suffice. When designing the wreaths, the dark leaves symbolize the fears and worries that one might encounter, while the yellow flowers represent the radiance of the sun and hope for new beginnings. Children and families might be asked to join together and form a wreath that symbolizes the events in their relationships and lives that are meaningful and essential to understand. Once the wreaths are formed, each family joins the circle and shares the meaning of the wreath. While reflecting on the process of wreath making, the facilitator might ask the following questions:

- What have been some of the toughest things that you encountered?
- How did the strengths within you and in the people in your family and community help you get through?
- How are you different now as a result of this experience?
- What kind of symbols did you come up with? What might those mean to you?
- What kind of strengths did you notice in you and your family members?
- If the flowers and branches could talk to you, what might they be saying?
- If the flowers and branches had a hearing heart, what would they hear from you?
- For you to feel safe and protected, which strengths within you will help you and those around you?

To gain awareness of one's cultural heritage, its experiences of privilege or oppression, its influence on identity formation through reciprocity, it is imperative to explore with clients several elements that influence cultural identity and wellness. Santiago-Rivera, Arredondo, and Gallardo-Cooper (2002a) identify the following elements as being essential for exploration: primary social networks (e.g., same ethnicity, mixed, other); their cultural dimensions such as place of nativity or acculturation level (e.g., integrated, assimilated, marginalized, rejecting); native culture contacts (e.g., high, moderate, low); immigration history (e.g., premigration dynamics, precipitating events, migration experience, postmigration); and language dimensions, psychocultural dimensions, and other sources of stress (e.g., residency, oppression, gender, immigration, racism, ethnosupport, educational, vocational, prejudice, familial, language, economic, marital). In addition, exploring regional cultural differences and living experiences is essential; someone residing in Los Angeles might have totally different experiences than an immigrant from rural Idaho.

SOCIAL JUSTICE COUNSELING   Another way counselors can work to alleviate stress associated with immigration while promoting wellness is to work from a social justice perspective. **Social justice counseling** represents an effort for counselors to promote general wellness and the common good through addressing systemic and cultural challenges to justice and equity, while helping individuals advocate for themselves within and successfully navigate systems where injustice and inequality exist (Counselors for Social Justice, 2004). Furthermore, social justice counselors identify four principles that guide their work: equity, access, participation, and harmony (Counselors for Social Justice, 2008).

The first principle, **equity,** pertains to involvement in culture-centered approach. Counselors and professional in the helping fields can be the catalysts for change by giving voice to dynamics that have been silenced and/or ignored. Counselors can become familiar with cultural practices that foster a sense of wellness for individuals representing various cultural groups. **Access,** the second principle, pertains to counselor's choosing to clarify identity construction in self and clients. How do we deconstruct deficiency models and reconstruct frameworks for counseling and educating based on differences model, not deficiencies? **Participation,** the third principle, underscores the importance of mutuality and authenticity. Orr and Hulse-Killacky (2006) offer a framework through which counselors are encouraged to note whose voice is heard, and how decisions are made through construction of meaning, leading to transfer of learning that is based on mutuality. It is important for counselors to offer active support to those who are discouraged from participating and whose contributions to society are minimized, devalued, and shut down. As consultants, we need to ask whose stories are celebrated throughout the educational systems, what images are portrayed, and what kind of policies are still not questions that dominant culture members take for granted. The fourth principle, **harmony,** pertains to searching for wellness by tapping into the cultural wisdom and deconstructing the process of devaluing that immigrants may be experiencing. An important aspect of harmony will be developing relationships with clients that are based on the principles of mutuality. Through honest reflections about our ways of relating with our clients—how we connect, how we take time and make time for valuing others, and how respect and care may be withheld from clients whom we serve—we can ensure that clients experience a sense of valuing within the counseling relationship that they may not be experiencing in other aspects of their lives. Through the process of unmasking who we are and what we do, and unmasking cultural camouflage that are a fertile soil for shame and isolation, counselors can provide for their clients an atmosphere of authenticity and permission to be who they desire to be. Moreover, as clients continue the process of questioning and tap into their own sense of wisdom and authenticity, counselors working from a social justice perspective can create and take advantage of opportunities to be the voice for those who have been silenced.

Summary

This purpose of this chapter was to highlight the need for and importance of multicultural counseling with individuals and families of European descent. It is not uncommon for many White Americans to be viewed as being acultural, even by themselves, and not uncommon for recent immigrants from European nations to be viewed as White. Both of these misunderstandings fail to take into account important cultural values and practices that are essential to fully understanding individuals and families. A brief history of European cultures was presented, along with an overview of how European immigrants during the colonial period brought their cultural values and traditions to the colonies, forming the beginnings of a White American ethnicity. Because the English dominated much of the social and political landscape, the developing ethnic identity of the new United States was based largely on English cultural norms, including individualism, self-reliance, strong work ethic, suspicion of others, and value of achievement and success. However, many other cultures added their own flavors, and in addition factors such as the geography of the country and larger social changes affected the evolution of ethnic identity as well. Concepts such as meritocracy, a national heritage, and the metaphor of the United States as a melting pot were both developed from and contributed to the ongoing evolution of the White American ethicity.

A central component of the White American ethnicity was the concept of Whiteness, yet the qualifications of who is considered White are vague and have changed over time and in response to various social and cultural factors, including immigration patterns. What has remained constant, however, is that certain people, based on physical, religious, or other criteria, are allowed or expected to become White, a process by which they adopt certain privileges reserved for White Americans, but are also expected to give up, to varying degrees, their former ethnic cultural traditions and values.

The goal of this chapter was to help counselors better conceptualize their clients of European descent. Particular attention was given to understanding that European immigrants to the United States face many of the same stressors that other immigrants face, including grief and loss, underemployment, educational difficulties, difficulties with language, and oppression. Understanding these stressors, as well as understanding their own ethnic and cultural values and practices, is crucial to effective counseling of European immigrants from a multicultural perspective.

At the same time, it is important to remember that White American ethnics, although often not included in multicultural conversations, are indeed cultural beings whose personal, social, emotional, career, educational, or relationship problems can be understood and addressed through a cultural lens.

In particular, feelings of inadequacy, incompetence, guilt, and shame within the White American ethnic population may be closely related to the cultural value of independence, success, and personal responsibility that is pervasive. Understanding these cultural values *as cultural values* can help counselors conceptualize their White American ethnic clients from a multicultural perspective, and work toward ameliorating the effects of these cultural conflicts with their clients.

However, as with all multicultural counseling, it is important to respect intragroup differences. Many variables of identity, such as gender, socioeconomic status, generation, geographic location, sexual/relationship orientation, ability status, and European country of origin can have profound impacts on the cultural identity of the individual, and all of these intersecting identities must be explored before an individual of European descent can be understood. This understanding is a crucial component of effective multicultural counseling with both recent European immigrants and White Americans, as is the process of cultural self-exploration that occurs within the counseling setting.

CHAPTER 15

Spiritual Diversity

CRAIG S. CASHWELL

PREVIEW

There is great religious and spiritual diversity within the United States. To the extent that a person's religious and spiritual beliefs, practices, and experiences shape his or her worldview, spirituality and religion are aspects of culture and are important in the counseling process. It is imperative that counselors understand a broad range of religious and spiritual beliefs, and are able to work within these beliefs to provide culturally sensitive counseling services. Eastern and Western religions are briefly reviewed in this chapter, as well as tenets common to all major world religions. The purpose of this chapter is to discuss spiritual and religious diversity within the United States and the pitfalls of working within a culturally encapsulated framework around religious and spiritual issues in counseling.

RELIGION AND SPIRITUALITY IN AMERICA

The United States as a nation was founded on religious tolerance, diversity, and freedom, in opposition to the historical religious oppression in England. As noted by any number of the founders of the United States, freedom of religion means the right to participate in *any* religion, including no religion at all. The separation of church and state was originally intended to avoid the imposition of one set of beliefs over others, as had been the case in England (Fukuyama, Siahpoush, & Sevig, 2005). It is important to remember, however, that religious diversity in the United States at that time essentially meant diverse forms of Protestantism. Prior to the early settlers' arrival, though, the spirituality of the Native Americans was already clearly in place (Garrett, 1998). Additionally, over the last 250 years there has been a steady influx of immigrant populations that have brought with them diverse spiritual and religious beliefs, rituals, and traditions. As a country, the United States has maintained its emphasis on Protestantism as the cultural norm and, as a result, "tensions have developed without a 'template' in which to incorporate an expanded sense of religious and cultural diversity" (Fukuyama et al., 2005, p. 124).

That spirituality and religion are important cultural aspects within the United States is clear. Researchers have found that 96% of Americans believe in a Higher Power, over 90% pray, 69% are members of a religious community, and 43% have attended a service at their church, synagogue, temple, or mosque within the past 7 days (Princeton Religion Research Center, 2000). The largest religious group, comprising just over 76% of the population, self-identifies as Christian (Largest Religious Groups in the United States, n.d.). The second largest group identifies as nonreligious or secular, and comprises 13.2% of the population. After these two groups, only Judaism includes more than 1% of the population (1.3%). Other religions in the United States, accounting for less than 1% of the population, include Islam (0.5%), Buddhism (0.5%), Agnosticism (0.5%), Atheism (0.4%), and Hinduism (0.4%). As evidence of the growing religious diversity in the United States, however, it bears mentioning that several religious groups have seen dramatic increases in recent history. For example, from 1990 to 2000, New Age Spirituality increased by 240%, Hinduism by 237%, Baha'i by 200%, Buddhism by 170%, Native

American Religion by 119%, and Islam by 109%. Beyond these numbers, however, is the fact that there is tremendous within-group variance among religious traditions. That is, knowing that someone is Jewish or Hindu or Protestant or Buddhist affords only cursory information about the religious and spiritual beliefs, practices, experiences, rituals, and traditions of the individual.

SPIRITUALITY AND RELIGION DEFINED

The terms *spirituality* and *religion* often are misunderstood. There are two potential ways in which cultural encapsulation occurs here. In the first, people assume that others hold the same beliefs and practices that they do. Accordingly, assumptions are made regarding beliefs about the presence of a deity or deities, what occurs after death, creation stories, and spiritual practices. The second form of cultural encapsulation around spirituality and religion occurs when an individual projects his or her experiences of a religious group onto an individual. For example, a person who has experienced fundamentalism only within a specific religious group assumes that everyone who practices that form of religion is, similarly, a fundamentalist. It is important to have a working understanding of spirituality and religion, and how the two may be related for individuals.

Toward Defining Spirituality

Spirituality is difficult, at best, to define, largely because it is highly personal, developmental, and often beyond verbal definition. That is, spirituality is personal in that it is unique and idiosyncratic to each individual. Because of this, it is not possible to provide a generic definition of spirituality that is sufficiently inclusive for all people. Further, spirituality is developmental in that a person's spiritual beliefs, practices, and experiences evolve and develop over time. That is, a true spirituality is far from a static way of being. To the contrary, it is highly dynamic and evolving. Finally, when discussing the **transformative aspects of religion** and spirituality (which will be discussed more fully later in this chapter), transformative spiritual experiences often defy verbal explanations. As one example of this, try Activity 15.1.

ACTIVITY 15.1

The following activity is adapted from Horovitz-Darby (1994).

Gather a set of art materials such as colored pencils, markers, or crayons, and some art paper. Once you have gathered these materials, follow these directions:

1. Many people believe in a Divine Creator. If you hold such a belief, represent this belief visually.
2. Once this image is complete, consider that many people believe there is an opposite power of a Divine Creator. If you hold such a belief, represent this belief visually.
3. Once this image is complete, journal or discuss with someone your answers to the following questions:
   a. What are the images you have created and what do they symbolize?
   b. How do you feel about each of the images you have created?
   c. Do you feel as though the image accurately represents your beliefs?
4. Journal or discuss how your image would have been different 5, 10, and 20 years ago, and how you expect it might evolve in the coming years.
5. Once you have completed this process, write a one- or two-sentence definition of this Divine Creator without using any of the imagery you have created in steps 1 through 4.

Note: Many people find the experience of visually representing the Divine Creator much easier than providing a verbal definition.

The challenges of defining spirituality notwithstanding, it seems important to provide a working definition of spirituality to serve as a starting place for discussion and to highlight the multidimensionality of the spiritual. **Spirituality**, then, is defined as a set of beliefs, practices, and experiences held by an individual that ultimately lead to a transcendence of self to be concerned with otherness (Otto, 1958). This compassion for others begins with self-compassion, and involves a search for wholeness and harmony in the universe (Cervantes & Ramirez, 1992). As such, this compassion occurs naturally as we realize that it is in giving that we receive. This framework distinguishes between compassion and codependency, where an individual helps others out of selfish reasons, albeit unconsciously, such as trying to feel worthwhile. Finally, because there needs to be a distinction between a spiritual life that is psychologically healthy and one that is not, this spiritual path allows the journeyer to mindfully and heartfully experience all emotions, even those that some religious groups might deem undesirable or a sign of weakness, and to create a collaborative relationship with a Higher Power or Higher Self. These last two points are to contrast a healthy spiritual life with a psychologically unhealthy spiritual life in which an individual is discouraged from feeling "negative" emotions, such as sadness, fear, and anger, by teachers or leaders, and a spiritual path that leads to an extreme external locus of control. It is important here to distinguish between a healthy construct, surrender, and unhealthy behaviors of abdicating personal responsibility either to a charismatic spiritual leader or a **Higher Power**. It is the cocreated and collaborative relationship with a Higher Power that has been found to be related to physical, emotional, and psychological health (Pargament, Ano, & Wachholtz, 2005).

Toward Defining Religion

In contrast to spirituality, religion is relatively easy to define. While spirituality is considered to be universal, ecumenical, internal, affective, spontaneous, and private, **religion** is considered to be denominational, external, cognitive, behavioral, ritualistic, and public (Richards & Bergin, 1997); that is, religion is organized spirituality (H. Smith, 2001). Smith further argued that religion was the container and spirit was the essence it contained. This definition works well for those who see their spiritual and religious lives as being harmonious and mutually supportive. Others, however, argue that "the essence" is too large for most of the containers that they have experienced. Such people likely define themselves as "spiritual but not religious." A more thorough discussion of the manner in which individuals experience the relationship between religion and spirituality likely is warranted.

Relationships Between Religion and Spirituality

The relationship between religion and spirituality differs for each individual and changes over time for each person. That is, this relationship is very personal and developmental. It is possible, however, to delineate four major relationships that have important implications for culturally sensitive counseling processes (see Reflection 15.1 on page 371).

HAND IN HAND   For some, the relationship between religion and spirituality is either complementary or coincidental. When viewed as complementary, the religious community is an important aspect of the individual's spiritual life, but also involves disciplined spiritual practice (or multiple practices) that support spiritual growth. That is, the exoteric (i.e., public) spiritual practice (religion) complements the esoteric (i.e., private) spiritual practice, and vice versa. For others, the relationship is more coincidental. For these people, their religious life is their spiritual life. Such people have a rich spiritual life that is almost exclusively experienced and expressed within their religious community. For both complementary and coincidental individuals, the religious community is vital to the spiritual life, and the exoteric and esoteric go hand in hand.

THE JUNGIAN PATH OF PRETENDING   Carl Jung (1959) once wrote that many people participate in religion to avoid having a religious experience. Essentially, this means that there are people who participate in organized religion, but more out of habit or fear of punishment than to connect to Spirit and integrate the sacred into their everyday life. For such people, religious participation is disconnected from the religious experience. In most cases, such people do not have a private spiritual practice and typically have limited spiritual experiences.

"SPIRITUAL BUT NOT RELIGIOUS"   A third category of people describe themselves as spiritual but not religious. Researchers have found that this category of people is rapidly growing in the United States (Princeton Religion Research Center, 2000). Such people recognize the importance of the spiritual journey. Either because they have never participated in organized religion or because they have had negative experiences with religion, they choose not to participate in an organized religion. Such people often find a nonreligious "community" an important aspect of religion, in other ways, such as through meditation or yoga groups.

There is an important distinction among two subtypes of people within this category. The first subtype, the *Accepting,* includes people who value religion and respect the place that it plays in the lives of others. That is, although they choose not to participate in organized religion themselves, they respect the importance of religion in the lives of others. The second subtype, the *Disdainful,* typically finish the phrase "I am spiritual but not religious" with a contemptuous tone. That is, they have had personal or vicarious negative experiences with organized religion. These experiences have led them not only to be nonreligious, but also to be antireligious.

Wilber (1998) provided a nice template for understanding the experiences of at least some people who describe themselves as spiritual but not religious. Within many religious communities, the focus is primarily on beliefs—that is, the translative aspect of religion is emphasized almost exclusively (i.e., the transformative potential of religion is deemphasized). In some religious communities, the focus is even more narrowly prescribed to a communal set of beliefs in which individual variation is discouraged. Often, people in the spiritual but not religious category have previous history with organized religion, but become disenfranchised with the emphasis on the translative aspects of religion. In search of transformative experiences, their spiritual journey moves away from organized religion. If this transition is done with some resentment toward the religious community, the person typically becomes disdainful of organized religion. If the transition is more peaceful, the person becomes accepting of the importance of religion for others, although the person does not participate in a religious community personally.

A second process that may lead to a person self-describing as spiritual but not religious occurs when religious wounding occurs. This occurs, for example, when a lesbian or gay man who has grown up within a faith community comes out to that community and is rejected by the community. In these instances, if the person is able to separate the experience in this religious community from personal spirituality, the person likely will either become disdainful of religion but maintain a private spiritual life, or find another religious community that supports the GLBT community (Cashwell & Marszalek, 2007). If people are unable, however, to separate this negative religious experience from their personal spiritual life, they likely operate within another category, the *Decliners.* These individuals consider themselves to be neither religious nor spiritual. Although religion is hardly universal, many argue that spirituality is innate and universal (Cashwell & Young, 2005). For a variety of reasons, though, some people develop neither their religious nor their spiritual lives.

As with the Accepting or Disdainful categories, there seems to be two subtypes of individuals in the Decliners category that are important to consider. The *Inexperienced Decliner* is a person who has never been exposed to the spiritual life or a religious community. Some may have grown up in a family that eschewed religion and spirituality or, at the very least, did not discuss such matters. When working with a client who is an Inexperienced Decliner, it is important to gently assess the openness to psychospiritual work that might be used within session (e.g., guided imagery) or between session (e.g., a referral to a meditation group).

The second subtype, the *Rejector,* has had some previous negative experience within a religious community that has led the individual to reject not only the religious life but also his or her own spirituality. That is, the religious and the spiritual become inseparable for the individual, and both are rejected. Understandably, a client with such a stance likely would be opposed to the integration of spirituality into the counseling process.

REFLECTION 15.1

Consider the various relationships between religion and spirituality previously chronicled and journal your responses to the following questions:

1. What type(s) would be most difficult with which to work?
2. What is it about this type that makes it a difficult match?
3. What is it about your own religious/spiritual history that makes it a difficult match?
4. Is it possible for you to be an effective counselor with a person of this type?
5. If so, what knowledge, self-awareness, and skills will be required for your work with this client to be sensitive to the client's view of religion and spirituality?

OVERVIEW OF MAJOR WORLD RELIGIONS

As the United States becomes increasingly diverse, it is imperative that counselors have at least a working knowledge of the major world religions. Although it is neither possible nor necessary that a counselor be an expert in all world religions, some basic working knowledge is important. In this spirit, some preliminary information about major world religions is offered. Clearly, though, it is beyond the scope of this chapter to provide an in-depth overview of the major world religions. The references contained within each section provide a nice starting place for additional reading. Further, there are many other sects (e.g., Wiccan, Aboriginal religions) that are not discussed here. It is simply not possible to capture the breadth and depth of belief systems in only a few scant pages. What follows, though, provides preliminary information about the most prominent wisdom traditions of the world.

Eastern World Religions

The major Eastern religions include Buddhism, Hinduism, Taoism, and Confucianism. It is important to keep in mind that some Eastern religious practitioners may integrate beliefs and traditions from various traditions. For example, some consider Confucianism to be a philosophical way of living and being rather than a religion per se and, as such, may practice another religious tradition as well as Confucianism.

BUDDHISM   **Buddhism** defines a religion organized around the teachings of Siddhartha Gautama, who was born into a wealthy Hindu family in Nepal around 563 BC. Siddhartha began his quest for enlightenment at age 19 years, originally by foregoing the luxuries of his rich family and living the life of an ascetic. He later realized that the ascetic life was no more a path to enlightenment than that of luxury, and began following a path he called *the middle way,* between asceticism and luxury, that remains a central tenet of contemporary Buddhism (Murgatroyd, 2001). Siddhartha developed the "divine eye" at age 35 years while meditating under a Bodhi tree and changed from a bodhisattva (i.e., enlightened person who has chosen to postpone Nirvana in order to help others become enlightened) to a **Buddha** (Awakened or Enlightened One). The Buddha died around 483 BC and, ostensibly in the same year, the first Buddhist Council of Rajagaha met to preserve the Buddha's teachings.

There are three major traditions of Buddhism: Theravada, Mahayana, and Vajrayana (Gethin, 1998). Theravada Buddhism, also referred to as "Southern Buddhism," is practiced primarily in Sri Lanka and Southeast Asia. It is based on the **Pali Canon**, which is regarded as the scriptures most closely following the Buddha's own words. Theravada Buddhism is practiced more by monks than laypeople, and has about 100 million followers. Mahayana (literally, "The Greater Ox-cart") Buddhism evolved as a schism from Theravada Buddhism, providing a form of Buddhism that could be practiced by the masses without requiring a monastic life. They considered enlightenment to be virtually unattainable, and so created two grades of attainment below becoming a Buddha. While the Buddha was the highest goal, one could become a pratyeka-buddha, one who has awakened to the truth but keeps it secret. Below the pratyeka-buddha is the arhant, or "worthy," who has learned the truth from others and has realized it as truth. Mahayana Buddhism establishes the arhant as the goal for all believers. Vajrayana Buddhism is an extension of Mahayana Buddhism, similar in philosophy but adding additional techniques, known as upaya or "skillful means," esoteric practices that should be learned only under the tutelage of a skilled spiritual teacher. Within the United States, there are slightly more than 1.5 million adherents to Buddhism (Largest Religious Groups in the United States of America, n.d.).

The most prominent teachings within Buddhism include The Four Noble Truths and The Eightfold Path (Buddha Dharma Education Association, 2007). **The Four Noble Truths** come from the first talk that the Buddha gave after his enlightenment. The Four Noble Truths are:

1. *Dukkha:* All existence is unsatisfactory and filled with suffering. Because this is the first Noble Truth of Buddhism, some falsely think that Buddhism is a "negative" religion. This is not so at all. Rather, Buddhism, perhaps more than other religion, acknowledges the struggles and challenges of life, and the path to transcend this suffering.
2. *Samudaya:* The root of suffering can be defined as a craving or clinging to the wrong things. Such a clinging is commonly referred to as an *attachment.*
3. *Dirodha:* It is possible to end suffering by abandoning our expectations of how things should be and, through this mindfulness, become more aware of how things really are.
4. *Magga:* Freedom from suffering is possible by following the Eightfold Path.

The **Eightfold Path**, then, is the key to practicing nonattachment and ending our suffering. Pain is inevitable, but suffering is said to occur when we resist pain. The Eightfold Path includes three major categories, Panna, Sila, and Samadhi:

Panna: Paths of discernment and wisdom
1. *Right view* occurs when we embrace the joy of life the way it is, without the maya (i.e., illusion) of hopes or fears.
2. *Right intention* occurs when we act with pure intention free of manipulation borne of our expectations, hopes, and fears.

Sila: Paths of virtue and morality
3. *Right speech* occurs when we speak from right intention in an honest, simple, and genuine way.
4. *Right discipline* occurs when we simplify life by surrendering all that complicates our life and our relationships.

5. *Right livelihood* occurs when we form a simple relationship with our job and perform it well and with attention to detail.

   Samadhi: Right concentration

6. *Right effort* occurs when we surrender our tendency to struggle and see things as they are and work with them without aggression.

7. *Right mindfulness* occurs when we are precisely and clearly aware of all of our experiences, without judgment.

8. *Right concentration* occurs when we are fully aware and completely absorbed in present moment experience, free of worries for the future and regrets from the past.

HINDUISM   **Hinduism** is the oldest known religion, with origins attributed as far back as 3200 BC, and it is the third largest religion in the world with over 762 million followers worldwide (Kinsley, 1993). It is the predominant religion of India, where over 80% of the population is Hindus. In the United States, there are just over 1 million Hindus (Largest Religious Groups in the United States of America, n.d.).

Hinduism is both a religion and a cultural way of life. It is sometimes mistakenly referred to as a polytheistic religion when, in fact, it is **henotheistic**, meaning that Hindus recognize a single Deity, but also recognize other gods and goddesses as facets, forms, manifestations, or aspects of that supreme God.

Central to Hindu beliefs are the concepts of karma and samsara. **Karma**, which translates as "works" or "deeds," refers to the notion that all actions have moral consequences that one must accept as a part of life. **Samsara** is the idea that one's present life is only the most recent in a long chain of lives extending far into the past. Hindus believe, then, in a continuous cycle of birth, life, death, and rebirth through many lifetimes, and that all past lives have some influence on the current life through karma. This cycle is represented in the Hindu trinity of Brahma (creator of the world), Vishnu (preserver of the world), and Shiva (destroyer of the world).

A final Hindu belief that may impact the counseling process is the belief that Atman (self or soul) is **Brahman** (God) and Brahman is Atman. Many religions separate the "self" from "God," and some mistakenly distinguish between the two when interpreting the Hindu belief system. By **Atman**, Hindus mean not a distinct or separate "self" as is often defined in Western traditions. Instead, by Atman Hindus are referring to that aspect of the universal consciousness that is contained within the mind, body, and soul of the individual (Shastri, n.d.). Thus, a core belief of Hindus is that the essence of the human personality is interchangeable with God and tat twam asi, that one is immutable and eternal.

TAOISM   **Taoism** is based on ancient Chinese beliefs that over centuries have become mixed with principles from Buddhism and Confucianism (Simpkins & Simpkins, 1999). Taoism originated with the teachings of Lao-tzu circa 604 BC, although there is some debate among scholars as to whether he really existed or whether the writings attributed to Lao-tzu were a compilation from many writers (Forstater, 2001). Regardless, the **Tao Te Ching**, one of the fundamental texts of Taoism attributed to Lao-tzu, has been translated into Western languages more than any other text with the exception of the Christian Bible (Ludwig, 1989).

There a number of concepts central to Taoist beliefs. These include:

1. *Tao:* the ultimate reality; literally, "The Way." The Tao is considered the intrinsic essence from which our existence and experience spring. The Tao is likened to water in that it is formless yet conforming, flows effortlessly yet changes, and is soft but powerful (Simpkins & Simpkins, 1999). It is through stillness and connectedness to nature that we are all connected with Tao.

2. *Te:* the life power that is the living expression of the Tao.
3. *Chi:* the life-force energy that is beyond intellectual understanding.
4. *Yin/Yang:* a symbol popularized in the West, the Yin/Yang represents opposites, most notably the masculine and feminine, that work together to bring wholeness.
5. *Wu-wei:* literally, "actionless action," the commitment of Taoists to avoid actions that go against the natural order or Tao.

Finally, it bears mentioning that many aspects of Taoism have been integrated into Western culture, although many people do not know the origins of these aspects. Martial arts such as *Tai Chi Chuan* and *Aikido*, healing practices such as *acupuncture* and *acupressure*, and the practice of removing energetic clutter in living spaces, known as *Feng Shui*, all have roots in Taoist principles.

CONFUCIANISM   **Confucianism** is a set of teachings from Confucius, whose formal name was Kong Qui (Yao, 2000). Confucius was reportedly born into royalty but was raised in poverty. He studied at the imperial capital of Zhou and became a renowned teacher and philosopher. He taught during a time in China considered by many to be a time of moral chaos, and his teachings were an effort to stem this moral decay—particularly among the nobility. Confucius initially attempted to teach the ruling class his doctrines, but he often was criticized and ignored, so he resigned from his formal positions and began to wander through China followed by a large group of disciples. It was during this 5 years of wandering through China that the majority of text that became the major sacred text of Confucianism, **The Analects**, was composed.

Although he was not accepted by the ruling class of China, Confucius gained a following of about 3,000 people, including about 70 disciples who followed him. He was not overly influential during his own generation, however, and it was not until much later that his teachings were implemented in China (Yao, 2000). To this day, the debate goes on as to whether Confucianism is indeed a religion, with some arguing that it clearly involves that which is holy and numinous (Yao), while others argue that it is more of a moral code than religion per se (Smith, 1991).

A fundamental practice among Neo-Confucianists is that of quiet-sitting, a practice that likely was inspired by Buddhist meditation (Yang, 1961). Distinct from other forms of meditation that have the intent to empty the mind or find the Self, quiet-sitting is intended to make the mind receptive to knowledge. Quiet-sitting has been likened to brightening up a mirror so that it can more clearly reflect the original nature within oneself (Kang, n.d.). As one becomes more fully oneself, the self can be united with God. Table 15.1 lists major observances of the religions discussed in this chapter.

Western World Religions

The three major Western religions are Christianity, Islam, and Judaism. Together, these three religions are professed by over 78% of the U.S. population and constitute the three largest organized religions in the United States (Largest Religious Groups in the United States of America, n.d.).

CHRISTIANITY   **Christianity** is overwhelmingly the largest religion in the United States, with estimates of over 224 million adherents, constituting 76.5% of the U.S. population (Largest Religious Groups in the United States of America, n.d.). It should be noted, however, that Christianity saw only a modest increase of 5% between 1990 and 2000. As such, it is growing much more slowly than other religions (e.g., Hinduism [237%] and Buddhism [170%]). Worldwide, estimates are that almost one out of every three persons consider themselves a Christian, bringing the number of worldwide adherents to greater than 1.5 billion (Smith, 1991).

TABLE 15.1 Major Religious Observances

Buddhism

Buddhist New Year: Celebrated on different days throughout the world. Theravada Buddhists celebrate the new year for 3 days from the first full moon day in April. Mahayana and Vajrayana Buddhists celebrate the new year on the first full moon day in January.

Vesak (Buddha Day): Vesak is the birthday of the Buddha and the most important festival in Buddhism. On the first full moon day in May, Buddhists celebrate the birth, enlightenment, and death of the Buddha in a single day. The name "Vesak" comes from the Indian month of that name in which it is held.

Dhamma Day: Observed on the full moon day of the eighth lunar month (July). Dhamma day commemorates the Buddha's first sermon.

Hinduism (The dates vary because the Hindu calendar is lunisolar.)

Ugadi: Hindu New Year

Holi: The festival of colors and spring (February–March)

Mashashivaratri: The sacred night for Shiva (February–March)

Rama Navami: Lord Rama's birthday (April)

Krishna Jayanti: Lord Krishna's birthday (July–August)

Raksabandhana: Renewing the bonds of brothers and sisters (July–August)

Kmbh Mela: The pilgrimage to the four cities of India (July–August, every 12 years)

Ganesh-Chaturthi: Ganesh festival (August–September)

Dassera: The victory of Ravana (September–October)

Navarati: The festival of Shakti (September–October)

Diwali: The festival of lights (September–October)

Taoism

Lao Tzu's Birthday: 15th day of the 2nd lunar month

Chinese New Year: First day of the first month of the Chinese calendar

Confucianism

Teacher's Day: Honors the birth of Confucius and the teaching profession (September 28)

Christianity

Christmas: Celebrates the birth of Jesus (December 25)

Easter: Spring festival that celebrates the resurrection of Jesus

Islam

Al-Hijra: The Islam New Year. It is celebrated on the first day of Muharram, the month in which Mohammed emigrated from Mecca to Medina in AD 622.

Ramadan: Considered a holy month in which the Qur'an was sent down as a guide for Muslims. Ramadan is the ninth month of the Muslim year.

Id Al-Fitr or *Eid al-Fitr*: Festival of the breaking of the fast, a celebration on the first 3 days of the month of Shawwal to mark the end of Ramadan.

Mawlid un-Nabi: The celebration of the birthday of Mohammed. Sunni Muslims celebrate on the 12th of Rabi'-ul-Awwal. Shi'a Muslims celebrate on the 17th of Rabi'-ul-Awwal. Many Muslims do not celebrate Mawlid as the consider it to be a *bidah*, or innovation, against Islam.

Judaism

Rosh Hashanah: Jewish New Year, occurring on the first and second days of Tishri. The Jewish New Year is a time to begin introspection, reflecting on the mistakes of the past year and planning the changes to make in the new year.

Yom Kippur: Literally "Day of Atonement," it is probably the most important holiday of the Jewish year. Yom Kippur occurs on the 10th day of Tishri.

Pesach (Passover): The primary observances of Pesach are related to the Exodus from Egypt after generations of slavery, and specifically the fact that God "passed over" the houses of the Jews when he was slaying the firstborn of Egypt. Pesach begins on the 15th day of the Jewish month of Nissan.

As with other major world religions, 2,000 years of history have resulted in a diverse religion. Within this diversity, however, there are three major divisions of Christianity: Roman Catholicism, Eastern Orthodoxy, and Protestantism. The common ground for all of these groups, however, is the historical Jesus, a man who

> was born in a stable, was executed as a criminal at age 33, never traveled more than ninety miles from his birthplace, owned nothing, attended no college, marshaled no army, and instead of producing books did his only writing in the sand. (Smith, 1991, p. 317)

Despite these humble roots, December 25 and the first Sunday after the first full moon of the vernal equinox in the Northern Hemisphere continue to be the holiest days of the year for Christians who each year remember the birth and death of their "Christ" at Christmas and Easter, respectively.

A central tenet of Christianity is the **Trinity**, or the representation of God the parent, Jesus the Son, and the presence of the Holy Spirit. For many Christians, Jesus was sent to earth by God to fulfill messianic prophecy foretold in what is now called the Old Testament, and that the life and death of Jesus created eternal life, as indicated in the Christian Bible:

> For God so loved the world that he gave his only Son, that whoever believes in Him should not perish but have eternal life. For God sent the Son into the world, not to condemn the world, but that the world might be saved through Him. (Oxford University Press, 1973, p. 1289)

Within each of the major divisions of Christianity (i.e., Roman Catholicism, Eastern Orthodoxy, and Protestantism) there remains great variation in the beliefs of adherents, with the most vocal divides arising between more conservative (often labeled "fundamentalist") factions and more moderate or liberal factions.

ISLAM   The religion of **Islam** currently has over 1.5 million adherents, known as Muslims, in the United States and, as such, is the third largest religion in the country, behind only Christianity and Judaism. Of note, however, is the fact that Islam grew by approximately 110% in the United States from 1990 to 2000 (Largest Religious Groups in the United States of America, n.d.). That is, Islam is by far the most quickly growing of the Western religions in the United States. Worldwide, estimates are that there are approximately 1.2 billion Muslims, making it the second largest religion in the world (Brown, 2004).

The central figure to Muslims, Mohammed Ibn Abdallah, was born in AD 570 in Mecca. In 610, Mohammed had his first vision and proclaimed Allah to be the one true God and condemned idol worship. Muslims later forced the city of Mecca to submit and accept Mohammed as a prophet. Mohammed destroyed all of the idols in the Kaba, or temple, in Mecca. From Mecca, Muslims waged **jihad**, or holy war, and forced surrounding cities to accept Islam and Mohammed as a prophet. Mohammed died in 632 (Robinson, 1999).

As with other religions, it is inaccurate to consider Islams to be a monolithic group. The primary historical division is between mainstream *Sunnis* (the word *sunni* drawn from *sunnah*, meaning "tradition") and *Shi'ites* (literally, "partisans" of Ali) who believed that Ali, Mohammed's son-in-law, should have succeeded Mohammed. Ali was appointed leader of the Muslims only after being passed over three times and was assassinated soon after assuming leadership. Shi'ites, comprising about 13% of all Muslims, are primarily located in Iraq and Iran. The Sunnis, comprising about 87% of all Muslims, flank the Shi'ites to both the West and the East (Smith, 1991). Recent events in Iraq have highlighted for Westerners the divide between Sunni and Shi'ite Muslims.

There is a third subgroup of Muslims, those who are primarily interested in the mystical aspects of Islam. These practitioners are called **Sufis**. Focused more on the inner life than the outer, they emphasized concepts such as meaning, inner reality, and contemplation. Westerners may be most familiar with the contemplative dancers among the Sufis (known as *Dervishes*) and the love poetry of the Persian Sufi, Jalal ad-Din Rumi.

The most central precepts of Islam are known as *The Five Pillars* (Kessler, 2000). The first pillar is Islam's creed, known as the *Shahadah*, that "There is no God but God, and Mohammed is His prophet." The second pillar of Islam is canonical prayer. Adherents are encouraged in the Koran to be constant in prayer. To this day, Muslims are required to pray five times a day, facing toward Mecca, a practice that reportedly was negotiated by Mohammed in his renowned Night Journey to Heaven (Smith, 1991). The third pillar of Islam is charity, with a simple message. Those who have much should help lift the burden of those who have less. The fourth pillar of Islam is the observance of **Ramadan**, Islam's holy month, considered holy because it was the month in which Mohammed both received his first revelation and, 10 years later, made his famous migration from Mecca to Medina. Tradition dictates that able-bodied Muslims fast during Ramadan, neither eating nor drinking from dawn until dusk, and only moderately after sunset. Islam's fifth pillar is pilgrimage, dictating that each Muslim who is physically and economically able should make a pilgrimage to Mecca to heighten devotion to God.

JUDAISM **Judaism** has almost 4 million adherents, constituting 1.3% of the U.S. population. This makes Judaism the second largest religion in the United States (Largest Religious Groups in the United States of America, n.d). Of the approximately 13 million Jews worldwide, approximately 4.7 million live in Israel. These numbers are greatly impacted by one of the greatest atrocities in history, the Holocaust, in which approximately 6 million Jews were murdered.

Judaism is a religion, but much more. Judaism is a culture and some consider it an ethnicity as well. That is, some consider themselves culturally or ethnically Jewish, but do not consider themselves to be Jewish in the religious sense. As with other religions, there are a variety of Jewish sects that hold distinct beliefs and practices. Of those Jews affiliated with a synagogue (on which such statistics can be kept), 45% consider themselves *Reformed Jews*, 42% consider themselves *Conservative Jews*, 9% consider themselves *Orthodox*, and 4% consider themselves *Reconstructivist*. Although it oversimplifies the differences somewhat, Orthodox Jews live by the *letter* of the Torah, the five books that comprise the central Jewish holy text, while Reform, Conservative, and Reconstructivist Jews live by the *spirit* of the Torah, with some variations between them.

The roots of Judaism began when God spoke to Abraham and promised a nation. This was followed some time later by a covenant between God and Moses on Mt. Sinai in which the Ten Commandments were given to Moses, land was promised, and Moses was commissioned to lead the Hebrews out of slavery.

Central to the Jewish tradition are rites of passage and the celebration of religious holy days. Important events in the life cycle include circumcision (and, in some instances, giving the child a Hebrew name), Bar or Bat Mitzvah, marriages, and funerals. The most important Jewish holy days often are referred to as the High Holy Days, celebrated during the first 10 days of the month of Tishri, usually in September or October. The first day is **Rosh Hashanah**, the Jewish New Year. For 10 days, from Rosh Hashanah until **Yom Kippur**, Jews think about how they have lived during the past year. They are asked to remember the wrongs they have to ask forgiveness from God and those they have hurt.

ALL IS ONE: ASPECTS COMMON TO ALL RELIGIONS

To this point, the emphasis of this chapter has been on the substantial variations of belief systems, both between and within world religions. One common precept of the spiritual life, however, is that all is connected, all is one. Within this framework, religious and spiritual diversity provides multiple paths that, at some point, converge. That is, all is connected and all is one, though the frameworks (or paths) that have evolved culturally may appear, on the surface, to be quite different. The seven tenets below are adapted from the work of Wilber (2001); these seven tenets are considered to be central to all religions.

Tenet 1: Spirit, by Whatever Name, Exists

Whether called God, Goddess, The Divine, The Absolute, Supreme Reality, Brahman, Tao, Allah, Shiva, Yahweh, Aton, Kether, Dharmakaya, or other names that have evolved from various wisdom traditions, Spirit exists. There is a certain ineffable quality to Spirit that makes the discourse around spirituality and counseling quite challenging. The proverbial hand pointing to the moon is not the moon, and the best that we can ever hope to do, given the numinous and ineffable quality of Spirit, is point toward its existence. Thousands of years of spiritual wisdom and experience across many cultural divides lead to the same conclusion. Spirit exists.

Tenet 2: Spirit Is Found "in Here," Within an Open Heart and Mind

Although some individual religious groups have worked to create a disconnection between Spirit and humankind, claiming that intercessories are required, or emphasizing the "unworthiness" of humans to be connected to Spirit, the wisdom of the ages suggests quite clearly, and across many different traditions, that Spirit, or at least some collective aspect of Spirit, resides within each of us. For example, the often quoted mantra of Hinduism, previously mentioned in this chapter, that "Atman is Brahman; Brahman is Atman" is indicative of this belief; that within each of us is a Divine spark. The Buddha is quoted as saying "We all have innate Buddha nature," and Jesus is quoted as saying that "The kingdom of heaven is within." Over time and across traditions, then, there is a recognition that we are, at the core of our being, spiritual in nature.

The second part of this tenet, "within an open heart and mind," reveals a more active process in which each of us has responsibility. Who, reading this text, could not more fully open their mind and heart? Increased mindfulness and heartfulness are fruits of the spiritual journey to wholeness. Opening the heart and mind is not something that is done "to us," but rather a journey co-constructed with Spirit, a journey in which each of us must accept the opportunity to discipline and tame the mind and open the heart more fully.

Tenet 3: Many/Most Don't Realize Spirit Within

There are many variations on this theme. For some, they have disavowed that they are spiritual beings. Such people may either be Inexperienced Decliners or Rejectors, as outlined earlier. Not acknowledging Spirit at all, they can hardly realize Spirit within. Others, though, see Spirit, using whatever name they have chosen as being an external entity, a being that (in most nomenclatures, at least) looks down on them from some ethereal realm. Such people see themselves, and label themselves, based solely on their mortal ego that hopes, at some point in the future, to be one with Spirit. Such a spirituality, which could be called a "there and then" spirituality, precludes the full experience of a "here and now" spirituality. As Ken Wilber noted,

> I cannot perceive my own true identity, or my union with Spirit, because my awareness is clouded and obstructed by a certain activity that I am now engaged in. And that activity,

although known by many different names, is simply the activity of contracting and focusing awareness on my individual self or personal ego. My awareness is not open, relaxed, and God-centered, it is closed, contracted, and self-centered. (Becoming Me, n.d., p. 1)

When this contraction occurs, it is not possible to live at one with Spirit and all that exists.

Tenet 4: There Is a Path to Liberation

The path to liberation involves transcendence of the individual self or personal ego. Although the path to liberation is unique to each individual, there are common aspects of this path. Although this list is intended to be neither exhaustive nor prescriptive, some common aspects of the path to liberation include:

1. Study of sacred texts, either within your personal faith tradition or across faith traditions, as befits personal preference.
2. Discussion of sacred texts in some form of community.
3. A mindfulness-based practice; this might include a practice such as vipassana meditation, **centering prayer**, breath prayer, or **Lectio Divina**. Many practitioners of mindfulness practices, particularly those just beginning a practice, find that a teacher and/or a supportive community of practitioners deepens the practice. Recommended readings on these practices include:
   - Meditation—Gunaratana (2002) and LeShan (1974)
   - Centering Prayer—Keating (2002)
   - Breath Prayer—Lewis (1998)
   - Lectio Divina—Merton (1986)

Note: Although these practices are discussed in the texts from a perspective that is either nonreligious or affiliated with a particular religion, any of these practices can easily be adapted to be consistent with different belief systems.

4. Heartfulness-based practices, such as the Buddhist practice of Loving Kindness Meditation (Chodron, 1996; Salzberg & Kabat-Zinn, 2004) and the conscious practice of forgiveness (Luskin, 2003; Tipping, 2002; Worthington, 2001).
5. Body-centered practices, such as focusing (Cornell, 1996; Gendlin, 1982), yoga (Desikachar, 1999), breathwork (Grof, 1988; Manne, 2004; Taylor, 1994) or T'ai Chi (Liao, 2001).
6. Acting on increased mindfulness with acts of social justice and compassion.

Tenet 5: If This Path Is Followed, the Result Is Rebirth or Enlightenment

Through disciplined spiritual practice and study, it is possible to experience a "death" of the old self and emergence, or rebirth, of a new self, more fully authentic and self-actualized (Maslow, 1971). This transcendence may include peak experiences and epiphanies, but overall the process of rebirth or enlightenment is a gradual and lifelong process.

It is important here to distinguish between the authentic spiritual path and that which is inauthentic. One distinction that has been made is the relationship of the spiritual path to the development of ego, known as the pre/trans fallacy, discussed by Wilber (2000). Although it oversimplifies Wilber's concepts greatly, in the interest of space, consider simply the difference between a codependent and Mother Teresa. If you watch from the "outside," both will appear dedicated to a life of service to others. The difference lies, however, in intention. The codependent behaves in a manner that solidifies a nonspiritual ego, one that clings desperately to the notion that in serving others, he or she will find love and acceptance, the proverbial "good enough" irony. Such behavior is prerational in that it is not borne of, nor does it contribute to, a "rebirth" of the self. On the other hand, the selfless giving of someone like Mother Teresa has the sole intent of service to God and humankind. Such behavior is said to be transrational, in that it involves a transcending of the personal ego in lieu of compassion and service. One key distinction between the two involves self-compassion. The person functioning at a prerational level literally lives to serve others, often at personal psychological expense. On the other hand, the person functioning at a transrational level of development recognizes that compassion for others must begin with self-compassion.

Tenet 6: Rebirth or Enlightenment Result in the End of Suffering

This concept is perhaps best discussed within the Buddhist tradition, where it is commonly acknowledged that pain is inevitable but suffering is not. That is, suffering occurs when we resist the physical, emotional, and psychological pain in life (Chodron, 2002). One of the fruits of the life of disciplined spiritual practice and study is not the eradication of pain; rather, it is the end of resistance to pain and, therefore, the end of suffering.

Tenet 7: The End of Suffering Manifests in Social Actions of Mercy and Compassion

Ultimately, rebirth or enlightenment, resulting in the end of suffering, is useful only if it manifests in acts of social justice, mercy, love, and compassion for others. Smith (2003) put this succinctly when he asserted that altered states are useful only if they lead to altered traits.

SPECIAL CONSIDERATIONS FOR COUNSELING

Having discussed diverse belief systems, and a framework that provides convergence of the world's wisdom traditions, attention is now directed toward special considerations in counseling with spiritual issues in counseling. Among these are issues related to approaching spiritual issues, ethical competence, and working with spiritual bypass.

Approaching Client Spiritual Issues

Whether clients bring their spiritual issues into counseling explicitly (i.e., identifying a crisis of faith or spiritual emergency) or implicitly (i.e., presenting issues that are underlaid with unspoken issues related to meaning and purpose), early responses of the counselor set the tone for the therapeutic process. Inherent in these responses from the counselor are meta-messages about the role that religious and spiritual beliefs, practices, or experiences can and should play in the counseling process.

In a seminal and frequently cited article, Zinnbauer and Pargament (2000) provide a nomenclature for the various approaches that counselors can take in working with spiritual issues that arise. In their categorization, counselors can take approaches that are rejectionist, exclusivist, constructivist, or pluralist. To this category system, I wish to add **impositional**, and will discuss this classification more fully. Reflection 15.2 on page 382 offers an opportunity to consider these categories and how they might relate to your work with clients.

The **rejectionist** counselor denies the sacred "truths" of the client. The counseling literature is replete with examples of the rejectionist approach. Freud reduced religion and spirituality to fantasy and wish fulfillment and characterized the religious experience as "infantile regression to a primitive state of limitless narcissism" (Freud 1930/1961, p. 19). This is far from a dated stance, however. In a recent interview (Master Psychotherapists, n.d.), Albert Ellis avowed that "Spirit and soul is horseshit of the worst sort" (p. 1). These are extreme examples in that they reduce the Sacred to psychological disturbance or defense (Zinnbauer & Pargament, 2000). There are, however, many examples of more tacit and implicit rejections. For example, in any given day, how many clients across the country choose not to talk about their religious and spiritual lives, largely because the counselor does not include this as an aspect of the initial assessment? Such a bias on the part of the counselor, although clearly less malicious than the quotes of Freud and Ellis, remains no less rejectionistic in impact (Harper & Gill, 2005).

The **exclusivist** counselor believes in a fundamental and exclusive reality of religious and spiritual experience. As such, the exclusivist is respectful of the client's religious and spiritual views, but only to the extent that these beliefs are consistent with the exclusivist's own understanding (Zinnbauer & Pargament, 2000). To the extent that the client's religious and spiritual worldview differ from that of the counselor, the exclusivist counselor sees it as within her or his purview to "bring the client around" to what they perceive as the "correct" belief system. As such, the exclusivist counselor proselytizes for a previously determined set of beliefs. Counselors using this approach have the potential to be as intolerant as a counselor working from a rejectionistic perspective. Clearly, then, both the rejectionist and exclusivist approaches to the sacred are problematic, and inconsistent with ethical standards of the counseling profession.

In contrast, the other two approaches to working with the Sacred, constructivist and pluralist approaches, are appropriate and consistent with counselor's ethical codes of conduct. Counselors working from a **constructivist** approach do not believe in an absolute reality, but that truth is constructed by humans in interactions with each other as they strive to understand their life experience. The focus, then, is on the quality of the constructions rather than whether the counselor agrees with the constructions (Neimeyer, 1995). When psychological symptoms appear, they are considered a manifestation of the breakdown of constructions and then, and only then, are the constructions considered problematic; at all times, the therapeutic work remains within the client's belief system and worldview (Zinnbauer & Pargament, 2000). There are, however, two substantive criticisms of the constructivist approach. First, when working with diverse religious and spiritual beliefs, it is important for the constructivist counselor to be authentic and sincere. It is possible that the impact of the constructivist counselor's work can be undermined by the client perception of insincerity on the part of the counselor. Second, the relativistic approach to client problems and perceptions can, in some instances be problematic. Zinnbauer and Pargament use the example of a parent who uses religious beliefs to justify physically abusing children as discipline. In such cases, it may be necessary for even the *constructivist* counselor to intervene on ethical and legal grounds.

The fourth approach to the Sacred, pluralism, involves an acceptance of diverse paths to Spirit as valid. Although there is agreement that Spirit exists, spiritual beliefs, practices, and experiences evolve within cultures and are expressed by different people in different ways. The **pluralistic** counselor holds personal beliefs, but at the same time prizes the different beliefs of a client. The pluralistic counselor differs from the constructivist counselor in one key way. Although the constructivist counselor works only within the religious and spiritual "template" of the client, the pluralistic counselor is willing to expose her beliefs with the client and "negotiate their social reality . . . and work to define the goals for therapy" (Zinnbauer & Pargament, 2000, p. 168). As with the constructivist approach, however, there are potential pitfalls to the pluralistic approach. Pluralistic counselors must be persistently aware of how their own beliefs and values might be impacting the therapeutic process and maintain a collaborative stance. A second problem, common to both pluralistic counselors and exclusivist counselors, occurs when the counselor and client come from a shared religious reality. In such cases, it is easy for one or both to assume that they share common beliefs and values when, in fact, there may be substantial variance between the two. In such cases, the counselor may fail to assess the client's religious worldview adequately, or the client may not sufficiently describe his problem. This occurs based on a faulty assumption that the other understands them more than they do.

Clearly, then, counselors who work with the Sacred need to work from either a constructivist or pluralist approach. To operate from a rejectionist or exclusivist approach risks violating the ethical and legal standards for professional conduct and, more importantly, has a high likelihood of, at best, minimizing the effectiveness of counseling and, at worst, causing iatrogenic harm.

With great respect toward the importance and impact of the Zinnbauer and Pargament (2000) categorization of approaches to the Sacred, with the increased attention to the important role of spirituality in the psychotherapeutic process, it may be useful to consider a fifth approach, potentially as problematic as either the rejectionist or exclusivist approaches. This approach might be labeled **impositional**, in that it involves the imposition of a religious or spiritual framework with a client who is either an atheist or nonreligious. Census data suggest that almost 40 million people, or 13.2% of the U. S. population, identify as nonreligious, and that this number grew 110% in the decade from 1990 to 2000 (Largest Religious Groups in the United States, n.d.). Further, more than 1.2 million Americans, or 0.4% of the U. S. population, self-identify as Atheist. For either of these groups, imposing a religious or spiritual view on the presenting problems and treatment process is a disavowal of their personal beliefs and values. This is akin to the exclusivist approach in that it imposes a set of beliefs on the client. The distinction, however, is that the impositional counselor is imposing the overarching framework of spirituality onto the counseling process when this is counter to the client's desires and expectations for counseling. Within this framework, it is necessary to consider that a counselor could be both impositional and exclusivist. Such a combined stance would involve imposing a specific religious reality on a client who not only does not agree with that specific reality, but also does not want spirituality to "intrude" into the secular counseling process.

REFLECTION 15.2

Using the Zinnbauer and Pargament category scheme, consider what approach you will most likely/frequently use when approaching the Sacred in counseling. Regardless of what category you place yourself, discuss the type of religious/spiritual beliefs with which you expect you will most struggle to work. Why?

Zinnbauer and Pargament have provided an invaluable schema for considering approaches to the sacred in counseling. It is important to realize, however, that this schema also might be applicable at more macro levels. In addition to working with individual clients, counselors must act to champion diversity and at minimum a tolerance, if not embracement, of religious diversity. Although such acts of social justice and advocacy might best be performed in a gentle and compassionate manner, such acts must also be emboldened by the knowledge that religious intolerance is detrimental to the clients we serve and society at large.

ETHICAL COMPETENCE   Ethical competence is at the heart of integrating spirituality and religion into the counseling process. Faiver and Ingersoll (2005) provide a nice framework for considering ethical competence in integrating spirituality and religion into counseling by considering Wilber's (1997, 1999) concepts of translation and transformation. **Translation** refers to those aspects of the spiritual experience such as beliefs, creeds, and dogma that the individual uses as a framework with which to find meaning and purpose in life. Ethical competence related to the translational aspects of the spiritual life follows the Zinnbauer and Pargament nomenclature discussed previously; that is, that the counselor works within either a constructivist or pluralist approach with the client's spiritual and religious beliefs and values.

Much more complex, however, is ethical competence related to **transformation**. According to Wilber (1997), the transformational aspect of spirituality involves progressions to higher levels of spiritual development, often accompanied by physical, emotional, cognitive, and spiritual break-throughs. An example of a transformational experience is a near death experience (NDE). People who have a NDE commonly become more altruistic, less materialistic, and more loving (Moody, 2001), attributes consistent with spiritual transformation. More subtle experiences of transformation may occur, for example, for a person who has developed and sustained a disciplined contemplative practice such as **vipassana meditation** or centering prayer. In the case of either a spontaneous transformation, such as an NDE, or a more gradual one, the central question is whether a counselor can accept and value the spiritual experiences of the individual. At the very least, a counselor who defines herself religiously from only a **translative** dimension may have difficulty working effectively with someone whose current practice and experiences are more transformational in nature. The converse of this likely also is true; that is, a counselor with a bias toward the transformational function of spirituality may run the risk of imposing this on a client whose primary interest is working at the translative (i.e., beliefs and meaning-making) level.

SPIRITUAL BYPASS   **Spiritual bypass** is a term coined by Whitfield (2003) to refer to a phenomenon in which a person attempts to heal psychological wounds by working at the spiritual level only. In so doing, "work" in the other realms, including the cognitive, emotional, physical, and interpersonal, is relegated to "less than" status and shunned. In short, the spiritual life of the individual serves an avoidance function, as the individual avoids other aspects of his problems.

Spiritual bypass is considered a common problem among people pursuing a spiritual path (Cashwell, Myers, & Shurts, 2004; Welwood, 1983). There are a number of common problems that emerge from spiritual bypass, including compulsive goodness, repression of undesirable emotions, spiritual narcissism, extreme external locus of control, spiritual addiction, blind faith in charismatic leaders, abdication of personal responsibility, and social isolation (Cashwell, 2005; Cashwell, Bentley, & Yarborough, 2007; Cashwell & Rayle, in press)

From a diversity perspective, the client in spiritual bypass presents a unique challenge. Such a client often presents in counseling with an explicit interest, if not desire, to integrate the Sacred into the counseling process. To fully support the wholeness and healing of such clients, though, it likely is necessary to encourage and challenge them to work at multiple levels (i.e., cognitive, emotional, physical, and interpersonal). To do so in a respectful manner is, at times, no small accomplishment. To highlight this, a case example is presented in Case Study 15.1.

CASE STUDY 15.1
The Case of Gail

Gail was a 44-year-old White female presenting in counseling with depression that she reported battling "off and on for all of my life." She had seen three counselors previously in the past 7 years, and had seen two counselors within the past 2 years, asserting that "they didn't really help me much." She specifically said that she was drawn to work with me because of my interest in spirituality.

Gail reported that she was a devout Christian who discovered in the past few years that references to reincarnation existed within early versions of the Christian Bible, and that these were deleted by the

(continued)

Council of Nicaea. She had begun studying reincarnation, and was convinced that her problems with depression stemmed from past-life experiences. I supported her in telling the story of her lifelong battle with depression, contracted for counseling services, and requested a release to talk to her previous counselor, a local counselor who I knew well.

Contacting her previous counselor proved an interesting experience. She spoke of Gail's preoccupation with past lives, and that Gail would spend a great deal of time ruminating in session about what her past lives must have been like to generate so much depression. She resisted referrals for medication evaluation because, as she said, "If I can just find the source of this depression, I believe that God and I can heal it." The client terminated after the counselor got frustrated with Gail and told her that "she shouldn't worry so much about past lives until this one wasn't so messed up," a response that the previous counselor admitted was unhelpful. Based on the initial session, I conceptualized Gail as struggling with spiritual bypass. She was, I believed, hyperfocused on karma as the cause of her depression. While I was not in a position to say if this was true or not, I expected that her counseling process would be more complex than this. In the next session, I further assessed what Gail thought the results might be of doing past-life work. Her answers seemed to make it clear that she was not looking to lessen her depression, but was rather looking for a reason (or, perhaps, an excuse) for why she was depressed. I was prepared to refer Gail to someone who did past-life hypnotherapy as this is not part of my counseling work. Based on my conceptualization, though, I was hopeful that I might be able to work with Gail in such a way that the problem was not seen as solely spiritual or karmic while still respecting her belief system.

My treatment approach was to remind Gail that she had been depressed for, as she reported, as long as she could remember, and that it was probably important to get better slowly. I told her that I thought it was important to go back in time, but that we should not start out by going straight back to past lives; I suggested we should work to understand the early part of this life as a stepping stone back to past lives. Although I think Gail was hoping to immediately do past-life work, she agreed that this made sense and we moved forward with our work together. Using an integrated combination of early life recollections from an Adlerian framework and phenomenological experiential approaches to work with those early recollections in the here and now, Gail began to unearth and heal some early trauma, including sexual and physical abuse. She began to connect with her anger, learned to channel that energy in appropriate ways, and began to be more assertive. As she reported at the end of the ninth session, "I feel like I have found my voice." I experienced Gail as a deeply spiritual woman, and we both spoke of feeling supported in our work together by something "beyond us." As her counseling progressed, she talked less about past lives. During our termination session (session 23), Gail laughed and said, "I still feel a little down sometimes, but nothing like I did. Maybe I'll do some past-life work sometime later, just for fun, but that doesn't seem nearly as important as it once did."

Gail did some amazing work as she began to heal some very old psychological wounds. If I did anything well with Gail, it was honoring her belief systems while still working in a way that seemed psychologically grounded and sound, by using her framework of past-life work to get her to work with her early childhood experiences. In her case, the work was largely at the cognitive and emotional levels, which resulted in some clear changes in interpersonal behaviors. To have supported her in her desire to work only at the spiritual level would have, in my opinion, been a therapeutic blunder as it would have supported her proclivity toward spiritual bypass.

ASERVIC COMPETENCIES   The **Association for Spiritual, Ethical, and Religious Values in Counseling**, or **ASERVIC** (2007) has developed competencies for integrating spirituality into the counseling process. Counselors may increase their levels of awareness, knowledge, and skills with respect to their own as well as their clients' spirituality by reflecting on each competence (see Activity 15.2). The nine competencies are:

1. The professional counselor can explain the difference between religion and spirituality, including similarities and differences.
2. The professional counselor can describe religious and spiritual beliefs and practices in a cultural context.
3. The professional counselor engages in self-exploration of religious and spiritual beliefs in order to increase sensitivity, understanding and acceptance of diverse belief systems.
4. The professional counselor can describe her/his religious and/or spiritual belief system and explain various models of religious or spiritual development across the lifespan.
5. The professional counselor can demonstrate sensitivity and acceptance of a variety of religious and/or spiritual expressions in client communication.
6. The professional counselor can identify limits of her/his understanding of a client's religious or spiritual expression, and demonstrate appropriate referral skills and generate possible referral sources.
7. The professional counselor can assess the relevance of the religious and/or spiritual domains in the client's therapeutic issues.
8. The professional counselor is sensitive to and receptive of religious and/or spiritual themes in the counseling process as befits the expressed preference of each client.
9. The professional counselor uses a client's religious and/or spiritual beliefs in the pursuit of the client's therapeutic goals as befits the client's expressed preference.

ACTIVITY 15.2

Form dyads and select three of the nine ASERVIC competencies. Brainstorm specific ways that you can increase your awareness, knowledge, and skills for each selected competence.

Competence ————:

_____

_____

_____

Competence ————:

_____

_____

_____

Competence ————:

_____

_____

_____

TABLE 15.2 Recommended Readings and Resources

For more information about the implementation of the ASERVIC competencies, read:

- *Integrating Spirituality and Religion into Counseling: A Guide to Competent Practice* (Cashwell & Young, 2005).

For further reading about the competent and culturally aware integration of spirituality into the counseling process, read:

- *Integrating Religion and Spirituality into Counseling: A Comprehensive Approach* (Frame, 2002).
- *Integrating Spirituality into Multicultural Counseling* (Fukuyama & Sevig, 1999).

The following online resources are recommended for additional information:

- www.religioustolerance.org
- www.beliefnet.com
- www.pluralism.org

Summary

If one believes, consistent with the majority of U.S. citizens, that Spirit exists in some form, and that one's religion or spirituality are aspects and expressions of culture, then counselors should be trained to address client issues related to religion and spirituality. This chapter has considered aspects of both the diversity of religious and spiritual beliefs and practices, as well as the unity that can be seen woven through the tapestry of the world religions.

Spirituality is difficult to define and has been described as a set of individual beliefs, practices, and experiences that lead to transcendence of self and connection with others. Religion may be viewed as organized spirituality. The relationship between spirituality and religion can be conceptualized in many ways: complementary or coincidental; religious practice not necessarily indicative of quality of religious or spiritual experience; or spirituality disconnected to an organized religion. Several major religions are described in this chapter, including Buddhism, Hinduism, Taoism, Confucianism, Christianity, Judaism, and Islam. While these religions are distinct from each other, there are several common tenets across religions.

The chapter discussed several approaches counselors may take in integrating spirituality into counseling. These include (a) rejectionist (counselor

dismisses or avoids discussions of spirituality); (b) exclusivist (counselor respects client's spiritual and religious beliefs to the degree they match the counselor's beliefs; (c) constructivist (counselor attends to how the spiritual or religious belief is constructed); (d) pluralist (counselor respects multiple beliefs and is willing to share his beliefs with the client); and (e) impositional (counselor imposes a spiritual or religious framework on the client who is either atheist or nonreligious).

An issue that may arise when working with clients involves spiritual bypass, in which clients attempt to solve psychological issues with spirituality alone. Finally, it is important to be ethically and culturally competent when integrating spirituality into counseling. The ASERVIC competencies are a useful framework to begin to think about ethical and cultural competence. Table 15.2 provides additional resources for facilitating multicultural counseling competence around spiritual diversity.

Within the ancient sanskrit language, there is a word that lacks a one-word translation in English. It characterizes one way in which spirituality can be integrated within the counseling process, that of seeing the client as more than a cluster of symptoms to be reduced. It translates as "the light within me bows to the light within you."

Namaste'.

The purpose of the following closing meditation is to allow people with diverse beliefs about spirituality to work with their Spirit connection.

1. Find a quiet place to sit in which you will not be interrupted during the meditation.
2. Soft, ambient background music may be used to support the meditation (e.g., *Shamanic Journey* by Anugama).
3. Begin the meditation with a few minutes of deep, full, and slow breathing in which you intentionally breathe fully both into the abdomen and then into the chest; the exhale should be used to release any remaining tension in the body.
4. After several minutes of full breathing, consider a problem or challenge that you currently face to come into your awareness. This should be done without overthinking the problem but, rather, allowing it to emerge naturally.
5. After considering this problem, see a connection to Spirit emerging before you. This may take the form of a person, a deity, an animal, or some other form. Look at your connection to Spirit closely. Study it.
6. Ask your connection to Spirit what He/She/It has to tell you about the problem that is before you. Allow the answer(s) to emerge slowly and fully without overthinking or judging the experience. After allowing this experience to play itself out fully for you, thank the connection to Spirit for providing you with this wisdom, and allow the image before you to fade.
7. Journal your experience or, if you are doing this within a class or other community, discuss your experience from the meditation and what it means for you in the coming days.

Multicultural Conceptualization

CHAPTER 16

Alternative Approaches to Counseling Theories

JONATHAN J. ORR

PREVIEW

Theory is the foundation upon which counselors build their professional identity and it is the knowledge base that defines mental health professions. As a fundamental dimension of counselor identity, theory also forms the backbone of clinical practice and informs how a counselor works with various types of clients. Given this primacy of theory to the work of counselors, it is important to understand how theory is created and supported in a multicultural context. Throughout this chapter, the development and implementation of theory will be viewed from a perspective of intersecting identities. This chapter assists readers to connect worldview to theory development, identify alternative sources for theory in multicultural contexts, trace cultural assumptions implicit to the major counseling theories, learn to use culture as a springboard for expanding the application of traditional counseling theories, and discover novel approaches to counseling that incorporate multicultural dimensions. Last, when examining the development, acquisition, and application of counseling theory in the context of culture, it is paramount to consider the cultural sources of information. This author's cultural identity consists of the following dimensions: White, male, educated, heterosexual, agnostic, lower-middle SES, living in an urban area in a southern U.S. region. Although this list is in no way exhaustive, readers are invited to consider how the author's cultural lenses through which information is passed may alternatively clarify and obscure included content.

SOCIAL AND CULTURAL FOUNDATIONS OF COUNSELING THEORY

Embarking on a journey to examine the cultural dimensions and relevance of counseling theory can indeed be a daunting task. In addition to specific theorists, many counselors have built entire careers developing, refining, or simply examining counseling theory. The basis for this challenge lies in the dynamic nature that is shared by both culture and theory. Both culture and theory are founded on persons' experiences, so as people experience more, including one another, their theoretical orientation changes. In addition to sharing similarities, culture and theory are at times at odds with one another. Theory in its most basic sense is reductionist and seeks to provide a consistent and all-encompassing response and explanation for various dimensions of a person's life (Hackney & Cormier, 2005; Seligman, 2006). However, counselors are not able to use the same type of theory to fit all people. Each is a unique person with unique perspectives and experiences that define an individual.

Theory cannot encompass all of human experience; likewise, it cannot account for all of the thoughts, feelings, behaviors, or contexts that contribute to individuals' identities. Counselors tend to get into trouble when they think of theory as an absolute or all-encompassing. In other words, a theory may indicate that things should be a certain way for a client, so counselors then grow to expect that from a client (Murdock, 2004).

Theory is something that belongs to us as counselors. It helps us organize what a client is saying, it provides us with direction for our questioning, and it helps us make sense of our work as counselors (Murdock, 2004). Our theory provides us with starting points in our work with clients. In this way, the phrase *theoretical orientation* describes both our rationale and our action. We use our theory to bring purpose to our work with clients, and theory helps us orient to our clients.

Worldview Shaping Counseling

Most people are unaware of the process underlying how they live their lives. That is, most humans do not give much thought to their philosophical or theoretical approach to life. For the most part, life proceeds for people in a more active rather than reflective manner. They are more involved and concerned with the function of their lives (i.e., what they need to get done) as opposed to the explanations, the motivations, or reasons for living their lives. At times of crisis or change, people may become more interested in the processes underlying their ways of life, and that is when they seek assistance from helpers such as counselors or spiritual leaders. It is in these times with a professional guide that most people discover their motivation for living or their personal theory for life.

Personal theories for life have been characterized in counseling literature as synonymous with *worldview* (Axelson, 1999; Ivey, D'Andrea, Ivey, & Simek-Morgan, 2002). A person's **worldview** is comprised of personal constructs that are created within familial, cultural, and societal contexts, and are typically constructed from five value orientations based on the Kluckhohn and Strodtbeck (1961) theoretical model. They are (a) human nature (evil, mixed, or good); (b) person/nature relations (subjugation to nature, harmony with nature, or mastery over nature); (c) social relations (lineal, collateral, or individual); (d) time sense (past, present, or future); and (e) human activity (being, being-in-becoming, or doing) (Yang, 1998). The extent to which individuals combine these orientations varies based on their identification with a particular cultural group and can account for both cross-cultural and within-group differences (Ivey et al., 2002; Ibrahim, Roysircar-Sodowsky, & Ohnishi, 2001; Yang, 1998). Refer to Reflection 16.1 and consider how you might integrate these orientations.

Building on these worldview orientations, Hjelle and Ziegler (1992) identify nine basic assumptions that counselors use to create and support their approaches to counseling. The nine assumptions are freedom/determinism, rationality/irrationality, holism/elementalism, constitutionalism/environmentalism, changeability/unchangeability, subjectivity/objectivity, proactivity/reactivity, homeostasis/heterostasis, and knowability/unknowability. These assumptions may be conceptualized along a continuum. Most people find themselves between the two poles and the combination of the assumptions dictates how persons see themselves and then view others. Counseling theorists are included among these and base the development of their approaches on these assumptions.

REFLECTION 16.1

Take a moment to answer the following questions based on the five dimensions of worldview set forth by Kluckhohn (1951, 1956). Then reflect on the value assigned to your own particular worldview:

- *Human Nature:* Do you consider humans to be essentially good, evil, or do we have equal capacity for good and evil at a given moment?
- *Person/Nature Relations:* Which of the following statements would you agree with most:
  - Humans are ultimately at the mercy of nature. We are not able to control how nature impacts us.
  - Humans are the masters of nature. We are meant to control it for our benefit.
  - Humans and nature rely on one another for coexistence. One cannot continue without the other keeping it in balance.
- *Social Relations:* Which of the following statements would you agree with most:
  - Ultimately, I need to take action for myself and do what is right for me in life.
  - Ultimately, I need to know how my actions might reflect on my family or community and act accordingly.
  - Ultimately, I need to know how my actions might reflect on my family and the legacy of those who have come before me.
- *Time Sense:* Are you more likely to be time-oriented to the past, present, or future?
- *Human Activity:* Which of the following statements would you agree with most:
  - I am most satisfied being acknowledged for my activities and accomplishments.
  - I am most satisfied being acknowledged for who I am and the aspirations I have for who I want to become.
  - I am satisfied being acknowledged for just being me.

Reflect for a moment on your responses. How is your worldview supported and/or challenged by your culture? How is it challenged and/or supported by your society? How might your worldview be similar and different from potential clients?

Transition From Worldview to Theory

From the foundation of personal worldviews, individuals begin to make sense out of their lives and account for the contexts in which they live. As people make meaning of their own life experiences, many may extend their worldview to others. Through observation, reflection, and refinement over time those individual worldviews may soon evolve into explanations for why things happen for groups of people. Gladding (2005b) points out that "a sound theory matches a counselor's personal philosophy of helping" (p. 4) and in this way, as worldview expands from the individual to larger groups, theory can be born. Indeed it has been suggested that most if not all of the counseling theories and techniques are derived from personal worldviews (Ibrahim, 1991; Ivey et al., 2002; Murdock, 2004; Trevino, 1996).

With worldviews forming the basis for individuals' personal philosophies as well as theoretical orientations in counseling, it seems that there exists potential for both success and folly. Take, for instance, counselors whose theories are congruent with both their own worldview and their clients' worldviews. In this pairing, counselor and client could share common ground in the characterization of challenges, motivations, and goals for living. This type of congruence facilitates stronger client–counselor alliance and counselor empathy (Kim, Ng, & Ahn, 2005). Alternatively, when clients and counselors differ on even one of the worldview dimensions, the therapeutic relationship can be affected negatively (see Activity 16.1).

ACTIVITY 16.1

Discuss the following case vignette involving competing worldviews in small groups:

A Japanese student studying as a visiting scholar attends a counseling session at a college counseling center complaining of general sadness and anxiety. During the session, the student describes to her counselor difficulty that she is having in some of her classes required for her major. As the counselor probes, he begins to realize that his client's sadness and anxiety seem to be directly linked to the courses with which she is struggling. However, when the counselor suggests that the student consider changing her major, she refuses saying that her parents would never approve of that action. The counselor is confident in his assessment and believes that the change in major would greatly improve his client's disposition. He continues to focus on encouraging her to change her major and challenge her parents' expectations. He sums his suggestions to her by saying, "After all, you are here living your life, not them. You need to make decisions that will work for you." The student left and upon returning asked for a different counselor citing that her previous one did not understand her.

How did this counselor's worldview affect his counseling?
Was his worldview congruent with his client's?
How might this counselor have approached his client differently?

From its more individualized beginnings in worldview, theory attempts to take on a more comprehensive explanation for human experience. Theory typically has been characterized as a collection of "interrelated ideas, constructs, and principles proposed to explain certain observations" (Hjelle & Ziegler, 1992, p. 7). In the field of counseling, these observations tend to be interpersonal in nature and deal with psychic rather than physical concerns. Furthermore, counseling theory commonly incorporates guidelines for human development and sets criteria for typical or desired functioning. It is in this area of defining typical human development and functioning that theory finds its limits. Human development is a social process (Bronfenbrenner, 1977; Erikson, 1978; Newman & Newman, 1999) that is impacted by persons' culture, ethnicity, gender, and socioeconomic status, among other things. Likewise, human functioning is also socially contextualized and infinite in its scope. Within these constant processes of evolution, human development and functioning can never be fully characterized by one theory. Regardless of its reported comprehensiveness, a counseling theory will work with particular clients under particular conditions (Ivey et al., 2002). To remain multiculturally competent in their application of theory, counselors need to understand the worldview of their clients as well as the worldview supported by particular counseling theories and strive to balance the two. It may behoove counselors to consider various conceptual systems (see Reflection 16.2).

REFLECTION 16.2

Based on cultural differences, worldviews have been variously characterized as representative of different groups. The following worldviews adapted from Jackson and Meadows (1991, p. 75) outline three conceptual systems that are prevalent among large populations in the United States.

European Conceptual System
- Material possession and the acquisition of objects are emphasized.
- External knowledge is emphasized and is supported through measuring and/or counting.

- Logic is based on a dichotomous system (e.g., things either are or are not).
- Identity and worth are based on external criteria.

Asian Conceptual System

- Cohesiveness of the group and cosmic unity (all life and energy is connected and inseparable) are emphasized.
- A blend of internal and external knowledge is emphasized and is supported by an integration of mind, body, and spirit.
- Logic is based on unity of mind and thought with a focus on interrelations.
- Identity and worth are based on being an integration of internal and external criteria.

African Conceptual System

- Spiritual and material dimensions are emphasized, and focuses on the relationship between women and men.
- Self-knowledge is emphasized and is supported through symbolic imagery and rhythm.
- Logic is based on the union of opposites, with a focus on interrelation of human and spiritual dimensions.
- Identity and worth are intrinsic.

Which of the conceptual systems is most in line with your own? Which is most different?
How might you use this information to inform your theoretical conceptualization of particular clients?
How might you use this information to empower your clients?
Based on these conceptual systems, match theories that you think would be most effective with particular clients. What evidence can you use to support your matches?

Alternative Sources of Theory in Multicultural Counseling

Theories of counseling have specific definitions for mental health and parameters for typical mental functioning. Exclusion from the targeted culture for counseling theory sets clients at a disadvantage. From the start, they run the risk of being considered somehow deficient because they do not fit the typical description of a client. Something that is actually a cultural difference can be misconstrued as a deficiency in the client. Take, for example, something as simple as language. If clients who do not speak English fluently as their first language were to visit an average counselor in the United States (the largest employer of counselors in the world), they run the risk of misdiagnosis based on counselors misunderstanding their presentations of issues. Furthermore, when counselors and clients do not share common language, their understanding of particular meanings for concepts as well as behaviors are affected. Simply stated, without some shared understanding of what it means to be mentally healthy, no counseling theory can be effective.

The difficulties that uncommon language bases present to the counseling relationship can be minor when compared to challenges that arise when worldviews of counselors and clients differ. When counselor and client differ on worldview dimensions, the very structure and basis for mental health can be called into question. When it comes to the defining and understanding of what it means to be a mentally healthy and functioning person in multicultural counseling contexts, counseling theory provides only a small part of a larger picture. In many cultures, the practice of counseling is relatively unknown, and the notion of mental health is incorporated into other social systems such as religion or familial relationships. These social systems influence people's beliefs about what it means to be a "normally" functioning member of a particular group. For counselors intending to be multiculturally competent, it is important that they understand the ways in which various social systems define a person's life. The social systems of religion, government, and family are three major systems found across cultures that impact clients and shape a culture's understanding of mental health.

RELIGION AND SPIRITUALITY   Religion and spirituality have alternatively been called the greatest unifier and the greatest divider of people. Nations have been built and wars have been waged on the bases of religious and spiritual beliefs. Religious and spiritual beliefs directly influence persons' worldviews in a number of ways that in turn affect how they define mental health. In many religions, the mind and functions of mental health are closely linked to the divine. Thoughts, emotions, and even motivations for behaviors are attributed to the influence of the divine. These beliefs in the influence of the divine in all matters beyond physical action predate any notion of counseling theory and fundamentally shape how persons shape their understanding of mental health.

When applying a particular theory of counseling it is important to consider how that theory interacts with clients' beliefs about the divine. Does the theory assume a humanistic perspective in that people can somehow control or influence their thoughts, behaviors, and emotions? Does the theory instead leave room for a deistic perspective in that the divine has some (if not primary) influence in people's lives? Answering these questions with each client and considering how clients conceptualize notions of the divine in their lives is an essential first step when integrating theory with religious and spiritual beliefs. A simple misunderstanding between counselor and client about the role of the divine can potentially lead to major differences in the perceptions of mental health. For example, while one may view hearing voices as an acceptable manifestation of the divine, the other may take it as a clear sign of Schizophrenia.

GOVERNMENT   In many ways particular forms of government are direct expressions of worldviews. Consider, for example, the American perspective of democracy. This form of democracy values equal representation in government based on certain inalienable rights that are attributed to all people. As the notions of democracy extend beyond this most basic understanding, there are certainly inequities that emerge and the definition of what a democracy might represent to different peoples begins to shift. These shifts in how democracy is represented are based in large part on worldviews. Within the United States democratic system, two of the primary opposing worldviews are represented by political parties. The Republican and the Democratic parties share a basic conceptualization for democratic governance, but differ greatly in how to define their roles in applying and supporting that government. The political differences between Republicans and Democrats in the United States are reflected in many lifestyle choices of individuals, and often these individuals pattern their own principles on the principles supported by their political affiliation.

Extending beyond the confines of an Amerocentric view of government, there are approximately nine systems of government in use throughout the world. Similar to democracy, each of these governments is based on worldview and lifestyle choices that are made within the context of government. Laws are created to support the structure of government and to reinforce the lifestyle choices for the governed. In this way the notions of acceptable human activity (i.e., normal functioning) are defined and shaped by government. Admittedly there is greater complexity to the intersection of government and lifestyle choices of the governed, but even in this most basic description, the impact that political or governmental views on mental health is evident (see Activity 16.2). Simply stated, governments set the parameters for what it means to be an accepted member of society and, by extension, how functional mental health is defined.

ACTIVITY 16.2

In dyads, consider the following definitions of mental health:

Mental health is the foundation for the well-being and effective functioning of individuals. It is more than the absence of a mental disorder. Mental health is the ability to think and learn, and the ability to understand and live with one's emotions and the reactions of others. It is a state of balance within a person and between a person and the environment. Physical, psychological, social, cultural, spiritual and other interrelated factors participate in producing this balance. (WHO, 2001)

Mental health is a state of successful performance of mental function, resulting in productive activities, fulfilling relationships with other people, and the ability to adapt to change and to cope with adversity. Mental health is indispensable to personal well-being, family and interpersonal relationships, and contribution to community or society. (United States Surgeon General, 1999)

- In what ways are these definitions similar?
- In what ways are they different?
- What are some of the assumptions that support these definitions?
- How might these definitions be influenced by worldview?
- How might these definitions be influenced by systems of government and/or social norms?
- Using these definitions of mental health, provide examples of culturally specific behavior that could be considered unhealthy.

FAMILY   Family is a social system that has the greatest potential for shaping notions of mental health. It serves as a filter through which the previously mentioned systems of religion and government are passed. Individuals learn how to connect with the divine and function socially from the members of their families. As such an influential social system, families play a primary role in shaping individuals' notions of mental health. Both the role of families in general within a society and the role of families in specific individuals' lives are significant factors. Specifically, how individuals relate to their particular families and how those familial relationships relate to the overall role of families are important to consider in multicultural counseling.

Families may play different roles within a particular society and understanding these roles will provide counselors with information about mental health. For example, what constitutes a family? Is family comprised of blood relations alone or does it include marital relations, close friends, and/or neighbors? How are family relations connected to social status? How are families created—by choice or arrangement? Who is allowed to be considered a family and under what conditions? What are some of the taboos related to marriage? These among other questions are important to explore with clients to achieve clear meaning for how their own families are viewed in particular societal contexts. Furthermore, exploration related to the general role of families in society will provide clues to the definitions for functional and dysfunctional familial relationships.

Moving to the individual level, it is important to explore how clients interact in their own families. Typically, clients get their first definition and subsequent reinforcement of mental health from their families. These familial characterizations may or may not reflect larger societal views of mental health, but regardless, their impact on individuals is significant. Relationships between clients and their family members are important to note as are other dimensions of family. How do clients' behaviors compare to others in the family? What roles are clients expected to play in their families and are they meeting those expectations? What is the role of ancestors in the family culture? Answers to these questions and others related to individuals' roles in family systems could illuminate the worldview that families use to shape notions of mental health.

APPLICATIONS OF COUNSELING THEORY ACROSS CULTURES

Traditional counseling theories are abundant in the counseling literature and the degree of their relevance across cultures is gaining increased attention. In this section, traditional theoretical approaches and Western assumptions of these approaches are discussed. In addition, adapting traditional approaches and integrating Eastern approaches in counseling practice are discussed.

Traditional Theoretical Approaches to Counseling

Over the last 50 years, the choices for therapeutic approaches to counseling have grown to reach over 400 in number (Corsini & Wedding, 2000). While this growth has been considerable, the foundational theories that support these approaches have grown at a more measured pace. The growth of major theoretical conceptualizations is typically characterized by the term *forces* and authors almost universally agree that the first three **forces in counseling** theory are comprised of psychodynamic, cognitive–behavioral, and humanistic–existential (Axelson, 1999; Gladding, 2005b; Hackney & Cormier, 2005, Ivey et al., 2002). The fourth force has been conceptualized as transpersonal (Peterson & Nisenholz, 1999), multicultural (Essandoh, 1996; Lee, 2006; Pedersen, 1999), systemic (Corey, 2005), and integrative (Seligman, 2006), among others. Regardless of the specific title for this fourth force, there is clearly a shared emphasis on contextual and systemic influences among all of the approaches.

Providing even a cursory overview of the major theoretical orientations in counseling is beyond the scope of this chapter. Indeed whole texts and even series of texts have been devoted to the discussion of theories and approaches to counseling. Turning instead to some of the underlying assumptions and constructs that support development of the four forces in counseling, similarities in worldview emerge. It has become a commonly accepted supposition that most of the major theories have been developed to serve White, middle-class men of European heritage (Atkinson, Morten, & Sue, 1979; Ivey, 1988; Katz, 1985; Ponterotto, 2001). Tracing much of counseling theory to its origins, theorists such as Freud, Adler, Perls, Ellis, and Rogers spring to mind and it would seem that, for the most part, this acknowledgment is supported and further reinforced by the demographic characteristics of the theorists themselves. However, besides the common target demographic for early theorists, there is something else that these theorists share in common. Their theories were developed to serve clients living particularly within Western European and American contexts (see Reflection 16.3). This means that counseling theories generally are developed in and support a particularly Westernized worldview.

REFLECTION 16.3

Consider the following examples of conventional Western assumptions in counseling theories:

- The universe was created spontaneously either through physical phenomenon (e.g., Big Bang) or creation by the divine.
- Through research and study all things can be known and reality is concrete and measurable.
- Empirical proof and intellectual knowledge and learning are highest valued.
- Consciousness is objective and only characteristic of humans.

- Personality provides unique individual identity and context is not as important as the intrinsic characteristics of an individual.
- Living is marked by growth and progress toward an inevitable end and value of one's life is based on the reflection of past experiences and future goals.
- Death is an inevitable end to human life. Consciousness, personality, and existence in the physical world end with death.
- Suffering is to be avoided and progress is marked by the alleviation of suffering.
- Emotions, learning, and consciousness are physical functions based on electrochemical systems.
- Mind, body, and spirit are divided and often at odds.
- Visual and/or auditory stimuli are more reliable than intuition (i.e., "Seeing is believing").
- Behavior, personality, and identity are individually created and modified.

To what extent do your own beliefs and worldviews match these assumptions?

Describe some of the alternative assumptions that might contradict these worldviews.

What cultural and/or social institutions support these assumptions?

How do mental health services create and perpetuate particular worldview assumptions?

What are some ways in which you might become aware of other assumptions underlying counseling theory? How might you best use those assumptions to serve your clients rather than to alienate them?

The relatively limited client base targeted by the majority of counseling theories proves difficult particularly when working with diverse client populations. Limiting theoretical and treatment options to approaches based solely on Western worldviews can prove to be both useless and potentially harmful to some clients (Pedersen, 2000). Furthermore, the almost singular worldview shared among most of the theories in counseling seems to imply that the psychological distress and its treatment are endemic to one culture or worldview in particular. Based on that implication, questions about mental health and theories of counseling come to mind. Are mental health and by extension mental distress universal concepts or is it that they are unique to a Westernized view of the world? Do other cultures and worldviews account for mental health through the development and application of theory? To fully answer these questions, it is necessary to expand the definitions of both mental health and counseling theory.

Although the traditional counseling theories that comprise the first three forces in counseling may have been developed and initially applied with specific clients in mind, they have expanded to meet the needs of a greater diversity of clients. This ability to evolve and adapt over time is one of the hallmarks of a grand theory in counseling. **Grand theories** in counseling are theories that seek to integrate all dimensions of human experience into a single overarching theoretical framework. Typically, these grand theories incorporate many different models for counseling and spawn variations on a particular theme. Psychodynamic theory provides a prime example of grand theory in counseling. From Freud's original conception of the human condition, theorists such as Jung, Adler, Erikson, Horney, and Stack-Sullivan have all developed their own unique interpretation of psychodynamic theory. The grand theories in counseling coincide with the "forces" described earlier and include psychodynamic, cognitive–behavioral, and humanistic–existential theories.

Culturally Responsive Use of Traditional Theories

Culturally responsive counseling is a concept that is gaining popularity and it marks a departure from typical "one size fits all" approaches to counseling. In **culturally responsive counseling**, the counselor includes diverse perspectives in the counseling process and recognizes contextual dimensions such as culture, class, gender, race, sexual orientation, religion, and geography (Day-Vines et al., 2003). When practicing this concept of culturally responsive counseling, counselors must also be aware of their own cultural identities and the cultural contexts for their approach to counseling. Incorporating awareness of self in the counseling process characterizes the notion of culturally responsible counseling (Pedersen, 1997). It is not enough for counselors to simply respond to culture in terms of their clients; they must also take responsibility for their own cultural contexts and the contexts of their chosen theoretical orientation.

To be culturally responsive, counselors must learn to be flexible in their theoretical approach. In this sense, counselors are expected to be chameleons, changing their theoretical approach as the therapeutic environment changes in much the same way lizards change appearance to match their surroundings. Typically, theoretical flexibility has been characterized as eclectic or integrative practice and in those characterizations counselors have been encouraged to utilize different theories based on the needs of clients. As clients present unique needs or cultural realities, an eclectic counselor might be tempted to shift from, say, a psychodynamic approach to a humanistic approach. This shift between theoretical approaches can be drastic and may bring most counselors to the brink of practicing beyond their competence. It is difficult for most counselors to fully master one theory, let alone several. The result of this type of approach can be quite harmful for clients and instead of meeting their needs, potentially could exacerbate their situation. After all, when a chameleon is faced with a new environment, it does not stop being a chameleon; instead, it simply changes color to adapt.

Adaptation of counseling theory is a more appropriate response to diverse clients. Through adaptation, counselors can expand their knowledge of particular theory and deepen their competence. **Theoretical adaptation** also allows counselors to remain grounded in their client conceptualization while exploring new ways to apply theory. If **eclecticism** or integration has a place in counseling it is in the techniques related to theory. Counselors are encouraged to practice technical eclecticism while maintaining a primary sense of theory across various settings and client groups.

Having introduced the concept of theoretical adaptation, it would seem natural to raise the question of how to adapt theories to fit unique client populations. Like the needs of clients, theoretical orientations are unique and their adaptation will depend largely upon the context in which they are applied. However, there are some general guidelines that counselors use to adapt particular theories to meet the dynamic needs of their clients. Refer to Reflection 16.4 on page 399 to consider how these general guidelines impact you personally.

1. *Illuminate Assumptions:* All theories are predicated on certain assumptions about mental health and worldview. Before using your chosen theory with any client you need to familiarize yourself with the associated underlying assumptions.
2. *Identify Limitations:* All theories do not fit all people, so explore the limitations of your chosen theory even before you begin working with clients. Pinpoint the gaps or gray areas in your theoretical orientation and strategize ways to compensate for them.
3. *Simplify Concepts:* Theories are notorious contributors to jargon. Quite often various theories will use multiple terms to refer to similar phenomena. Consider the concept of the therapeutic alliance as first described by Freud. Subsequent theorists have used any number of terms such as *partnering, rapport building,* and so on to describe the same process. Develop a lay explanation for your chosen theory that contains easily recognizable concepts in the place of jargon.
4. *Diversify Interventions:* Many theories are accompanied by a particular set of interventions. These interventions may be primary to the theory, but they are by no means the only way to apply that theory. Consider the commonly recognized empty chair technique that involves

clients imagining and role-playing a conversation with someone whom they are in conflict with as if that person is actually present. This technique is typically attributed to Gestalt theory but it can be adapted for use with a wide range of theoretical orientations. The empty chair technique can be especially useful with clients who have a more collectivist worldview regardless of counselors' primary theoretical orientation. In those situations the empty chair can be occupied by imagined family or community members, elders, or other supporters who might be needed to endorse the particular treatment.

In leaving this topic of adapting theories to address diverse populations, there are two things to keep in mind. First, theories are intended to address the questions of why: Why is the client here? Why is the client having difficulty? and so forth. Alternatively, interventions are intended to address the client's needs. The second thing to keep in mind is that human experience is finite, but interpretation and perception of experience is infinite. In other words, there is a specific range of emotions that humans are capable of expressing; however, the meaning that is assigned to those emotions is dynamic and based on the ever-evolving variables of culture and context.

REFLECTION 16.4

Identify your beliefs about human development and change and link those to a specific counseling theory. Consider the following questions in terms of adapting your chosen theory for work with diverse populations:

1. *Determine Assumptions.* Who is credited with developing the theory? What were the circumstances surrounding development of the theory (e.g., what was happening in history at that time, where was it developed, etc.)? The theory was developed to address which particular populations or issues?
2. *Identify Limitations.* For which populations or issues is the theory considered inappropriate? Which populations or issues related to the theory are missing from research, and why were they overlooked or excluded? How has professional knowledge and contextual (e.g., social, historical, political, scientific, etc.) knowledge changed since development of the theory?
3. *Simplify Concepts.* Explain the major concepts of your theory to noncounselors. Partners, friends, and family members are all good audience members for this type of explanation of your theory. Ask them which parts were easiest to understand and which were most difficult. Once you have managed to simplify the theory for those adults, try communicating the major theoretical concepts to a child under the age of 10. The process of adapting the theoretical orientation for a young child will assist in simplifying your theory for communication and application with clients who have limited language comprehension and fluency.
4. *Diversify Interventions.* Can all clients participate in the chosen interventions regardless of their physical ability? Can all clients participate in the chosen intervention regardless of their mental and comprehension abilities? What is your expected outcome for the intervention? Under what conditions would this intervention "fail" or not produce the desired result? How would you react if the intervention did not work as planned?

Culturally Responsive Counseling Theories

In terms of multicultural competence, the fourth force in counseling has taken on a more global perspective in its use of worldview and offers the most opportunity when working with diverse populations. Supported by constructivist rather than positivist paradigms, contextual–systemic models in counseling use diverse worldviews to create theory and incorporate resources from many different approaches to healing. Another unique characteristic of the fourth force in counseling is that it supports and encourages what Gilligan (1982) terms alternative ways of knowing. There is an acknowledgment that all persons are unique and because of their uniqueness, they require flexible and adaptable approaches to counseling. That flexibility includes both the conceptualization of alternative explanations for psychic distress and the use of alternative ways to heal that distress.

Approaches to counseling that are included in this fourth force range from evolved progeny of previous counseling theories to traditional healing practices associated with a specific culture to newly developed approaches that combine the two. Besides use of an expanded worldview, cultural responsiveness is common among all of these approaches. In theoretical terms, being culturally responsive means that culture and differences between cultures are primary considerations in counseling relationships. The issue of culture may have entered into previous approaches to counseling as a secondary or tertiary concern, but for approaches included in the context–systemic movement in counseling cultural identity is the starting point. As in earlier sections, a complete discussion of all approaches that are considered to be culturally responsive cannot be adequately covered in this limited space. Instead, discussion will be devoted to a grand theory that has risen to prominence as the foremost approach to multicultural counseling.

MULTICULTURAL COUNSELING AND THERAPY (MCT)   Similar to the grand theories that comprise the first three forces in counseling, **multicultural counseling and therapy (MCT)** has been presented as a metatheory that encompasses many different conceptual models and approaches to counseling (Ivey et al., 2002). Although the organizational structure and title for this metatheory are relatively new, many of the conceptual models and approaches are quite old and in the case of many indigenous healing practices long predate Freud's inception of psychodynamic theory. Conceptual models that are included in MCT are numerous and include feminist theory, Afrocentric theory, Naikan, and indigenous healing practices just to name a few. In addition to the varied conceptualizations, MCT includes extensive numbers of interventions and approaches to counseling ranging from meditation to social consciousness-raising. These various conceptual models and approaches to counseling are unified under the MCT theory by their shared recognition for the importance of cultural context in the application of counseling theory and techniques (Ivey et al., 2002).

In addition to bringing the cultural contexts to the foreground, Sue (1995) states that MCT adheres to the following six propositions: (1) MCT is an integrative metatheory; (2) counselor and client identities are formed based on differing levels of experience and context and the combination of these are the focus of counseling; (3) cultural identity development determines client and counselor attitudes toward self and others; (4) counseling is more effective when approaches and interventions are consistent with cultural values of the clients and no one approach to counseling will appropriately meet the needs of all clients; (5) the traditional approach to counseling is only one of many strategies for helping clients; and (6) liberation of consciousness (individual, familial, community, and organizational) is a basic goal of MCT. When reviewing some of these propositions it is easy to see where MCT shares common ground in its approach with other metatheories such as humanistic theory. However, MCT uses cultural context as the springboard for change and provides maximum flexibility for working with diverse clientele. See Build Your Knowledge 16.1 to create a personal foundation for MCT.

BUILD YOUR KNOWLEDGE 16.1

CREATING A FOUNDATION FOR MCT

As the case tends to be with most counseling theory, MCT does not provide specific procedural guidelines for working with clients. Instead, the MCT propositions provide a framework in which culturally responsible counselors can use a variety of therapeutic approaches and interventions. To put the MCT propositions into action, counselors must initially become aware of both themselves and their clients. This awareness is the foundation of MCT and is essential to implementing any counseling theory with any client population. To reach an initial level of self-awareness and awareness of self in relation to others, consider the following questions adapted from Hulse-Killacky, Killacky, and Donigian (2001):

Who am I?

- What do I value?
- What dimensions of my identity do I consider to be fundamental?
- What beliefs do I consider to be absolute or universally true?
- What kinds of people and institutions have contributed to and supported my development both personally and professionally?
- What are the defining moments and experiences in my life?

Who am I with you?

- How do counselor–client similarities facilitate the counseling process? How do they inhibit it?
- How do counselor–client differences facilitate the counseling process? How do they inhibit it?
- Historically, how have relationships been characterized between individuals of similar cultural identity as counselor and client?
- What is the dynamic of power, privilege, and oppression between counselor and client in this relationship?
- Besides counselor, what other role might I inadvertently portray in this relationship (e.g., parent, sibling, authority, subordinate)?

Who are we together?

- How will the counselor–client relationship change my life (professional development, personal development, social/contextual development)?
- How will the counselor–client relationship change my clients' lives?
- How might counseling bring greater difficulty and/or challenges for my clients?
- How will the counselor–client relationship support societal norms?
- How will the counselor–client relationship challenge societal norms?

Source: Adapted with written permission from Hulse-Killacky, Killacky, and Donigian (2001).

COUNSELING APPROACHES BASED ON NON-WESTERN WORLDVIEWS   Every culture has a means and manner for addressing the mental health needs of its residents. For example, it has been observed as a Westernized phenomenon that mind, body, and spirit are separated and compartmentalized. Furthermore, some have argued that it is due to this segregation that many find themselves in crisis (Carr, 1996; Wolsko, Eisenberg, Davis, & Phillips, 2004). For many cultures, mental health is incorporated in religious or spiritual belief systems. The functions of the mind are linked to the characteristics of the soul, and in this way, problems of conscious are conceptualized as problems of conscience. Other cultures believe that the problems of an individual are linked more often to their role and participation in a larger social group or society than to intrapersonal dynamics. These different conceptualizations of mental health require unique approaches to counseling based on different worldviews. The following sections will outline three alternative approaches to counseling that have been demonstrated as effective in counseling literature. These examples are provided as snapshots of possibilities that await counselors who consider approaches to counseling that are based on non-Western worldviews. It is important to recognize that all cultures have unique approaches to healing and establishing one's mental well-being. Exploration of those varied approaches to healing can fill the life span of several careers and integration of them into counseling practice can provide enrichment for both counselors and clients. For additional information on approaches to counseling based on a non-Western worldview explore the resources listed in Table 16.1.

Naikan Therapy.   **Naikan** is a formalized and structured method of self-reflection intended to provide clients with understanding themselves as well as their relationships with others in order to gain meaning of their existence. Developed by a Jodo Shinshu Buddhist, Yoshimoto Ishin, Naikan is based on a Confucian worldview that emphasizes familial and social obligations and sustaining the harmony of social order (Hedstrom, 1994). In keeping with this Confucian worldview, the practice of Naikan encourages individuals to consider their roles in and reliance on larger social systems. Inward reflection leads to a greater understanding and appreciation for the benefits of an external system.

The basic process of Naikan is fairly simple and for the most part self-guided. The meditative self-reflection is initiated by three questions: (a) What have I received from _____; (b) What have I given to _____; and (c) What troubles or difficulties have I caused _____ (Krech, 2002). The blanks are filled in with names of people the client has a relationship with. For instance, the blanks could be filled in with names of loved ones or business associates. The blanks could also be filled in with names of institutions, such as a place of employment. Whatever relationship is chosen, the goal of reflection in Naikan is self-in-relation. In approaches that emphasize **self-in-relation** the clients are encouraged to consider how their own behaviors and attitudes contribute or detract from a greater social system. In other words, challenges faced by an individual affect larger social systems such as family and community and those greater systems play an integral role in healing the individual. In this way the relationship remains the primary beneficiary of reflection and social order can be maintained (Hedstrom, 1994). Once a subject is identified for reflection, clients consider their responses to the three questions for a period of approximately 50 to 60 minutes, with the frequency of reflection varying from daily to monthly practice (Krech, 2002).

The practice of Naikan as a therapeutic intervention has been shown effective in the treatment of a variety of issues including anxiety (Hong-Xin, Zao-Huo, & Hong-Xiang, 2006), anorexia nervosa (Morishita, 2000), and alcoholism (Suwaki, 1979, 1985). Although clients are engaged in meditative self-reflection, individualism is devalued with a goal of shifting clients' attention away from internal symptoms and blaming others to an external appreciation for interdependence and the benefits that others have brought to them (Reynolds, 1983).

TABLE 16.1   Internet Resources

- American Counseling Association (ACA) Division, Association for Multicultural Counseling and Development (AMCD): www.amcdaca.org
- American Psychological Association (APA) Division 52, International Psychology: www.internationalpsychology.net
- International Association for Cross-Cultural Psychology (IACCP): www.iaccp.org

---

Morita Therapy.   **Morita therapy** is an approach to counseling that shares some similarities with Naikan and is often used in conjunction with it when working with clients. Like Naikan, Morita is based on Buddhist values but is not linked to the practice of Buddhism. It also emphasizes the importance of self-in-relation.

Dr. Shoma Morita created Morita therapy. He was a contemporary of Sigmund Freud and Carl Jung, practicing psychiatry in the early part the 20th century. While serving in the Department of Psychiatry at Jikei University School of Medicine in Tokyo, Japan, he created Morita therapy as treatment for a Japanese culturally bound anxiety disorder known as shinkeishitsu (Reynolds, 1983). Dr. Morita practiced Zen Buddhism, and the principles of that religion, especially the focus on mindfulness and an understanding of what a person can and cannot control, influenced his development of theory. The overall approach to Morita therapy can be described as purpose-centered, response-oriented, and active. Instead of attempting to reduce or alleviate symptoms, as is typical for most counseling approaches, Morita therapy stresses building clients' character in order to empower them to accept and respond to their life regardless of the circumstances. Clients practicing Morita therapy can expect that their behaviors will be emphasized more than thoughts or feelings and their decision making will be influenced by purpose rather than intuition.

Ntu Psychotherapy.   Based on an African conceptual system and worldview, **Ntu** (pronounced in-too) psychotherapy incorporates ancient Eastern principles of healing and New Age conceptualizations of mind–body integration (Gregory & Harper, 2001). Beyond being simply an approach to counseling, it is a holistic philosophy and lifestyle that also provides conceptualizations for human behavior and functioning. The concept of Ntu comes from Central Africa (Bantu) and refers to universal energy or sense of being that is shared by all things (Gregory & Harper, 2001). In Ntu psychotherapy this energy is presumed to be essential to the therapeutic process and becomes the focus of the approach. As the Ntu is increased, so is the well-being of the client and vice versa. The functions of counselors in Ntu psychotherapy are that of spiritual guides as they help clients become aware of and stimulate their own self-healing processes (Gregory & Phillips, 1997).

The Ntu approach was developed by Fredrick Phillips and the staff of the Progressive Life Center. With a goal of restoring harmony, genuineness, and interconnectedness, this approach is characterized by six contextual suppositions (Phillips, 1990). As a therapeutic approach Ntu is:

1. *Family-focused:* Gregory and Harper (2001) characterize this dimension of Ntu in the following way, "The family focused approach acknowledges that families are always emotionally present within each of us" (p. 306). Extending this acknowledgment, it is assumed that the entire family is with the client even if an individual presents alone for counseling. In the Ntu approach, family is typically defined based on both psychological and biological relationships, so clients are responsible for self-defining their familial group.
2. *Culturally competent:* The counselor–client relationship is collaborative and based on clients' needs. The Ntu counselor is expected to gain understanding about client populations being served and tailor interventions accordingly. Similar to any culturally competent counselor, those using the Ntu approach are expected to be self-aware and aware of any environmental circumstances (e.g., socioeconomic factors, political climate) that may impact the counseling relationship.
3. *Competence-based:* Ntu is a wellness-based approach that seeks to highlight strengths rather than deficits. In focusing on competence, an Ntu counselor can more easily avoid imposition of personal or culturally based assumptions about mental health.
4. *Holistic/systemic:* To live a full and productive life, clients must care for all dimensions of themselves (i.e., body, mind, and spirit). In addition to caring for themselves, clients must also care for

the environments that support them. Ntu uses various interventions to address clients and their systems. These interventions range from traditional individual talk therapy to integrative and indigenous healing techniques such as meditation, herbology, acupuncture, and so on.

5. *Values-driven:* Unlike some typical counseling approaches that strive to suspend values in the counseling relationship and focus on unconditional regard for clients, the Ntu approach defines appropriate behavior according to particular principles. Using an Afrocentric worldview, Ntu counselors assume that contribution to family and community is essential and clients' behaviors are assessed in terms of this contribution. In terms of specific value systems inherent to the Ntu approach, the counseling relationship focuses on the Nguzo Saba (seven principles of Kwanza). These seven principles are Umoja (unity), Kujichagulia (self-determination), Ujima (collective work and responsibility), Ujamaa (cooperative economy), Kuumba (creativity), Nia (purpose), and Imani (faith).

Operating from these six suppositions, Phillips (1990) describes five distinct phases in Ntu psychotherapy through which client and counselor collaborate. The first phase is harmony in which rapport is built and the counselor–client relationship is established. The next phase is awareness and counselor and client work together to identify and clarify the reason for counseling. Alignment is the third phase and core of Ntu counseling. Alignment can be alternatively characterized as congruence in that consistency among thoughts, behaviors, and feelings are sought so that family members experience one another and the presenting challenge from a common base. Actualization follows alignment and consists of putting into practice the changes learned during the preceding phase. The Ntu process concludes with the synthesis phase in which client and counselor reflect on and evaluate the overall Ntu experience. Research on the successful application of the Ntu approach is ongoing and to date it has been used to help clients in foster care and juvenile justice systems, family counseling, school-based counseling, and in-home counseling (Gregory & Harper, 2001).

Having discussed some culturally responsive counseling approaches, it is very important to recognize that they, too, are not without their own potential pitfalls. As is the case when using theories from the psychodynamic, cognitive–behavioral, and humanistic–existential movements, counselors must be cognizant of the underlying assumptions for their chosen approaches to counseling. Most of the counseling approaches based on traditional healing practices are culture specific and require initial acceptance of particular cultural assumptions.

Summary

When using a counseling theory, flexibility in the approach and nimbleness of the counselor using the approach are of the highest importance. This requires adaptations in both conceptualization and intervention based on the diversity that clients bring to sessions. In any case, when working as a multiculturally competent counselor, it is critical to note that all counseling approaches ascribe to a specific worldview. These worldviews may alternatively be liberating to some and oppressive to others. Recognition of how a chosen approach to counseling impacts clients is essential to ethical practice and will determine the effectiveness of therapy.

This chapter has provided a brief overview of some of the components necessary to developing and applying counseling theory in a culturally responsible manner. The influences that worldview and cultural assumptions have on conceptualizations of mental health have been explored and you had the opportunity to reflect on how your own worldview interacts with your definition of mental health and your chosen theory of counseling. The affects that the social systems of religion and spirituality, government, and family have on mental health were also discussed in this chapter. Building on diverse definitions of mental health, we identified alternative sources for counseling theory and linked worldview to the development of traditional counseling theory. In terms of applying specific theory to counseling clients across cultures, MCT was reviewed as a viable approach to counseling clients from many different cultures. Techniques were introduced for adapting traditional counseling theories, and several approaches to counseling, such as Naikan, Morita, and Ntu, have been identified and discussed as alternatives to typical counseling theory.

On a final note, this chapter has included basic information about the development and application of counseling theory that responds to diverse groups of clients. It can be a common misconception among novice counselors and even those who are more advanced that the conceptualization and application of counseling theory is somehow static. Nothing could be further from the truth. Counseling theory is as alive and dynamic as the counselors who use it and the clients who benefit from it. As clients face new challenges and counselors develop a better understanding for these clients and their challenges, theory evolves.

CHAPTER 17

Multicultural Diagnosis and Conceptualization

KAREN ERIKSEN, VICTORIA E. KRESS, ANDREA DIXON, AND STEPHANIE J. W. FORD

PREVIEW

Ample evidence exists that nondominant groups are disadvantaged in U.S. society in many ways, including mental health treatment. This chapter focuses on cultural- and gender-sensitive diagnosis because critiques of the diagnostic process have been particularly intense for women and people of color. In addition to reviewing these critiques, this chapter offers strategies for diagnosis, assessment, and case conceptualization that are sensitive to such cultural factors as age, gender, and race.

THE CHALLENGE OF ETHICAL PRACTICE

All mental health professionals' ethical codes prohibit discrimination on the basis of such factors as age, disability, sex, race, ethnicity, religion, socioeconomic class, sexual orientation, or any other difference of the client from the mainstream. Additionally, all ethical practitioners are to commit themselves to gaining knowledge, personal awareness, sensitivity, and skills pertinent to working with a diverse client population. Yet how do these mandates play out in the actual diagnostic practice of mental health providers?

According to some authors (Mezzich, 1999a, 1999b; Mezzich, Kleinman, Fabrega, & Parron, 1996b; Tseng, 2001), competence to work with diverse client groups when diagnosing, assessing, and providing subsequent treatment means knowing how to do an overall cultural assessment. From their perspective, this means understanding the cultural framework of the client's identity, cultural explanations of illness experiences and help-seeking behavior, cultural meanings of adaptive functioning and social context, and cultural elements in the counselor–client relationship. Although it seems unlikely that a counselor could accomplish these ideals relative to many cultures, counselors should certainly develop these abilities for the cultures of the clients whom they predominantly serve, and should develop a referral base of counselors for clients from cultures with which they are less familiar (Welfel, 2002).

Furthermore, counselors should avoid jumping to conclusions about clients on the basis of their cultural groups; should acquire knowledge about different cultures' norms and interaction styles; and should commit to ongoing awareness about their own biases, assumptions, and cultural encapsulation (American Psychological Association, 2003; Ivey, D'Andrea, Ivey, & Simek-Morgan, 1999; Sue et al., 1996; Welfel, 2002). Such cultural awareness extends beyond the usual attention to race and ethnicity to differences related to religion, age, socioeconomic class, gender, ethnicity, disability, and sexual orientation.

Fully actualizing these sorts of knowledge, skills, and awareness can be challenging. Culturally sensitive diagnosis and conceptualization, in particular, is easier to talk about than to do, especially when diagnosing clients from cultures different from the dominant culture. Wide variations exist among people from different cultures in perspectives about "normal" behavior; for example, how interpersonal relationships should be conducted, especially in families. In some cases, the ways in which relationships are conducted (e.g., parents using physical discipline with children, or husbands physically abusing their wives because their wives "belong" to them and are their possessions) differ from those of North American culture or are in conflict with North American laws (Garcia, Cartwright, Winston, & Borzuchowska, 2003; Lo & Fung, 2003; McGoldrick, Giordano, & Garcia-Preto, 2005). If we extend this thinking to other areas of diversity, we might ask, how can men fully understand women, or women men? How can a counselor fully understand the challenges of being an immigrant if she is not one herself? Can counselors ever completely eliminate the influence of systemic oppressions—such as institutionalized racism and sexism—on themselves, the client, or the relationship when diagnosing people who differ from the majority (Bhugra & Bhui, 1999; McLaughlin, 2002)? What forum is available for discussing the "illness" or diagnosis of contexts or systems? How do counselors find funding for correcting such systems, rather than expecting individual clients to correct the oppressions that may be weighing them down?

Questions about the counselor's cultural and gender sensitivity are not the only questions raised by those pursuing culturally sensitive diagnosis and case conceptualization. The usefulness of the *Diagnostic and Statistical Manual of Mental Disorders* (DSM–IV–TR; American Psychiatric Association, 2000) system has been challenged for people who differ from the dominant culture. Critics ask whether counselors can draw any definite conclusions about people of color, gays or lesbians, or women based on a diagnostic system whose development was grounded in the knowledge of European American men and that claims to be based on evidence from research studies that did not include diverse participants (McLaughlin, 2002; Rogler, 1996).

Some may wonder whether any counseling or diagnostic system can be free of such potential bias and problems. This is a legitimate query. One response might be is that the *DSM* or any particular diagnostic or counseling system can only be considered one story among many; however, no story contains the whole or absolute "truth." From this perspective, counselors might tentatively explore a number of stories in an egalitarian manner with clients, rather than imposing a truth. Such an approach may help counter the harm that has been, and could potentially continue to be, caused by applying the *DSM* or any particular diagnostic or counseling system to historically oppressed groups.

NORMAL VERSUS ABNORMAL

Fundamental to any diagnostic process are questions about where the line is between normal and abnormal. Relatedly, who gets to draw the line, to decide what is abnormal? On what basis do they get to decide these things? At what point do we decide that a person is mentally ill? In answer to these questions, some have asserted that people in power make the decisions—people such as doctors or psychiatrists (Kutchins & Kirk, 1997; Richardson, 1999; Sarbin, 1997)—and that agreements about such decisions change over time, depending on who is in power, and on the spirit of the times (Caplan, 1995; Cermele, Daniels, & Anderson, 2001; Duffy, Gillig, Tureen, & Ybarra, 2002; Sadler, 2002). For instance, Kutchins and Kirk (1997) state that political processes decide who is considered abnormal or normal. They trace the political debates and battles over the inclusion in the *DSM* of homosexuality, masochistic personality disorder, borderline personality disorder, and posttraumatic stress disorder (PTSD). They persuade readers that the political process involved in *DSM* development has consisted of debates, hearings, pressure by interest groups, keeping track of and worrying about public opinion, "horse trading," protests, manipulation, invalid studies thrown together by those with conflicts of interest, and falsified research.

Szasz (1974) and others (Burr & Butt, 2000; Caplan, 1995; Kutchins & Kirk, 1997) point to the impact of market forces on inclusions in the *DSM*. That is, they indicate that increasing the number of reimbursable diagnoses serves to increase the treatment domain and profits of mental health providers. Their perspective is that moving "problems in living"—such as worrying, feeling blue, having obsessive thoughts, bearing grudges, lacking sexual interest, not sleeping, smoking, being alone, having trouble in school, being hung over—into the realm of diagnosable mental illness or pathology results in the increased pathologizing of everyday life (Chrisler & Caplan, 2002; Duffy et al., 2002; Kutchins & Kirk, 1997; Pilgrim & Bentall, 1999; Sperry, 2002).

Increased pathologizing or "psychologization," in turn, places daily difficulties into the framework of counseling theory, which then locates problems at the level of the individual (Burr & Butt, 2000). As a result, the responsibility for problems and for change becomes solely the individual's, despite the availability of alternative, more systemic explanations—such as sexism, racism, and poverty—and remediation. This increasing pathologization of everyday life and the expansion of the boundaries of abnormality mean that it becomes harder and harder to be assessed as "normal" and more and more likely that individuals, rather than dysfunctional social systems, will be blamed for abnormality (Cermele et al., 2001; Chrisler & Caplan, 2002; Duffy et al., 2002; Kleinman, 1996; Lewis, Lewis, Daniels & D'Andrea, 2003).

Further, Lewis-Fernandez and Kleinman (1994) declare that "North American professional constructs of personality and psychopathology are mostly culture bound, selectively reflecting the experiences of particular cohorts—those who are White, male, Anglo-Germanic, Protestant, and formally educated and who share a middle- and upper-class cultural orientation" (p. 67). They further indicate that diagnostic criteria ignore 80% of the world's population and the most rapidly increasing segments of U.S. society (see also Gaines, 1992; Kleinman, 1988). These culturally specific ways of viewing individuals and their personality development result in an ethnocentrism (Markus & Kitayama, 1991). They ignore the influence of cultural norms and social context on human behavior (Nuckolls, 1992), and they take cultural diversity into consideration when evaluating psychological symptoms (Mezzich et al., 1993). For instance, Latino clients, particularly those who have recently immigrated, are poorly acculturated into the dominant culture, are economically disadvantaged, and rarely have cultural meanings about their distress considered in the diagnostic process. Such practices result in a "category fallacy"—that is, the application of diagnostic categories to cultural groups for which they were not developed and have never been validated (Rogler, 1996).

Historically, people who have not conformed to societal conventions have been psychiatrically hospitalized, ostracized from their communities as deviants and witches, and prevented from marrying and working (Bever, 2002; Forsythe & Melling, 1999; Porter, 2003). Consider the following list of those who did or do not fit social conventions: Until recently, gay people were diagnosable as mentally ill (American Psychiatric Association, 1980; Penfold & Walker, 1983; Sadler, 2002). African Americans and other people of color were considered subhuman animals, so any pursuit of human "rights" was considered abnormal (Szasz, 2002; Tynerm & Houston, 2002); African American slaves' pursuit of freedom was given the diagnosis of drapetomania (Woolfolk, 2001). Women of the upper classes who masturbated (and were sometimes considering divorce) were said to be treading on dangerous ground, risking idiocy, mania, and death, and therefore were "treated" with clitoridectomies (Chesler, 1973). More generally, masturbation was considered a diagnosable problem (Woolfolk, 2001). Women pursuing higher education and/or athletics would become sterile, according to "objective" research (Chesler, 1973). Women who chose not to marry, not to have children, to divorce, or to have sex outside marriage were considered abnormal and were ostracized (Cohen & Casper, 2002; Gordon, 2003). Those women who expressed left-leaning politics were considered disordered more often than left-leaning men (Brodsky & Holroyd, 1975). And Christian European Americans sought to convert the "heathen savages" (e.g., Native Americans, Africans, Asians) who dressed differently, had different customs, and perhaps used opiates or other drugs in their spiritual activities. Few today would attribute mental illness to these groups of people, and yet, such attributions were made within the 20th century.

Some readers may assert that such past "uncivilized" and "uninformed" behavior should not worry us; that now that science has advanced our knowledge, we no longer treat people inhumanely; that such misbehavior is part of the distant past. However, recent history indicates a continuing lack of cultural and gender sensitivity that results in harm to those who differ from Western norms or the dominant cultural group. Harm results from overdiagnosis, underdiagnosis, misdiagnosis, and sampling bias. Use Activity 17.1 to discuss the impact of context on people's behavior and subsequent diagnosis.

ACTIVITY 17.1

In small groups, discuss the relationship between a particular diagnosis and the cultural milieu. For example, in the United States during the late 20th century, Anorexia Nervosa was most commonly diagnosed in young European American females. What contextual situations might contribute to this fact? The demographics of this diagnosis appear to be changing, with more people of color and males being diagnosed with anorexia nervosa and bulimia nervosa. What contextual situations might contribute to this fact? Other examples for similar discussions might be antisocial personality disorders, dependent personality disorders, and conduct disorders in children.

Overdiagnosis, Underdiagnosis, and Misdiagnosis

Because behavior that does not match Western norms is sometimes labeled as pathological (Blankfield, 1987; Draguns, 1985; Fabrega, 1989; Mwaba & Pedersen, 1990; Snyder, 1992), gay men, lesbians, racial/ethnic minorities, women, and nontraditional men may be overdiagnosed with certain disorders or misdiagnosed entirely (Cook, Warnke, & Dupuy, 1993; Enns, 1993; Lewis, Croft-Jeffreys, & David, 1990; Loring & Powell, 1988; Robertson & Fitzgerald, 1990). Specifically, research indicated that African Americans were overdiagnosed with psychosis and underdiagnosed with depression (Jones & Gray, 1986; King, Coker, Leavey, Hoare, & Johnson-Sabine, 1994). Afro-Caribbean patients who were actually suffering from affective disorders were misdiagnosed with schizophrenia (Jones & Gray, 1986; Keisling, 1981). People of varying ethnic populations received more frequent diagnoses of schizophrenia (Jones & Gray, 1986; Keisling, 1981; King et al., 1994; Lewis et al., 1990). Asian clients were underdiagnosed for mood disorders and overdiagnosed for dependency (Lin, 1996).

According to Cook et al. (1993), the problem of misdiagnosis of those from nondominant cultural groups occurs because diagnostic decisions rely on mental health professionals' own judgments of excessiveness or inappropriateness rather than on more precise criteria. A great deal of evidence indicates that such misdiagnosis occurs as a result of stereotyping and overlooking the perspectives of women and the poor (Good, 1993; Lin, 1990; Parron, 1982). Furthermore, bias seems to occur when one cultural group tolerates a higher level of misbehavior than another (Fisher, Storck, & Bacon, 1999) or when clinicians classify client characteristics into stereotypical categories (Brown, 1986). An additional concern related to sex and diagnosis is that if mental health professionals view certain problems as more prevalent in one sex, they may stop gathering information before they recognized occurrence in the other sex (e.g. PTSD in men following rape, women's substance abuse problems;

Boyd & Mackey, 2000; Brown, 1990a, 1990b; Cook et al., 1993; Ely, Hardy, Longford, & Wadsworth, 1999; Mintz & Wright, 1992; Warren, 1983).

Sampling Bias

Of further concern is the impact on women and those from nondominant groups of sampling bias in the research upon which many *DSM* claims are based. Research has ignored many of the people most in need of counselors' services (e.g., lower-SES individuals, women, non-Whites, and the unemployed; Osipow & Fitzgerald, 1993; Reid, 1993). Sampling has also included a disproportionate representation of the sexes. These research omissions raise questions about success in developing unbiased diagnostic criteria (Gannon, Luchetta, Rhodes, Pardie, & Segrist, 1992; National Institutes of Health, 1994), questions about the relevance of applying current diagnoses to women and people of color, and questions about the appropriateness and availability of treatments that are based on such diagnoses.

Such sampling bias also raises questions about power and social control. What impact might there be, for example, on truths about mental illness when they are created by a small group of predominantly White, middle- or upper-class males and when they are practiced largely on a female population? Caplan, McCurdy-Myers, and Gans (1992) claim that a small group of people maintain a great deal of sanctioned power over what happens to less powerful groups. They define such disproportionate power as the exercise of social control and further claim that without addressing the social context of diagnosis, our culture will tend "to use any sign of difference in a low-status group as proof that it deserves its low status" (p. 31) (see also Hoagwood & Jensen, 1997; Howard, 1991). Use Reflection 17.1 to discuss the development of psychological difficulties.

REFLECTION 17.1

Using the example of major depression (or other disorders such as phobias, generalized anxiety disorder, conduct disorder, etc.), explore how sociocultural factors could legitimately lead to a diagnosis of depression in anyone who experienced symptoms. Consider what family dynamics, geographical region, language difficulties, religion, socioeconomic status (SES), folk beliefs, quality of life, immigrant experiences, disabilities, discriminations, or work experiences might contribute to depression (or other disorders). Name all of the possible life circumstances that might lead someone to feel depressed. A discussion of these changes and contexts may help to highlight the complexities of bias in diagnosis. How might understanding context alter practitioners' ways of knowing beyond the typical perception that only certain people, with certain genetic predispositions, "get" certain "diseases" or diagnoses?

CULTURE AND PSYCHOPATHOLOGY

Culture defines, expresses, and interprets the dynamic beliefs, values, and customs of a social group (Cole & Cole, 1996). It offers explanations for problematic behavior that are culturally congruent, and may influence (a) what symptoms are allowed as expressions of suffering (Serafica, 1997) and (b) how individuals cope with distress (Cohler, Stott, & Musick, 1995). Culture determines how those around the individual respond to distress or problematic behaviors; in particular, deciding the intensity or severity of the problem that must be evident before intervention is deemed necessary (Weisz & Weiss, 1991). Culture prescribes what are considered acceptable help-seeking responses and interventions, and who may intervene (Harkness & Super, 1990). Within a specific culture, psychological sophistication and education influence the understanding and perception of problems, as well as beliefs about what should be done about problems (Lambert et al., 1992). Class and social position may also influence how people respond to psychological problems. Thus, Engelsmann (2000) urges counselors to consider not only the interaction of race and ethnicity with the development of problems, but also the influence of "minority status, experiences of prejudice, social and economic disadvantages, and language and communication barriers" (p. 429).

Overall, then, culture influences clients in many ways, including clients' experiences of problems and internal sense of distress, their interpretations of problems after experiencing symptoms, and their presentation of the complaint (Constantine & Ladany, 2000; Mezzich, Kleinman, Fabrega, & Parron, 1996a, 1996b). Culture also impacts counselors' perceptions of the disorder, their style of interviewing, their choice of theoretical perspectives, the classification system that they use, and the purpose for making a diagnosis (Cooper, Kendall, Gurland, Sartorius, & Farkas, 1969; Tseng, Asai, Kitanish, McLaughlin, & Kyomen, 1992; Tseng, McDermott, Ogino, & Ebata, 1982).

Cross-cultural studies reveal intricacies of culture and diagnosis, exposing behaviors that may be characteristic of particular cultures, and that clinicians need to be aware of to prevent misdiagnosis or under- or overdiagnosis. For example:

a. Plains Indians hear the voices of recently departed relatives calling them from the afterworld. This is considered normative and not evidence of psychopathology. However, in an adult European American North America, counselors would be concerned that hearing such voices was evidence of serious mental illness.

b. Anorexia nervosa primarily exists in Western societies "that regard slim female bodies as beautiful, sexually desirable, and commercially significant" (Kleinman, 1996, p. 18).

c. Peasant societies have much lower rates of schizophrenia than "economically and technologically advanced, urbanized, and bureaucratized societies" (Kleinman, 1996, pp. 18–19). The World Health Organization has shown in several major studies that "schizophrenia, regardless of age at onset, is a less serious illness and has a better outcome in poor countries, despite their limited health services, apparently because families and communities provide better support for schizophrenic patients" (Kleinman, 1996, pp. 18–19) (see also Hopper, 1991; Jablensky, Sartorius, Ankar, & Korten, 1992; Jenkins & Karno, 1992; Kleinman, 1988; WHO, 1979).

d. The 35 million immigrants (legal and illegal) in the United States (Center for Immigration Studies, 2005) face tremendous challenges in adjusting to their new lives. Yet counselors may be challenged by the vast diversity of immigrant cultures (Downs-Karkos, 2004) and by language limitations in describing psychological problems. For example, depression may be described as "soul loss" (Shweder, 1985) or "congestion" (Anagnostopoulos, Vlassopoulou & Rotsika, 2004), which could result in misdiagnosis and inappropriate treatment.

e. African American and Hispanic adolescents in high-crime, inner-city neighborhoods may normatively demonstrate many of the *DSM* criteria for Conduct Disorder or Antisocial Personality Disorder (Kleinman, 1986). Because violence is routine in these locales, criteria for this disorder may be considered normative coping styles that aid survival.

Thus, culture is inextricably linked with both normal and abnormal behavior. Discerning the line between normal and abnormal; assessing development, experience, and expression of abnormal behavior; understanding the ways in which diagnosed people are perceived and treated; and making decisions about diagnosis and treatment all require consciousness of cultural norms, values, and typical behaviors. It is well documented that those from nondominant cultural groups underuse mental health services (Fugita, 1990; Root, 1985; Sue & McKinney, 1975). Perhaps multicultural diagnostic insensitivity can be at least partially faulted for the alienation and reluctance of some cultural groups to receive needed psychological help.

Valasquez, Johnson, and Brown-Cheatham (1993) specify the particular ways in which the *DSM* fails culturally:

a. No discussion exists in the *DSM* of how specific diagnoses present or manifest themselves in people of color. The *DSM* could include data about key features, unique symptoms, or prevalence of specific diagnoses in specific ethnic minorities.

b. No empirical evidence indicates that using the *DSM* is valid or reliable with ethnic minorities, but there is evidence that diagnosis of ethnic minorities is highly susceptible to human error, errors that are particularly compounded when diagnosing a linguistically different client.

c. There is an absence in the *DSM* of culture-specific syndromes or culture-bound syndromes related to alienation, acculturation difficulty, migration and immigration trauma, ethnic/racial identity confusion, gang involvement, PTSD caused by socially sanctioned racism or violence, or familial intergenerational distress.

d. Ethnic minority professionals have generally not been included in the development of the *DSM*, which may mean that minimal attention was paid to the role of ethnicity or culture in the development of the diagnostic system, particularly in earlier *DSM* editions.

These limitations seem to indicate that the *DSM* represents Western thought and assumptions, and thus currently represents a minority bias cross-culturally (Kleinman, 1996; Kress, Eriksen, Rayle, & Ford, 2005). Consider the difficulties in relating to Michael in Case Study 17.1, in determining whether a particular diagnosis or treatment might be helpful to him.

CASE STUDY 17.1

Michael, a 35-year-old man with no criminal record, was brought into a community mental health clinic after a verbal confrontation with a police officer. When asked why he refused to pay a parking fee for a local event, he responded angrily, "I offered the parking attendant my credit card, and he said that they only take cash. I never carry cash! Why does everyone have to make things so difficult?"

Michael noted that he does not like to go to banks, and he refuses to ever enter a bank. He handles all of his finances over the phone and through writing and depositing checks at an ATM. Furthermore, he indicates that he never carries or handles cash.

"When I have to use an ATM," Michael reported, "I have a pocket knife in the passenger seat, ready to use, just in case." Michael also reported that he is leery of others and becomes suspicious when discussions involve the subject of money. He has one credit card and his driver's license in his wallet, and he carries a list of his allergies just in case he is ever wounded and unconscious. He has also posted on his refrigerator the phone number for the local police, as well as the phone number of the credit card company, in the event that his card is ever stolen.

Michael's suspicious behaviors appear bizarre, and you begin to suspect that he may be paranoid or psychotic. Address the following questions before moving on:

• What diagnoses might you be considering at this point in the interview?
• What additional questions do you need to ask Michael?

After further inquiry about past events, Michael explains that while he was in a bank approximately 2 years ago, he witnessed an armed robbery during which a man was shot and killed. Almost every night since then, Michael has nightmares about the event, so vivid that he can smell the money and feel the man's blood spatter onto his face. He indicates that he was afraid to tell the interviewer this because of fears that he will be found and hurt by the family of the bank robber.

- How does the context surrounding Michael's presenting problem change the aforementioned case scenario?
- What additional traumas might a counselor ask about when assessing a client and ascribing diagnoses?
- Discuss the importance of specifically asking clients about their context versus assuming that they will tell you?
- Why might clients not tell you about their varying contextual situations?
- How might Michael's ethnicity or gender impact his situation?

FEMINIST CHALLENGES

Feminist theorists believe that women's anger, depression, and discontent have been reframed as medical or psychiatric symptoms, and that, as a result, the often difficult and distressing life circumstances of women have been disregarded. They state that it is often forgotten that the roots of women's so-called psychological problems have many times been social and political, rather than individual and intrapsychic in origin (Caplan et al., 1992; Koss, 1990; Ussher, 2000; Wakefield, 1992). Feminists also point out the stigmatizing effects of diagnostic labels; the classist, sexist, racist, and homophobic assumptions that they consider to be embedded in both the *International Classification of Diseases (ICD)* and the *DSM;* the resulting pathologizing of behaviors that may be normative within particular gender contexts; the underdiagnosing of problematic behaviors; and, finally, the inability to find any use in the classification system for treatment or for conceptualizing the counseling process (Brown, 1990a, 1990b). Reflection 17.2 may be helpful in stimulating readers' thinking on gender socialization, its advantages or disadvantages for men and women, boys and girls, and possible biases in diagnosis that might emerge from socialization rather than biology.

REFLECTION 17.2

Complete the following statements as they apply to your gender. If you are female:

> As a woman/girl, I am a failure if I don't . . .
> Real women/girls do . . .
> Real women/girls don't . . .

If you are a male:

> As a man/boy, I am a failure if I don't . . .
> Real men/boys do . . .
> Real men/boys don't . . .

How might the diagnostic process be influenced by a counselor's responses to these statements? Based on your responses, consider the following questions:

- What diagnoses might you be more likely to give to men than to women because of the beliefs inherent in your responses to these statements?
- What diagnoses might you be more likely to give to women than to men?
- What behaviors would you be likely to consider abnormal or diagnosable in men, but not in women?
- What behaviors would you be likely to consider abnormal or diagnosable in women, but not in men?

Prevalence Data of Diagnoses by Gender

Research on the prevalence of mental illness by gender yields contradictory results. Some evidence seems to confirm that more women than men are mentally ill and that women's prevalence rates are higher than those for men on far more disorders (Cook et al., 1993; Gove, 1980; Hartung & Widiger, 1998). Others indicate that men and women experience mental illness at comparable rates for personality disorders (17.4% and 18%, respectively; Bijl, deGraaf, Ravelli, Smit, & Vollebergh, 2002; Horsfall, 2001; Kass, Spitzer, & Williams, 1983). The reasons proposed for the conflicting results include differing definitions of mental illness (Gove, 1980; Johnson, 1980), differing research strategies (Gove, 1980), and sex bias (Abramowitz, 1973; Brodsky & Holroyd, 1975; Broverman, Broverman, Clarkson, Rosenkrantz, & Vogel, 1970; Broverman, Vogel, Broverman, Clarkson, & Rosenkrantz, 1972; Cook et al., 1993; Fabrikant, 1974; Maslin & Davis, 1975; Sherman, 1980).

However, when examining prevalence of specific diagnoses rather than overall rates of mental illness, it does seem fairly clear that men predominate in some disorders, while women predominate in others. For instance, men's prevalence rates are higher for substance abuse and sexually related disorders, whereas women's prevalence rates are higher for all forms of mood and anxiety disorders (Bijl et al., 2002; Hartung & Widiger, 1998; Horsfall, 2001; Wetzel, 1991). Furthermore, women have been found to predominate in borderline, dependent, and histrionic personality disorders (Nehls, 1998), although Reich, Nduaguba, and Yates (1988) found little difference between men and women on dependent personality disorders for any age groups other than 31 to 40 years of age. Men predominate in antisocial, compulsive, paranoid, schizoid, and passive aggressive personality disorders in all age groups except 31 to 40 years of age (Kass et al., 1983; Reich et al., 1988).

Developmental Shifts in Prevalence Rates

Interestingly, gender prevalence studies indicate that there are few gender differences in diagnosis prevalence before school age. Once children begin school, however, boys are more frequently diagnosed in the elementary years, and girls in adolescence and beyond (Keenan & Shaw, 1997). Keenan and Shaw hypothesized that young girls with difficulties are socialized to channel them into internalized distress that is not as identifiable by teachers and parents, whereas boys are not. Therefore, they suggest, young boys' more externalized problems disrupt families and school rooms, increasing their frequency of diagnosis and referral (see also Caplan, 1992). Caplan (1992) indicated that girls' problems are more likely to be overlooked, underdiagnosed, and untreated because of the (a) lack of ability to observe young girls' distress when it is present and (b) the traditional notion that it is less important for girls to succeed academically (Caplan, 1973, 1977; Caplan & Kinsbourne, 1974). Although it may be difficult to firmly ascertain differential incidence of diagnoses during childhood by gender, beliefs about the differences seem to affect policy and funding decisions, making less money available for services for girls who remain unreferred and undiagnosed (Kimball, 1981). The very apparent needs of boys would, in contrast, result in the overpathologizing of young boys (Caplan, 1992).

Children are, in general, often overdiagnosed or misdiagnosed. Children under age 13 years are currently overdiagnosed for attention deficit disorder (ADD) and attention deficit/hyperactivity disorder (ADHD) and often misdiagnosed with depression and antisocial personality disorder (Roberts, Attkisson, & Rosenblatt, 1998). Adolescents are overdiagnosed for conduct disorders and depression as well as substance abuse disorders (Gumbiner, 2003). Inappropriate diagnosis may result in labels that follow children into adulthood, and thus, it presents a serious ethical concern.

For those children whose problematic behavior does continue into adulthood, however, it is interesting that childhood mental disorders with male predominance, such as conduct disorder, oppositional defiant disorder, and ADHD, have only three correlates in adulthood: Antisocial Personality Disorder, ADHD, and Intermittent Explosive Disorder (Hartung & Widiger, 1998). Only two of these are Axis I disorders. Those children with disorders of female predominance find a full range of diagnoses available to them as adults. Caplan (1995), in an attempt to explain the research results that indicate that more women than men are mentally ill argued that "the failure to include [other reimbursable] diagnoses for adults with disorders of dyscontrolled anger or aggression has reflected a masculine bias in the recognition of psychopathology or denial of psychopathology that would be more common in men than in women" (p. 264). From her perspective, then, the reason fewer men are considered mentally ill when they continue their problematic childhood/adolescent behavior into adulthood is that young girls' problems seem to evolve into adult problems that can receive a wide range of DSM diagnoses, while young boys' problems seem to evolve into criminality, which is not "mental illness", per se. Review Case Study 17.2 to stimulate your thinking on how male/female prevalence rates and practitioner expectations might affect assessment and treatment.

CASE STUDY 17.2

Jordan is a 41-year-old African American male. He has a long history of receiving services within the mental health system. Jordan meets with you during a recent hospitalization for a suicide attempt. He seems uninterested during the interview, is not forthcoming with information, and states he's "been through this a million times and that you can't help him." You are aware that you feel annoyed with Jordan.

In reviewing his charts, you see that he has historically been diagnosed with Borderline Personality Disorder, Major Depression - recurrent, pathological gambling, impulsive self-mutilation, and adult antisocial behavior. Jordan has attempted suicide multiple times and is perceived by many health care providers as "difficult" and "manipulative." Jordan often fails to follow through on recommendations made by providers and can appear "needy," "volatile," and "helpless," as documented in many of his providers' progress notes.

Jordan is aware of the annoyance that many providers feel toward him. He is bitter about the multiple diagnoses and "uncaring" treatment he receives. He feels very misunderstood and has not been open with his providers about his past experiences. In reality, his father and mother were sexually and physically abusive. His football coach also raped him in the ninth grade. He suffers many trauma reactions secondary to his childhood experiences and many of his behaviors are attempts to keep him from committing suicide and spiraling into a deep depression.

- How might Jordan's reactions be adaptive given his life circumstances?
- What impact did Jordan's diagnoses have on his situation?
- How might the stigma of the diagnoses have made his situation worse?
- How might Jordan's diagnoses help him or the treatment process?
- If you were the practitioner, how would you manage your feelings of annoyance toward Jordan?
- What strengths or resources might Jordan have and how could you assess these and use them in your work together?
- How might Jordan's behaviors be expectable developmental reactions to abnormal situations?
- How might Jordan's gender affect his situation, his perception of his past and present situation, and your understanding of his situation?

Although often unconsidered, additional concerns about the assessment and diagnosis process emerge from prevalence studies with older adult clients. Counselors may struggle with differentiating normal aging concerns from symptoms of depression or mild dementia. Disinterest and forgetfulness, for instance, may result from advancing age rather than from psychological problems (Ginter, 1995). Psychological symptoms may also be caused by a physical disorder or medications aimed at treating a medical problem. Indeed, over 80% of those over the age of 65 have a chronic physical condition and may take several medications on a regular basis. Thus, psychological disorders may be overlooked among older clients. Psychological disorder may also be assumed inappropriately when a medical, aging, or medication interaction is really responsible for symptoms (Pouget, Yersin, Wietlisbach, Bumand, & Bula, 2000), and in fact, studies have demonstrated that the detection and treatment of depression with older adults have been unsatisfactory (Pearson et al., 1999).

Sex Bias in Diagnosis

Sex bias may also potentially harm both women and men. Many have found that women are given diagnoses for both underconforming and overconforming to sex-role stereotypes (Abramowitz, 1973; Brodsky & Holroyd, 1975; Broverman et al., 1970; Broverman et al., 1972; Cook et al., 1993; Cormak & Furman, 1998; Fabrikant, 1974; Maslin & Davis, 1975; Seem & Johnson, 1998; Sherman, 1980). Additionally, traditional masculinity is generally associated with strength of mind, while traditional femininity is associated with frailty and irrationality (Galliano, 2003). Broverman et al. (1970) demonstrated that the qualities that practitioners consider to be healthy male characteristics (e.g., independence, personal assertion, and goal-directed activity) were also considered to be healthy adult characteristics. However, both differed substantially from what practitioners considered to be healthy female characteristics. Thus, being a healthy woman in 1970, according to societal, or at least practitioners' standards, made it impossible to be a healthy adult. Women were supposed to be "more submissive, less independent, less adventurous, more easily influenced, less aggressive, less competitive, more excitable in minor crises, having their feelings hurt more easily, being more emotional, more conceited about their appearance, less objective, disliking math and science" (Broverman et al., 1970, p. 4). If women wanted to be considered healthy adults, they had to behave like men and lose their status as healthy (or desirable) women. Of course, men operating within this context also ran the risk of underdiagnosis; that is, they might have all of Broverman and colleagues' identified characteristics of a healthy adult, but the very bias about these characteristics being "healthy" might cause practitioners to overlook males' suffering. Research, in fact, confirms that well-socialized White men run the risk of underdiagnosis with the possible implication that they do not receive the services that they may need (Ganley, 1987; Kaplan, 1983b).

One might assume that "times have changed" since Broverman et al.'s 1970 study. However, study after study continues to demonstrate sex bias in diagnoses. Angermeyer, Matschinger, and Hotzinger (1998), for instance, when asking participants to respond to vignettes of men and women with alcohol dependence, major depression, or schizophrenia, found that women who acted in unfeminine ways received very strong negative reactions, but that men who behaved similarly did not. Cook et al. (1993) pointed out further that mental health professionals have been found to label people disturbed if their behavior does not fit the professional's gender ideals. Researchers have also found that simply knowing a client's sex can influence the diagnostic process, even among experienced practitioners (Loring & Powell, 1988). Female and male clients may earn different diagnoses even when they present with identical symptomatology (Becker & Lamb, 1994; Hamilton, Rothbart, & Dawes, 1986). Seem and Johnson (1998) found that counselor trainee responses on case vignettes indicated that trainees had significant gender bias toward both men and women who displayed nontraditional gender role behavior. Even 35 years after Broverman et al.'s classic research, these biases continue to be evident.

Women from traditionally marginalized groups find themselves pathologized to an even greater extent. Women of color (e.g., racial/ethnic women, immigrant women) and lesbians in the United States may experience political, legal, cultural, and personal risk factors, but may not have regular access to counseling and diagnosis that is sensitive to their particular cultural, emotional, or language needs (Caplan, 2006). As a result, women of color have been found more likely to be sexualized when diagnosed (Cermele et al., 2001). Lesbian women may be diagnosed with Sexual Dysfunction Not Otherwise Specified by insensitive counselors who are justifying their personal or religious prejudices, even though homosexuality is no longer listed as a mental disorder in the *DSM* (Smart & Smart, 1997). Women with multiple identities from traditionally oppressed groups may find themselves "pathologized" through the lenses of the upper-class-driven *DSM* characteristics when their behavior would be considered "normal" in ethnic/racial minority, immigrant, and/or lesbian cultures (Cermele et al., 2001). Reflect on Case Study 17.3 as a means to assess your own tendencies toward bias in diagnosing.

CASE STUDY 17.3

Jada is a 17-year-old girl brought to counseling by her parents because of the concerns and anxieties that Jada has about her English class. She indicates that it is hard for her to pay attention because her teacher is boring. She adds that she does not like her teacher because the teacher calls on her when she doesn't have her hand up. She says that the teacher tries to pick on her, knowing that it will upset her. Jada is embarrassed when this happens because she does not like to be put on the spot when she doesn't know the answer. She says that it is not normal for teachers to call on girls in class. She indicates that in her other classes, it is the boys who mostly talk in class.

Jada feels that it is not important for her to learn English. She says she speaks English just fine and doesn't understand the point of the class. She adds that she doesn't plan on working when she graduates and has no intentions of going to college. She wants to get married and support her husband in his work while she develops as a homemaker.

Jada says that she hates school because she has no friends and people pick on her because she is different. She wishes she could drop out of school, but her parents won't let her. She says she has only one friend, but that she and her friend don't have much in common. Jada says that the only reason that they are friends is because they are both losers. Jada adds that she is used to being a "nerd," so this really doesn't bother her. The only problem is her mean English teacher.

Jada indicates mounting anxiety prior to attending her English class. She says that her stomach starts to hurt about one hour before English class everyday. She used to go to the school nurse instead of going to class, but the nurse told her that she couldn't come anymore. She says that sometimes she doesn't even want to go to school because she hates English so much. When she's in English class her palms are sweaty and she has trouble breathing. She says that her chest feels tight and she is afraid she is going to have a heart attack.

Jada says she has trouble eating lunch because she is so nervous about going to English class. She also says that if she thinks about English class before bed, she cannot sleep and often has nightmares about going to her class. Jada wishes that she could drop out of English class and take something else so that she can get rid of her anxiety.

- Provide a diagnosis or diagnoses for Jada.
- Now, reread the case inserting "boy" and "he." How does your assessment differ if the client is a boy?

- Now reread the case with the assumption that Jada of Asian descent from an upper-middle-class family. Her father is a doctor and her mother is a housewife. How does that change your impressions?
- How would your reactions have been different if this client were from the "barrio"?
- How would ascribing a *DSM* diagnosis potentially impact the client?
- How would your values impact your conceptualization of the client's situation?
- How might some of the client's issues be related to developmental issues?

PREMENSTRUAL DYSPHORIC DISORDER   The battle over the inclusion of the Premenstrual Dysphoric Disorder (PDD or LLPDD) draws particular attention to the political and gender struggles inherent in the development of *DSM* classifications. Some believe that Premenstrual Dysphoric Disorder has been supported as a "diagnosis under further study" without any scientific support (Caplan et al., 1992). Caplan et al. (1992), for instance, suggest that, although women may experience dysphoria related to their menstrual cycle, such dysphoria may result from culturally determined, negative associations with menstruation or from physiological, hormonal changes. Further, Gallant and Hamilton (1988) indicate "the overabundance of methodological problems in this literature" (p. 273). As Caplan et al. (1992) point out, "there is no evidence that [women's hormonal changes] are any more severe than men's hormonally based mood or behavior changes [and yet] . . . there is no DSM equivalent for males" (p. 28; see also Caplan, 1992). Caplan and her colleagues thus question why women's changes in moods caused by hormonal changes are considered psychiatric abnormalities, but men's are not.

PERSONALITY DISORDERS AND SOCIALIZATION   Personality disorder diagnoses have been examined more frequently for sex bias because they represent medical diseases least of all and therefore could be more likely to reflect social conventions (Kroll, 1988). As mentioned previously, women seem to predominate in borderline, dependent, and histrionic personality disorders, and men seem to predominate in compulsive, paranoid, antisocial, schizoid, and passive–aggressive personality disorders.

It seems a major concern to many feminists that women who are well socialized receive a diagnosis, but that men who are well socialized do not (Brown, 1991a, 1992; Caplan, 1992; Kaplan, 1983a; Pantony & Caplan, 1991; Russell, 1986a; Wine, Moses, & Smye, 1980). For instance, Caplan (1992), when challenging a proposed self-defeating personality disorder (SDPD), and Kaplan (1983a), when questioning the assumptions underlying the dependent personality disorder diagnosis, suggested that the criteria for each matched the "good wife syndrome" (p. 74), or the ways that North American women are socialized to be unselfish and to put others' needs ahead of their own. Both authors declared that it seemed unreasonable to raise women to behave in certain ways and then to diagnose them for complying. In addition, Kaplan questions the notions that dependency is unhealthy, that extreme dependence in women indicates a disorder rather than merely that women are subordinate in our society, and that women's dependency deserves a diagnosis, but that men's dependency (e.g., relying on others to clean their houses, cook for them, take care of their children) does not. Caplan (1992) questions why the *DSM* does not consider the inability to express a wide range of emotions, or other forms of extreme male socialization, to be disordered (e.g., macho personality disorder). Use Activity 17.2 to consider possible sex biases in personality disorders.

ACTIVITY 17.2

Consider the following two diagnoses in dyads:

Antisocial Personality Disorder

1. Failure to conform to social norms with respect to lawful behaviors as indicated by repeatedly performing acts that are grounds for arrest.
2. Deceitfulness, as indicated by repeated lying, use of aliases, or conning others for personal profit or pleasure.
3. Impulsivity or failure to plan ahead.
4. Irritability and aggressiveness, as indicated by repeated physical fights or assaults.
5. Reckless disregard for safety of self or others.
6. Consistent irresponsibility, as indicated by repeated failure to sustain consistent work behavior or honor financial obligations.
7. Lack of remorse, as indicated by being indifferent to or rationalizing having hurt, mistreated, or stolen from another. (American Psychiatric Association, 2000, p. 706)

Dependent Personality Disorder

1. Has difficulty making everyday decisions without an excessive amount of advice and reassurance from others.
2. Needs others to assume responsibility for most major areas of his or her life.
3. Has difficulty expressing disagreement with others because of fear of loss of support or approval.
4. Has difficulty initiating projects or doing things on his or her own (because of a lack of self-confidence in judgment or abilities rather than a lack of motivation or energy).
5. Goes to excessive lengths to obtain nurturance and support from others, to the point of volunteering to do things that are unpleasant.
6. Feels uncomfortable or helpless when alone because of exaggerated fears of being unable to care for himself or herself.
7. Urgently seeks another relationship as a source of care and support when a close relationship ends.
8. Is unrealistically preoccupied with fears of being left to take care of himself or herself. (American Psychiatric Association, 2000, p. 725)

Now, address the following:

- Imagine a man diagnosed with Antisocial Personality Disorder and then imagine a man diagnosed with Dependent Personality Disorder.
- Now imagine a woman diagnosed with Antisocial Personality Disorder and then a woman diagnosed with Dependent Personality Disorder.
- How do your perceptions of men and women differ even when they are diagnosed with the same disorder?
- What would the opposite of each of the disorders be? Develop the specific "opposite" criteria.
- Why are there not *DSM* diagnoses associated with these opposite criteria?
- What are some other "opposites" that are not included in the *DSM* (e.g., stoic to parallel histrionic)?
- Why do you suppose such opposites are left out?

In reaction to what they consider an imbalance in pathologizing, Pantony and Caplan (1991) proposed Delusional Dominating Personality Disorder (DDPD) as a challenge to practitioners and diagnosticians to pay attention to those stereotypical male characteristics that harm men and those around them. The criteria include characteristics such as difficulties establishing and maintaining interpersonal relationships; difficulties expressing and attending to emotions; the choice of violence, power, silence, withdrawal, and/or avoidance as solutions to conflict; the need to be around younger women who are shorter, weigh less, make less money, and are conventionally physically attractive; a tendency to be threatened by women who don't disguise their intelligence; and resistance to efforts to establish gender equity.

Landrine (1989), however, points to the lack of empirical success of studies that examine such feminist hypotheses. She proposes instead that the personality disorders received by men most represent role stereotypes for men of a certain age, class, and marital status, while the personality disorders received most by women represent female role stereotypes for females of a certain age, class, and marital status. Her research has found support for her "social role" hypothesis, a hypothesis that includes gender, age, and socioeconomic class as interacting variables. The research results indicate that stereotypes of young, lower-class men were labeled antisocial; stereotypes of single middle-class young women were labeled histrionic/hysterical; stereotypes of married middle-class middle-aged women were labeled dependent; stereotypes of the "ruling class," that is, middle-class men, were labeled prototypically normal, or corresponded with the criteria for compulsive, paranoid, and narcissistic descriptions. Borderline and schizoid descriptions were not attributed to either sex. Landrine indicates, therefore, that the gender distribution of personality disorders does not result from the misogyny of practitioners, but from the overlap between personality disorder characteristics and gender role stereotypes of both sexes.

Socialization and Mental Health

Research and theory on the mental health implications of socialization have further clarified some of the ways that gender-specific socialization harms people or causes them distress. Gilligan and her colleagues' research on "voice" (Brown & Gilligan, 1992; Gilligan, 1982; Taylor, Gilligan, & Sullivan, 1995) found that girls silence themselves and their desires, abilities, and interests (i.e., they give up their "voice") as they move into adolescence because they believe that such silence is necessary for intimate relationships. Smolak's (2002) research on voice and psychopathology found that voice was negatively correlated to femininity, and that the "lack of voice" and psychopathology link was documented more clearly for women than for men. Rather than voice being related strictly to being male or female, however, higher voice ratings were related to higher ratings on masculinity, and lower voice ratings to lower ratings on masculinity and higher ratings on femininity. Her findings confirmed previous findings that higher levels of masculinity were related to better mental health (Murnen & Smolak, 1998).

Kirsh and Kuiper (2002) discuss individualism and relatedness, comparing these to masculinity and femininity, in their discussions of why women in North America are twice as likely to experience depression in their lives than men. They explained the difference in prevalence rates as a –function of cultural factors, claiming that such explanations are validated by the fact that in other countries such gender differences are not as dramatic (Nolen-Hoeksema, 1995). Their explanations are also supported because gender differences seem to begin during adolescence, just at the time when girls' socialization becomes different from boys' (Sprock & Yoder, 1997; Steinberg, 1990). During adolescence, boys are taught that men are to be "active, masterful, and autonomous" (p. 77), whereas girls are taught that women are to be passive, compliant, and committed to interpersonal relationships (Helgeson & Fritz, 1998; Kaplan, 1987).

Bem (1974) indicated that suppression of the non-sex-typed part of oneself was unhealthy, and that androgyny resulted in better mental health and adjustment. Helgeson and Fritz's (Helgeson, 1994; Helgeson & Fritz, 1998) later research confirmed Bem's findings that poor health and relationship difficulties result from a lack of balance between individualism (maleness) and relatedness (femaleness). However, being male or female turned out to be less relevant than the person's degree of masculinity and femininity. Higher femininity scores and lower masculinity scores correlated with higher depression in both sexes, and higher levels of masculinity resulted in lower levels of depression in both men and women.

What then are women to do about the conflict between their needs to adopt masculine characteristics in order to be mentally healthy and society's demands that they adopt feminine characteristics in order to be desirable? Feminists assert that answers to these questions are unlikely to emerge from a focus on diagnosing and medically reducing the symptoms of these conflicts. At the very least, part of counselors' focus ought to be on changing a biased society.

Social Conditions

Beyond the socialization questions are questions about the impact of societal conditions on women's mental health, trauma experiences in particular. For instance, environmental factors that many researchers (Carmen, Russo, & Miller, 1981; Collins, 1998; Cook et al., 1993; Gove & Tudor, 1973; Horsfall, 1998; Howell, 1981; Jordanova, 1981; Root, 1992; Rothblum, 1982; Vance, 1997; Weissman & Klerman, 1981; Wetzel, 1991) have hypothesized to account for the high rates of depression and other disorders in women include (a) the greater restrictiveness of women's roles, which result in less financial, occupational, or social gratification; (b) the inability to measure up to standards of women who are held up as examples of those who have "made it"; (c) a lack of social networks and supports; (d) marriage, as married women are more depressed than never-married women, possibly as a result of isolation and not having their needs met in their roles as homemakers, or as a result of being employed yet also carrying most of childcare and household responsibilities; (e) separation or divorce (because women are less likely to remarry and more likely to live longer than men); (f) single motherhood and its attendant stresses (Rothblum, 1982); (g) more frequent experiences of gender-based discrimination (Cook et al., 1993; Root, 1992); (h) higher prevalences of living in poverty with its stressors; (i) inequities related to marriage, family relationships, reproduction, child rearing, divorce, aging, education, and work (Carmen et al., 1981); (j) work outside the home that is low status or low pay; and (k) women's roles being defined in terms of the needs of others, which serves to leave their own needs secondary and unmet. Carmen and colleagues (1981) believe that the current circumstances of inequality for women "set the stage for extraordinary events that may heighten vulnerability to mental illness: the frequency with which incest, rape, and marital violence occur suggests that such events might well be considered normative developmental crises for women" (p. 1321; see also Caplan, 1992; Lee, Lentz, Taylor, Mitchell, & Woods, 1994; Libbus, 1996).

Thus, it may be more accurate to say that disorder exists in the relationships between certain people and those with whom they relate, or between those people and societal norms and demands, rather than existing in individual biology. Focusing on the individual may result in failure to "cure" the problem, while focus on societal situations (e.g., providing child care, opening up employment for women, changing the definitions of proper female behavior) may succeed in reducing the incidence of the problems.

Collins (1998) examines the effects of being in subordinate roles, and indicates that the effects can be generated in any subordinate group, not only in women. For instance, in Zimbardo's Stanford prison experiment (Musen, 1992), the effects of subordination and domination were artificially generated in White males. In the experiment, psychologically healthy White male college students were assigned to be prison guards or prisoners. The "prisoners" developed symptoms that are associated with the *DSM* diagnoses typically ascribed to women; they became depressed, suicidal, anxious, and developed eating problems. The "guards" developed symptoms that are associated with *DSM* diagnoses typically ascribed to men; they became verbally abusive, violent, and otherwise antisocial. Collins's (1998) conclusions were that "even psychologically healthy White males will exhibit the 'psychopathology' that is typically ascribed to subordinates when placed in a subordinate role, even for a short period of time" (p. 108). She remarks that the results of this experiment demonstrate that these disorders probably result more from social position (subordinate/dominant) than from biology, as is typically assumed.

WOMEN'S TRAUMA EXPERIENCES   Some authors have indicated that the ongoing experiences of subordination and oppression and the previously cited negative social conditions that surround female daily existence are a type of insidious trauma (Brown, 1990a, 1991a, 1991b, 1992; Root, 1989, 1992). Gender differentiation in our society (Cook, 1992a, 1992b) results in violence against women in the form of incest, rape, and battering, observing the abuse of other women, and sexual abuse in childhood, all of which approach normative status in girls and women. Others from nondominant groups are also repeatedly exposed to trauma and victimization (Brown, 1986, 1992; Committee on Women in Psychology, 1985; Rosewater, 1986, 1987; Russell, 1986b; Walker, 1985, 1986). Reflect on "Angela's" situation in Case Study 17.4 to get a sense of how considering or not considering context affects your diagnostic impressions.

CASE STUDY 17.4

You begin counseling Angela, a 28-year-old female. Angela reports that she'd like help in decreasing her anxiety. She indicates constant tension, irritableness, tiredness, worrying, and occasional panic reactions. She notes that she has a history of strained relationships and has difficulty trusting others. She also reports that she self-injures by cutting her arms and legs and has difficulty feeling at ease and "real." She states, "I don't know who I am or where I'm going. Life feels so chaotic." During your intake interview you notice that Angela is difficult to connect with and seems very distracted and agitated.

- At this point, what *DSM* diagnostic labels might apply?
- What additional information do you need before applying a formal diagnosis?

You obtain a release of information to talk with Angela's mom. "Since the rape and the time she moved in with me 3 months ago, she begs me everyday to never make her leave," says Ms. Connor about her daughter.

- How does this information change your initial diagnostic impressions?

Angela appears to be somewhat restless and guarded during your second session, but when you ask about the rape and validate her experience, she relaxes and shares her story. She reports that she was raped while walking home from work 3 months ago, and the rape triggered memories of early sexual abuse inflicted by her father. Now driving everywhere rather than walking, she continues to function well at work, but finds herself unable to live on her own.

When asked what prompted her to pursue counseling, Angela reluctantly pulls up the sleeves of her shirt, revealing multiple slash type cuts and scars. In tears, Angela explains that when she feels overwhelmed by thoughts of her abuse as a child and recent rape, she distracts herself by making superficial cuts on her arms. She explains that she continually thinks about what has happened to her, especially when she's alone, and that she feels sad most of the time.

Angela reports that she was able to trust men earlier in her life. However, she has felt uncomfortable around men since her rape, and now believes that they are untrustworthy. She has recently begun working in a women's clothing store, and as a result rarely has to deal with men. Angela carries pepper spray in the event that she should ever find herself alone with a man.

- Based on this additional information, what *DSM* diagnoses best apply?
- What additional information do you need to make a formal diagnosis?

The impacts of sexual abuse and sexual assault on women's mental health and development are well documented (Ferrara, 2002; James & Gilliland, 2001). For instance, women and girls who have experienced such traumas display despair, anger, and retraumatization, and are given diagnoses of PTSD, depression, anxiety, eating disorder, and borderline personality disorder (Busfield, 1996; Gallop, McKeever, Toner, Lancee, & Lueck, 1995; Lego, 1996; Nehls, 1998). These disorders and experiences seriously impede women from "effectively performing and enjoying activities of daily living such as work, parenting, recreation, partnerships, and friendships" (Horsfall, 2001, p. 429).

Many authors challenge the notion that women who have been victims of sexual or physical abuse should be diagnosed or labeled as flawed in any way, because whatever distressed or distressing resultant behavior that they may display is usually understandable and normative in the context of the experience of trauma (Brown, 1991a; Johnson, 1980). An Abuse/Oppression Artifact Disorder diagnosis has thus been proposed, hypothesizing that it would help clients make sense of their behaviors, placing ultimate responsibility for distress on the oppression or abuse that they experienced. The diagnosis would clarify etiology for counselors. Symptoms could be considered as understandable, "survival-oriented" responses to horrible circumstances, rather than as a form of pathology. Further, such a diagnosis might correct for the undertreatment of women who experience trauma. Use Reflection 17.3 to stimulate your thinking about diagnosing women with histories of abuse. Then consider Case Study 17.5 and discuss the diagnostic and treatment dilemmas you might experience were you the clinician.

REFLECTION 17.3

The trauma that women experience is often related to mental health and developmental well-being. Professional counselors who work with women with histories of abuse must assess and consider social conditions. List and describe the salient variables a counselor must consider before providing a diagnosis for these women.

CASE STUDY 17.5

Lourdes is a 30-year-old immigrant from Puerto Rico who says that she is unhappy in her life because she has not made many friends in the United States. She feels very lonely and isolated. She is sad and would like to work on feeling more grateful and happy while learning how to become a better wife. She misses all of her old friends in Puerto Rico and longs to see them again.

Lourdes and her husband arrived in the United States 2 years ago. They have no children, but do have a few other family members who came to the United States with them. Lourdes is unemployed, but her husband owns a convenience store. She works for her husband at the store when he requests her service. When she is not working for her husband, she is at home cooking and cleaning and tending to home matters. She says that this is what women "do," and she feels comfortable with this arrangement.

However, she feels lonely being in the house for days at a time. She says that in Puerto Rico when she had to stay at home all day, she could at least socialize with her neighbors and family, but she has had difficulty connecting with her neighbors here in the United States.

Lourdes says that she is having trouble sleeping and has had appetite changes, as she is often worrying about various issues. She says that she worries that she did not make the right thing for dinner or that the house will not be clean enough for her husband. She also worries that she will never make any new friends. She indicates that she often is jumpy because she is afraid she is forgetting something or will make a mistake and upset her husband. She says that when she is not cooking or cleaning she feels lethargic and feels sad and worried.

Lourdes wishes that her husband had more time for her, but "realizes" that she is being selfish with his time. She says that she knows that it is important for him to be at work and to tend to his social life. She indicates that her husband has several girlfriends and while she sometimes feels jealous, she would never challenge his behaviors. She is not upset that her husband has girlfriends. Her husband gets mad at her and sometimes becomes violent if she asks him to spend more time with her. She said she also feels guilty that she has not been able to provide her husband with children, and she notes that he often castigates her for not being able to get pregnant.

The next time Lourdes comes into the office she has a black eye. The counselor also notices several bruises on her arms. When questioned about the bruises, she says that her husband hit her the night before because she was in a bad mood and asked him to stay home instead of going out with his friends. She says that she came to this appointment to tell the counselor that it would be her last appointment. Her husband does not want her to come anymore because he feels that it is disrespectful to him for her to see the counselor. He also doesn't want her participating in anything that takes away from his time with her.

- Without the context of domestic violence, what diagnoses might have best fit this client?
- How does the domestic violence context change your diagnostic impressions?
- How do you think that long-term contexts, such as living in a domestic violence situation, affect a client's *DSM* profile?
- How might your values affect your conceptualization of the client's situation?
- How might the client's gender/culture affect her perceptions of her situation?
- If the client ever needed to go to court to obtain a restraining order, press domestic violence charges, obtain a divorce, and the like, and the court ordered your files, what would the implications be of the different diagnoses you mentioned above?
- If the client continues in counseling, how might you play a preventative role with this client?

TOWARD SOLUTIONS

In the literature, much of the critical discourse around professionals' use of the *DSM* has focused on what "not to do" versus "what to do," on problems rather than solutions. This section offers strategies with activities, exercises, and cases that are designed to increase counselors' incorporation of systemic, developmental, and multicultural "stories" about client problems and solutions to these problems. Begin by developing a case vignette with the prompts in Activity 17.3.

ACTIVITY 17.3

Develop a case vignette. Include the client's demographics, presenting concerns, and a brief psychosocial history. Provide a diagnosis for the client using the most current version of the *DSM*. In addition, write a couple of paragraphs about multicultural considerations when giving the client a particular diagnosis.

Discuss the vignette along with your peers' vignettes in small groups. Record notes on the multicultural considerations and possible diagnoses for each client. Discuss as a class themes in multicultural diagnosis using the "clients" presented in your small group as a framework.

Comprehensive Assessment

Diagnosis should not just identify a disorder or differentiate one disorder from another. Counselors should always remain aware that *DSM* diagnosis is only one piece of a comprehensive assessment. Not only do other diagnostic considerations beyond the *DSM* exist, but the *DSM* can be considered helpful to the degree only that it helps counselors in their work with clients (e.g., triggering referrals for medication or hospitalization or special programs). For example, Sadler and Hulgus (1994), Lo and Fung (2003) and Nelson (2002) state that for assessment to contribute effectively to client care, it must include a careful description and operationalization of all relevant phenomena (e.g., individual symptoms, functional abilities, family interactions, contextual factors, longitudinal-historical information). Further, Mezzich (1995, 2002) and others (e.g., McLaughlin, 2002) suggest that a comprehensive diagnosis should integrate the perspectives of the client, the counselor, and significant others, such as friends and family members. A counselor might therefore consider the *DSM* as a first step toward helping clients, while being aware of the *DSM*'s intended (and limited) scope, and extending the assessment process beyond *DSM* diagnosis.

Other conceptualizations of diagnoses, perceptions that consider the *DSM* in context, have also been proposed. For example, McAuliffe and Eriksen (1999) and others (e.g., Anderson & Goolishian, 1992; Tomm, 1989) state that diagnosis is a construction of meaning that is accomplished during a dynamic process and that diagnoses should be co-created with all who are involved in the clinical relationship. Tomm (1989) also recommends considering diagnoses as case-and-situation specific, as though there is a wide array of potential descriptions and explanations for the presenting difficulties. These diagnoses should further be considered to be evolving as new information becomes available over time, rather than remaining static, objective truths. The counselor is, then, according to Tomm and others (Dietz, 2000; Larner, 2000) not an expert *doing* diagnosis to the client, but a facilitator in forming diagnostic meanings. To get a sense of how practitioners in the field ensure that their assessments are comprehensive, conduct Activity 17.4.

ACTIVITY 17.4

In your local community, select a mental health professional to interview. Ask the individual if he or she would be interested in discussing multicultural issues and diagnosis. Select two or three areas from the chapter and develop five questions related to comprehensive assessment to ask the practitioner. Interview the practitioner. After the interview identify the similarities or differences between the literature and the practices of the mental health professional.

Universal and Culturally Specific Diagnoses

Cultural and diagnostic scholars seem to pursue two different poles or models: one that suggests that there are universal diagnostic categories and descriptors that apply regardless of situational and cultural factors, and the other that claims that "it is impossible to extract an individual's lifestyle from the culture that helps to mold it and through which it is expressed" (Thomas & Sillen, 1972, p. 59) (To review further discussions of the two different models, see Fabrega [1996], Hoagwood & Jensen [1997], Hughes [1996], Kirmayer & Minas [2000], Lopez [1997], and Sayed, Collins, & Takahashi [1998].) Large-scale epidemiological studies that may support universal diagnostic categories has often suppressed "the voices of small groups," which has, according to Kirmayer and Minas (2000, p. 447), contributed "to the homogenization and standardization of world cultures and traditions of healing. What we gain in methodological rigor," they claim, "we lose in diversity". The relevance of culture is then undermined, which results in interpreting those behaviors that do not conform to a Western model as abnormal or maladaptive (Sayed et al., 1998).

However, attempts to hear "the voices of small groups" by adding cultural data to the *DSM* has also generated criticism. Hughes (1996) points out that separating culture-bound syndromes in the *DSM* and giving them special, restricted status puts them at risk or makes them vulnerable to being dismissed, discounted, or not taken seriously. By separating culture-bound syndromes into a separate section, *DSM* developers are assuming that the European American perspective is somehow superior or the standard or the point of reference against which all other psychiatry (including cultural psychiatry) is compared (Hughes, 1996).

The Culture and Diagnosis Group believes further that a culturally sensitive *DSM* would include more extensive guidelines in the *DSM*'s introduction about how to use the *DSM* in a culturally sensitive manner; a cultural axis; a cultural issues section under each disease condition or chapter; specific examples of culturally normative client experiences that might look like disease or of disorders that are expressed in unexpected ways for cultural reasons; culture-bound syndromes; and an appendix related to expectable problems in working with interpreters (Kleinman, 1996). The *DSM* should also, according to Thompson (1996), (a) include information to assist the counselor to address the interactions between the client's culture and the counselor's culture; (b) assist the counselor to distinguish between pathology and culturally different (i.e., normal cultural practices that appear strange to dominant-culture practitioners); (c) clearly state that pathology should not be dismissed just because it occurs with high frequency in a particular culture; and (d) encourage counselors to avoid the temptation to assume that they cannot treat clients with culture-bound syndromes—counselors should instead assess what part of a client's psychopathology that they can treat.

Sinacore-Guinn (1995) outlines what more culturally sensitive assessment would look like. She recommends that counselors begin by exploring cultural systems and structures (i.e., community structure, family, schools, interaction styles, concepts of illness, life-stage development, coping patterns, and immigration history; Bahr & Sinacore-Guinn, 1993; Sinacore-Guinn, 1992; Sinacore-Guinn & Bahr, 1993a, 1993b); cultural values (i.e., time, activity, relational orientation, person–nature orientation, basic nature of people; Kelly, 1990); gender socialization; and the effect of trauma. In the process, the counselor (and perhaps the client as well) would gain an understanding of the impact of race, class, gender, sexual orientation, and ethnicity on the presenting problem, on the client's understanding of the problem, and on the client's expression of the problem.

Other Culturally Astute Strategies

Castillo (1997) contends that an accurate assessment of emotion or behavior is not possible without an assessment of cultural schemas. The counselor, therefore, needs to know what types of emotions a particular cultural group experiences, which emotions are elicited by what situations, what particular emotions mean to indigenous observers, what means of expression of particular emotions exist in that culture, what emotions are considered proper or improper for a person of a particular social status, and how unexpressed emotions are handled. Castillo further urges practitioners to treat both the illness (i.e., client's subjective experience of being sick) *and* the disease (i.e., practitioner's diagnosis).

Castillo (1997) provides the following guidelines to enable mental health professionals to offer clients a culturally sensitive diagnosis:

1. Assess the client's cultural identity.
2. Identify sources of cultural information relevant to the client.
3. Assess the cultural meaning of a client's problem and symptoms.
4. Consider the impacts and effects of family, work, and community on the complaint, including stigma and discrimination that may be associated with mental illness in the client's culture.
5. Assess personal biases.
6. Plan treatment collaboratively. He adds the following specific suggestions for the assessment and treatment process:
   a. Adjust the interviewing style (i.e., eye contact, personal space, rate of speech) to the norms of the client.
   b. Do not use symptom scales without validating them in the new culture.
   c. Remember that different symptoms mean different things in different cultures.
   d. Consult with and work in collaboration with qualified folk healers.
   e. Use symbols from the client's culture as part of the treatment.
   f. Reduce the unknown by supporting the client's own understanding of the illness, as long as his or her understanding includes the possibility of treatment and eventual cure.
   g. Increase the manageability or the client's sense of "control or competence to meet the demands of the illness" (p. 80).
   h. Increase understanding of the function of the illness, its purpose, and the moral or religious reason behind it.
   i. Use symbolic, ritualistic healing in order to shift clients' cognitions about the problem, the client meanings, and thus their emotions.

Kress et al. (2005) further suggest questions that culturally sensitive counselors should ask themselves before diagnosing any client:

- Have I been able to separate what is important to me and what is important to this particular client?
- What do I know about this client's cultural heritage?
- What do I *not* know about this client's cultural heritage?
- What is this client's relationship with his or her culture from his or her perspective?
- How acculturated is the client?
- What are my stereotypes, beliefs, and biases about this culture, and how might these influence my understandings?
- What culturally appropriate strategies or techniques should be incorporated in the assessment process?
- What is my philosophy of how pathology is operationalized in individuals from this cultural group?
- Have I appropriately consulted with other mental health professionals, members from this particular culture, and/or members of this client's family or extended family?
- Has this client aided in the co-construction of my understanding of this problem? (p. 103)

Kress et al. (2005) also suggest an increased emphasis on Axis IV as a means by which counselors may ensure more culturally sensitive diagnosis. An increased focus on Axis IV information can carve out a better contextual understanding of psychosocial and environmental problems that may impact the diagnosis, treatment, and prognosis of clients. Table 17.1 summarizes recommendations for diversity-sensitive diagnoses.

TABLE 17.1 Summary of Recommendations for Diversity-Sensitive Diagnoses: A Proactive Approach to Limiting *DSM* Biases

---

Counselor Awareness

- Commit to assessing and overcoming personal biases and stereotypes.
- Commit to ongoing awareness about personal assumptions and cultural encapsulation, including continually questioning assumptions about what is usual or normal with respect to gender.
- Overcome own tendency to diagnose early, or to stop assessing when "usual" understandings are reached.
- Avoid jumping to conclusions about clients on the basis of their cultural group.

Counselor Knowledge

- Know and use only symptom scales validated in the client's culture.
- Remember that different symptoms mean different things in different cultures.
- Acquire knowledge about different cultures' norms and interactions styles.
- Be aware of the wide variations and conflicts that may exist among people from different cultures, and the conflicts that may exist between North American law and other culture's practices.
- Avoid accepting conclusions of research if it does not include lower socioeconomic status, women, non-Whites, and the unemployed.
- Identify sources of cultural information relevant to the clients currently being seen.

Counselor Skills

- Assess the client's cultural identity.
- Assess the cultural meaning of a client's problem and symptom.
- Reduce the unknown by supporting the clients' own understanding of the illness, as long as their understanding includes the possibility of treatment and eventual cure.
- Understand fully what happens in the mind and body of the person who presents for care (i.e., comprehensive assessment), rather than just identifying a disorder or differentiating one disorder from another.
- Carefully describe and operationalize all relevant phenomena (e.g., individual symptoms, functional abilities, family interactions, contextual factors, and longitudinal historical information).
- Consider the effects of family, work, and community on the development and continuance of the complaint, including stigma and discrimination that may be associated with mental illness in the client's culture.
- Plan treatment collaboratively.
- Incorporate the perspective of clients and their cultures, the practitioner, and significant others, such as friends and family members.
- Adjust the interviewing style (i.e., eye contact, personal space, rate of speech) to the norms of the client.
- Work in collaboration with qualified folk healers.
- Use symbols from the client's culture as part of the treatment.
- Increase the manageability or the client's sense of control or competence.
- Conduct feminist clinical assessments, including questions about gender issues and experiences within the client's milieu and experiences of culture and cultural oppression.
- Attend to factors that may influence the expression of gender.
- Question the meaning to the client and to the practitioner of gendered behavior.
- Avoid error of overdiagnosis and misdiagnosis of gay men, lesbians, African Americans, ethnic minorities, women, and nontraditional men when their behavior does not match Western norms.
- Attend to reports of somatic symptoms (e.g., headache, trouble sleeping, stomach ache), which in most societies indicate depression.

Feminist Analysis

Feminist analysis proposes that traditional approaches to diagnosis and treatment overfocus on idiosyncratic life experiences, biology, or personality traits as causes of problems and thus hold individuals responsible for solving these problems to too large a degree. Feminists thus begin from the position that the personal cannot be separated from the political or social, and so make no apologies for envisioning the therapy process as a political process aimed at solving social problems, which they blame for many client problems (Brown, 1991b).

Brown (1990b) urges all counselors to conduct feminist clinical assessments, to continually question their own assumptions about what is usual or normal with respect to gender, to attend to factors that may influence the expression of gender, and to question the meaning to both the client and to the counselor of gendered behaviors. Counselors conducting feminist clinical assessments purposefully ask about gender issues and other aspects of the client's experiences (Brown, 1990b), assessing whether the presenting problems are functional and serve positive purposes or if they fail to be useful to the individual in her or his social context (Brown, 1990b). For instance, the counselor may assess what it means to the client to be a failure or a success as a man or a woman within her or his social environment.

Counselors also need to be aware of issues, patterns, or behavior that occur with high frequency in one gender or the other, of the cultural reasons for men and women's positions in a society, and of the impact on men and women's expressions of distress or types of problems (Brown, 1990b). They intentionally and directly inquire into life events whose base rates are related to gender (e.g., interpersonal violence, sexual assault, covert discrimination) (Bass & Davis, 1988; Brown, 1990b; Bryer, Nelson, Miller, & Krol, 1987). Use Reflection 17.4 to consider what to do to overcome some of feminists' concerns.

REFLECTION 17.4

Professional counselors who adhere to the feminist perspective challenge the current processes used to diagnose clients. Select one diagnostic challenge identified by the feminist perspective (as listed previously) and make recommendations to address the challenge.

Function of Symptoms in Context

Counselors may experience difficulties in fully including social and environmental influences in the *DSM*'s multiaxial system. In fact, if we maintain a contextual perspective, can we consider any disorder to be located within the individual? It would seem that counselors who fully consider social and environmental influences, rather than locating dysfunction in individuals, will extend their assessments beyond the individual to communities, neighborhoods, and families, and will define the "problem" in terms that include such entities (Gottschalk, 2000; Hoagwood & Jensen, 1997). Where does one find room for such definitions in the *DSM*'s five-axis system?

In fact, when thinking systemically, counselors may also realize that what the *DSM* considers to be psychopathology may actually be a very functional attempt on a person's part to adapt to or cope with a dysfunctional context (Allwood, 2002; Ivey & Ivey, 1998, 1999; Webb, 2002; Yahav & Sharlin, 2002). A compulsively overeating teenager may be offering herself nurturance when she experiences negative emotions because no one in her family is able or willing to comfort her when she needs it. A little boy may hide under his bed and refuse to see or speak to anyone as an escape from incessant parental fighting and abuse. A firefighter may dissociate in some way following the horror of having removed bodies from the collapsed World Trade Center. Including the context (e.g., rape, incest, abuse, battering) in the diagnostic discussion thus creates a very different diagnostic picture than considering symptoms without the context (e.g., PTSD vs. major depression).

Conceptualizing symptoms as adaptations or coping strategies may also result in a different counselor–client relationship than might emerge within a medical-model assessment relationship. That is, when viewing symptoms as coping strategies that are already being employed, a counselor might acknowledge and recognize the value of the symptom/coping strategy, might appreciate all that the client is doing to manage, and might encourage the client to use the symptom until another, less damaging or more helpful coping strategy becomes apparent or useful. In contrast, when client problems are viewed traditionally, the counselor immediately focuses on how to reduce symptoms, viewing the client's way of handling life as inadequate or as demonstrating deficits (Hoagwood & Jensen, 1997).

Relational (and Other Theoretical) Systems of Diagnosis

The *DSM* has, in fact, become more relationally oriented as a result of efforts by the Coalition on Family Diagnosis (CFD), a multidisciplinary conglomeration of professionals representing mental health-related organizations (Kaslow, 1993). The CFD encouraged *DSM* developers to expand the V Codes at the end of the *DSM* to include Relational Problems and Other Conditions That May Be a Focus of Clinical Attention.

They also promoted the Global Assessment of Relationship Functioning (GARF; see also Mash & Johnston, 1996). The GARF is located in the *DSM–IV* appendix, and focuses counselors on clients' relationships. "The GARF scale permits the practitioner to rate the degree to which a family or ongoing relational unit meets the affective or instrumental needs of its members" (American Psychiatric Association, 2000, p. 814). Like the GAF, the GARF's numerical ratings range from 0 to 100. Higher scores indicate satisfactory relationship functioning and imply that the client's perspectives are included in relational decisions. The GARF rates a family's levels of organization, emotional climate, and problem solving, and thus also offers direction to counselors when they develop interventions about these areas (Ivey & Ivey, 1999; Mottarella, Philpot, & Fritsche, 2001; Sporakowski, 1995).

However, despite improvements provided by the GARF, Hoagwood and Jensen (1997), in their review of the constraints of the current *DSM* system, conclude that the current system fails to address the complex nature of the interactions between individuals and their environments. In response to this criticism, some theorists have developed assessment models that more predominantly include relational factors that are pertinent to *DSM* diagnoses. For example, these theorists propose that it might be helpful to include an Axis VI for family evaluation as part of the traditional multiaxial system. Such an inclusion would make the *DSM* more useful to family therapists (and other systemically oriented professionals) whose implicit paradigm currently contradicts that of the *DSM* (Denton; 1990; Kaslow, 1993; Mash & Johnston, 1996). The axis could include a narrative case formulation from a family systems perspective, a family typology, a global assessment of family health, or a rating of families on various dimensions such as enmeshment or power (Denton, 1990). Inclusion of an axis relevant to their work might also challenge family counselors to more fully use the *DSM*, and thus to acknowledge the "individual system" in their considerations of the family (Mash & Johnston, 1996; Sporakowski, 1995). Full multiaxial diagnosis that includes such an Axis VI on each family member would also provide critical information to more individually oriented mental health professionals who often need encouragement to acknowledge the impact of contextual factors. Use Activity 17.5 to discuss the possible impact of this chapter on your future work as a counselor.

ACTIVITY 17.5

With two or three of your classmates, discuss how multicultural diagnosis will influence your work as a counselor. In addition, list concerns you may have regarding multiculturalism and diagnosis. After discussing these issues for 20 to 30 minutes, share the highlights of your discussion with the class.

Summary

It is only by standing back from one's own beliefs and experiences, by taking oneself as object (Kegan, 1982, 1994), that one can truly evaluate the pluses and minuses of various assumptions and behaviors. The ability to do so is a developmental achievement (Kegan, 1982, 1994; Kohlberg, 1981; Loevinger, 1976; Perry, 1970; Rest, 1979). It is our position that critically reflecting on the data and the questions posed in this chapter may assist counselors to step back from automaticity and become aware of the broader societal influences on *DSM* development, on diagnostic decision making, and on treatment, more generally, of those groups in our society that have less power. Furthermore, considering the possibilities presented here focuses attention on who benefits from diagnosis. Ethical counselors seek ultimately to benefit their clients with their counseling procedures. However, they cannot extract themselves from the broader social and economic milieus within which they operate. Constant attention to the impact of these broader milieus on their work and balancing the benefits to the multiple stakeholders may be fundamental to ethical diagnosis. In addition, experiencing other cultures also often assists people to take their own as object; thus, cross-cultural experiences and sensitivities can be very helpful to those attempting to deconstruct a *DSM* diagnosis (or any other mental health practice).

Further, with so many questions being raised about the cultural and gender limitations of diagnoses, it seems to us that it becomes more clearly necessary for practitioners to be tentative in diagnosing those from diverse backgrounds, and to, as part of a more egalitarian relationship, co-construct an understanding of the problem *with* the client,

rather than imposing a diagnosis *upon* the client. The questions of diagnostic accuracy that haunt all research on diagnostic reliability and validity apply doubly to counselors who diagnose clients from diverse backgrounds. That is, how can counselors be accurate when assuming only an individual description of a problem, without describing strengths, support systems, and positive characteristics, and without including a broader understanding of the cultural contexts in which the person was raised and in which the person currently resides? Beyond diagnosing the client's context and its impact lies the broader social constructionist question of the impact of culture on the mental health professional and on the counseling relationship. Social constructionists, for example, indicate that the questions asked while diagnosing tell us more about the diagnoser and the culture in which diagnosis takes place, than about the client (Dickerson & Zimmerman, 1995; Parker, Georgaca, Harper, McLaughlin, & Stowell-Smith, 1995; Wakefield, 1992).

So, what does culturally sensitive and feminist diagnosis mean? Might it mean *not* diagnosing? Might it mean more broadly assessing the problem situation in conversation with the client, without entertaining the *DSM* system? Does it mean considering the *DSM* as one minor part of the broader scheme of diagnosis and assessment—a part currently necessary for obtaining funding for services—while considering all of the parts of a typical intake interview to be the more important guides to further treatment? Might *DSM* diagnosis be considered one story among many and, in the particular case of clients from groups who have historically had less power, might that story be less relevant or more harmful than other stories? Might culturally sensitive and feminist diagnosis require mental health professionals to diagnose and act to change oppressive systems, instead of confining themselves to their offices and requiring clients to change? These are difficult questions, but questions that need to be asked, and asked, and asked again, as mental health professionals struggle with the ethical dilemmas posed by mandates to be culturally sensitive while engaging in the diagnostic process.

Note: This chapter includes some reorganized information from K. Eriksen and V. Kress (2006), *Beyond the DSM story: Quandaries, challenges and best practices.* Pacific Grove, CA: Sage. Reprinted by permission from Sage Publications.

CHAPTER 18

Themes and Future Directions in Multicultural Counseling Theory, Practice, and Research

DANICA G. HAYS AND TAMMI F. MILLIKEN

PREVIEW

Developing multicultural competence within and across various social, cultural, and historical systems involves an ongoing effort of integrating and transforming multicultural counseling theory, practice, and research. This chapter highlights key themes within the text as a framework for future directions in multicultural counseling in general and counselors' multicultural competence development more specifically. First, themes regarding cultural identity, social advocacy and oppression, cultural diversity, and multicultural case conceptualization are presented. Second, self-reflection questions are presented for each theme. Finally, future directions for multicultural theory, practice, and research are described.

MOVING TOWARD MULTICULTURAL COMPETENCE

Developing multicultural competence has been significantly at the forefront of counseling theory, practice, and research only within the last couple of decades, even though the counseling profession called attention in the 1960s and 1970s to the importance of cultural variables in counseling (e.g., Sue, 1978; Sue, 1977; Wrenn, 1962). During this time most of the discussion in our profession centered on disproportionate use and the impact of mental health care services among racial and ethnic minorities, primarily African Americans. Scholars have since brainstormed ways by which counselors could close the gap in differential access to and use of mental health services for various racial and ethnic individuals and their families within a variety of settings including agencies and schools. One solution was to develop competencies and standards that all counselors could use to be effective and sensitive when counseling diverse populations (i.e., multiculturally competent). The counseling profession has seen great strides with the development and subsequent revision and operationalization of multicultural counseling competencies (i.e., Arredondo et al., 1996; Sue et al., 1982, 1992). These competencies have since sparked several initiatives in academia and clinical practice, from evaluating and revising key multicultural counseling constructs (e.g., identity development, diversity, multiculturalism, acculturation), to increasing attention on the role of systemic forces and the impact of privilege and oppression experiences in clients' lives, to differentiating as well as searching for commonalities among various cultural group memberships (e.g., race/ethnicity, gender, sexual orientation, spirituality), to critically examining and transforming counseling theory and case conceptualization for better serving an

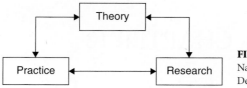

FIGURE 18.1   The Interdependent Nature of Multicultural Competence Development.

increasingly diverse U.S. population. Each of these initiatives is described throughout the text for various cultural groups and systemic phenomena. In addition, we would like to summarize in this chapter some of the major themes of these initiatives.

As these themes are presented, it is important to note that multicultural counseling theory, practice, and research are interdependent constructs (see Figure 18.1). As counselors strive for increased multicultural competence within various client systems, we cannot focus solely on one of these areas. Developing multicultural competence is a dynamic and cyclical process. When we work with culturally diverse clients, we collect informal and formal process and outcome data that influence how we think about certain populations or clinical issues. Our practice thus drives theory to be tested empirically. Further empirical tests or research is integrated into practice leading to further theory formulation. This cycle continues as we gain a clearer understanding of what and why interventions work in multicultural counseling (Ridley, 2005). It is important to note that multicultural competencies we gain for working with particular individuals and families do not necessarily apply to others with similar cultural characteristics and social experiences. New knowledge must be tested and verified for each individual and family system with which we work, taking into account their unique experiences within systems.

Themes in Cultural Identity Development

In practice, traditional models of client conceptualization were insufficient for assessing the worldview of many diverse clients. As described in Chapter 2 (Moore-Thomas), oppression, enculturation, acculturation, and culture shock are a few of the unique influences on the **cultural identity development** of individuals with minority statuses. Neither did traditional therapy consider the cultural-related perceptions, attitudes, and behaviors of White clients. In response, research was conducted to develop models of cultural identity development through the examination of individuals' evolving sense of self in the context of race, ethnicity, gender, sexuality, and spirituality.

Moore-Thomas (Chapter 2) describes several seminal models stemming from this research including, among others, Helms's (1995) people of color and White racial identity models, Downing and Roush's (1985) feminist identity development model, Cass's (1990) model of sexual identity, and Fowler's (1981) theory of faith development. These models are commonly used as tools for culturally competent practice. By assessing a client's cultural identity, counselors can deliberately normalize perceptions and foster continued cultural identity development. Additionally, they can explore their own cultural identity development process and reflect on how the match (or mismatch) among various statuses impacts their attitudes and actions toward clients that are both culturally similar and different from them.

Understanding our own as well as our clients' cultural identity development process is thus an important foundation for multiculturally competent work: it gives us a sense of how we as well as clients view memberships in various cultural groups, others within those groups, and those outside a particular combination of cultural groups. Cultural identity models described in Chapter 2 serve additional purposes. First, it normalizes the process and associated advantages or challenges that we as humans face as we come to know ourselves as cultural beings. Second, the mere fact that cultural self-understanding is developmental ties into the holistic, growth-oriented philosophy to which counselors follow. In essence, we as cultural beings can advance to higher statuses and have a more systemic perspective of our worlds.

Reflect on the following regarding the theme of cultural identity:

- Which cultural identity development processes are more salient for you at this stage of your multicultural competence development? Why?
- How and when might you integrate discussions of cultural identity development in the counseling process?
- Using the systems approach model presented in Chapter 1 (Hays & McLeod), how might various systems influence each of the cultural identity development processes described in Chapter 2?
- Many of the cultural identity development models include the experience or acknowledgment of systemic oppression in the development of a more defined identity. (See racial/ethnic, feminist, and sexual identity development models, specifically.) To what extent do you believe that oppression plays in the identity development process?
- In what ways might cultural identity development impact work with the different multicultural populations described throughout the text?
- How might you integrate clients' cultural identity development statuses in case conceptualization?

Themes in Social Advocacy and Oppression

Models of cultural identity take into consideration the impact of oppression on members of all racial, ethnic, and cultural groups. This conceptualization has helped guide our understanding of clients' experiences of **oppression**, which in turn has contributed to the shaping of empowerment and **social advocacy** efforts. The *–isms* and corresponding privileges that encompass this theme (i.e., racism and White privilege, sexism and male and binary gender classification privilege, heterosexism and heterosexual privilege, classism and social class privilege, ableism, ageism) are interdependent. Both counselors and clients have to negotiate a variety of privileges and forms of oppression depending on cultural group membership and degree of identification with those groups. These negotiations shape our cultural values and psychological, social, and physical experiences, to name a few. Thus, it is imperative that social advocacy and oppression be integrated into the multicultural counseling experience.

Chang and Gnilka (Chapter 3) describe the evolution of social advocacy as the "fifth force" in counseling. This force stemmed from research in multicultural counseling that expanded our knowledge of social injustices, oppression, and majority status privilege. Research and conceptual writings reveal that racism, sexism, heterosexism, classism, ableism, and ageism, as discussed in Chapters 4 through 8 (Hays & Grimmett; Cannon & Singh; Chaney & Marszalek; Newton; and Berens, respectively) are forms of oppression that are perpetuated and sustained by society. The deleterious effects of these social injustices require interventions that expand beyond individual clients to the broader community and societal levels. As such, multiculturally competent counselors are tasked with becoming change agents advocating for equal access to resources and equitable distribution of power for all people.

To guide these efforts at change, research and effective practice has introduced the advocacy competencies, which were adopted by the ACA Governing Council in 2003. These competencies specify efforts counselors can and should take to empower clients at the individual or microlevel and advocate for systemic change at the macrolevel.

Social justice counseling may require a paradigm shift for many counselors. Traditional counseling approaches may need to be abandoned for approaches that are more systemic, efforts may need to be taken to avoid burnout from ongoing work that often results in only minor change, and an investment in learning new approaches to countering oppression may need to be taken. However, the satisfaction that can come from social justice work typically outweighs the costs.

As you consider the theme of social advocacy and oppression, reflect on the following:

- To what degree should multicultural counseling incorporate social advocacy efforts? What are the benefits of this?
- How might the values associated with social advocacy as a force in counseling conflict with the fourth force of counseling: multiculturalism?
- Using the systems approach model presented in Chapter 1 (Hays & McLeod), describe ways by which privilege and oppression is evident within and across systems. What are some specific advocacy strategies that could address social injustice?

Themes in Cultural Diversity

To be successful social advocates, counselors must have self-awareness and knowledge of diverse individuals and families. As such, it is necessary to understand **cultural diversity** or unique characteristics of various racial, ethnic, and other cultural groups. This heightened knowledge and awareness alerts counselors to universal shared experiences, values and customs specific to diverse groups, variations within groups, and individual differences stemming from a multitude of factors including intersecting identities, degree of enculturation and acculturation, and level of identity development.

Chapters 9 through 15 (Helm & James; Nassar-McMillan, Gonzalez, & Mohamed; Inman & Alvarez; Villalba; Garrett; McMahon, Paisley, & Molina; and Cashwell, respectively) offer an overview of several distinct cultural groups that counselors are likely to encounter in the United States. These groups include those of African descent, Arab descent, Asian descent, Latin descent, and European descent, as well as Native Americans, and those of various spiritual orientations. As stated in the chapters, a combination of research and practical experience has shaped and continues to shape understanding of these groups.

Each chapter describes the impact of past and present experiences on current functioning, common cultural values, typical presenting issues, and suggestions for culturally competent therapeutic interventions. For each group, the authors stress the importance of considering subpopulation variations as well as individual variations. A common thread in every chapter is the need to recognize, acknowledge, and respect the influence of culture on clients' experiences. In addition, the chapters model culturally sensitive terminology and provide guidelines for ethical practice.

While there is significant overlap in the information provided in each chapter, practical experience and research have led to an awareness of distinct differences in cultural groups. For example, Helm and James (Chapter 9) assert that many individuals of African descent value a kinship to other African Americans and as such counselors might utilize these support systems as valuable therapeutic resources. Nassar-McMillan and colleagues (Chapter 10) discuss the unique immigration patterns of individuals and families of Arab descent due to political and religious reasons. These immigration trends and associated acculturation experiences have led to increased importance placed on family, education, and religion in counseling.

Inman and Alvarez (Chapter 11) note that there are 43 distinct Asian groups with a range of immigration histories that impact enculturation and acculturation, and subsequently, counseling interventions. However, it is common for those of Asian descent to hold a nonconfrontational, collectivistic perspective in which elders are given the utmost respect. This perspective is counter to many theories of counseling based in U.S. ideology and may require the counselor to utilize alternative healing practices.

Villalba (Chapter 12) describes *machismo* and *marianismo* as distinct terms describing customary behaviors of Latinos/as. Respecting these and other values, and honoring language preference is important for counselors to consider when working with those of Latin descent. For many Native American clients, the eagle feather and medicine symbolize distinct perspectives that shape this group's cultural experience. Garrett (Chapter 13) suggests that integrating these perspectives and respecting the role of spirituality are important considerations for counselors working with many Native Americans.

An example of a characteristic of individuals of European descent described in Chapter 14 (McMahon et al.) is this group's common belief that they are culture-free. To assist White American ethnics in heightening awareness of cultural aspects of self, the authors suggest counselors utilize the RESPECTFUL model. This model includes an assessment of religious/spiritual identity, social class background, sexual identity, psychological maturity, ethnic/racial identity, chronological/developmental challenges, trauma and other threats to one's well-being, family background and history, unique physical characteristics, and location of residence and language differences.

Cashwell (Chapter 15) describes spirituality as an influential aspect of culture that warrants consideration in the counseling process. Primary traditions within major Eastern and Western religions are discussed. Common threads throughout religion and spirituality are also specified. Whereas various counseling approaches are described, an emphasis is placed on the need to be pluralistic with clients. In this manner, counselors remain committed to their own beliefs while honoring the beliefs of their clients, even when in stark opposition to one another.

The distinct characteristics of each group described here provide only a sample of the multitude of characteristics described in Chapters 9 through 15. These examples are offered to illustrate the value of research in assisting to shape our understanding of diverse cultural groups. This research has often been guided by practice. As counselors made empathic failures, found traditional theoretical approaches to be ineffective and even harmful, and "lost" (both literally and figuratively) culturally diverse clients, many turned to research. This research aimed to enhance knowledge of diverse others and subsequently modify existing theories of counseling and develop new theories that consider the unique worldviews of various racial and cultural groups. The process is ever evolving and requires the ongoing pursuit of knowledge that will contribute to the continued shaping of culturally alert theories and interventions. In thinking about cultural diversity, reflect on the following:

- What are some common cultural values among racial/ethnic minorities? How do these compare to common cultural values among White American ethnics?
- To what degree has the "culture of counseling" reflected the value systems of racially/ethnically diverse individuals and families, including White American ethnics? What trends are you familiar with regarding how the "culture of counseling" has changed to reflect more multiculturally competent practice?
- How do cultural values for racial and ethnic group membership diverge as you consider intersecting identities such as social class, gender, sexual orientation, and spirituality?
- This theme highlights experiences and values that may be group-specific. To what degree do you believe that cultural values described for various cultural, racial, and ethnic groups be explained as reactions to privilege and oppression experiences?

Themes in Multicultural Conceptualization

Counselors' understanding of clients is often shaped by the theoretical models and diagnostic criteria most commonly taught. Unfortunately, these traditional theories and mechanisms for diagnosis are predominantly based on the meaning-making systems of White middle-class men of European heritage. As such, diverse clients with values, beliefs, and behaviors typical of their culture yet in contrast to the norms on which these models were based risk being perceived as deviant and mentally unhealthy.

Orr (Chapter 16) states that cultural norms and theoretical principles can be at odds. Limitations of the three forces of counseling theory (i.e., psychodynamic, cognitive–behavioral, humanistic–existential) for adequately understanding the worldviews of diverse clients are described. Similarly, Eriksen, Kress, Dixon, and Ford (Chapter 17) illustrate how use of the *Diagnostic and Statistical Manual of Mental Disorders (DSM)* can result in the underdiagnosis, overdiagnosis, or misdiagnosis of people of color and those who are culturally underprivileged. Research indicates that misconceptualizations and faulty diagnoses result in client dissatisfaction and either early termination from counseling services or a resistance to seeking help in times of need. The results of this research have lead to recognition of the need to depart from the norms and instead adopt a systemic approach to **client conceptualization**.

Chapter 16 describes a multicultural approach that takes into account intersecting identities such as culture, class, gender, race, sexual orientation, religion, and geography. The differential influence on worldview of social institutions such as religion, family, and government are considered. Rather than an eclectic approach, counselors are encouraged to adapt their theory of choice to suit the conditions and worldview of their diverse clients by considering these variables. Within this multicultural theoretical framework, a variety of culturally sensitive interventions can be used. This contemporary approach to conceptualizing diverse clients has positively affected counseling practice.

Likewise, diagnosis in counseling practice has been influenced by research revealing the relevance of a systemic approach to culturally competent assessment. Rather than ascribing problems at the individual level, counselors are encouraged, in Chapter 17, to recognize problems within the social system that impact client functioning. Strict adherence to a diagnostic system, such as the *DSM,* is discouraged. Instead, consideration of multiple influences and individual variations is recommended. This awareness can contribute to culturally sensitive diagnosis as well as a commitment to advocate for change in the dysfunctional system.

Since cultural groups are socially constructed, and as such, ever evolving and changing, it is necessary to continue researching effective approaches to multicultural conceptualization and diagnosis to ensure that counseling practice is best meeting the needs of all clients. While research has had an impact on multicultural theory and diagnosis in counseling practice, counseling practice offers direction for future research in client conceptualization as well. For example, persistent diagnostic failures with diverse clients speak to the need for research that includes a more diverse sample when identifying criteria in diagnostic systems. As you think about how to more effectively conceptualize cases from a multicultural perspective, reflect on the following:

- Consider your counseling theoretical orientation. To what degree does it integrate constructs and processes described throughout this text?
- Multicultural case conceptualization includes multiculturally competent clinical assessment, diagnosis, and treatment plan framing within a culturally sensitive theoretical orientation while attending to cultural values and privilege and oppression experiences. Using the systems approach model presented in Chapter 1 (Hays & McLeod), consider case conceptualization strategies that address various components of the model.

WHERE DO WE GO FROM HERE? FUTURE DIRECTIONS FOR DEVELOPING MULTICULTURAL COMPETENCE

The four major themes presented (i.e., cultural identity development, social advocacy and oppression, cultural diversity, and multicultural case conceptualization) refer often to the interdependence and complexity of theory, practice, and research in multicultural counseling. Where do we as practitioners and researchers go from here? In the following sections, future directions in multicultural counseling theory, practice, and research are presented to assist in demystifying the unknown in multicultural counseling and as a result facilitate the development of multicultural competence of counselors at all levels of training and education.

Future Directions in Multicultural Counseling Theory

Future directions in multicultural counseling theory involve two separate discussions: the appropriateness and expansion of current theoretical orientations (primarily Western counseling theories with European American values, see Chapter 16); and our "theory" or conceptualization of what constitutes multicultural counseling and thus multicultural counseling competence.

COUNSELING THEORIES AND MULTICULTURAL POPULATIONS

There was no "one, two, three, and away," but they began running when they liked, and left off when they liked, so that it was not easy to know when the race was over. However, when they had been running half an hour or so, and were quite dry again, the Dodo suddenly called out "The race is over!" and they all crowded round it, panting, and asking, "But who has won?" This question the Dodo could not answer without a great deal of thought, and it sat for a long time with one finger pressed upon its forehead . . . while the rest waited in silence. At last the Dodo said, "*everybody* has won, and all must have prizes."

—LEWIS CARROLL'S *ALICE IN WONDERLAND*

Wampold (2001) proposed the **Dodo hypothesis** named after the character in *Alice in Wonderland* to describe the validity and efficacy of counseling theories. Basically, it states, "we have all won prizes"; that is, counseling theoretical approaches may be equally efficacious for optimal client outcomes to the degree they possess certain "common factors." Traditional counseling theories share many **common factors** or core conditions of a therapeutic alliance that may be useful for work with diverse populations (Gaston, 1990). They include the client's affective relationship to the counselor; the client's capacity to purposefully work in therapy; the counselor's empathic understanding and involvement; and client–counselor agreement on goals and tasks of therapy.

There has been competition among theoretical camps as to which counseling theory is most effective in general and with culturally diverse clients specifically. On one hand, discourse on theory has suggested that some Western counseling theories are ineffective and culturally insensitive. But, on the other hand, as the Dodo hypothesis asserts, there is value among several if not all major counseling theories. Thus, we do not have to get rid of Western counseling theories. If we attend to these core conditions and adapt existing counseling theories in a culturally sensitive manner, Western theoretical approaches may be useful with diverse clients. However, caution must be exercised as indicated by Ridley (2005): "there is a paucity of research comparing the effectiveness of theories across cultures . . . there is little evidence to support the claim that theories' Eurocentric bias adversely affects minorities. At the same time, however, there is little evidence to contradict the claim" (p. 184).

Multicultural counseling theory is different from what has been traditionally defined as counseling theory because it integrates the client's social and historical context (Pope-Davis, Liu, Toporek, & Brittan-Powell, 2001). However, multicultural counseling theory and traditional counseling theory may be more alike than we think. To expand scholarship on optimal theoretical approaches for diverse clientele, we need to explore the degree to which diverse populations perceive common factors that comprise a therapeutic alliance. Are these factors culturally biased or universal phenomena? To what degree do cultural identity development, social injustices, and cultural values "change" these common factors? Finally, although current theoretical approaches have potential validity with diverse individuals, they must continue to evolve as our roles within the profession expand. This calls counselors to integrate some Eastern or nontraditional approaches depending on a client's cultural makeup, particularly if these approaches relate to the common factors proposed by Gaston (1990).

THE "THEORY" OF MULTICULTURAL COMPETENCE   The other future direction in theory is related to how we conceptualize multicultural competence. Our general competence as counselors is closely related to the degree to which we are multiculturally competent (Coleman, 1998; Constantine, 2002b). The MCC standards (Sue et al., 1992) provide 31 competence statements that have been operationalized (Arredondo et al., 1996) to guide and encourage counselors to conduct ethical and culturally sensitive practice with diverse clientele. These standards were proposed for work with racially/ethnically diverse populations with a primary mission of cultural sensitivity. While there is some mention in the standards of counselors being knowledgeable of clients' oppression experiences and how these experiences affect counseling process and outcome, Reynolds (1999) notes a "conspiracy of silence about racism and oppression within the counseling profession" (p. 182). That is, while we focus on awareness of cultural traits and competent skills for meeting diverse clients' needs, we as counselors are disregarding or minimizing the role oppression has on clients' daily lives.

In addition to attention to oppression and social advocacy, multicultural counseling as a theory should continue to be expanded to apply these standards to work with individuals of minority statuses other than race/ethnicity, as well as an increased attention on how racial or ethnic statuses intersect with other cultural identities. As such, it is an aim of this text to incorporate the role of social advocacy and intersecting identities and the critical evaluation of current practices in case conceptualization. However, much more work needs to be done. Before we can accurately assess our own multicultural competence, the theory of multicultural competence needs to increase in scope and be refined.

In sum, future directions in multicultural counseling theory include:

- Assessing how "common factors" for a therapeutic alliance may be universal across culturally diverse populations
- Refining traditional counseling theories and integrating Eastern and nontraditional approaches
- Rethinking multicultural competence as a concept to include a focus on social advocacy and intersecting identities

Future Directions in Multicultural Counseling Practice

One of the most significant questions related to multicultural counseling practice is: "How does the client view the counselor's multicultural competency?" (Pope-Davis et al., 2001, p. 122). We have several studies that have explored how counselors perceive themselves as multiculturally competent: for example, Dunn, Smith, and Montoya (2006) located only 137 published and unpublished empirical studies of 800 manuscripts written on multicultural competence after 1990. Of the 137 empirically based articles, only 17 (12%) studies relied on observer ratings of counselors' multicultural competence, with just a handful of these observers being actual clients. Much more focus is needed on clients' perceptions of what makes a counselor multiculturally competent. And, if clients perceive a counselor to be multiculturally competent, what do they cite as the benefits? More specifically, how does a counselor's increased multicultural competence (as perceived by the client) impact treatment process and outcome?

Multicultural counseling practice also involves integrating several roles: working with individuals, families, and groups in traditional clinical settings and educational environments; empowering clients; linking social and community services; providing guidance and support across the life span; and consulting and collaborating with other health professionals as well as social and community members. These are just some of the roles we serve. As the U.S. population becomes increasingly diverse, a more traditional scope of counselors working with clients within the confines of a counseling office will lessen. Given the myriad of culturally specific symptomology, oppression experiences, and developmental challenges sometimes associated with identity development processes, the way we practice counseling must change. We must "leave our offices" (Kiselica & Robinson, 2000) and attend to systemic issues in an innovative way to maximize positive counseling experiences for culturally diverse clientele.

As counselors, how much do we attend to context? This question relates not only to how we conceptualize and diagnose client symptomology but also to the degree to which we integrate culture and context into client interventions. Ridley (2005) states that there is some debate to whether the etic or emic perspective is more appropriate for interventions. On one hand, scholars propose that interventions may be applied without harm universally to all clients if a counselor is competent (i.e., etic perspective). On the other hand, scholars note that identical application of interventions is actually discriminatory because it disregards individual and cultural differences and using culturally specific interventions (i.e., emic perspective) is more equitable.

In sum, future directions in multicultural counseling practice include:

- Increasing attention to clients' perceptions of counselors' multicultural competence and related benefits for treatment process and outcome
- Expanding counselors' roles to include more attention to context and social injustice in clients' lives
- Negotiating the extent to which counseling interventions should be universally or more specifically applied to particular clients

Future Directions in Multicultural Counseling Research

As we become more multiculturally competent practitioners and researchers, two key issues complicate the study of the clinical and daily experiences of culturally diverse populations: (a) varying definitions of multiculturalism, multicultural counseling, and multicultural research; and (b) methodological issues in research design and data interpretation. In addition, collaboration between researchers and participants is a concern as we move toward engaging in multiculturally competent research.

DEFINITIONAL AND METHODOLOGICAL ISSUES IN COUNSELING RESEARCH DESIGN   Before we can explore cross-cultural dynamics in counseling, we have to operationally define the constructs of multiculturalism, multicultural counseling, and multicultural research. What groups and identities are included in the definition of *multicultural* varies throughout literature, from a narrow definition that restricts membership to select cultural groups, such as race and ethnicity, to a broader definition that encompasses several cultural groups, including race/ethnicity, gender, socioeconomic status (SES), ability status, spiritual affiliation, sexual orientation, and so forth. While the counseling profession is moving more toward a discussion of multicultural counseling using a broader definition of *multicultural,* a majority of multicultural counseling literature has historically described and examined racial and ethnic differences only. To this end, multicultural counseling has been defined primarily as practice involving racially or ethnically different counselors and clients. The traditional definitions of multicultural and multicultural counseling have thus influenced multicultural research, limiting scholarship to primarily the interface of race/ethnicity with psychological constructs and counseling process and outcome. In essence, multicultural research has been interested in understanding both etic and emic aspects of behavior and attitudes; however, this understanding has been restricted to racially or ethnically specific and universal cultural dynamics within the United States and some international comparative research. Future research must examine these variables in reference to groups included in more contemporary definitions of *multicultural,* as well as diverse groups constructed by intersecting identities.

Second, there are methodological issues inherent in published research involving racially/ethnically diverse populations. A major methodological concern relates to research design in itself. **Validity threats**, or the degree of risk that the relationship between an independent variable and some outcome is not valid, may be particularly relevant in multicultural research. When finding cultural differences for some variable of interest, there may be factors in the research design that mask or distort these differences. Some factors include instruments that yield unreliable and invalid scores due to minimal or insufficient norms or other test construction issues for a particular group; history and maturation bias in that cultural groups will differentially experience events based on their cultural makeup and other intersecting variables such as values, communication patterns, and spirituality; and selection bias in that analyzing data by cultural groups such as race or ethnicity fails to control for either general confounding variables such as SES or language differences, significant within-group variation that may exist, or limitations of the sample in itself (Cokley & Awad, 2008). These fallacies lead to not only misinterpretation of findings, but also to misapplication of results to a larger population.

As an example of research design issues in multicultural research, imagine that you uncover racial differences in mean depression scores among college students. Perhaps the inventory used to assess depression may not be appropriate because it does not have psychometric data available for all cultural groups sampled in your study, the language of the instrument is not understood by some of the participants, or the construct of depression has different meanings for participants' cultural statuses. Perhaps individuals of one racial group (e.g., Asian Americans) recently were exposed to a traumatic event that might temporarily elevate depression or there may be other variables that better account for differences in depression scores than race (e.g., lower-SES individuals or females having higher scores for a particular race). Maybe one racial group has more within-group variation (e.g., diversity in spiritual beliefs, level of acculturation, SES) with respect to depression such that it gets "canceled out" in comparison to another racial group with less within-group variation, or racial differences in mean depression scores may be either underestimated or overestimated due to sampling a college population. Thus, in such ways, racial differences may be explained by many other variables or intricacies of research design rather than by race itself.

Another methodological concern involves the way we interpret findings across multicultural populations. Most research articles describe cultural differences for various counseling constructs (e.g., SES, acculturation level, identity development status, education level) without providing a theoretical basis for why those differences exist. Thus, demographic information is often used as proxy variables and may not be appropriate. For example, when several cultural groups are included in a sample, several studies have mistakenly interpreted mean scores among these groups for constructs such as intelligence or self-esteem as attributable to cultural group membership alone rather than considering underlying, more complex explanations as causing observed differences, such as level of acculturation or oppression experiences. Additionally, multicultural research has often used Whites or European Americans as the norm in interpreting constructs of interest. Thus, cross-comparative multicultural research, which most commonly compares racial/ethnic minorities to Whites or European Americans, has tended to highlight cultural differences as evidence of deficiency for those groups that differ significantly from a White or European standard of normality.

RESEARCHER–PARTICIPANT COLLABORATION   Throughout U.S. history Europeans, Whites, and members from dominant cultural statuses in general (e.g., male, heterosexual, Christian) have evaluated and conceptualized groups that differed from them in a variety of ways, often in a manner that pathologized or ignored certain groups. In counseling many practitioners have developed, implemented, and interpreted culturally biased (e.g., discriminatory based on sample used or items included) clinical and academic assessments that produced results that "supported" deficiency and pathology for minority statuses. As a result, several groups or cultural processes are not understood accurately and sufficiently. For those interested in engaging in multiculturally competent research it may be difficult to study culturally diverse populations or cultural phenomena because there may be distrust based on historically discriminatory research practices.

To gain necessary knowledge for effective multicultural counseling, counseling researchers need to collaborate *and cooperate* with members of minority communities. Several suggestions for engaging minority communities in research have been proposed (Norton & Manson, 1996; Quintana, Troyano, & Gaylor, 2001; Ridley, 2005):

- Outline and weigh the benefits and challenges for the scientific and participant communities prior to beginning research
- Offer incentives to potential participants
- Network and gain support from community leaders
- Have some familiarity with the population you would like to study
- Maintain personal contact and build rapport with participants throughout the research process
- Give something back to communities instead of just benefiting from researching them
- Make research a two-way learning process

As the counseling profession continues to focus on social advocacy and a systems approach, counseling researchers may want to use **participatory action research (PAR)** methods incorporating the previous strategies. PAR involves a collaborative approach to problem solving between the researcher and other key stakeholders (e.g., community leaders, members of minority communities). Theory, previous research, and collaborative interaction between the researchers and stakeholders provide the foundation for PAR inquiry and guide formulation of research questions. In essence, researchers and participants work together to identify the needs of a community, study processes related to a particular group or phenomenon, ensure findings are "true" for that community, present findings to a variety of communities at various levels (e.g., scientific, academic, social, cultural), and work to create beneficial changes in communities based on the findings. Counseling researchers should continually reflect on how the research design may be biased in terms of voices that are present and absent in the collaborative process of research.

Building on issues and strategies presented for multicultural counseling research, future research directions could include the following:

- Develop research on cultural identity development. Most existing research focuses on describing racial identity and client preferences. Future research might examine modalities for promoting cultural identity for clients as well as practitioners. Further, because cultural identities are socially constructed, it is necessary to engage in ongoing research assessing shifts in societal and cultural beliefs, customs, values, and behaviors and its subsequent impact on identity development.
- Multicultural counseling research is a social justice imperative. Counselors should collaborate with participants and attend to systemic influences and their impact on variables under investigation.
- Expand scholarship to include what clients perceive as multiculturally competent counseling practice (Pope-Davis et al., 2001). Much of research that examines multicultural counseling competence has focused on counselors' and counselors-in-training's perceptions of their competence levels and not on clients' perceptions. The scholarship that does exist exploring culturally diverse clients' perceptions primarily focuses on counseling expectations before counseling

begins. It seems that clients may perceive different skills as more favorable depending on cultural identities and values.

- Extend research efforts to address how intersecting cultural identities influence identity development, help-seeking attitudes, counseling process and outcome, and privilege and oppression experiences.
- Increase use of qualitative research methods. In their survey examining multicultural counseling articles, Ponterotto and Casas (1991) note that there was an overreliance on paper-and-pencil measures that often possess an ethnocentric bias in their construction, administration, and interpretation. Existing quantitative measures limit opportunities to explore client context in conjunction with presenting problems (Pope-Davis et al., 2001).

Summary

Developing multicultural competence within a systems approach requires a concerted effort by counselors to view multicultural counseling theory, practice, and research as interdependent constructs. That is, theory, practice, and research drive each other to solidify ideas about what constitutes a multiculturally competent counselor and thus culturally focused and effective treatment. This chapter begins by describing four key themes described throughout this text: cultural identity development, social advocacy and oppression, cultural diversity, and multicultural case conceptualization. As these themes are presented, each is shown to build upon or intersect with each other.

The study and practice of multicultural counseling within the past few decades has helped illuminate complex constructs in multicultural counseling, such as identity development, privilege, oppression, and diversity. However, there is much to be learned regarding theory, practice, and research. The last half of the chapter provides examples of ways in which multicultural counseling theory, practice, and research might be expanded to address some of the limitations of previous scholarship.

As indicated in suggested future directions in multicultural counseling theory, counselor practitioners and researchers are encouraged to critically examine and refine traditional counseling theories as well as the way multicultural competence is conceptualized as a theory. These two efforts are not independent. The more we come to agree on (with the help of clients) the definition of multicultural competence and how to best facilitate it, the more we may understand how best to adapt and develop counseling theoretical approaches.

Future directions in multicultural counseling practice echo and expand upon the directions for multicultural counseling theory. Specifically, what does multicultural competence look like in the counseling setting? How does it impact treatment process and outcome? These questions as discussed in the chapter should be primarily addressed from the perspectives of clients. Additionally, multicultural counseling practice involves expanding the roles we possess as counselors to address the "fifth force" in counseling, social advocacy. Context, particularly oppression experiences, may be important aspects of determining what counseling interventions should look like for culturally diverse clientele.

Finally, future directions in multicultural counseling research are presented. Two key issues include (a) conflicts in how *multicultural* has been defined in research studies; and (b) methodological issues in research design such as validity threats and an overreliance on cross-racial comparative research that is primarily descriptive. As counselors consider the sample of research topics and general strategies for more multiculturally competent research, participatory action research, whereby counseling researchers and participants collaborate to verify and strengthen the validity of findings, becomes more helpful and imperative.

APPENDIX
AMCD Multicultural Counseling Competencies

I. COUNSELOR AWARENESS OF OWN CULTURAL VALUES AND BIASES

A. Attitudes and Beliefs

1. Culturally skilled counselors believe that cultural self-awareness and sensitivity to one's own cultural heritage is essential.
2. Culturally skilled counselors are aware of how their own cultural background and experiences have influenced attitudes, values, and biases about psychological processes.
3. Culturally skilled counselors are able to recognize the limits of their multicultural competency and expertise.
4. Culturally skilled counselors recognize their sources of discomfort with differences that exist between themselves and clients in terms of race, ethnicity and culture.

B. Knowledge

1. Culturally skilled counselors have specific knowledge about their own racial and cultural heritage and how it personally and professionally affects their definitions and biases of normality/abnormality and the process of counseling.
2. Culturally skilled counselors possess knowledge and understanding about how oppression, racism, discrimination, and stereotyping affect them personally and in their work. This allows individuals to acknowledge their own racist attitudes, beliefs, and feelings. Although this standard applies to all groups, for White counselors it may mean that they understand how they may have directly or indirectly benefited from individual, institutional, and cultural racism as outlined in White identity development models.
3. Culturally skilled counselors possess knowledge about their social impact upon others. They are knowledgeable about communication style differences, how their style may clash with or foster the counseling process with persons of color or others different from themselves based on the A, B, and C dimensions and how to anticipate the impact it may have on others.

C. Skills

1. Culturally skilled counselors seek out educational, consultative, and training experiences to improve their understanding and effectiveness in working with culturally different populations. Being able to recognize the limits of their competencies, they (a) seek consultation, (b) seek further training or education, (c) refer out to more qualified individuals or resources, or (d) engage in a combination of these.
2. Culturally skilled counselors are constantly seeking to understand themselves as racial and cultural beings and are actively seeking a non racist identity.

II. COUNSELOR AWARENESS OF CLIENT'S WORLDVIEW

A. Attitudes and Beliefs

1. Culturally skilled counselors are aware of their negative and positive emotional reactions toward other racial and ethnic groups that may prove detrimental to the counseling relationship. They are willing to contrast their own beliefs and attitudes with those of their culturally different clients in a nonjudgmental fashion.

2. Culturally skilled counselors are aware of their stereotypes and preconceived notions that they may hold toward other racial and ethnic minority groups.

B. Knowledge

1. Culturally skilled counselors possess specific knowledge and information about the particular group with which they are working. They are aware of the life experiences, cultural heritage, and historical background of their culturally different clients. This particular competency is strongly linked to the "minority identity development models" available in the literature.
2. Culturally skilled counselors understand how race, culture, ethnicity, and so forth may affect personality formation, vocational choices, manifestation of psychological disorders, help seeking behavior, and the appropriateness or inappropriateness of counseling approaches.
3. Culturally skilled counselors understand and have knowledge about sociopolitical influences that impinge upon the life of racial and ethnic minorities. Immigration issues, poverty, racism, stereotyping, and powerlessness may impact self esteem and self concept in the counseling process.

C. Skills

1. Culturally skilled counselors should familiarize themselves with relevant research and the latest findings regarding mental health and mental disorders that affect various ethnic and racial groups. They should actively seek out educational experiences that enrich their knowledge, understanding, and cross-cultural skills for more effective counseling behavior.
2. Culturally skilled counselors become actively involved with minority individuals outside the counseling setting (e.g., community events, social and political functions, celebrations, friendships, neighborhood groups, and so forth) so that their perspective of minorities is more than an academic or helping exercise.

III. CULTURALLY APPROPRIATE INTERVENTION STRATEGIES

A. Beliefs and Attitudes

1. Culturally skilled counselors respect clients' religious and/ or spiritual beliefs and values, including attributions and taboos, because they affect worldview, psychosocial functioning, and expressions of distress.
2. Culturally skilled counselors respect indigenous helping practices and respect helping networks among communities of color.
3. Culturally skilled counselors value bilingualism and do not view another language as an impediment to counseling (monolingualism may be the culprit).

B. Knowledge

1. Culturally skilled counselors have a clear and explicit knowledge and understanding of the generic characteristics of counseling and therapy (culture bound, class bound, and monolingual) and how they may clash with the cultural values of various cultural groups.
2. Culturally skilled counselors are aware of institutional barriers that prevent minorities from using mental health services.
3. Culturally skilled counselors have knowledge of the potential bias in assessment instruments and use procedures and interpret findings keeping in mind the cultural and linguistic characteristics of the clients.

4. Culturally skilled counselors have knowledge of family structures, hierarchies, values, and beliefs from various cultural perspectives. They are knowledgeable about the community where a particular cultural group may reside and the resources in the community.

5. Culturally skilled counselors should be aware of relevant discriminatory practices at the social and community level that may be affecting the psychological welfare of the population being served.

C. Skills

1. Culturally skilled counselors are able to engage in a variety of verbal and nonverbal helping responses. They are able to send and receive both verbal and nonverbal messages accurately and appropriately. They are not tied down to only one method or approach to helping, but recognize that helping styles and approaches may be culture bound. When they sense that their helping style is limited and potentially inappropriate, they can anticipate and modify it.

2. Culturally skilled counselors are able to exercise institutional intervention skills on behalf of their clients. They can help clients determine whether a "problem" stems from racism or bias in others (the concept of healthy paranoia) so that clients do not inappropriately personalize problems.

3. Culturally skilled counselors are not averse to seeking consultation with traditional healers or religious and spiritual leaders and practitioners in the treatment of culturally different clients when appropriate.

4. Culturally skilled counselors take responsibility for interacting in the language requested by the client and, if not feasible, make appropriate referrals. A serious problem arises when the linguistic skills of the counselor do not match the language of the client. This being the case, counselors should (a) seek a translator with cultural knowledge and appropriate professional background or (b) refer to a knowledgeable and competent bilingual counselor.

5. Culturally skilled counselors have training and expertise in the use of traditional assessment and testing instruments. They not only understand the technical aspects of the instruments but are also aware of the cultural limitations. This allows them to use test instruments for the welfare of culturally different clients.

6. Culturally skilled counselors should attend to as well as work to eliminate biases, prejudices, and discriminatory contexts in conducting evaluations and providing interventions, and should develop sensitivity to issues of oppression, sexism, heterosexism, elitism and racism.

7. Culturally skilled counselors take responsibility for educating their clients to the processes of psychological intervention, such as goals, expectations, legal rights, and the counselor's orientation.

Source: Sue, Arredondo, and McDavis (1992), pp. 477–486.

REFERENCES

Abe-Kim, J., Takeuchi, D. T., Hong, S., Zane, N., Sue, S., Spencer, M. S., et al. (2007). Use of mental health related services among immigrant and U.S. born Asians: Results from the National Latino and Asian American Study. *American Journal of Public Health, 97*(1), 91–98.

Abramowitz, S. (1973). The politics of clinical judgment. *Journal of Consulting and Clinical Psychology, 41,* 385–391.

Abreu, M. M., & Giordano, F. G. (1996). An examination of power as it is embedded in language. *Journal of Humanistic Education and Development, 35,* 40–50.

Abu-Ali, A., & Reisen, C. A. (1999). Gender role identity among adolescent Muslim girls living in the U.S. *Current Psychology, 18,* 185–192.

Abudabbeh, N. (1996). Arab families. In M. Goldrick, J. Giordano & J. K. Pearce (Eds.), *Ethnicity and family therapy* (2nd ed., pp. 333–346). New York: Guilford.

Abudabbeh, N., & Aseel, H. A. (1999). Transcultural counseling and Arab Americans. In J. McFadden (Ed.), *Transcultural counseling* (pp. 283–296). Alexandria, VA: American Counseling Association.

Abu El-Haj, T. R. (2002). Contesting the politics of culture, rewriting the boundaries of inclusion: Working for social justice with Muslim and Arab communities. *Anthropology & Education Quarterly, 33,* 308–316.

Adams, G., & Markus, H. R. (2001). Culture as patterns: An alternative approach to the problem of reification. *Culture and Psychology, 7,* 283–296.

Addis, M. E., & Mahalik, J. R. (2003). Men, masculinity, and the contexts of help-seeking, *American Psychologist, 58*(1), 5–14.

Adebimpe, V. R. (1981). Overview: White norms and psychiatric diagnosis and Black patients. *American Journal of Psychiatry, 138,* 279–285.

Adler, A. (1964). *Problems of neurosis.* New York: Harper & Row.

Agronick, G., O'Donnell, L., Stueve, A., Doval, A. S., Duran, R., & Vargo, S. (2004). Sexual behaviors and risks among bisexually and gay-identified young Latino men. *AIDS and Behavior, 8,* 185–197.

Ahrens, L. (Writer), & Warburton, T. (Director). (1977). Great American melting pot. In *School House Rock.* New York: American Broadcasting Company.

Ajrouch, K. J. (2000). Place, age, and culture: Community living and ethnic identity among Lebanese American adolescents. *Small Group Research, 31,* 447–469.

Akutsu, P. D. (1997). Mental health care delivery to Asian Americans: Review of the literature. In E. Lee (Ed.), *Working with Asian Americans: A guide for clinicians* (pp. 464–476). New York: Guilford Press.

Akutsu, P. D., & Chu, J. P. (2006). Clinical problems that initiate professional help-seeking behaviors from Asian Americans. *Professional Psychology: Research and Practice, 37,* 407–415.

Akutsu, P. D., Lin, C. H., & Zane, N. W. (1990). Predictors of utilization intent of counseling among Chinese and White students: A test of the proximaldistal model. *Journal of Counseling Psychology, 37,* 445–452.

Albee, G. W. (2006). Historical overview of primary prevention of psychopathology: Address to the 3rd World Conference on the Promotion of Mental Health and Prevention of Mental and Behavioral Disorders, September 15–17, 2004, Auckland , New Zealand. *The Journal of Primary Prevention, 27,* 449–456.

Albrecht, D. E., & Albrecht, S. G. (2007). The benefits and costs of inequality for the advantaged and the disadvantaged. *Social Science Quarterly, 88,* 382–403.

Al-Krenawi, A., & Graham, J. R. (2000). Culturally sensitive social work practice with Arab clients in mental health settings. *Health & Social Work, 25*(1), 9–22.

Allen, D. J., & Oleson, T. (1999). Shame and internalized homophobia in gay men. *Journal of Homosexuality, 37,* 33–43.

Allen, T. W. (1994). *The invention of the White race* (Vol. 1). London: Verso.

Allen, T. W. (1997). *The invention of the White race* (Vol. 2). London: Verso.

Allwood, M. A. (2002). Children's trauma and adjustment reactions to violent and nonviolent war experiences. *Journal of the American Academy of Child and Adolescent Psychiatry, 41,* 450–457.

Almeida, R. (1996). Hindu, Christian, and Muslim families. In M. McGoldrick, J. Giordano, & J. K. Pearce (Eds.), *Ethnicity and family therapy* (pp. 395–423). New York: Guilford Press.

Alvarez, A. N., & Chen, G. A. (2009). Ruth as an Asian American: A multicultural and integrative perspective. In G. Corey (Ed.), *Case approach to counseling and psychotherapy* (7th ed., pp. 304–312). Belmont, CA: Wadsworth Press.

Alvarez, A. N., & Helms, J. E. (2001). Racial identity and reflected appraisals as influences on Asian Americans' racial adjustment. *Cultural Diversity and Ethnic Minority, 7,* 217–231.

Alvarez, A. N., Juang, L., & Liang, C. (2006). Asian Americans and racism: When bad things happen to "model minorities." *Cultural Diversity and Ethnic Minority Psychology, 12,* 477–492.

American-Arab Anti-Discrimination Committee. (2005). Web site home page. Retrieved July 6, 2005, from http://www.adc.org

American Association for Counseling and Development. (1990). *Gerontological competencies for counselors and human development specialists.* Alexandria, VA: Author.

American Association of University Women Educational Foundation. (1993). *Hostile hallways: The AAUW survey on sexual harassment in America's schools* (Research Report 923012). Washington, DC: Harris/Scholastic Research.

American Civil Liberties Union. (2006). *Too high a price: The case against restricting gay parenting* (2nd ed.). New York: Author.

American Counseling Association. (2005). *ACA code of ethics* (3rd ed.). Alexandria, VA: Author.

American Psychiatric Association. (1973a). *Diagnostic and statistical manual of mental disorders* (2nd ed.). Washington, DC: Author.

American Psychiatric Association. (1973b). Position statement on homosexuality and civil rights. *American Journal of Psychiatry, 131,* 497.

American Psychiatric Association. (1980). *Diagnostic and statistical manual of mental disorders* (3rd ed.). Washington, DC: Author.

American Psychiatric Association. (2000). *Diagnostic and statistical manual of mental disorders* (4th ed., text revision). Washington, DC: Author.

American Psychological Association. (2000). *Resolution on poverty and socioeconomic status.* Retrieved August 31, 2007, from http://www.apa.org/pi/urban/povres.html

American Psychological Association. (2003). Guidelines on multicultural education, training, research, practice, and organizational change for psychologists. *American Psychologist, 58,* 337–402.

American Psychological Association. (2006a). *Guidelines for psychological practice with girls and women: A joint task force of APA divisions 17 and 35.* Washington, DC: Author.

American Psychological Association. (2006b). *Lesbian and gay parenting.* Retrieved August 23, 2007, from http://www.apa.org/pi/parent.html

American School Counselor Association. (2005). *ASCA position statement: The professional school counselor and gay, lesbian, bisexual, transgendered and questioning youth.* Retrieved on May 30, 2007, from http://www.schoolcounselor.org/content.asp?contentid=217

America's Second Harvest. (2006). *Hunger study—2006 (key findings).* Retrieved April 19, 2007, from http://www.hungerinamerica.org/key_findings

Ammar, N. H. (2000). Simplistic stereotyping and complex reality of Arab-American immigrant identity: Consequences and future strategies in policing wife battery. *Islam and Christian-Muslim Relations, 11*(1), 51–70.

Anagnostopoulos, D. C., Vlassopoulou, M., & Rotsika, V. (2004). Psychopathology and mental health service utilization by immigrants' children and their families. *Transcultural Psychiatry, 41,* 465–486.

Ancis, J. R. (Ed.). (2004). *Culturally responsive interventions: Innovative approaches to working with diverse populations.* New York: Brunner-Routledge

Ancis, J. R., & Szymanski, D. M. (2001). Awareness of White privilege among White counseling trainees. *The Counseling Psychologist, 29,* 548–569.

Anderson, D. (1994). *Homosexuality in adolescence.* New York: Norton.

Anderson, H., & Goolishian, H. (1992). The client is the expert: A not-knowing approach to therapy. In S. McNamee & K. Gergen (Eds.), *Therapy as social construction* (pp. 25–39). London: Sage.

Angermeyer, M., Matschinger, H., & Holzinger, A. (1998). Gender and attitudes towards people with schizophrenia. *International Journal of Social Psychiatry, 44,* 107–116.

Anminifu, H. R. (1995). The issue of skin color in psychotherapy with African Americans. *Families in Society, 76,* 3–12.

Arab American Institute. (2002). *Healing the nation: The Arab American experience after September 11.* Washington, DC: Author.

Arab American Institute. (n.d.). *Demographics.* Retrieved February 22, 2008, from http://www.aaiusa.org/arab-americans/22/demographics

Arminio, J. (2001). Exploring the nature of race-related guilt. *Journal of Multicultural Counseling and Development, 29,* 239–252.

Arredondo, P. (1999). Multicultural counseling competencies as tools to address oppression and racism. *Journal of Counseling and Development, 77,* 102–108.

Arredondo, P., Toporek, R., Brown, S. P., Jones, J., Locke, D., Sanchez, J., et al. (1996). Operationalization of the multicultural counseling competencies. *Journal of Multicultural Counseling and Development, 24,* 42–78.

Asante, M. (1987). *The Afrocentric idea.* Philadelphia: Temple University Press.

Ashman, A. (2004). Same-sex attracted youth: Suicide and related factors. *Australian Journal of Guidance and Counseling, 14,* 48–64.

Association for Gay, Lesbian, Bisexual and Transgender Issues in Counseling. (2005). *Competencies for counseling gay, lesbian, bisexual and transgendered (GLBT) clients.* Retrieved December 4, 2006, from http://www.aglbtic.org/resources/competencies.html

Association for Spiritual, Ethical, and Religious Values in Counseling. (2007). *Competencies for integrating spirituality in counseling.* Retrieved June 7, 2007, from http://www.aservic.org/CompetenciesforIntegrating SpiritualityintoCounseling.pdf

Atkinson, D. R., & Gim, R. H. (1989). Asian-American cultural identity and attitudes toward mental health services. *Journal of Counseling Psychology, 36,* 209–212.

Atkinson, D. R., & Hackett, G. (2004). *Counseling diverse populations* (3rd ed.). New York: McGraw-Hill.

Atkinson, D. R., & Lowe, S. M. (1995). The role of ethnicity, cultural knowledge, and conventional techniques in counseling and psychotherapy. In J. G. Ponterotto, J. M., Casas, L. A. Suzuki, & C. M. Alexander (Eds.), *Handbook of multicultural counseling* (pp. 387–414). Thousand Oaks, CA: Sage.

Atkinson, D. R., Morten, G., & Sue, D. W. (1979). *A cross-cultural perspective.* Dubuque, IA: William C. Brown.

Atkinson, D. R., Morten, G., & Sue, D. W. (1989). *Counseling American minorities.* Dubuque, IA: William C. Brown.

Atkinson, D. R., Morten, G., & Sue, D. W. (1998). *Counseling American minorities* (5th ed.). Boston: McGraw-Hill.

Atkinson, D. R., Ponterotto, J. G., & Sanchez, A. R. (1984). Attitudes of Vietnamese and Anglo-American students toward counseling. *Journal of College Student Personnel, 25,* 448–452.

Atkinson, D. R., Thompson, C. E., & Grant, S. K. (1993). A three-dimensional model for counseling racial/-ethnic minorities. *The Counseling Psychologist, 21,* 257–277.

Atkinson, D. R., Whiteley, & Gim, R. H. (1990). Asian American acculturation and preferences for help providers. *Journal of College Student Development, 31,* 155–161.

Attneave, C. L. (1969). Therapy in tribal settings and urban network intervention. *Family Process, 8,* 192–210.

Attneave, C. L. (1985). Practical counseling with American Indian and Alaska Native clients. In P. Pedersen (Ed.), *Handbook of cross-cultural counseling and therapy* (pp. 135–140). Westport, CT: Greenwood Press.

Axelson, J. A. (1999). *Counseling and development in a multicultural society* (3rd ed). Pacific Grove, CA: Brooks/Cole.

Azayem, G. A. E., & Hedayat-Diba, Z. (1994). The psychological aspects of Islam: Basic principles of Islam and their psychological corollary. *The International Journal for the Psychology of Religion, 4*(1), 41–50.

Badgett, M. V. L. (1995). The wage effects of sexual-orientation discrimination. *Industrial and Labor Relations Review, 48,* 726–739.

Badinter, E. (1989). *The unopposite sex: The end of the gender battle.* New York: Harper & Rowe.

Bagley, C., & Tremblay, P. (1997). Suicidal behaviours in homosexual and bisexual males. *Crisis: The Journal of Crisis Intervention and Suicide Prevention, 18,* 24–31.

Bahr, M., & Sinacore-Guinn, A. L. (1993, April). *Assessment of Attention Deficit Hyperactivity Disorder: Integrating a cultural framework.* Paper presented at the annual convention of the National Association of School Psychologists, Washington, DC.

Baker, K. A. (1999). Acculturation and reacculturation influence: Multilayer contexts in therapy. *Clinical Psychology Review, 19,* 951–967.

Balkovic, B. (2008, Spring). *Statistics of income bulletin: High-income tax returns for 2005.* Retrieved July 28, 2008, from http://www.irs.gov/pub/irs-soi/05inhigh-incomebul.pdf

Banks, J. A. (2003). *Teaching strategies for ethnic studies* (7th ed.). Boston: Allyn & Bacon.

Barbara, A. M. (2002). Substance abuse treatment with lesbian, gay, and bisexual people: A qualitative study of service providers. *Journal of Gay and Lesbian Social Services, 14,* 1–17.

Barclay, S., & Fisher, S. (2003). The states and the differing impetus for divergent paths on same-sex marriage, 1990–2001. *The Policy Studies Journal, 31,* 331–352.

Barker-Hackett, L. (2003). African Americans in the new millennium: A continued search for our true identity. In J. S. Mio & G. Y. Iwamasa (Eds.), *Culturally diverse mental health: The challenges of research and practice* (pp. 155–170). New York: Brunner-Routledge.

Barlow, E. (1995, Winter). Middle East facts and fictions. *The Journal of the International Institute, 2*(2). Available at: http://www.umich.edu/~iinet/journal/vol2no2/v2n2_Middle_East_Facts_and_Fictions.html

Barret, B., & Logan, C. (2002). *Counseling gay men and lesbians: A practice primer.* Pacific Grove, CA: Brooks/Cole.

Barrett, D. C., & Pollack, L. M. (2005). Whose gay community? Social class, sexual self-expression, and gay community involvement. *The Sociological Quarterly, 46,* 437–456.

Barry, C. Y., & Motoni, K. (1998). Ethnic and sexual identity development of Asian-American lesbian and gay adolescents. *Professional School Counseling, 1,* 21–25.

Bartholomew, C. (2003). *Gender-sensitive therapy: Principles and practices.* Chicago: Waveland Press.

Bartlett, R. (1993). *The making of Europe: Conquest, colonialism, and cultural change.* Princeton, NJ: Princeton University Press.

Bass, E., & Davis, L. (1988). *The courage to heal.* New York: Harper & Row.

Baum, B. (2006). *The rise and fall of the Caucasian race: A political history of racial identity.* New York: New York University Press.

Baumgardner, J., & Richards, A. (2000). *Manifesta.* New York: Farrar, Straus, and Giroux.

Beagan, B. (2007). Experiences of social class: Learning from occupational therapy students. *Canadian Journal of Occupational Therapy, 74,* 125–133.

Beard, J., & Glickauf-Hughes, C. (1994). Gay identity and sense of self: Rethinking male homosexuality. *Journal of Gay and Lesbian Psychotherapy, 2*(2), 21–37.

Becker, D., & Lamb, S. (1994). Sex bias in the diagnosis of Borderline Personality Disorder and Posttraumatic Stress Disorder. *Professional Psychology: Research and Practice, 25*(1), 55–61.

Becoming Me. (n.d.). *An interview with Ken Wilber on the seven points of timeless wisdom.* Retrieved April 10, 2007, from http://www.becomingme.com/timeless_wilber.html

Beiser, M. N., & Hou, F. (2006). Ethnic identity, resettlement stress and depressive affect among Southeast Asian refugees in Canada. *Social Science and Medicine, 63,* 137–150.

Bell, A., & Weinberg, M. (1978). *Homosexualities: A study of diversity among men and women.* New York: Simon and Schuster.

Bem, S. (1974). The measurement of psychological androgyny. *Journal of Cognitive Psychotherapy, 1,* 2–27.

Bemak, F., & Chung, R. C. (2003). Multicultural counseling with immigrant students in schools. In P. B. Pedersen, & J. C. Carey (Eds.), *Multicultural counseling in schools: A practical handbook* (pp. 84–101). Boston: Allyn & Bacon.

Bemak, F., & Chung, R. C. (2008). New professional roles and advocacy strategies for school counselors: A multicultural/social justice perspective to move beyond the nice counselor syndrome. *Journal of Counseling and Development, 86,* 372–383.

Bemporad, J. R. (1997). Cultural and historical aspects of eating disorders. *International Journal of Eating Disorders, 17,* 147–152.

Benedetto, A., & Olisky, T. (2001). Biracial youth: The role of the school counselor in racial identity development. *Professional School Counseling, 5,* 66–69.

Bennett, L., Jr. (2003). *Before the Mayflower: A history of Black America* (7th ed). Chicago: Johnson Publishing.

Berens, D. (1994). Workers' compensation. In R. Weed & T. Field (Eds.), *Rehabilitation consultant's handbook* (pp. 45–56). Athens, GA: E & F, Inc.

Berger, J. M., Levant, R., McMillan, K. K., Kelleher, W., & Sellers, A. (2005). Impact of gender role conflict, traditional masculinity ideology, alexithymia, and age on men's attitudes towards psychological help seeking. *Psychology of Men and Masculinity, 6*(1), 73–76.

Bergman, J. (2005, June 22). Drugs, disease, denial. *New York Press, 18*(25). Retrieved March 17, 2007, from http://www.nypress.com

Berry, J. W. (1980). Acculturation as varieties of adaptation. In A. M. Padilla (Ed.), *Acculturation: Theory, models and some new findings* (pp. 9–25). Boulder, CO: Westview Press.

Berry, J. W. (1993). Ethnic identity in plural societies. In M. E. Bernal, & G. P. Knight (Eds.), *Ethnic identity: Formation and transmission among Hispanics and other minorities* (pp. 271–296). Albany: State University of New York Press.

Beutler, L. E. (2000). David and Goliath: When empirical and clinical standards of practice meet. *American Psychologist, 51,* 1050–1058.

Bever, E. (2002). Witchcraft, female aggression, and power in the early modern community. *Journal of Social History, 35,* 955–989.

Bhugra, D., & Bhui, K. (1999). Racism in psychiatry: Paradigm lost—paradigm regained. *International Review of Psychiatry, 11,* 236–244.

Bijl, R. V., deGraaf, R., Ravelli, A., Smit, F., & Vollebergh, W. A. M. (2002). Gender and age-specific first incidence of *DSM–III–R* psychiatric disorders in the general population: Results from the Netherlands Mental Health Survey and Incidence Study (NEMESIS). *Social Psychiatry and Psychiatric Epidemiology, 37,* 372–379.

Black, D., Gates, G., Sanders, S., & Taylor, L. (2000). Demographics of the gay and lesbian population in the United States: Evidence from available systematic data sources. *Demography, 37,* 139–154.

Black, D., Gates, G., Sanders, S., & Taylor, L. (2002). Why do gay men live in San Francisco? *Journal of Urban Economics, 51,* 54–76.

Blair, S. L., & Qian, Z. (1998). Family and Asian students' educational performance: A consideration of diversity. *Journal of Family Issues, 19,* 355–374.

Blankfield, A. (1987). The concept of dependence. *The International Journal of the Addictions, 22,* 1069–1081.

Bliatout, B. T. (1993). Hmong death customs: Traditional and acculturated. In D. P. Irish, K. F. Lundquist, &

V. J. Nelsen, (Eds.), *Ethnic variations in dying, death, and grief: Diversity in universality* (pp. 79–100). Philadelphia: Taylor & Francis.

Blum, D. (1998). *The school counselor's book of lists.* West Nyack, NY: Center for Applied Research.

Blumenfeld, W. J., & Raymond, D. (1988). *Looking at gay and lesbian life.* Boston: Beacon.

Bobbe, J. (2002). Treatment with lesbian alcoholics: Healing shame and internalized homophobia for ongoing sobriety. *Health and Social Work, 27,* 218–223.

Borowsky, I. W., Ireland, M., & Resnick, M. D. (2001). Adolescent suicide attempts: Risks and protectors. *Pediatrics, 107,* 485–494.

Boyd, M., & Mackey, M. (2000). Alienation from self and others: The psychosocial problem of rural alcoholic women. *Archives of Psychiatric Nursing, 14*(3), 134–141.

Boyd-Franklin, N. (1989). *Black families in therapy: A multisystems approach.* New York: Guilford Press.

Boyd-Franklin, N., & Hafer-Bry, B. (2000). *Reaching out in family therapy: Home-based, school, and community interventions.* New York: Guilford Press.

Boysen, G. A., Vogel, D. L., Madon, S., & Wester, S. R. (2006). Mental health stereotypes about gay men. *Sex Roles, 54,* 69–82.

Brace, C. (1995). Race and political correctness. *American Psychologist, 50,* 725–726.

Bradley, C., & Kiselica, M. (1998). Understanding racial identity development among school age children. *Professional School Counseling, 2,* 83–84.

Brannon, R. (1985). Dimensions of the male sex-role in America. In A. G. Sargent (Ed.), *Beyond sex roles* (2nd ed., pp. 296–316). New York: West.

Brendtro, L. K., Brokenleg, M., & Van Bockern, S. (1990). *Reclaiming youth at risk: Our hope for the future.* Bloomington, IN: National Education Service.

Briere, J. (2002). *Psychological assessment of adult posttraumatic states.* Washington, DC: American Psychological Association.

Brodsky, A. M., & Holroyd, J. (1975). Report on the task force on sex bias and sex-role stereotyping in psychotherapeutic practice. *American Psychologist, 30,* 1169–1175.

Brodzinsky, D. M., Patterson, C. J., & Vaziri, M. (2002). Adoption agency perspectives on lesbian and gay prospective parents: A national study. *Adoption Quarterly, 5*(3), 5–23.

Bronfenbrenner, U. (1977). Toward an experimental ecology of human development. *American Psychologist, 32,* 513–531.

Brooks, D. (2005, October 6). Pillars of cultural capital. *New York Times,* p. A37.

Brooks, G. R. (1998). *A new psychotherapy for traditional men.* San Francisco: Jossey-Bass.

Broverman, I. K., Broverman, D. M., Clarkson, F. E., Rosenkrantz, P. S., & Vogel, S. R. (1970). Sex-role stereotypes and clinical judgments of mental health. *Journal of Consulting and Clinical Psychology, 34*(1), 1–7.

Broverman, I. K., Vogel, S. R., Broverman, D. M., Clarkson, F. E., & Rosenkrantz, P. S. (1972). Sex-role stereotypes: A current appraisal. *Journal of Social Issues, 28*(2), 59–78.

Brown, D., & Srebalus, D. J. (2003). *Introduction to the counseling profession* (3rd ed.). Upper Saddle River, NJ: Pearson Education.

Brown, D. W. (2004). *A new introduction to Islam.* Malden, MA: Blackwell.

Brown, L. (Ed.). (1997). *Two spirit people: American Indian lesbian women and gay men.* Binghamton, NY: Haworth Press.

Brown, L. S. (1986, August). Diagnosis and the zeitgeist: The politics of masochism in the *DSM–III–R.* In R. Garfinkel (Chair), *The politics of diagnosis: Feminist psychology and the* DSM–III–R. Symposium presented at the Convention of the American Psychological Association, New York.

Brown, L. S. (1990a). Feminist therapy perspectives on psychodiagnosis: Beyond the *DSM* and *ICD.* In L. Walker, N. J. Nicolaï, & J. Sayers (Eds.), *Feminist diagnosis and therapy* (pp. 45–66). Amsterdam: Stichting de Maan.

Brown, L. S. (1990b). Taking account of gender in the clinical assessment interview. *Professional Psychology: Research and Practice, 21,* 12–17.

Brown, L. S. (1991a). Diagnosis and dialogue. *Canadian Psychology, 2,* 142–144.

Brown, L. S. (1991b). Not outside the range: One feminist perspective on psychic trauma. *American Imago, 48,* 119–133.

Brown, L. S. (1992). A feminist critique of the personality disorders. In L. S. Brown & M. Ballou (Eds.), *Personality and psychopathology: Feminist reappraisals* (pp. 206–228). New York: Guilford Press.

Brown, L. S., & Gilligan, C. (1992). *Meeting at the crossroads.* Cambridge, MA: Harvard University Press.

Browning, C., Reynolds, A. L., & Dworkin, S. H. (1991). Affirmative psychotherapy for lesbian women. *The Counseling Psychologist, 19,* 177–196.

Bryan, L. A., Dersch, C., Shumway, S., & Arredondo, R. (2004). Therapy outcomes: Client perception and similarity with therapist view. *The American Journal of Family Therapy, 32,* 11–26.

Bryer, J. B., Nelson, B. A., Miller, J. B., & Krol, P. A. (1987). Childhood sexual and physical abuse as factors in adult psychiatric illness. *American Journal of Psychiatry, 144,* 1426–1430.

Buddha Dharma Education Association. (2007). *Buddhist information and education network.* Retrieved April 9, 2007, from http://www.buddha.net

Burns, J. S. (Writer), & Anderson, B. (Director). (2007). Marge the gamer [Television series episode]. In J. L. Brooks, M. Groening, & S. Simon (Producers), *The Simpsons.* Los Angeles: 20th Century Fox Television.

Burr, V., & Butt, T. (2000). Psychological distress and post-modern thought. In F. Fee (Ed.), *Pathology and the postmodern* (pp. 186–206). London: Sage.

Burstow, B. (2003). Toward a radical understanding of trauma and trauma work. *Violence Against Women, 9,* 1293–1317.

Busfield, J. (1996). Men, women, and madness: Understanding gender and mental disorder. London: Macmillan.

Bush, G. H. W. (1990). *Remarks of President George Bush at the signing of the Americans with Disabilities Act.* Retrieved May 4, 2007, from http://www.eeoc.gov/ada/bushspeech.html

Butler, J. (1990). *Gender trouble: Feminism and the subversion of identity.* New York: Routledge.

Cable News Network. (2007, September). *Census: More Blacks, Latinos live in cells than dorms.* Retrieved July 18, 2007, from http://www.cnn.com/2007/us/09/07census.prisions.ap/index.html

Cabrera, N. L., & Padilla, A. M. (2004). Entering and succeeding in the "culture of college": The story of two Mexican heritage students. *Hispanic Journal of Behavioral Sciences, 26,* 152–170.

Cainkar, L. (2002). Arabs, Muslims, and race in America. *Middle East Report, 224.* Retrieved October 14, 2004, from http://www.merip.org/mer224/224_cainkar.html

Camarota, S. A. (2002). *Immigrants from the Middle East: A profile of the foreign-born population from Pakistan to Morocco.* Retrieved July 7, 2005, from http://www.cis.org/articles/2002/back902.html

Cameron, S. C., & Wycoff, S. M. (1998). The destructive nature of the term race: Growing beyond a false paradigm. *Journal of Counseling and Development, 76,* 277–285.

Campo-Flores, A. (2006, April 10). America's divide. *Newsweek,* 28–38.

Caplan, P. J. (1973). The role of classroom conduct in the promotion and retention of elementary school children. *Journal of Experimental Education, 41,* 45–51.

Caplan, P. J. (1977). Sex, age, behavior, and subject as determinants of reporting of learning problems. *Journal of Learning Disabilities, 10,* 314–316.

Caplan, P. J. (1992). Gender issues in the diagnosis of mental disorder. *Women & Therapy, 12*(4), 71–82.

Caplan, P. J. (1995). *They say you're crazy: How the world's most powerful psychiatrists decide who's normal.* Reading, MA: Addison-Wesley.

Caplan, P. J. (2006). *Psychiatric labels plague women's mental health.* Retrieved September 30, 2006, from http://womenofcolor.blogspot.com/2006/05/psychiatric-labels-plague-womens.html

Caplan, P. J., & Kinsbourne, M. (1974). Sex differences in response to school failure. *Journal of Learning Disabilities, 7,* 232–235.

Caplan, P. J., McCurdy-Myers, J., & Gans, M. (1992). Should "Premenstrual syndrome" be called a psychiatric abnormality? *Feminism and Psychology, 2*(1), 27–44.

Carli, L. L. (1990). Gender, language, and influence. *Journal of Personality and Social Psychology, 59,* 941–951.

Carmen, E. H., Russo, N. F., & Miller, J. B. (1981). Inequality and women's mental health: An overview. *American Journal of Psychiatry, 138,* 1319–1330.

Carr, J. E. (1996). Psychology and mind-body segregation: Are we part of the problem? *Journal of Clinical Psychology in Medical Settings, 3,* 141–144.

Carroll, L. (2001). Teaching "outside the box": Incorporating queer theory in counselor education. *Journal of Humanistic Counseling, Education, and Development, 40,* 49–57.

Carroll, L., & Gilroy, P. J. (2002). Transgender issues in counselor preparation. *Counselor Education and Supervision, 41,* 233–242.

Carson, J., & Sperry, L. (1999). *The intimate couple.* Philadelphia: Brunner/Mazel.

Carter, R. T. (1990). Does race or racial identity status attitudes influence counseling process in Black/White dyads? In J. Helms (Ed.), *Black and White racial identity: Theory, research, and practice* (pp. 145–163). New York: Greenwood Press.

Casas, J. M., Furlong, M. J., & Ruiz de Esparza, C. (2003). Increasing Hispanic parent participation in schools: The role of the counselor. In P. B. Pedersen, & J. C. Carey (Eds.), *Multicultural counseling in the schools: A practical handbook* (pp. 105–130). Boston: Allyn & Bacon.

Cashwell, C. S. (2005). Spirituality and wellness. In J. E. Myers, & T. J. Sweeney (Eds.), *Counseling for wellness: Theory, research, and practice* (pp. 197–206). Alexandria, VA: American Counseling Association.

Cashwell, C. S., Bentley, D. P., & Yarborough, J. P. (2007). The only way out is through: The peril of spiritual bypass. *Counseling and Values, 51,* 139–148.

Cashwell, C. S., & Marszalek, J. (2007, March). *Spiritual identity of lesbians, gay men, and bisexuals: Implications for counseling*. Paper presented at the meeting of the American Counseling Association, Detroit, MI.

Cashwell, C. S., Myers, J. E., & Shurts, M. (2004). Using the Developmental Counseling and Therapy Model to work with clients in spiritual bypass: Some preliminary considerations. *Journal of Counseling and Development, 82*, 403–409.

Cashwell, C. S., & Rayle, A. D. (in press). Spiritual bypass. In D. S. Sandhu (Ed.), *Spirituality as the 5th force in counseling and psychology: Implications for research, training, and practice*. Alexandria, VA: American Counseling Association.

Cashwell, C. S., & Young, J. S. (2005). *Integrating spirituality and religion into counseling: A guide to competent practice*. Alexandria, VA: American Counseling Association.

Cass, V. C. (1979). Homosexual identity formation: A theoretical model. *Journal of Homosexuality, 4*, 219–235.

Cass, V. C. (1990). The implications of homosexual identity formation for the Kinsey model and scale of sexual preference. In D. P. McWhirter, S. A. Sanders, & J. M. Reinisch (Eds.), *Homosexuality/heterosexuality: Concepts of sexual orientation* (pp. 239–266). New York: Oxford University.

Castillo, R. J. (1997). *Culture and mental illness: A client centered approach*. Pacific Grove, CA: Brooks/Cole.

Cavanaugh, J. C., & Blanchard-Fields, F. (Eds.). (2006). *Adult development and aging* (5th ed.). Belmont, CA: Thomson Wadsworth.

Center for Immigration Studies. (2005). *Current numbers*. Retrieved November 27, 2006, from http://www.cis.org/topics/currentnumbers.html#Publications

Central Intelligence Agency. (2007). *The world factbook 2007: Rank order—Infant mortality rate*. Retrieved August 31, 2007 from http://www.cia.gov/library/publications/the-world-factbook/rankorder/2091rank.html

Cermele, J. A., Daniels, S., & Anderson, K. L. (2001). Defining normal: Constructions of race and gender in the *DSM–IV* casebook. *Feminism & Psychology, 11*, 229–247.

Cervantes, J. M., & Ramirez, O. (1992). Spirituality and family dynamics in psychotherapy with Latino children. In L. A. Vargas, & J. D. Koss-Chioino (Eds.), *Working with culture: Psychotherapeutic interventions with ethnic minority children and adolescents* (pp. 103-128). San Francisco: Jossey-Bass.

Chambless, D. L., & Williams, K. E. (1995). A preliminary study of the effects of exposure *in vivo* for African Americans with agoraphobia. *Behavior Therapy, 26*, 501–515.

Chan, A. Y. (1998). Factors promoting marital resilience among interracial couples. In H. L. McCubbin, E. A. Thompson, A. L. Thompson, & E. J. Fromer (Eds.), *Resiliency in Native American and immigrant families* (pp. 71–87). Thousand Oaks, CA: Sage.

Chan, C. S. (1989). Issues of identity development of Asian-American lesbians and gay men [Special issue]. *Journal of Counseling and Development, 68*(1), 16–20.

Chan, S. (1991). *Asian Americans: An interpretive history*. Boston: Twayne.

Chandler, C. K., Holden, J. M., & Kolander, C. A. (1992). Counseling for spiritual wellness: Theory and practice. *Journal of Counseling and Development, 71*, 168–175.

Chang, C. Y., Hays, D. G., & Milliken, T. F. (in press). Addressing social justice issues in supervision. *The Clinical Supervisor*.

Chapman, A. B. (2007). In search of love and commitment: Dealing with the challenging odds of finding romance. In H. P. McAdoo (Ed.), *Black families* (pp. 97–124). Thousand Oaks, CA: Sage.

Chapman, B. E., & Brannock, J. C. (1987). Proposed model of lesbian identity development: An empirical examination. *Journal of Homosexuality, 14*, 69–80.

Chappell, M. S., & Overton, W. F. (2002). Development of logical reasoning and school performance of African American adolescents in relation to socioeconomic status, ethnic identity, and self esteem. *Journal of Black Psychology, 28*, 295–317.

Chen, S., Sullivan, N. Y., Lu, Y. E., & Shibusawa, T. (2003). Asian Americans and mental health services: A study of utilization patterns in the 1990s. *Journal of Ethnic & Cultural Diversity in Social Work, 12*, 19–42.

Chen-Hayes, S. (1997). Counseling LGB persons in couple and family relationships. *The Family Journal, 5*, 236–240.

Chernin, J. N., & Johnson, M. R. (2002). *Affirmative psychotherapy and counseling for lesbians and gay men*. Thousand Oaks, CA: Sage.

Cheryan, S., & Bodenhausen, G. V. (2000). When positive stereotypes threaten intellectual performance: The psychological hazards of "model minority" status. *Psychological Science, 11*, 399–402.

Cheryan, S., & Tsai, J. L. (2007). Ethnic identity. In F. T. Leong, A. Ebreo, L. Kinoshita, A. G. Inman, & L. H. Yang (Eds.), *Handbook of Asian American psychology* (2nd ed., pp. 125–139). Thousand Oaks, CA: Sage.

Chesler, P. (1973). *Women and madness*. New York: Avon Books.

ChildStats. (2006). *America's children in brief: Key national indicators of well-being*. Retrieved April 1, 2007, from http://childstats.gov/americaschildren

Child Welfare League of America. (2003). *A quick trip through CWLA's history*. Retrieved October 15, 2007, from http://www.cwla.org/whowhat/CWLAtimeline.pdf

Chiu, E., Ames, A., Draper, B., & Snowdon, J. (1999). Depressive disorders in the elderly: A review. In M. Maj, & N. Sartorius (Eds.), *Depressive disorders* (pp. 485–504). Thousand Oaks, CA: Sage.

Chodron, P. (1996). *Awakening loving-kindness*. Boston: Shambhala.

Chodron, P. (2002). *Comfortable with uncertainty: 108 teachings*. Boston: Shambhala.

Choney, S. K., Berryhill-Paapke, E., & Robbins, R. (1995). The acculturation of American Indians: Developing frameworks for research and practice. In J. G. Ponterotto, J. M. Casas, L. A. Suzuki, & C. M. Alexander (Eds.), *Handbook of multicultural counseling* (pp. 73–92). Thousand Oaks, CA: Sage.

Chow, J. C.-C., Jaffee, K., & Snowden, L. (2003). Racial/ethnic disparities in the use of mental health services in poverty areas. *American Journal of Public Health, 93,* 792–797.

Chrisler, J. C., & Caplan, P. (2002). The strange case of Dr. Jekyll and Ms. Hyde: How PMS became a cultural phenomenon and a psychiatric disorder. *Annual Review of Sex Research, 13,* 274–307.

Chua, P., & Fujino, D. C. (1999). Negotiating new Asian-American masculinities: Attitudes and gender expectations [Special issue]. *The Journal of Men's Studies, 7,* 391–413.

Chun, K. M., & Akutsu, P. D. (2003). Acculturation among ethnic minority families. In K. M. Chun, P. B. Organista, & G. Marin (Eds.), *Acculturation: Advances in theory, measurement, and applied research* (pp. 95–120). Washington, DC: American Psychological Association.

Chun, K. M., Eastman, K. L., Wang, G. C., & Sue, S. (1998). Psychopathology. In L. C. Lee, & N. W. Zane (Eds.), *Handbook of Asian American psychology* (pp. 457–483). Thousand Oaks, CA: Sage.

Chung, R. C., & Bemak, F. (2007). Asian immigrants and refugees. In F. Leong, A. G. Inman, A. Ebreo, L. Lang, L. Kinoshita, & M. Fu (Eds.), *Handbook of Asian American psychology* (2nd ed., pp. 227–244). Thousand Oaks, CA: Sage.

Chung, Y. B., & Katayama, M. (1998). Ethnic and sexual identity development of Asian-American lesbian and gay adolescents. *Professional School Counseling, 1,* 21–25.

Chung, Y. B., & Singh, A. A. (2008). Lesbian, gay, bisexual, and transgender Asian Americans. In A. Alvarez & N. Tewari (Eds.), *Asian American psychology: Current perspectives* (pp. 233–246). Mahwah, NJ: Erlbaum.

Clance, P. C. (1985). *The impostor phenomenon: When success makes you feel like a fake*. New York: Bantam Books.

Clance, P. C., & Imes, S. A. (1978). The impostor phenomenon in high achieving women: Dynamics and the therapeutic intervention. *Psychotherapy: Theory, Research, and Practice, 15,* 241–247.

Clance, P. C., & O'Toole, M. A. (1988). The impostor phenomenon: An internal barrier to empowerment and achievement. *Women and Therapy, 6,* 51–54.

Clark, R., Anderson, N. B., Clark, V. R., & Williams, D. R. (1999). Racism as a stressor for African Americans: A biopsychosocial model. *The American Psychologist, 54,* 805–816.

Class Action. (n.d.). *Self-awareness & consciousness raising*. Retrieved February 25, 2009, from http://www.classism.org/action_self.html

Clemente, R., & Collison, B. B. (2000). The relationship among counselors, ESL teachers, and students. *Professional School Counseling, 3,* 339–349.

Clements-Nolle, K., Marx, R., Guzman, R., & Katz, M. (2001). HIV prevalence, risk behaviors, health care use, and mental health status of transgender persons: Implications for public health intervention. *American Journal of Public Health, 91,* 915–921.

Coatsworth, J. D., Maldonado-Molina, M., Pantin, H., & Szapocznik, J. (2005). A person-centered and ecological investigation of acculturation strategies in Hispanic immigrant youth. *Journal of Community Psychology, 33,* 157–174.

Cochran, S. D., & Mays, V. M. (2000a). Lifetime prevalence of suicide symptoms and affective disorders among men reporting same-sex sexual partners: Results from the NHANES III. *American Journal of Public Health, 90,* 573–578.

Cochran, S. D., & Mays, V. M. (2000b). Relation between psychiatric syndromes and behaviorally defined sexual orientation in a sample of the U.S. population. *American Journal of Epidemiology, 151,* 516–523.

Cohen, P. N., & Casper, L. M. (2002). Stigma management among the voluntarily childless. *Sociological Perspectives, 45,* 21–46.

Cohler, B. J., Stott, F. M., & Musick, J. (1995). Adversity, vulnerability, and resilience: Cultural and developmental perspectives. In D. Cicchetti, & D. J. Cohen (Eds.), *Developmental psychopathology* (Vol. 2, pp. 753–800). New York: Wiley.

Cokley, K., & Awad, G. H. (2008). Conceptual and methodological issues related to multicultural research. In P. P. Heppner, B. E. Wampold, & D. M. Kivlighan (Eds.), *Research design in counseling* (3rd ed., pp. 366–384). Belmont, CA: Thomson Brooks/Cole.

Cole, M., & Cole, S. R. (1996). *The development of children* (3rd ed.). New York: Freeman.

Cole, S. W., Kemeny, M. E., Taylor, S. E., & Visscher, B. R. (1996). Accelerated course of human immunodeficiency virus infection in gay men who conceal their homosexual identity. *Psychosomatic Medicine, 58,* 219–231.

Coleman, E. (1981/1982). Developmental stages of the coming out process. *Journal of Homosexuality, 7*, 31–43.

Coleman, E. (1990). Toward a synthetic understanding of sexual orientation. In D. P. McWhirter, S. A. Sanders, & J. M. Reinisch (Eds.). *Homosexuality/ heterosexuality: Concepts of sexual orientation* (pp. 267–276). New York: Oxford University.

Coleman, H. L. K. (1998). General and multicultural counseling competency: Apples and oranges? *Journal of Multicultural Counseling and Development, 26*, 147–156.

Collins, L. H. (1998). Illustrating feminist theory: Power and psychopathology. *Psychology of Women Quarterly, 22*, 97–112.

Colman, P. (1995). *Rosie the riveter: Women working on the home front in WWII.* New York: Crown.

Committee on Women in Psychology. (1985). *Critique of proposed new diagnoses for the DSM–III–R.* Unpublished manuscript.

Conger, J. J. (1975). Proceedings of the American Psychological Association, Incorporated, for the year 1974: Minutes of the annual meeting of the Council of Representatives. *American Psychologist, 30*, 620–651.

Conner-Edwards, A. F., & Spurlock, J. (Eds.). (1988). *Black families in crisis: The middle class.* New York: Brunner/Mazel.

Constantine, M. G. (2002a). The intersection of race, ethnicity, gender, and social class in counseling: Examining selves in cultural contexts. *Journal of Multicultural Counseling and Development, 30*, 210–215.

Constantine, M. G. (2002b). Predictors of satisfaction with counseling: Racial and ethnic minority clients' attitudes toward counseling and their ratings of their counselors' general and multicultural counseling competence. *Journal of Counseling Psychology, 49*, 255–263.

Constantine, M. G., Hage, S. M., Kindaichi, M. M., & Bryant, R. M. (2007). Social justice and multicultural issues: Implications for the practice and training of counselors and counseling psychologists. *Journal of Counseling and Development, 85*, 24–29.

Constantine, M. G., & Ladany, N. (2000). Self-report multicultural counseling competence and scales: Their relation to social desirability attitudes and multicultural case conceptualization ability. *Journal of Counseling Psychology, 47*, 155–164.

Cook, E. P. (1992a). Gender and psychological distress. *Journal of Counseling and Development, 68*, 371–380.

Cook, E. P. (Ed.). (1992b). *Women, relationships, and power: Implications for counseling.* Alexandria, VA: American Counseling Association.

Cook, E. P., Warnke, M., & Dupuy, P. (1993). Gender bias and the *DSM–III–R. Counselor Education and Supervision, 32*, 311–322.

Cooper, J. E., Kendall, R. E., Gurland, B. J., Sartorius, N., & Farkas, T. (1969). Cross-national study of diagnosis of the mental disorders: Some results from the first comparative investigation. *American Journal of Psychiatry, 125*, 21–29.

Corey, G. (2005). *Theory and practice of counseling and psychotherapy* (7th ed.). Pacific Grove, CA: Brooks/ Cole.

Cormack, S., & Furnham, A. (1998). Psychiatric labeling, sex role stereotypes and beliefs about the mentally ill. *International Journal of Social Psychiatry, 44*, 235–247.

Cornelius, J. R., Fabrega, H., Cornelius, M. D, Mezzich, J., & Maher, P. J. (1996). Racial effects on the clinical presentation of alcoholics at a psychiatric hospital. *Comprehensive Psychiatry, 37*, 102–108.

Cornell, A. W. (1996). *The power of focusing: A practical guide to emotional self-healing.* New York: MJF Books.

Corrigan, P. W. (2004). Don't call me nuts: An international perspective on the stigma of mental illness. *Acta Psychiatrica Scandinavica, 109*, 403–404.

Corsini, R. J., & Wedding, D. (2000). *Current psychotherapies* (6th ed.). Itasca, IL: F. E. Peacock.

Costantino, G., Malgady, R. G., & Rogler, L. H. (1986). Cuento therapy: A culturally sensitive modality for Puerto Rican children. *Journal of Consulting and Clinical Psychology, 54*, 639–645.

Council on Islamic Education. (1995). *Teaching about Islam and Muslims in the public school classroom.* Fountain Valley, CA: Council on Islamic Education.

Counselors for Social Justice (2004). *What is Counselors for Social Justice?* Retrieved August 27, 2008, from Counselors for Social Justice Web site: http:// counselorsforsocialjustice.com

Cozzarelli, C., Wilkinson, A. V., & Tagler, M. J. (2001). Attitudes toward the poor and attributions for poverty. *The Society for the Psychological Study of Social Issues, 57*, 207–27.

Crawford, J. (1999). *Bilingual education: History, politics, theory, and practice* (4th ed.). Los Angeles: Bilingual Educational Services, Inc.

Cross, W. E., Jr. (1971a). Discovering the Black referent: The psychology of Black liberation. In J. Dixon & B. Foster (Eds.), *Beyond Black or White.* Boston: Little, Brown.

Cross, W. E., Jr. (1971b). The Negro-to-Black conversion experience: Toward a psychology of Black liberation. *Black World, 20*, 13–27.

Cross, W. E., Jr. (1991). *Shades of Black: Diversity in African-American identity.* Philadelphia: Temple University Press.

Cross, W. E., Jr. (1995). The psychology of nigrescence: Revising the Cross model. In J. M. Ponterotto, J. M. Casas, L. A. Suzuki, & C. M. Alexander (Eds.), *Handbook of multicultural counseling* (pp. 93–122). Thousand Oaks, CA: Sage.

Cross, W. E., Jr., & Vandiver, B. J. (2001). Nigrecence theory and measurement: Introducing the Cross Racial Identity Scale (CRIS). In J. Ponterotto, J. Casas, L. Suzuki, & C. Alexander (Eds.), *Handbook of multicultural counseling* (2nd ed., pp. 371–393). Thousand Oaks, CA: Sage.

Cummins, J. (1994). Knowledge, power, and identity in teaching ESL. In F. Genesee (Ed.), *Educating second language children* (pp. 33–58). New York: Press Syndicate of the University of Cambridge.

Curtis-Boles, H., & Jenkins-Monroe, V. (2000). Substance abuse in African American women. *Journal of Black Psychology, 26*, 450–469.

D'Andrea, M. (2000). Postmodernism, constructivism, and multiculturalism: Three forces reshaping and expanding our thoughts about counseling. *Journal of Mental Health Counseling, 22*, 1–16.

D'Andrea, M., & Daniels, J. (1997). RESPECTFUL counseling: A new way of thinking about diversity counseling. *Counseling Today, 40*(6), 30, 31, 34.

D'Andrea, M., & Daniels, J. (1999). Understanding the different psychological dispositions of White racism: A comprehensive model for counselor educators and practitioners. In M. Kiselica (Ed.), *Confronting prejudice and racism during multicultural training* (pp. 59–87). Alexandria, VA: American Counseling Association.

D'Andrea, M., & Daniels, J. (2001). Expanding our thinking about White racism: Facing the challenge of multicultural counseling in the 21st century. In J. G. Ponterotto, J. M. Casas, L. A. Suzuki, & C. M. Alexander (Eds.), *Handbook of multicultural counseling* (2nd ed., pp. 289–310). Thousand Oaks, CA: Sage.

Daniels, J. A. (2001). Conceptualizing a case of indirect racism using the White racial identity development model. *Journal of Mental Health Counseling, 23*, 256–268.

Dank, B. M. (1973). The development of a homosexual identity: Antecedents and consequents (Doctoral dissertation, tUniversity of Wisconsin, 1973). *Dissertation Abstracts International*, pp. 423A–424A.

Das, A., & Kemp, S. (1997). Between two worlds: Counseling South Asian Americans. *Journal of Multicultural Counseling and Development, 25*, 23–33.

Dasgupta, S. D. (1998). Gender roles and cultural continuity in the Asian Indian immigrant community in the U.S. *Sex Roles, 38*, 953–974.

Dasgupta, S. D., & Dasgupta, S. (1996). Private face, private space: Asian Indian women and sexuality. In N. B. Maglin & D. Perry (Eds.), *Bad girls, good girls: Women, sex, and power in the nineties* (pp. 226–243). New Brunswick, NJ: Rutgers University Press.

Davenport, D. S., & Yurich, J. M. (1991). Multicultural gender issues. *Journal of Counseling and Development, 70*, 64–71.

Davies, N. (1996). *Europe: A history.* New York: Harper Perennial.

Day-Vines, N. L., Patton, J. M., & Baytops, J. L. (2003). Counseling African American adolescents: The impact of race, culture, and middle class status. *Professional School Counseling, 7*, 40–51.

Dearing, E., Taylor, B. A., & McCartney, K. (2004). Implications of family income dynamics for women's depressive symptoms during the first 3 years after childbirth. *American Journal of Public Health, 94*, 1372–1377.

Deater-Deckard, K., Dodge, K. A., Bates, J. E., & Pettit, G. S. (1996). Physical discipline among African American and European American mothers: Links to children's externalizing behaviors. *Developmental Psychology, 32*, 1065–1072.

DeLamotte, E., Meeker, N., & O'Barr, J. (1997). *Women imagine change: A global anthology of women's resistance from 600 B.C.E. to present.* New York: Routledge.

de las Fuentes, C. (2003). Latinos and mental health. In J. S. Mio & G. Y. Iwamasa (Eds.), *Culturally diverse mental health: The challenges of research and resistance* (pp. 159–172). New York: Routledge.

Delgado-Romero, E. A. (2001). Counseling a Hispanic/Latino client—Mr. X. *Journal of Mental Health Counseling, 23*, 207–221.

Deloria, V., Jr. (1988). *Custer died for your sins: An Indian manifesto.* Norman: University of Oklahoma Press.

de Mente, B. L .(1996). *NTC's dictionary of Mexican cultural code words.* Chicago: NTC Publishing Group.

Demo, D. H., & Hughes, M. (1990). Socialization and racial identity among Black Americans. *Social Psychology Quarterly, 53*, 364–374.

DeNavas-Walt, C., Proctor, B. D., & Lee, C. H. (2006). *Income, poverty and health insurance coverage in the United States: 2005* (U.S. Census Bureau, *Current Population Reports*, P60-231). Retrieved March 3, 2007, from http://www.census.gov/prod/2006pubs/p60-231.pdf

Denton, W. H. (1990). A family systems analysis of DSM–III–R. *Journal of Marital and Family Therapy, 16*(2), 113–125.

Desikachar, T. K. V. (1999). *The heart of yoga: Developing a personal practice.* Rochester, VT: Inner Traditions.

Dhruvarajan, V. (1993). Ethnic cultural retention and transmission among first generation Hindu Asian Indians in a Canadian prairie city. *Journal of Comparative Family Studies, 24*, 63–79.

Díaz, R. M., Ayala, G., Bein, E., Henne, J., & Marin, B. V. (2001). The impact of homophobia, poverty, and racism on the mental health of gay and bisexual Latino men: Findings from 3 U.S. cities. *American Journal of Public Health, 91*, 927–932.

Dickerson, V. C., & Zimmerman, J. L. (1995). A constructionist exercise in anti-pathologizing. *Journal of Systemic Therapies, 14*(1), 33–45.

Dietz, C. A. (2000). Reshaping clinical practice for the new millennium. *Journal of Social Work Education, 36*, 503–521.

Dinsmore, J. A., Chapman, A., & McCollum, V. J. C. (2000, April). *Client advocacy and social justice: Strategies for developing trainee competence.* Paper presented at the annual conference of the American Counseling Association, Washington, DC.

DiPlacido, J. (1998). Minority stress among lesbians, gay men, and bisexual: A consequence of heterosexism, homophobia, and stigmatization. In G. M. Herek (Ed.), *Stigma and sexual orientation: Understanding prejudice against lesbians, gay men, and bisexuals* (pp. 138-159). Thousand Oaks, CA: Sage.

Disability. (n.d.). In *Merriam-Webster's online dictionary.* Retrieved from http://www.merriam-webster.com

Doswell, W., Kouyate, M., & Taylor, J. (2003). The role of spirituality in preventing early sexual behavior. *American Journal of Health Studies, 18*, 195–202.

Downing, N. E., & Roush, K. L. (1985). From passive-acceptance to active commitment: A model of feminist identity development for women. *The Counseling Psychologist, 13*, 695–709.

Downs-Karkos, S. (2004). *Addressing the mental health needs of immigrants and refugees.* Retrieved September 30, 2006, from http://www.gih.org/usr_doc/Immigrant_Mental_Health.pdf#search=%22immigrants%20and%20mental%20health%22

Draguns, J. (1985). Psychological disorders across cultures. In P. Pedersen (Ed.), *Handbook of cross-cultural counseling and therapy* (pp. 55–62). Westport, CT: Greenwood Press.

Duberman, M. (1993). *Stonewall.* New York: Penguin Press

DuBray, W. H. (1985). American Indian values: Critical factor in casework. *Social Casework: The Journal of Contemporary Social Work, 66*, 30–37.

Duffy, M., Gillig, S. E., Tureen, R. M., & Ybarra, M. A. (2002). A critical look at the *DSM–IV. Journal of Individual Psychology, 58*, 363–374.

Dufrene, P. M. (1990). Exploring Native American symbolism. *Journal of Multicultural and Cross-Cultural Research in Art Education, 8*, 38–50.

Dunn, T. W., Smith, T. B., & Montoya, J. A. (2006). Multicultural competency instrumentation: A review and analysis of reliability generalization. *Journal of Counseling and Development, 84*, 471–482.

Dwairy, M. (2002). Foundations of psychosocial dynamic personality theory of collective people. *Clinical Psychology Review, 22*, 343–360.

Dworkin, S. H., & Yi, H. (2003). LGBT identity, violence, and social justice: The psychological is political. *International Journal for the Advancement of Counselling, 25*, 269–279.

Elaasar, A. (2004). *Silent victims: The plight of Arab and Muslim Americans in post 9/11 America.* Bloomington, IN: Authorhouse.

Elizur, Y., & Mintzer, A. (2003). Gay males' intimate relationship quality: The roles of attachment security, gay identity, social support, and income. *Personal Relationships, 10*, 411–435.

Ellis, K., & Eriksen, K. (2002). Transsexual and transgenderist experiences and treatment options. *The Family Journal, 10*, 289–299.

Eltner, R. (1999). *Gender loving care: A guide to counseling gender-variant clients.* New York: Spectrum.

Ely, M., Hardy, R., Longford, N., & Wadsworth, M. E. J. (1999). Gender differences in the relationship between alcohol consumption and drink problems are largely accounted for by body water. *Alcohol and Alcoholism, 34*, 894–902.

Engelsmann, F. F. (2000). Transcultural psychiatry: Goals and challenges. *Canadian Journal of Psychiatry, 45*, 429–430.

Enns, C. (1993). Twenty years of feminist counseling and therapy: From naming biases to implementing multifaceted practice. *The Counseling Psychologist, 21*, 3–87.

Erickson, C. D., & Al-Timimi, N. R. (2001). Providing mental health services to Arab Americans: Recommendations and considerations. *Cultural Diversity and Ethnic Minority Psychology, 7*, 306–327.

Eriksen, K., & Kress, V. E. (2004). *Beyond the DSM story: Ethical quandaries, challenges, and best practices.* Thousand Oaks, CA: Sage.

Erikson, E. H. (1978). Reflections on Dr. Borg's life cycle. In E. H. Erikson (Ed.), *Adulthood* (pp. 1–31). New York: Norton.

Espiritu, Y. L. (1997). *Asian American women and men: Labor, laws, and love.* Thousand Oaks, CA: Sage

Essandoh, P. K. (1996). Multicultural counseling as the "fourth force": A call to arms. *The Counseling Psychologist, 24*, 126–137

Evans, G. W. (2004). The environment of childhood poverty. *American Psychologist, 59,* 77–92.

Fabrega, H. (1989). Cultural relativism and psychiatric illness. *The Journal of Nervous and Mental Disease, 177,* 415–425.

Fabrega, H. (1996). Cultural and historical foundations of psychiatric diagnosis. In J. E. Mezzich, A. Kleinman, H. Fabrega, & D. L. Parron (Eds.), *Culture and psychiatric diagnosis: A* DSM–IV *perspective* (pp. 3–14). Washington, DC: American Psychiatric Press.

Fabrikant, B. (1974). The psychotherapist and the female patient: Perceptions, misperceptions, and change. In V. Franks, & V. Burtle (Eds.), *Women and therapy* (pp. 83–110). New York: Brunner/Mazel.

Fairburn, C. G., Cooper, Z., Doll, H. A., Norman, P., & O'Connor, M. (2000). The natural course of Bulimia Nervosa and Binge Eating Disorder in young women. *Archives of General Psychiatry, 57,* 659–665.

Faiver, C., & Ingersoll, R. E. (2005). Knowing one's limits. In C. S. Cashwell & J. S. Young (Eds.), *Integrating spirituality and religion into counseling: A guide to competent practice* (pp. 169–183). Alexandria, VA: American Counseling Association.

Fall, K. A., Howard, S., & Ford, J. E. (1999). *Alternatives to domestic violence: A homework manual for battering intervention groups.* Philadelphia: Accelerated Development.

Faragallah, M. H., Schumm, W. R., & Webb, F. J. (1997). Acculturation of Arab-American immigrants: An exploratory study. *Journal of Comparative Family Studies, 28,* 182–204.

Fassinger, R. E. (1991). The hidden minority: Issues and challenges in working with lesbian women and gay men. *The Counseling Psychologist, 19,* 151–176.

Fassinger, R. E. (1995). From invisibility to integration: Lesbian identity in the workplace. *Career Development Quarterly, 44,* 148–167.

Fassinger, R. E., & Miller, B. A. (1996). Validation of an inclusive model of sexual minority identity formation on a sample of gay men. *Journal of Homosexuality, 32,* 53–78.

Feagin, J. R. (2006). *Systematic racism: A theory of oppression.* New York: Routledge.

Federal Bureau of Investigation. (2001). *Hate crime statistics.* Retrieved June 10, 2007, from http://www.fbi.gov/ucr/ucr/htm#hate

Fennelly, K., Mulkeen, P., & Giusti, C. (1998). Coping with racism and discrimination: The experience of young Latino adolescents. In H. McCubbin, E. Thompson, A. Thompson, & J. Fromer (Eds.), *Resiliency in Native American and immigrant families* (pp. 343–366). Thousand Oaks, CA: Sage.

Ferrara, F. F. (2002). *Childhood sexual abuse: Developmental effects across the yes lifespan.* Pacific Grove, CA: Brooks/Cole.

Fields, J., & Casper, L. M. (2001). *America's families and living arrangements* (*Current Population Report,* P20-537). Washington, DC: U.S. Census Bureau.

Fisher, P. A., Storck, M., & Bacon, J. G. (1999). In the eye of the beholder: Risk and protective factors in rural American Indian and Caucasian adolescents. *American Journal of Orthopsychiatry, 69,* 294–304.

Flaskerud, J. H., & Hu, L. (1992). Relationship of ethnicity to psychiatric diagnosis. *Journal of Nervous and Mental Disease, 180,* 296–303.

Flaskerud, J. H., & Hu, L. (1994). Participation in and outcome of treatment for major depression among low income Asian-Americans. *Psychiatry Research, 53,* 289–300.

Foner, E. (1998). Who is an American? In P. S. Rothenberg (Ed.), *Race, class, and gender in the United States: An integrated study* (pp. 84–91). New York: St. Martin's Press.

Forstater, M. (2001). *The Tao: Finding the way of balance and harmony.* New York: Penguin Books.

Forsythe, B., & Melling, J. (1999). *Insanity, institutions and society, 1800–1914: A social history of madness in comparative perspective.* New York: Routledge.

Fouad, N. A., Gerstein, L. H., & Toropek, R. L. (2006). Social justice and counseling psychology in context. In R. L. Toropek, L. H. Gerstein, N. A. Fouad, G. Roysircar, & T. Israel (Eds.), *Handbook for social justice in counseling psychology* (pp. 1–16). Thousand Oaks, CA: Sage.

Fowler, J. W. (1981). *Stages of faith: The psychology of human development and the quest for meaning.* San Francisco: Harper & Row.

Fox, R. C. (1995). Bisexual identities. In L. Garnets and D. C. Kimmel (Eds.), *Psychological perspectives on lesbian, gay and bisexual experiences* (pp. 86–129). New York: Columbia University Press.

Fox, S., & Stallworth, L. E. (2005). Racial/ethnic bullying: Exploring links between bullying and racism in the U.S. workplace. *Journal of Vocational Behavior, 66,* 438–456.

Frable, D. E. S. (1997). Gender, racial, ethnic, sexual, and class identities. *Annual Review of Psychology, 48,* 139–163.

Frable, D. E. S., Wortman, C., & Joseph, J. (1997). Predicting self-esteem, well-being, and distress in a cohort of gay men: The importance of cultural stigma, personal visibility, community networks, and positive identity. *Journal of Personality, 65,* 599–624.

Frame, M. (2002). *Integrating religion and spirituality into counseling: A comprehensive approach.* Belmont, CA: Wadsworth.

Frankl, V. (1959). *Man's search for meaning.* New York: Simon and Schuster.

Franklin, J. H., & Moss, A. A., Jr. (2002). *From slavery to freedom: A history of African Americans* (8th ed.). New York: Knopf.

Freeman, J. (1995). *Women: A feminist perspective* (5th ed.). Mountain View, CA: Mayfield.

Freeman, S. C. (1993). Client-centered therapy with diverse populations: The universal within the specific. *Journal of Multicultural Counseling and Development, 21,* 248–254.

Freud, S. (1924). *A general introduction to psychoanalysis.* New York: Washington Square Press.

Freud, S. (1961). *Civilization and its discontents* (J. Strachey, Ed. and Trans.). New York: Norton. (Original work published 1930)

Frey, L. L., & Roysircar, G. (2004). Effects of acculturation and worldview for White American, South American, South Asian, and Southeast Asian students. *International Journal for the Advancement of Counseling, 26,* 229–248.

Friedan, B. (1963). *The feminine mystique.* New York: Norton.

Friedman, S., Paradis, C. M., & Hatch, M. (1994). Characteristics of African-American and White patients with Panic Disorder and agoraphobia. *Hospital and Community Psychiatry, 45,* 795–803.

Froggett, L. (2001). From rights to recognition: Mental health and spiritual healing among older Pakistanis. *Psychoanalytic Studies, 3,* 177–186.

Frye, M. (1983). Oppression. In M. Frye (Ed.), *The politics of reality* (pp. 1–16). Trumansburg, NY: Crossing Press.

Fuertes, J. N., Bartholomeo, M., & Nichols, C. M. (2001). Future research directions in the study of counselor multicultural competency. *Journal of Multicultural Counseling and Development, 70,* 86–90.

Fuertes, J. N., & Brobst, K. (2002). Clients' ratings of counselor multicultural competency. *Cultural Diversity and Ethnic Diversity Psychology, 8,* 214–233.

Fugita, S. (1990). Asian/Pacific-American mental health: Some needed research in epidemiology and service utilization. In F. C. Serafica, A. I. Schwebel, R. K. Russell, P. D. Isaac, & L. B. Myers (Eds.), *Mental health of ethnic minorities* (pp. 66–84). New York: Praeger.

Fujino, D. C., Okazaki, S., & Young, K. (1994). Asian-American women in the mental health system: An examination of ethnic and gender match between therapist and client [Special issue]. *Journal of Community Psychology, 22,* 164–176.

Fukuyama, M. A., & Sevig, T. D. (1999). *Integrating spirituality into multicultural counseling.* Thousand Oaks, CA: Sage.

Fukuyama, M. A., Siahpoush, F., & Sevig, T. D. (2005). Religion and spirituality in a cultural context. In C. S. Cashwell, & J. S. Young (Eds.), *Integrating spirituality and religion into counseling: A guide to competent practice* (pp. 123–142). Alexandria, VA: American Counseling Association.

Gaines, A. D. (1992). From *DSM–I* to *II–R:* Voices of self, mastery, and the others: A cultural constructivist reading of the U.S. psychiatric classification. *Social Science and Medicine, 35,* 3–24.

Gallant, S. J., & Hamilton, J. A. (1988). On a premenstrual psychiatric diagnosis: What's in a name? *Professional Psychology: Research and Practice, 19,* 271–278.

Galliano, G. (2003). Gender and mental health: On labels, culture, and boundary violations. *Gender: Crossing boundaries* (pp. 261–282). Belmont, CA: Wadsworth.

Gallop, R., McKeever, P., Toner, B., Lancee, W., & Lueck, M. (1995). Inquiring about childhood sexual abuse as part of the nursing history: Opinions of abused and non-abused nurses. *Archives of Psychiatric Nursing, 9*(3), 146–151.

Ganley, A. L. (1987). Perpetrators of domestic violence: An overview of counseling the court-mandated client. In D. J. Sonkin (Ed.), *Domestic violence on trial: Psychological and legal dimensions of family violence* (pp. 155–173). New York: Springer.

Gannon, L., Luchetta, T., Rhodes, K., Pardie, L., & Segrist, D. (1992). Sex bias in psychological research: Progress or complacency? *American Psychologist, 47,* 389–396.

Garcia, J. G., Cartwright, B., Winston, S. M., & Borzuchowska, B. (2003). A transcultural integrative model for ethical decision making in counseling. *Journal of Counseling and Development, 81,* 268–277.

Garcia, R. L., & Ahler, J. G. (1992). Indian education: Assumptions, ideologies, strategies. In J. Reyhner (Ed.), *Teaching American Indian students* (pp. 13–32). Norman: University of Oklahoma Press.

García Coll, C., & Magnuson, K. (1997). The psychological experience of immigration: A developmental perspective. In A. Booth, A. Crouter, & N. Landale (Eds.), *Immigration and the family: Research and policy on U.S. immigrants* (pp. 91–132). Mahwah, NJ: Erlbaum.

Garrett, J. T. (2001). *Meditations with the Cherokee: Prayers, songs, and stories of healing and harmony.* Rochester, VT: Bear & Company.

Garrett, J. T., & Garrett, M. T. (1994). The path of good medicine: Understanding and counseling Native Americans. *Journal of Multicultural Counseling and Development, 22,* 134–144.

Garrett, J. T., & Garrett, M. T. (1996). *Medicine of the Cherokee: The way of right relationship.* Santa Fe, NM: Bear & Company.

Garrett, M. T. (1995). Between two worlds: Cultural discontinuity in the dropout of Native American youth. *The School Counselor, 42,* 186–195.

Garrett, M. T. (1996a). Reflection by the riverside: The traditional education of Native American children. *Journal of Humanistic Education and Development, 35,* 12–28.

Garrett, M. T. (1996b). "Two people": An American Indian narrative of bicultural identity. *Journal of American Indian Education, 36,* 1–21.

Garrett, M. T. (1998). *Walking on the wind: Cherokee teachings for harmony and balance.* Santa Fe, NM: Bear & Company.

Garrett, M. T. (1999a). Soaring on the wings of the eagle: Wellness of Native American high school students. *Professional School Counseling, 3,* 57–64.

Garrett, M. T. (1999b). Understanding the "medicine" of Native American traditional values: An integrative review. *Counseling and Values, 43,* 84–98.

Garrett, M. T., & Carroll, J. (2000). Mending the broken circle: Treatment and prevention of substance abuse among Native Americans. *Journal of Counseling and Development, 78,* 379–388.

Garrett, M. T., & Garrett, J. T. (1997). Counseling Native American elders. *Directions in Rehabilitation Counseling: Therapeutic Strategies with the Older Adult, 3,* 3–18.

Garrett, M. T., & Garrett, J. T. (2002). Ayeli: Centering technique based on Cherokee spiritual traditions. *Counseling and Values, 46,* 149–158.

Garrett, M. T., & Garrett, J. T. (2003). *Native American faith in America.* New York: Facts on File.

Garrett, M. T., Garrett, J. T., & Brotherton, D. (2001). Inner circle/outer circle: Native American group technique. *Journal for Specialists in Group Work, 26,* 17–30.

Garrett, M. T., Garrett, J. T., Wilbur, M., Roberts-Wilbur, J., & Torres-Rivera, E. (2005). Native American humor as spiritual tradition: Implications for counseling. *Journal of Multicultural Counseling and Development, 33,* 194–204.

Garrett, M. T., & Myers, J. E. (1996). The rule of opposites: A paradigm for counseling Native Americans. *Journal of Multicultural Counseling and Development, 24,* 89–104.

Garrett, M. T., & Osborne, W. L. (1995). The Native American sweat lodge as metaphor for group work. *Journal for Specialists in Group Work, 20,* 33–39.

Garrett, M. T., & Pichette, E. F. (2000). Red as an apple: Native American acculturation and counseling with or without reservation. *Journal of Counseling and Development, 78,* 3–13.

Garrett, M. T., & Wilbur, M. P. (1999). Does the worm live in the ground? Reflections on Native American spirituality. *Journal of Multicultural Counseling and Development, 27,* 193–206.

Gaston, L. (1990). The concept of the alliance and its role in psychotherapy: Theoretical and empirical considerations. *Psychotherapy, 27,* 143–153.

Gates, G. J. (2006, October). *Same-sex couples and the gay, lesbian, bisexual population: New estimates from the American Community Survey.* Retrieved May 25, 2007, from the Williams Institute, UCLA School of Law Web site: http://www.law.ucla.edu/williamsinstitute/publications/SameSexCouplesandGLBpopACS.pdf

Gee, G. C., Delva, J., & Takeuchi, D. T. (2006). Relationships between self-reported unfair treatment and prescription medication use, illicit drug use, and alcohol dependence among Filipino Americans. *American Journal of Public Health, 96*(8), 1–8.

Gelman, C. R. (2003). Psychodynamic treatment of Latinos: A critical review of the theoretical literature and practice outcome research. *Psychoanalytic Social Work, 10,* 79–102.

Gendlin, E. (1982). *Focusing.* New York: Bantam.

Gethin, R. (1998). *The foundations of Buddhism.* New York: Oxford University Press.

Ghaffarian, S. (1998). The acculturation of Iranian immigrants in the United States and the implications for mental health. *Journal of Social Psychology, 138,* 645–654.

Gilligan, C. (1982). *In a different voice: Psychological theory and women's development.* Cambridge, MA: Harvard University Press.

Gilman, S. E., Cochran, S. D., Mays, V. M., Hughes, M., Ostrow, D., & Kessler, R. C. (2001). Risk of psychiatric disorders among individuals reporting same-sex sexual partners in the National Cormorbidity Study. *American Journal of Public Health, 91,* 933–938.

Gim, R. H., Atkinson, D. R., & Kim, S. J. (1991). Asian-American acculturation, counselor ethnicity and cultural sensitivity, and ratings of counselors. *Journal of Counseling Psychology, 38,* 57–62.

Gim, R. H., Atkinson, D. R., & Whiteley, S. (1990). Asian-American acculturation, severity of concerns, and willingness to see a counselor. *Journal of Counseling Psychology, 37,* 281–285.

Ginter, G. G. (1995). Differential diagnosis in older adults: Dementia, depression, and delirium. *Journal of Counseling and Development, 73,* 346–351.

Giordono, J., McGoldrick, M., & Klages, J. G. (2005). Italian families. In M. McGoldrick, J. Giordano, & J. K. Pearce (Eds.), *Ethnicity and family therapy* (3rd ed., pp. 616–628). New York: Guilford.

Gladding, S. (2001). *The counseling dictionary: Concise definitions of frequently used terms.* Upper Saddle River, NJ: Prentice Hall.

Gladding, S. T. (2005a). *Counseling as an art: The creative arts in counseling* (3rd ed.). Alexandria, VA: American Counseling Association.

Gladding, S. T. (2005b). *Counseling theories: Essential concepts and applications.* Upper Saddle River, NJ: Pearson Merrill Prentice Hall.

Gomes, S. L. (2000). Factors affecting Asian Indian selection of psychotherapy: Therapist ethnicity and therapy modality. *Dissertation Abstracts International, 61*(2B), 1081.

Gonsiorek, J., & Weinrich, J. (1991). *Homosexuality: Research implications for public policy.* Newbury Park, CA: Sage.

Good, B. J. (1993). Culture, diagnosis, and comorbidity. *Culture, Medicine and Psychiatry, 16,* 427–446.

Goodman, D. J. (2001). *Promoting diversity and social justice: Educating people from privileged groups.* Thousand Oaks, CA: Sage.

Gopaul-McNicol, S., & Thomas-Presswood, T. (1998). *Working with linguistically and culturally different children: Innovative clinical and educational approaches.* Boston: Allyn & Bacon.

Gordon, K. A. (1996). Resilient Hispanic youths' self-concept and motivational patterns. *Hispanic Journal of Behavioral Sciences, 18,* 63–73.

Gordon, P. A. (2003). The decision to remain single: Implications for women across cultures. *Journal of Mental Health Counseling, 25,* 33–45.

Gorst-Unsworth, C., & Goldenberg, E. (1998). Psychological sequalae of torture and organised violence suffered by refugees from Iraq. *The British Journal of Psychiatry, 172,* 90–94.

Gottschalk, S. (2000). Escape from insanity. In D. Fee (Ed.), *Pathology and the postmodern: Mental illness as discourse and experience* (pp. 18–48). London: Sage.

Gove, W. R. (1980). Mental illness and psychiatric treatment among women. *Psychology of Women Quarterly, 4,* 345–362.

Gove, W. R., & Tudor, J. (1973). Adult sex roles and mental illness. *American Journal of* Sociology, *77,* 812–835.

Greene, B. (1997). Psychotherapy with African American women: Integrating feminist and psychodynamic models. *Journal of Smith College Studies in Social Work—Theoretical, Research, Practice and Educational Perspectives for Understanding and Working with African American Clients, 67,* 299–322.

Greene, B. (2005). Psychology, diversity, and social justice: Beyond heterosexism and across the cultural divide. *Counseling Psychological Quarterly, 18,* 295–306.

Greene, M. L., Way, N., & Pahl, K. (2006). Trajectories of perceived adult and peer discrimination among Black, Latino, and Asian American adolescents: Patterns and psychological correlates. *Developmental Psychology, 42,* 218–238.

Greenwood, G. L., Paul, J. P., Pollack, L. M., Binson, D., Catania, J. A., Chang, J., et al. (2005). Tobacco use and cessation among a household-based sample of U.S. urban men who have sex with men. *American Journal of Public Health, 95,* 145–151.

Gregory, S. D. P., & Phillips, F. B. (1997). Of mind, body and spirit: Therapeutic foster care—An innovative approach to healing from an NTU perspective. *Child Welfare Journal, 76,* 127–142.

Gregory, W. H., & Harper, K. W. (2001). The NTU approach to health and healing. *Journal of Black Psychology, 27,* 304–320.

Griffin, B. (1993). Promoting professionalism, collaboration, and advocacy. *Counselor Education and Supervision, 33,* 2–9.

Griffith, B. A., & Griggs, J. (2001). Religious identity status as a model to understand, assess, and interact with client spirituality. *Counseling and Values, 46,* 14–25.

Groce, N. (2005). Immigrants, disability and rehabilitation. In J. H. Stone (Ed.), *Culture and disability: Providing culturally competent services* (pp. 1–13). Thousand Oaks, CA: Sage.

Grof, S. (1988). *The adventure of self-discovery.* New York: State University of New York Press.

Guindon, M. H., Green, A. G., & Hanna, F. J. (2003). Intolerance and psychopathology: Toward a general diagnosis for racism, sexism, and homophobia. *American Journal of Orthopsychiatry, 73,* 167–176.

Gumaer, J. (1987). Understanding and counseling gay men: A developmental perspective. *Journal of Counseling and Development, 66,* 144–146.

Gumbiner, J. (2003). *Adolescent assessment.* Hoboken, NJ: Wiley.

Gunaratana, B. H. (2002). *Mindfulness in plain English.* Somerville, MA: Wisdom.

Guthrie, R. V. (1998). *Even the rat was White: A historical view of psychology.* Boston: Allyn & Bacon.

Guzman, M. R., Santiago-Rivera, A. L., & Haase, R. F. (2005). Understanding academic attitudes and achievement in Mexican-origin youth: Ethnic identity, other-group orientation, and fatalism. *Cultural Diversity and Mental Health, 11,* 3–15.

Hackney, H., & Cormier, S. (2005). *The professional counselor: A process guide to helping* (5th ed). Boston: Allyn & Bacon.

Haddad, Y. Y. (2004). *Not quite American? The shaping of Arab and Muslim identity in the United States.* Waco, TX: Baylor University Press.

Hakim-Larson, J., & Nassar-McMillan, S. C. (2006). *Identity development in Arab American youth: Implications for practice and research.* Paper presented at the annual American Counseling Association Conference, Montreal, Canada.

Hakim-Larson, J., & Nassar-McMillan, S. C. (2008). Middle Eastern Americans and counseling. In G. McAuliffe (Ed.), *Culturally alert counseling: A comprehensive introduction* (pp. 293–322). Thousand Oaks, CA: Sage.

Hall, A. S., & Fradkin, H. R. (1992). Affirming gay men's mental health: Counseling with a new attitude. *Journal of Mental Health Counseling, 14,* 362–374.

Hall, G., & Okazaki, S. (2002). *Asian American psychology: The science of lives in context.* Washington, DC: American Psychological Association

Hall, M. (2004). Psychotherapy with African American women. [Review of the book *Psychotherapy with African American women: Innovations in psychodynamic perspectives in practice*]. *Smith College Studies in Social Work, 74,* 453–455.

Hamilton, S., Rothbart, M., & Dawes, R. M. (1986). Sex bias, diagnosis, and *DSM–III. Sex Roles, 15,* 269–274.

Hanna, F. J., Talley, W. B., & Guindon, M. H. (2000). The power of perception: Toward a model of cultural oppression and liberation. *Journal of Counseling and Development, 78,* 430–441.

Hargrow, A. (2001). Racial identity development: The case of Mr. X, an African American. *Journal of Mental Health Counseling, 23,* 222–237.

Harkness, S., & Super, C. M. (1990). Culture and psychopathology. In M. Lewis & S. Miller (Eds.), *Handbook of developmental psychopathology* (pp. 41–52). New York: Plenum.

Harley, D., Alston, R., & Middleton, R. (2007). Infusing social justice into rehabilitation education: Making a case for curricula refinement. *Rehabilitation Education, 21,* 41–52.

Harper, G. W., & Schneider, M. (2003). Oppression and discrimination among lesbian, gay, bisexual, and transgendered people and communities: A challenge for community psychology. *American Journal of Community Psychology, 31,* 243–252.

Harper, M., & Gill, C. (2005). Assessing the client's spiritual domain. In C. S. Cashwell, & J. S. Young (Eds.), *Integrating spirituality and religion into counseling: A guide to competent practice* (pp. 31–62). Alexandria, VA: American Counseling Association.

Harrell, S. (2000). A multidimensional conceptualization in racism-related stress: Implications for the well-being of people of color. *American Journal of Orthopsychiatry, 70,* 42–57.

Harrison, N. (2000). Gay affirmative therapy: A critical analysis of the literature. *British Journal of Guidance and Counseling, 28,* 24–53.

Hartman, A. (1995). Diagrammatic assessment of family relationships. *Families in Society, 76,* 111–122.

Hartung, C. M., & Widiger, T. A. (1998). Gender differences in the diagnosis of mental disorders: Conclusions and controversies of the *DSM–IV. Psychological Bulletin, 123,* 260–278.

Hartung, P. J., & Blustein, D. L. (2002). Reason, intuition, and social justice: Elaborating on Parson's career decision-making model. *Journal of Counseling and Development, 80,* 41–47.

Hashem, M. (1991). Assimilation in American life: An Islamic perspective. *The American Journal of Islamic Social Sciences, 8*(1), 83–97.

Havighurst, R. J. (1961). The learning process. *American Journal of Public Health, 51,* 1694–1697.

Haynes, E. S. (2002). *League of Arab states, Winthrop University.* Retrieved February 22, 2008, from http://faculty.winthrop.edu/haynese/_index.html

Hays, D. G., & Chang, C. Y. (2003). White privilege, oppression, and racial identity development: Implications for supervision. *Counselor Education and Supervision, 43,* 134–145.

Hays, D. G., Chang, C. Y., & Chaney, M. P. (2007). *Counselor trainees' social justice awareness, readiness and initiatives.* Manuscript submitted for publication.

Hays, D. G., Chang, C. Y., & Dean, J. K. (2004). White counselors' conceptualization of privilege and oppression: Implications for counselor training. *Counselor Education and Supervision, 43,* 242–257.

Hays, D. G., Dean, J. K., & Chang, C. Y. (2007). Addressing privilege and oppression in counselor training and practice: A qualitative analysis. *Journal of Counseling and Development, 85,* 317–324.

Hays, D. G., & Gray, G. (2010). Multicultural counseling. In B. T. Erford (Ed.), *Orientation to the counseling profession: Advocacy ethics, and essential professional foundations* (pp. 163–192). Columbus, OH: Pearson/Merrill.

Hedstrom, L. J. (1994). Morita and Naikan therapies: American applications. *Psychotherapy, 31,* 154–160.

Heflin, C. M., Siefert, K., & Williams, D. R. (2005). Food insufficiency and women's mental health: Findings from a 3-year panel of welfare recipients. *Social Science & Medicine, 61,* 1971–1982.

Heinrich, R. K., Corbine, J. L., & Thomas, K. R. (1990). Counseling Native Americans. *Journal of Counseling and Development, 69,* 128–133.

Helgeson, V. S. (1994). Relation of agency and communion to well-being: Evidence and potential explanations. *Psychological Bulletin, 116,* 412–428.

Helgeson, V. S., & Fritz, H. L. (1998). A theory of unmitigated communion. *Personality and Social Psychology Review, 2*(3), 173–183.

Helms, J. E. (1990). *Black and White racial identity: Theory, research, and practice.* New York: Greenwood Press.

Helms, J. E. (1995). An update of Helms' White and people of color racial identity. In J. G. Ponterotto, J. M. Casas, & C. M. Alexander (Eds.), *Handbook of multicultural counseling* (pp. 181–198). Thousand Oaks, CA: Sage.

Helms, J. E., & Carter, R. T. (1990). Development of the *White Racial Identity Inventory.* In J. E. Helms (Ed.), *Black and White racial identity attitudes: Theory, research and practice* (pp. 67–80). Westport, CT: Greenwood Press.

Helms, J. E., & Carter, R. T. (1991). Relationships of White and Black racial identity attitudes and demographic similarity to counselor preferences. *Journal of Counseling Psychology, 38,* 446-457.

Hencken, J. D., & O'Dowd, W. T. (1977). Coming out as an aspect of identity formation. *Gai Saber, 1,* 18–22.

Herman, J. L. (1992a). Complex PTSD: A syndrome in survivors of prolonged and repeated trauma. *Journal of Traumatic Stress, 5,* 377–391.

Herman, J. L. (1992b). *Trauma and recovery: The aftermath of violence—From domestic abuse to political terror.* New York: Basic Books.

Herring, R. D. (1990). Non-verbal communication: A necessary component of cross-cultural counseling. *Journal of Multicultural Counseling and Development, 18,* 172–179.

Herring, R. D. (1994). The clown or contrary figure as a counseling intervention strategy with Native American Indian clients. *Journal of Multicultural Counseling and Development, 22,* 153–164.

Herring, R. D. (1999). *Counseling with Native American Indians and Alaska Natives: Strategies for helping professionals.* Thousand Oaks, CA: Sage.

Hill, C., & Corbett, M. (1993). A perspective on the history process and outcome research in counseling psychology. *Journal of Counseling Psychology, 40,* 3–24.

Hill, R. (1972). *The strengths of Black families.* New York: Emerson-Hall.

Hilton, B. A., Grewal, S., Popatia, N., Bottorff, J. L., Johnson, J. L., & Clarke, H. (2001). The desi way: Traditional health practices of South Asians women in Canada. *Health Care for Women International, 22,* 553–567.

Hirayama, H., & Hirayama, K. K. (1986). The sexuality of Japanese Americans. *Journal of Social Work and Human Sexuality, 4,* 81–98.

Hirschfelder, A., & Kreipe de Montano, M. (1993). *The Native American almanac: A portrait of Native America today.* New York: Macmillan.

Hjelle, L. A., & Ziegler, D. J. (1992). *Personality theories: Basic assumptions, research, and applications* (3rd ed.). New York: McGraw-Hill.

Hoagwood, K., & Jensen, P. S. (1997). Developmental psychopathology and the notion of culture: Introduction to the special section on "The fusion of cultural horizons: Cultural influences on the assessment of psychopathology in children and adolescents." *Applied Developmental Science, 1*(3), 108–112.

Hochschild, J. L. (1995). *Facing up to the American Dream: Race, class, and the soul of the nation.* Princeton, NJ: Princeton University Press.

Hodgkinson, H. L. (1990). *The demographics of American Indians: One percent of the people; fifty percent of the diversity.* Washington, DC: Institute for Educational Leadership.

Hoffman, R. M. (2006). Gender self-definitions and gender self acceptance in women: Intersections with feminist, womanist, and ethnic identities. *Journal of Counseling and Development, 84,* 358–372.

Holcomb-McCoy, C. (2005). Ethnic identity development in early adolescence: Implications and recommendations for middle school counselors. *Professional School Counseling, 9,* 120–127.

Holstein, M., & Minkler, M. (2003). Self, society, and the "new gerontology." *The Gerontologist, 43,* 787–796.

Hong, G., & Ham, M. (2001). *Psychotherapy and counseling with Asian American clients: A practical guide.* Thousand Oaks, CA: Sage.

Hong, Y., Morris, M. W., Chiu, C., & Benet-Martinez, V. (2000). Multicultural minds: A dynamic constructivist approach to culture and cognition. *American Psychologist, 55,* 709–720.

Hong-Xin, W., Zao-Huo, C., & Hong-Xiang, M. (2006). Intensive Naikan therapy cure six patients with mental disorder. *Chinese Journal of Clinical Psychology, 14,* 324–325.

hooks, b. (1984). *Feminist theory: From margin to center.* Boston: South End Press.

Hopper, K. (1991). Some old questions for the new cross-cultural psychiatry. *Medical Anthropology, 5,* 299–330.

Horovitz-Darby, E. G. (1994). *Spiritual art therapy: An alternate path.* Springfield, IL: Charles C Thomas.

Horsfall, J. (1998). Mainstream approaches to mental health and illness: An emphasis on individuals and a de-emphasis of inequalities. *Health: An Interdisciplinary Journal for the Social Study of Health, Illness, and Medicine, 2*(2), 217–231.

Horsfall, J. (2001). Gender and mental illness: An Australian overview. *Issues in Mental Health Nursing, 22,* 421–438.

Howard, G. S. (1991). Culture tales: A narrative approach to thinking, cross-cultural psychology, and psychotherapy. *American Psychologist, 46,* 187–197.

Howell, E. (1981). The influence of gender on diagnosis and psychopathology. In E. Howell & M. Bayes (Eds.), *Women and mental health* (pp. 153–159). New York: Basic Books.

Hudson, C. G. (2005). Socioeconomic status and mental illness: Tests of the social causation and selection hypothesis. *American Journal of Orthopsychiatry, 75*(1), 3–18.

Hughes, C. C. (1996). The culture-bound syndromes and psychiatric diagnosis. In J. E. Mezzich, A. Kleinman, H. Fabrega, & D. L. Parron (Eds.), *Culture and psychiatric diagnosis: A* DSM–IV *perspective* (pp. 289–305). Washington, DC: American Psychiatric Press.

Hulse-Killacky, D., Killacky, J., & Donigian, J. (2001). *Making task groups work in your world.* Upper Saddle River, NJ: Merrill Prentice Hall.

Human Rights Campaign Fund. (2006). *The state of the workplace for gay, lesbian, bisexual, and transgender Americans: 2005–2006.* Washington, DC: Author.

Human Rights Campaign Fund. (2007). *Custody and visitation laws: State by state.* Retrieved March 4, 2007, from http://www.hrc.org/Template.cfm?Section= Custody_Visitation

Hunt, M. O. (2002). Religion, race/ethnicity, and beliefs about poverty. *Social Science Quarterly, 83,* 810–831.

Hunt, M. O. (2004). Race/ethnicity and beliefs about wealth and poverty. *Social Science Quarterly, 85,* 827–853.

Ibrahim, F. A. (1991). Contribution of culture worldview to generic counseling and development. *Journal of Counseling and Development, 70,* 13–19.

Ibrahim, F. A., Ohnishi, H., & Sandhu, D. (1997). Asian American identity development: A culture specific model for South Asian Americans. *Journal of Multicultural Counseling and Development, 25,* 34–50.

Ibrahim, F. A., Roysircar-Sodowsky, G., & Ohnishi, H., (2001). Worldview: Recent developments and needed directions. In J. G. Ponterotto, J. M. Casas, L. A. Suzuki, & C. M. Alexander (Eds.), *Handbook of multicultural counseling* (2nd ed., pp. 425–456). Thousand Oaks, CA: Sage.

Igartua, K. J., Gill, K., & Montoro, R. (2003). Internalized homophobia: A factor in depression, anxiety, and suicide in the gay and lesbian population. *Canadian Journal of Community Mental Health, 22,* 15–30.

Ina, S. (1997). Counseling Japanese Americans: From internment to reparation. In C. C. Lee (Ed.), *Multicultural issues in counseling: New approaches to diversity* (2nd ed., pp. 189–206). Alexandria, VA: American Counseling Association.

Inman, A. G. (2006). South Asian women: Identities and conflicts. *Cultural Diversity and Ethnic Minority Psychology, 12,* 306–319.

Inman, A. G., Constantine, M., & Ladany, N. (1999). Cultural value conflict: An examination of Asian Indian women's bicultural experience. In D. S. Sandhu (Ed.), *Asian Pacific Islander Americans: Issues and concerns for counseling psychotherapy* (pp. 31–41). Commak, NY: Nova Science Publishers.

Inman, A. G., Howard, E. E., Beaumont, L. R., & Walker, J. (2007). Cultural transmission: Influence of contextual factors in Asian Indian immigrant parent's experience. *Journal of Counseling Psychology, 54,* 93–100.

Inman, A. G., Rawls, K. N., Meza M. M., & Brown, A. L. (2002). An integrative approach to assessment and intervention with adolescents of color. In R. F. Massey & S. D. Massey (Eds.), *Comprehensive handbook of psychotherapy: Vol. 3. Interpersonal, Humanistic, Existential Approaches* (pp. 153–178). New York: Wiley.

Inman, A. G., & Tewari, N. (2003). The power of context: Counseling South Asians within a family context. In G.Roysircar, D. S. Sandhu, & V. B. Bibbins (Eds.), *A guidebook: Practices of multicultural competencies* (pp. 97–107). Alexandria, VA: American Counseling Association.

Inman, A. G., & Yeh, C. (2007). Stress and coping. In F. Leong, A. G. Inman, A. Ebreo, L. Lang, L. Kinoshita, & M. Fu (Eds.), *Handbook of Asian American psychology* (2nd ed., pp. 323–340). Thousand Oaks, CA: Sage.

Inman, A. G., Yeh, C. J., Madan-Bahel A., & Nath, S. (2007). Bereavement and coping of South Asian families post 9/11. *Journal of Multicultural Counseling and Development, 35,* 101–115.

Institute of Medicine. (2002). *Unequal treatment: Confronting racial and ethnic disparities in health care.* Retrieved July 22, 2007, from http://www.iom.edu/ ?id=16740

Intersex Society of North America. (n.d.). *How common is intersex?* Retrieved June 29, 2007, from http://www. isna.org/faq/frequency

Israel, T. (2003). Integrating gender and sexual orientation into multicultural counseling competencies. In G. Roysircar, P. Arredondo, J. Fuentes, J. Ponterotto, & R. Toporek (Eds.), *Multicultural counseling competencies 2003* (pp. 69–78). Alexandria, VA: American Counseling Association.

Ivey, A. E. (1988). *Intentional interviewing and counseling: Facilitating client development.* Pacific Grove, CA: Brooks/Cole.

Ivey, A. E. (1993). *Developmental strategies for helpers: Client, family, and network interventions.* North Amherst, MA: Mictrotraining Associates.

Ivey, A. E. (1995). Psychology as liberation: Toward specific skills and strategies in multicultural counseling and therapy. In J. G. Ponterotto, J. M. Casas, L. Suzuki, & C. M. Alexander (Eds.), *Handbook of multicultural counseling* (pp. 53–72). Thousand Oaks, CA: Sage.

Ivey, A. E., D'Andrea, M., Ivey, M. B., & Simek-Morgan, L. (2002). *Theories of counseling and psychotherapy: A multicultural perspective* (5th ed.). Boston: Allyn & Bacon.

Ivey, A. E., & Ivey, M. B. (1998). Reframing *DSM–IV:* Positive strategies from developmental counseling and therapy. *Journal of Counseling and Development, 76,* 334–350.

Ivey, A. E., & Ivey, M. B. (1999). Toward a developmental diagnostic and statistical manual: The vitality of a contextual framework. *Journal of Counseling and Development, 77,* 484–491.

Ivey, A. E., & Ivey, M. B. (2007). *Intentional interviewing and counseling: Facilitating client development in a multicultural society* (6th ed.). Belmont, CA: Brooks/Cole.

Iyer, D. S., & Haslam, N. (2003). Body image and eating disturbance among South Asian-American women: The role of racial teasing. *International Journal of Eating Disorders, 34,* 142–147.

Jablensky, A., Sartorius, N., Ankar, M., & Korten, A. (1992). Schizophrenia: Manifestations, incidence, and course in different cultures. *Psychology and Medicine, 26,* 1–97.

Jackson, A. P., & Meadows, F. B., Jr. (1991). Getting to the bottom to understand the top. *Journal of Counseling and Development, 70,* 72–76.

Jackson, L. C., & Greene, B. (Eds.) (2000). *Psychotherapy with African American women: Innovations in psychodynamic perspectives and practice.* New York: Guilford.

Jackson, M., & Nassar-McMillan, S. C. (2006). Counseling Arab Americans. In C. C. Lee (Ed.), *Counseling for diversity* (3rd ed., pp. 235–247). Alexandria, VA: American Counseling Association.

Jacobs, E .E., Masson, R. L., & Harvill, R. L. (2006). *Group counseling: Strategies and skills* (5th ed.). Belmont, CA: Brooks/Cole.

Jacobs, M. A., & Brown, L. B. (1997). American Indian lesbians and gays: An exploratory study. *Journal of Gay and lesbian Social Services, 6*(2), 29–41.

Jakubowska, E. (2003). Everyday rituals in Polish and English. In K. M. Jaszcolt & K. Turner (Eds.), *Meaning through language contrast* (Vol. 2). Philadelphia: John Benjamins.

James, R. K., & Gilliland, B. E. (2001). *Crisis intervention strategies* (4th ed.). Belmont, CA: Brooks/Cole.

Jamil, H., Nassar-McMillan, S. C., & Lambert, R. G. (2007). Immigration and attendant psychological sequalae: A comparison of three waves of Iraqi immigrants. *Journal of Orthopsychiatry, 77,* 199–205.

Janus, S. S., & Janus, C. L. (1993). *The Janus Report on Sexual Behavior.* New York: Wiley.

Jenkins, J. H., & Karno, M. (1992). The meaning of expressed emotion: Theoretical issues raised by cross-cultural research. *American Journal of Psychiatry, 149,* 9–21.

Jezewski, M. A., & Sotnik, P. (2005). Disability service providers as culture brokers. In J. H. Stone (Ed.), *Culture and disability: Providing culturally competent services* (pp. 37–64). Thousand Oaks, CA: Sage.

Johnson, B. W., & Raub, B. G. (2001). *SOI Bulletin: Personal wealth, 2001.* Retrieved August 31, 2007, from http://www.irs.gov/taxstats/indtaxstats/article/0,,id=9 6426,00.html#3

Johnson, H. B. (2006). *The American Dream and the power of wealth: Choosing schools and inheriting inequality in the land of opportunity.* New York: Routledge.

Johnson, J. J. (1986). *Developmental clinical psychology and psychiatry: Vol. 8. Life events as stressors in childhood and adolescence.* Beverly Hills, CA: Sage.

Johnson, M. (1980). Mental illness and psychiatric treatment among women: A response. *Psychology of Women Quarterly, 4,* 363–371.

Johnston, A. (1996). *Eating in the light of the moon.* Carlsbad, CA: Gurze Books.

Jones, B. E., & Gray, B. A. (1986). Problems in diagnosing schizophrenia and affective disorders among Blacks. *Hospital and Community Psychiatry, 37,* 61–65.

Jones, C. P. (2000). Levels of racism: A theoretic framework and a gardener's tale. *American Journal of Public Health, 90,* 1212–1215.

Jones, J. M. (1997). *Prejudice and racism* (2nd ed.). New York: McGraw-Hill.

Jones, J. M., & Carter, R. T. (1996). Racism and White racial identity. In B. P. Bowser & R. G. Hunt (Eds.), *Impacts of racism on White Americans* (2nd ed., pp. 1–23). Thousand Oaks, CA: Sage.

Jordan, J., & Hartling, L. (2002). New developments in relational-cultural theory. In M. Ballou & L. S. Brown (Eds.), *Rethinking mental health and disorders: Feminist perspectives* (pp. 48–70). New York: Guilford Press.

Jordanova, L. J. (1981). Mental illness, mental health: Changing norms and expectations. In Cambridge Women's Studies Group (Ed.), *Women and society* (pp. 95–114). London: Virago.

Josephson, J. (2005). The intersectionality of domestic violence and welfare in the lives of poor women. In N. J. Sokoloff & C. Pratt (Eds.), *Domestic violence at the margins: Readings on race, class, gender, and culture* (pp. 83–101). New Brunswick, NJ: Rutgers University Press.

Jung, C. G. (1959). *The undiscovered self.* New York: Signet.

Kakar, S. (1982). *Shamans, mystics, and doctors: A psychological inquiry into India and its healing traditions.* New Delhi, India: Oxford University Press.

Kambon, K. K. (1998). *African/Black psychology in the American context: An African-centered approach.* Tallahassee, FL: Nubian Nation Publications.

Kang, T. (n.d.). *Meditation.* Retrieved April 9, 2007, from http://www.wam.umd.edu/~tkang/meditation.html

Kaplan, A. (1987). Reflections on gender and psychotherapy. *Women and Therapy, 6,* 11–24.

Kaplan, M. (1983a). The issue of sex bias in the *DSM–III:* Comments on articles by Spitzer, Williams, and Kass. *American Psychologist, 38,* 802–803.

Kaplan, M. (1983b). A woman's view of the *DSM–III.* *American Psychologist, 38,* 786–792.

Kaslow, F. (1993). Relational diagnosis: Past, present and future. *The American Journal of Family Therapy, 21,* 195–204.

Kass, F., Spitzer, R. L., & Williams, J. B. W. (1983). An empirical study of the issues of sex bias in the diagnostic criteria of the *DSM–III* Axis II personality disorders. *American Psychologists, 7,* 799–801.

Katz, J. H. (1985). The sociopolitical nature of counseling. *The Counseling Psychologist, 13,* 615–624.

Katz, J. H. (2003). *White awareness: Handbook for anti-racism training* (2nd ed.). Norman: University of Oklahoma Press.

Kauhlwein, K. T. (1992). Working with gay men. In A. Freeman & F. M. Dattilio (Eds.), *Comprehensive casebook of cognitive therapy* (pp. 1–19). New York: Plenum.

Kawahara, D. M., & Fu, M. (2007). The psychology and mental health of Asian American women. In F. T. Leong, A. Ebreo, L. Kinoshita, A. G. Inman, & L. H. Yang (Eds.), *Handbook of Asian American psychology* (2nd ed., pp. 181–196). Thousand Oaks, CA: Sage.

Kawanga-Singer, M., & Chung, R. C. Y. (2002). A paradigm for culturally based care in ethnic minority populations. *Journal of Community Psychology, 22,* 192–208.

Kaye-Kantrowitz, M. (2000). Jews in the U.S.: The rising cost of Whiteness. In M. Adams, W. J. Blumenfeld, R. Castaneda, H. W. Hackman, M. L. Peters, & X. Zuniga (Eds.), *Readings for diversity and social justice: An anthology on racism, anti-Semitism, heterosexism, ableism, and sexism* (pp. 138–143). New York: Routledge.

Keating, T. (2002). *Open mind, open heart: The contemplative dimension of the gospel.* New York: Continuum International.

Keenan, K., & Shaw, D. (1997). Developmental and social influences on young girls' early problem behavior. *Psychological Bulletin, 121,* 95–113.

Kegan, R. (1982). *The evolving self.* Cambridge, MA: Harvard University Press.

Kegan, R. (1994). *In over our heads: The mental demands of modern life.* Cambridge, MA: Harvard University Press.

Keisling, R. (1981). Under diagnosis of manic-depressive illness in a hospital unit. *American Journal of Psychiatry, 138,* 672–673.

Kelly, G. (1990). The cultural family of origin: A description of a training strategy. *Counselor Education and Supervision, 30,* 77–84.

Kelly, S. (2003). African American couples: Their importance to the stability of African American families and their mental health issues. In J. S. Mio, & G. Y. Iwamasa (Eds.), *Culturally diverse mental health: The challenges of research and practice.* New York: Brunner-Routledge.

Kennedy, M. R. (1991). Homeless and runaway youth mental health: No access to the system. *Journal of Adolescent Health, 12,* 576–597.

Kent, M. M. (2007, December). *Immigration and America's Black population.* Retrieved July 18, 2008, from http://www.prb.org/PublicationBulletins/2007/blackimmigration.aspx

Kent, M. M. (2007). *Immigration and America's Black population.* Population Reference Bureau, 62 (4), 2-15.

Kerber, L. K., & DeHart, J. S. (2003). *Women's America: Refocusing the past* (6th ed.). New York: Oxford University Press.

Kerwin, C., & Ponterotto, J. (1995). Biracial identity development: Theory and research. In J. Ponterotto, J. Casas, L. Suzuki, & C. Alexander (Eds.), *Handbook of multicultural counseling* (pp. 199–217). Thousand Oaks, CA: Sage.

Keshishian, F. (2000). Acculturation, communication, and the U.S. mass media: The experience of an Iranian immigrant. *The Howard Journal of Communications, 11,* 93–106.

Kessler, G. E. (2000). *Ways of being religious.* Mountain View, CA: Mayfield.

Kessler, R. C., Berglund, P., Demler, O., Jin, R., Koretz, D., Merikangas, K. R., et al. (2003). The epidemiology of

Major Depressive Disorder: Results from the National Comorbidity Survey Replication (NCS-R). *Journal of the American Medical Association, 289*, 3095–3105.

Kessler, R. C., Mickelson, K. D., & Williams, D. R. (1999). The prevalence, distribution, and mental health correlates of perceived discrimination in the United States. *Journal of Health and Social Behavior, 40*, 208–230.

Kessler, R. C., Sonnega, A., Bromet, E., Hughes, M., & Nelson, C. B. (1995). Posttraumatic Stress Disorder in the national comorbidity survey. *Archives of General Psychiatry, 52*, 1048–1060.

Kilpatrick, M., Ohannessian, C., & Bartholomew, J. B. (1999). Adolescent weight management and perceptions: An analysis of the National Longitudinal Study of Adolescent Health. *Journal of School Health, 69*, 148–152.

Kim, B., & Aberu, J. (2001). Acculturation measurement: Theory, current instruments, and future directions. In J. G. Ponterotto, J. M. Casas, L. A. Suzuki, & C. M. Alexander (Eds.), *Handbook of multicultural counseling* (2nd ed., pp. 394–424). Thousand Oaks: CA: Sage.

Kim, B. S., Atkinson, D. R., & Umemoto, D. (2001). Asian cultural values and counseling process: Current knowledge and directions for future research. *The Counseling Psychologist, 29*, 570–603.

Kim, B. S. K., Hill, C. E., Gelso, C. J., Goates, M. K., Asay, P. A., & Harbin, J. M. (2003). Counselor self-disclosure, East Asian American client adherence to Asian cultural values, and counseling process. *Journal of Counseling Psychology, 50*, 324–332.

Kim, B. S. K., Ng, G. F., & Ahn, A. J. (2005). The Asian American Values Scale—Multidimensional: Development, reliability, and validity. *Journal of Counseling Psychology, 52*, 67–76

Kim, I. J., Lau, A. S., & Chang, D. F. (2007). Family violence among Asian Americans. In F. Leong, A. G. Inman, A. Ebreo, L. Lang, L. Kinoshita, & M. Fu (Eds.), *Handbook of Asian American psychology* (2nd ed., pp. 363–378). Thousand Oaks, CA: Sage.

Kimball, M. (1981). Women and science: A critique of biological theories. *International Journal of Women's Studies, 4*, 318–335.

King, M., Coker, E., Leavey, G., Hoare, A., & Johnson-Sabine, E. (1994). Incidence of psychotic illness in London: A comparison of ethnic groups. *British Medical Journal, 309*, 1115–1119.

Kingman, L. A. (1997). European American and African American men and women's valuations of feminist and natural sciences research methods in psychology. In K. M. Vaz (Ed.), *Oral narrative research with Black women* (pp. 250–259). Thousand Oaks, CA: Sage.

Kinsey, A. C., Pomeroy, W. B., & Martin. C. E. (1948a). *Sexual behavior in the human female.* Philadelphia: W. B. Saunders.

Kinsey, A. C., Pomeroy, W. B., & Martin. C. E. (1948b). *Sexual behavior in the human male.* Philadelphia: W. B. Saunders.

Kinsley, D. R. (1993). *Hinduism: A cultural perspective* (2nd ed.). Upper Saddle River, NJ: Prentice Hall.

Kirmayer, L. J., & Minas, H. (2000). The future of cultural psychiatry: An international perspective. *Canadian Journal of Psychiatry, 45*, 438–446.

Kirsh, G. A., & Kuiper, N. A. (2002). Individualism and relatedness themes in the context of depression, gender, and a self-schema model of emotion. *Canadian Psychology, 4*(2), 76–90.

Kiselica, M. S. (2004). When duty calls: The implications of social justice work for policy, education, and practice in the mental health professions. *The Counseling Psychologist, 32*, 838–854.

Kiselica, M. S., & Robinson, M. (2000). Bringing advocacy counseling to life: The history, issues, and human dramas of social justice work in counseling. *Journal of Counseling and Development, 79*, 387–397.

Kivel, P. (1996). *Uprooting racism: How White people can work for racial justice.* Philadelphia: New Society Publishers.

Klein, F. (1990). The need to view sexual orientation as a multivariable dynamic process: A theoretical perspective. In D. P. McWhirter, S. A. Sanders, & J. M. Reinisch (Eds.), *Homosexuality/heterosexuality: Concepts of sexual orientation* (pp. 277–282). New York: Oxford University.

Kleinman, A. (1986). *Social origins of distress and disease: Depression, neurasthenia and pain in modern China.* New Haven, CT: Yale University Press.

Kleinman, A. (1988). *Rethinking psychiatry: From cultural category to personal experience.* New York: Free Press.

Kleinman, A. (1996). How is culture important for *DSM–IV?* In J. E. Mezzich, A. Kleinman, H. Fabrega, & D. L. Parron (Eds.), *Culture and psychiatric diagnosis: A DSM–IV perspective* (pp. 15–25). Washington, DC: American Psychiatric Press.

Klonoff, E. A., Landrine, H., & Ullman, J. B. (1999). Racial discrimination and psychiatric symptoms among Blacks. *Cultural Diversity and Ethnic Minority Psychology, 5*, 329–339.

Kluckhohn, C. (1951). Values and value orientations in the theory of action. In T. Parsons, & E. A. Shields (Eds.), *Toward a general theory of action* (pp. 388–433). Cambridge, MA: Harvard University Press.

Kluckhohn, C. (1956). Towards a comparison of value-emphasis in different cultures. In L. D. White (Ed.), *The state of social sciences* (pp. 116–132). Chicago: University of Chicago Press.

Kluckhohn, F. R., & Strodtbeck, F. L. (1961). *Variations in value orientations.* Evanston, IL: Row, Petersen.

Kohlberg, L. (1981). *The philosophy of moral development.* San Francisco: Harper & Row.

Kosciw, J. G., & Cullen, M. K. (2001). *The GLSEN 2001 national school climate survey: The school-related experiences of our nation's lesbian, gay, bisexual, and transgender youth.* New York: Office of Public Policy of the Gay, Lesbian, and Straight Education Network.

Koss, M. (1990). The women's mental health research agenda: Violence against women. *American Psychologist, 45,* 374–380.

Krech, G. (2002). *Naikan: Gratitude, grace and the Japanese art of self-reflection.* Berkeley, CA: Stone Bridge.

Kress, V. E., Eriksen, K. P., Rayle, A. D., & Ford, S. J. W. (2005). The *DSM–IV–TR* and culture: Considerations for counselors. *Journal of Counseling and Development, 83,* 97–104.

Kroll, J. K. (1988). *The challenge of the borderline patient: Competency in diagnosis and treatment.* New York: Norton.

Kulczycki, A., & Lobo, A. P. (2002). Patterns, determinants, and implications of intermarriage among Arab Americans. *Journal of Marriage and Family, 64,* 202–210.

Kuo, W. H. (1995). Coping with racial discrimination: The case of Asian Americans. *Ethnic and Racial Studies, 18,* 109–127.

Kutchins, H., & Kirk, S. A. (1997). *Making us crazy:* DSM: *The psychiatric bible and the creation of mental disorders.* New York: Free Press.

Kwan, K. (2001). Models of racial and ethnic identity development: Delineation of practice implications. *Journal of Mental Health Counseling, 23,* 269–277.

Kwan, K. K., & Sodowsky, G. R. (1997). Internal and external ethnic identity and their correlates: A study of Chinese American immigrants. *Journal of Multicultural Counseling and Development, 25,* 51–67.

Ladany, N., Brittan-Powell, C. S., & Pannu, R. K. (1997). The influence of supervisory racial identity interaction and racial matching on the supervisory working alliance and supervisee multicultural competence. *Counselor Education and Supervision, 36,* 284–304.

LaFromboise, T. D., Coleman, H. L. K., & Gerton, J. (1993). Psychological impact of biculturalism: Evidence and theory. *Psychological Bulletin, 114,* 395–412.

Lai, P., & Arguelles, D. (2003). *The new face of Asian Pacific America: Numbers, diversity & change in the 21st century.* San Francisco: UCLA's Asian American Studies Center Press.

Lake, M. G. (1991). *Native healer: Initiation into an ancient art.* Wheaton, IL: Quest Books.

Lambert, M., & Bergin, A. (1994). The effectiveness of psychotherapy. In A. Bergin & S. Garfield (Ed.), *Handbook of psychotherapy and behavior change* (4th ed., pp. 143–189). New York: Wiley.

Lambert, M. C., Weisz, J. R., Knight, F., Desroisiers, M., Overly, K., & Thesiger, C. (1992). Jamaican and American adult perspectives on child psychopathology: Further exploration of the threshold model. *Journal of Consulting and Clinical Psychology, 60,* 146–149.

Lambert, S. (2005). The experience of gay male and lesbian faculty in counselor education departments: A grounded theory. *Dissertation Abstracts International, 66* (06A), 2113. (UMI No. 3177885)

Landrine, H. (1989). The politics of personality disorder. *Psychology of Women, 13,* 324–339.

Landrine, H., & Klonoff, E. A. (1996). *African American acculturation: Deconstructing race and reviving culture.* Thousand Oaks, CA: Sage.

Langman, P. F. (2000). Including Jews in multiculturalism. In M. Adams, W. J. Blumenfeld, R. Castaneda, H. W. Hackman, M. L. Peters, & X. Zuniga (Eds.), *Readings for diversity and social justice: An anthology on racism, anti-Semitism, heterosexism, ableism, and sexism.* New York: Routledge.

LaPlante, M. (2002). Panel presentation to the Center for an Accessible Society. Retrieved May 8, 2007, from http://www.accessiblesociety.org/topics/demographics identity/census2000.htm

Largest Religious Groups in the United States of America. (n.d.). *Top twenty religions in the United States, 2001.* Retrieved April 9, 2007, from http://www.adherents. com/rel_USA.html#religions

Larner, G. (2000). Towards a common ground in psychoanalysis and family therapy: On knowing not to know. *Journal of Family Therapy, 22*(1), 61–83.

Laungani, P. (2004). Counselling and therapy in a multicultural setting. *Counselling Psychology Quarterly, 17,* 195–207.

Lazarus, R. S., & Folkman, S. (1984). *Stress, appraisal, and coping.* New York: Springer.

Lee, C. C. (1994). *Counseling for diversity: A guide for school counselors and related professionals.* Needham Heights, MA: Allyn & Bacon.

Lee, C. C. (2001a). Culturally responsive school counselors and programs: Addressing the needs of all students. *Professional School Counseling, 4,* 257–261.

Lee, C. C. (2001b). Defining and responding to racial and ethnic diversity. In D. C. Locke, J. E. Myers, & E. L. Herr (Eds.), *The handbook of counseling* (pp. 581–588). Thousand Oaks, CA: Sage.

Lee, C. C. (2006). *Multicultural issues in counseling: New approaches to diversity* (3rd ed.). Alexandria, VA: American Counseling Association.

Lee, C. C. (Ed.). (2007). *Counseling for social justice* (2nd ed.). Alexandria, VA: American Counseling Association.

Lee, C. C., & Walz, G. R. (Eds.). (1998). *Social action: A mandate for counselors*. Alexandria, VA: American Counseling Association.

Lee, E. (1997). Overview: The assessment and treatment of Asian American families. In E. Lee (Ed.), *Working with Asian Americans: A guide for clinicians* (pp. 3–36). New York: Guilford Press.

Lee, E., & Lu, F. (1989). Assessment and treatment of Asian-American survivors of mass violence. *Journal of Traumatic Stress, 2*, 93–120.

Lee, J. A. (1977). Going public: A study into the sociology of homosexual liberation. *Journal of Homosexuality, 3*(1), 49–78.

Lee, K., Lentz, M., Taylor, D., Mitchell, E., & Woods, N. (1994). Fatigue as a response to environmental demands in women's lives. *Image, 26*, 149–154.

Lee, R. M., & Liu, H. T. (2001). Coping with intergenerational family conflict: Comparison of Asian American, Hispanic, and European American college students. *Journal of Counseling Psychology, 48*, 410–419.

Lee, S. J. (1996). Perceptions of panethnicity among Asian American high school students. *Amerasia Journal, 22*, 109–125.

Lego, S. (1996). The client with Borderline Personality Disorder. In S. Lego (Ed.), *Psychiatric nursing. A comprehensive reference* (pp. 234–245). Philadelphia: Lippincott.

Lemieux, A. F., & Pratto, F. (2003). Poverty and prejudice. In S. C. Carr, & T. S. Sloan (Eds.), *Poverty and psychology: From global perspective to local practice* (pp. 147–162). New York: Kluwer Academic/Plenum.

Leonardo, A. (2004). The color of supremacy: Beyond the discourse of "White privilege." *Educational Philosophy and Theory, 36*, 137–152.

Leong, F. T. (1986). Counseling and psychotherapy with Asian-Americans: Review of the literature. *Journal of Counseling Psychology, 33*, 196–206.

Leong, F. T., Chang, D. F., & Lee, S. (2007). Counseling and psychotherapy with Asian Americans: Process and outcomes. In F. T. Leong, A. Ebreo, L. Kinoshita, A. G. Inman, & L. H. Yang (Eds.), *Handbook of Asian American psychology* (2nd ed., pp. 429–447). Thousand Oaks, CA: Sage.

Leong, F. T., & Lau, A. S. (2001). Barriers to providing effective mental health services to Asian Americans. *Mental Health Services Research, 3*, 201–214.

Leong, F. T., Wagner, N. S., & Tata, S. P. (1995). Racial and ethnic variations in help-seeking attitudes. In J. G. Ponterotto, J. M. Casas, L. A. Suzuki, & C. M. Alexander (Eds.), *Handbook of multicultural counseling* (pp. 415–438). Thousand Oaks, CA: Sage.

Leong, F. T. L., & Gim, R. H. C. (1995). Career assessment and intervention with Asian Americans. In F. T. L. Leong (Ed.), *Career development and vocational behavior of racial and ethnic minorities* (pp. 193–226). Hillsdale, NJ: Erlbaum.

Leopold, M., & Harrell-Bond, B. (1994). An overview of the world refugee crisis. In M. A. J. Marsella, T. Bornemann, T. S. Edblad & J. Orley (Eds.), *Amidst peril and pain: The mental health and well-being of the world's refugees* (pp. 17–31). Washington, DC: American Psychological Association.

Lerner, G. (1986). *The creation of patriarchy*. New York: Oxford University Press.

Lerner, G. (1993). *The creation of feminist consciousness: From the middle ages to eighteen-seventy*. New York: Oxford University Press.

LeShan, L. (1974). *How to meditate: The acclaimed guide to self-discovery*. New York: Bantam.

Leupp, G. P. (1995). *Male colors: The construction of homosexuality in Tokugawa Japan*. Berkley, CA: University of California Press.

Levant, R. F. (1996). The crisis of connection between men and women. *Journal of Men's Studies, 5*(1), 1–12.

Leventhal, T., & Brooks-Gunn, J. (2003). Moving to opportunity: An experimental study of neighborhood effects on mental health. *American Journal of Public Health, 93*, 1576–1582.

Levine, H., & Evans, N. (1991). The development of gay, lesbian, and bisexual identities. In N. Evans & V. Wall (Eds.), *Beyond tolerance: Gays, lesbians, and bisexuals on campus* (pp. 1–24). Washington, DC: American College Personnel Association.

Lewis, G., Croft-Jeffreys, C., & David, A. (1990). Are British psychiatrists racist? *British Journal of Psychiatry, 157*, 410–415.

Lewis, G. B. (2003). Black-White differences in attitudes toward homosexuality and gay rights. *Public Opinion Quarterly, 67*, 59–78.

Lewis, J. A., Arnold, M. S., House, R., & Toporek, R. (2003). *Advocacy competencies*. Retrieved June 21,

2007, from http://counselorsforsocialjustice.com/advocacycompetencies.html

Lewis, J. A., Lewis, M. D., Daniels, J. A., & D'Andrea, M. J. (2003). *Community counseling: Empowerment strategies for a diverse society.* San Francisco: Brooks/Cole.

Lewis, K. (1998). *Prayer without ceasing: Breath prayer.* Bellevue, WA: Prescott Press.

Lewis, S. (1925). *Arrowsmith.* New York: Harcourt, Brace, & World.

Lewis-Fernandez, R., & Kleinman, A. (1994). Culture, personality, and psychopathology. *Journal of Abnormal Psychology, 103*(1), 67–71.

Liang, C. T., Alvarez, A. N., Juang, L. J., & Liang, M. X. (2007). The role of coping in the relationship between perceived racism and racism-related stress for Asian Americans: Gender differences. *Journal of Counseling Psychology, 54*(2), 132–141.

Liang, C. T., Li, L. C., & Kim, B. S. (2004). The Asian American racism-related stress inventory: Development, factor analysis, reliability, and validity. *Journal of Counseling Psychology, 51*, 103–114.

Liao, W. (2001). *T'ai Chi classics.* Boston: Shambhala.

Libbus, M. K. (1996). Women's beliefs regarding persistent fatigue. *Issues in Mental Health Nursing, 17*, 589–600.

Lichtenberg, P. A., Kimbarow, M. L., Morris, P., & Vangel, S. J. (1996). Behavioral treatment of depression in predominantly African-American medical clients. *Clinical Gerontologist, 17*, 15–33.

Lieberstein, P., Fino, J. (Writers), & Shinagawa, C. (Director). (1997). Luanne's saga [Television series episode]. In M. Judge & G. Daniels (Producers), *King of the hill.* Los Angeles: 20th Century Fox Television.

Liebkind, K., Jasinskaja-Lathi, I., & Solheim, E. (2004). Cultural identity, perceived discrimination, and parental support as determinants of immigrants' school adjustments: Vietnamese youth in Finland. *Journal of Adolescent Research, 19*, 635–656.

Lin, K. M. (1990). Assessment and diagnostic issues in the psychiatric care of refugee patients. In W. H. Holzman (Ed.), *Mental health of immigrants and refugees* (pp. 198–206). Austin: University of Texas Press.

Lin, K. M. (1996). Asian American perspectives. In J. E. Mezzich, A. Kleinman, H. Fabrega, & D. L. Parron (Eds.), *Culture and psychiatric diagnosis: A* DSM–IV *perspective* (pp. 35–38). Washington, DC: American Psychiatric Press.

Lind, A. (2004). Legislating the family: Heterosexist bias in social welfare policy frameworks. *Journal of Sociology and Social Welfare, 31*, 21–35.

Linkowski, D. C., & Sherman, S. G. (2006). Ethics: Aging population. In Commission on Rehabilitation Counselor Certification (Ed.), *Ethics for Rehabilitation Counselors, Program II* (pp. 18–22). Retrieved September 14, 2007, from http://www.crccertification.com/pages/25home_study.html

Littlefield, A., Lieberman, L., & Reynolds, L. (1982). Redefining race: The potential demise of a concept in physical anthropology. *Current Anthropology, 23*, 641–656.

Little Soldier, L. (1992). Building optimum learning environments for Navajo students. *Childhood Education, 68*, 145–148.

Liu, P. K. (1997). *Population policy and programs in Taiwan.* Honolulu, HI: East-West Center.

Liu, W. (2004). A new framework to understand social class in counseling: The Social Class Worldview Model and Modern Classism Theory. *Journal of Multicultural Counseling and Development, 32*, 95–122.

Liu, W. M., & Chang, T. (2007). Asian American men and masculinity. In F. Leong, A. Inman, A. Ebreo, L. Yang, L. Kinoshita, & M. Fu (Eds.), *Handbook of Asian American psychology* (2nd ed., pp. 197–212). Thousand Oaks: Sage.

Liu, W. M, & Iwamoto, D. K. (2006). Asian American men's gender role conflict: The role of Asian values, self-esteem, and psychological distress. *Psychology of Men & Masculinity, 7*, 153–164.

Liu, W. M., & Pope-Davis, D. B. (2004). Understanding classism to effect personal change. In T. B. Smith (Ed.), *Practicing multiculturalism: Affirming diversity in counseling and psychology* (pp. 294–310). Boston: Allyn & Bacon.

Liu, W. M., Pope-Davis, D. B., Nevitt, J., & Toporek, R. (1999). Understanding the function of acculturation and prejudicial attitudes among Asian Americans. *Cultural Diversity and Ethnic Minority Psychology, 5*, 317–328.

Llorente, E. (2002, August 12). Arabs debate need for minority status. *North Jersey News.*

Lo, H., & Fung, K. P. (2003). Cultural competent psychotherapy. *Canadian Journal of Psychiatry, 48*(3), 161–171.

Locust, C. (1988). Wounding the spirit: Discrimination and traditional American Indian belief systems. *Harvard Educational Review, 58*, 315–330.

Loevinger, J. (1976). *Ego development.* San Francisco: Jossey-Bass.

Loewen, J. W. (1995). *Lies my teacher told me.* New York: New Press.

Loftin, J. D. (1989). Anglo-American jurisprudence and the Native American tribal quest for religious freedom. *American Indian Culture and Research Journal, 13,* 1–52.

Logan, C. (1996). Homophobia? No, homoprejudice. *Journal of Homosexuality. 31,* 31–53.

Loiacano, D. (1989). Gay identity issues among Black Americans: Racism, homophobia, and the need for validation. *Journal of Counseling and Development, 68,* 21–25.

Lollar, D. (2002). *Panel presentation to the Center for an Accessible Society.* Retrieved May 8, 2007, from http://www.accessiblesociety.org/topics/demographics-identity/census2000.htm

Loo, C., Tong, B., & True, R. (1989). A bitter bean: Mental health status and attitudes in Chinatown. *Journal of Community Psychology, 4,* 283–296.

Loo, C. M., Fairbank, J. A., Scurfield, R. M., Ruch, L. O., King, D. W., Adams, L. J., et al. (2001). Measuring exposure to racism: Development and validation of a Race-Related Stressor Scale (RRSS) for Asian American Vietnam veterans. *Psychological Assessment, 13,* 503–520.

Lopez, S. R. (1997). Cultural competence in psychotherapy: A guide for clinicians and their supervisors. In C. E. Watkins Jr. (Ed.), *Handbook of psychotherapy supervision* (pp. 570–588). New York: Wiley.

Lopez-Baez, S. (1999). Marianismo. In J. S. Mio, J. E. Trimble, P. Arredondo, H. E. Cheatham, & D. Sue (Eds.), *Key words in multicultural interventions: A dictionary* (p. 183). Westport, CT: Greenwood Press.

Loring, M., & Powell, B. (1988). Gender, race, and *DSM–III:* A study of the objectivity of psychiatric diagnostic behavior. *Journal of Health and Social Behavior, 29,* 1–22.

Lott, B. (2001). Low-income parents and the public schools. *Journal of Social Issues, 57,* 247–259.

Lott, B. (2002). Cognitive and behavioral distancing from the poor. *American Psychologist, 57,* 100–110.

Lott, B., & Bullock, H. E. (2007). *Psychology and economic injustice: Personal, professional, and political intersections.* Washington, DC: American Psychological Association.

Love, P. (2001). Spirituality and student development: Theoretical connections. *New Directions For Student Services, 95,* 7–16.

Lowe, S. M., & Mascher, J. (2001). The role of sexual orientation in multicultural counseling: Integrating bodies of knowledge. In J. G. Ponterotto, J. M. Casas, L. A. Suzuki, & C. M. Alexander (Eds.), *Handbook of multicultural counseling* (pp. 755–778). Thousand Oaks, CA: Sage.

Lubecka, A. (2000). *Requests, invitations, apologies and compliments in American English and Polish.* Krakow: Ksiegarnia Akademicka.

Ludwig, T. M. (1989). *The sacred paths: Understanding the religions of the world.* New York: Macmillan.

Luskin, F. (2003). *Forgive for good.* San Francisco: Harper.

Madon, S. (1997). What do people believe about gay males? A study of stereotype content and strength. *Sex Roles, 37,* 663–685.

Manne, J. (2004). *Conscious breathing: How shamanic breathwork can transform your life.* Berkeley, CA: North Atlantic Books.

Maples, M. F., & Abney, P. C. (2006). Baby boomers mature and gerontological counseling comes of age. *Journal of Counseling and Development, 84*(1), 3–9.

Maples, M. F., Dupey, P., Torres-Rivera, E., Phan, L. T., Vereen, L., & Garrett, M. T. (2001). Ethnic diversity and the use of humor in counseling: Appropriate or inappropriate? *Journal of Counseling and Development, 79,* 53–60.

Marín, G., & Triandis, H. C. (1985). Allocentrism as an important characteristic of the behavior of Latin Americans and Hispanics. In R. Diaz-Guerrero (Ed.), *Cross-cultural and national studies in social psychology* (pp. 85–104). Amsterdam: North Holland.

Marinoble, R. (1998). Homosexuality: A blind spot in the school mirror. *Professional School Counseling, 1,* 4–7.

Markoff, L. S., Finkelstein, N., Kammerer, N., Kreiner, P., & Prost, C. A. (2005). Implementing a model of change in integrating services for women with substance abuse and mental health disorders and histories of trauma. *Journal of Behavioral Health Services and Research, 32,* 227–240.

Marks, J. (1995). *Human biodiversity: Genes, race, and history.* New York: Aldine de Gruyter.

Markus H. R., & Kitayama, S. (1991). Culture and the self: Implications for cognition, emotion, and motivation. *Psychological Review, 98,* 224–253.

Marris, J., & Jagers, R. (2001). A relational framework for the study of religiosity and spirituality in the lives of African Americans. *Journal of Community Psychology, 29,* 519–539.

Marsella, A. J. (1993). Counseling and psychotherapy with Japanese Americans: Cross-cultural considerations. *American Journal of Orthopsychiatry, 63,* 200–208.

Marshall G. N., Schell T. L., Elliott M. N., Berthold S. M., & Chun C. A. (2005). Mental health of Cambodian refugees 2 decades after resettlement in the United States. *Journal of the American Medical Association, 294,* 571–579

Marszalek, J. F., III, & Cashwell, C. S. (1998). A parallelism of Ivey's developmental therapy and Cass' homosexual identity formation model: Promoting positive gay and lesbian identity development. *Journal of Adult Development and Aging: Theory and Research, 1,* 13–31.

Marszalek, J. F., III, Dunn, M. S., & Cashwell, C. S. (2002). The relationship between gay and lesbian identity development and psychological adjustment. *"Q": The Journal of the Association for Lesbian, Gay, Bisexual and Transgender Issues in Counseling, A Division of the American Counseling Association* [Online journal], *2*(1).

Mash, E. J., & Johnston, C. (1996). Family relational problems: Their place in the study of psychopathology. *Journal of Emotional and Behavioral Disorders, 4,* 240–254.

Maslin, A., & Davis, J. (1975). Sex-role stereotyping as a factor in mental health standards among counselors-in-training. *Journal of Counseling Psychology, 22,* 87–91.

Maslow, A. (1971). *The farther reaches of human nature.* New York: Penguin.

Master Psychotherapists (n.d.). Master Psychotherapists discuss their lives and work: An interview with Albert Ellis, PhD. Retrieved March 12, 2009, from http://www.psychotherapy.net/interview/Albert_Ellis

Matheny, K. B., & McCarthy, C. J. (2000). *Write your own prescription for stress.* Oakland, CA: New Harbinger.

Matheson, L. (1996). Valuing spirituality among Native American populations. *Counseling and Values, 41,* 51–58.

Mathy, R. M., Lehmann, S. K., & Kerr, B. A. (2003). Mental health implications of same-sex marriage: Influences of sexual orientation and relationship status in Canada and the United States. *Journal of Psychology and Human Sexuality, 15*(2/3), 117–141.

Matsuoka, J., Breaux, C., & Ryujin, D. (1997). National utilization of mental health services by Asian Americans and Pacific Islanders. *Journal of Community Psychology, 25,* 141–145.

Matthews, A. K., & Peterman, A. H. (1998). Improving provision of effective treatment for racial and ethnic minorities. *Psychotherapy, 35,* 291–305.

Maylon, A. K. (1993). Psychotherapeutic implications of internalized homophobia in gay men.

In C. Cornett (Ed.), *Affirmative dynamic psychotherapy with gay men* (pp. 77–92). Northvale, NJ: Jason Aronson.

Maynard, C., Ehreth, J., Cox, G. B., Peterson, P. D., & McGann, M. E. (1997). Racial differences in the utilization of public mental health services in Washington state. *Administration and Policy in Mental Health, 24,* 411–424.

Mau, W., & Jepsen, D. A. (1988). Attitudes toward counselors and counseling processes: A comparison of Chinese and American graduate students. *Journal of Counseling and Development, 67,* 189–192.

McAdoo, H. P. (Ed.). (2007). *Black families.* Thousand Oaks, CA: Sage.

McAuliffe, G. J. & Eriksen, K. P. (1999). Toward a constructivist and development. Identity for the counseling profession: The context-phase-stage-style model. *Journal of Counseling and Development, 77,* 267–280.

McCabe, K., Yeh, M., Hough, R. L., Landsverk, J., Hurlburt, M. S., Culver, S. W., et al. (1999). Racial/ethnic representation across five public sectors of care for youth. *Journal of Emotional and Behavioral Disorders, 7,* 72–82.

McCarn, S. R. & Fassinger, R. E. (1996). Re-visioning sexual minority identity formation: A new model of lesbian identity and its implications for counseling and research. *The Counseling Psychologist, 24,* 508–534.

McClure, B. A., & Russo, T. R. (1996). The politics of counseling: Looking back and forward. *Counseling and Values, 40,* 162–175.

McClure, F. H., Chavez, D. V., Agars, M. D., Peacock, M. J., & Matosian, A. (2008). Resiliente in sexually abused women: Risk and protective factors. *Journal of Family Violence, 23,* 81–88.

McDonald, J. D., & Chaney, J. M. (2003). Resistance to multiculturalism: The "Indian problem." In J. S. Mio & G. Y. Iwamasa (Eds.), *Culturally diverse mental health: The challenges of research and resistance* (pp. 39–53). New York: Brunner-Routledge.

McGill, D. W., & Pearce, J. K. (2005). American families with English ancestors from the colonial era: Anglo Americans. In M. McGoldrick, J. Giordano, & N. Garcia-Preto (Eds.), *Ethnicity and family therapy* (3rd ed., pp. 520–533). New York: Guilford.

McGilley, B. M., & Pryor, T. L. (1998). Assessment and treatment of Bulimia Nervosa. *American Family Physician, 57,* 2743–2750.

McGoldrick, M. (Ed.). (1998). *Ethnicity and family therapy* (2nd ed.). New York: Guilford Press.

McGoldrick, M., Gerson, R., & Shellenberger, S. (1999). *Genograms: Assessments and interventions* (2nd ed.). New York: Norton.

McGoldrick, M., Giordano, J., & Garcia-Preto, N. (2005). *Ethnicity and family therapy* (3rd ed.). New York: Guilford Press.

McHenry S., & Johnson, J. W. (1993). Homophobia in the therapist and gay or lesbian client: Conscious and unconscious collusions in self-hate. *Psychotherapy, 30,* 141–151.

McIntosh, P. (1988). *White privilege and male privilege: A personal account of coming to see correspondences through work in women's studies*. Working papers #189, Wellesley College Center for Research on Women, Wellesley, MA.

McIntosh, P. (1989, July/August). White privilege: Unpacking the invisible knapsack. *Peace and Freedom*, 10–12.

McLaughlin, D. (1994). Critical literacy for Navajo and other American Indian learners. *Journal of American Indian Education, 33*, 47–59.

McLaughlin, J. E. (2002). Reducing diagnostic bias. *Journal of Mental Health Counseling, 24*, 256–270.

McWhirter, E. H. (1994). *Counseling for empowerment*. Alexandria, VA: American Counseling Association.

McWhirter, E. H. (1997). Empowerment, social activism, and counseling. *Counseling and Human Development, 29*, 1–14.

Merton, T. (1986). *Spiritual direction and meditation*. Collegeville, MN: Liturgical Press.

Meyer, I. H. (1995). Minority stress and mental health in gay men. *Journal of Health and Social Behavior, 36*, 38–56.

Meyer, I. H. (2003). Prejudice, social stress, and mental health in lesbian, gay, and bisexual populations: Conceptual issues and research evidence. *Psychological Bulletin, 129*, 674–697.

Mezzich, J. E. (1995). International perspectives on psychiatric diagnosis. In H. I. Kaplan & B. J. Sadock (Eds.), *Comprehensive textbook of psychiatry* (6th ed.). Baltimore: Williams and Wilkins.

Mezzich, J. E. (1999a). Ethics and comprehensive diagnosis. *Psychopathology, 32*, 135–140.

Mezzich, J. E. (1999b). The place of culture in *DSM–IV. Journal of Nervous and Mental Disease, 187*(18), 457–464.

Mezzich, J. E. (2002). Comprehensive diagnosis: A conceptual basis for future diagnostic systems. *Psychopathology, 35*(2–3), 162–165.

Mezzich, J. E., Kleinman, A., Fabrega, H., Good, B., Johnson-Powell, G., Lin, K. M., et al. (1993). *Cultural proposals and supporting papers for* DSM–IV (3rd rev.). Washington, DC: National Institute of Mental Health Culture and Diagnosis Committee.

Mezzich, J. E., Kleinman, A., Fabrega, H., & Parron, D. L. (1996a). *Culture and psychiatric diagnosis: A* DSM–IV *perspective*. Washington, DC: American Psychiatric Press.

Mezzich, J. E., Kleinman, A., Fabrega, H., & Parron, D. L. (1996b). Introduction. In J. E. Mezzich, A. Kleinman, H. Fabrega, & D. L. Parron (Eds.), *Culture and psychiatric diagnosis: A* DSM–IV *perspective* (pp. xvii–xxiii). Washington, DC: American Psychiatric Press.

Miles, M. (1999). Some influences of religions on attitudes towards disabilities and people with disabilities. In R. Leavitt (Ed.), *Cross-cultural rehabilitation: An international perspective* (pp. 49–57). London: W. B. Saunders.

Minow, M. (1990). *Making all the difference: Inclusion, exclusion and American law*. Ithaca, NY: Cornell University Press.

Mintz, L. B., & Wright, D. (1992). Women and their bodies: Eating disorders and addiction. In E. P. Cook (Ed.), *Women, relationships, and power: Implications for counseling* (pp. 211–246). Alexandria, VA: American Counseling Association.

Miranda, J., & Storms, M. (1989). Psychological adjustment of lesbians and gay men. *Journal of Counseling and Development, 68*, 41–45.

Miville, M. M., Constantine, M. G., Baysden, M. F., & So-Lloyd, G. (2005). Chameleon changes: An exploration of racial identity themes of multiracial people. *Journal of Counseling Psychology, 52*, 507–516.

Mobley, M., & Cheatham, H. (1999). R. A. C. E.—Racial affirmation and counselor educators. In M. S. Kiselica (Ed.), *Confronting prejudice and racism during multicultural training* (pp. 89–105). Alexandria, VA: American Counseling Association.

Mock, G. (1985). Reflections on feminine sexuality. *Journal of Social Work and Sexuality, 4* 135–150.

Molina, B., Brigman, G., & Rhone, A. (2003). Fostering success through group work with children who celebrate diversity. *Journal for Specialists in Group Work, 28*, 166–184.

Molina, B., Monteiro-Leitner, J., Garrett, M. T., & Gladding, S. (2005). Four ways of group counseling: An integrated approach for strengthening the human spirit through the multicultural traditions. *Journal for Creativity in Counseling, 1*, 5–15.

Monk, D., & Ricciardelli, L. A. (2003). Three dimensions of the male gender role as correlates of alcohol and cannabis involvement in young Australian men. *Psychology of Men and Masculinity, 4*(1), 57–69.

Moody, R. (2001). *Life after life: The investigation of a phenomenon-survival of bodily death*. San Francisco: Harper.

Moon, M. W., McFarland, W., Kellogg, T., & Baxter, M. (2000). HIV risk behavior of runaway youth in San Francisco: Age of onset and relation to sexual orientation. *Youth and Society, 32*, 184–201.

Moradi, B., & Hasan, N. T. (2004). Arab American persons' reported experiences of discrimination and mental health: The mediating role of personal control. *Journal of Counseling Psychology, 51,* 418–428.

Morales, E. S. (1989). Ethnic minority families and minority gays and lesbians. *Journal of Homosexuality, 17,* 217–239.

Moreira, V. (2003). Poverty and psychopathology. In S. C. Carr & T. S. Sloan (Eds.), *Poverty and psychology: From global perspective to local practice* (pp. 69–86). New York: Kluwer Academic/Plenum.

Morishita, S. (2000). Treatment of Anorexia Nervosa with Naikan therapy. *International Medical Journal, 7*(2), 151.

Morris, E. W. (2005). From "middle class" to "trailer trash": Teacher's perceptions of White students in a predominantly minority school. *Sociology of Education, 78,* 99–121.

Morrissey, M. (1997). The invisible minority: Counseling Asian Americans. *Counseling Today, 40,* 21–22.

Morten, G., & Atkinson, D. R. (1983). Minority identity development and preference for counselor race. *Journal of Negro Education, 52,* 156–161.

Mottarella, K. E., Philpot, C. L., & Fritzsche, B. A. (2001). Don't take out this appendix! Generalizability of the Global Assessment of Relational Functioning Scale. *American Journal of Family Therapy, 29,* 271–279.

Mui, A. C., Kang, S. Y., Chen, L. M., & Domanski, M. D. (2003). Reliability of the Geriatric Depression Scale for use among elderly Asian immigrants in the USA. *International Psychogeriatrics, 15,* 253–271.

Mullatti, L. (1995). Families in India: Beliefs and realities. *Journal of Comparative Family Studies, 26,* 11–25.

Murdock, N. L. (2004). *Theories of counseling and psychotherapy: A case approach.* Upper Saddle River, NJ: Pearson Merrill Prentice Hall.

Murgatroyd, W. (2001). The Buddhist spiritual path: A counselor's reflection on meditation, spirituality, and the nature of life. *Counseling and Values, 45,* 94–102.

Murnen, S., & Smolak, L. (1998). Femininity, masculinity, and disordered eating: A meta-analytic approach. *International Journal of Eating Disorders, 22,* 231–242.

Murphy, H. B. (1977). Migration, culture and mental health. *Psychological Medicine, 7,* 677–684.

Musen, K. (Producer). (1992). *Quiet rage: The Stanford prison experiment* [Videotape]. New York: Harper-Collins.

Mwaba, K., & Pedersen, P. (1990). Relative importance of intercultural, interpersonal, and psychopathological attributions in judging critical incidents by multicultural counselors. *Journal of Multicultural Counseling and Development, 18,* 107–117.

Myers, J. E. (1992). Competencies, credentialing and standards for gerontological counselors: Implications for counselor education. *Counselor Education and Supervision, 32*(1), 34–42.

Myers, J. E., Sweeney, T. J., & White, V. E. (2002). Advocacy for counseling and counselors: A professional imperative. *Journal of Counseling and Development, 80,* 394–402.

Naber, N. (2006). Arab American femininities beyond Arab/virgin and American(ized). *Feminist Studies, 1,* 13–21.

Naff, A. (1994). The early Arab immigrant experience. In E. McCarus (Ed.), *The development of Arab American identity* (pp. 23–35). Ann Arbor: University of Michigan Press.

Nagayama-Hall, G., & Barongan, C. (2002). *Multicultural psychology.* Upper Saddle River, NJ: Prentice Hall.

Nagi, S. Z. (1965). Some conceptual issues in disability and rehabilitation. In M. B. Sussman (Ed.), *Sociology and rehabilitation* (pp. 100–113). Washington, DC: American Sociological Association.

Nagi, S. Z. (1991). Disability concepts revisited: Implications for prevention. In A. M. Pope & A. R. Tarlov (Eds.), *Disability in America: Toward a national agenda for prevention* (pp. 309–327). Washington, DC: National Academy Press.

Narikiyo, T. A., & Kameoka, V. A. (1992). Attributions of mental illness and judgments about help seeking among Japanese-American and White American students. *Journal of Counseling Psychology, 39,* 363–369.

Nassar-McMillan, S. C. (2003). Counseling Arab Americans: Counselors' call for advocacy and social justice. *Counseling and Human Development, 35*(5), 2–12.

Nassar-McMillan, S. C. (2007). Applying the multicultural guidelines to Arab American populations. In D. W. Sue & M. G. Constantine (Eds.), *Multicultural competencies for working with people of color: Clinical practice implications* (pp. 85–103). New York: Teachers College Press.

Nassar-McMillan, S. C. (in press). *Counseling Arab Americans.* Boston: Houghton Mifflin/Lahaska Press.

Nassar-McMillan, S. C., & Hakim-Larson, J. (2003). Counseling considerations among Arab Americans. *Journal of Counseling and Development, 81,* 150–159.

National Asian Pacific American Legal Consortium. (2003). *Remembering: A ten year retrospective.* Washington, DC: Author.

National Asian Women's Health Organization. (2002). *Silent epidemic: A survey of violence among young Asian American women.* San Francisco: Author.

National Center for Education Statistics. (2000). *Educational attainment of Hispanic 25-29-year-old high school graduates, by citizenship status.* Washington, DC: U.S. Department of Education.

National Center for Health Statistics. (2001). *Health, United States, 2001, with urban and rural health chartbook.* Hyattsville, MD: Author.

National Center for Health Statistics. (2002). *Sexual behavior and selected health measures: Men and women 15–44 years of age, United States, 2002.* Retrieved June 25, 2007, from http://www.cdc.gov/nchs/products/pubs/pubd/ad/361-370/ad362.htm

National Coalition for LGBT Health. (2004). *An overview of Trans health priorities.* Retrieved June 1, 2007, from http://nctequality.org/healthpriorities.pdf

National Coalition for Women and Girls in Education. (2002). *Title IX at 30: Report card on gender equity.* Retrieved on July 1, 2007, from http://www.ncwge.org/pubs-reports.html

National Coalition of Anti-Violence Programs. (1994). *1994 Report on anti-GLBT violence.* New York: Author.

National Commission on Asian American and Pacific Islander Research in Education. (2008). *Asian American and Pacific Islanders—Facts not fiction: Setting the record straight.* New York: Author.

National Council of La Raza. (2005). *Critical disparities in Latino mental health: Transforming research into action.* Washington, DC: Author.

National Gay and Lesbian Task Force. (2007). *Hate crime laws in the U.S.* Retrieved on June 10, 2007, from http://www.thetaskforce.org/reports_and_research_/hate_crimes_laws

National Institutes of Health. (1994). NIH guidelines on the inclusion of women and minorities as subjects in clinical research. *NIH Guide, 23*(10), 1–34.

National Law Center on Homelessness and Poverty. (2005). *Key data concerning homeless persons in America.* Retrieved May 11, 2007, from http://www.nlchp.org/FA_HAPIA/HomelessnessFactsJune2006.pdf

National Organization for Women Foundation. (2001). *Lesbians and smoking: Fact sheet for the women's health project.* Retrieved March 18, 2007, from http://www.nowfoundation.org/issues/health/whp/lesbs-factsheet.html

Negy, C., & Eisenman, R. (2005). A comparison of African-American and White college students' affective and attitudinal reactions to lesbian, gay, and bisexual individuals: An exploration study. *The Journal of Sex Research, 42,* 291–298.

Nehls, N. (1998). Borderline Personality Disorder: Gender stereotypes, stigma, and limited system of care. *Issues in Mental Health Nursing, 19,* 97–112.

Neimeyer, R. A. (1995). An appraisal of constructivist psychotherapies. In M. J. Mahoney (Ed.), *Cognitive and constructive psychotherapies* (pp. 163–194). New York: Stringer.

Nelson, M. L. (2002). An assessment-based model for counseling strategy selection. *Journal of Counseling and Development, 80,* 416–423.

Neulicht, A. T., & Berens, D. E. (2004). The role of the vocational counselor in life care planning. In S. R. Grisham (Ed.), *Pediatric life care planning and case management* (pp. 277–324). Boca Raton, FL: CRC Press.

Neville, H. A., Spanierman, L. B., & Doan, B. (2006). Exploring the association between color-blind racial ideology and multicultural counseling competencies. *Cultural Diversity and Ethnic Minority Psychology, 12,* 272–290.

Neville, H. A., & Walters, J. M. (2004). Contextualizing Black Americans' health. In D. R. Atkinson (Ed.), *Counseling American minorities* (pp. 83–143). Boston: McGraw-Hill.

Neville, H. A., Worthington, R. L., & Spanierman, L. B. (2001). Race, power, and multicultural counseling psychology: Understanding White privilege and color-blind racial attitudes. In J. G. Ponterotto, J. M. Casas, & C. M. Alexander (Eds.), *Handbook of multicultural counseling* (pp. 257–288). Thousand Oaks, CA: Sage.

Newlin, K., Knafl, K., & Melkus, G. D. (2002). African American spirituality: A concept analysis. *Advances in Nursing Science, 25,* 57–70.

Newman, B. M., & Newman, P. R. (1999). *Development through life: A psychological approach* (7th ed.). Belmont, CA: Wadsworth.

Nobles, A. Y., & Sciarra, D. T. (1997). *Cultural determinants in the treatment of Arab Americans: A primer for mainstream therapists.* Paper presented at the American Psychological Association, Chicago, IL.

Nolen-Hoeksema, S. (1995). Epidemiology and theories of gender differences in unipolar depression. In M. Seeman (Ed.), *Gender and psychopathology* (pp. 63–87). Washington, DC: American Psychiatric Press.

Nolen-Hoeksema, S. (2002). Gender differences in depression. In I. H. Gotlib & C. L. Hammen (Eds.), *Handbook of depression* (pp. 492–509). New York: Guilford Press.

Nolen-Hoeksema, S., & Girgus, J. S. (1994). Mediators of the gender differences in depression during adolescence. *Psychological Bulletin, 115,* 424–443.

Northrup, J. (1997). *The rez road follies: Canoes, casinos, computers, and birch bark baskets.* New York: Kodansha International.

Norton, I. M., & Manson, S. M. (1996). Research in American Indian and Alaska Native communities: Navigating the cultural universe of values and process. *Journal of Consulting and Clinical Psychology, 64,* 856–860.

Nuckolls, C. W. (1992). Toward a cultural history of the personality disorders. *Social Science and Medicine, 35,* 37–47.

Nydell, M. (1987). *Understanding Arabs: A guide for Westerners.* Yarmouth, ME: Intercultural Press.

Oaklander, V. (1988). *Windows to our children.* Highland, NY: Gestalt Journal Press.

Office of Management and Budget. (1997). *Revisions to the standards for the classification of federal data on race and ethnicity.* Retrieved June 18, 2007, from http://health.state.ga.us/pdfs/ohip/fdre.pdf

Office of Minority Health and Health Disparities. (2007, June). *Eliminate disparities in infant mortality.* Retrieved September 4, 2007, from the Centers for Disease Control and Prevention (CDC) Web site: http://www.cdc.gov/omhd/AMH/factsheets/infant.htm

Older Americans Act. (n.d.). *Older Americans Act of 1965.* Retrieved September 9, 2007, from http://www.aoa.gov/oaa2006/Main_Site/oaa_full.asp#_Toc153957624

Olson, J. (2004). *The abolition of White democracy.* Minneapolis: University of Minnesota Press.

O'Neil, J. M., Good, G. E., & Holmes, S. (1995). Fifteen years of theory and research on men's gender role conflict. In R. F. Levant & W. S. Pollack (Eds.), *The new psychology of men* (pp. 164–206). New York: Basic Books.

O'Neil, J. M., Helms, B. J., Gable, R. K., Davis, L., & Wrightsman, L. (1986). Gender Role Conflict Scale: College men's fear of femininity. *Sex Roles, 14,* 335–350.

Operario, D., Adler, N., & Williams, D. R. (2004). Subjective social status: Reliability and predictive utility for global health. *Psychology and Health, 19,* 237–246.

Oppedal, B., Rysamb, E., & Sam, D. L. (2004). The effect of acculturation and social support on change in mental health among young immigrants. *International Journal of Behavioral Development, 28,* 481–494.

Orfalea, G. (1988). *Before the flames: A quest for the history of Arab Americans.* Austin: University of Texas Press.

Orr, J. J., & Hulse-Killacky, D. (2006). Using voice, meaning, mutual construction of knowledge, and transfer of learning to apply an ecological perspective to group work training. *Journal of Specialists in Group Work, 12,* 189-200.

Osipow, S., & Fitzgerald, L. (1993). Unemployment and mental health: A neglected relationship. *Applied and Preventative Psychology, 2,* 59–63.

Ostrove, J. M., Feldman, P., & Adler, N. E. (1999). Relations among socioeconomic status indicators and health for African Americans and Whites. *Journal of Health Psychology, 4,* 451–463.

Oswalt, W. H. (1988). *This land was theirs: A study of North American Indians* (4th ed.). Mountain View, CA: Mayfield.

Otto, R. (1958). *The idea of the holy.* New York: Oxford University Press.

Outlaw, L. (1990). Towards a critical theory of race. In D. T. Goldberg (Ed.), *Anatomy of racism* (pp. 58–82). Minneapolis: University of Minnesota Press.

Oxford University Press. (1973). *The New Oxford annotated bible: Revised standard version.* New York: Author.

Pack-Brown, S. P. (1999). Racism and White counselor training: Influence of White racial identity theory and research. *Journal of Counseling and Development, 77,* 87–95.

Palmer, L. K. (2004). The call to social justice: A multidiscipline agenda. *The Counseling Psychologist, 32,* 879–885.

Palsane, M. N., & Lam, D. J. (1996). Stress and coping from traditional Indian and Chinese perspectives. *Psychology and Developing Societies, 8,* 29–53.

Paniagua, F. A. (2005). *Assessing and treating culturally diverse cliente: A practical guide* (3rd ed.). Thousand Oaks, CA: Sage.

Pantony, K., & Caplan, P. J. (1991). Delusional dominating personality disorder: A modest proposal for identifying some consequences of rigid masculine socialization. *Canadian Psychology, 2,* 120–135.

Pargament, K. I., Ano, G. G., & Wachholtz, A. B. (2005). The religious dimension of coping: Advances in theory, research, and practice. In R. F. Paloutzian & C. L. Park (Eds.), *Handbook of the psychology of religion and spirituality* (pp. 479–495). New York: Guilford.

Parham, T. A. (1989). Cycles of psychological nigrescence. *Counseling Psychologist, 17,* 187–226.

Parham, T. A. (2001). Beyond intolerance: Bridging the gap between imposition and acceptance. In J. Ponterrotto, J. M. Casas, L. A. Suzuki, & C. M. Alexander (Eds.), *Handbook of multicultural counseling* (pp. 871–882). Thousand Oaks, CA: Sage.

Parham, T. A. (2002a). Counseling models for African Americans: The what and how of counseling. In T. A. Parham (Ed.), *Counseling persons of African descent: Raising the bar of practitioner competence* (pp. 100–118). Thousand Oaks, CA: Sage.

Parham, T. A. (Ed.). (2002b). *Counseling persons of African descent: Raising the bar of practitioner competence.* Thousand Oaks, CA: Sage.

Parham, T. A., & Helms, J. E. (1981). The influence of Black students' racial identity attitudes on preferences or counselor's race. *Journal of Counseling Psychology, 28,* 250–257.

Parham, T. A., White, J. L., & Ajamu, A. (2000). *The psychology of Blacks: An African-centered perspective* (3rd ed.). Upper Saddle River, NJ: Prentice Hall.

Parker, I., Georgaca, E., Harper, D., McLaughlin, T., & Stowell-Smith, M. (1995). *Deconstructing psychopathology.* Thousand Oaks, CA: Sage.

Parks, C. A., & Hughes, T. L., & Matthews, A. (2004). Race/ethnicity and sexual orientation: Intersecting identities. *Cultural Diversity and Ethnic Minority Psychology, 10,* 241–254.

Parks, S. D. (2000). *Big questions, worthy dreams: Mentoring young adults in their search for meaning, purpose, and faith.* San Francisco: Jossey-Bass.

Parron, D. L. (1982). An overview of minority group mental needs and issues as presented to the President's Commission on Mental Health. In President's Commission on Mental Health (Ed.), *Perspectives in minority group mental health* (pp. 52–67). Washington, DC: University Press of America.

Parrott, S., & Sherman, A. (2006). *TANF at 10: Program results are more mixed than often understood.* Retrieved September 3, 2007, from http://www.cbpp.org/8-17-06tanf.pdf

Pearson, Q. (2003). Breaking the silence in the counselor education classroom: A training seminar on counseling sexual minority clients. *Journal of Counseling and Development, 81,* 292–300.

Pearson, S. D., Katzelnick, D. J., Simon, G. E., Manning, W. G., Helstad, C. P., & Henk, H. J. (1999). Depression among high utilizers of medical care. *Journal of General Internal Medicine, 14,* 461–468.

Pedersen, P. (1991). Multiculturalism as a generic approach to counseling. *Journal of Counseling and Development, 70,* 6–12.

Pedersen, P. (1997). *Culture-centered counseling interventions: Striving for accuracy.* Thousand Oaks, CA: Sage.

Pedersen, P. (1999). Culture-centered interventions as a fourth dimension of psychology. In P. Pedersen (Ed.), *Multiculturism as a fourth force* (pp. 3–17). Philadelphia: Brunner/Mazel.

Pedersen, P. (2000). *A handbook for developing multicultural awareness* (3rd ed.). Alexandria, VA: American Counseling Association.

Pedersen, P. B., & Ivey, A. (1993). *Culture-centered counseling and interview skills: A practical guide.* Westport, CT: Praeger.

Penfold, S. P., & Walker, G. A. (1983). *Women and the psychiatric paradox.* Montreal, Quebec, Canada: Eden Press.

People for the American Way. (2003). *Hostile climate: Report on anti-gay activity, 2003 edition.* New York: Author.

Perkins-Dock, R. E. (2005). The application of Adlerian family therapy with African American families. *The Journal of Individual Psychology, 61,* 233–248.

Perry, W. G. (1970). *Forms of intellectual and ethical development in the college years.* Troy, MO: Holt, Rinehart & Winston.

Peters, M. F. (2007). Parenting of young children in Black families. In H. P. McAdoo (Ed.), *Black families* (pp. 97–124). Thousand Oaks, CA: Sage.

Peters, R. M. (2004). Racism and hypertension among African Americans. *Western Journal of Nursing Research, 26,* 612–631.

Peterson, J. V., & Nisenholz, B. (1999). *Orientation to counseling* (4th ed.). Boston: Allyn & Bacon.

Pew Hispanic Center. (2002a). *Counting the "other Hispanics": How many Colombians, Dominicans, Ecuadorians, Guatemalans and Salvadorans are there in the United States?* Washington, DC: Author.

Pew Hispanic Center. (2002b). *U.S.-born Hispanics increasingly drive population developments.* Washington, DC: Author.

Pew Hispanic Center. (2005). *Hispanics: A people in motion.* Washington, DC: Author.

Pew Hispanic Center. (2006a). *Hispanics at mid-decade.* Washington, DC: Author.

Pew Hispanic Center. (2006b). *2006 national survey of Latinos: The immigration debate.* Washington, DC: Author.

Pew Research Center for the People and the Press. (2003). *Religious beliefs underpin opposition to homosexuality.* Retrieved March 4, 2007, from http://peoplepress.org/reports/display.php3?ReportID=197

Pharr, S. (1988). *Homophobia: A weapon of sexism.* Little Rock, AR: Women's Project.

Phillips, F. B. (1990). NTU psychotherapy: An Afrocentric approach. *The Journal of Black Psychology, 17,* 55–74.

Phinney, J. S. (1990). Ethnic identity in adolescents and adults. *Psychological Bulletin, 108,* 499–514.

Phinney, J. S. (1992). The Multigroup Ethnic Identity Measure: A new scale for use with diverse groups. *Journal of Adolescent Research, 13,* 171–184.

Phinney, J. S. (1996). When we talk about American ethnic groups, what do we mean? *American Psychologist, 51,* 918–927.

Phinney, J. S., & Alipuria, L. L. (1990). Ethnic identity in college students from four ethnic groups. *Journal of Adolescence, 13,* 171–183.

Phinney, J. S., Horenczyk, G., Liebkind, K., & Vedder, P. (2001). Ethnic identity, immigration, and well-being: An interactional perspective. *Journal of Social Issues, 57,* 493–510.

Pilgrim, D., & Bentall, R. (1999). The medicalisation of misery: A critical realist analysis of the concept of depression. *Journal of Mental Health, 8,* 262–276.

Pina, A., Silverman, W., Fuentes, R., Kurtines, W., & Weems, C. F. (2003). Exposure-based cognitive-behavioral treatment for phobic and anxiety disorders: Treatment effects and maintenance for Hispanic/Latino relative to European-American youths. *Journal of the American Academy of Child and Adolescent Psychiatry, 42,* 1179–1187.

Pinderhughes, E. E., Dodge, K. A., Bates, J. E., Pettit, G. S., & Zelli, A. (2000). Discipline responses influences of parents' socioeconomic status, ethnicity, beliefs about parenting, stress, and cognitive-emotional processes. *Journal of Family Psychology, 14,* 380–400.

Plank, G. A. (1994). What silence means for educators of American Indian children. *Journal of American Indian Education, 34,* 3–19.

Plummer, K. (1975). *Sexual stigma: An interactionist account.* London: Routledge and Kegan Paul.

Poliakov, L (1974). *The Aryan Myth: A history of racist and nationalist ideas in Europe.* London: Sussex University Press.

Polivy, J., & Herman, C. P. (2002). Causes of eating disorders. *Annual Review of Psychology, 53,* 187–213.

Poll, J. B., & Smith, T. B. (2003). The spiritual self: Toward a conceptualization of spiritual identity development. *Journal of Psychology and Theology, 31,* 129–142.

Pollack, W. S., & Levant, R. F. (Eds.). (1998). *New psychotherapy for men.* New York: Wiley.

Ponterotto, J. G. (1988). Racial consciousness development among White counselor trainees: A stage model. *Journal of Multicultural Counseling and Development, 16,* 146–156.

Ponterotto, J. G. (1991). The nature of prejudice revisited: Implications for counseling intervention. *Journal of Counseling and Development, 70,* 216–224.

Ponterotto, J. G. (2001). *Handbook of multicultural counseling.* Thousand Oaks, CA: Sage.

Ponterotto, J. G., Anderson, W. H., & Grieger, I. Z., (1986). Black students' attitudes toward counseling as a function of racial identity. *Journal of Multicultural Counseling and Development, 22,* 50–59.

Ponterotto, J. G., & Casas, J. M. (1991). *Handbook of racial/ethnic minority counseling research.* Springfield, IL: Charles C Thomas.

Pope, A. M., & Tarlov, A. R. (Eds.). (1991). *Disability in America: Toward a national agenda for prevention.* Washington, DC: National Academy Press.

Pope, M. (1995). The "salad bowl" is big enough for us all: An argument for the inclusion of lesbians and gay men in any definition of multiculturalism. *Journal of Counseling and Development, 73,* 301–304.

Pope, M., & Chung, Y. B. (1999). From bakla to tongzhi: Counseling and psychotherapy with gay and lesbian Asian and Pacific Islander Americans. In D. S. Sandhu (Ed.), *Asian and Pacific Islander Americans: Issues and concerns for counseling and psychotherapy* (pp. 283–300). Commack, NY: Nova Science Publishers.

Pope-Davis, D. B., & Coleman, H. L. (Eds.). (1997). *Multicultural counseling competencies: Assessment, education and training.* Thousand Oaks, CA: Sage.

Pope-Davis, D. B., Liu, W. M., Toporek, R. L., & Brittan-Powell, C. S. (2001). What's missing from multicultural competency research: Review, introspection, and recommendations. *Cultural Diversity and Ethnic Minority Psychology, 7,* 121–138.

Portela Myers, H. (2005, April). *Immigrant identity development model.* Paper presented at the annual American Counseling Association Conference, Atlanta, GA.

Porter, R. (2003). *Madness: A brief history.* New York: Oxford University Press.

Poston, W. S. C. (1990). The biracial identity development model: A needed addition. *Journal of Counseling and Development, 69,* 152–155.

Pouget R., Yersin B., Wietlisbach, V., Bumand, B., & Bula, C. J. (2000). Depressed mood in a cohort of elderly medical inpatients: Prevalence, clinical correlates and recognition rate. *Aging, 12,* 301–307.

Prathikanti, S. (1997). East Indian American families. In E. Lee (Ed.), *Working with Asian Americans: A guide for clinicians* (pp. 79–100). New York: Guilford.

President's Advisory Commission on Educational Excellence for Hispanic Americans. (2003). *From risk to opportunity: Fulfilling the educational needs of Hispanic Americans in the 21st century.* Washington, DC: Author.

Prilleltensky, I., & Gonick, L. (1996). Politics change, oppression remains: On the psychology and politics of oppression. *Journal of Political Psychology, 17,* 127–148.

Princeton Religion Research Center. (2000). Americans remain very religious, but not necessarily in conventional ways. *Emerging Trends, 22*(1), 2–3.

Prochaska, J. O., & Norcross, J. C. (2007). *Systems of psychotherapy: A transtheoretical analysis* (6th ed.). Belmont, CA: Thomson Brooks/Cole.

Qualls, S. H. (1999). Mental health and mental disorders in older adults. In J. C. Cavanaugh & S. K. Whitbourne (Eds.), *Gerontology: An interdisciplinary perspective* (pp. 305–328). New York: Oxford University Press.

Quintana, S. M., Troyano, N., & Gaylor, G. (2001). Cultural validity and inherent challenges in quantitative methods for multicultural research. In J. G.

Ponterotto, J. M. Casas, L. A. Suzuki, & C. A. Alexander (Eds.), *Handbook of multicultural counseling* (pp. 604–630). Thousand Oaks, CA: Sage.

Ramisetty-Mikler, S. (1993). Asian Indian immigrants in America and sociocultural issues in counseling. *Journal of Multicultural Counseling and Development, 21,* 36–49.

Ratts, M., D'Andrea, M., & Arredondo, P. (2004, July). Social justice counseling: A "fifth force" in the field. *Counseling Today, 47*(1), 28–30.

Rawls, J. A. (1971). *A theory of justice.* Cambridge, MA: Harvard University Press.

Rayle, A. D., & Myers, J. E. (2003). Counseling older persons. In N. A. Vacc, S. B. DeVaney, & J. M. Brendel (Eds.), *Counseling multicultural and diverse populations: Strategies for practitioners* (pp. 253–282). New York: Taylor & Francis.

Read, J. G. (2003). The sources of gender role attitudes among Christian and Muslim Arab-American women. *Sociology of Religion, 64,* 207–222.

Read, J. G., & Bartkowski, J. P. (2000). To veil or not to veil? A case study of identity negotiation among Muslim women in Austin, Texas. *Gender & Society, 14,* 395–417.

Real, T. (1997). *I don't want to talk about it: Overcoming the secret legacy of male depression.* New York: Fireside.

Red Horse, J. G. (1997). Traditional American Indian family systems. *Families, Systems, & Health, 15,* 243–250.

Rees, D. (2001). *Death and bereavement: The psychological, religious, and cultural interfaces* (2nd ed.). Philadelphia: Whurr Publishers.

Reeves, T. J., & Bennett, C. E. (2004). *We the people: Asians in the United States, Census 2000 special reports CENSR-17.* Washington, DC: U.S. Department of Commerce.

Reich, J., Nduaguba, M., & Yates, W. (1988). Age and sex distribution of *DSM–III* personality cluster traits in a community population. *Comprehensive Psychiatry, 29,* 298–303.

Reid, P. T. (1993). Poor women in psychology research: Shut-up and shut-out. *Psychology of Women Quarterly, 17,* 133–150.

Reis, B. F., & Brown, L. G. (1999). Reducing psychotherapy dropouts: Maximizing perspective convergence in the psychotherapy dyad. *Psychotherapy: Theory, Research, Practice, and Training, 36*(2), 123–136.

Rest, J. (1979). *Development in judging moral issues.* Minneapolis: University of Minnesota Press.

Rew, L., Taylor-Seehafer, M., Thomas, N. Y., & Yockey, R. D. (2001). Correlates of resilience on homeless adolescents. *Journal of Nursing Scholarship, 33,* 33–40.

Reyhner, J., & Eder, J. (1992). A history of Indian education. In J. Reyhner (Ed.), *Teaching American Indian students* (pp. 33–58). Norman: University of Oklahoma Press.

Reynolds, A. L. (1999). Challenging our profession, challenging ourselves: Further reflections on multicultural counseling and training. In M. Kiselica (Ed.), *Confronting prejudice and racism during multicultural training.* Alexandria, VA: American Counseling Association.

Reynolds, D. K. (1983). *Naikan psychotherapy: Meditation for self-development.* Chicago: University of Chicago Press.

Richards, P. S., & Bergin, A. E. (1997). *A spiritual strategy for counseling and psychotherapy.* Washington, DC: American Psychological Association.

Richardson, J. (1999). Response: Finding the disorder in gender identity disorder. *Harvard Review of Psychiatry, 7,* 43–50.

Richardson, M. A., Myers, H. F., Bing, E. G., & Satz, P. (1997). Substance use and psychopathology in African American men at risk for HIV infection. *Journal of Community Psychology, 25,* 353–370.

Ridley, C. R. (Ed.). (2005). *Overcoming unintentional racism in counseling and therapy: A practitioner's guide to intentional intervention* (2nd ed.). Thousand Oaks, CA: Sage.

Ridley, C. R., Li, L. C., & Hill, C. L. (1998). Multicultural assessment: Reexamination, reconceptualization, and practical application. *Counseling Psychologist, 26,* 827–910.

Rivers, I. (2004). Recollections of bullying at school and their long-term implications for lesbians, gay men, and bisexuals. *Crisis, 25,* 169–175.

Roberts, R. E., Attkisson, C. C., & Rosenblatt, A. (1998). Prevalence of psychopathology among children and adolescents. *American Journal of Psychiatry, 155,* 715–725.

Robertson, J., & Fitzgerald, L. F. (1990). The (mis)treatment of men: Effects of client gender role and life-style on diagnosis and attribution of pathology. *Journal of Counseling Psychology, 37,* 3–9.

Robinson, N. (1999). *Islam: A concise introduction.* Washington, DC: Georgetown University Press.

Robinson, T. L., & Howard-Hamilton, M. F. (2000). *The convergence of race, ethnicity and gender: Multiple identities in counseling.* Upper Saddle River, NJ: Prentice Hall.

Robinson, T. N., Killen, J. D., Hammer, L. D., Wilson, D. M., Haydel, K. F., & Taylor, C. B. (1996). Ethnicity and body dissatisfaction: Are Hispanic and Asian girls at increased risk for eating disorders? *Journal of Adolescent Health, 19,* 384–393.

Roediger, D. R. (1991). *The wages of Whiteness.* New York: Verso.

Rogler, L. H. (1996). Hispanic perspectives. In J. E. Mezzich, A. Kleinman, H. Fabrega, & D. L. Parron (Eds.), *Culture and psychiatric diagnosis: A DSM–IV perspective* (pp. 39–41). Washington, DC: American Psychiatric Press.

Root, M. P. P. (1985). Guidelines for facilitating therapy with Asian American clients. *Psychotherapy, 22,* 349–356.

Root, M. P. P. (1989). *A model for understanding variations in the experience of traumata and their sequelae.* Paper prepared for the Eighth Advanced Feminist Therapy Institute, Banff, Canada.

Root, M. P. P. (1992). Reconstructing the impact of trauma on personality. In L. S. Brown & M. Ballou (Eds.), *Personality and psychopathology: Feminist reappraisals* (pp. 229–265). New York: Guilford Press.

Root, M. P. P. (1995). The psychology of Asian American women. In H. Landrine (Ed.), *Bringing cultural diversity to feminist psychology: Theory, research, and practice* (pp. 265–301). Washington, DC: American Psychological Association.

Root, M. P. P. (1998). Experiences and processes affecting racial identity development: Preliminary results from the biracial sibling project. *Cultural Diversity and Mental Health, 4,* 237–247.

Root, M. P. P. (Ed.). (1990). *Racially mixed people in America.* Newbury Park, CA: Sage.

Rosario, M., Schrimshaw, E., & Hunter, J. (2004). Ethnic/racial differences in the coming-out process of lesbian, gay, and bisexual youths: A comparison of sexual identity development over time. *Cultural Diversity and Ethnic Minority Psychology, 10,* 215–228.

Rosewater, L. B. (1986, August). Ethical and legal implications of the *DSM–III–R* for feminist therapists. In R. Garfinkel (Chair), *The politics of diagnosis: Feminist psychology and the* DSM–III–R. Symposium presented at the Convention of the American Psychological Association, Washington, DC.

Rosewater, L. B. (1987). A critical analysis of the proposed Self Defeating Personality Disorder. *Journal of Personality Disorders, 1,* 190–195.

Rothblum, E. D. (1982). Women's socialization and the prevalence of depression: The feminine mistake. In the New England Association for Women in Psychology (Ed.), *Current feminist issues in psychotherapy* (pp. 5–13). New York: Haworth Press.

Rowe, J. L., & Kahn, R. L. (1998). *Successful aging.* New York: Pantheon.

Ruan, F. F. (1991). *Sex in China: Studies in sexology in Chinese culture.* New York: Plenum.

Ruiz, A. S. (1990). Ethnic identity: Crisis and resolution. *Journal of Multicultural Counseling and Development, 18,* 29–40.

Russell, D. (1986a). Psychiatric diagnosis and the oppression of women. *Women and Therapy, 5,* 83–89.

Russell, D. (1986b). *The secret trauma: Incest in the lives of girls and women.* New York: Basic Books.

Russell, G. (1997). *American Indian facts of life: A profile of today's tribes and reservations.* Phoenix, AZ: Russell.

Russell, G. (2004). *American Indian facts of life: A profile of today's tribes and reservations.* Phoenix, AZ: Native Data Network.

Ryan, C. C., & Futterman, D. (1998). *Lesbian and gay youth: Care and counseling.* New York: Columbia University Press.

Ryder, A. G., Alden, L. E., & Paulhus, D. L. (2000). Is acculturation unidimensional or bidimensional? A head-to-head comparison in the prediction of personality, self-identity, and adjustment. *Journal of Personality and Social Psychology, 79*(1), 49–65.

Sack, W. H., Him, C., & Dickason, D. (1999). Twelve-year follow-up study of Khmer youths who suffered massive war trauma as children. *Journal of the American Academy of Child and Adolescent Psychiatry, 38,* 1173–1179.

Sack, W. H., McSharry, S., Clarke, G. N., Kinney, R., Seeley, J., & Lewinsohn, P. (1994). The Khmer adolescent project: I. Epidemiologic findings in two generations of Cambodian refugees. *Journal of Nervous and Mental Disease, 182,* 387–395.

Sacks, K. B. (1998). How Jews became White. In P. S. Rothenberg (Ed.), *Race, class, and gender in the United States: An integrated study.* New York: St. Martin's Press.

Sadler, J. Z. (2002). *Descriptions and prescriptions: Values, mental disorders, and the* DSMs. Baltimore: Johns Hopkins University Press.

Sadler, J. Z., & Hulgus, Y. F. (1994). Enriching the psychosocial context of a multiaxial nosology. In J. Z. Sadler, O. P. Wiggins, & M. A. Schwartz (Eds.), *Philosophical perspectives on psychiatric diagnostic classification* (pp. 261–278). Baltimore: Johns Hopkins University Press.

Said, E. W. (1978). *Orientalism.* New York: Random House.

Salvador, D. S., Omizo, M. M., & Kim, B. S. (1997). Bayanihan: Providing effective counseling strategies with children of Filipino ancestry. *Journal of Multicultural Counseling and Development, 25,* 201–209.

Salzberg, S., & Kabat-Zinn, J. (2004). *Lovingkindness: The revolutionary art of happiness.* Boston: Shambhala.

Samhan, H. H. (2001). *Arab Americans.* Retrieved June 23, 2008, from http://gme.grolier.com

Sanchez, E., Cronick, K., & Wiesenfeld, E. (2003). Poverty and community. In S. C. Carr & T. S. Sloan (Eds.), *Poverty and psychology: From global perspective to local practice* (pp. 123–146). New York: Kluwer Academic/Plenum.

Sanders, M. M. (2007). Family therapy: A help-seeking option among middle-class African Americans. In H. P. McAdoo (Ed.), *Black families* (pp. 97–124). Thousand Oaks, CA: Sage.

Sandfort, T. G. M., de Graaf, R., Bijl, R. V., & Schnabel, P. (2001). Same-sex sexual behavior and psychiatric disorders: Findings from the Netherlands Mental Health Survey and Incidence Study (NEMESIS). *Archives of General Psychiatry, 58,* 85–91.

Sandhu, D. S. (1999). *Asian and Pacific Islander Americans: Issues and concerns for counseling and psychotherapy.* Commack, NY: Nova Science Publishers.

Sandoval, S. R., Gutkin, T. B., & Naumann, W. C. (1997). Racial identity attitudes and school performance among African American high school students: An exploratory study. *Research in Schools, 4,* 1–8.

Santiago-Rivera, A., Arredondo, P. M., & Gallardo-Cooper, M. (2002a). The middle and last stages of counseling. In A. Santiago-Rivera, P. M. Arredondo & M. Gallardo-Cooper (Eds.), *Counseling Latinos and la familia: A practical guide* (pp. 129–145). Thousand Oaks, CA: Sage.

Santiago-Rivera, A., Arredondo, P., & Gallardo-Cooper, M. (Eds.). (2002b). *Counseling Latinos and la familia: A practical guide.* Thousand Oaks, CA: Sage.

Santisteban, D. A., Coatsworth, J. D., Perez-Vidal, A., Kurtines, W. M., Schwartz, S. J., LaPerriere, A., et al. (2003). Efficacy of brief strategic family therapy in modifying Hispanic adolescent behavior problems and substance use. *Journal of Family Psychology, 17,* 121–133.

Santisteban, D. A., & Mitrani, V. B. (2003). The influence of acculturation processes on the family. In K. Chun, P. B. Organista, & G. Marin (Eds.), *Acculturation: Advances in theory, measurement, and applied research.* (pp. 121–136). Washington, DC: American Psychological Association.

Sarbin, T. R. (1997). On the futility of psychiatric diagnostic manuals (*DSMs*) and the return of personal agency. *Applied and Preventive Psychology, 6,* 233–243.

Sarroub, L. K. (2002). From neologisms to social practice: An analysis of the wanding of America. *Anthropology & Education Quarterly, 33,* 297–307.

Savin-Williams, R. C. (2001). *Mom, Dad, I'm gay: How families negotiate coming out.* Washington, DC: American Psychological Association.

Sayed, M. A. (2003). Psychotherapy of Arab patients in the West: Uniqueness, empathy, and otherness. *American Journal of Psychotherapy, 57,* 445–459.

Sayed, M. A., Collins, D. T., & Takahashi, T. (1998). West meets East: Cross-cultural issues in inpatient treatment. *Bulletin of the Menninger Clinic, 62,* 439–454.

Schriner, K. F., & Batavia, A. I. (1995). Disability law and social policy. In A. E. Dell Orto & R. P. Marinelli (Eds.), *Encyclopedia of disability and rehabilitation* (pp. 260–270). New York: Macmillan.

Sciarra, D. T. (1999). *Multiculturalism in counseling.* Itasca, IL: F. E. Peacock.

Scott, D. A., & Robinson, T. L. (2001). White male identity development: The key model. *Journal of Counseling and Development, 79,* 415–421.

Seem, S. R., & Johnson, E. (1998). Gender bias among counseling trainees: A study of case conceptualization. *Counselor Education and Supervision, 37,* 257–268.

Seligman, L. (2006). *Theories of counseling and psychotherapy: Systems, strategies, and skills* (2nd ed.). Upper Saddle River, NJ: Pearson Prentice Hall.

Serafica, F. C. (1997). Psychopathology and resilience in Asian American children and adolescents. *Applied Developmental Science, 1*(3), 145–155.

Sered S. S., & Fernandopulle, R. (2005). *Uninsured in America: Life and death in the land of opportunity.* Los Angeles: University of California Press.

Sevig, T. D., Highlen, P., & Adams, E. (2000). Development and validation of the Self-Identity Inventory (SII): A multicultural identity development instrument. *Cultural Diversity and Ethnic Minority Psychology, 6,* 168–182.

Seymour, S. (1993). Sociocultural contexts: Examining sibling roles in South Asia. In C. W. Nuckolls (Ed.), *Siblings in South Asia: Brothers and sisters in cultural context* (pp. 45–69). New York: Guilford Press.

Shackel, P. A. (Ed.). (2001). *Myth, memory, and the making of the American landscape.* Gainesville: University Press of Florida.

Shaheen, J. G. (1997). *Arab and Muslim stereotyping in American popular culture.* Washington, DC: Center for Muslim-Christian Understanding.

Shain, Y. (1996). Arab-Americans at a crossroads. *Journal of Palestine Studies, 25*(3), 46–59.

Shakir, E. (1997). *Bint Arab: Arab and Arab American women in the United States.* Westport, CT: Praeger.

Shannon, J. W., & Woods, W. J. (1991). Affirmative psychotherapy with gay men. *The Counseling Psychologist, 19,* 197–215.

Shastri, H. P. (n.d.). *Brahman and Atman.* Retrieved on April 9, 2007, from http://www.self-knowledge.org/latest/05sum/brahmanAndAtman.htm

Shea, M., Ma, P. W., & Yeh, C. J. (2007). Development of a culturally specific career exploration group for urban Chinese immigrant youth. *The Career Development Quarterly, 56,* 62–73

Sherman, J. A. (1980). Therapist attitudes and sex-role stereotyping. In A. M. Brodsky & R. T. Hare-Mustin (Eds.),

Women and psychotherapy: An assessment of research and practice (pp. 35–45). New York: Guilford Press.

Shively, M. G., & DeCecco, J. P. (1993). Components of sexual identity. In L. D. Garnets & D. C. Kimmel (Eds.), *Psychological perspectives on lesbian and gay male experiences* (pp. 80–88). New York: Columbia University Press.

Shorris, E. (1992). *Latinos: A biography of the people.* New York: Norton.

Shreeve, J. (2006, March). The greatest journey. *National Geographic,* 61–69.

Shweder, R. (1985). Menstrual pollution, soul loss, and the comparative study of emotions. In A. Kleinman & B. Good (Eds.), *Culture and depression* (pp. 182–215). Berkeley: University of California Press.

Simpkins, C. A., & Simpkins, A. (1999). *Simple Taoism: A guide to living in balance.* Boston: Tuttle.

Sinacore-Guinn, A. L. (1992, October). *Cultural considerations in diagnosis: A multi-faceted approach.* Paper presented at the conference of the Chicago School of Professional Development on "Cultural Impact: Meeting the Challenge of Growing Up in a Changing America," Chicago, IL.

Sinacore-Guinn, A. L. (1995). The diagnostic window: Culture-and gender-sensitive diagnosis and training. *Counselor Education and Supervision, 35,* 18.

Sinacore-Guinn, A. L., & Bahr, M. (1993a, April). *Diagnosis and culture: Working toward an integrative assessment model.* Paper presented at the annual meeting of the Great Lakes Regional Conference for Counseling Psychology, Division 17, American Psychological Association, Bloomington, IN.

Sinacore-Guinn, A. L., & Bahr, M. (1993b, August). *Cultural considerations in the assessment of children.* Paper presented at the national convention of the American Psychological Association, Division 16, Toronto, Ontario, Canada.

Singh, A. A. (2006). Resilience strategies of South Asian women who have survived child sexual abuse. *Dissertation Abstracts International: Section B: The Sciences and Engineering, 67*(8-B), 4722.

Singh, A. A., & Hays, D. G. (2008). Feminist group counseling with South Asian women who have survived intimate partner violence. *Journal of Specialists in Group Work, 33*(1), 84–102.

Singh, A. A., Hays, D. G., & Watson, L. S. (2008). *Strength in the face of adversity: Resilience strategies of transgender individuals.* Manuscript submitted for publication.

Skillings, J. H., & Dobbins, J. E. (1991). Racism as a disease: Etiology and treatment implications. *Journal of Counseling and Development, 70,* 206–212.

Sloan, T. S. (2003). Poverty and psychology: A call to arms. In S. C. Carr & T. S. Sloan (Eds.), *Poverty and psychology: From global perspective to local practice* (pp. 301–314). New York: Kluwer Academic/Plenum.

Smart, D. W., & Smart, J. F. (1997). DSM–IV and culturally sensitive diagnosis: Some observations for counselors. *Journal of Counseling and Development, 75,* 392–398.

Smart, J. F., & Smart, D. W. (2006). Models of disability: Implications for the counseling profession. *Journal of Counseling and Development, 84*(1), 29–40.

Smedley, A. (1999). *Race in North America: Origin and evolution of a worldview* (2nd ed.). Boulder, CO: Westview Press.

Smedley, A. (2006). *Race in North America: Origin and evolution of a worldview* (3rd ed.). Boulder, CO: Westview Press.

Smedley, A., & Smedley, B. D. (2005). Race as biology is fiction, racism as a social problem is real: Anthropological and historical perspectives on the social construction of race. *American Psychologist, 60,* 16–26.

Smith, D. (2001). Assessing the needs of lesbian, gay, and bisexual youth. *Monitor on Psychology, 32,* 42–43.

Smith, D., & Smith, G. (1998). The ideology of "fag": The school experience of gay students. *Sociological Quarterly, 39,* 309–316.

Smith, H. (1991). *The world's religions: Our great wisdom traditions.* San Francisco: Harper.

Smith, H. (2001). *Why religion matters: The fate of the human spirit in an age of disbelief.* San Francisco: Harper.

Smith, H. (2003). *Cleansing the doors of perception: The religious significance of entheogenic plants and chemicals.* Boulder, CO: Sentient.

Smith, L. (2005). Psychotherapy, classism, and the poor: Conspicuous by their absence. *American Psychologist, 60,* 687–696.

Smith, N. G., & Ingram, K. M. (2004). Workplace heterosexism and adjustment among lesbian, gay, and bisexual individuals: The role of unsupportive social interactions. *Journal of Counseling Psychology, 51,* 57–67.

Smolak, L. (2002). The relationship of gender and voice to depression and eating disorders. *Psychology of Women Quarterly, 26,* 234–242.

Snyder, D. (1992). *The misdiagnosis of men in gender nontraditional roles.* Unpublished manuscript.

Social Security Online. (2007). *The full retirement age is increasing.* Retrieved September 9, 2007, from http://www.ssa.gov/pubs/ageincrease.htm

Sodowsky, G. R., Kwan, K. K., & Pannu, R. (1995). Ethnic identity of Asians in the United States. In J. G. Ponterotto,

J. M. Casas, L. A. Suzuki, & C. M. Alexander (Eds.), *Handbook of multicultural counseling* (pp. 123–154). Thousand Oaks, CA: Sage.

Solberg, V. S., Ritsma, S., Davis, B. J., Tata, S. P., & Jolly, A. (1994). Asian-American students' severity of problems and willingness to seek help from university counseling centers: Role of previous counseling experience, gender, and ethnicity. *Journal of Counseling Psychology, 41,* 275–279.

Sophie, J. (1986). A critical examination of stage theories of lesbian identity development. *Journal of Homosexuality, 12*(2), 39–51.

Sotnik, P., & Jezewski, M. A. (2005). Culture and the disability services. In J. H. Stone (Ed.), *Culture and disability: Providing culturally competent services* (pp. 15–36). Thousand Oaks, CA: Sage.

Spanierman, L. B., & Heppner, M. J. (2004). Psychosocial costs of racism to White scale (PCRW): Construction and initial validation. *Journal of Counseling Psychology, 51,* 249–262.

Spanierman, L. B., Poteat, V. P., Beer, A. M., & Armstrong, P. I. (2006). Psychosocial costs of racism to Whites: Exploring patterns through cluster analysis. *Journal of Counseling Psychology, 53,* 434–441.

Speight, S. L., & Vera, E. M. (2004). A social justice agenda: Ready or not? *The Counseling Psychologist, 32,* 109–118.

Sperry, L. (2002). From psychopathology to transformation: Retrieving the developmental focus in psychotherapy. *Journal of Individual Psychology, 58,* 398–421.

Sporakowski, M. J. (1995). Assessment and diagnosis in marriage and family counseling. *Journal of Counseling and Development, 74,* 60–64.

Springer, D. W., Lynch, C., & Allen, R. (2000). Effects of a solution-focused mutual aid group for Hispanic children of incarcerated parents. *Child and Adolescent Social Work Journal, 17,* 431–442.

Sprock, J., & Yoder, C. (1997). Women and depression. *Sex Roles, 36,* 269–303.

Steinberg, L. (1990). Autonomy, conflict, and harmony in the family relationship. In S. Freedman & G. Elliott (Eds.), *At the threshold: The developing adolescent* (pp. 255–276). Cambridge, MA: Harvard University Press.

Stephens, D., & Phillips, L. (2003). Freaks, gold diggers, divas, and dykes: The sociohistorical development of adolescent African American Women's sexual scripts. *Sexuality and Culture, 7,* 3–49.

Stone, C. B. (2003). Counselors as advocates for gay, lesbian, and bisexual youth: A call for equity and action. *Journal of Multicultural Counseling and Development, 31,* 143–155.

Stone, J. H. (Ed.). (2005). *Culture and disability: Providing culturally competent services.* Thousand Oaks, CA: Sage.

Story, M., French, S. A., Neumark-Sztainer, D., Downes, B., Resnick, M. D., & Blum, R. W. (1997). Psychosocial and behavioral correlates of dieting and purging in Native American adolescents. *Pediatrics, 99,* 1–8.

Striegel-Moore, R. (1997). Risk factors for eating disorders. *Annual New York Academy of Sciences, 817,* 98–109.

Striepe, M. I., & Tolman, D. L. (2003). Mom, Dad, I'm straight: The coming out of gender ideologies in adolescent sexual identity development. *Journal of Clinical and Adolescent Psychology, 32,* 523–530.

Suan, L. V., & Tyler, J. D. (1990). Mental health values and preference for mental health resources of Japanese-American and Caucasian-American students. *Professional Psychology: Research and Practice, 21,* 291–296.

Sue, D. W. (1978). Eliminating cultural oppression in counseling: Toward a general theory. *Journal of Counseling Psychology, 25,* 419–428.

Sue, D. W. (1994). Mental health. In N. Zane, D. T., Takeuchi, & K. Young (Eds.), *Confronting critical health issues of Asian and Pacific Islander Americans* (pp. 266–288). Newbury Park, CA: Sage.

Sue, D. W. (1995). Towards a theory of multicultural counseling and therapy. In J. A. Banks & C. A. M. Banks (Eds.), *Handbook of research multicultural education* (pp. 647–659). New York: Macmillan.

Sue, D. W. (1997). Counseling strategies for Chinese Americans. In C. C. Lee (Ed.), *Multicultural issues in counseling: New approaches to diversity* (2nd ed., pp. 173–187). Alexandria, VA: American Counseling Association.

Sue, D. W. (2001). Surviving monoculturalism and racism: A personal and professional journey. In J. G. Ponterotto, J. M. Casas, L. A. Suzuki, & C. M. Alexander (Eds.), *Handbook of multicultural counseling* (2nd ed., pp. 289–310). Thousand Oaks, CA: Sage.

Sue, D. W. (2004). Whiteness and ethnocentric multiculturalism: Making the "invisible" visible. *American Psychologist, 59,* 759–769.

Sue, D. W., Arredondo, P., & McDavis, R. J. (1992). Multicultural counseling competencies and standards: A call to the profession. *Journal of Counseling and Development, 70,* 477–486.

Sue, D. W., Bernier, J. E., Durran, A., Feinberg, L., Pedersen P., Smith, E. J., et al. (1982). Position paper: Cross-cultural counseling competencies. *The Counseling Psychologist, 10,* 45–52.

Sue, D. W., Bucceri, J., Lin, A. L., Nadal, K. L., & Torino, G. C. (2007). Racial microaggressions and the Asian American experience. *Cultural Diversity & Ethnic Minority Psychology, 13,* 72–81.

Sue, D. W., Capodilupo, C. M., Torino, G. C., Bucceri, J. M., Holder, A. M. B., Nadal, K. L., et al. (2007). Racial microaggressions in everyday life: Implications for clinical practice. *American Psychologist, 62,* 271–286.

Sue, D. W., Ivey, A. E., & Pedersen, P. B. (Eds.). (1996). *A theory of multicultural counseling and therapy.* Pacific Grove, CA: Brooks/Cole.

Sue, D. W., & Sue, D. (2003). *Counseling the culturally diverse: Theory and practice* (4th ed.). New York: Wiley.

Sue, S. (1977). Community mental health services to minority groups: Some optimism, some pessimism. *American Psychologist, 32,* 616–624.

Sue, S. (1999). Asian American mental health: What we know and what we don't know. In W. J. Lonner, D. L., Dinnel, D. K. Forgays, & S. A. Hayes (Eds.), *Merging past, present, and future in cross-cultural psychology: Selected papers from the Fourteenth International Congress of the International Association for Cross-Cultural Psychology* (pp. 82–89). Lisse, Netherlands: Swets & Zeitlinger.

Sue, S., Fujino, D. C., Hu, L., Takeuchi, D. T., & Zane, N. (1991). Community mental health services for ethnic minority groups: A test of the cultural responsiveness hypothesis. *Journal of Consulting and Clinical Psychology, 59,* 533–540.

Sue, S., & McKinney, H. (1975). Asian-Americans in the community health care system. *American Journal of Orthopsychiatry, 45,* 111–118.

Sue, S., & Okazaki, S. (1990). Asian American educational achievements: A phenomenon in search of an explanation. *American Psychologist, 45,* 913–920.

Sue, S., Sue, D. W., Sue, L., & Takeuchi, D. T. (1995). Psychopathology among Asian Americans: A model minority? *Cultural Diversity and Mental Health, 1,* 39–51.

Suggs, D. N., & Miracle, A. W. (1993). *Culture and human sexuality: A reader.* Belmont, CA: Thomson Brooks/Cole.

Suwaki, H. (1979). Naikan and Danshukai for the treatment of Japanese alcoholic patients. *British Journal of Addiction, 74,* 15–19.

Suwaki, H. (1985). International review series: Alcohol and alcohol problems research: II. Japan. *British Journal of Addiction, 80,* 127–132.

Swim, J. K., & Miller, D. L. (1999). White guilt: Its antecedents and consequences for attitudes toward affirmative action. *Personality and Social Psychology Bulletin, 25,* 500–514.

Szapocznik, J., Kurtines, W., & Fernandez, T. (1980). Biculturalism and adjustment among Hispanic youths. *International Journal of Intercultural Relations, 4,* 353–375.

Szasz, T. S. (1974). *The myth of mental illness.* New York: Harper & Row.

Szasz, T. S. (2002). *Liberation by oppression: A comparative study of slavery and psychiatry.* New Brunswick, NJ: Transaction.

Szymanski, D. M. (2005). Heterosexism and sexism as correlates of psychological distress in lesbians. *Journal of Counseling and Development, 83,* 355–360.

Szymanski, D. M., & Chung Y. B. (2001). The Lesbian Internalized Homophobia Scale: A rational/theoretical approach. *Journal of Homosexuality, 41,* 37–52.

Szymanski, D. M., & Chung, Y. B. (2003). Internalized homophobia in lesbians. *Journal of Lesbian Studies, 7,* 115–125.

Takaki, R. (1998). *A history of Asian Americans: Strangers from a different shore.* New York: Little, Brown.

Takaki, R. (2002a). The "Indian question": From reservation to reorganization. In R. Takaki (Ed.), *Debating diversity: Clashing perspectives on race and ethnicity in America* (3rd ed., pp. 228–244). New York: Oxford University Press.

Takaki, R. (2002b). Reflections on racial patterns in America. In R. Takaki (Ed.), *Race and ethnicity in America* (3rd ed., pp. 23–36). New York: Oxford University Press.

Takeda, J. (2000). Psychological and economic adaptation of Iraqi adult male refugees: Implications for social work practice. *Journal of Social Service Research, 26,* 1–21.

Takeuchi, D. T., Cheng, R. C. Y., Lin, K. M., Shen, H., Kurasaki, K., Chun, C., et al. (1998). Lifetime and twelve-month prevalence rates of major depressive episodes and dysthymia among Chinese Americans in Los Angeles. *American Journal of Psychiatry, 155,* 1407–1414.

Takeuchi, D. T., Sue, S., & Yeh, M. (1995). Return rates and outcomes from ethnicity-specific mental health programs in Los Angeles. *American Journal of Public Health, 85,* 638–643.

Takeuchi, D. T., Zane, N., Hong, S., Chae, D. H., Fang, G., Gee, G. C., et al. (2007). Immigration-related factors and mental disorders among Asian Americans. *American Journal of Public Health, 97*(1), 84–90.

Tang, H., Greenwood, G. L., Cowling, D. W., Lloyd, J. C., Roeseler, A. G., & Bal, D. G. (2004). Cigarette smoking among lesbians, gays, and bisexuals: How serious a problem? *Cancer Causes and Control, 15,* 797–803.

Tatum, B. D. (2003). *Why are all the Black kids sitting together in the cafeteria? And other conversations about race.* New York: Basic Books.

Taylor, J., Gilligan, C., & Sullivan, A. (1995). *Between voice and silence: Women and girls, race and relationship.* Cambridge, MA: Harvard University Press.

Taylor, K. (1994). *The breathwork experience: Exploration and healing in nonordinary states of consciousness.* Santa Cruz, CA: Hanford Mead.

Taylor, R. J., Hardison, C. B., & Chatters, L. M. (1996). Kin and nonkin as sources of informal assistance. In H. W. Neighbors & J. S. Jackson (Eds.), *Mental health in Black America* (pp. 130–160). Thousand Oaks, CA: Sage.

Tewari, N., Inman, A. G., & Sandhu, D. S. (2003). South Asian Americans: Culture, concerns and therapeutic strategies. In J. Mio & G. Iwamasa (Eds.), *Culturally diverse mental health: The challenges of research and resistance* (pp. 191–209). New York: Brunner-Routledge.

Thomas, A., & Sillen, S. (1972). *Racism and psychiatry.* New York: Brunner/Mazel.

Thomason, T. C. (1991). Counseling Native Americans: An introduction for non-Native American counselors. *Journal of Counseling and Development, 69,* 321–327.

Thompson, C. E., & Isaac, K. (2004). African Americans: Treatment issues and recommendations. In D. R. Atkinson (Ed.), *Counseling American minorities* (pp. 125–143). Boston: McGraw-Hill.

Thompson, C. E., & Jenal, S. T. (1994). Interracial and intraracial quasi-counseling interactions when counselors avoid discussing race. *Journal of Counseling Psychology, 41,* 484-491.

Thompson, C. E., & Neville, H. A. (1999). Racism, mental health, and mental health practice. *The Counseling Psychologist, 27,* 155–223.

Thompson, C. E., Worthington, R., & Atkinson, D. R. (1994). Counselor content orientation, counselor race and Black women's cultural mistrust and self-disclosures. *Journal of Counseling Psychology, 41,* 155–161.

Thompson, J. W. (1996). Native American perspectives. In J. E. Mezzich, A. Kleinman, H. Fabrega, & D. L. Parron (Eds.), *Culture and psychiatric diagnosis: A* DSM–IV *perspective* (pp. 31–33). Washington, DC: American Psychiatric Press.

Thompson, W., & Hickey, J. (2005). *Society in focus.* Boston: Pearson.

Tiefer, L. (1995). *Sex is not a natural act, and other essays.* Boulder, CO: Westview Press.

Tiggeman, M., & Pinkering, A. S. (1996). Role of television in adolescent women's body dissatisfaction and drive for thinness. *International Journal of Eating Disorders, 20,* 199–203.

Tipping, C. (2002). *Radical forgiveness: Making room for the miracle.* Northboro, MA: Quest.

Tisdell, E. J., (2007). In the new millennium: The role of spirituality and the cultural imagination in dealing with diversity and equity in the higher education classroom. *Teachers College Record, 109,* 531–560.

Tjadden, P., & Thoennes, N. (2000). *Extent, nature and consequences of intimate partner violence: Findings from the National Violence Against Women Survey.* Washington, DC: U.S. Department of Justice.

Tolman, D. (2002). *Dilemmas of desire: Teenage girls talk about sexuality.* Cambridge, MA: Harvard University Press.

Tomm, K. (1989). Externalizing the problem and increasing personal agency. *Journal of Strategic and Systemic Therapies, 8,* 54–59.

Toporek, R. L., & Williams, R. A. (2006). Ethics and the professional issues related to the practice of social justice in counseling psychology. In R. L. Toropek, L. H. Gerstein, N. A. Fouad, G. Roysircar, & T. Israel (Eds.), *Handbook for social justice in counseling psychology* (pp. 17–34). Thousand Oaks, CA: Sage.

Toro-Morn, M. I. (1998). The family and work experiences of Puerto Rican women migrants in Chicago. In H. McCubbin, E. Thompson, A. Thompson, & J. Fromer (Eds.), *Resiliency in Native American and immigrant families* (pp. 277–294). Thousand Oaks, CA: Sage.

Torres-Rivera, E. (2004). Psychoeducational and counseling groups with Latinos. In J. DeLucia-Waack, D. Gerrity, C. Kalodner, & M. Riva (Eds.), *Handbook of group counseling and psychotherapy* (pp. 213–223). Thousand Oaks, CA: Sage.

Tracey, T. J., Leong, F. T., & Glidden, C. (1986). Help seeking and problem perception among Asian Americans. *Journal of Counseling Psychology, 33,* 331–336.

Travis, C. B., & Compton, J. D. (2001). Feminism and health in a decade of behavior. *Psychology of Women Quarterly, 25,* 312–323.

Trevino, J. G. (1996). Worldview and change in cross-cultural counseling. *The Counseling Psychologist, 24,* 198–215.

Troiden, R. (1979). Becoming homosexual: A model of gay identity acquisition. *Psychiatry, 42,* 362–373.

Troiden, R. (1984). Self, self-concept, identity, and homosexual identity: Constructs in need of definition and differentiation. *Journal of Homosexuality, 10*(3/4), 97–109.

Troiden, R. (1988). Homosexual identity development. *Journal of Adolescent Health Care, 9,* 105–113.

Troiden, R. R. (1989). The formation of homosexual identities. *Journal of Homosexuality, 17,* 159–178.

Truitner, K., & Truitner, N. (1993). Death and dying in Buddhism. In D. P. Irish, K. F. Lundquist, & V. J. Nelsen (Eds.), *Ethnic variations in dying, death, and grief:*

Diversity in universality (pp. 125–136). Philadelphia: Taylor & Francis.

Tse, L. (1999). Finding a place to be: Ethnic identity exploration of Asian Americans. *Adolescence, 34,* 121–138.

Tseng, W. S. (2001). *Handbook of cultural psychiatry.* San Diego: Academic Press.

Tseng, W. S., Asai, M. H., Kitanish, K. J., McLaughlin, D., & Kyomen, H. (1992). Diagnostic pattern of social phobia: Comparison in Tokyo and Hawaii. *Journal of Nervous and Mental Disease, 180,* 380–385.

Tseng, W. S., McDermott, J. F., Jr., Ogino, K., & Ebata, K. (1982). Cross-cultural differences in parent-child assessment: U.S.A. and Japan. *International Journal of Social Psychiatry, 145,* 1538–1543.

Tuan, M. (1998). *Forever foreigners or honorary Whites? The Asian ethnic experience today.* New Brunswick, NJ: Rutgers University Press.

Turk, M. (2004). The question of rent: The emerging urban housing crisis in the new century. *International Journal of Urban and Regional Research, 28,* 909–918.

Turner, R. J., & Gil, A. G. (2002). Psychiatric and substance use disorders in South Florida: Racial/ethnic and gender contrasts in a young adult cohort. *Archives of General Psychiatry, 59,* 43–50.

Turner, T., & Collinson, S. (2003). From Enlightenment to eugenics: Empire, race, and medicine 1780-c1950. In D. Ndegwa & D. Olajide (Eds.), *Main issues in mental health and race* (pp. 1–29). Burlington, VT: Ashgate.

Tynerm J., & Houston, D. (2002). Controlling bodies: The punishment of multiracialized sexual relations. *Antipode, 32,* 387–410.

Uba, L. (1994). *Asian Americans: Personality patterns, identity, and mental health.* New York: Guilford Press.

Uba, L. (2002). *A postmodern psychology of Asian Americans: Creating knowledge of a racial minority.* Albany: State University of New York.

U.S.Bureau of Indian Affairs. (1988). *American Indians today.* Washington, DC: Author.

U.S. Bureau of Labor Statistics. (n.d.). *Occupational outlook handbook.* Retrieved October 15, 2007, from http://www.bls.gov/oco/ocos067.htm

U.S. Census Bureau. (1997). *National crime victimization survey.* Retrieved June 27, 2007, from http://webapp.icpsr.umich.edu/cocoon/NACJD-SERIES/00095.xml.

U.S. Census Bureau. (2000a). *Population profile of the United States: 2000.* Retrieved November 29, 2007, from http://www.census.gov/population/popprofile/profile2000.html

U.S. Census Bureau. (2000b). *Population profile of the United States: 2000, Overview of race and Hispanic ori-*gin. Retrieved August 23, 2007, from http://www.census.gov/prod/2001pubs/c2kbr01-1.pdf

U.S. Census Bureau. (2000c). *We the People: Asians in the United States.* Retrieved from http://www.census.gov/prod/2004pubs/censr-17.pdf

U.S. Census Bureau. (2001a). *Population profile of the United States.* Washington, DC: U.S. Government Printing Office.

U.S. Census Bureau. (2001b). *Poverty in the United States: 2000 (Current population reports,* Series P60-214). Washington, DC: Author.

U.S. Census Bureau. (2001c). *2000 census counts of American Indians, Eskimos, or Aleuts and American Indian and Alaska Native areas.* Washington, DC: Author.

U.S. Census Bureau. (March, 2003). *Disability status: 2000 Census Bureau brief.* Retrieved May 8, 2007, from http://www.census.gov/prod/2003pubs/c2kbr-17.pdf

U.S. Census Bureau. (2003). *The older population in the United States: March 2002.* Retrieved November 29, 2007, from http://www.census.gov/prod/2003pubs/p20-546.pdf

U.S. Census Bureau (2004a). *The foreign-born population in the United States: 2003.* Retrieved November 29, 2007, from http://www.census.gov/prod/2004pbs/p20-551.pdf

U.S. Census Bureau. (2004b). *Census Bureau projects tripling of Hispanic and Asian populations in 50 Years; Non-Hispanic Whites may drop to half of total population.* Retrieved February 20, 2007, from http://www.census.gov/PressRelease/http://www/releases/archives/population/001720.html

U.S. Census Bureau (2004c). *U.S. interim projections by age, sex, race, and Hispanic origin.* Retrieved November 29, 2007, from http://www.census.gov/ipc/ http://www/usinterimproj

U.S. Census Bureau. (2006a). *Educational attainment in the United States: 2006.* Retrieved August 31, 2007, from http://www.census.gov/population/ http://www/socdemo/education/cps2006.html

U.S. Census Bureau. (2006b). *Press release: More than 50 million Americans report some level of disability.* Retrieved September 9, 2007, from http://www.census.gov/Press-Release/ http://www/releases/archives/aging_population/006809.html

U.S. Census Bureau. (2007a). *The American community— Hispanics: 2004.* Retrieved April 18, 2007, from http://www.census.gov/prod/2007pubs/acs-02.pdf

U.S. Census Bureau. (2007b). *Historical poverty tables: Table 18.* Retrieved October 8, 2007, from http://www.

census.gov/hhes/ http://www/poverty/histpov/hstpov 18.html

U.S. Census Bureau. (2008). *U.S. Hispanic population surpasses 45 million: Now 15 percent total.* Retrieved on May 27, 2008 from http://www.census.gov/Press-Release/ http://www/releases/archives/population/011910.html

U.S. Commission on Civil Rights. (1992). *Civil rights issues facing Asian Americans in the 1990s.* Washington, DC: Author.

U.S. Department of Agriculture. (2007). *Briefing rooms: Food security in the United States.* Retrieved September 1, 2007, from http://www.ers.usda.gov/Briefing/FoodSecurity

U.S. Department of Commerce. (1998). *Statistical abstract of the United States 1998* (118th U.S. Department of Commerce, 1998 ed.). Washington, DC: U.S. Bureau of the Census.

U.S. Department of Education. (2007). *The condition of education 2007* (National

Center for Education Statistics report 2007-064). Retrieved September 5, 2007, from http://nces.ed.gov/ pubsearch/pubsinfo.asp?pubid=2007064

U.S. Department of Health and Human Services. (1995). *National College Health Risk Behavior Survey.* Retrieved June 26, 2007, from http://www.cdc.gov/ mmwr/preview/mmwrhtml/00049859.htm

U.S. Department of Health and Human Services. (2001a). *Mental health: Culture, race and ethnicity—A supplement to mental health: A report of the surgeon general.* Rockville, MD: Author.

U.S. Department of Health and Human Services (2001b). *A provider's introduction to substance abuse treatment of lesbian, gay, bisexual, and transgender individuals.* (DHHS Publication No. SMA 01-3498). Rockville, MD: Author.

U.S. Department of Health and Human Services. (2002). *Child maltreatment summary: Report from Administration for Children and Families,* National Clearinghouse on Child Abuse and Neglect. Rockville, MD: Author.

U.S. Department of Health and Human Services, Administration on Aging. (2003a). *Facts and figures: Statistics on minority aging in the U.S.* Retrieved July 6, 2007, from http://www.aoa.gov/prof/Statistics/minority_ aging/facts_minority_aging.asp#PopulationbyRace

U.S. Department of Health and Human Services, Administration on Aging. (2003b). *Older population by age: 1900–2050.* Retrieved July 6, 2007, from http://www.aoa.gov/prof/Statistics/online_stat_data/A gePop2050.asp

U.S. Department of Health and Human Services, Administration on Aging. (2004). *A profile of older*

Americans: 2004. Retrieved July 6, 2006, from http:// assets.aarp.org/rgcenter/general/profile_2004.pdf

U.S. Department of Health and Human Services, Centers for Disease Control and Prevention. (2007). *Health information for older adults.* Retrieved October 15, 2007, from http://www.cdc.gov/aging/info.htm#top

U.S. Department of Health and Human Services, Centers for Disease Control and Prevention, National Center for Health Statistics. (2006). Table 27, Life expectancy at birth, at 65 years of age, and at 75 years of age, by race and sex: United States, selected years 1900–2004. *Health, United States 2006.* Retrieved October 20, 2007, from http://www.cdc.gov/nchs/fastats/lifexpec.htm

U.S. Department of Health and Human Services, Office on Women's Health. (2001). *Women's health issues: An overview.* Washington, DC: National Women's Health Information Center.

U.S. Department of Labor. (2007). *Wages: Minimum wage.* Retrieved August 31, 2007, from http://www.dol. gov/dol/topic/wages/minimumwage.htm

U.S. Department of Labor, Bureau of Statistics. (2001). *Highlights of women's earnings in 2000* (Report 952). Retrieved June 22, 2007, from http://www.bls.gov/ wb/jobs6497.htm

U.S. Social Security Administration. (1983). *Social Security Amendments of 1983, P.L. 98-21, (H.R. 1900).* Retrieved September 9, 2007, from http://www.ssa.gov/history/1983amend.html

U.S. Surgeon General. (1999). *Mental health: A report of the surgeon general.* Retrieved November 12, 2006, from http://www.surgeongeneral.gov/library/ mentalhealth/home.html

Ussher, J. (2000). Women's madness: A material–discursive–intrapsychic approach. In D. Fee (Ed.), *Pathology and the postmodern: Mental illness as discourse and experience* (pp. 205–230). London: Sage.

Ustun, T. B., Chatterji, S., Bickenbach, J. E., Trotter R. T., II, Room, T., Rehm, J., et al. (Eds.). (2001). *Disability and culture: Universalism and diversity.* Seattle, WA: Hogrefe & Huber.

Utsey, S. O., McCarthy, E., Eubanks, R., & Adrian, G. (2002). White racism and suboptimal psychological functioning among White Americans: Implications for counseling and prejudice prevention. *Journal of Multicultural Counseling and Development, 30,* 81–95.

Uy, M. (2004). Tax and race: The impact on Asian Americans. *Asian Law Journal, 11,* 129–138.

Valasquez, R. J., Johnson, R., & Brown-Cheatham, M. (1993). Teaching counselors to use the *DSM–III–R* with ethnic minority clients: A paradigm. *Counselor Education and Supervision, 32,* 323–331.

Vance, E. T. (1997). A typology of risks and the disabilities of low status. In G. W. Albee & J. M. Joffee (Eds.), *The primary prevention of psychopathology: The issues.* Hanover, NH: University Press of New England.

Vandiver, B. J., Fhagen-Smith, P. E., Cokley, K. O., Cross, W. E., Jr., & Worrell, F. C. (2001). Cross' nigrescense model: From theory to scale to theory. *Journal of Multicultural Counseling and Development, 29,* 174–200.

Verbrugge, L. M., & Jette, A. M. (1994). The disablement process. *Social Science and Medicine, 38,* 1–14.

Via, T., Callahan, S., Barry, K., Jackson, C., & Gerber, D. E. (1997). Middle East meets Midwest: The new health care challenge. *The Journal of Multicultural Nursing and Health, 3*(1), 35–39.

Villalba, J. A. (2003). A psychoeducational group for limited-English proficient Latino/Latina Children. *Journal for Specialists in Group Work, 28,* 261-276.

Villalba, J. A. (2007). Culture-specific assets to consider when counseling Latina/o children and adolescents. *Journal of Multicultural Counseling and Development, 35,* 15–25.

Vodde, R. (2001). De-centering privilege in social work education: Whose job is it anyway? *Race, Gender & Class, 7,* 139–160.

Vygotsky, L. (1978). *Mind in society.* London: Harvard University Press.

Wakefield, J. C. (1992). The concept of mental disorder: On the boundary between biological facts and social values. *American Psychologist, 47,* 373–388.

Walker, L. E. A. (1985). Feminist therapy with victims/survivors of interpersonal violence. In L. B. Rosewater & L. E. A. Walker (Eds.), *Handbook of feminist therapy: Women's issues in psychotherapy* (pp. 210–221). New York: Springer.

Walker, L. E. A. (1986, August). Diagnosis and politics: Abuse disorders. In R. Garfinkel (Chair), *The politics of diagnosis: Feminist psychology and the* DSM–III–R. Symposium presented at the Conference of the American Psychological Association, Washington, DC.

Walters, K. L., & Simoni, J. M. (1993). Lesbian and gay male group identity attitudes and self-esteem: Implications for counseling. *Journal of Counseling Psychology, 40,* 94–99.

Wampold, B. E. (2001). *The great psychotherapy debate: Models, methods, and findings.* Mahwah, NJ: Erlbaum.

Warren, L. W. (1983). Male intolerance of depression: A review with implications for psychotherapy. *Clinical Psychology Review, 3,* 147–156.

Washington, H. A. (2002). Burning love: Big tobacco takes aim at LGBT youths. *American Journal of Public Health, 92,* 1086–1095.

Webb, L. (2002). Deliberate self-harm in adolescence: A systematic review of psychological and psychosocial factors. *Journal of Advanced Nursing, 38,* 235–245.

Weinberg, M. S., Williams, C. J., & Pryor, D. W. (1996). *Dual attraction: Understanding bisexuality.* New York: Oxford University Press.

Weissman, M. M., & Klerman, G. L. (1981). Sex differences and the epidemiology of depression. In E. Howell & M. Bayes (Eds.), *Women and mental health* (pp. 160–195). New York: Basic Books.

Weisz, J. R., & Weiss, B. (1991). Studying the "referability" of child clinical problems. *Journal of Consulting and Clinical Psychology, 59,* 266–273.

Welfel, E. (2002). *Ethics in counseling and psychotherapy: Standards, research, and emerging issues* (2nd ed.). Pacific Grove, CA: Brooks/Cole.

Welwood, J. (1983). *Awakening the heart: East-west approaches to psychotherapy and the healing relationship.* Boston: Shambhala.

Wester, S. R., & Lyubelsky, J. (2005). Supporting the thin blue line: Gender-sensitive therapy with male police officers. *Professional Psychology: Research and Practice, 36*(1), 51–58.

Westwood, M. J., & Ishiyama, F. J. (1990). The communication process as a critical intervention for client change in cross-cultural counseling. *Journal of Multicultural Counseling and Development, 18,* 163–171.

Wetzel, J. W. (1991). Universal mental health classification systems: Reclaiming women's experience. *Affilia, 6*(3), 8–31.

Whaley, A. L. (2001). Cultural mistrust: An important psychological construct for diagnosis and treatment of African Americans. *Professional Psychology: Research and Practice, 32,* 555–562.

Whitefield, W., McGrath, P., & Coleman, V. (1992, October). *Increasing multicultural sensitivity and awareness.* Paper presented at the annual conference of the National Organization for Human Services Education, Alexandria, VA.

Whitfield, C. L. (2003). *My recovery: A personal plan for healing.* Deerfield Beach, FL: HCI.

Wicker, L. R., & Brodie, R. E., II (2004). The physical and mental health needs of African Americans. In D. R. Atkinson (Ed.), *Counseling American minorities* (pp. 105–124). Boston: McGraw-Hill.

Wilber, K. (1997 Fall/Winter). A spirituality that transforms. *What Is Enlightenment?, 12,* 22–32.

Wilber, K. (1998). *The essential Ken Wilber reader.* Boston: Shambhala.

Wilber, K. (1999). *The collected works of Ken Wilber* (Vol. 3). Boston: Shambhala.

Wilber, K. (2000). *Sex, ecology, spirituality*. Boston: Shambhala.

Wilber, K. (2001). *Grace and grit: Spirituality and healing in the life and death of Treya Killam Wilber*. Boston: Shambhala.

Wilbur, M. P. (1999a). Finding balance in the winds. *Journal for Specialists in Group Work, 24*, 342–353.

Wilbur, M. P. (1999b). The rivers of a wounded heart. *Journal of Counseling and Development, 77*, 47–50.

Williams, C. L., & Berry, J. W. (1991). Primary prevention of acculturative stress among refugees: Applications of psychological theory and practice. *American Psychologist, 46*, 632–641.

Williams, D. R., & Williams-Morris, R. (2000). Racism and mental health: The African American experience. *Ethnicity and Health, 5*, 234–268.

Willie, C. V., & Reddick, R. J. (2003). *A new look at Black families* (5th ed.). Walnut Creek, CA: AltaMira Press.

Winawer, H., & Wetzel, N. A. (2005). German families. In M. McGoldrick, J. Giordano, & N. Garcia-Preto (Eds.), *Ethnicity and family therapy* (3rd ed., pp. 555–572). New York: Guilford.

Wine, J. D., Moses, B., & Smye, M. D. (1980). Female superiority in sex different competence comparisons: A review of the literature. In C. Stark-Adamec (Ed.), *Sex roles: Origins, influences, and implications for women* (pp. 148–163). Montreal, Quebec, Canada: Eden Press Women's Publishers.

Winslade, J., Monk, G., & Drewery, W. (1997). Sharpening the critical edge: A social constructionist approach in counselor education. In T. L. Sexton & B. L. Griffin (Eds.), *Constructivist thinking in counseling practice, research, and training* (pp. 228–245). New York: Teachers College Press.

Witmer, J. M., Sweeney, T. J., & Myers J. E. (1994). A holistic model of wellness and prevention over the life span. *Journal of Counseling and Development, 71*, 140–148.

Wolsko, P. M., Eisenberg, D. M., Davis, R. B., & Phillips, R. S. (2004). Use of mind–body medical therapies: Results of a national survey. *Journal of General Internal Medicine, 19*(1), 43–50.

Woolfe, S. H., Johnson, R. E., Phillips, R. L., Jr., & Philipsen, M. (2007). Giving everyone the health of the educated: An examination of whether social change would save more lives than medical advances. *American Journal of Public Health, 97*, 679–683.

Woolfolk, R. L. (2001). "Objectivity" in diagnosis and treatment. In B. D. Slife, R. N. Willimans, & S. H. Barlow (Eds.), *Critical issues in psychotherapy: Translating new ideas into practice* (pp. 2887–2898). London: Sage.

Worell, J., & Remer, P. (2003). *Feminist perspectives in therapy: Empowering diverse women* (2nd ed.). Hoboken, NJ: Wiley.

World Bank. (2005). *World development report 2006: Equity and development (overview)*. Retrieved August 15, 2007, from http://web.worldbank.org/WBSITE/EXTERNAL/EXTDEC/EXTRESEARCH/EXTWDRS/EXTWDR2006/0,,menuPK:477658~pagePK:64167702~piPK:64167676~theSitePK:477642,00.html

World Health Organization. (1979). *Schizophrenia: An international follow-up study*. Chichester, England: Wiley.

World Health Organization. (1980). *International classification of impairments, disabilities, and handicaps*. Geneva: Author.

World Health Organization. (2001). *The world health report 2001—Mental health: New understanding, new hope*. Retrieved November 12, 2006, from http://www.who.int/whr/2001/en/

Worrell, F., Cross, W., & Vandiver, B. (2001). Nigrescence theory: Current status and challenges for the future. *Journal of Multicultural Counseling and Development, 29*, 201–213.

Worrell, F., Vandiver, B., Schaefer, B., Cross, W., & Fhagen-Smith, P. (2006). Generalizing nigrescense profiles: Cluster analyses of Cross Racial Identity Scale (CRIS) scores in three independent samples. *The Counseling Psychologist, 34*, 519–547.

Worthington, E. (2001). *Five steps to forgiveness: The art and science of forgiveness*. New York: Crown.

Wrenn, C. G. (1962). The culturally encapsulated counselor. *Harvard Educational Review, 32*, 444–468.

Wu, F. H. (2002). *Yellow: Race in America beyond Black and White*. New York: Basic Books.

Xie, Y., & Goyette, K. A. (2004). *A demographic portrait of Asian Americans*. New York: Russell Sage Foundation.

Yahav, R., & Sharlin, S. A. (2002). Blame and family conflict: Symptomatic children as scapegoats. *Child and Family Social Work, 7*(2), 91–99.

Yang, C. K. (1961). *Religion in Chinese society: A study of contemporary social functions of religion and their historical factors*. Los Angeles: University of California Press.

Yang, J. (1998). Counseling in the 21st century: Multicultural and postmodernist perspectives. In Chinese Guidance Association (Ed.), *Trends of counseling* (pp. 73–102). Taipei, Taiwan: Psychological Publishing.

Yang, L. H., & WonPat-Borja, A. J., (2007). Psychopathology among Asian Americans. In F. Leong, A. G. Inman, A. Ebreo, L. Lang, L. Kinoshita, & M. Fu (Eds.), *Handbook of Asian American psychology* (2nd ed., pp. 379–405). Thousand Oaks, CA: Sage.

Yao, X. (2000). *An introduction to Confucianism.* Cambridge, England: Cambridge University Press.

Yared, C. (1997). Where are the civil rights for gay and lesbian teachers? *Human Rights: American Bar Association, 24*(3). Retrieved March 1, 2002, from http://www.abanet.org/irr/hr/summer97/hrsum97.html

Yarhouse, M. (2001). Sexual identity development: The influences of valuation frameworks on identity synthesis. *Psychotherapy, 38,* 331–341.

Yee, A., Fairchild, H., Weizmann, F., & Wyatt, G. (1993). Addressing psychology's problems with race. *American Psychologist, 48,* 1132–1142.

Yee, B., DeBaryshe, B., Yuen, S., Kim, S., & McCubbin, H. (2007). Asian American and Pacific Islander families: Resiliency and life-span socialization in a cultural context. In F. Leong, A. G. Inman, A. Ebreo, L. Lang, L. Kinoshita, & M. Fu (Eds.), *Handbook of Asian American Psychology* (2nd ed., pp. 69–86). Thousand Oaks, CA: Sage.

Yeh, C., Inose, M., Kobori, A., & Chang, T. (2001). Self and coping among college students in Japan. *Journal of College Student Development, 42,* 242–256.

Yeh, C. J., Inman, A., Kim, A. B., & Okubo, Y. (2006). Asian American families' collectivistic coping strategies in response to 9/11. *Cultural Diversity and Ethnic Minority Psychology, 12,* 134–148.

Yeh, C. J., & Wang, Y. W. (2000). Asian American coping attitudes, sources, and practices: Implications for indigenous counseling strategies. *Journal of College Student Development, 41,* 94–103.

Ying, Y., & Hu, L. (1994). Public outpatient mental health services: Use and outcome among Asian Americans. *American Journal of Orthopsychiatry, 64,* 448–455.

Ying, Y., Lee, P. A., & Tsai, J. L. (2000). Cultural orientation and racial discrimination: Predictors of coherence in Chinese American young adults. *Journal of Community Psychology, 28,* 427–442.

Ying, Y., & Miller, L. S. (1992). Help-seeking behavior and attitude of Chinese Americans regarding psychological problems. *American Journal of Community Psychology, 20,* 549–556.

Yip, T., & Fulgni, A. J. (2002). Daily variation in ethnic identity, ethnic behaviors, and psychological well-being among American adolescents of Chinese descent. *Child Development, 73,* 1557–1572.

Yoshikawa, H., Wilson, P. A. D., Chae, D. H., & Cheng, J. F. (2004). Do family and friendship networks protect against the influence of discrimination on mental health and HIV risk among Asian and Pacific Islander gay men? *AIDS Education and Prevention, 16*(1), 84–100.

Young, D. M. (1997). Depression. In W.-S. Tseng & J. Streltzer (Eds.), *Culture and psychopathology: A guide to clinical assessment* (pp. 46–66). New York: Brunner/Mazel.

Zane, N., Hatanaka, H., Park, S., & Akutsu, P. (1994). Ethnic-specific mental health services: Evaluation of the parallel approach for Asian American clients. *Journal of Community Psychology, 22,* 68–81.

Zhang, A. Y., & Snowden, L. R. (1999). Ethnic characteristics of mental disorders in five U.S. communities. *Cultural Diversity and Ethnic Minority Psychology, 5*(2), 134–146.

Zhang, A. Y., Snowden, L. R., & Sue, S. (1998). Differences between Asian and White Americans' help-seeking and utilization patterns in the Los Angeles area. *Journal of Community Psychology, 26,* 317–326.

Zinn, H. (1999). *A people's history of the United States 1492–present.* New York: HarperCollins.

Zinnbauer, B. J., & Pargament, K. I. (2000). Working with the sacred: Four approaches to religious and spiritual issues in counseling. *Journal of Counseling and Development, 78,* 162–171.

Zlotnick, C., Elkin, I., & Shea, M. T. (1998). Does the gender of a patient or the gender of a therapist affect the treatment of patients with major depression? *Journal of Consulting and Clinical Psychology, 66,* 655–659.

Zogby, I. (2001). *Who we are and how we live* (Survey/Report). New York: Zogby International.

Zogby, J. (2000, May). *Are Arab Americans people like us?* Retrieved November 24, 2004, from http://www.aaiusa.org/zogby/people_like_us.htm

Zsembik, B. A., & Fennell, D. (2005). Ethnic variation in health and the determinants of health among Latinos. *Social Science and Medicine, 61,* 53–63.

Zuckerman, M. (1990). Some dubious premises in research and theory on racial differences: Scientific, social, and ethical issues. *American Psychologist, 45,* 1297–1303.

INDEX

A

Ableism, 166
  awareness of, 174–175
  counseling process and, 173–174
  defining, 173
  resources related to, 188
Abuse, sexual, 108, 422–423
ACA. *See* American Counseling Association
Access, 365
Acculturation, 198, 322, 344
  Arab Americans and, 226–227
  Asian American, 255–256
  assessing, 318
  children and, 361
  European American, 351
  immigration and, 18
  level of, 19
  models of, 18–19, 30–31
  of Native Americans, 311, 318
  visualization, 227
ADA. *See* Americans with Disabilities Act
ADC. *See* American-Arab
    Anti-Discrimination Committee
Adolescents
  counseling, 292–293
  ethnic identity/academic achievement
    relation for, 39–40
Adultism, 182
Advocacy. *See also* Social advocacy
  competencies of, 61–62, 110–111
  by counselors, 9–10, 60–62, 272
  as defined, 9–10
  in disability/rehabilitation, 180
  ideas for, 162–163
  national plan for, 63
  resources for learning and, 164
  responsibility of, 9–10
  in schools, 163
Affectional orientation, 114
Affirmative action, 91–92
African Americans. *See also* African descent
  culture/values, 199–200
  elderly, 205
  gay/lesbian, 205
  gender roles of, 105, 204–206
  historical effects on, 193–194
  history, 195–196
  identity and, 35, 198
  mental health and, 205
  sexual orientation of, 125–126
  terminology used for, 195
African descent. *See also* African
    Americans
  children of, 203–204
  counseling people of, 194, 208–209, 214

couples of, 202
demographics of people of, 195
discrimination experiences of people
  from, 196–197
guidelines for work with clients of,
  210–213
history with, 193–194
individuals/families of, 193–215
media resources for individual/family
  of, 214
mental health issues of individuals of,
  205–206
support systems for individuals of, 207
Age, 2. *See also* Ageism
  awareness and, 186–187
  counseling process and, 185–190
  demographics, 181
  disclosure of sexual orientation and, 124
  discrimination, 184
  economics of, 184
  issues associated with, 183
  physical changes with, 183
  skills and, 187–188
  trends, 3–4
Ageism, 166, 191
  awareness of, 186–187
  counseling process and, 185–190
  as defined, 182
  older Americans and, 183–185
  resources related to, 190–191
  skills and, 187–188
Alderian counseling, 356
Alexithymia, normative male, 100
ALGBTIC. *See* Association for Lesbian,
  Gay, Bisexual, and Transgender Issues
  in Counseling
American Counseling Association (ACA)
  advocacy competencies of, 110–111, 140
  aging projects by, 185
  Code of Ethics, 110
  gerontological competencies of, 186–187
American dream, 340
American-Arab Anti-Discrimination
  Committee (ADC), 220
Americans with Disabilities Act
  (ADA), 167
Androgyny, 7
Anxiety, 261
Arab Americans
  acculturation and, 226–227
  collectivism and, 222, 239–240
  communication styles of, 225–226
  complexity of existence for, 219
  considerations for counseling, 238–244
  culture/values, 222–226

discrimination experiences of,
  219–221, 235
economic status of, 225
education of, 225
ethnic/gender identity development
  of, 236–237
ethnicity and, 228–229
family/community involvement in
  counseling, 239–240
famous, 219
gender roles of, 106–107, 232–234
help-seeking behaviors of, 240
heterogeneity, 216–219
identifying as, 221
identity development of, 226
immigration history of, 216–218
mental health issues among, 234–238
as Muslim, 217
oppression and, 235
parenting style of, 222
perceptions about, 216
PTSD of, 237–238
religion/faith of, 223–225
resources for counseling, 244
social perceptions of, 219–221
stereotypes of, 220
stigmas for, 240
veiling practice by, 234
women, 229, 232–234
Arab descent. *See also* Arab Americans
  individuals/families of, 216–245
ASERVIC. *See* Association for Spiritual,
  Ethical, and Religious Values in
  Counseling
Asian American(s), 276
  acculturation and, 255–256
  barriers in help-seeking for, 263–264
  community of, 246–248
  culture/values, 252–255
  death/dying and, 254–255
  depression among, 260
  discrimination of, 248–250
  diversity among community
    of, 251–252
  domestic violence among, 261
  education of, 254
  enculturation and, 255–256
  ethnicity and, 256–257
  family and, 252–253
  gender roles of, 106, 253, 257–258
  help seeking/coping by, 262–263
  heterogeneity, 250–252
  history, 247–248
  identity, 255–259, 268
  immigration histories of, 251–252